Hong Kong Public Housing

Hong Kong Public Housing provides the first comprehensive history of one of the most dramatic episodes in the global history of the modern built environment: the vast public housing programme sponsored by successive Hong Kong governments from the 1950s, in a quest to build up the territory into a lasting 'people's home'. And unlike many of its counterparts elsewhere, this is a programme still ongoing today – a case of 'history in progress' – as Hong Kong now boasts one of the world's longest-lasting public housing programmes. During that time, it has been not just a mirror of the cultural and economic values of Hong Kong society but also a reflection of more nebulous, fast-changing perceptions of identity – and a testament to the community-building achievements of Hongkongers over these years.

This authoritative study combines architectural history with the broader social, political, and cultural aspects of housing production – particularly the geo-political issues of sovereignty and decolonisation that uniquely, and fundamentally, structured the trajectory of Hong Kong public housing and territory development. Exploring the relationship between built form, ideology, and administrative governance, it shows how massive state intervention interacted at times uneasily with Hong Kong's dominant laissez-faire ethos, to help maintain the legitimacy of successive administrations during an era of 'auto-decolonisation', and support an interstitial society suspended between two sovereignties. Following more recent political changes, Hong Kong's public housing heritage has also become a focus of nostalgic community pride – a monumental achievement of 'home building' which this book documents and celebrates for posterity.

Miles Glendinning is Professor of Architectural Conservation at the University of Edinburgh, Scotland.

Hong Kong Public Housing

An Architectural and Policy History

Miles Glendinning

Routledge
Taylor & Francis Group
LONDON AND NEW YORK

Designed cover image: Wah Fu Estate Twin Tower Block: Miles Glendinning

First published 2025
by Routledge
4 Park Square, Milton Park, Abingdon, Oxon OX14 4RN

and by Routledge
605 Third Avenue, New York, NY 10158

Routledge is an imprint of the Taylor & Francis Group, an informa business

British Library Cataloguing-in-Publication Data
A catalogue record for this book is available from the British Library

ISBN: 978-1-138-68022-7 (hbk)
ISBN: 978-1-032-87725-9 (pbk)
ISBN: 978-1-315-56370-1 (ebk)

DOI: 10.1201/9781315563701

Typeset in Times New Roman
by Newgen Publishing UK

Contents

Acknowledgements

Grateful thanks are due to the following individuals and organisations for helping me in this project. In some cases, the help was immediately and specifically related to the text or illustrations, including commenting on drafts or bringing new points to my attention. In other cases, the input was more indirect, including organisational assistance, general advice on Hong Kong housing matters, or more general support, sometimes over a period of years. Those whose names are asterisked contributed or partly contributed through participation in historical interviews, mostly in the last 15 years. Special thanks are due in particular to Rosman Wai for advice and help throughout; Joyce Fu Si Qi for the production of many drawings for the book; and finally, to Donald Liao for inspiring the entire project through his illustrious career as Hong Kong's 'Mr Housing'.

* Sir David Akers-Jones; Agnes and Robert Allcock; Jeroen van Ameijde; Bodleian Library of Commonwealth and African Studies at Rhodes House, Oxford; * Philip Boyle; Bernard Brennan; * Nicholas Burns; Stephen Cairns; * Iris Chan; Chang Jiat-Hwee; * Cheng Hon-kwan; * Ken Cheung; Cecilia Chu; Lynne DiStefano; Joyce Fu Si Qi; * Ada Fung; * Fung Tung; * Chris Gabriel; * Dave Hall; Patrick Hetherington; Jess Hindle; Puay-peng Ho; Hong Kong Central Library; Hong Kong Public Records Office; Alison, Amy-Felicity, Kitty, Margaret and Sali Horsey; Helena Hurd; Jane Jacobs; Kei Yat-shun; * Denis Ko; * John Lambon; Jennifer Lang; Moly Lau; * Patrick Lau; Francis Law; Rui Leao; Lee Chui Mei; Lee Ho-Yin; * Donald Liao; * Ian and Norian Lightbody; * Liu Thai Ker; Theresa Love; Martha Luke; Sharen Mak; * Tony Miller; Stefan Muthesius; The National Archives (Kew); Ed Needle; * John Ng; Ken Nicolson; Hongbin Ouyang; Duncan Pescod; * Stephen Poon; * Bob Pritchard; Cole Roskam; Eunice Seng; Linda Shetabi; *South China Morning Post* (Steven Hon); John and Archie Stirling; Ian Tan Yuk-Hong; Hendrik Tieben; Carmen Tsui; Brian and Rosemary Turner; Ola Uduku; Florian Urban; * Rosman C C Wai; Rémi Wei-Chou Wang; * Bernard Williams; * Lord Wilson; * L C Wong; * Rosanna Wong; * Michael Wright;* Connie Yeung; Yu Ka-sing; Zhao Xiaofeng; Zhou Ying; Zhu Rong.

The assistance of the Society of Architectural Historians of Great Britain in grant aid towards image reproduction costs is specifically, and gratefully, acknowledged.

Introduction

A mirror of identity? Public housing in Hong Kong

Hong Kong – a 'hot-spot' in the global history of mass housing

This book is concerned with one of the most dramatic episodes in the global history of the modern built environment: the vast public housing programme sponsored by the Hong Kong government from the 1950s onwards. And unlike many of its counterparts elsewhere, this is a programme still ongoing today – a case of 'history in progress'.

Like all histories of the built environment, this book is concerned with both buildings and the society that created them. However, although built environments are certainly in many ways a mirror of the culture that produces them, their monumental solidity means they can also outlast their parent society. That was certainly the fate of *ancien-régime* monuments such as Versailles, which long outlasted the French Revolution. More relevantly to Hong Kong, the same applies to the colonial monuments that survived the fall of the European empires, and whose heritage can now be both problematised and positively re-appropriated. Yet built heritage is also itself transient, subject to decay and ultimate disappearance, as Viennese conservation theorist Alois Riegl stressed over a century ago.[1] In Hong Kong, for cultural and political reasons, perceptions of transience have been especially acute, but the same ultimately applies to all built environments: even such a vast and seemingly all-conquering movement such as mass housing has in many places almost disappeared. In fact, Hong Kong, although something of a latecomer, now boasts one of the world's longest-lasting public housing programmes, spanning nearly three-quarters of a century. During that time, it has been not just a mirror of Hong Kong society but also a reflection of more nebulous perceptions of identity – and a testament to the achievements of Hong Kong and its people.

At a global level, during the 20th century mass housing became one of the most ubiquitous patterns of urban development. Complexes of state-sponsored homes for lower-income citizens, especially in tall apartment blocks, came to dominate many cities across the developed world, and, more uncertainly, in some 'developing' countries. Yet despite this ubiquity, modernist mass housing was a global landscape of kaleidoscopic variety, reflecting both the diversity of the modern state and the many permutations of modernist architecture, interacting with each other in countless 'micro-ecologies'. And of all these ecologies, Hong Kong's public housing programme was one of the most extreme and fantastic. Culturally and organisationally, it was shaped by Hong Kong's unique interstitial status, suspended between two geo-political poles. And architecturally, the soaring towered clusters of Hong Kong's public housing dramatised international modernism's ability to balance its claims of universal applicability with elements of national and local place-specificity (Figure 0.1).[2]

To properly appreciate the distinctiveness of the Hong Kong story, we need first to review the wider global panorama of late-20th-century mass housing. Organisationally, within the developed world, almost all states, capitalist and socialist, developed their own distinctive patterns of social provision and housing production, energised by strong state intervention and collective values. Mass housing helped define membership of the 'imagined community' of national society, but the results varied radically between countries, and within these national structures, a further layer of micro-regional diversity stemmed from the power of key cities – a pattern of housing autonomy that would later be hugely elaborated in Hong Kong and Singapore.[3]

These ideological patterns constantly interplayed with shared themes, not least the fluctuating social-political definitions of the 'housing problem'. There was constant debate about the targeting of state-led housing campaigns: who should be the recipients? A balance of affordability and ethical prioritisation was struck between the poorest citizens and middling income groups. In the United States, public housing was targeted at the poorest 'slum-dwellers', with strong racial overtones, whereas in Western and Eastern Europe a broader-based collective approach applied. In the west, doctrines such as the Catholic-dominated Christian Democracy competed with social democrats, and in the east, communism appropriated capitalist organisational ideologies such as Fordist hierarchical mass-production in support of 'classless' provision. Organisationally, there was a limitless variety of financing and organisational regimes. Typical in Continental Europe were private, philanthropic or co-operative agencies enjoying state support, or arm's length public agencies, although some systems were highly centralised, such as France's programme of *grands ensembles*. 'Public housing' in the strict sense – built by direct agencies of the state itself – was uniquely dominant in Anglophone countries, where it was mostly built by area-based national or municipal 'housing authorities' or 'commissions' (as in Australia or the USA). An extreme variant of this was the 'council housing' system of direct municipal provision in Britain and Ireland.[4]

In architecture, too, individual countries developed their own variants of the 'universal' formulae of international modernism. Of course, mass housing architecture everywhere was influenced in some way by the avant-garde concepts of modernist pioneers, notably Le Corbusier, or the younger Team 10 grouping, with their advocacy of dense cluster planning and 'brutalist' concrete. However, we must beware of excessive reification of 'artistic' architectural creativity here: far more significant were impersonal, contextual factors such as land control, density pressures or building-industry organisation. The multiple modernities of mass-housing architecture as built, simplified and mixed together the main avant-garde concepts, especially tall towers in open space, in countless local permutations. Most fundamental in these were basic choices of building patterns, such as between high apartment blocks and single-family dwellings, or between different locations. Straightforward new development on city peripheries was the assumed norm in the overwhelming majority of Western and Eastern European states, especially in the vast planned settlements of the Soviet Union, but equally in countries such as France or Italy with their high-status inner-apartment zones and peripheral *bidonvilles* – whereas English-speaking countries, with their dilapidated inner-urban industrial housing, laid much more emphasis on radical, surgical 'slum clearance' in inner cities.[5]

In the developing world, there were also multiple modernities, but these stemmed from different conceptions of modernity and nationalism, and were often bound up with countries' specific experiences of colonialism and imperialism: here Hong Kong vividly highlights the strong local diversities within what has been termed 'the new global history of modernization'.[6] Some countries emerged from colonisation dogged by poverty and governmental incapacity, and could produce little or no mass housing, while others managed to match, or even exceed, the political-organisational cohesion of the developed capitalist and socialist worlds – as in the case of Hong Kong and Singapore. In many decolonising and developing countries, most low-income housing was organised on an informal, self-help basis – an approach significantly endorsed by US-led international development aid agencies in the post-War era.[7] In Hong Kong, however, although this approach formed a significant minority theme, it was increasingly dwarfed by the state-organised public housing programme. But was Hong Kong actually an example of colonialism at all? Although some post-2020 government school textbooks now deny that, branding the coercive 19th-century treaties ceding the territory as illegitimate and therefore to be historically disregarded, the pre-1997 chapters of this book are based on the pragmatic position that if a territory *looked* like a European colony in its governance, then it probably *was* one – albeit in this case with some very special characteristics.[8]

What is undeniable, though, is that post-War Hong Kong certainly also belonged to another grouping linked with this, and especially with the legacy of both European and Japanese imperialism: the 'developmental capitalist' societies of Eastern Asia. In the same decades that saw the heyday of European mass housing, a small group of states and territories embarked on modernisation programmes calculated to catapult them from Third to First World status. These were programmes where mass housing was as central as in Western welfare states, but enshrined a very different aim: the rapid development of organised capitalism, within a more cohesive, collectivist cultural framework sometimes claimed to reflect 'Confucian' values. In housing, the undisputed pioneer of this developmentalism, post-War Japan, was also an exception, not least in its avoidance of large-scale 'grand ensemble' developments – partly owing to Japan's traditionally fragmented urban fabric and its earthquake vulnerability. It was, instead, the later 'Asian tigers', especially Hong Kong, Singapore and South Korea, which established from the 1950s a link between Asian developmental capitalism and large-scale mass housing.

They adopted a strongly interventive response to rural–urban migration and informal housing, through redevelopment and state housing for rental and home-ownership – an innovative combination of the US mass owner-occupier ideal with high-density Modernist public housing.[9] In late-colonial Hong Kong and newly decolonised Singapore, the 'Anglo' traditions of 'public authority' housing, and of high-rise urban slum clearance with tall towers, were transformed in distinctive and divergent ways, one emphasising a respect for laissez-faire values and the other prioritising state planning – setting the scene for a 'sibling rivalry' in housing and city building that has endured to the present day, and which was a constant point of reference for contemporary actors in our story.

Public housing and the historiography of Hong Kong

We will return to that global picture, and Hong Kong public housing's place in it, later in this introduction. But first we need to stress that this book is also a specialist built-environment contribution to the general history of Hong Kong, and thus fits into quite a dense landscape of writings touching on public housing as a part of the territory's modern society and cultural heritage. It argues that public housing in Hong Kong has a life of its own, intertwined with concepts such as identity or sovereignty, or with various economic paradigms, but never entirely consumed by them. In that sense the book can be seen as a rather specialised commemoration of the achievements of generations of Hongkongers in building up a globally distinctive social and cultural system. Although its focus is on the material reality of the built environment – with buildings and estates never far away from discussion – and thus forms part of the 'material turn' in history, it also constantly cross-refers to these wider cultural, economic and political discourses.[10] Public housing was not only itself a key policy area, but also gives us a window into the heart of government decision-making processes, strongly executive-led both before and after 1997.

In that respect, the book is different from most previous historical accounts of Hong Kong housing. Among these, some have treated public housing chiefly as a constituent element in the city's overall political-economic fabric.[11] Housing is also commonly touched on in studies of public administration under colonialism, which mostly highlight the surprising amount of autonomy that Hong Kong achieved under late-colonial rule, to the point of virtual 'auto-decolonisation'.[12] Housing also plays a more incidental role in general histories of Hong Kong, or in general current affairs accounts of the 2010s' political unrest.[13] Other books have focused more narrowly on Hong Kong housing itself, and on the discourse of the housing problem, whether from a practical, policy-analysis or critical viewpoint, or in the form of reminiscences of key actors.[14] Publications by housing organisations themselves have varied from commemorative or celebratory books to more factual compendia, notably Yeung and Wong's HA-sponsored *Fifty Years of Public Housing in Hong Kong – A Golden Jubilee Review and Appraisal* (2003).[15] However, the deliberately low political profile adopted by Hong Kong's late-colonial governments – for reasons we will explore especially in Chapter 5 – discouraged the publication of official texts of a self-glorifying or propagandist character, as seen in Singapore from the 1960s and 1970s onwards. Attempts to tackle housing issues from a specifically architectural or built-environment perspective have been more intermittent, but a handful of scholarly books have successfully integrated the housing built-environment with its wider architectural or cultural context.[16]

Arrangement, methodology and key themes

To communicate straightforwardly the spectacular story of Hong Kong's public housing achievement, while also paying proper regard to its broader political and cultural context, the book is structured as a chronological narrative. This focuses on the policy background and architecture of 'permanent' public housing (as opposed to temporary or emergency accommodation), while setting the subject matter in its broader political and social context, for the benefit of readers not familiar with Hong Kong. The text is divided into four Parts: Part 1 (Chapters 1–4) covers its prehistory and beginnings up to 1971; Part 2 (Chapters 5–8) the seminal and in some ways revolutionary 1971–82 governorship of Sir Murray MacLehose; Part 3 (Chapters 9–12) the remainder of British rule; and Part 4 (Chapters 13 and 14) the HKSAR era from 1997. Most chapters follow a standard plan, beginning with the geo-political, domestic political, administrative and economic context of mass housing and then homing in on more specific questions of housing policy and organisation, followed finally by architectural and construction matters. Reflecting the 'executive-led' character of Hong Kong government, both before and after 1997, most chapters correspond to the term of office of a single governor or chief executive, with a few exceptions. Pre-1997, although governors were selected by London for a variety of reasons, and stemmed from various backgrounds, they almost invariably mutated rapidly into staunch defenders of Hong Kong's autonomy against London pressures. The first and last chapters (1, 14) feature two governors and four chief executives respectively; the four focal chapters of the book, 5–8, are devoted to the governorship of Sir Murray MacLehose, and combine three broadly chronological chapters and one thematic chapter (7, on the Home Ownership Scheme); Chapters 10–11, covering the governorship of Sir David Wilson, are divided between policy (Chapter 10, on the Long-Term Housing Strategy) and architectural innovation (Chapter 11, on the emergence of the crucial 'Harmony' standard block series). The largest single chapters are 12 and 13, covering the wealth of political and administrative controversies over housing during the administrations of Chris Patten and C H Tung.

The book draws on three main source-material categories: firstly, government files and newspaper cuttings, in the Hong Kong Public Records Office (HKPRO) and the National Archives in Kew; secondly, factual source-books, publications and annual reports; and thirdly, interviews with key historical actors in the fields of administration, planning and architecture (see list at end). Some key methodological challenges in the use of this material need to be emphasised 'up-front'. Firstly, the effect of the 30-year access rule in the HKPRO and National Archives, combined with the author's regrettable lack of Chinese reading ability, has largely restricted research for Chapters 12–14 to published sources, English-language newspapers and interviews – with inevitable consequent issues of potential bias and omission. In particular, those chapters make extensive use of the *South China Morning Post,* which was described in 1992 as 'an exclusive in-house newsletter of the Government' (by journalist Bernard Fong) and yet was also somewhat internally conflicted during the 1990s, owing to the tensions between Governor Chris Patten and the traditional colonial establishment.[17] Many of the earlier newspaper references cited in the book stemmed from cuttings in the HKPRO 'HKRS' collection, with no page references, hence their sometimes highly abbreviated reference format.

Having set out all these contextual and methodological considerations, we can now finally turn to the main themes of the book, covering them in the order in which they normally feature in each chapter.

The first and foremost theme is the way in which geopolitical factors in Hong Kong, unlike most other societies, played an extraordinarily strong role in forming public housing. Above all, it was framed by a long process of decolonisation. Brought into being in the first place as an indirect consequence of the 1949 revolution and the floods of refugees and economic reorientation that it triggered, the housing drive was constantly shaped by apprehensions concerning the likely manner in which Hong Kong would be claimed back by Beijing in, or perhaps before, 1997. This predicament dictated an urgent, yet oddly restricted agenda of social action by the Hong Kong government, shaped by a combination of necessarily low political profile and lack of coercive power over private market forces – in both respects strikingly diverging from the state-coordinated, aggressively propagandistic pattern of decolonisation in post-1959/1965 Singapore. Both before and after 1997, the Hong Kong government system was unambiguously 'executive-led' – a position reflected in the chapter arrangement – yet in some respects was deficient in real executive power, other than in the exceptional case of Sir Murray MacLehose. The argument of this book is based on the idea that the Hong Kong colonial regime after 1945 was an unusual kind of colonialism. This was a 'caretaker' regime without the usual driving certainties of self-determination and independence, yet whose ruling elite managed to carve out a very substantial autonomy from their nominal London masters. The very uncertainties and ambiguities of that system allowed an 'interstitial space' to form, within which both native Hongkongers and expatriates could participate in the shared creation of identity in the built environment – a process of identity formation within which public housing played an ever more central role.[18] This role underwent a succession of fundamental transformations, partly reflecting the self-protective instincts of late colonialism, from the containment of unrest in the 1950s and '60s, and the self-legitimising promotion of civic pride in the '70s, to its absorption into capitalist globalisation in the 1980s and '90s. The result, arguably, was a far more variegated landscape of public housing, both organisationally and architecturally, than Singapore's coordinated homogeneity – its bold outcrops of soaring towers vividly reflecting Hong Kong's turbulent post-War history.

Secondly, public housing also reflected the more specific internal politics of Hong Kong. Up until the 1980s, the role of public housing as a vehicle for collective identity and pride was highlighted by the strong ruling-elite consensus against 'democratisation', owing to Hong Kong's unique geopolitical position. Correspondingly, when a degree of political democracy then began to emerge, both before and after 1997, the prestige of public housing went into significant decline, partly as a simple counterbalancing reaction, and also as a result of the specific housing complaints that arose within the new and raucously critical climate of public discourse. Also new were some political interpretations of the role of public housing that began to emerge in the more polarised circumstances of the 2010s, including establishment claims that housing problems, rather than lack of democratic rights, were the true underlying cause of popular unrest. This book, with its explicitly housing-centric perspective, takes no position on the virtues of specific political ideologies or standpoints, instead treating phenomena such as the democracy movement, and its opponents, strictly as part of the cultural background to housing debates – especially in Chapters 12–14.

The third main theme of the book is the way that, alongside these political factors, the workings of the Hong Kong economy – as interpreted by government – also strongly shaped the housing programme. On the one hand, the territory's precarious position and the perceived paramount need to maintain 'business confidence' dictated a constant emphasis on the primacy of laissez-faire principles and the private sector. The arrangement of the book also reflects fundamental shifts within this capitalist economic context, from post-1945 export-led manufacturing to post-1980s global financial metropolis – in each case generating distinctive housing policies, beginning with the clearing of development land with Resettlement blocks from 1954. The role of housing was always seen as ancillary to capitalist needs in Hong Kong, unlike state-dominated Singapore. But the primacy attributed to the private sector was associated not with cut-throat competition and fragmentation but with the growth of a monopolistic cartel of speculative developers, whose power steadily increased in the last quarter of the century and culminated after 1997, allowing figures such as Li Ka-shing to exert an effective veto over public housing policy. Their influence culminated in the 2002 scrapping of the Home Ownership Scheme (Chapter 13), but was increasingly called into question during the late-2010s.

Fourthly, the organisation of public housing production is a constant theme of this volume. In parallel with the rise of the great private-sector tycoons, the public housing sector became organised on increasingly coordinated lines, especially in the 1970s – partly reflecting the shift from reactive containment policies to more comprehensive, planned visions. The focus of the book is on the process of housing development, not of management or resident experience (which would be another book in its own right), and hence topics such as rent levels or tenant eligibility criteria are only touched on when relevant to the organisation of production. Here, there was a radical shift from fragmented and privatised solutions, exemplified by the initial prominence of the philanthropic Housing Society, towards a coordinated government 'Housing Authority' structure typical of Anglophone countries – although preserving the normal British colonial division between

Housing and Public Works, and between both of these and the Lands Department. Although planning in Hong Kong was multi-headed in character, unlike the unitary programme of the Ministry of National Development in Singapore, in practice this did not significantly impede the development of the New Territories, whose New Towns were steered by multi-agency project teams. And the 1987 shift from ad-hoc 10-year housing drives to a permanent, onward-rolling Long Term Housing Strategy (Chapter 10) allowed a similar coordinated approach to be applied to a vast redevelopment programme of early public housing estates in urban Hong Kong and Kowloon. Throughout our entire period, however, acute shortage of housing development land exerted a constant constraint on decision-making, and a stimulus to ever more dramatically compressed built landscapes, very different from the orderly yet undeniably less exciting 'precincts' of the Housing and Development Board (HDB) in Singapore.

The role of home ownership as an ideology and a cultural 'hope mechanism' (Chung-kin Tsang) is a more specific theme, linked both to the expansion of governmental vision into the field of identity, and to the growth of the real-estate sector. The cult of home ownership took hold in Hong Kong rather later than in the main Anglophone countries, especially the United States, England and Australia, but it made up for that late start in the passionate enthusiasm with which the public embraced it, and the way in which it was bound up with speculative profit-making from the beginning. Shared with many Anglophone countries, and with Singapore, was the integration of state-promoted home ownership into public policy. The polarisation between rental and home ownership contrasted strongly with the prevalence of 'third-sector' systems in Western European countries, especially Scandinavia, Germany and the Low Countries. Although Hong Kong's Home Ownership Scheme (HOS – Chapter 7) had a more uncertain status than its Singapore antecedent, being constantly accused of trespassing on private-sector territory, that was nothing to the outright marginalisation of any real 'third-sector' solutions in the face of the public-housing juggernaut. As a result, this book's coverage of the Hong Kong Housing Society, and other philanthropic interventions – with their semi-detached, rather marginal relationship to strictly defined 'public housing' – has necessarily had to be relatively cursory.

Finally, in the built form, or architecture, of the public housing programme, a key role was played by the British-style preference for standard block-types. The initially two distinct streams of resettlement/Public Works Department and Housing Authority were integrated after 1973, and the design emphasis shifted from slab blocks to spectacularly verticalised towers – culminating in the renowned 'Harmony' series, designed from 1987 and the special focus of Chapter 11 – and then finally to a 'site-specific' approach. Within the blocks, there was an inexorable shift from basic serviced shelter-spaces to self-contained flats with domestic conveniences, a shift led by the Housing Authority (pre- and post-1973) and Housing Society, and with a particular stress on expansion in flat sizes and room numbers under the post-1976 Home Ownership Scheme. In building construction, the initially underdeveloped state of building technology in Hong Kong was reflected in the prevalence of crude in situ construction of even high slab blocks at least until the 1980s, and the shock effect of the '26 Blocks' concrete decay scandal that erupted in those years. It was that quality crisis, rather than just building capacity or speed issues, as in Europe, that lay behind the steady shift thereafter towards mechanised and then prefabricated construction, with use of precast slabs spreading in the 'Harmony era' from exterior cladding to the interior of the block, including significant elements such as bathroom pod units.

Rather like the Long-Term Housing Strategy that inspired the Harmony project (Chapter 10), these trends proved so enduring that they have continued undiminished to the present – another striking demonstration of the underlying organisational and cultural continuities of Hong Kong's autonomous mass-housing system, continuities that preclude any attempt to polarise the mass housing story between a heroic late-colonial 'golden age' and a disillusioned present. In Part 1 of this book, we trace the first, halting steps taken in the early 1950s towards the establishment of that globally unique system.

Notes

1 M Glendinning, *The Conservation Movement – A History of Architectural Preservation*, Routledge, London, 2013, 147; George Dehio, *Denkmalschutz under Denkmalpflege im 19. Jahrhundert*, 1905 (courtesy of Jonathan Blower)

2 S N Eisenstadt, 'Multiple modernities', *Daedalus*, vol. 129, no. 1, Winter 2000, 1–29. Richard Evans, *In Defence of History,* Granta, London, 1997 (2001 edition), 291. Microecologies and microregions in ancient history: Peregrine Horden and Nicholas Purcell, *The Corrupting Sea: A Study of Mediterranean History*, Blackwell, Oxford, 2, 64, 78–80 (microregions and 'la trame du monde'), 464, 523, 548–9.

3 Eisenstadt, 'Multiple modernities', 2. Greg Castillo, *Cold War on the Home Front*, University of Minnesota Press, Minneapolis, 2010; Etienne Balibar and Immanuel Wallerstein, *Race, Nation, Class*, Verso, New York, 1991. Y Allweil, 'Nation-Building in Israel', in K Kılınç and M Gharipour, *Social Housing in the Middle East*, Indiana University Press, Bloomington, 2019, 144.

4 M Glendinning, *Mass Housing, Modern Architecture and State Power – a Global History*, Bloomsbury, London, 2021, 141–2.

5 Glendinning, *Mass Housing, 20,* 83, 171, 180, 270, 306–8. Jim Yelling, 'The incidence of slum-clearance in England and Wales', *Urban History*, 27:2, August 2000, 234–54.

6 S-M Shih, *The Lure of the Modern,* Berkeley, University of California Press, 2001, 3-4. D C Engerman and C R Unger, 'Introduction: towards a global history of modernization', *Diplomatic History*, 33:3, June 2009, 375–85.

7 Glendinning, *Mass Housing,* 442; Carmen Tsui, 'Minimum government assistance – planning cottage resettlement areas in post-war Hong Kong', *Planning Perspectives*, 38:6, 2023, 1257–80.

8 Helen Davidson, 'New Hong Kong textbooks will claim city never was a British colony', *Guardian,* 15-6-2022, online edition (consulted 11-1-2023). Given the general recognition today that any sort of colonialism or imperialism, past or present, is an intrinsically illegitimate phenomenon, invariably resting on violence and the 'right of the stronger', the argument that Hong Kong was not a colony potentially carries the implication that no colonies can ever have existed anywhere in the world, whether in 20th-century Asia, 19th-century Africa, or 5th-century BC Greece.

9 D Drakakis-Smith, *High Society – Housing Provision in Metropolitan Hong Kong*, University of Hong Kong, 1979, 1–22.

10 T Bennett and P Joyce (eds), *Material Powers: Cultural Studies, History and the Material Turn*, Routledge, London, 2010; C Tilley, W Keane, S Küchler, M Rowlands, P Spyer (eds), *Handbook of Material Culture*, Sage, London, 2013.

11 An approach exemplified in Castells, Goh and Kwok's authoritative *Shek Kip Mei Syndrome* (1990 – a comparison with Singapore), but also in articles such as by Kockelkorn et al (2023): see full references in Bibliography. See also R Forrest and N Yip, 'The future for reluctant intervention: the prospects for Hong Kong's public rental sector', *Housing Studies*, 2014, 9:4, 551–65.

12 E.g. S Tsang's *Governing Hong Kong* (2007), Monnery's *Architect of Prosperity* (2017), Ure's *Governors, Politics and the Colonial Office* (2012), Goodstadt's *Uneasy Partners* (2005) or Scott's *Political Change and the Crisis of Legitimacy in Hong Kong* (1999): see Bibliography. 'Auto-decolonisation': C-K Mark, 'Development without Decolonisation? Hong Kong's future and relations with Britain and China 1969–1972', *Journal of the Royal Asiatic Society*, 24:2, April 2014, 327.

13 General histories of Hong Kong: see e.g. Tsang's *Modern History of Hong Kong* (2004). Overview memoir-style accounts: Patten's *Hong Kong Diaries* (2022) or Dimbleby's *The Last Governor* (1997). More recent 'unrest studies' or books covering the 2010s 'democracy debate': e.g. Cheung's *Hong Kong's Watershed* (2009); Bickers and Yep's *May Days in Hong Kong (2009)* on the 1966-7 riots; Ho-fung Hung's *City on the Edge* (2022); Fong and Lui's *Hong Kong 20 Years after the Handover* (2018); Ng and Wong's *Civil Unrest and Governance in Hong Kong* (2017): see Bibliography.

14 Policy-orientated accounts of housing, factual or critical: see e.g. Pryor's *Housing in Hong Kong* (1983); D Drakakis-Smith's *High Society* (1979); J Lee's *Housing, Home Ownership and Social Change in Hong Kong* (1999); Nissim's *Land Administration and Practice in Hong Kong* (2021 edition); Richard Wong's *Hong Kong Land for Hong Kong People* (2015); Poon's *Land and the Ruling Class in Hong Kong* (2011); Brown and Loh's *Hong Kong– the Political Economy of Land* (2002); Chung-kin Tsang's *Homeownership in Hong Kong* (2021). Memoirs and reminiscences: e.g. Akers-Jones's *Feeling the Stones* (2004); Elsie Tu's 2003 *Colonial Hong Kong in the Eyes of Elsie Tu*; or collections of reminiscences of diverse actors such as Blyth & Wotherspoon's *Hong Kong Remembers* (1996): see Bibliography.

15 Y M Yeung and T K Y Wong (eds), *Fifty Years of Public Housing in Hong Kong – A Golden Jubilee Review and Appraisal*, HKHA, Hong Kong, 2003; see also the annual reviews of the Housing Authority or Housing Society, and occasional compendia such as the HA's 2010 *Planning, Design and Delivery of Quality Public Housing in the New Millennium*.

16 Recent examples include Cecilia Chu's *Building Colonial Hong Kong, Speculative Development and Segregation in the City* (2022); Rosman Wai's *Design DNA of Mark I, Hong Kong's Public Housing Prototype* (2019); Smart's *Shek Kip Mei Myth* (2006), which focuses on the specific discourse of squatter fires and outcomes of resettlement; or the 2016 special housing-themed journal issue of the Hong Kong Institute of Architects, *Occupy Housing*: see Bibliography.

17 Chan Yuen-ying, 'The English-language media in Hong Kong', in Kingsley Bolton (ed), *Hong Kong English – Autonomy and Creativity*, HKUP 2002, 101–16.

18 Caretaker imperialism' B C H Fong, T L Lui (eds) *Hong Kong 20 Years after the Handover*, Palgrave Macmillan, London 2018, 238.

Part I

Towards a public housing drive

1 1945–1953

Laying the foundations

Politics and geo-politics in the early postwar years

A central theme of this book is that public housing has served as a key vehicle for the repeated attempts by successive government administrations to construct or reconstruct collective identity within modern Hong Kong – efforts structured both by the external dynamic of protracted decolonisation, and by the internal tension between free-trade capitalism and government intervention.[1] Part I of this book traces how this role emerged after World War II, gradually and hesitantly at first, but rapidly gathering pace in the flurry of innovation around the Shek Kip Mei squatter fire of December 1953 – a period when its main role was to protect the colonial regime from demographic pressures and help build up a new structure of export-orientated industry.[2] This chapter, however, covers the period immediately before that: the mid and late 1940s, the period of British military administration in 1945–6, led by D M MacDougall, and the governorships of Mark Young from May 1946 to 1947 (retaining MacDougall as colonial secretary), and Alexander Grantham from 1947 to 1957 – the years in which Hong Kong transformed from entrepot city to Cold-War border outpost.[3] In those years, although the steep rise in Hong Kong's population, from 1.6 million in 1946 to 2.4 million in 1950, was already laying the groundwork for a future radical change in attitudes, before 1950 housing was not yet a central or existential concern of government.[4]

Against the backdrop of suspicion from China's nationalist government prior to its Civil War defeat, and the continuing permeability of the mainland border and the temporary residence patterns of many immigrants, MacDougall and Young embarked on a high-profile reformist initiative aimed at fostering a sense of Hong Kong identity, but confined to the area of political representation, with little effort devoted to social reconstruction as such: there was no attempt to echo the contemporary British welfare state, although a building reconstruction advisory committee set up in April 1946 by the British military administration clearly pointed towards some reformist efforts in the built environment.[5] Young's main concern was to establish what he termed a 'diarchy' under which the central government and secretariat would share power with an elected 'super municipal council', to give the permanent inhabitants of Hong Kong 'a fuller and more responsible share in the management of their own affairs'.[6] However, the initiative was doomed not just by

DOI: 10.1201/9781315563701-2

its complexity and by general public apathy, but by the likelihood that any elected 'democracy' in Hong Kong at that stage would degenerate into a 'political cockpit' of fighting between Kuomintang and communist sympathisers.[7]

On the accession to the governorship of the more cautious Grantham, a career colonial administrator who had previously served as Governor of Fiji, the threat to the Legislative Council (LegCo) posed by Young's 'ill-thought-out proposals' (Akers-Jones) prompted their rapid abandonment.[8] Instead, a more cautious policy of tinkering around the edges was adopted, badged as a constructive partnership with existing local institutions, including in particular the Urban Council.[9] Within this framework, as we will see, both Grantham's administration and the unofficials showed no interest in formulating any kind of coherent housing policy, as before 1948 the great waves of permanent refugees were yet to come. Housing was still seen as an exclusively private-sector responsibility, more like 19th-century Britain than the contemporary Britain of mass municipal-built 'council housing'. Michael Wright, the longstanding chief government architect within the PWD (and later its director) recollected that 'the government didn't really want to know about it'.[10] Laissez-faire Hong Kong was already striking out in a different direction from Singapore, where the Singapore Improvement Trust was integrating planning and housing strategy in a way unmatched in any other colonial territory – a dirigiste approach that would be perpetuated and hugely expanded by the post-1959 government of Lee Kuan Yew.[11]

The beginnings of decolonisation

While the 1945 restoration of British control of Hong Kong – in the face of counter-manoeuvres by the Chinese Nationalist government – represented on the face of it a successful reassertion of the colonial status quo, not unlike the 'restoration' aftermath of the 1814–15 Council of Vienna, it was accompanied by significant harbingers of change, and mounting challenges of containment. The 1941–2 debacle had destroyed any notion of British control through military power in eastern Asia, and the Hong Kong Planning Unit, established 1943 in London, and headed from 1944 by David MacDougall, argued that Britain could only convincingly re-establish its presence in Hong Kong if significant political and social reform were attempted.[12]

Within Hong Kong society as a whole, the turbulent earlier decades had already witnessed an upsurge in trade-union militancy, linked to the sovereignty question and the interwar rise in Chinese nationalism, especially in the strikes of 1920–2, the 1925–6 general strike orchestrated by the Kuomintang and the CCP, and the 1948 riots over the perennially controversial status of the Kowloon Walled City.[13] And the wartime Colonial Development and Welfare (CDW) Bill of 1940 had begun to provide funds for modernisation schemes in 'all parts of the Colonial Empire', with a CDW Committee and Fund later established in Hong Kong.[14] Any corresponding shifts in the configuration of Hong Kong government administration, however, were only gradual. This remained dominated by the 'cadet' elite of administrators, a system established in 1862 and ultimately stretching back before then to the British East India Company, whose 'intense conservatism', Gavin Ure argued, resembled the Chinese imperial system in its strong 'bureaucratic autonomy'.[15] The cadets' generalist orientation gave them great versatility: in the words of Ian Lightbody (later Secretary for Housing), 'whenever we got a big new problem in Hong Kong, we always put in one of my service to get it going – a very sound decision'.[16] But they were also increasingly criticised, for example by liberal reformists such as Bishop Hall (in 1942), as 'parochial'.[17] Their relationship to the new professional class of technical experts was uneasy. Michael Wright argued that they still remained on top in the traditional government system: 'The cadets were the thoroughbreds, the racehorses, of the Colonial Service', while 'the professional officers were the carthorses'. Yet their 'mystique' was increasingly challenged by modernisation: the cadets 'all could be experts in everything, but knew about nothing'.[18] (Figure 1.1)

The military administration regime of MacDougall had also begun to challenge the ingrained racism in the system, in the beginnings of a shift towards so-called 'localisation' in the government service, and among the 'unofficials' who played a growing role in LegCo and the Urban Council, established in 1935 as a successor to the Sanitary Board.[19] Under Young, that shift gathered pace a little: in a May 1947 speech, for example, Sir Man Kam Lo hailed the vision of what 'self-government' would bring.[20]

With Grantham's abandonment of Young's municipalisation strategy and any conception of universal suffrage, the Urban Council took on, by default, an uncertain role as a surrogate 'opposition' force, including high-profile public figures such as lawyer Brook Bernacchi, and Hong Kong's closest to a reform 'firebrand', Elsie Elliott.[21] It was chaired ex-officio by the head of the Department of Urban Services – from 1950, Kenneth Barnett (see below).[22] The cadet elite regarded Urban Council members with derision, as seen in the recollections of a middle-ranking administrator, George Rowe: Bernacchi

Figure 1.1 Michael Wright, seen in 2015, aged 105, in his Kensington flat. (MG).

simply got this mistaken idea he was God's gift to parliamentary opposition – he was simply a chap who wanted to make a name and shout about it. I doubt his good intentions, I really do. They were solely concerned to make a public criticism and they were really dreadful – they often didn't even trouble to find out what was being done before they got up to shout about it'.[23]

Likewise, any suggestion that the Reform Club and Civic Association (also dominated by Bernacchi) played a constructive role was dismissed by Rowe: 'That's a barmy statement. Their contribution was nil. They were a bloody awful block in the way of anything getting done'.[24]

David Akers-Jones, a leading administrative innovator in later years, more thoughtfully argued that the Reform Club and Civic Association valiantly 'tried to excite an indifferent electorate'.[25] Yet as we will see later, the contribution of the Urban Council and the unofficials to housing policy, in the early 1950s, increasingly gained in prominence, and became bound up with pressure for establishment of a 'Housing Authority' charged with building low-income housing, and with the parallel, but far more dramatically growing crisis of the mushrooming refugee squatters from 1948 onwards.[26] In both of these issues, as we will see – despite its constant disparagement by the cadet elite – the Council initially intervened with surprising success, laying the groundwork for prominent unofficial contributions to the Authority, which continued even after radical reforms in 1973 and 1988.

In economic terms, the postwar picture was again initially one of return to tradition, including the ingrained polarisation between rich and poor, with an 'almost non-existent' middle class in between, and a rapid return to financial self-sufficiency and surplus from 1947–8.[27] Under the regime of financial secretary Sir Geoffrey Follows, while Hong Kong followed the 1948 system of London financial controls 'to the letter', a repeated pattern began to emerge of Hong Kong governments fending off pressure from London administrations (especially if Labour-controlled) to converge with British-style welfare-state and social-service provisions.[28] But while Hong Kong determinedly stuck with laissez-faire, the latter was itself now moving with the times. The cutting-off of mainland China after the revolution, and the later imposition of economic sanctions at US instigation, terminated Hong Kong's traditional role as an entrepot economy. Instead, a shift to a manufacturing-based economy was heralded by the unexpected, massed transfer of textile machinery and manufacturing from Shanghai in 1949 by manufacturers such as C C Lee or P Y Tang: they resourcefully moved key personnel and diverted new machinery on order and already at sea to Hong Kong. It soon became clear that the old port-based commercial areas were no longer sufficient, and that land for industrial development would now be at a premium – not least because of the mass influxes of refugees, and concomitant invasions of potential development land by squatters.[29]

In these years, housing, far from the central and burning concern of the Hong Kong Government that it became by the 1970s, was only one of many social policy areas in which Hong Kong was under pressure from London governments. In housing, the pattern in the first five post-war years was of cajoling from London and reluctance and policy deadlock in Hong Kong – the cajoling being initially transmitted via the Anglican Bishop Hall.[30] In December 1949, Arthur Creech-Jones, Secretary of State for the Colonies, following an intervention by the Archbishop of Canterbury, asked exasperatedly, 'Am I right in assuming that there is no social policy in Hong Kong at all? The housing policy seems non-existent. Why has the Department allowed this drift to go on?'[31] From Governor Grantham's perspective, however, the picture seemed very different. To him, the Colonial Office permanent officials recalled 'the words of a popular song, "Little man, you've had a busy day!" – I always thought that should have been written up over the portals of the Colonial Office. They did work terribly hard, but they didn't understand Hong Kong's problems.'[32] Creech-Jones, he felt, 'meant very well and was kindly, but I think he was held in very little esteem by his Prime Minister, Clement Attlee'. And in any case Hong Kong was considered 'very small beer' in Whitehall, in comparison for instance to Malaya.[33] By June 1950, the Colonial Office's attitude was mellowing, and Creech-Jones's successor, Griffiths, instructed Grantham to establish a 'housing authority', tasked with 'the preparation and execution of a programme of housebuilding, and the management of low-cost housing'. However, as we will see, it took a long time to agree what form that 'housing authority' should take.[34]

Planning and slum clearance in Hong Kong – a prehistory

If housing was far from the forefront of the attention of the Hong Kong government in the immediate postwar years, the same could even more be said of 'planning' – an activity that would later vitally underpin housing construction in the massive development programmes from the 1970s. From the beginning of the colonial history of Hong Kong, a laissez-faire land-use system was assumed to apply, although in the original urban areas of Hong Kong Island and Kowloon, an 1844 Ordinance allowed 'resumption' of land for public purposes.[35] In the New Territories, as we will see, the entrenched rights of indigenous occupants and villagers would require a more cautious, negotiated approach, mainly through the agency of the Heung Yee Kuk, a British-managed association of local leaders.[36]

This system's potential sensitivity to emergency pressures had been demonstrated at the turn of the century, when Hong Kong, then containing a population of 210,000, found itself in 1894 an epicentre of a significant bubonic plague pandemic. In the 1840s, immediately following the colonial government's establishment, serious malaria outbreaks had established a popular association between high densities and diseased 'miasmas'; but the 1890s plague crisis was of a different order of magnitude altogether. By the late 19th century, despite their low-rise configuration, the typical colonial system of shop-houses was already generating significantly high densities.[37] A pair of reports prepared in 1882 and 1902 by Osbert Chadwick, son of the famous reformer Edwin Chadwick, laid the groundwork for a 1903 Public Health and Buildings Ordinance. This brought significant reforms to the urban core. Rear lanes were opened up in the dense fabric, and limits on the depth and height of individual developments were imposed. In the densest district, Taipingshan, a more

Figure 1.2 (a) View of Taipingshan *c.* 1869, prior to the 1894 resumptions. (b) Aerial view of Western District immediately after World War II.

ambitious blanket redevelopment was attempted. An 1894 Resumption Ordinance, and a 1894–5 executed scheme, involved resumption of 6.2 acres from private owners and demolition of 400,000 sq ft; land available for private development was reduced from 272,000 sq ft to 97,000, and a standard of 21 sq ft living-space per person was imposed for new development.[38] (Figure 1.2a,b)

In the early 20th century, reflecting the parallel movements within Britain of garden-city planning on the urban periphery and slum clearance in central areas, renewed initiatives in urban and suburban planning were attempted in Hong Kong. Following the 1898 New Territories lease, a huge extension area became available within Kowloon, and attracted efforts at zoning and layout plans, especially following the government's 1922 formation of a committee to facilitate urban-extension schemes. This policy culminated in promulgation of a town planning ordinance in 1939. Individual schemes included a garden suburb at Kowloon Tong (from 1922),[39] and some reflected racial zoning principles, including garden-suburbs for Europeans and wealthy Chinese at Kadoorie Estate and for Portuguese at Kowloon Tong, and middle-class Chinese at Kowloon Bay.[40] Commercial firms also made tentative efforts at 'improved' workers' housing, notably in projects built between 1883 and the 1930s by Butterfield & Swire for the Taikoo Sugar Refinery at Quarry Bay, in ventilated fireproof construction.[41]

Paralleling this, slum clearance and sub-standard housing in the existing urban core were addressed by a Housing Commission, headed by secretary Wilfred Owen. (Figure 1.3) Owen's initial report in 1935 suggested the government should establish a Town Planning and Housing Committee, and finance slum clearance and upgrading of substandard housing. However, with the influx of war refugees from 1937, 'like so many reports, [it] had been shoved away and forgotten!'[42] Also overtaken by war were the 1939 Town Planning Committee and Ordinance, and Owen's second report in 1940 (the Report on Town Planning and Housing). This suggested population redistribution into the New Territories, and the combining of planning and housing into a single organisation, preferably a Trust modelled on the post-1927 operations of the Singapore Improvement Trust.[43] This was the first

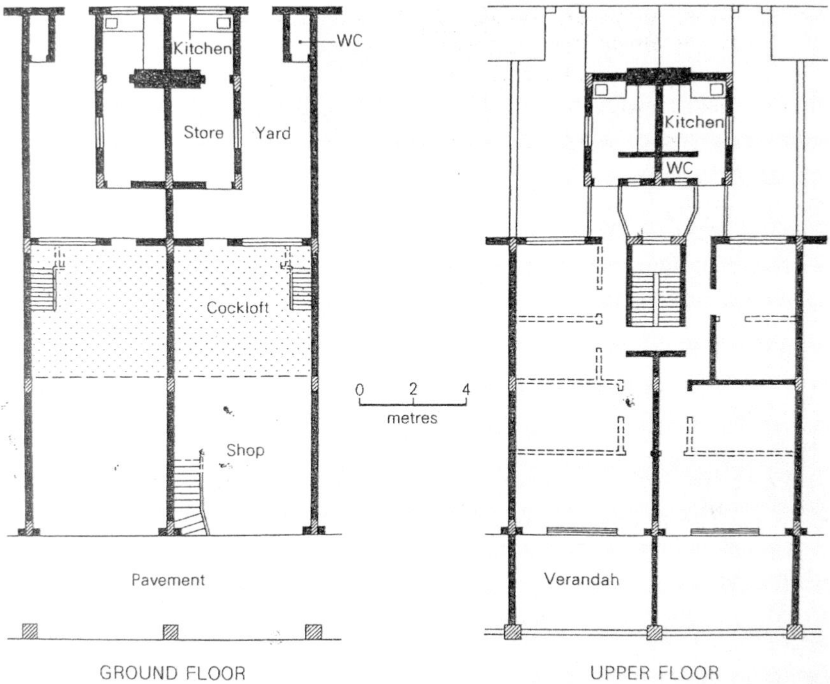

Figure 1.3 Floor-plan of typical tenement block, reproduced in the 1935 Owen Report, showing verticalised density and intermingling of residential and commercial uses.

time that this double policy recipe – planned expansion into the New Territories, coupled with unification of government planning and mass housing – was proposed as a formal agenda. And it would not be the last – until this 'pincer strategy' was finally implemented in the 1970s under the reformist regime of Governor Sir Murray MacLehose.

At first glance, unlike Britain and Western Europe, World War II did not decisively boost the planning reconstruction cause: the work of MacDougall's Hong Kong Planning Unit from 1943/4 was concerned with a broader politico-social agenda of re-establishment of colonial legitimacy via 'development'.[44] Owen, brought back to Hong Kong in January 1947, drafted a Development Ordinance that reiterated the need for a public housing 'Trust', citing the recent British precedents of the Uthwatt Committee on land betterment and the Town Planning Bill (later the 1947 Act). Later that year the *Times* urged a 5–10 -ear development programme for the colony.[45]

These pressures resulted in one outcome in Hong Kong that significantly echoed the British planning approach: the 1947 appointment of planning doyen Sir Patrick Abercrombie, author of countless city and regional reconstruction plans within

Britain, to prepare a planning report on the territory.[46] Abercrombie was a strong defender of population decentralisation away from 'overcrowded' old cities to planned, self-contained 'new towns', coupled with radical redevelopment of the old 'slum' areas. This modernist update of the Ebenezer Howard turn-of-century philosophy had recently been enshrined in his own 1944 Greater London Plan and given significant national policy backing in the 1946 New Towns Act. Hong Kong, even before the post-1948 influx of refugees, might well have seemed a suitable, albeit challenging, setting in which to apply this concept. Abercrombie's Preliminary Planning Report, submitted in 1948, enthusiastically endorsed Owen's 1947 proposals and suggested they should form the basis of a strategic blueprint, combining a satellite-town programme in the New Territories with curbs on net densities in any redevelopment areas in the urban core. He proposed reductions from the prevalent 2,000 persons per acre (ppa) to only 500, and 285 maximum in new development areas – although the latter was itself far above anything considered acceptable in Britain.[47]

By 1949–50, however, Abercrombie's proposals for Hong Kong had been comprehensively vitiated, by a combination of the vast refugee influxes in 1948–9 and the economic consequences of sharply increased defence spending in 1950 following the outbreak of the Korean War. The claim of the *China Mail* in May 1949 that 'the time is now ripe for town planning in Hong Kong' now seemed distinctly inopportune. Wright argued that Abercrombie's report 'was out of date before it was finished'.[48] Additionally, the assumed primacy of private property interests undermined any proposals for strategic controls. A January 1950 meeting presided over by Grantham decided nothing could be spent on town planning, and that as low-income housing was such 'a formidable question', it 'had not been possible to make much headway' on it either.[49] Wright recalled that

> until 1954 the Government didn't want to get involved with housing the masses. I remember Sir Alexander Grantham's catchphrase was, "We must have maximum development everywhere in order to house these people" – and so the Building Ordinance was rewritten and reliance was put on private enterprise. This was quite wrong – it led to the dreadful tenements that were built in the early 1950s. But the Government didn't really want to know about it. And then luckily, they had the Shek Kip Mei fire in Christmas 1953, and then the Government had to do something to rehouse the fire victims.[50]

Abercrombie's Hong Kong exercise left in its wake an unintended staffing legacy, in the form of three Town Planning Officers who had been engaged for a three-year follow-up contract within the Public Works Department. Wright recalled the story at length, including the unexpected role played by the influential colonial housing-planning adviser George Atkinson, an indefatigable proselytiser of 'enlightened modernist' solutions:

> Atkinson had an odd sort of job, he was at the Building Research Station, and was Colonial Representative – he used to come out sometimes, but he never got

> involved in design work. The one useful thing he did do was, in the immediate post-war years, in the aftermath of Abercrombie's plan, when three planners came out for three years: Molloy, Fraser and Darke. The Hong Kong government were too down-to-earth to be concerned about the Abercrombie plan, and they decided to shelve it. But what were they to do about Messrs. Molloy, Fraser and Darke? Darke, who was a town planner only, was made redundant – he camped on the cricket court in the park by the Supreme Court, but he was forcibly ejected from Hong Kong eventually. Molloy and Fraser, who were both town planners and architects, joined the architects' department, where they worked on police stations in the New Territories. Then their town planning department was shut down. Then Atkinson came out, and we said, "We still need a town planning department!" He very sensibly advised we should put it into the Crown Lands Office. Then we got a couple of planners: one of them was Hadland, who had less grandiose ideas then Abercrombie had had.[51]

The involvement of Atkinson was intended to correct not just an administrative anomaly, but a potential source of political embarrassment. In November 1950, following the trio's departure, Follows had minuted Colonial Secretary John Nicoll that the accidental inclusion of Town Planning Officer salaries in the C D & W Estimates risked implying readiness to embark on town-planning schemes requiring costly resumptions. In his view, city planning was a hare-brained mirage associated mainly with dictators: 'Large-scale planning of a big city which has been allowed to grow up anyhow has always proved to be impracticable. Hitler tried it in Berlin and failed, even with his immense resources'.[52] A year later, the can was kicked further down the road, with a decision to defer the question of town planning until Atkinson's next visit. Atkinson's pragmatic solution of re-establishing planning, but in the practical setting of the CLO, proved surprisingly enduring: 'It was quite a good idea, to ensure that the Crown Lands Office disposed of land sensibly'.[53]

From planning to housing reform

The legacy of Abercrombie also included further impetus towards addressing the worsening problem of poor housing. In November 1949, a minute from the chairman of the C D & W Committee to Nicoll reported on post-Abercrombie discussions with Bishop Hall and Father Ryan about a potential 'housing scheme'.[54] Compared with the grandiose planning schemes, low-income housing seemed more prosaic and low-key in those years, with relatively little sense of the moral panic that would begin to swirl around it after the explosion in refugee squatting in 1948–9. The Hong Kong government prioritised laissez-faire housing not least because it was financially dependent on the revenues from private sector land sales.[55] The only significant exception to this approach was the policy of rent control, first introduced in 1921 with considerable political support – albeit opposed by Sir Paul Chater – and renewed in 1945.[56]

Despite his reformist leanings, Young made little headway in housing. A Housing Committee was appointed in 1950 under the chairmanship of W J

Carrie, and later George Rowe.[57] But in April 1946, following the report of the Building Reconstruction Advisory Committee, Young bemoaned lack of finance and housing supply, as preventing decisive action. The policy vacuum was filled by unofficials such as Sir Man Kam Lo, who in May 1946 requested a government LegCo policy statement on the housing problem.[58] In June/July 1947, during the interregnum between Young and Grantham, acting Colonial Secretary Todd argued that the government was 'deeply conscious of its obligations to the citizens of this colony in the present prolonged housing crisis' and might respond by building low-income housing 'on a large scale, uneconomic as that might be'.[59] In response, in a July 1947 LegCo meeting, enraged unofficials called on the government to treat the housing issue as 'one of utmost urgency', arguing that far from being conscious of its housing obligations, the government was, 'in fact, not conscious of them at all'.[60] The period between this LegCo debate and McDougall's eventual departure in 1949 saw little progress.[61] An initial proposal for low-income private-sector housing ran into distrustful opposition from the Colonial Office, which in January 1948 refused to commit the funds necessary to support it.[62]

Squatters and resettlement

The main reason why housing shot into prominence in the following years, however, had very little to do with this conventional reformist discourse of 'fighting the slums' and 'combating bad housing', and everything to do with a far more urgent, overriding crisis – the explosion of squatters in 1948–9, from around 200,000 to around 300,000 in a single year, and more subsequently.[63]

As Grantham later recalled, 'previously refugees had come swarming in. But the moment the trouble was over they had gone swarming back to China, and the Hong Kong Government had done nothing about them – for the simple reason that if they had done something about them, given them free food and free lodging, hundreds of thousands would have come swarming in'. Now, however, 'they wouldn't go streaming back again, they didn't want to go back to China and there was nowhere else they could go'. In response, 'probably we waited too long in seizing the nettle, in realising that we had to accept these people within Hong Kong and do our best to absorb them into the community'.[64] But the refugees posed a more urgent challenge than that of galvanising collective loyalty: the 'stacks and stacks of squatter villages all around the city, almost to a certain extent blocking the roads', were sterilising swathes of developable land that would be vital to support the ongoing turn from entrepot trade to manufacturing: thus only 30 acres of land were freed up between 1945 and 1954.[65] The political overtones of the problem became clear in January 1948 when tentative efforts began to evict squatters from the Kowloon Walled City, the results being riots not only in Hong Kong but also in Shanghai and Canton: a report by an Urban Council committee, commissioned by MacDougall, suggested responding with 'a short term policy of gradual attrition followed up by measures to ensure that sites once cleared are kept cleared', backed up by potential building of government-subsidised private four-storey flats.[66]

The response that rapidly began to emerge for this complex problem was known under the shorthand term: ‘resettlement’. This was initially just an umbrella term that covered a wide range of physical and organisational solutions and agencies, and aimed purely at containment of the problem.[67] The first phase, in 1948–50, saw a successful programme of clearance in the main urban area, linked with government-organised displacement to aided self-help cottage resettlement areas such as Homantin (1950). Initially, in the less extreme immigration conditions of 1948–9, a significant impact was made by private welfare organisations, which set up cottage resettlement sites for specific refugee groups or cleared squatters.[68] In this first phase the resettlement programme seemed surprisingly effective: by the end of 1949, 45,000 dwellings had been cleared. But during that year the number of squatters soared to 330,000, far outstripping the clearance rate, with an overall tenfold increase over three years.[69]

Thus the second phase of resettlement, from 1950 to 1953, was very different, as it vainly attempted to extend the containment and aided self-help cottage-building policy to cope with far more extreme circumstances.[70] Initially, the central figure in this confused situation was another, far-more-senior cadet, Kenneth M A Barnett, appointed Director of Urban Services in 1950 and thus ex-officio chair of the Urban Council.[71] His reign was later characterised by Leo Goodstadt as one of ‘bureaucratic bungling’.[72] His first efforts, during 1950, simply attempted to ‘persuade new arrivals to leave the colony by making them as uncomfortable as possible. Having driven squatters to the outskirts of the urban area, to try to pen them in still closer and again to make them as uncomfortable as possible.’ But the lack of economic prospects back in China meant that this was a vain hope, and meantime the fire and public health risks mounted, and development land was swamped by new arrivals.[73] Chief Assistant Social Welfare Officer David Alexander recalled suggesting, perhaps jokingly, to firefighters after one Kowloon fire, ‘“Have you any matches? Any huts left? Give me some matches!” But they wouldn’t do so. I felt there was no point in leaving a few more huts to set fire to later on’.[74]

The erratic development of resettlement policy in 1950–3 is traced in detail in Smart and Ure’s books: however, the essentials are as follows.[75] Firstly, a report on squatting in April 1951 by cadet officer J T Wakefield recommended expanding the existing 1948 clearances policy to remove 210,000 squatters, bolstering it by gazetting the entire Hong Kong/Kowloon urban area.[76] There would be one ‘approved’ and one ‘tolerated’ area in both Kowloon and Hong Kong Island (including the ‘tolerated’ Ngau Tau Kok in Kowloon); from 1951, the USD set up a system of ‘Approved’ and ‘Tolerated’ Areas (i.e. cottage areas and re-site areas), approved by Executive Council (ExCo) resolution in January 1952. Wakefield also recommended establishing a ‘Housing Trust’ to accommodate government employees.[77]

Having successfully seen off the Young ‘super-municipal council’ proposal, the Urban Council naturally attempted to carve out a central role for itself by setting up an emergency executive committee dedicated to resettlement.[78] A leading role in these debates was played by the unofficials in the Council and the Reform Club, including Brook Bernacchi, and especially Douglas Clague: the latter’s most decisive contribution would, however, come following the December 1953

Shek Kip Mei fire, when the government policy vacuum allowed him to become an unofficial 'secretary for Resettlement'.[79] In these discussions, the Hong Kong professional interest was represented by the Public Works Department: architect George P Norton designed temporary huts and re-organised water supply.[80]

The result of these efforts, however, was a confused succession of conflicting initiatives and 'turf wars' that failed to impact decisively on the problem. In November 1952, Barnett admitted that only 7,000 of 23,000 planned resettlement huts had been completed.[81] The following year brought a growing storm of protests from unofficials and the Urban Council, but little improvement, despite numerous multi-agency meetings and memos, including some (e.g. a December 1952 minute from the Commissioner of Police) arguing for a slowing-down of clearances and use of 6–7-storey tenements instead of cottages. In the seven months ending November 1953, the number of successfully resettled squatters had only increased by 10,000 – from 35,000 to 45,000.[82] It was still unclear who was responsible – the Urban Council, its Resettlement Committee, or the government? The government's general reputation for competence was at stake, and Grantham had the awkward task of managing public expectations: he later acknowledged that 'probably we waited too long in seizing the nettle'. This impasse would only be resolved in 1954 following the Shek Kip Mei fire, as we will see, by the establishment of a dedicated Resettlement Department headed by a talented but junior cadet, Ronald Holmes, who 'rescued' the government from the consequences of its previous vacillations.[83]

It should be emphasised at this point that squatting and organised temporary resettlement in low-rise cottage-type developments is not specifically covered in this book, which is concerned exclusively with the 'permanent' housing programme – although many temporary settlements lasted far longer than planned, and there was some overlap in cases such as today's multi-storey 'transitional' or 'light' public housing (see Chapter 14). To be sure, the self-help cottage resettlement programme continued in operation right through the 1960s, in areas such as Choi Wan and Chuk Yuen and also, especially, in the New Territories, eventually housing over 87,000 settlers and with the last areas only finally cleared between 1988 and 2001. But the introduction of state-built high-density public rental housing, as we will see later, nevertheless represented a decisive change in the narrative of Hong Kong housing, both in terms of efficiency of land use and maximisation of output.[84]

Towards 'mainstream' low-cost housing: from Society to Authority

Alongside the dramatic and often chaotic debates about resettlement and squatting, the cause of mainstream low-income housing for the time being enjoyed a lower profile, and was propelled forward as much by external pressure from the Colonial Office as by demand within Hong Kong. The initial stage was a succession of proposals for the founding of philanthropic or indirectly state-supported housing societies.

First came a succession of cottage garden-suburb societies, partly inspired by an interwar mainland programme of 'common people's villages' (pingmin cun) sponsored by the Nationalist government from 1919 to 1936. These began in 1926 with a YMCA-sponsored model village in Shanghai (Pudong laogong xincun) and expanded after 1928 to villages in ten cities, organised by YMCA engineers.[85] After 1946, the government began granting land to the private sector, including philanthropic and Christian organisations, to build low-cost working-class housing. This measure stimulated construction of several dozen Christian villages from 1950, all single-storey cottages, for example the Methodist-built Asbury Village of 1962 at Tai Wo Hau.[86]

These villages often had a resettlement aspect, somewhat muddying the distinction from the self-help cottage resettlement sites mentioned above – an overlap that also applied to the succession of state-supported philanthropic societies that began in 1948 with proposals drawn up by Bishop Hall for the founding of a Hong Kong Housing Society. This was followed by the foundation of the Hong Kong Model Housing Society in 1950, the Hong Kong Settlers' Housing Corporation in 1952, and the Economic Building Society in 1954.[87] Originally, there was considerable overlap between the intended tasks of the Hong Kong Housing Society and the Hong Kong Model Housing Society. 1950 had seen the formation of W J Carrie's government-sponsored Housing Committee, to advise whether the remainder of C D & W funds earmarked for Hong Kong should be spent on emergency housing for the poor – one of its first acts being to report on a proposal by the Hong Kong Housing Society for barrack-like five-storey tenement blocks with communal kitchens and toilets (see below).[88] Increasingly, the idea began to emerge both within the Colonial Office in London, and within Hong Kong, that a coordinating 'authority' should be established under Hong Kong government auspices, to bring all these low-cost housing initiatives together. But there was no consensus what form that 'authority' should take, how it should be organised, and in particular what its relation should be to the Urban Council – especially considering the prevalent view in Britain, shaped by its internationally distinctive 'council' system of mass housing, that low-income housing was 'generally a municipal responsibility'. As late as 1953, the Financial Secretary, Arthur Clarke, vetoed any open-ended government housing construction, and instead suggested establishment of a semi-private 'Development and Housing Corporation'.[89]

A key role in this process of cajoling the reluctant Hong Kong government to take a more serious interest in general low-income housing was played not only by lobbying from unofficials within Hong Kong, and Bishop Hall,[90] but also by Colonial Office political pressure from London, and especially from the professional influence of Atkinson, who kept in close touch with the Public Works Department and leading administrators. A 1952 visit by Atkinson, while eliciting negative news on planning from the Colonial Secretary and from PWD chief T L Bowring – specifically, that Hong Kong was 'not interested in a further Report' from Abercrombie – also significantly helped push forward the agenda of the establishment of a 'housing authority', as we will see shortly.[91]

The Housing Society's first development after its 1948 formation was planned for a site at North Point, which was to be granted at nil premium, with loan finance from the Hong Kong and Shanghai Bank. However, when the bank, whose head personally disliked Hall, insisted on its contribution being

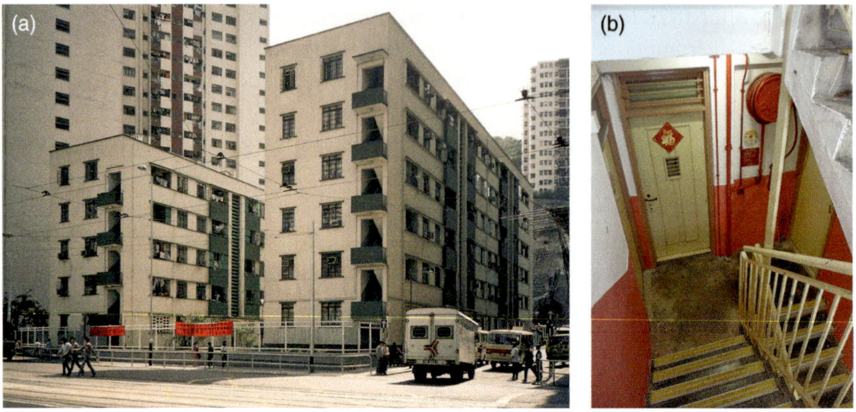

Figure 1.4 (a) The Hong Kong Model Housing Society's development at North Point: 1983 photo (MG) of the six-storey staircase-access tenements. (b) Internal view of the Model Estate, showing internal staircase-access plan: 2018 photo (MG).

ring-fenced, a different society, the Hong Kong Model Housing Society, was formed to develop the site instead, several years later, with six-storey staircase-access flats. (Figure 1.4a,b)

Eventually, the Hong Kong Housing Society began its own work with a small site of 270 flats at Sheung Li Uk.[92] Just as he would later act as a 'bureaucratic entrepreneur' in consolidating the Resettlement programme from 1954, Urban Councillor and entrepreneur Douglas Clague played a key role in the Housing Society's subsequent survival and growth: PWD chief architect Michael Wright argued that 'he deserved a lot of the credit for the Housing Society and for the Housing Society's influence on government' – he 'did his homework'.[93] Another small stand-alone organisation, the Hong Kong Settlers Housing Corporation, was the first of these efforts to run into terminal difficulties, in early 1952. In May of that year Barnett remarked that its troubles 'provided a skid mark to warn other vehicles': the HKSHC eventually built only one development, at Tai Hang Sai, as late as 1965–77 (see Chapter 8). 1952 saw equally convoluted discussions about the relationship between the Hong Kong Model Housing Society and the Hong Kong Housing Society.[94] All these initiatives continued to experience major difficulties in raising private finance, compared to the government's easy access to the C D & W Fund for squatter clearance.[95]

At one remove from the agonised worries concerning the escalating squatter crisis, discussion slowly gathered pace about the need for a government organisation that could act as a 'competent authority' to coordinate low-cost housing efforts in general. Here, the precedent of Singapore's Improvement Trust, with its coordinating responsibility for both planning and low-income housing, loomed constantly in the background. The first firm proposal approved by ExCo, in July 1951, following a December 1950 study visit to the SIT by Chief Resettlement Officer

Wakefield, explicitly envisaged the establishment of an 'Improvement Trust': later in 1951 another officer was sent to Singapore.[96]

However, following 1950–1 pressure from the Colonial Office to instead proceed down a 'housing-only' route, April 1952 saw discussions in Government House and ExCo that pointed towards establishment of a coordinating 'Housing Authority'. In August 1952, following the report of the Ad-hoc Committee on Housing, a small steering group chaired by Colonial Secretary (later Governor) Robert Black and including three unofficials, agreed to set up a 'Housing Authority' rather than a housing-planning Improvement Trust.[97] There was considerable debate about its powers and its relationship to the Urban Council, and whether it should oversee resettlement: Barnett warned that 'it would be extremely difficult to keep the Urban Council out of Housing'.[98] It was recommended by Black's committee that, on the British 'council housing' model, the UC should simply be vested as the new Housing Authority.[99] It was proposed that the Authority should take over all existing HKHS/HKMHS properties, but that the PWD would retain sole responsibility for erecting buildings.[100] Michael Wright argued to Bowring in July 1952 that a new 'Housing Division' would be required to support a programme of a thousand new low-cost flats a year.[101] But even in March 1953 the Financial Secretary was railing against 'Government Housing': to which Barnett acerbically responded that he 'hasn't been able to build up a case' against it, 'though given the opportunity by HE' – it was 'merely a "hunch"'.[102] Follows proposed as an alternative an arm's-length 'Development and Housing Corporation'.[103] However, both Follows and the UC Chairman rebuffed a 1953 proposal by R C Lee for a rival private-enterprise-based alternative to the Housing Authority.[104] In the event, though, it took Grantham three years to bring the Housing Authority proposal to fruition, as it was only finally implemented in 1954. Here, unlike resettlement, the relative lack of impetus meant that pressure from London was required all the time to nudge the government forward – a striking contrast to later years![105]

Towards an architecture of mass housing: garden suburbs and tenements

Today, with Hong Kong's status as one of the world's redoubts of very high-density, very high-rise housing, it is difficult to imagine a time, before the 1950s, when its housing was exclusively low-rise – and at a time when significant pioneering efforts in Modern Movement mass housing were underway elsewhere, not just in isolated pioneering projects, such as the Berlin schemes of Gropius or the Drancy project of slender, high towers, but in large-scale practical urban programmes directed by powerful specialist institutions.[106] Of these, among the earliest were the famous 'Red Vienna' programme mounted by the 1920s/early 30s social-democratic municipality, and the public rental programme of the New York City Housing Authority ('NYCHA') from 1935 onwards, rising to a climax in the early 1950s. Neither were of orthodox 'International Modern' architectural style, and they contrasted significantly – the Viennese programme comprising massive courtyard complexes inserted into large and small urban gap-sites, and NYCHA's housing comprising densely arrayed but architecturally utilitarian brick-clad towers and slabs scattered on irregular layouts very different from CIAM Zeilenbau.[107] But what they had in common was a focus on dense urban slum redevelopment rather than the spacious peripheral 'grands ensembles' and 'mikrorayons' that would characterise much post-1945 mass housing internationally.[108]

In 1940s and early 1950s Hong Kong, multi-storey flats of social housing in any shape or form remained unknown, even though the first towers of 'council housing' were already being built in staunchly pro-cottage England, especially by the London County Council from 1950.[109] Instead, the solutions adopted in Hong Kong remained faithful to more traditional British and European precedents, especially the low-rise garden suburb, as presaged in interwar planning schemes such as Kowloon Tong, and continued in the single-storey Christian villages of 1950 onwards; 1949 also saw proposals to build prefabricated caravan houses in the New Territories.[110] As late as 1952, low-density solutions still seemed possible: Barnett wrote to Black that the Urban Council and Housing Authority should not be confined to flats, and hopefully could build villas or bungalows eventually too.[111] The PWD architects were painfully aware the garden city model had now been replaced in Britain by the somewhat more modernist Mk I New Town model, with its articulated, dispersed neighbourhood units. Following a 1953 tour by the PWD's A R Giles of several London-area New Towns, Bowring implausibly claimed in 1953 that the PWD's own planning schemes followed most of the New Town principles 'where the physical conditions permit'.[112] The principles of terrace housing would also, in a way, be incorporated in the 'Bowring Bungalows', designed by Norton's PWD team in the aftermath of the 1953 Shek Kip Mei fire (see Chapter 2), but the name 'bungalow' was here an extreme misnomer, the blocks being two-storey flatted rows of hyper-high-density, single-room dwelling units.[113]

As the 1950s began, the alternative formula of mass housing in flats was beginning to be increasingly discussed in Hong Kong, but not yet in a form significantly influenced by orthodox international modernist patterns of towers and parallel *Zeilenbau* slabs in open space – even though the SIT in Singapore had already attempted something like this, for example at its Tiong Bahru estate of 1935. (Figure 1.5)[114]

Although the Housing Society in 1950 put forward an abortive proposal of this general kind for five-storey, internal staircase-access 'barrack' blocks of single-room units, the nearest architectural equivalent actually built in Hong Kong in those years was a series of blocks of flats for expatriate government employees. This began with the HK$5m Leighton Hill project in 1948: two large cruciform flat-roofed seven-storey blocks of modernist flats, designed by Wright's PWD architects, and rapidly dubbed the 'Leighton Hill Taj Mahals'... built 'for a few privileged families'.[115] Further expatriate blocks followed, all on the same basic plan, for example at Queen's Gardens, King's Park, Peak Pavilions, and in 1953 at Pokfulam Road. By 1949, housing for around 150–200 expatriates had been completed.[116] Wright recalled that

> the highest priority, and this caused a great deal of argument and criticism in Hong Kong, was to provide quarters to house expatriate civil servants. There

Figure 1.5 The Singapore Improvement Trust's Tiong Bahru estate, 1935: 2011 photo (MG).

> was nowhere to house families and a great deal had to be done to get ready for wives coming out. So the first priority was, in fact, not housing for the masses, but housing for expatriate civil servants.[117]

Far more prescient of the first generation of Hong Kong mass housing, in their balcony access (or 'verandah') arrangement of low- and medium-rise blocks, were two schemes of quarters for the families of Chinese police officers, beginning in 1951 with an eight-storey scheme of 168 flats in two slab blocks in Hollywood Road, designed by PWD architects Norton and Reid within Wright's team in the PWD Architectural Office, and continuing with a larger scheme of 1953 in Canton Road, again gallery-access, and designed by Norton and Reid on the basis of sketches supplied by Duncan W MacIntosh, Commissioner of Police 1946–53. (Figure 1.6a,b,c)[118]

As Wright himself freely acknowledged, and as is explained in detail in Rosman Wai's 2019 monograph, it was above all these schemes, which recalled not avant-garde international modernism but the more conservatively designed interwar 'block dwellings' of the London County Council or Liverpool Corporation, or the 'chawls' of colonial India, that would help shape the first large-scale mass-housing complex commissioned by the Hong Kong government: the Shek Kip Mei fire site rebuilding scheme of 1954–5 – as we will see in Chapter 2.[119]

Figure 1.6 (a) 1951 perspective (published in SCMP) of the seven-storey Hollywood Road Married Police Quarters. (b) External view of living-room façade of Hollywood Road Quarters: 2009 photo (MG). (c) January 1953 SCMP perspective of Canton Road Police Quarters, showing similar gallery-access arrangement to Hollywood Road.

Notes

1 A Kockelkorn, C Schmid, M Streule, K P Wong, 'Peripheralisation through mass housing urbanisation in Hong Kong, Mexico City, and Paris', *Planning Perspectives*, 38 (3), 2023, 603–642.

2 F Mizuoka, Contrived Laissez-Faireism: *The Politico-Economic Structure of British Colonialism In Hong Kong*, Springer, Cham, 2018.

3 M Holdsworth and C Munn, *Dictionary of Hong Kong Biography*, Hong Kong University Press (HKUP), Hong Kong, 2012, 162–4, 207–9, 484–6; MacDougall, 1983 interview, Bodleian Library Rhodes House collection of transcribed Hong Kong interviews (hereafter 'Bodleian interview'); C-K Mark, *Hong Kong and the Cold War*, Oxford University Press, Oxford, 2004.

4 Bernard Williams, 'Administration of public housing in Hong Kong', 1982 manuscript (courtesy B Williams, 2012).
5 Gavin Ure, *Governors, Politics and the Colonial Office, Public Policy in Hong Kong 1918–1958*, HKUP, 2012, 140–3.
6 Holdsworth and Munn, *Dictionary of Hong Kong Biography*, 484–6; S Tsang, *A Modern History of Hong Kong*, HKUP, 2004, 145–7.
7 Holdsworth and Munn, *Dictionary of Hong Kong Biography*, 484–6; Ure, *Governors, Politics and the Colonial Office*, 33–6.
8 Holdsworth and Munn, *Dictionary of Hong Kong Biography,* 162–4; David Akers-Jones, *Feeling the Stones – Reminiscences by David Akers-Jones*, HKUP, 2004, 55.
9 Tsang, *Modern History of Hong Kong*, 68, 148.
10 Wright, 2011 interview. Ure, *Governors, Politics and the Colonial Office*, 136
11 HKRS523-2-1 1952 memo on J T Wakefield visit to Singapore to study SIT's work.
12 Ure, *Governors, Politics and the Colonial Office*, 67; Holdsworth and Munn, *Dictionary of Hong Kong Biography*, 297–9. David Edgerton, *The Rise and Fall of the British Nation,* Allen Lane, London, 2018, 66.
13 Tsang, *Modern History of Hong Kong*, 88; Akers-Jones, *Feeling the Stones*, 28–9.
14 Hansard, House of Commons Debate, 28-1-1942, vol 377, cols 699–701.
15 Ure, *Governors, Politics and the Colonial Office*, 5.
16 Lightbody, 2011 interview.
17 Ure, *Governors, Politics and the Colonial Office*, 67.
18 Wright, 2011 interview.
19 HKRS896-1-71 3-1952 Settlers Meeting; Holdsworth and Munn, *Dictionary of Hong Kong Biography*, 297–9. E Tu, *Colonial Hong Kong in the Eyes of Elsie Tu*, HKUP 2003, 19; HKRS523-2-1 4-1952 debate re 'competent Authority', 20-5-1953 memo from CS to Urban Council Chairman K Barnett, 1-6-1953 Urban Council debate on creation of Housing Division. Runhe Liu, *A History of the Municipal Councils of Hong Kong, 1883–1999*, Leisure and Cultural Service Department, Hong Kong, 2002.
20 L Goodstadt, *Journal of the Royal Asiatic Society* (JRAS), Hong Kong Branch, vol 53, 2013, 327–8.
21 Ure, *Governors, Politics and the Colonial Office*, 261; Holdsworth and Munn, *Dictionary of Hong Kong Biography*, 28; Akers-Jones, *Feeling the Stones*, 30; HKRS523-2-1 Bernacchi to Barnett and speech at Reform Club, both 11–1953; HKRS163-1-781 11-1952 report by Bernacchi; Tu, *Colonial Hong Kong,* 19.
22 Holdsworth and Munn, *Dictionary of Hong Kong Biography*, 19–20.
23 Rowe, 1987 Bodleian interview.
24 Rowe, 1987 Bodleian interview.
25 Akers-Jones, *Feeling the Stones*, 30.
26 Ure, *Governors, Politics and the Colonial Office*, 144–9; HKRS523-2-1 11–1953 Bernacchi to CUC Barnett.
27 Wright, 1988 Bodleian interview; Hong Kong Census and Statistics Department, *Hong Kong Statistics 1947–1967,* Hong Kong, 1969, 74.
28 Ure, *Governors, Politics and the Colonial Office*, 194, 213; L Goodstadt, *Uneasy Partners – the Conflict between Public Interest and Private Profit in Hong Kong*, HKUP 2005; L Goodstadt, 'Fiscal freedom and the making of Hong Kong's capitalist society', *China Information*, vol 24:3, 2010, 273–294.
29 'Sir Ronald: 40 great years' (cutting), SCMP 30-4-1977; Bernard Williams, 'Housing in Hong Kong', 1987 manuscript for World Bank course (courtesy B Williams).
30 Ure, *Governors, Politics and the Colonial Office*, 222–8, 150–1.

31 Ure, *Governors, Politics and the Colonial Office*, 135, 261.
32 Grantham, 1968 Bodleian interview.
33 Grantham, 1968 Bodleian interview.
34 Ure, *Governors, Politics and the Colonial Office*, 136–8, 153–6; Atkinson as 'colonial representative': Wright, 2011 interview.
35 HKRS895-1-55.
36 Akers-Jones, *Feeling the Stones*, 29.
37 Christopher Cowell, *Form Follows Fever – Malaria, Architecture, and the Building of Hong Kong 1841–1849*, Chinese UP, Hong Kong, 2023; Cecilia Chu, *Building Colonial Hong Kong, Speculative Development and Segregation in the City*, Routledge, Abingdon, 2022, 34–41. HY Lee and L DiStefano, 'The Hong Kong Shophouse', *Context*, 145, July 2016, 13–15.
38 Chu, *Building Colonial Hong Kong*, 34–41, 73–85; Pui-Yin Ho, *Making Hong Kong – a History of its Urban Development*, Elgar Online, Cheltenham, 2018, 6–68; C Xue, H Zou, B Li, K C Hui, 'The shaping of early Hong Kong – transplantation and adaptation by British professionals, 1841–1941', *Planning Perspectives,* vol 27:4, October 2013, 549–568.
39 Chu, *Building Colonial Hong Kong,* 154–160, 187. Pui-Yin Ho, *Making Hong Kong.*
40 Chu, *Building Colonial Hong Kong,* 154–160.
41 Jennifer Lang, 'Taikoo Sugar Refinery workers' housing: progressive design by a pioneering commercial enterprise', *Journal of the Royal Asiatic Society,* vol 57, 2017, 130–157.
42 Xue et al, 'The shaping of early Hong Kong', 563; Wright, 2015 interview.
43 Xue et al, 'The shaping of early Hong Kong', 562–3, 568.
44 Ure, *Governors, Politics and the Colonial Office*, 67–8; Holdsworth and Munn, *Dictionary of Hong Kong Biography*, 297–9.
45 Xue et al, 'The shaping of early Hong Kong', 562–3, 568.
46 HKRS156-1-3425 (especially Bryce DPW to Chairman of CDW Committee 1–1950); HKRS232-1-1, cutting from SCMP 23-9-1949.
47 HKRS156-1-3425 (e.g. 11–1949 Chairman of CDW Committee to CS); Xue et al, 568.
48 Wright, 1988 Bodleian interview; Junwei Li, 'Immigration, employment, and new town initiatives in Hong Kong', *Planning Perspectives*, 38:5, 2023, 997.
49 HKRS156-1-3425 1-1950 Bryce DPW to CDW Committee Chairman; HKRS41-1-796 1–1950 meeting.
50 Wright, 1988 Bodleian interview.
51 Wright, 2011 interview; Wright, 1988 Bodleian interview.
52 HKRS156-1-3425 11–1950 Financial Secretary to CS.
53 Wright, 1988 Bodleian interview.
54 HKRS156-1-3425 11–1949 Chairman of CDW Committee to CS.
55 Wright, 1988 Bodleian interview.
56 Ure, *Governors, Politics and the Colonial Office*, 140.
57 Ure, *Governors, Politics and the Colonial Office*, 152; HKRS232/1/7 Rowe lecture 2–1958; Alan Smart, *The Shek Kip Mei Myth – Squatters, Fires and Colonial Rule in Hong Kong, 1950–1963*, Hong Kong UP, 2006, 48.
58 Ure, *Governors, Politics and the Colonial Office*, 142–3.
59 Ure, *Governors, Politics and the Colonial Office*, 143.
60 Ure, *Governors, Politics and the Colonial Office*, 144.
61 Ure, *Governors, Politics and the Colonial Office*, 150.
62 Ure, *Governors, Politics and the Colonial Office*, 146.

63 Ure, *Governors, Politics and the Colonial Office*, 164–171; Smart, *The Shek Kip Mei Myth*, ix, 47–105, 170–1; HKRS232-1-1 cutting of SCMP 14-7-1948; HKRS163-1-781, 11–1952 to 12–1953, including 12–1953 Bray paper for DCS; HKRS896-1-71; HKRS523-2-1 8-1952 report of ad-hoc committee on housing.
64 Grantham, 1968 Bodleian interview.
65 Rowe, 1987 Bodleian interview. 'Sir Ronald: 40 great years', SCMP 30-4-1977.
66 Ure, *Governors, Politics and the Colonial Office*, 167.
67 HKRS896-1-71; Ure, *Governors, Politics and the Colonial Office*, 164–5.
68 Tsui, 'Minimum government assistance', 1262–8; Ure, *Governors, Politics and the Colonial Office*, 168–9, 186–7.
69 Ure, *Governors, Politics and the Colonial Office*, 163, 170.
70 Ure, *Governors, Politics and the Colonial Office*, 163–4.
71 Holdsworth and Munn, *Dictionary of Hong Kong Biography*, 19–20.
72 Goodstadt, JRAS 2013, 327.
73 Ure, *Governors, Politics and the Colonial Office*, 187.
74 Alexander, 1988 Bodleian interview.
75 Alan Smart, *The Shek Kip Mei Myth – Squatters, Fires and Colonial Rule in Hong Kong, 1950–1963*, Hong Kong UP, 2006; Ure, *Governors, Politics and the Colonial Office*, 169–189.
76 Tsui, 'Minimum government assistance', 1264–5; Ure, *Governors, Politics and the Colonial Office*, 171, Smart, *The Shek Kip Mei Myth,* 85–8; Wakefield Report, HKRS1017-3-6.
77 Ure, *Governors, Politics and the Colonial Office*, 170–5; Smart, *The Shek Kip Mei Myth,* 85–7
78 HKRS163-1-781 passim; Ure, *Governors, Politics and the Colonial Office*, 171–3.
79 HKRS163-1-781, including 31-12-1952 note, 'Squatter Resettlement', by Chief of Police.
80 Liao, 2010 interview; Cheng, 2014 interview; Lightbody, 2011 interview (on Wright, 'An amazing chap!'); Wright, 2011 interview (on Donnithorne, Bramwell). HKRS896-1-71 memo of 19-5-1952 from K Barnett CUC, to CS.
81 Ure, *Governors, Politics and the Colonial Office*, 171.
82 HKRS163-1-781 1–1953 correspondence and 12–1953 report by Bray to DCS; Barnett 11–1952 report and 12–1952 note by Chief of Police; Smart, *The Shek Kip Mei Myth,* 101; Ure, *Governors, Politics and the Colonial Office*, 175.
83 HKRS232-1-2 SCMP 30-12-1953 cutting; 'Seizing the nettle', Grantham, 1968 Bodleian interview; SCMP 30-4-1977 (on Holmes); Ure, *Governors, Politics and the Colonial Office*, 188–9, 221–4; Goodstadt, JRAS 2013, 327.
84 Tsui, 'Minimum government assistance', 1270–4.
85 Qian Zhu, 'The Production of Everyday Space for Workers: The New Village Movement in China, 1919–1936', *Positions,* vol 30:3, 2022, 429–453; see also J T L Lee, 'God's villages – Christian communities in late-19th-century South China', *Journal of Ritual Studies*, vol 19:1, 2005, 31–46.
86 Carmen Tsui, 'Can NGOs still provide affordable houses to Hong Kong?', Hong Kong Institute of Architects, *Occupy Housing – HKIA Journal 72*, HKIA, Hong Kong, 2016, 76–9; see also Chu, *Building Colonial Hong Kong*, 166–172. HKHA, *The First Two Million*, HKHA, Hong Kong, 1980, 53. Tsui, 'Minimum government assistance'; Carmen Tsui, 'Cottage areas: squatter resettlements and the making of self-built communities in post-war Hong Kong', lecture to 18th International Planning History Society, Yokohama, 2018.

87 Tsui, 'Minimum government assistance', 1268–70; Carmen Tsui, 'Welfare housing in colonial Hong Kong – the contributions of philanthropic organisations', Association of Critical Heritage Studies, 2016. (https://sites.grenadine.co/sites/patrimoine/en/ACHS2016/) HKRS896-1-71 memo of 19-5-1952 from K Barnett CUC, to CS. Rosman C C Wai, *Design DNA of Mark I – Hong Kong's Public Housing Prototype*, MCCM Creations, Hong Kong, 2019, 49–52.
88 Ure, *Governors, Politics and the Colonial Office*, 152; Smart, *The Shek Kip Mei Myth,* 48–50.
89 Ure, *Governors, Politics and the Colonial Office*, 156–7.
90 Ure, *Governors, Politics and the Colonial Office*, 222–6.
91 HKRS156-1-3812, report on 1952 Atkinson visit (combining with stops at Aden, Malaya, and Singapore). HKRS156-1-4079-1, 1953 report by Director of Public Works on London New Towns. Ure, *Governors, Politics and the Colonial Office*, 153–6.
92 Smart, *The Shek Kip Mei Myth,* 48–9; Ure, *Governors, Politics and the Colonial Office*, 150–1; 523-2-1 4-52, 11–52 discussions on HS, MHS, HA; Wright, 2015 interview; Wright, 1988 Bodleian interview, L C Wong, 2011 interview. *Hong Kong Housing Society Annual Report 1955*, Hong Kong, 1956, 16 (information from Carmen Tsui).
93 Tsui, 'Minimum government assistance', 1274; Wright, 2015 interview; Holdsworth and Munn, *Dictionary of Hong Kong Biography,* 101; Ure, *Governors, Politics and the Colonial Office*, 222.
94 HKRS232-1-1 on 1948 discussions; HKRS523-2-1 4-1952, 11–1952 discussions on Housing Society, Model Housing Society, Housing Authority; HKRS896-1–71 discussions on HK Settlers Housing Corporation. Wai, *Design DNA of Mark I,* 53–6.
95 Ure, *Governors, Politics and the Colonial Office*, 222–4
96 HKRS523-2-1 1952 on Wakefield visit to Singapore.
97 Ure, *Governors, Politics and the Colonial Office*, 153–8.
98 HKRS523-2-1 discussion on August 1952 report of Ad-Hoc Committee on Housing.
99 HKRS523-2-1 1951–3 discussions on Housing Authority; Ure, *Governors, Politics and the Colonial Office*, 156–8; Smart, *The Shek Kip Mei Myth,* 48–9.
100 HKRS523-2-1 3–1952 to May 1953 discussions on HA-HS takeover of assets; Ure, *Governors, Politics and the Colonial Office*, 156–8.
101 HKRS523-2-1 1951-3 discussions on Housing Authority.
102 HKRS523-2-1 3–1953 Barnett memo.
103 Ure, *Governors, Politics and the Colonial Office*, 157.
104 HKRS523-2-1 25-1-1953 memo for ExCo by Financial Secretary, UC Chairman.
105 Ure, *Governors, Politics and the Colonial Office*, 159–161.
106 M Glendinning, *Mass Housing, Modern Architecture and State Power – a Global History*, Bloomsbury, London, 2021, 32–3, 54–5.
107 Glendinning, *Mass Housing*, 34–40, 64–6, 97–107.
108 Glendinning, *Mass Housing*, 97–107.
109 S Muthesius and M Glendinning, *Towers for the Welfare State – an Architectural History of British Multi-Storey Housing 1945–1970*, SCCS, Edinburgh, 2017, 35–67.
110 SCMP 9-4-1949; Chu, *Building Colonial Hong Kong.*
111 HKRS523-2-1 6–1952 Barnett to Black.
112 HKRS156-1-4079-1 1953 report by DPW on London New Towns.
113 Wright, 1988 Bodleian interview.
114 Glendinning, *Mass Housing*, 71, 503–5 (Tiong Bahru, etc.).
115 HKRS232-1-1, cuttings from Sunday Herald 18-7-1948 and SCMP 4-11-1948.

116 SCMP 3-10-1953; Wright, 1988 Bodleian interview. Later housing for expatriate officers designed by PWD, with similar plans: Chatham Garden, HKRS232-1-5-1 4-1956 and 5-1956 cuttings; Chater Hall, 1955, HKRS232-1-1 28-11-1955 cutting, and HKRS232-1-3; Arsenal St, 1956, HKRS232-1-5-2 10-1956 cutting; Waterloo Rd HKRS232-1-5-2.

117 Wright, 1988 Bodleian interview, Wright, 2011 interview; Lightbody, 2011 interview. The linked subject of housing co-operatives in Hong Kong, as a 'third way' between Hong Kong's two poles of private and public housing, is currently subject of a major RGC research project by Dr Carmen Tsui of Lingnan University ('The Third Way of Housing Production: A History of Housing Cooperatives in Post-War Hong Kong, 1940s–1980s').

118 SCMP 16-4-1951, 11-11-1951, 17-1-1953. Wai, *Design DNA of Mark I,* 107.

119 Links from Canton Road Police Quarters to Mk I Resettlement design: Cheng, 2014 interview. Wai, *Design DNA of Mark I*, 107-115. R Home, *Of Planting and Planning: the Making of British Colonial Cities*, Spon, London, 1997.

2 1953–1957

Shek Kip Mei and the Resettlement revolution

Shek Kip Mei – a symbolic and practical watershed

The previous chapter set out a story of well-intended, but ultimately ineffective, efforts at containment of the squatting and housing crises of post-war Hong Kong from within the established laissez-faire framework. That phase decisively ended with the Shek Kip Mei squatter fire of Christmas Day 1953. It caused relatively few casualties (three deaths and 40 injuries), but marked a sharp symbolic and organisational break from all that went before, and a foundation narrative for what eventually followed, as did the Bukit Ho Swee fire seven years later in Singapore. It achieved that not least by the dramatic way it attracted government attention, imprinting itself directly on the consciousness of individual cadets. Ian Lightbody recalled that '60,000 or so were made homeless in one night. Norian and I had come out of a party somewhere on the Peak, and from the top of Hong Kong Island, we could see this great fire burning in Kowloon – it was spectacular stuff!'[1] (Figure 2.1)

The fire was started about 9:30 pm by the upsetting of a kerosene lamp into a bucket of rubber solution for shoe manufacture, and was fanned by strong wind: it burned for five hours and devastated 41 acres of temporary timber structures. Denis Bray recalled that 'it was much more severe than anything we had seen. Shek Kip Mei was the largest squatter area by far. It might have contained up to one third of all squatters'. The social welfare office and philanthropic aid services mobilised to provide food and screen and register the homeless, initially estimated at 58,000.[2] At 10.30 on the following morning, Boxing Day, Governor Grantham called an emergency meeting at Government House. Dennis Bray again:

> I was able to tell the gathering that it would be impossible… to try to build temporary shelter for some 60,000 people. The Governor then turned to the Director of Public Works and asked him to make proposals for some permanent shelter. So the momentous step was taken for the Government itself to build something for the fire victims.[3]

Within four months of that meeting, the decision had been taken to rehouse the displacees in permanent government-built multi-storey blocks, and within a

DOI: 10.1201/9781315563701-3

Figure 2.1 Contemporary photograph of the Christmas 1953 Shek Kip Mei fire.

year, a general policy decision had been taken that all cleared squatters should be rehoused likewise. What the shock of Shek Kip Mei achieved was, firstly, a revolution in the policy and practice of resettlement; secondly, a general supercharging of the squatter issue within the colonial government's consciousness as a threat requiring enhanced containment; and thirdly, a new readiness to tackle the issue in a concerted, well-resourced manner. In the process, the government's overall attitude to housing shifted from regarding it as an issue to be avoided, or tackled only reluctantly under external pressure from London, to seeing it as a potential field for administrative innovation, and accretion of policy autonomy for Hong Kong.[4]

Building on surplus: Hong Kong in the early '50s

The government's laissez-faire orientation in the early 1950s resulted not just from ideological preference but also from simple shortage of numbers: even later in the decade there were less than fifty administrative officers, so the government simply had no staff resources to support strategic planning. Hence unplanned economic growth prevailed, by the principle of the survival of the fittest. Only following the McKinsey report of 1972/3 would a developed system of administrative and professional structures emerge within government.[5] Governor Grantham, although wedded in general to the laissez-faire system, could be prodded into action on individual issues – such as resettlement, where, as we will see, he was happy to allow Douglas Clague to take the initiative on behalf of the government.[6] He was more interested in high-prestige projects such as that for a new City Hall, where he engaged the charismatic Hong Kong University Architecture Professor, Gordon Brown. Wright recalled that Grantham had 'a very difficult American wife, who thought she was an interior decorator!'[7]

But in the key matter of external relations with London, it was Grantham's years of office that saw the emergence of the phenomenon of 'Hong Kong chauvinism', particularly in industrial policy, where Hong Kong's new textile industry generated both economic strength and controversy. He recollected that the Shanghai firms were technologically far more advanced than Hong Kong, and that they 'saved the day' for the territory – even though Britain drastically restricted textile imports from Hong Kong, fearing the impact in marginal constituencies: 'I took a very poor view of that'. Lightbody agreed that 'we really fell on our feet' industrially.[8] Grantham felt that in the Colonial Office in London, Alan Lennox-Boyd (Secretary of State for the Colonies 1954–9) was 'the outstanding man – quite obviously interested in each and every colony, including Hong Kong', whereas his predecessor Oliver Lyttelton (1951–4) was 'far more interested in Malaya'.[9] The government soon realised that London's concern to avoid political embarrassment from Hong Kong's emergency conditions could be harnessed to domestic advantage. For example, in April 1957, following a United Nations intervention concerning Chinese refugees, and initial abortive proposals to ship refugees to Formosa, Grantham proposed to Lennox-Boyd that defence cutback savings be diverted to refugee and housing relief.[10]

More generally, these were the years when the post-war formula of soaring government surpluses, and social programmes financed by those rather than from increased taxation, became established. In the 1955 budget, which included the Urban Council's plan for a big Housing Authority programme of multi-storey flats, Financial Secretary Clarke noted that he had abandoned producing a five-year plan, given the inability to forecast prices or unexpected events such as Shek Kip Mei. But between 1950 and 1962, government reserves nearly tripled, from HK$384m to $1,030m, and annual spending also jumped, from $312m to $953m. Between 1953/4 and 1957/8 alone, government revenue rose from $397m to 584m, expenditure from $355m to $533m, and the surplus from $42m to $52m: the 1957 budget allocated over $300m to housing.[11] Playing a significant role in the expanding surplus were the soaring revenues from premiums from sale of Crown land – from $6m in 1953/4 to $33m in 1958/9, and $107m in 1961/2.[12]

In the professional arena, George Atkinson's liaison role continued, on visits paid for out of CDW funds. With Housing Authority projects now actively in the offing, these visits now focused more specifically on built form, especially housing density and design. In late 1955, Atkinson was consulted by the Authority on its second project, a cluster of balcony-access blocks on a precipitously sloping site at Cadogan Street, Kennedy Town (Sai Wan – see below), and declined to give it his 'unqualified professional blessing'.[13] Accordingly, early the following year, London expressed reluctance to approve a £43,750 CDW grant for Sai Wan, arguing Atkinson was 'slightly uneasy about the high density of recent building in Hong Kong', and that Cadogan Street especially had an 'unreasonably high density' (1,300 persons per acre, or 'ppa') – although in fact the first HA scheme, North Point, was even denser (2,310 ppa).[14] In March 1956, Atkinson visited to give a lecture and further 'advice' on high flats, especially to the newly established Housing Authority, and, throughout the mid- and late 1950s, followed the progress of the two major Special Committee investigations of Hong Kong housing (see below). But in practice, the HA's high-density, high-rise policy continued to develop virtually unimpeded.[15]

A revolution in resettlement

In reality, the immediate decisions taken at the Governor's Boxing Day 1953 meeting were modest: to permit fire victims to sleep on the streets of Sham Shui Po, and to clear the whole Shek Kip Mei site so they could build replacement housing structures themselves, with government assistance of about HK$200 per family plus free building materials.[16] The obvious inadequacy of that formula led to an upgrading of the proposed intervention, as approved by ExCo three days later, to direct government construction of 'lines of small temporary housing units' each comprising 'a room 10ft by 10ft with door and window,' and costing $800 each. These eventually materialised as the 'Bowring bungalows' – on which see below.[17]

At this point, the Public Works Department was envisaged as the lead authority in tackling the Shek Kip Mei crisis. But in a demonstration of the volatility of housing policy at this stage, that immediately changed following a dramatic intervention from the unofficials of the Urban Council and, in particular, from businessman and war hero Col. Douglas Clague, appointed chairman of the Council's Emergency Resettlement Sub-committee in January 1954.[18] Clague, the Rhodesian-born and Manx-educated chairman of John D Hutchison & Co Ltd – the real-estate and port conglomerate later taken over by Li Ka-shing in 1979 – was a driving figure with a strong philanthropic conscience, who chaired the Housing Society for 29 years.[19] Wright recalled Clague as 'like an old Jardine Matheson buccaneer – a go-getting businessman – who was later, for instance, behind the idea of the Cross-Harbour Crossing'.[20]

Clague's committee immediately started looking for sites for resettlement developments, flats as well as cottages, and preparing a report for publication in March 1954. In parallel with this, Colonial Secretary Burgess adumbrated a concept of experimental government-built multi-storey resettlement tenements, including 'convertible' six-storey blocks designed by the PWD and approved by the Urban Council's Emergency Resettlement Sub-committee in January. Their single-room basic units could supposedly later be merged into self-contained flats, thus becoming 'a permanent asset to the Colony'.[21] Burgess successfully argued for inclusion of these at a meeting with the Governor in February, claiming that six-storey blocks could provide a way of exploiting ad-hoc gap sites without 'applying to the whole squatter resettlement problem the direct action which had been forced upon it as a result of the Shek Kip Mei disaster'. He suggested the coordination problem could be rectified by appointing a senior cadet as a Commissioner of Resettlement, charged with oversight of the PWD's work, including rebuilding of the Shek Kip Mei site partly with multi-storey tenements.[22]

These recommendations were endorsed by Clague's committee in February/March. It backed decanting and multi-storey construction as a way of freeing land for other uses, rejecting the alternative of retained but regulated structures: 'Why should squatters, who have no particular claim, be rehoused on land worth in some cases $30–$40 per square foot?'[23] The committee acclaimed the PWD's plans for 'convertible' structures, and recommended experimental six-storey blocks should be built at Shek Kip Mei, alongside the two-storey Bowring Bungalows already planned (see below), and that a senior government officer should oversee the programme, becoming a temporary ex-officio member of the Urban Council.[24] Although Barnett had argued that the Resettlement department should be incorporated within the new Housing Authority, Clague disagreed.[25] It was duly set up in July 1954 as an autonomous department, incorporating the PWD squatter control section, the USD cottage-areas management, and the SWD clearance and screening section. The accompanying Resettlement Ordinance of 1954 focused on clearance of Crown land and squatter-resettlement procedures.[26]

The first Commissioner for Resettlement was senior cadet Ronald Holmes, who headed the new Resettlement Department from the beginning of 1954 to late 1955.[27] Owing to the head-start established and cleverly maintained by Clague, Holmes had to allow the Urban Council to oversee the entire operation. He expressed reservations about this, arguing ‘it would be unfortunate if the Urban Council were able to extend its authority into a new sphere of administration’. He suggested it should be a ‘once-for-all, emergency operation’ with the Resettlement Department existing for two years maximum.[28] But he soon stamped his authority on the process, his enthusiasm (according to Wright) distinguishing him from normal cadets: as a temporary Urban Council member, he duly became chairman of the Council’s three decision-making resettlement committees. From 1955, Holmes subsequently became chairman of the Council and of the Housing Authority (see below).[29]

Figure 2.2 (a) Director of Public Works T L Bowring lays the ‘first shovelful of concrete’ for Bowring Bungalows at the Shek Kip Mei site: SCMP article, January 1954. (b) 1954 view of Bowring Bungalows under construction, showing gallery access and blockwork construction; included in a heritage exhibition in Mei Ho House: 2014 photo (MG).

The programme was remarkably cost-effective, as it used far less space than HS or HA projects (2.2 sq m, rather than 3.3 sq m, per inhabitant), and successfully cleared large numbers of squatters. For the first contract, 'Operation Boxing Day', Bowring himself laid the 'first shovel of concrete' on 27 January 1954.[30] (Figure 2.2a, b) This included the first two six-storey 'Experimental Blocks' as well as the low-rise Bowring Bungalows. The six-storey blocks proved far cheaper per unit than the two/three-storey Bowring Bungalows.[31] This allowed contractors to be paid significant bonuses ($1,200 per block per day) for early completion of the Shek Kip Mei blocks: Bowring argued in August 1954 that this would also save $300,000 on the feeding costs of fire victims, costing $1 each per day.[32] Rents were based on the construction costs of the first block (as with later 'Mark' variants) amortised over 40 years at 3% p.a. This worked out at $10–$14 per month: a six-storey block would cost $600,000 and generate $85,000 annual rent income. Following deliberations in mid-1954 about how to finance the new programme, it was claimed by Holmes in an October memo to ExCo that accommodation for 120,000 squatters could be built in 18 months, at a cost of $40–$45 million.[33]

The hunt for land: justifying and criticising the resettlement programme

Despite quibbles within the Secretariat and the PWD, for example in October 1954 (Wright) about committee members' constant pressure 'to improve in many small ways the amenities connected with the flats', the new system was so generally effective that by November 1954 the government could contemplate the far more ambitious concept of a permanent programme of multi-storey resettlement. This began at another recent fire site at Lei Cheng Uk, whose 'H' blocks were completed from November 1955 (see below).[34] (Figure 2.3a) In October 1954, Holmes told ExCo that the new blocks offered 'a practical, successful and permanent solution to the squatter problem. Many distinguished and well-informed visitors have already seen the occupied buildings at Shek Kip Mei and it is safe to say that the six-storey resettlement programme is making an important contribution to the prestige of the Colony as well as to the standards of public health and public order'.[35] By mid-1955, 18 months after his appointment, Holmes proclaimed that 'we now know that resettlement in multi-storey buildings… can be successfully carried out on a very large scale (we were far from being certain of this 18 months ago)'. Colonial Secretary Lennox-Boyd visited Resettlement estates in July 1955 and praised the programme's 'magnificent scale' and 'stupendous achievement': Holmes was pictured explaining an estate layout to him.[36] (Figure 2.3b) Yet behind the scenes the programme was always perceived by Holmes and colleagues as being on a knife-edge of viability. During 1955, he felt optimism about progress, so long as clearance of development land was 'ruthlessly' prioritised: he justified the Resettlement programme not on the basis of humanitarianism towards squatters but exclusively 'when the interests of the community *as a whole* demand that we should do so', above all to protect the colony's development land. Referring to Shek Kip Mei, Holmes argued that if government 'had not taken vigorous and effective action, the streets of Kowloon and the fire area itself would have been in a

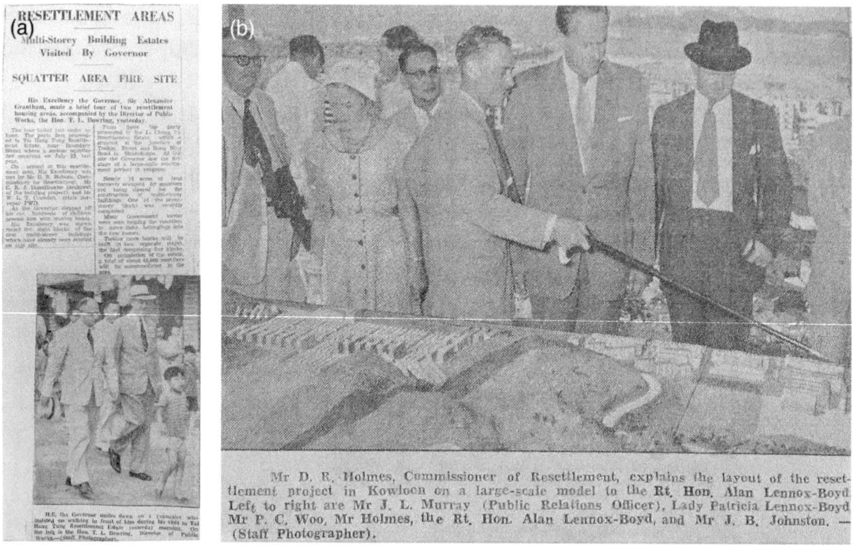

Figure 2.3a Governor Grantham and Bowring visiting Tai Hang Tung Resettlement estate in 1955: SCMP article, May 1955.

Figure 2.3b Resettlement Commissioner Holmes showing a model of Resettlement estates to Colonial Secretary Lennox-Boyd: SCMP article, July 1955. Shek Kip Mei is visible on the left of the model, including both Mk I 'H' blocks and low-rise lines of Bowring Bungalows, and Lei Cheng Uk is on the right.

state of chaos for an indefinite period and the fire area would eventually have been re-squatted and ready for another fire. Considerations of public health, public order and public prestige made this quite unacceptable, and the *general* interest therefore demanded that we embark on the construction of semi-permanent and permanent resettlement accommodation'.[37]

This was a very different, less idealistic understanding of the term 'community' from contemporary Britain and other welfare-state societies of Western Europe. But the organic link between resettlement and land policy was well understood by all actors in the system, within and outside the establishment. Denis Bray argued in 1991 that resettlement had been the only way to clear land for development.[38] In 1960 Colonial Secretary Burgess opposed extension of rehousing eligibility to roof and street squatters: the only criterion for priority in resettlement should be 'the freeing of land for proper development', as with the 'hard facts' and 'grim realities' of Hong Kong, 'a squatter moved from a rooftop, or a street, contributes nothing to the community as a whole. A squatter moved under existing priorities makes the priceless contribution of a few square feet of developable land'.[39]

The Urban Council unofficials, in keeping with their self-appointed 'opposition' role, had a different perspective on the squatter issue. They maintained an approach that was robust and voluble, even if erratic in focus. The most militant was housing activist Elsie Elliott. 'She was convinced that every government official was a crook, including me', recalled Wright.[40] But this was a philanthropic rather than socialist militancy. Bad housing conditions were fearlessly critiqued, including squatters' huts and overcrowded tenements, but Elliott acknowledged the paradox that while the resettlement programme was 'not purely altruistic' – land sales being a major source of revenue for the government – this provided a key foundation for Hong Kong's prosperity.[41] The 1954 'demolish on sight' policy, she argued, 'brought more suffering to the most underprivileged who were not catered for in the public housing scheme, and created more opportunities for corruption by officials, and bullying and "squeeze" by triads'; yet 'the rehousing of fire victims and redevelopment displacees was in large measure responsible for the development of Hong Kong's economy'.[42] The worst aspect of the system, Elliott argued, was that it was tied into injustice and criminality. The squatter huts, which seemed like luxury to their squatter occupants, were originally built on hillsides controlled by 'ba wong' triad leaders, but after Shek Kip Mei the start of the large-scale resettlement programme led to an upsurge in fires.[43] Some were started by the squatters themselves to secure public housing, others by the triad bosses for the resale of plot rights, and others, allegedly, by the government, to ease the acquisition of development land. This was tantamount to a stimulus to corruption in the sale of land for private development; following a proven arson attack in Tai Po Road in 1954, fire victims were expressly excluded from resettlement accommodation.[44] (Figure 2.4)

Within roughly a decade, the Resettlement legacy of Shek Kip Mei would become generally seen in critical terms, as a flawed solution born of excessive haste, but in policy discussions in the mid/late-1950s it was acclaimed by many as an unexpected achievement of the colonial administration – although it should be reiterated that the smaller scale self-help cottage resettlement programme continued alongside it, especially in the New Territories.[45] This interpretation foregrounded a humanitarian rationale for the programme, while not denying the underlying land-supply motive. The complex tensions between these were set out in 2011 recollections by Ian Lightbody, who later headed the Resettlement Department. He argued that Resettlement housing was

> Basic, cheapie, economical – we were paying *all* this out of revenue, and we wanted to maximise the number of people resettled. The Resettlement programme was all about clearing squatters off valuable land. Before 1953 we couldn't find enough large sites. Then, along came redemption on Christmas Day 1953! A great squatter fire in Kowloon left about 53,000 people homeless – but there was the site! Our people moved in, and stopped any attempts to rebuild the squatter huts. That's how we managed to start the Resettlement programme. But one needs to remember that, from the point of view of these squatters, once they'd got the message that the government intended to rehouse them in fireproof blocks, where they'd be safe, from fire, storms and landslides – the old Hong Kong problems – and would have status as residents of Hong Kong, they became relaxed. They were Government tenants [and their houses were] fireproof, rainproof, everything-proof! It was very basic, but it solved a problem. So, that

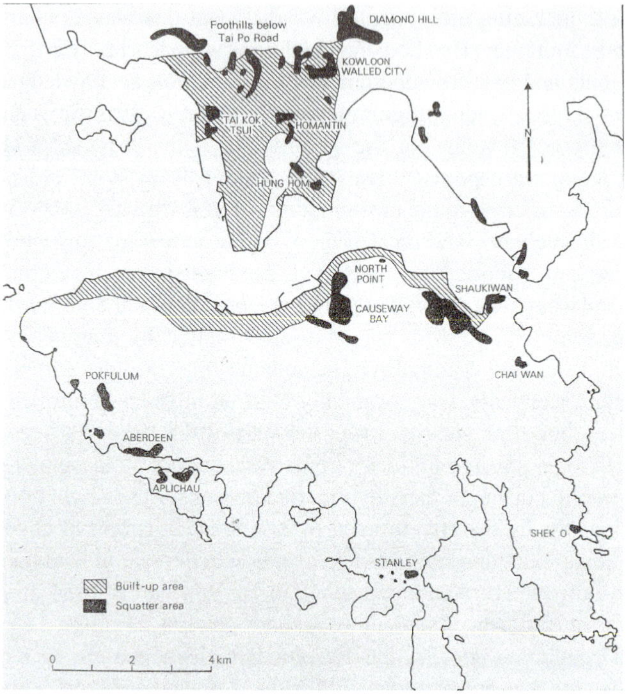

Figure 2.4 Distribution of squatter settlements in 1955.

> brought in its train the process of getting more sites to build the Resettlement blocks. Early on, a few 2-storey buildings were built, but they didn't make sensible use of the valuable land. So the aim became 6 or 7 storeys. Design was done in-house, in the Public Works Department – they were very good. The aim was to maximise the number of residents in each block. The kitchens and loos were communal but the tenants were happy. So – this particular first building development could accommodate more people than had been burnt out at the Christmas fire. That let our people clear more areas of squatters, and open up more sites for Resettlement blocks – so the process rolled on. For these ex-squatters, they were in seventh heaven, as they were Government tenants, completely safe in the concrete blocks. These Resettlement blocks were, then, the basic public housing – the lowest standards, but doing a wonderful job.[46]

The first Commissioner in charge of the new Housing Authority (see below), George Rowe, highlighted a humanitarian justification for Resettlement:

> What do you take first? Is it best to give people somewhere to live… where at least it's fireproof? It's a bloody sight better than living out in the hills. And you haven't got any ground. What do you do? You've no alternative. It doesn't

matter what else comes from it. You can get all sorts of scallywags in any Resettlement estate but 90 out of 100 are not, they're just ordinary, bloody good citizens thankful to get somewhere. You've got to care for the 90%.[47]

But from the outset, discordant elements were prominent, for example in approaches to management problems: Fung Tung (later Director of Housing), then a junior housing assistant in the Housing Authority, recoiled at the 'disciplinarian' approach of Resettlement's 'policeman-like', often ex-military staff. Yet at the same time, any social-containment effects of Resettlement were severely restricted in effectiveness.[48]

Resettlement architecture and its PWD designers

The first emergency government-built flats at Shek Kip Mei at the beginning of 1954 were the two-storey terraced 'Bowring Bungalows', with their unserviced one-room units of up to 130 sq ft.[49] Designed by PWD architect George Norton and built in precast concrete blockwork with corrugated asbestos roofs, their construction resembled previous squatter cottages, but they were very differently arranged, in long rows with staircases at each end: the upper-floor units were shallower, to allow continuous balcony access at the front. Although relatively few records of them survive, they are documented in Rosman Wai's seminal 2019 monograph, *Design DNA of Mark I – Hong Kong's Public Housing Prototype* (2019). Built by Fook Lee & Co, they and the first two six-storey blocks comprised the first contract for the area.[50] By late 1954, with the shift underway to multi-storey blocks which essentially rearranged similar units in a larger and taller form, the Bungalows were branded 'now a very bad slum area', to be demolished as soon as possible.[51]

Michael Wright recollected in 2011 that 'the big watershed came with the Shek Kip Mei fire. Now the Government had to do something, and the Resettlement blocks were designed. I was on leave, but the first few blocks built were the Bowring Bungalows, two-storey walk-ups. They were quickly followed by the design of the Resettlement blocks. These were worked out on the basis of 24 sq ft per person. Each room measured 12 by 10 ft – that is, 120 sq ft, to house a family of four. They were very, very substandard – they had no cooking facilities, and there were communal toilets!' During late 1954, improvements to the basic design, suggested by Wright and his staff, were approved, including communal bathrooms and drying facilities.[52]

The origin and design of the Mk I blocks is covered exhaustively in Wai's book, and so is only summarised here in outline. The six- (later seven-) storey 'H' plan blocks were constructed of reinforced-concrete load-bearing walls and floor slabs, with cantilevered access balconies and hollow-block balustrades, and link blocks (containing communal toilets and washing spaces) of separate framed construction. Each upper storey originally contained 64 units of 120 sq ft, designated for five-adult occupancy, and with no internal water supply or electricity, but later estates featured longer blocks with up to 120 units, and six rather than four staircases. The roofs were used for schools or recreation and the ground floors could be used for shops or workshops: cooking was done on the balconies.[53] (Figure 2.5a, b)

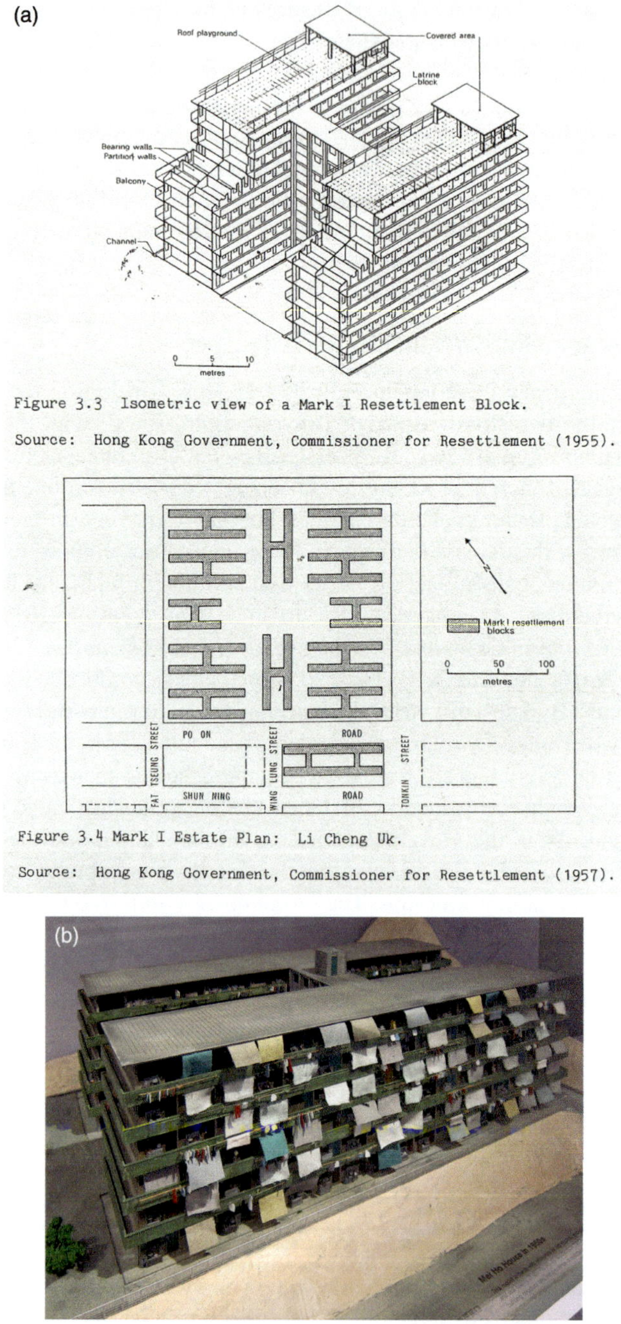

Figure 2.5 (a) 1955 cutaway view of Mk I block (seven-storey variant) and 1957 layout plan of Lei Cheng Uk estate. (b) Model of Mei Ho House six-storey Mk I block in use (complete with washing), in Mei Ho House exhibition. 2014 photo (MG).

In March 1954, Ken Barnett, the Director of Urban Services, claimed there was a strong overlap between the Mk I and 'low-cost-housing' designs under discussion for the Housing Authority, the only significant differences being intensity of occupancy and squatter tenancy: he argued housing and resettlement were separated by an 'artificial barrier… forced on us by emergency conditions'; 'the two tasks differ in key and tempo, but they are both tunes played in the same orchestra, and must have one conductor if we are to avoid frightful discord'. Barnett even claimed slightly bafflingly that the Mk I was 'based on a design evolved in the UK by me for "Low Cost Housing."'[54] However, the likely immediate inspiration for the Mk I was closer at hand, within the PWD: Wright argued that

> for their design, an inspiration was possibly, if anything, the Canton Road Police Quarters. That was one of the first jobs I did as PWD Chief Architect, and it also had kitchens and communal WCs. The idea of having a staircase at each end, and the corridors, was already in use in Hong Kong. I've never heard any suggestion it was copied from the UK – although there are some halls of residence of Imperial College, built back in the 50s – by Norman & Dawbarn – which were very reminiscent of the Government Low Cost Housing and Police quarters.

Asked if they were influenced by other colonial patterns such as the Calcutta 'chawls', Wright responded, 'No, they were designed in Hong Kong! I remember reading about Shek Kip Mei when I was on leave in England. I wrote to Norton and said, "This is a terrific opportunity to put the Architectural Office on the map!" It would win great prestige for the office!'[55]

Cheng Hon-Kwan, a young engineer who joined the PWD Architectural Office in June 1953, recollected at length in 2014 the urgent design efforts for the six-storey 'experimental blocks' for Shek Kip Mei in early 1954:

> The architects responsible for the design, the sketches of these buildings, were working in the same room as me. I remember Donnithorne in particular. He was also new in the Architectural Office. He was an architect. I came over to have a look at his drawing board. I said, "Oh, this is something the government would like to build for the fire victims!" It was very simple, six storeys high, for Shek Kip Mei. On plan, it was a sort of H-shaped layout. All I could see was all these little compartments. So I said, "Where are the kitchens and toilets?" He said, "No, they're all communal – communal toilets, hygiene and latrines". So it was very, very simple. And very soon all these buildings were built, and the homeless residents were accommodated. One of those first blocks is still here, it's been preserved – and back in 1954, there was Donnithorne drawing it out, for the government's approval! It was a very economical type: a very low-cost building. At that time it was thought these could be temporary – not knowing the same buildings would still be standing several decades later. I think his idea for the "H" type, with the link in the middle, with all the facilities in the link – quite an effective idea, a cost-effective layout – I think he just thought it up himself. Maybe, from various options, he thought, "This is the simplest and most economical".

But Cheng also agreed that the Canton Road Police Quarters had had an impact, as it

> showed the sort of layout the government architects of the time would like to adopt… They thought it was the most efficient, with long corridors, access to each room and so on. I understood in those days that it didn't mean that one room would accommodate just one family; it could be two families or even three – more than one certainly. At the time, that land in Hong Kong was precious. We couldn't afford to build two storeys (i.e., the Bowring Bungalows) to occupy that piece of land. But in those days, six or seven storeys was quite a height! They were six storeys high, wall-bearing, with RC frames; at the time, those were already advanced multi-storey buildings.[56]

Within the PWD, the architect C R J Donnithorne had been transferred to the multi-storey experimental project (from designing a remand home) in February 1954.[57] Within the hierarchy above him, the decision to embark on the project was chiefly the responsibility of George P Norton, described by Wright as 'a very, very competent architect, very down-to-earth, not arty-crafty'; he had also led on the design of the Bowring Bungalows. One of Wright's prewar colleagues and fellow wartime internees, the Aberdonian architect William Shewan, was also involved.[58] Cheng recalled that

> Norton was the Acting Chief Architect, in 1953, and the chief architect was Michael Wright. He was Acting Assistant Director of Public Works, in charge of buildings, so George Norton became Acting Chief Architect. So of course he had a role, to make the final decision. There must have been very thorough discussions between them – they must have decided that this was the most simple way to do it, as time was of the essence. Michael Wright had the final say: he was in charge of two offices – the Architectural Office (AO) and the Building Ordinance Office (BOO), which deals with private buildings.

Lightbody described Wright as 'an amazing chap… always wonderfully helpful'.[59] The Director of Public Works (1950–7, in succession to E A Boyce), T L Bowring, was not involved in these specifics. From the perspective of the young Donald Liao, Bowring was 'regarded as God in those days… a towering figure' (Liao 2010). Wright was more lukewarm: Bowring 'was all right, but a bit of a publicity-seeker – you got little, in fact no, interference' from him.[60]

In later phases of the Resettlement programme, Donnithorne continued his design role for several years, until he was displaced by a more forceful and opportunistic architect colleague, Colin Bramwell. Cheng again:

> All along, Donnithorne was in charge of the design of housing and resettlement blocks. But the expat officers, every two years or so, went on home leave. On one occasion, Donnithorne was on home leave, so Colin Bramwell was the

> architect taking over from him while he was away. At first it was meant to be temporary, but even after Donnithorne's return, Colin continued to work on it. This was how Colin Bramwell got in. He was junior to Donnithorne, and came later. From then on, Colin carried on working on it for a number of years, till he retired. He designed the various housing types, from resettlement to Low Cost Housing – it was all very standard, all very quick.[61]

Wright recalled that 'doing Resettlement estates was not a particularly popular job. A lot of them didn't think it was "Architecture". That was where Bramwell was different. He always had another job, and so he could continue doing "Architecture" – for instance, he did the Hong Kong Crematorium. With Resettlement blocks the task was mainly that of levelling hillsides, sites and so forth'.[62] Bramwell subsequently took responsibility for design of the later 'Mark' variants of Resettlement blocks.[63]

By November 1954, as part of the shift to a permanent, ongoing programme of resettlement flat construction in Hong Kong, beginning at Lei Cheng Uk, it was proposed to add an extra storey to new estates, raising net density from 3,310 ppa to an 'absolute maximum' of 3,862 ppa (9,543 ppha) – nearly 20 times higher than the London County Council residential maximum.[64] The planned low-rise portion of the programme would be replaced by seven-storey blocks for 120,000 on the same sites, and the temporary houses at Shek Kip Mei would be redeveloped. However, Holmes argued in November 1954 against a proposal for open ground floors, which would cause 'severe' management problems, and recommended 'recreational' use of rooftops instead.[65] (Figure 2.6)

But here, in August/September 1955, Donnithorne made another, unexpected intervention. Not only was Lei Cheng Uk the first location of Hong Kong's new,

Figure 2.6 Newspaper article of August 1960 illustrating the cycle of decanting once fully operational, with the seven-storey Mk I blocks of Jordan Valley receiving displaced squatters from the site of the Housing Authority's Clearwater Bay Road (Choi Hung) development. (cf. Fig. 3.6b).

ongoing resettlement programme, but it became the site of the first setback to the new programme – for reasons of Chinese cultural heritage. Wright recalled that

> when we were doing Lei Cheng Uk, on the Kowloon side, we uncovered a tomb. I immediately put a stop to the work, and a professor from Hong Kong University was notified. He got inside it. Ronnie said, "To hell with this tomb, let's pull the bloody thing down and get on with my Resettlement programme!"[66]

But the original impetus actually stemmed not from Wright himself but from Donnithorne. Wright recalled the same episode again on another occasion:

> This tomb was unearthed, and oddly enough it was Donnithorne, who was doing Resettlement, who did it. He came to see me in the office to say he'd discovered this tomb. I said, "Stop all work – we can't demolish a tomb of that sort!" About two hours later, Ronnie Holmes was on the phone: "What the hell have you told them to stop work for? Come on – we're going to lose a Resettlement block – get rid of the damn thing, dig it out before anybody [notices]!" I said, "No, I won't do that – it is far too important!" Anyway, we'd by now phoned the Professor of Chinese at Hong Kong University and he was going over there. Then somebody else from the Secretariat, Aserappa, phoned up, and he too was a bit cross because we were holding up the Resettlement programme on account of this tomb. Anyway, the tomb is still there, and I'm very glad. I think it would have been a terrible thing to have lost it – and the PWD – in that case, Donnithorne the architect – acted very, very responsibly against pressure from senior people in the Secretariat who would willingly have seen it demolished.[67]

That pressure was, in the event, all the greater as the find eventually led to two rather than one Mk I Resettlement blocks being cancelled. Prof. Frederick S Drake, the head of the Chinese Department at Hong Kong University, led the excavations, and while the original plan had been to demolish the remains after recording, it was eventually permanently preserved and opened to visitors from May 1957, complete with official guide-leaflet.[68] (Figure 2.7a, b, c)

Other obstacles to construction were of a more traditional kind within PWD. Corruption in the construction of the PWD's Resettlement schemes was endemic, but mainly of an incremental, ad-hoc kind: Wright recalled that 'On the construction side of the PWD, I think that the main source of corruption was fiddling the measurements and accounts'. For example,

> when we were doing Resettlement flats, the government wanted them to be built very, very quickly and very, very cheaply. If we'd had enough foremen to watch every bit of concrete being mixed to make sure it was exactly

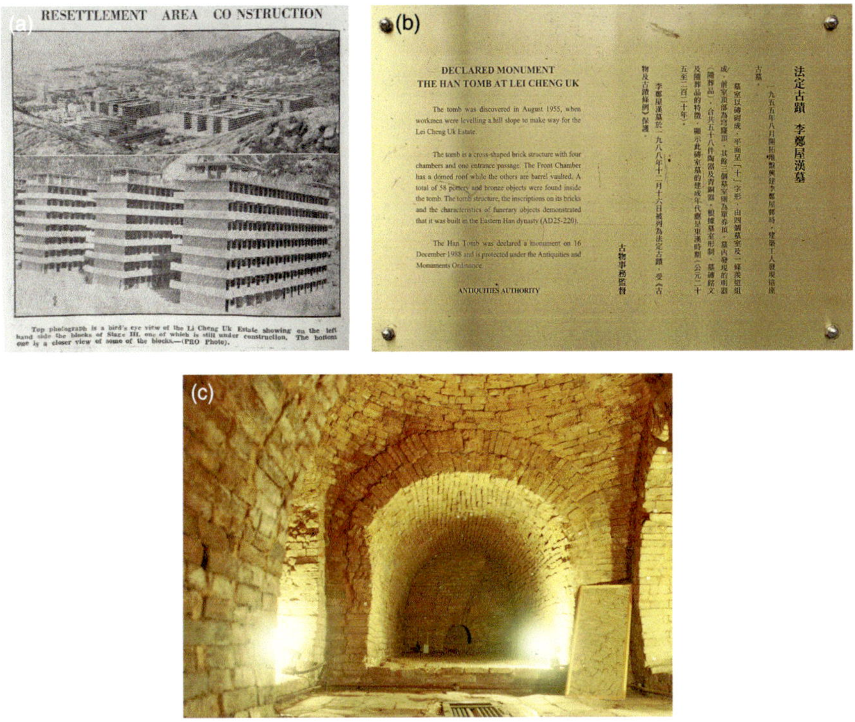

Figure 2.7 (a) Newspaper article of 1957 on Lei Cheng Uk Estate: the gap in the centre of the development is the section abandoned, to Holmes's dismay, to protect the Han tomb. (cf. Fig. 9.12b) (b) Lei Cheng Uk, commemorative plaque at preserved Han Tomb. (c) Lei Cheng Uk, interior of Han Tomb.

> according to specification, we'd have had to have about eight on each site because there was so much concrete mixing going on [which would have slowed the work].
> So probably … the concrete was substandard in mix, but there's a terrific factor of safety in concrete. But… the biggest danger of poor concrete is putting too much water in. Concrete sets by chemical action, not by the water drying out… and to get really good quality concrete you've got to have a very dry mix… Now this again slows down the work.

Post-completion, management of the estates was minimal, with consequent accretions of refuse and clutter that began even at this early stage to trouble the authorities, negating any attempt by the colonial authorities to use Resettlement as a tool of containment or 'discipline'.[69] (Figure 2.8)

Figure 2.8 1955 cartoon by Resettlement staff mocking the ineffectiveness of the department's militaristic management style.

Consolidating the Housing Society

The mid-1950s, which saw the emergence and consolidation of Hong Kong's Resettlement drive, also witnessed the parallel consolidation of the far smaller, philanthropic programme of the Hong Kong Housing Society, as well as the establishment, at last, of the government's long-debated low-cost housing initiative, a Hong Kong 'Housing Authority' closely bound up, like Resettlement, with the Urban Council.[70]

The first Housing Society scheme, at Sheung Li Uk (1954), was designed by expatriate architect Terence Stanley Feltham, and comprised 360 self-contained flats in five-storey blocks with end staircases, including internal kitchens and toilets: it cost HK$2.5 million and its overall appearance was not dissimilar to contemporary SIT schemes in Singapore. It was followed by two similar, larger schemes at Hung Hom (completed 1955/8) with corridor-access six-storey blocks, and Healthy Village I and II, North Point (1956–9, 10/11-storey slab blocks). (Figure 2.9a, b) Construction of further schemes had to wait several years, until the government extended its loans to the HS to a total of $38 million.[71] A prominent role in consolidating the Society was played by Douglas Clague, whose go-getting

Figure 2.9 (a) The Housing Society's Sheung Li Uk development, 1954: 1983 photo (MG). (b) The HS's Hung Hom Estate (1955/8): 1983 photo (MG).

attitude and networking connections proved vital in carving out and protecting a niche role for the new body, and for unofficials in general within housing.[72] Wright recalled that

> the Housing Society was first suggested by Bishop Hall in 1948 and formally set up in 1951. They got their land from government but they had to borrow money to build: they were not able to do it in the massive way in which the PWD could after they were given the go-ahead. The Housing Society was, before the Shek Kip Mei fire, pressing the government to do more for the rehousing of the squatters and the poor people. But again, I think the government didn't want to get committed financially, they were still very uncertain about the financial future of Hong Kong. The Shek Kip Mei fire really forced their hand. The Housing Society was given limited support by the Hong Kong government. The Housing Society got land for practically nothing, and had to pay for formation costs. The man I give credit for getting the Housing Society going was Dougie Clague – a controversial figure who did a great job for the Society. He thought he knew how to be a good chairman. He always did his homework, and knew what decision he wanted to get. He should have a lot of the credit for the Housing Society, and for the Housing Society's influence on government.

Equally crucial was the role of Bishop Hall, 'a very fine man' who had previously worked in Stevenage and 'was very familiar with the housing management movement in England… . He insisted on having housing management when he started the Housing Society'. The Society's chief housing manager, Ms Sanderson, later Miss Glover, was 'a forceful lady steeped in the Octavia Hill ethos.'[73] Other philanthropic general-needs housing organisations established at this time included the Hong Kong Economic Housing Society, founded September 1954 for a lower middle-income clientele. Its first project was the Lady Grantham Villas, in Tai Kok Tsui, Kowloon, opened July 1955, and comprising five-storey blocks of self-contained flats for salaried employees: designed on 'strictly practical, utilitarian and serviceable' lines, these were sold, not rented.[74]

Housing Authority, Urban Council and Resettlement – an uneasy partnership

Early 1954 saw not only the sudden eruption of the Shek Kip Mei crisis but also the slower maturing of the proposals to establish a 'Housing Authority' to oversee low-cost housing in general – the beginning of a parallel discourse of housing as an instrument of welfare betterment rather than colonial containment and control. As we saw in Chapter 1, it had been agreed in Colonial Secretary (subsequently Governor) Robert Black's Ad-Hoc Committee report in July-August 1952, that this new body should not merely come under the aegis of the Urban Council but should comprise the entire Council membership, constituted as the 'Hong Kong Housing Authority'.[75] Black introduced the bill establishing the Housing Authority (HA) in LegCo in April 1954, stressing that 'the establishment of such an organisation is no light undertaking. The most searching investigations and the most careful deliberations have been necessary'. He conceded, however, contrary to the recommendations of the Ad-Hoc Committee, that the new Authority would not take over the Housing Society and other philanthropic societies. The bill only received lukewarm support from unofficials, concerned at disruption of the private housing market and excessive costs – even though throughout the preliminary discussions, it was stressed the HA would build only basic flats that did not conflict with private enterprise.[76]

The new HA had 30 members (i.e. all Urban Councillors and some officials) and in practice – as we will see in Chapter 3 – built for white-collar workers and some medium-income tenants. It was given powers to acquire land, which were never fully used, and was to be self-financing, with capital expenditure met by loans from the government Development Loan Fund, and obligated to balance revenue and expenditure over three years. Shortly afterwards, a Housing Division was set up within the Urban Services Department to provide professional support for the Authority.[77] The time-honoured principle of entrusting a new initiative to a generalist cadet was followed here, but with different results to Holmes's impact at Resettlement: the first Commissioner for Housing, George Rowe, was a distinctly hands-off character. Wright recalled that 'Ron Firth, who was Housing Architect, told me that Rowe, as Commissioner for Housing, did bugger-all – he was very good at delegating, whereas I was a bad delegator!' And Liao concurred: 'G T Rowe was merely as Administrative Officer, brought in when they wanted to set up the department – he didn't make any contributions'.[78] Rowe himself recalled rather flippantly that 'as the first Commissioner for Housing, the problem for me was that nobody knew what the job was, how big it was. All their judgements were stupid, entirely subjective: "My friend tells me it's very bad in Wan Chai". What does he mean by "very bad"? What's he comparing it with?'[79] Rowe had little tolerance for the impassioned language of some Urban Council members, especially their (in his view) insistence on excessively high standards: 'Every move in that field had to be put to the housing authority of the Urban Council. They, unfortunately in my opinion, settled for a large standard, not luxurious, but more than basic, saying that that was only "reasonable". It's silly to use terms like that when people are in dire need. And they would say, for instance, "We have now housed 12,500 people" – in the first estate, Java Road – "and this standard is better than Resettlement". The answer, which they would never look at, was, "Yes, but you've left 6,000 out, who are now living at standards far *worse* than Resettlement, so why the bloody hell don't you bring your sights down?" They wouldn't, they never did'. Asked why, in that case, the Housing Authority had been set up in the first place, Rowe quipped, 'Good question! Good Lord! I don't know the answer… [I suppose] the Urban Council had a certain overall authority in the urban area'.[80]

From late 1955, Holmes became chairman of the Urban Council and ex-officio chair of the new Authority, and attempted to distance the latter from the former, in reflection of the traditional government disparagement of unofficials. Lightbody recalled that 'we also had an "Urban Council" which built a certain number of better-grade flats for lower and middle income people: affordable housing. They were building in small numbers: we in Resettlement were the big providers: they didn't have much money'.[81] And from Wright's perspective,

> The Housing Authority was, in effect, the Urban Council with changed hats. By that time I was Deputy Director of Public Works – so ex-officio I became vice-chairman of the Housing Authority. I never enjoyed the Housing Authority as much as the Housing Society. The Housing Society was non-political – it was made up of private-sector people who were socially keen on doing something about housing. The Housing Authority was always quarrelling with the Government. Brook Bernacchi, Elsie Elliott, [Arnaldo de Oliveira] Sales – they thought it was their job to be "The Opposition", politically – but Hong Kong doesn't work that way! I didn't enjoy going to the Housing Authority meetings: they were always quarrelling, there was no team spirit. In my first year or so on the Housing Authority I didn't attend [many meetings]. Their first architect, Donald Liao, was followed by Ron Firth. They were good, and I would work closely and happily with them – it was my fellow-members of the Authority that I found a pain in the neck![82]

In the architectural design of the first Housing Authority estates, the governing principle, in explicit contrast to Resettlement, was family self-containment. Each household would have a one-roomed flat with its own cooking and toilet facilities, at a per-person space standard (35 sq ft per adult) nearly 50% higher than Resettlement, and thus somewhat lower net density. The aim was to give families a 'home of their own', to 'give dignity and a sense of security vital to their own participation in Hong Kong's continuing social and economic progress'.[83] There was also an implicit or explicit link between Resettlement designs and the discussions concerning the formation of the Housing Authority, as seen in Barnett's

Figure 2.10 Inspection of model of the Housing Authority's Java Road development (North Point Estate) in April 1957. From left in foreground: Cheung Chan-hon (head of contractor Cheong Lee); Kenneth Fung; Ronald Holmes (then HA Chairman); Philip Au (Urban Council member); Governor Grantham; and architect Eric Cumine.

March 1954 orchestra analogy.[84] In 1955 Brook Bernacchi, in his capacity as Urban Council member and Reform Club chairman, returned from a visit to the UK and Ceylon, proudly boasting that public housing blocks currently being built in London were 'definitely inferior in design to those now being constructed at North Point and Kennedy Town'.[85] In managing these small, self-contained family flats, and their lower-income white-collar occupants, the HA explicitly followed an Octavia Hill-inspired formula of housing management, with Elizabeth Bedwell as Chief Housing Manager.[86]

The first HA estate, on a prominent harbour-side site at Java Road, North Point, was built in 1955–7, and comprised three long, U-shaped blocks with six detached or semi-detached 'towers' adjoining – all 12 storeys high, and at a net density of 2,300 ppa: the balcony access arrangement and dispersed, staggered accommodation clusters ensured excellent cross-ventilation and variegated architectural modelling.[87] With its mainly two-bedroomed flats of four types, North Point long remained 'one of the jewels in the crown' of the Authority (Akers-Jones), and its rents were calculated to cover half of the land and building costs at 5% over 40 years, plus management and maintenance costs, and a 15% surplus. (Figures 2.10, 2.11, 2.12a, b)

The second estate, at Cadogan Street, Kennedy Town (Sai Wan), designed by Stanley Feltham, which featured a cross-contour layout of splayed-out

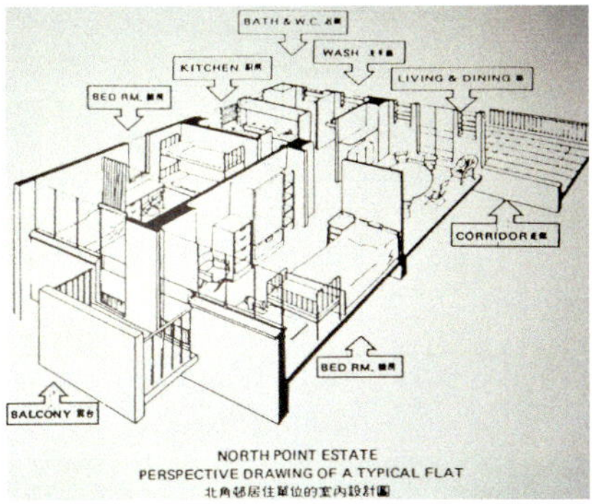

Figure 2.11 Axonometric of typical two-bedroom flat at North Point, showing self-contained facilities and through ventilation.

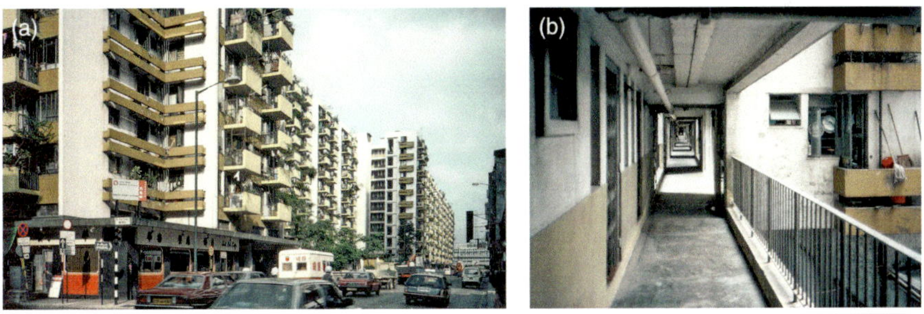

Figure 2.12 (a) The exterior of North Point Estate in 1983 (MG). (b) Access gallery in North Point Estate, pictured 1983 (MG), showing 'staggered' arrangement of accommodation towers on either side.

balcony-access slabs up to 13 storeys high, only yielded 1,300 ppa owing to its steeply sloping site, as we saw above: the ground level at the NE corner was 72 m higher than at the SW. It cost $402,000 for land, $700,000 for site development and $7 million for building costs, with a CDW grant covering the entire site development cost.[88] (Figure 2.13a, b, c, 2.14a, b)

In the following years, gradually the estate designs 'became more ambitious' (Cheng), and eventually, by the time of its supersession in the 1973 reorganisation (Chapter 5), the Housing Authority-cum-Urban Council had built 34,393 self-contained flats in nine estates, far less than Resettlement's 225,000 units in 25 estates.[89] Overall, the new Authority suffered from a three-way split in responsibility, between the Housing Division's professional approach to development and management, Rowe's generalist administrative leadership, and the often gestural political interventions of the Urban Council members. That fragmentation would be gradually addressed during the 1960s, but only finally remedied in the comprehensive unification reform of 1973.

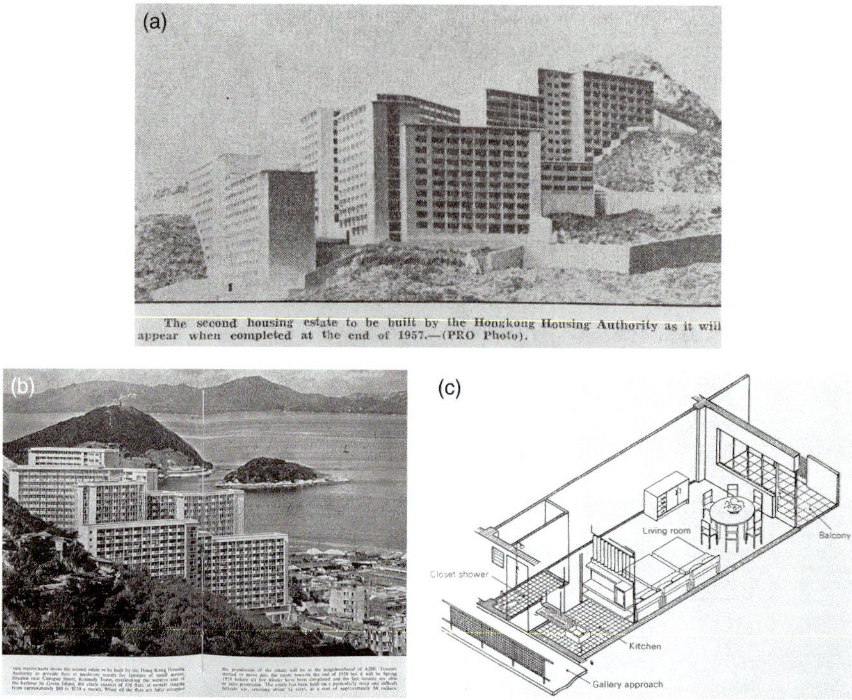

Figure 2.13 (a) Pre-construction perspective of Cadogan Street (Sai Wan) development: in SCMP article of January 1955. (b) Sai Wan under construction in 1955, illustration in 1955 *Hong Kong Annual Report.* (c) Sai Wan Estate, 1958 axonometric of typical one-room flat, with kitchen and shower unit.

Figure 2.14 (a) Sai Wan as completed, perspective view in a 1964 Government Information Services brochure on the HA, showing the extremely difficult site and the coloured balcony panels. (b) Sai Wan Estate, 2014 view (MG) from upper access gallery.

Resettlement, the Housing Authority and the Special Committees on Housing

Before the revolutionary developments of 1954, there had been incessant discussion within government (and within the Urban Council) of how the two new organisations might fit together, and in particular about whether Resettlement should come under the aegis of the Housing Authority – which would pose awkward questions about the coordination of tenant eligibility criteria, especially regarding income levels. We saw above how Barnett in March 1954 likened Housing and Resettlement to 'tunes played in the same orchestra', and that Clague, the DCS and Holmes had debated in the same month whether the Resettlement Department should become a subsidiary part of the Housing Authority or kept autonomous but under the aegis of the Urban Council. There were also differences over points of principle, as with Urban Council objections to plans to hold Housing Authority meetings in private.[90] Free-ranging organisational debates within the cadet elite continued over the following year, with Holmes now arguing in November 1955 that the Resettlement Department must retain its autonomous existence, despite the risk of '*imperium in imperio*' ('a state within a state'): the 1954 squatting policy report had recommended a permanent resettlement programme.[91] Equally contentious was potential overlap between the new Housing Authority and the private sector: John Cowperthwaite, later an intransigent defender of the colony's free-market system as Financial Secretary (1961–71), complained at LegCo in 1954 that Housing Authority-subsidised flats 'will compete with private low-cost housing. We do not want to get to the stage where subsidised housing will kill private housing.' Yet 1956 also saw opposition by Bowring to a proposal by Bernacchi for a programme of private redevelopment. And the 1955 Budget fleshed out the Urban Council's plan for a programme of low-cost high flats.[92]

Thus, a wide range of possibilities was still in play, together with tensions about the roles of the two new departments. These tensions, however, were put in suspense for the remainder of the decade by a decision to channel further debate through a Special Committee on Housing, which would enable the ruling administrative generalists to co-opt specialist advice. It was to be chaired by Rowe, as Commissioner for Housing – in itself a mildly 'unifying' gesture – and with middle-ranking executive officer W E Collard as secretary.[93]

The committee's First Interim Report, in May 1956, pronounced itself 'deeply impressed' with the scale of the Resettlement programme, but insisted there still must be 'a new and positive policy' for housing development, including building of 'the equivalent of one [British Mark 1] New Town, not much smaller than York, each year'. This, the Report emphasised, would require expansion of development into the New Territories. In response, a Development Office was established within PWD to oversee the building of the proposed satellite towns, followed by the 1957 appointment of Scott Wilson Kirkpatrick to report on potential sites.[94] In that year – showing how geo-political considerations were increasingly lurking in the background of Hong Kong housing controversies – the Special Committee's deliberations became embroiled with the embarrassing public controversy about Hong Kong's refugee problem at the United Nations: Atkinson at the Colonial Office pressurised Burgess in January 1957 about the committee's progress, suggesting that the two were seen as clearly linked. The committee's Second Interim Report, in February 1957, accordingly went rather further, and now proposed establishment of a separate Housing Department under a new 'Commissioner for Housing'. This would take over the Housing Division of the Urban Services Department – a proposal rapidly accepted by the government.[95] A 1957 survey of private housing showed 70% of households occupied a dwelling of less than 120 sq ft – the Resettlement space standard.[96] Eventually, the Committee would issue its final report in 1958, but this, rather than ending the ongoing debate, would further escalate reform demands, by proposing the unification of all public housing agencies into a single organisation, that would somehow unify the 'containment' and 'welfare' strands of colonial housing policy (see Chapter 3).

Towards town planning and new towns

A principal concern of the Special Committee was the relation between housing, especially 'emergency' housing, and town planning, especially in relation to the growing calls for modernisation of the territory as a whole, and development in the New Territories. Here the precedent of Singapore's SIT, with its coordinated oversight of planning and housing, seemed relevant, despite the visceral hostility of many Hongkongers towards any kind of planned coordination. Comparisons between the two were made constantly by officials. In 1956, for example, Bowring highlighted not only Singapore's more easily developable and plannable 'hinterland' but also the greater staffing resources dedicated to planning within the SIT, with no fewer than eight expatriate planners and 72 other planning staff.[97]

During the 1950s, as the principles of spacious, if unexciting, 'colony master-planning' were developed by the SIT, the chief focus of 'planning' innovation within Hong Kong was instead one of laissez-faire-based density intensification. Here the set-piece was a 1956 amendment to the Buildings Ordinance, paralleling the removal of tenant protection in the 1956 Landlord and Tenant Ordinance Amendment. It allowed a much higher density in private-sector redevelopment schemes, and building up to 20 storeys or more in freer, more verticalised configurations– the result being a boom in private production, peaking in 1959 (12,000 flats).[98] But with the 'path-dependency' towards very small flats already firmly established, the result was a dramatic explosion of ultra-dense site cramming in both Kowloon and Hong Kong, often in enormously massive blocks tapered-off at the top in accordance with building-envelope regulations. This prompted a cutback in permitted densities in 1962, but with a 'period of grace' until 1966 that in reality only further encouraged densification.[99]

Beyond these exchanges, the status of planning in Hong Kong remained precarious in the extreme, and generally disregarded by administrators: Rowe recalled that all plans for Hong Kong by then 'were out of date, and they were all bloody barmy anyway', Wright likewise claimed Abercrombie's report 'was out of date before it was finished', and Liao argued the floods of refugees had rendered

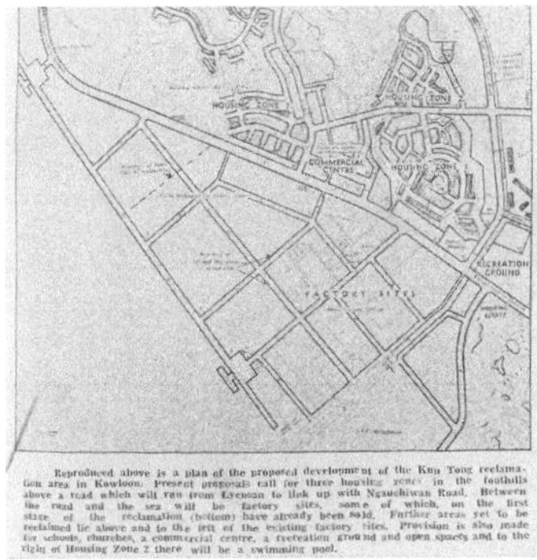

Figure 2.15 Layout plan in December 1956 for industrial 'new town' at Kwun Tong, including housing for 120,000 inhabitants in three zones arranged in garden-city fashion.

Abercrombie immediately obsolete.[100] In 1953, Grantham had effectively vetoed any immediate progress with Abercrombie's agenda, arguing that 'to carry out large-scale town planning schemes will not be possible until the present congestion of the urban areas is reduced by the… . resettlement of squatters in outlying areas or by the end of emergency conditions.'[101] The two satellite communities actually started now, Tsuen Wan and Kwun Tong, were essentially high-density industrial suburbs of flatted factories, bound up with both resettlement clearances and land reclamation.[102] (Figure 2.15)

But the Abercrombie agenda of strategic population dispersal and satellite towns did not go away. As we saw above, the Special Committee's First Interim Report in May 1956 had advocated the building of new towns in the New Territories.[103] In July 1956, against opposition from the Director of Public Works, who argued against putting planning 'on a more elaborate basis', the report of a Civic Association town-planning special committee on New Territories sites proposed five specific sites for potential 'self contained' new towns: at Gin Drinkers Bay (later more tactfully renamed Kwai Chung), Tai Po, Sha Tin, Junk Bay (later Tseung Kwan O) and Castle Peak (later Tuen Mun).[104] Most of these were still undeveloped: Sha Tin, for example, was 'a completely rural area in the late '40s – it had a little river, with fish, and rice plantations'.[105] In December 1957, nearing the end of his governorship, Grantham significantly qualified his previous laissez-faire stance and predicted to LegCo that there was a 'limitless task ahead of the Colony' in New Territories satellite town development, and that 'planning will have to go on and on'.[106]

Into this 1956/7 debate weighed the colourful figure of HKU architecture professor Gordon Brown, who predictably compared Hong Kong unfavourably to Singapore, arguing that it 'has no plan for development' and was indeed 'the largest unplanned city in the world'; and that the new town strategy recommended by the Special Committee was likely to be excessively expensive and 'more arresting than constructive'.[107] (Figure 2.16) Instead, Brown advocated more intensive

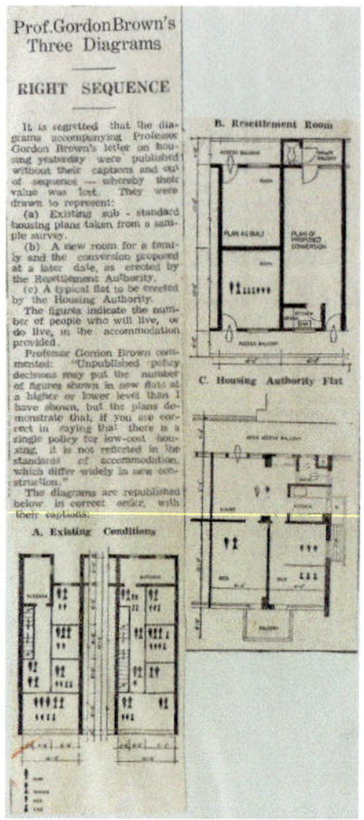
Prof. Gordon Brown's Three Diagrams

RIGHT SEQUENCE

It is regretted that the diagrams accompanying Professor Gordon Brown's letter on housing yesterday were published without their captions and out of sequence — whereby their value was lost. They were drawn to represent:

(a) Existing sub - standard housing plans taken from a sample survey.

(b) A new room for a family and the conversion proposed at a later date, as erected by the Resettlement Authority.

(c) A typical flat to be erected by the Housing Authority.

The figures indicate the number of people who will live, or do live, in the accommodation provided.

Professor Gordon Brown commented: "Unpublished policy decisions may put the number of figures shown in new flats at a higher or lower level than I have shown, but the plans demonstrate that, if you are correct in saying that there is a single policy for low-cost housing, it is not reflected in the standards of accommodation, which differ widely in new construction."

The diagrams are republished below in correct order, with their captions.

A. Existing Conditions

B. Resettlement Room

C. Housing Authority Flat

Figure 2.16 1956 comparative plans of mixed-function pre-World War II tenement with Mk I Resettlement and Housing Authority (North Point) flats, drawn in 1956 by Prof. Gordon Brown of HKU.

Figure 2.17 1957 exhibition of HKU 5th-year architecture students' proposal for new town at Tai Po – expressing 'economy, imaginative realism, and planning for the people'. This November 1957 SCMP view shows student Fanny So explaining the scheme to DPW Inglis (left) and New Territories District Commissioner Ken Barnett.

redevelopment of prime urban sites such as Ho Man Tin, where proposals for 150 ppa redevelopment of a large squatter area were 'hardly economic' and should be intensified to 600 ppa instead.[108] Stimulated by the government-backed proposal for the five New Territories sites, a group of HKU architecture students in late 1957 prepared a studio concept project for a New Town at Tai Po, guided by 'economy, imaginative realism and planning for the people', and duly forwarded it to Barnett (by now District Commissioner, New Territories) and the PWD planners. (Figure 2.17) The SCMP argued that any new town strategy 'will demand a massive cooperative effort by government and private enterprise'. In the event, as we will see in the following chapters, it soon became clear that the state would need to play a far larger and more interventionist role in the mature new towns programme.[109]

Notes

1 Lightbody, 2011 interview.
2 Ure, *Governors, Politics and the Colonial Office*, 176–8, 265, 268–9.
3 Ure, *Governors, Politics and the Colonial Office*, 163.
4 Ure, *Governors, Politics and the Colonial Office*, 188–9, 222–4.
5 Tsang, *Modern History of Hong Kong*, 165; Ian Scott, *Political Change and the Crisis of Legitimacy in Hong Kong*, Hurst, London, 1999, 133–6.
6 Ure, *Governors, Politics and the Colonial Office*, 222–4
7 Miles Glendinning, *Modern Architect, the Life and Times of Robert Matthew*, RIBA, London, 2008, 134–5, on Gordon Brown's previous controversies; Wright, 2011 interview.
8 Grantham, 1968 Bodleian interview.
9 Grantham, 1968 Bodleian interview.
10 HKRS158-1-62 1-1957 Colonial Office to Burgess, 4–1957 Governor to Secretary of State for the Colonies.
11 Neil Monnery, *Architect of Prosperity, Sir John Cowperthwaite and the Making of Hong Kong*, London Publishing Partnership, 2017, 113–9; Scott, *Political Change and the Crisis of Legitimacy*, 74.
12 Hong Kong Public Works Department, *Annual Departmental Report for the Financial Year 1961–62*, Hong Kong, 1962, 21–2.
13 HKRS156-1-5264 12-1955 to 2-1956 Colonial Office-Hong Kong exchange.
14 HKRS156-1-5264 memo 3-1956 on Atkinson visit; HKRS232-1-5-1 cuttings of SCMP 3-2-1956 and 6-3-1956.
15 HKRS156-1-5264 Lightbody, AS (Lands), memo of 3–1956; HKRS158-1-62 Atkinson to Burgess; HKRS156-1-5264 12-1955 Colonial Office memo and 3–1956 memo on Atkinson visit.
16 Ure, *Governors, Politics and the Colonial Office*, 176–8
17 Wright, 2011 interview; Cheng, 2014 interview; Ure, *Governors, Politics and the Colonial Office*, 177.
18 Tsui, 'Minimum government assistance', 1274; Ure, *Governors, Politics and the Colonial Office*, 178–9.
19 Ure, *Governors, Politics and the Colonial Office*, 178–9, 269 L C Wong 2011
20 Wright, 2011 interview.
21 HKRS163-1-781 1–1954 papers of Urban Council emergency sub-committee; Commissioner for Resettlement, *Report for 1955–56*, 33–5. Wai, *Design DNA of Mark I*, 93.
22 Ure, *Governors, Politics and the Colonial Office*, 179–81.
23 Ure, *Governors, Politics and the Colonial Office*, 181.
24 Ure, *Governors, Politics and the Colonial Office*, 181.
25 HKRS163-1-781, DCS memo of 3–1954; Holmes memo of 3–1954.

26 Williams, 'Administration of Public Housing in Hong Kong' and 'Housing in Hong Kong'; 'Sir Ronald: 40 great years', SCMP 30-4-1977 cutting.
27 Ure, *Governors, Politics and the Colonial Office*, 270; 'Sir Ronald', SCMP 30-4-1977; HKRS163-1-791 4–1954 note by Holmes; 163-3-20 appointment discussions 3–1954; Ure, *Governors, Politics and the Colonial Office*, 181–3; Elsie Tu, *Colonial Hong Kong in the Eyes of Elsie Tu*, Hong Kong UP, 2003, 50; Steve Tsang, *Governing Hong Kong – Administrative Officers from the Nineteenth Century to the Handover to China, 1861–1997*, I B Tauris, London, 2007, 68.
28 HKRS163-1-781 12–1953 discussion about transferring resettlement from Urban Services to Public Works; 3–1954 note by Holmes.
29 Steve Tsang, *Governing Hong Kong, 20;* Ure, *Governors, Politics and the Colonial Office*, 181–3; Wright, 2015 interview (Holmes 'very keen' and 'charming Eurasian wife'; cadets 'experts in everything, but knew nothing'); Williams, 'Administration of Public Housing in Hong Kong'. HKRS 163-1-791 4–1954 memo from Holmes.
30 Williams, 'Housing in Hong Kong'; SCMP 27-1-1954; HKRS163-1-781 1–1954 DCS to CS.
31 HKRS163-1-781 memos of 7–1954 and 8–1954; HKRS310-1-1 1-1954 and 2–1954 comparative cost breakdowns.
32 HKRS310-3-1: 1954 memos, detailed schedule and progress reports for completions at Shek Kip Mei for Contract 63/53.
33 HKRS163-1-781 memos of 5-7-1954, 26-10-1954 by Holmes for ExCo; Williams, 'Administration of Public Housing in Hong Kong', 1–2.
34 HKRS310-1-1, 10-1954 Wright note; Ure, *Governors, Politics and the Colonial Office*, 183–6; HKRS232-1-4, 18-11-55 SCMP cutting. Progress of Shek Kip Mei scheme and follow-ons: HKRS 163-1-781, HKRS310-1-1, HKRS310-3-1, HKRS232-1-3.
35 Ure, *Governors, Politics and the Colonial Office*, 184.
36 HKRS232-1-4 SCMP 29-7-1955 cutting of Holmes and Lennox-Boyd.
37 Ure, *Governors, Politics and the Colonial Office*, 186.
38 Yue Chim Richard Wong, *Hong Kong Land for Hong Kong People – Fixing the Failures of our Housing Policy*, Hong Kong UP, 2015, 60–61.
39 HKRS163-3-20, 1960 Hon. CS speech; Williams, 'Housing in Hong Kong'; P-Y Ho, *Challenges for an Evolving City: 160 Years of Port and Land Development in Hong Kong*, Commercial Press, Hong, Kong, 2004; Ure, *Governors, Politics and the Colonial Office*, 269–70.
40 Wright, 2015 interview.
41 Ho, *Challenges*; Tu, *Colonial Hong Kong*, 41–6; Y C Jao, 'The rise of Hong Kong as a financial center', *Asian Survey*, 19 (7), 1979, 674–694.
42 Tu, *Colonial Hong Kong*, 47.
43 Tu, *Colonial Hong Kong*, 41–5.
44 Tu, *Colonial Hong Kong*, 50; Alan Smart, *The Shek Kip Mei Myth – Squatters, Fires and Colonial Rule in Hong Kong, 1950–1963*, Hong Kong UP, 2006, 140–4.
45 HKRS 163-1-791, 310-3-1, 310-3-1. Resettlement targets: Williams, 'Public Housing and I', 'Administration of Public Housing'; Ure, *Governors, Politics and the Colonial Office*, 179–187. Grantham set a target of 500,000 persons resettled in ten years from 1954 – i.e. 50,000 per year (Williams 'Public Housing and I'), but in fact 600,000 were resettled by 1964, plus 240,000 in GLCH (Y C R Wong, *Hong Kong Land*, 60–1). Actual Resettlement units completions in 1954/5 = 6,196, 1955/6 = 5,424, 1956/7 = 8,853, 1957/8 = 5,557 (M Castells, L Goh, R Y W Kwok, *The Shek Kip Mei Syndrome – Economic*

Development and Public Housing in Hong Kong and Singapore, Pion, London, 1990, 10). Cottage programme: Tsui, 'Minimum government intervention', 1275–6.
46 Lightbody, 2011 interview.
47 Rowe, 1987 Bodleian interview.
48 Fung Tung, 2010 interview; Mizuoka, *Contrived Laissez-Faireism*; J M Carroll, *A Concise History of Hong Kong*, Rowman & Littlefield, Lanham, 2007.
49 Wright, 1988 Bodleian interview; Liao, 2010 interview.
50 Wright, 2011 interview; HKRS163-1-781, 24-3-1954 papers. Wai, *Design DNA of Mark I*, 69–74. HKHA, *The First Two Million*, 1980, 36.
51 HKRS163-3-20 9-11-1954 memo for ExCo by Colonial Secretariat; HKRS163-1-781 1954 note; HKRS232-1-3 SCMP 30-5-1955 cuttings on single-storey huts at Ngau Tau Kok, costing HK$1,189 each, completed May 1955 in an area 'until recently' a mess. Wai, *Design DNA of Mark I*, 69–74.
52 Wright, 2011 interview; HKRS310-1-1 9–1954 correspondence. Bowring Bungalows: Wai, *Design DNA of Mark I*, 67–74.
53 Wai, *Design DNA of Mark I*, 75–86, 121–137; HKRS 310-1-1; *The Hong Kong and Far East Builder*, 11:5, 1955, 61–4.
54 HKRS163-3-20 DUS Barnett note to CS 24-3-1954.
55 Wai, *Design DNA of Mark I*, 89–107. Wright, 2011 interview; HKRS 896-1-72 3–1954, Canton Road Police Quarters, report of special sub-committee of Urban Council with detailed description.
56 Cheng, 2014 interview.
57 HKRS310-1-1 8-2-1954 note.
58 Wright, 2011 interview; Wai, *Design DNA of Mark I*, 67–74. Shewan, www.scottisharchitects.org.uk/architect_full.php?id=204768.
59 Lightbody, 2011 interview.
60 Wright, 2011 interview; SCMP 8-12-1955, 1-7-1956, 9-1-1957; Hong Kong Public Works Department, *Annual Departmental Report for the Financial Year 1961–62*, 71–2.
61 Cheng, 2014 interview.
62 Wright, 2011 interview.
63 Cheng, 2014 interview. J R Firth, 'Housing in Hong Kong', *Builder*, 9-2-1962, 298
64 HKRS232-1-4 11-12-1954 and 18-11-1955 SCMP cuttings; HKRS63-3-20, 9-11-1954 ExCo Memo by Colonial Secretariat. Wai, *Design DNA of Mark I*, 85.
65 HKRS163-3-20 CfR to DCS.
66 Wright, 2015 interview.
67 Wright, 1988 Bodleian interview.
68 HKRS232-1-4, SCMP 19-9-1955 and 1-10-1955 cuttings; HKRS232-1-6 SCMP 5–1957 cuttings.
69 Wright, 1988 Bodleian interview; Kockelkorn et al, 'Peripheralisation', 618.
70 Housing Society: Wai, *Design DNA of Mark I*, 53–6.
71 Wai, *Design DNA of Mark I*, 53–6.
72 L C Wong, 2011 interview; HKRS896-1-72 3–1954 report of special sub-committee of Urban Council; HKRS232-1-3, SCMP 14-10-1954 cutting.
73 Wright, 2011 interview and 1988 Bodleian interview. Wai, *Design DNA of Mark I*, 53.
74 Wai, *Design DNA of Mark I*, 47–52; *The Hong Kong and Far East Builder*, 11:4, 1955, 57–8. Eunice Seng, 'The City in a Building', *Studies in the History and Theory of Architecture*, vol 5, 2015, 85; Carmen Tsui, 'Welfare housing in colonial Hong Kong – the contributions of philanthropic organisations', Association of Critical Heritage Studies,

2016. (https://sites.grenadine.co/sites/patrimoine/en/ACHS2016/) HKRS896-1-71 memo of 19-5-1952 from K Barnett CUC, to CS. Hong Kong Civil Servants' Housing Society quadrangle by Szeto: HKRS 232-1-5-1 6-1-1956 tour of co-operative enterprises.
75 Ure, *Governors, Politics and the Colonial Office*, 156-8, Monnery, *Architect of Prosperity*, 105.
76 Ure, *Governors, Politics and the Colonial Office*, 158–9.
77 Williams, 'Administration of Public Housing in Hong Kong'; HKRS158-1-62 Special Committee 2nd Interim Report, 4–1957 note from Governor to Lennox-Boyd.
78 Wright, 2011 interview; Liao, 2010 interview.
79 Rowe, 1987 Bodleian interview.
80 Rowe, 1987 Bodleian interview.
81 Lightbody, 2011 interview.
82 Wright, 2011 interview.
83 HKRS156-3-6, HA brochure of c.1970.
84 HKRS 163-1-78 3-1954 papers, and HKRS163-3-20.
85 HKRS232-1-4 18-9-1955 *South China Sunday Post* cutting.
86 Fung Tung, 2010 interview ('Carroll came later from Singapore because Fraser knew him'; HA's 'phenomenal' rent collection approach, zero arrears).
87 *HKIA Journal* 72, 2016, 'Occupy Housing', 144–5. E Bedwell, 'Low cost housing in Hong Kong, 1958', *Housing Review*, 11/12–1958, 181–3. *Municipal Journal*, 6-2-1959, 374. W E Collard, 'Housing in Hong Kong', *Housing Review*, 3-1960, 51–63.
88 North Point: *Hong Kong & Far Eastern Builder*, vol 11:1, 1955, 27. J R Firth, 'Three new Hong Kong housing projects', *Builder*, 6-9-1957, 398–9. J R Firth, 'Housing in Hong Kong', *Builder,* 9-2-1962, 298. Akers-Jones, 2014 interview; HKRS 156-1-5264 3–1956 memo, and 12–1955 Colonial Office memo; HKRS156-3-6 file on Cadogan St; HKRS 232-1-4 26-10-55 cutting with detailed account. Cadogan St: W E Collard, 'Housing in Hong Kong', *Housing Review*, 3-1960, 51–63; *Architectural Review*, 7–1960, 74. *Municipal Journal,* 20-3-1964, 932. *Architect and Building News*, 10-5-1956, 489, and 12-7-1956, 74.
89 Williams, 'Administration of Public Housing in Hong Kong'.
90 HKRS163-3-20 31-3-1954 Barnett to DCS; HKRS163-1-781 12–1952 discussion on responsibility for resettlement, and 3–1954 Urban Council discussion on 'open debates'.
91 HKRS163-3-20 23-11-1955 Holmes to Hon. CS; Monnery, *Architect of Prosperity*, 103.
92 HKRS163-1-781, 12–1956 DPW paper; Monnery, *Architect of Prosperity*, 107.
93 HKRS158-1-62, 27-5-1956 First Interim Report of the Special Committee on Housing (members T L Bowring, M W Lo, R C Lee, Brook Bernacchi, J D Clague, B C Field, J J Cowperthwaite). Ure, *Governors, Politics and the Colonial Office*, 185; HKRS156-1-4809, 7–1956 interim report papers.
94 HKRS158-1-62 27-5-1956, First Interim Report.
95 HKRS158-1-62 5-2-1957, Second Interim Report of the Special Committee on Housing; HKRS232-1-7 SCMP 18-12-1958 cutting.
96 HKRS158-1-62 1-1957 message from Colonial Office to Burgess; Williams, 'Public Housing and I'.
97 HKRS156-1-3425 Bowring 7–1956 memo; HKRS232-1-5-1 9-2-1956 paper on Singapore.
98 HKRS232-1-6 9-1957 PWD Report.

99 Path dependency: Y C R Wong, *Hong Kong Land*, 63; Williams, 'Public Housing and I'.
100 Rowe, 1987 Bodleian interview; Wright, 1988 Bodleian interview.
101 HKRS156-1-3425 AS1 note to DCS 7–1956.
102 Wright, 2015 interview; Junwei Li, 'Immigration, employment and New Town initiatives in Hong Kong', 998–1001.
103 HKRS158-1-62 27-5-1956 First Interim Report.
104 HKRS156-1-3425, 7–1956 and 8–1956 correspondence; HKRS158-1-62; HKRS232-1-6 10-12-1957 Special Committee July 1956 report.
105 Liao, 2010 interview.
106 HKRS232/1/6 22-12-1957 note by Grantham.
107 Liao, 2010 interview; HKRS232-1-5-2 18-8-1956 letter.
108 HKRS232-1-5-2 18-8-1956 Gorden Brown letter on Ho Man Tin.
109 HKRS232-1-6 11-1957, 12–1957 clippings.

3 1958–1964

Robin Black and incremental reform

Between January 1958 and March 1964, Hong Kong was governed by Sir Robert ('Robin') Black, previously Colonial Secretary in 1952–5, the years of the Shek Kip Mei revolution. In between (1955–8), he had been Governor of Singapore in the lead-up to self-rule, and was reputed to have favoured Lee Kuan Yew as 'the best prospect to lead an independent Singapore'. Born and brought up in Edinburgh, where he attended George Watson's College and Edinburgh University, Robin Black combined insider familiarity with Hong Kong's governmental system and the issues of decolonisation, with a practical, 'hands-on', low-key approach. He framed himself as a 'nuts and bolts Governor' who 'hated pomp and pomposity', making unannounced visits to community and housing projects.[1] Although he downplayed 'grandiose schemes' in favour of an incremental approach, housing was at the core of his personal agenda, which focused on limited social provision to support the expanded labour force needed for Hong Kong's switch from entrepot to manufacturing city: an expansion of Grantham's restricted colonial agenda of containment and control. Thus a central policy aim was to speed up resettlement and clearance of squatter areas: 'His aim was to make sure that the average man in the street would have somewhere to live'.[2]

This restricted social agenda was, as always in Hong Kong, grounded in the geopolitical realities of the territory's position, whose precariousness had been vividly impressed on Black by his previous Hong Kong and Singapore experiences. He acknowledged frankly that 'we hold our position in Hong Kong at China's sufferance' and thus must avoid 'rocking the boat'.[3] Thus in January 1963 he backed away from confrontation with Kowloon Walled City residents over planned demolition of 200 dwellings there, a plan attacked by Beijing as a 'gross violation of China's sovereignty'. While denying that China had sovereignty over the enclave, he pragmatically shelved the redevelopment plans indefinitely.[4] The previous year (1962), he wrote to the Permanent Under-Secretary of State for the Colonies that there was no explanation for China's failure to press its claims on Hong Kong other than that 'her immediate interests counsel restraint' and the conviction that 'time will not derogate from these claims': 'it is on this slim thread that the stability and, indeed, the security of Hong Kong depend'.[5]

DOI: 10.1201/9781315563701-4

Alongside Hong Kong's political dependency, he well appreciated its absolute *material* dependence on China for key essentials, ranging from bricks for building (70% of Hong Kong's needs in 1962) to water supply, which began to feature ever more problematically in his worries.[6] Although official contacts with the Po On Regional People's committee just over the border were established in 1960, and the first mainland water supplies followed from 1962, supply became increasingly precarious and highly rationed in the following years. Deputy Director of Public Works Robson travelled to Guangzhou for further negotiations, while a proportion of supply needs were supported by a Hong Kong fleet of tankers. Occasional weather calamities such as Typhoon Wanda (September 1962) further disrupted administrative order.[7]

Like Grantham, Black combined opposition to the Young agenda of internal political self-determination, for which he was convinced there was 'emphatically no emotional popular support', with vigorous pursuit of administrative self-determination from London. Within weeks of his arrival he had persuaded the Colonial Office to agree it need no longer approve the government's Annual Estimates.[8] A key supporting role in 1958–1963 was played by Colonial Secretary Claude Burgess. He argued to the Secretary of State in London in 1962 for a strongly inclusive approach to the one million immigrants of the previous 12 years, with Resettlement as a key building-block: seven years ago the government had 'decided to integrate every immigrant into our community – the new people become our people'.[9]

In pursuit of this ideal, the government elite witnessed the first organisational reforms. The cadets were retitled the 'Administrative Service' in 1962, following a 1959 review, and what would later be known as 'localisation' got underway, the first Chinese female administrative officer being appointed in 1961.[10] The growing specialisation of government business foregrounded the work of professional staff, but they remained of lesser status, and resented the gentlemanly, generalist pretensions of the administrators.[11] Michael Wright vividly recalled this uneasy relationship.

> The Administrative Service thought they could do anything. Ian Lightbody, for example, was a good friend of mine, but he felt that, as an Administrative Officer, he could do anything. Or George Rowe: my wife and Mrs Rowe were friends, we were neighbours in the Pavilion Flats, but he was an administrator, and his approach was to sit back, and read the newspaper, and let the hoi polloi do the work.[12]

Old, racist ways still persisted within the service: Akers-Jones recalled that despite his talent and drive, Ronald Holmes could never become governor or colonial secretary because 'he had a Eurasian wife, which was frowned on'.[13] There was also the question of corruption, which was reputedly rife among lower-grade officials such as estate managers or police officers, both expatriate and Chinese, but even occasionally within the Administrative Service: Wright recalled that 'When I became [PWD] assistant director, I had no respect for the PACS Lands, because I didn't think that he was honest'.[14]

Externally, the pattern became established of better relations with Conservative-controlled London governments than with the Labour Party – for both industrial-relations and political-ideological reasons. The multi-headedness of the Hong Kong housing apparatus confronted visitors with an obstacle-course of overlapping tour destinations: Lord and Lady Perth, for example, in October 1960, visited a squatter resettlement area, a new Resettlement estate, and a Housing Authority estate, and in September 1963, Lord Lansdowne, the Minister of State at the Colonial Office, visited Resettlement estates with the Commissioner for Resettlement, and the HA's So Uk estate with the Commissioner for Housing and the Executive Committee of the Housing Authority: it was specified for the tour that 'shorts should be worn'.[15] Senior civil servants came in their wake: following a 1962 visit, Sir Edward Muir, Permanent Secretary to the Ministry of Works, declared himself 'amazed' at the PWD's housing projects.[16]

For architectural and housing professionals, the most important external visitor was still George Atkinson, now head of the Tropical Section of the Building Research Station at Watford, but the continuing strength of Hong Kong 'chauvinism' within the Secretariat meant the welcome given him by administrators was not unqualified.[17] On a November-December 1960 visit, he met not only architectural staff such as Firth or Wright (as DDPW) but also Housing Authority housing managers. In September of that year, Firth, as acting Commissioner for Housing (see below), reported that Atkinson had asked to see completed Authority estates, and 'to examine what is planned for the future, in order that he shall be better able to advise the Secretary of State on the provision of low-cost housing here' – at which point Colonial Secretary Burgess scrawled two large exclamation marks in the margin. Firth continued enthusiastically that 'I myself frequently consult on various aspects of the work, and his advice is always sound and comprehensive'.[18] Caught up in the heady atmosphere, the Deputy Colonial Secretary minuted Burgess in September 1960, 'I think it would be a good idea to get Mr Atkinson here and try and impress him, so that we can be sure of an up-to-date friend at court'.[19] To this Burgess replied acidly that 'there may be benefit to Mr Atkinson in the proposed visit, but I'm not so sure about benefit to us' – and thus the visit should be merely 'a courtesy call' rather than 'a full-dress detailed discussion'.[20] Reciprocally, professional staff visited Atkinson in London: for example, Bedwell called on him and Woodhouse at the Colonial Office in November to discuss housing management, and they gave Bedwell a copy of an influential paper by Stone and Reiners on building costs which claimed multi-storey flats cost disproportionately more than low-rise housing – hardly a relevant argument for Hong Kong, as it would turn out in due course! Colonial Office ministers and staff were expected to defend their Hong Kong colleagues from criticisms by UK-based commentators: for example, in November 1960, Lord Perth reported to Black that he had had a visit from National Liberal MP Joan Vickers, who was anxious to improve minimum housing standards in resettlement schemes, but had told her of the 'overriding concern' in Hong Kong 'that they must build to a rent of $14 per month, and that any increase would cause grave unrest': he warned the Governor that people like Vickers were likely 'to press the issue pretty hard'.[21]

Government self-sufficiency and higher public spending

The late 1950s and 1960s were the years in which Hong Kong's textile-led industrial export boom reached maturity. Rising urban land prices were helping to fuel Hong Kong's manufacturing industry, by encouraging enterprises to relocate to areas such as Kwun Tong, where they could build large modern factories with their capital gains. For example, Sir S Y Chung built a two-storey, 10,000-square-foot factory at To Kwa Wan in the 1950s at a cost of $750,000, and sold this in the 1960s for over $3 million, with which he bought a 35,000 ft^2 plot in San Po Kong – and so the process of aggrandisement went on.[22] To avoid jeopardising this process, successive Financial Secretaries and governors continued to pursue 'the goal of total financial independence'.[23] As mentioned above, Black finally achieved this through the March 1958 agreement that the Colonial Office would no longer require the annual estimates to be submitted for their approval. This position had already applied *de facto* for several years, as the Colonial Office could hardly intervene effectively if Hong Kong required no financial assistance from Britain, but it now became official policy, announced by Black at ExCo soon after his arrival. However, Hong Kong's sudden eruption of manufacturing industry, combined with its laissez-faire economic internationalism, would rapidly come into conflict with the postwar trade protectionism and state-coordinated 'national capitalism' of the 'mother country' – ironically once the world's leading redoubt of the free-trade values now championed by Hong Kong, but now deeply committed to import controls against Commonwealth textiles, supported for different reasons by both Tory and Labour politicians.[24]

The dedication of successive administrations to a laissez-faire economic policy ensured there would continue to be suspicion of anything smacking of strategic planning. In his 1960 budget, Financial Secretary Clark rhetorically asked whether the government should 'do something to plan our economy', but his successor from 1961, John Cowperthwaite, vigorously reaffirmed the traditional policy. In January 1962, for example, Cowperthwaite opposed any general rent-control policy, arguing it risked suppressing private enterprise building; and in March 1962, in a speech to LegCo, he emphatically rejected the idea of five-year plans, stressing 'my deep-seated dislike and distrust of anything of this sort in Hong Kong', redolent as it was of 'Papa knows best'.[25] Yet he freely admitted that the government was aiming to resettle 100,000 people each year, and on top of this to house 60,000 in HA and Government Low-Cost dwellings, and emphatically supported state involvement in water supply planning and provision.[26] In education, a goal was set of schooling all primary-age children by 1961, while medical/health expenditure rose from 6% to 10% of the government's total expenditure between 1951 and 1964.[27] In his 1963 and 1965 budget speeches, Cowperthwaite set out this balance between laissez-faire and basic intervention. In 1963, 'I do not think that when one is speaking of hardships or benefits, one can reasonably speak in terms of classes or social groups but only in terms of individuals'. And in 1965,

> whatever we do for the middle-income groups must not be such as to prejudice, by diversion of resources or energy, the continuation of our maximum housing

> effort at the lower end of the scale. It is normal in richer countries that government moves into the field of state-aided housing for the middle classes, only where demand lower down the income scale is nearing satisfaction.[28]

Government statistics emphatically demonstrated the inter-relationship between rising government income and expenditure. Whereas government revenue, expenditure, and surplus in 1957/8 comprised $584, $533 and $51 million, respectively, in 1962/3 those three figures had risen to $1,253, $1,113 and $140 million. Housing expenditure rose sharply in absolute terms, from $106 million to $207 million between 1960/1 and 1963/4, but remained constant as a percentage of total social expenditure and overall government expenditure: from 33% and 12% in 1960/1 to 38% and 15% in 1963/4.[29]

Rising expectations and the Special Committee Final Report

Black's governorship saw the start of an inexorable reversal in the public and political reputation of the Resettlement scheme, an initiative that had seemed such a triumphant outcome of his time as Colonial Secretary. And correspondingly, those years also saw the start of an inexorable rise in the demands for mainstream low- and middle-income housing.

At first, in the late-1950s years of relatively limited refugee influxes, all seemed well, and the Resettlement programme was scaled up into something more like a very-low-income housing programme. 1958 saw a proposal by the Commissioner for Resettlement to raise the annual rehousing rate from 30,000 to a 'reasonable' target of 100,000, and the following year an immediate annual target of 75,000 was set, equating to 30 seven-storey H-blocks.[30] November 1959 saw the opening by Burgess of the hundredth Resettlement scheme, at Wong Tai Sin. (Figure 3.1)

His speech stressed 'the sense of purpose, the daring experimentation' of the programme, and enthused that Hong Kong was 'in a way, the richest city on earth.

Figure 3.1 Colonial Secretary Claude Burgess opens the 100th Resettlement scheme, at Wong Tai Sin, in November 1959.

Rich with human life, rich with human energy'. At the end of 1959, the total Resettlement population stood at 310,342.[31]

Meanwhile, however, the deliberations of the Special Committee on Housing were generating proposals that pointed in a very different direction – towards the sidelining and eventual abolition of the Resettlement programme.[32] As we saw in Chapter 2, the 1956 First Interim report had stepped up the pressure for more integrative measures.[33] Now the Final Report went considerably further. Released in December 1958, with a covering summary letter from Rowe, it included 42 recommendations, foremost among them the unification of all public housing into one coordinating programme for housing, rehousing and resettlement, overseen by the Housing Department. The latter would become a formal government department headed by the Commissioner for Housing, 'combined or closely associated with the Resettlement Department' and with an 'architectural section common to both'. It would be tasked with implementing a ten-year housing programme and a planned programme of New Towns.[34]

These bold headline recommendations concealed the wide 'divergence of views' within the Committee, which helped sustain a vigorous debate within government after the report's initial publication.[35] The chief stimulus for this was the impending transformation of the Commissionership for Housing into a professional rather than generalist cadet post, assigned as from February 1959 to a highly experienced expatriate Scottish architect, Jim Fraser. Fraser had previously headed the Singapore Improvement Trust for many years until his abrupt departure the previous July as part of the chaotic decolonisation process there, as we will see below. In November 1958, responding to a suggestion to convene a new working party on housing to follow up the Special Committee's findings, Burgess responded that this would mean 'piling Pelion on Ossa' (i.e. adding further to existing difficulty). In extended discussion within ExCo, Black suggested that a formal response should await Fraser's arrival in February 1959.[36] In March, Woodhouse of the Colonial Office chipped in, stressing that Atkinson would want to scrutinise the report, but generally endorsing the concept of 'coordination of all housing efforts under a unified department'.[37]

For Fraser, whose SIT post had combined chief architect-planner and chief-executive roles, and who was steeped in the Singapore ethos of comprehensive, planning-led housing policy, the Hong Kong laissez-faire philosophy of minimalist government intervention in general, and the restricted role of the Commissioner for Housing in particular, came as something of a shock.[38] Invited to contribute to the discussion on the Special Committee Final Report, he took that as his cue to wade into the debate.[39] In notes of May 1959 on the Report and on various aspects of the housing programme, Fraser argued the Housing Authority was 'unwieldy' in its present Urban Council-linked form: 'too many people have too much to say about too little'. In view of its professional efficiency, the remedy was not contraction but Singapore-style expansion: it should take over the Housing Department from Urban Services, and Resettlement must not be allowed to continue 'ad infinitum': it should be allowed to run for only three more years and then the Commissioner for Housing should take it over. Subsequent tasks would include preparation of a

Master Plan, and it must *not* build down to a standard the poor can afford, but build 'fewer but better'. In effect, Fraser was proposing to recreate the SIT (or HDB) within the very different context of Hong Kong.[40] In further notes of February 1960 on the Special Committee's planning recommendations, he argued that 'We need a Master Plan', and a 'unitary body'.[41] And in a comparative overview of Singapore and Hong Kong housing at a 1960 Town Planning Institute conference at St Andrews, he stressed how, as manager-chairman of the SIT, he had been responsible for both housing and planning and had drawn up a Master Plan, approved in 1958, including three satellite towns.[42]

Fraser's argumentation served to demonstrate that the Singaporean superiority complex vis-à-vis Hong Kong housing – an all-too-familiar discourse throughout the period covered by our story – was not a propaganda creation of the post-1959 PAP regime, but actually stemmed from colonial precedents. And understandably, the private reactions of the Hong Kong administrative elite were less than enthusiastic. In July 1959, Black and senior staff discussed Fraser's advocacy of HA reorganisation and the phasing out of Resettlement, and the Financial Secretary criticised his observations as 'patronising'.[43] Not surprisingly, the government eventually decided to turn down or defer every one of the Special Committee's recommendations.[44] They were 'not acceptable at present', partly because of the radically different financing regimes of the various housing organisations and programmes – an obstacle, or pretext, already highlighted at a March 1959 meeting. Instead, the Resettlement Department should 'continue its specialised activities for the immediate future'.[45] The Special Committee's suggestion of a specific ten-year programme for all social housing was also dismissed, as it was 'not felt that a programme related to any specific period is advisable'.[46] With all these debates, only in July 1960 could a definitively approved version of the Special Committee final report be sent to the Colonial Office in London.[47]

A sop to the Special Committee: Government Low-Cost Housing

The main positive outcome would be far more modest than all this: the establishment of a 'Government Low-Cost Housing' (GLCH) programme targeted at an income bracket between Resettlement and Housing Authority eligibility, reflecting the initial government preference for a fragmented social rental housing sector subdivided by income-based eligibility criteria – a policy that would only be decisively ended in 1973 with the creation of a unitary Housing Authority and the move towards a more comprehensive, need-based eligibility structure.

At ExCo in September 1959 it was decided that at this stage, far from any unification of housing, the picture should be complicated still further by setting up yet another semi-autonomous public housing organisation.[48] In the Financial Secretary's February 1960 budget, it was emphasised that this GLC programme was a direct outcome of the Special Committee report, and would target the over-50% of the population who were overcrowded or living in slums, and whose monthly income was less than $300 (slotting in exactly below the HA lower eligibility limit of $300 minimum – the HA maximum being $600). It was hoped to house

20,000 per annum at a maximum monthly rent of \$40.[49] The new 20,000 annual programme would be launched from October 1959.[50] Originally it was assumed the GLC programme would be directly run by Resettlement but by September 1961 it had instead been decided that the HA, not RSD, should manage the completed estates – a first modest step towards interconnection, if not yet merger, between the RSD and HA.[51] The PWD would continue to design and build the estates, preserving an indirect link to the Resettlement programme through a general architectural similarity.[52] Six months earlier, in the March 1961 Budget debate, Burgess had argued there was 'little to be gained' by the HA taking over management of Resettlement, but that more integration in management of GLC was possible.[53] Now, that decision was effectively reversed.[54]

In March 1961 a fire-demolished site at Hung Hom had been identified as a first potential GLC site. In the event, however, the first completed estate, of seven 7-storey blocks at Yau Tong Road, Kwun Tong, was handed over in 1963, followed by a larger development of fourteen 7-storey blocks at Wong Tai Sin, comprising, on plan, a central corridor flanked by single-room living units with self-contained facilities. (Figure 3.2) Also approved in 1963 at Wong Tai Sin was a second phase of two taller blocks, one of 13 and one of 20 storeys, accommodating 14,000 inhabitants overall.[55] By December of that year nearly a million people had applied for GLC flats. In 1963 it was decided that for the Cheung Sha Wan GLC estate, 5,000 out of 96,000 applicants would be selected by ballot.[56] GLC dwelling

Figure 3.2 One of the first Government Low-Cost schemes completed, at Upper Wong Tai Sin (1963), with the taller Phase 2 visible behind the initial seven-storey blocks: 1983 photo (MG).

standards were initially based on Housing Society norms, with an external corridor and 35 sq ft space per person (as opposed to 24 sq ft for Resettlement), in self-contained units with simple squat WCs and shower above. Fung Tung was transferred from the HA to manage the first let GLC estate, at Lei Yue Mun in east Kowloon – which in fact actually comprised Mk III blocks with no WCs or kitchens.[57] Eventually, a total of 62,380 flats in 18 GLC developments would be completed by PWD, at the same 35 sq ft per person standard and at an income limit (eventually) of $500 monthly.[58] Within PWD, the same team involved in the later Resettlement 'Mark' series – Bramwell for architectural design, Claassen for engineering – also oversaw GLC design, and because of the extra work generated by the programme, Deputy Financial Secretary Clinton allowed the Public Works Department's Architectural Office to set up a separate Tender Board to expedite expenditure on its building projects.[59]

The Housing Authority: an uncertain consolidation

The Black years were two-edged for the Housing Authority. On the one hand, its programme was fully established, and the Housing Division was widely respected for its professional competence, both in building and management. But the efficiency-sapping impact of its dual-headed structure, integrally linked to the entire UC membership, remained undiminished, and played a very large role in limiting the output contribution of the Authority to the housing problem.

In February 1962, Housing Architect J R Firth characterised the Authority as a 'non-profit-making commercial enterprise', supported by a revolving fund. In November of that year, with 6,780 dwellings completed, and sites found for an ongoing programme of 1,600/2,000 flats per year, the Government announced it would top up its loan to the HA by $80m over the next eight years.[60] In an April 1960 *Housing Review* article, W E Collard explained that the Housing Authority received Crown land at one third of its value, plus DLF loans. In December 1963, an editorial in the *SCMP*, marking the completion of the newly opened Choi Hung estate, hailed the Authority's self-financing revolving-fund organisation for having generated $165m to finance construction of 17,850 flats: the Governor declared in opening Choi Hung that the Housing Authority had 'developed into a unique institution, working on an impressive programme'.[61] To others, this output seemed meagre. Akers-Jones recalled that 'the old Housing Authority was a world of its own, building these very nice, comfortable small flats, but making a very small contribution to tackling the housing problem'.[62] At the time of Fraser's arrival in February 1959, the HA's offices were still very small-scale, located on the top floor of the GPO Building.[63] Writing in November 1962 to the Minister of State in London concerning Urban Council interventions in the squatter problem, Black wrote that the Housing Authority, after six years of existence, 'cannot really be proud of the scale of its achievements'.[64] The core of the problem, as we saw in Chapter 2, was the interconnection of the HA with the Urban Council, the HA being 'in effect, the Urban Council with changed hats'.[65] Owing to its link to the UC it was widely 'felt to be ineffective: this was one of those administrative problems that were too difficult to sort out'.[66] Rowe argued later that every significant decision concerning the Authority in effect had to be put to the Urban Council. But in built quality terms, Rowe conceded, 'they had some very good housing estates, they were very popular.'[67]

Unease at the HA's low output within government was exacerbated by the growing pressure from Urban Council members to extend the Authority's remit under the banner of housing/planning coordination and strategic planning in general, demands brandished ever more boldly after Fraser's arrival. This created growing tension with administrators. In April 1960, Collard even suggested that Resettlement Department officials should conceal information on Resettlement work in the New Territories from Hilton Cheong-Leen, despite the latter being a member of the Urban Council's Resettlement Committee – in order to prevent the Urban Council from potentially extending its remit into New Territories development.[68] The Urban Council members were undaunted, and following a November 1962 debate in which Cheong-Leen echoed the Special Committee by calling for a ten-year unitary housing plan, in February 1963 the HA approved for itself the more restricted aim of a ten-year 'progressive building programme' of 24,500 flats: Fraser argued that one-third of the cost would be self-financed, out of Housing Authority rents.[69] The Urban Council's annual debate in December 1963 saw a chorus of demands to widen the UC's authority, while 1963 also saw the establishment of the UMELCO office as an institutional support for LegCo unofficials' activities: it remained a small-scale organisation until 1970. We will see in Chapter 5 that unofficials would gain significantly greater powers within housing in the 1970s – but only once the UC had, in effect, been expelled from the housing 'system'.[70]

That all lay in the future, however. From 1963, a more activist note was introduced by Elsie Elliott, who was elected in that year to the Urban Council, representing the Reform Club.[71] As we saw in Chapter 2, she brought a more assertively anti-establishment approach to housing debates, combining a protest stance in meetings, and denunciations of official corruption, with highly publicised interventions in individual housing controversies. Michael Wright recalled that 'she was convinced that every government servant was a crook, including me. She just pulled down the shutters – you just couldn't convince her. She was her own worst enemy'.[72] Although Elliott was treated as a disruptive force within officialdom, reporting that 'visiting MPs were briefed not to listen to me', and that housing officials gave a 'cold' reception to her plea for rehousing for hawkers, she eventually succeeded in securing approval for a new policy of temporary housing areas.[73] Key individual controversies with which she became involved included a 1963 clearance crisis in the Jordan Valley, and a September 1963 near-uprising at Diamond Hill, where she defended squatters from clearance and attacked resettlement as 'in conflict with the principle of human rights'.[74]

Elliott's interventions also provoked results outside Hong Kong, especially by exploiting Labour Party connections in London – although she was herself no socialist, but rather a 19th-century-style philanthropic activist. In 1963, she contrived to get through a letter to Harold Wilson and Labour MPs about squatter problems, with the result that the government was compelled to press for 'a full and frank Report' on the topic.[75] December 1963 saw 'strong criticism' by Elliott in UC meetings against the Resettlement Department's 'outdated' policy, as exclusively concerned with the value of redevelopment land, and its treatment of squatters as 'second-grade human beings'. She asked, 'Why cannot Resettlement policy be based on need as well?'... 'What, after all is resettlement policy based on – people or money?'[76] The impact of Elliott's interventions not only anticipated the later more institutionalised power of unofficials within housing in the 1970s, but also highlighted the contradiction within colonial housing policy between demographic containment and industrial promotion on the one hand and growing welfare aspirations on the other – a contradiction that the government was not yet willing to address.

Professionals as decision-makers in the Housing Authority – from Fraser to Liao

The early 1960s saw the beginnings of an enduring swing towards an enhanced executive role for architects and other professionals within the Housing Department. Previously, a dominant role had been played by colourful private-practice figures such as Eric Cumine, lead architect at So Uk (see below). Born in Shanghai and of mixed Chinese-British ethnicity, he studied at the AA, and came to Hong Kong in 1948; his firm eventually employed 174 staff. He became a racing jockey, and was widely travelled.[77] A decisive change came with the arrival of Fraser as the new Commissioner for Housing in February 1959. As mentioned above, he had left Singapore in July 1958 at the height of the anti-colonial militancy stirred up by Lee Kuan Yew's PAP, especially following the 1957 election of PAP firebrand Ong Eng Guan as head of the city council. Ong's agitations reduced SIT operations to a shambles, and although Fraser had worked in the SIT since 1927, and had managed it from the 1940s, and had done most of the groundwork for the pre-1959 Labour Front government's plan to transform the SIT into a far more powerful 'Housing and Development Board', his position rapidly became untenable and he left the SIT before the transition to the HDB – which was then appropriated and expanded by the new regime. It seems more than likely that Black brokered Fraser's transfer, given his own exactly contemporary shift from Singapore to Hong Kong.[78] David Akers-Jones recalled of the post-1959 Housing Authority that, 'as usual, there was a big Scot who was head of it – Fraser. He was a very able man, yet they in Singapore had dismissed him as rubbish'. And the direction the HA took from that point, Akers-Jones felt, was increasingly 'based on Singapore precedent'.[79] (Figure 3.3)

Working under Fraser as Commissioner was a specialist Housing Architect, J R Firth, formerly based in Trinidad, who had moved to Hong Kong in the late 1950s, bringing Caribbean preferences for low-rise, low-density housing: for example, in a 1962 lecture to the Reform Club, Firth argued unrealistically that the HA's latest set piece at Choi Hung, at 35 sq ft per person, was 'not a satisfactory home in which to bring up a family' but only tolerable as a transitional space.[80] Far more important

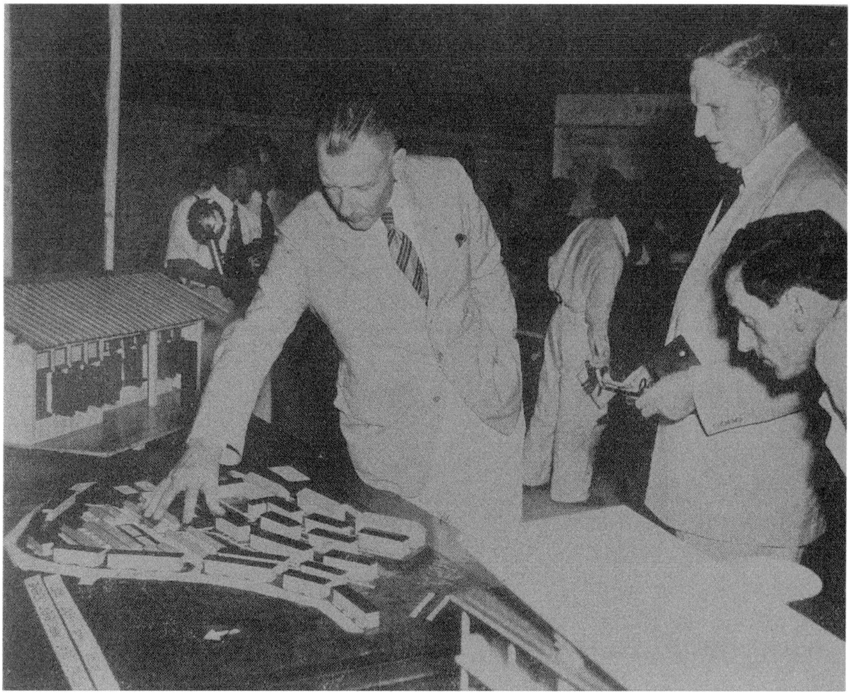

Figure 3.3 J M Fraser (centre) explains a model of Kampung Silat Estate to the Governor of Singapore, Sir Franklin Gimson, and G G Thomson, SIT Public Relations Secretary, in an image from the 1951 SIT *Annual Report*: the SIT's relatively low-rise, low-density developments contrasted strongly with Hong Kong, or for that matter with post-1959 Singapore under the HDB.

for the future, however, was a much younger architect, Donald Liao, who joined the HA's newly established Architectural Division in 1960 and rapidly began to rise to prominence – eventually becoming the leading innovator in the dramatic story of Hong Kong public housing.

Liao originally came to Hong Kong in 1947 from his native Taiwan. Illustrating the cultural flux in mid-20th-century Eastern Asia, during World War II he had been left behind in his ancestral house in Xiluo, Yunlin County, in central Taiwan: two brothers and sisters were in Tokyo, one brother having been conscripted into the Japanese army. Liao recalled the attempts to 'Japanise' Taiwan, under which he was forced to speak Japanese at school. In 1949, he had been about to go to Princeton but, after family pressure to stay in Asia, had instead signed up in 1950 as an architecture undergraduate at HKU, recalling Gordon Brown as 'a very impressive figure – we respected him immensely'.[81] Liao's contact with housing as a student was minimal: 'to us, the Unité was just an image!' However, within the Hong Kong context, by the late 1950s he was becoming 'aware of public housing' in general and the HA's work in particular, North Point having just been completed. In September 1957–8, having won a British Council scholarship, Liao signed up for a postgraduate diploma in Landscape Architecture at King's College, Durham University, travelling beforehand around Britain and Europe. Trips included (as we will see below) a 1957–8 tour of New Towns around London: 'my first encounter with social housing and comprehensive planning'.[82] The legacy of those travels and encounters would powerfully shape Hong Kong, especially in the 1970s and '80s as Liao rose rapidly to assume the focal decision-making role in the planning and design of its public housing.

In 1960, despite offers at promotion from Gordon Brown and private practice opportunities, Liao joined the Housing Authority. He recalled,

> A fellow HKU lecturer, Ron Firth, had left and joined the Authority, and became *the* only architect there. He said, "We have an opening – we're about to set up a little architectural section – why don't you come?" I duly applied. My wife (at that stage my girl-friend) helped me type the application letter. There were a dozen applicants. I applied and got in, in 1960 – and in those days, there were very few local civil servants who'd got into government with a three years contract: I got in as a contract officer. Cheung Sing-Hoi also applied and became an assistant architect – he was working in the Public Works Department getting a meagre salary. We had one apprentice architect – a new graduate from HKU – and two draughtsmen.[83]

Liao's first job was as project architect for the Ma Tau Wai Estate, a 2,075-flat infill development restricted to 14 storeys by airport height curbs but still reaching a density of 1,886 ppa, in linked slab blocks in in situ reinforced-concrete construction. There 'I was given the very challenging problem of getting over 2,000 units on a very small site: W E Collard, the Housing Authority Secretary, had been out walking his dog one day and spotted the site, and managed to secure it'. Liao took strenuous efforts to prevent trees from being felled, and the design was also complicated by feng shui constraints: 'Facing the street, I left two units on the 14 storeys empty, for the full height of the building, to avoid a road appearing to come straight into the block'.[84] (Figure 3.4a, b)

Liao recollected in 2010 the close relations he rapidly established with Fraser:

> Jim Fraser had been in Singapore during the war, and was captured by the Japanese. When the war ended, he became head of the Singapore Improvement Trust. Under him was architect Teh Cheang Wan. He was from Penang, a Hokkien. Later, Cheang Wan [who became chief architect after the PAP takeover of the HDB] came to see his former boss in Hong Kong – and he used to compare notes with me, as we moved up in our careers. Jim Fraser never told me his life history, other than about the SIT and the war years: he was put in captivity, I'm not sure if he was tortured. The SIT was very much his baby – he came to Hong Kong from there, started with one architect – the buildings were

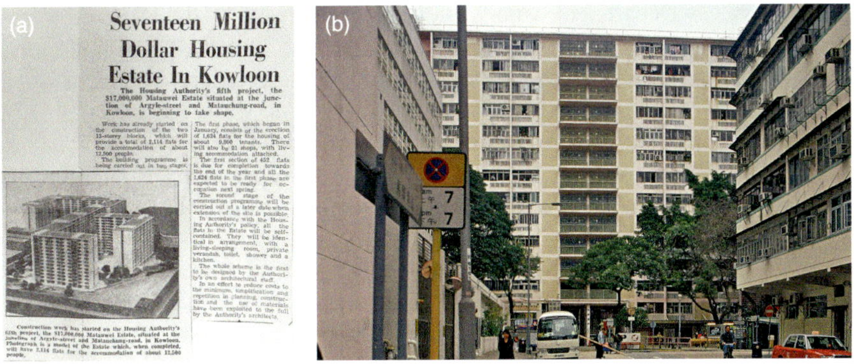

Seventeen Million Dollar Housing Estate In Kowloon

The Housing Authority's fifth project, the $17,000,000 Matauwei Estate situated at the junction of Argyle-street and Matauchung-road, in Kowloon, is beginning to take shape.

Work has already started on the construction of the two 13-storey blocks, which will provide a total of 2,114 flats for the accommodation of about 12,500 people.

The building programme is being carried out in two stages. The first phase, which began in January, consists of the erection of 1,624 flats for the housing of about 9,800 tenants. There will also be 21 shops, with living accommodation attached.

The first section of 452 flats is due for completion towards the end of the year and all the 1,624 flats in the first phase are expected to be ready for occupation next spring.

The second stage of the construction programme will be carried out at a later date when extension of the site is possible.

In accordance with the Housing Authority's policy, all the flats in the Estate will be self-contained. They will be identical in arrangement, with a living-sleeping room, private verandah, toilet, shower and a kitchen.

The whole scheme is the first to be designed by the Authority's own architectural staff.

In an effort to reduce costs to the minimum, simplification and repetition in planning, construction and the use of materials have been exploited to the full by the Authority's architects.

Construction work has started on the Housing Authority's fifth project, the $17,000,000 Matauwei Estate, situated at the junction of Argyle-street and Matauchung-road, in Kowloon. Photograph is a model of the Estate which, when completed, will have 2,114 flats for the accommodation of about 12,500 people.

Figure 3.4 (a) 1961 newspaper article on Ma Tau Wai (1961–3): the first designed by the HA's own architects, including 14-storey slab blocks, with Donald Liao as project architect. (b) 2011 view of Ma Tau Wai, showing the full-height non-residential bay of this 14-storey block, incorporated by Liao in his design for feng shui reasons. (MG).

rather basic in the '50s. In Hong Kong he was trying to go beyond that, and was looking forward to doing something greater in Hong Kong.[85]

Liao recalled that 'Fraser definitely had an influence. He came and built the HA estates, Singapore-style'.[86] 'He said, "Hell, why should we be paying whacking great fees to private architects?" That's how the HA architecture department started. Fraser was Commissioner, then Ron Firth as Housing Architect, with five staff beneath him, although Fraser was himself also a qualified architect. Elizabeth Bedwell was the housing manager, and brought in the principles of the old Octavia Hill style of management: it was a bit strong-arm. I liked Fraser immensely. He was a very straightforward man – he liked me very much, treated me as "his son". He was a Scottish Presbyterian, and very typical of that culture'. Liao recalled one reconnaissance visit to what would later become his showpiece project, at Wah Fu:

> Although you could use government cars for fieldwork, on a visit to Wah Fu with Jim Fraser, I drove us in my little Morris 1100. We walked round the uncultivated vegetable grounds there, and he said, "Lad, you're very lucky at your age to have a scheme of this size!"[87]

To entrench an Octavia Hill style of intensive housing management, in 1962 Fraser secured the appointment of chartered surveyor F J Carroll to succeed Bedwell: he too had previously worked in the SIT, and, like Fraser, experienced some culture-shock on arrival in Hong Kong. The fragmented structure of housing agencies seemed to him 'odd and unsatisfactory'. Below him was Fung Tung (later Director of Housing in the 1990s) who had joined the HA as housing assistant in 1960, and worked in So Uk in 1962–3. By contrast, the Head of the Urban Services Department, who was officially in charge of the HD, was a less reliable supporter of Fraser, at least until later years.[88] Overall, whereas Fraser's position in Singapore had resembled the coordinating role later played in Hong Kong by figures such as David Akers-Jones or Dominic Wong (Chapters 10, 12), as Commissioner for Housing within Hong Kong's polycentric system he had to distinctly scale down his aspirations, and exercise influence by persuasion: he retired in 1965 and was replaced by Firth as Commissioner for four years, with Liao as Housing Architect.

In their built form, unlike the contemporary trend towards prefabricated 'industrialised' building in both Western Europe and the Soviet bloc, the Housing Authority's developments exclusively used conventional in situ construction. In discussion following a February 1958 lecture in London just prior to the transfer of the Commissioner post to Fraser, Rowe argued that prefabricated construction 'would be more costly in Hong Kong' owing to the low technology level of the building industry. Nor did very high buildings yet seem to be on the agenda: in reply to a question as to whether it would be possible to go up to 100 feet higher than existing blocks, Rowe replied it would be too expensive – although in a glimpse of the future, the *SCMP* reported in May 1958 that 'monster' 18-storey commercial office buildings, even 38 storeys, were being planned, and that Hong Kong was becoming 'more and more like New York every day!'[89] The HA's programme in general was described by the *Builder* in 1961 as 'ultra-high-density housing, without monotony and serious overcrowding'.[90]

The two major HA developments of these years, So Uk (1957–63) and Choi Hung (1962–4) differed sharply in their design approach.[91] So Uk was built on a steep and dramatic 19-acre site, allocated to the Authority in 1954 and formed into four broad terraces. It featured a masterplan coordinated by private architect Eric Cumine, with design split between four architects, Leigh & Orange, Luk Him Sau, Szeto Wai, and Chau & Lee: its 5,313 flats were said to be the largest integrated housing project in South-East Asia. The Szeto Wai section, at the centre of the site, comprised five Y-plan towers, not dissimilar to the HA's later 'Trident' towers, but (at 16 storeys) less than half their height; whereas the other three sections, around the outside, comprised variations on the theme of slab blocks, some linear and some L-plan, some with central corridors and some with balcony access. The project also included two primary schools and shops.[92] (Figure 3.5a–e)

Choi Hung, by contrast, was built on a flat site near Kowloon Bay and featured a far more unified design by architects Palmer & Turner, the project architects being Ian Campbell and Dick N Pang. It entirely comprised slab blocks in a rectilinear arrangement, varying from 7 to 20 storeys, with the tall blocks lining the periphery, and the lower blocks and community facilities, such as schools, concentrated in the centre. All blocks had central corridor-access and the taller slabs each had two play areas on each floor, denoted on the facades by patterned ventilation blocks. Although the name 'Choi Hung' means 'rainbow' in Cantonese, the blocks were originally all-grey, and only transformed into 'rainbow' colours in the late 1980s.[93] (Figure 3.6a–c, 3.7a–c)

Figure 3.5 (a) So Uk (1957–63), a project for 33,000 inhabitants masterplanned by Eric Cumine and distributed from implementation among a consortium of four firms: Leigh & Orange, Szeto Wai, Luk Him Sau and Chau & Lee. This 2010 view (MG) shows the towers by Szeto Wai: Hong Kong's first Y-planned high towers. (b) So Uk, 1983 view (MG) of Szeto Wai towers. (c) So Uk, 1983 view (MG) from diagonal wing of one of Szeto Wai's towers, looking north towards the Chau & Lee section. (d) So Uk, 2010 view (MG) across Luk Him Sau section. (e) So Uk, medium-rise section along Po Un Road, designed by Leigh & Orange: 1983 photo (MG).

Figure 3.6 (a) 1961 model of the HA's Choi Hung estate (1962–4), illustrated in 1961 SCMP article. (b) Aerial view of the nearly completed Choi Hung from 1964 Government Information Services brochure on the HA, showing its originally all-grey colouring – despite its name ('Rainbow'). (c) Plaque commemorating Governor Black's December 1963 inauguration of Choi Hung: 2011 photo (MG).

Towards middle-income mass housing: the Housing Society and home-ownership

While the Government Low-Cost Housing programme was beginning to fill the gap, in income terms, between Resettlement on the one hand and Housing Authority or Housing Society programmes on the other, the government had no immediate plans to address the needs of the next income tier up, the lower-middle-income group, as its overwhelming concern was still the existential challenges posed by squatting.

Instead, the Housing Society had been trying to intervene, but on a very limited scale. Overall, the main orientation of the Society was similar to that of the HA, namely medium-low rental. But it was the Society that had first pioneered the Octavia Hill-style management tradition, through its successive Housing Managers such as Joan Sanderson, a tradition then appropriated by the HA.[94] The early 1960s saw a dribble of further low-cost HS rental sites, developed on a piecemeal basis dependent on individual loans from government, which started to dry up from the mid-1960s: the first four 13-storey blocks were completed on a steeply sloping site at Ming Wah Dai Ha, and the first nine-storey balcony-access block of the Yue Kwong Chuen development at Aberdeen was finished in December 1962. (Figure 3.8a, b) September 1963 saw a 10–15% rise in HS rents, owing to higher maintenance costs – the Society's rent levels already being markedly higher than those of the HA. This was the first rent rise since the beginning of its programme, which had now completed a modest 4,335 flats, all self-contained, and housing 27,426 inhabitants overall. However, the HS also built directly for middle-income groups as well, including blocks for civil servants built by contract to government, as, for example, Ming Wah Dai Ha Block A.[95]

For middle-income housing, some kind of home-ownership, rather than rental, solution seemed most plausible; but the lack of political urgency meant that nothing could be done for now. In December 1963, an SCMP editorial reported bitter complaints that the government's resettlement focus had led it to ignore everything else. And in the same week, following claims of government inaction in the Urban Council annual debate, Financial Secretary Cowperthwaite reported to LegCo that although the government could not afford to divert efforts from lower-income to middle-income housing, the Commonwealth Development Corporation might potentially support a home-ownership scheme: the Corporation's property consultant had visited Hong Kong in October to draw up a proposal.[96] However, there seemed no clarity on the economic fundamentals of any potential home-ownership initiative, and in particular whether it should be philanthropic or private sector. For example, in July 1960, opening the Island Garden estate for the Hong Kong Chinese Civil Servants Association, Black hailed the civil servants' cooperative societies – which had completed 2,931 flats in 142 schemes since the first example, Belcher Gardens, in 1952 – as 'an integral part of our comprehensive plans for housing the people of Hong Kong'. In June 1963, on the other hand, it was announced that the Hong Kong Land Investment Company was to build low-cost private housing in 12-storey blocks in Hong Kong and the new Tsuen Wan satellite town.[97]

Figure 3.7 (a) 2023 view of Choi Hung, showing more recent polychromatic colour scheme (MG). (b) Plan of two sizes of one-roomed flats at Choi Hung, and flat interior, from 1964 GIS brochure. (c) 2023 interior view of upper-floor corridor in 20-storey Tan Fung House, Choi Hung (MG).

Experience in the United States, especially in New York City, seemed to point to the potential for government-aided private enterprise in this sector, and in September 1963, a visit by prominent New York developer Samuel J Lefrak highlighted this approach. Lefrak, however, cast the entire discourse in aggressively ideological terms: Hong Kong was 'small but important, and Americans should do whatever they can to provide education and shelter – to prove that private enterprise pays.' Khrushchev had reputedly said that communism would survive as long as cesspits survived, to which Lefrak responded that 'we want to eliminate the cesspits and put in a good sewage system'. What was essential was to 'let free enterprise do the job that is needed. Let government-dominated and socialised construction be left out of it'. For this, Lefrak declared, he would need 'cheap land' and partnership with government, but a SCMP editorial ridiculed this proposal, given Hong Kong's endemic

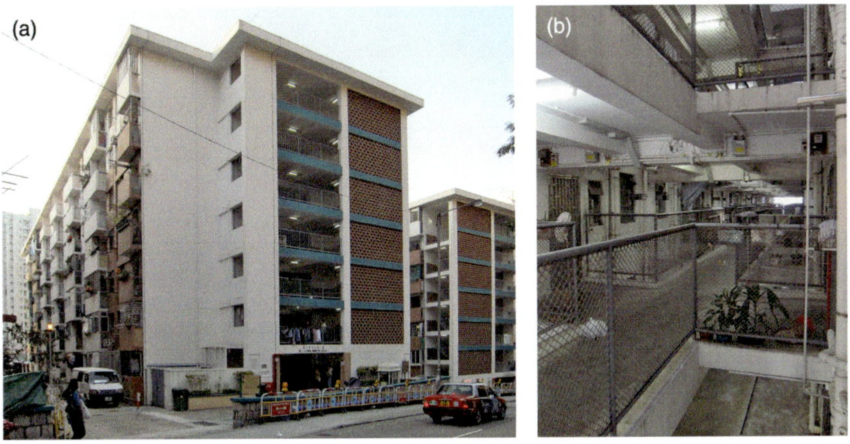

Figure 3.8 (a) The Housing Society's Ming Wah Dai Ha development, completed 1965/6: 2014 photo (MG). (b) View of the linking access balconies between the paired seven-storey blocks of Ming Wah Dai Ha: 2014 photo. (MG).

land shortages: the project would 'in effect parallel the Housing Authority's operation', and private enterprise would be unlikely to significantly improve on the latter.[98] More generally, Lefrak's confrontational tone was glaringly inconsistent with the low-profile political approach followed by all Hong Kong governments up to 1992. Later experience in Singapore would show that an ideologically laden home-ownership initiative of a very different kind, government-dominated and socialised, could significantly contribute to the development of collective 'identity' – but such a strategy, as we will see in Chapter 7, would necessarily take a different form in Hong Kong.

Early 1960s Resettlement – a new squatter explosion

All these initiatives were, of course, small in scale compared to the huge, ongoing machine of the Resettlement programme. (Figure 3.9) Here, however, there was growing dissatisfaction among both the colonial establishment and the public. The RSD's 1961 Annual Review envisaged building of 440 further Resettlement blocks. But within two years the picture was instead one of shortfall; by November 1962 the ambitious new 100,000 annual target was being significantly under-fulfilled, by 30,000 – a position worsened by the Typhoon Wanda disruption – and voices advocating a convergence with the HA's approach started to be raised.[99] Overall, the Director of Medical and Health Services protested in a November 1958 memo, the cubic-space standard of Resettlement accommodation was 'probably the lowest in the world' for new public housing, having been adopted despite warnings from his department. The foremost object of complaints was the lack of management. This, Police Commissioner Maxwell reported in 1958, left estates such as Shek Kip

Figure 3.9 Resettlement Department map of estates and cottage areas in Hong Kong as at August 1963.

Mei susceptible to triad infiltration, which also dominated the local kaifong associations: Maxwell suggested countering this with 'floor representatives'.[100] Village redevelopment controversies also continued to rumble: 1962–3, for example, saw protests at resumption of shops and an informal settlement in Tung Tau Village,

Figure 3.10 (a) 1961 aerial photo showing dilapidated village housing on a site planned for four Mk. II Resettlement blocks at Tung Tau II, with the first phase under construction behind. (b) Mk I blocks at Kwun Tong Resettlement Estate immediately prior to conversion work in 1983, showing the still-persisting chaos of informal structures and hawker stalls around and between the blocks (MG).

very near to Kowloon Walled City, and a representation to the Secretary for Chinese Affairs by a delegation from the 5,000 villagers and Tung Tau and Sai Tau; and August 1962 saw official proposals that surviving Wan Chai 'villages' should be 'bulldozed out of existence… liquidated'.[101] (Figure 3.10a, b)

What was to be done to address these qualitative and quantitative challenges? The government's rejection of the Special Committee's merger recommendation left it little scope for organisational reform. In a March 1961 budget debate, R C Lee argued the HA could gradually take over completed Resettlement estates, to generate efficiencies, to which Burgess replied that while there was 'little to be gained' by that, the government could certainly consider integration at a 'higher level', in relation to the GLC programme. HKU planning professor W G Gregory in May 1961 argued it was 'absolutely vital' that planning and development powers were coordinated by one body.[102]

But by then the level of Resettlement production activity was starting to seem almost an irrelevance, as the number of squatters was escalating rapidly out of control once again. During Black's governorship the territory's total population increased by one million – a vital labour-force support for Hong Kong's manufacturing boom, but including inevitably a high number of squatters. This prompted a stern re-statement by Burgess in 1960 of the principle that 'The primary object of clearance is to free land for permanent development'. Later, Burgess warned in 1962 that 'nothing could wreck both our plans and our achievements more rapidly or certainly than a further flood of immigrants'.[103] And that was exactly what happened, as the number of squatters soared again between 1961 and 1963, despite the stuttering Resettlement output. In April 1963, James Sweetman of the Resettlement Department reported to the DCS that despite the completion of

Resettlement accommodation for 60,000 people in 1962, between late 1961 and late 1962 there had actually been a 9% increase in rooftop squatters and 8.6% in ground-squatters: to 75,921 and 414,618, respectively. Paul Tsui, Assistant Commissioner for Resettlement at this stage, noted in May 1963 that squatter-pitch demolitions had risen from 3,000 in 1955/6 to 10,500 in 1961/2, and stressed that 'clearance' was 'not a nice job – in fact it's a nasty job, but it has to be done'.[104] A paper on 'The Squatter Problem', discussed in the Urban Council in May 1963, argued Resettlement had changed from 'a solution to the squatter problem' to 'much more a mass re-housing scheme'.[105] Later that year, Elliott vociferously criticised the Resettlement Department in a UC debate, and in debates on Resettlement, DPW Wright declared himself 'greatly disappointed' by the failure to reach the 'elusive figure' of 100,000 rehousees, and noted that resettlement policy was to be reviewed by a subcommittee of the Urban Council.[106]

Elliott's agitations in Hong Kong and London further ramped up pressure concerning the deficiencies of Resettlement. The outcome of that pressure was the 1963 instigation of yet another inquiry – a Working Party on Resettlement and Low-Cost Housing, prompted by 'the growing dissatisfaction, and civil and security risks inherent in the present squatter clearance and resettlement policy'.[107] The 1963 Working Party, chaired by John McDouall, Secretary for Chinese Affairs, investigated the reasons for growth of the squatter population, which it now estimated as 580,000. The key immediate reason was the perceived failure of the 'clear on sight' 1954 policy and its 1959 revision. Reflecting this, and under some pressure from the Secretary of State in London, the Working Party made a second estimate of housing needs: 0.8 million in Government-subsidised housing, 1.1 million in temporary housing, 1.6 million in private building (all of which was *existing*). It recommended the introduction of 'licensed' squatter areas and proposed that 130,000 Resettlement 'units' should be built each year – a 'unit' corresponding not to a dwelling but to a notional 24 sq ft living space for one resettled adult. In July 1964, it was argued that a 'technical planning target' of 1.9 million such 'units' should be set for the period April 1964 to April 1974, plus 300,000 GLCH 'units'. This slightly confusing concept of a ten-year housing programme of a certain number of 'living units' would repeat itself with different figures in the 1970s, in the 10-year plan of Sir Murray MacLehose. At a March 1964 meeting, Michael Wright (now Director of Public Works) had argued that production of 150,000 Resettlement units per annum was achievable but that any further boost towards 200,000 would require additional resources.[108]

Increasingly, various permutations of the principle of coordination were proposed. The Working Party considered but rejected a government take-over of the Housing Society, while Sales proposed amalgamation of the HA and Resettlement – an idea which Barty labelled 'very doubtful'.[109] An alternative 'coordinating' sop was to found a completely new central organisation for policy-level strategic oversight, such as an advisory Housing Board. In an August 1962 Urban Council debate about establishment of such a body, Hilton Cheong-Leen argued the government should appoint a centralised authority with advisory, and perhaps executive, powers over housing policy: 'The time is long past when

Government's housing policy and public housing programme should continue to be directed by two or three persons in the Colonial Secretariat, no matter how able, sincere and efficient those individuals might be' … 'A centralised Housing and Resettlement Authority with overriding jurisdiction in planning and administration was the obvious answer'. To this, De Sales cautioned that the UC must not try to 'stampede' government into precipitate action, while in a November 1962 UC debate Cheong-Leen reiterated that a ten-year plan for both government and private housing was needed.[110]

As we will see in Chapter 4, a 'Housing Board' would eventually be created in 1965, following recommendations of the 1964 White Paper on the 'Review of Policies for Squatter Control, Resettlement and Government Low-Cost Housing'.[111] Largely ineffective in practice, the Board was nevertheless Hong Kong's first overarching housing-policy initiative, and as such presaged several similar policies in later years, such as the 'Housing Branch' re-established in 1994 under Housing Secretary Dominic Wong (see Chapter 12).

Architectural developments in the Resettlement programme

Of the PWD's 7,138 staff overall in 1961/2, 404 were in the Architectural Office (83 of whom professional). The PWD's total expenditure was $366 million – up 15.5% on the previous year – which accounted for 38% of total government spending.[112] The Architectural Office operated largely free of political/administrative interference. Wright recalled that 'as DPW my main contact with the Secretariat was the AS Lands, successively Lightbody and Wakefield. Fortunately they didn't interfere'.[113]

In the design of the 'Mark' variants in the mainstream Resettlement programme, Bramwell had by now displaced Donnithorne.[114] He 'had his charisma: he was a good friend of the Governor, and of Bowring, who was regarded as God in those days'. A E (Ted) Claassen, head of the PWD Structural Engineering Division, worked with Bramwell closely.[115] Bramwell developed close links with the Financial Secretary in securing incremental design improvements, and also with the PACS (Lands). In 1960, the Financial Secretary's budget for the next year incorporated a prediction by the DPW that he could build 40 blocks each year, and thus achieve an annual rate of 100,000 people resettled for the next five years. A detailed report in 1960 set out comprehensive financial information, including rent affordability.[116] In the 1961 budget debate, R C Lee expressed concern about the rising costs of Resettlement – $7.5m in 1958/9 to rehouse 37,000, but $11.2m in 1960/1 to rehouse only 32,000. He suggested yet again that the HA should gradually take over the RSD.[117]

By 1960–1, demolition of the last twelve Bowring Bungalows at Shek Kip Mei was said to be imminent,[118] but only in March 1962 did the Resettlement Department demolish the final four Bungalows of the total of 97 built in February 1954, and which originally housed 36,000 people: the remaining 984 people were rehoused in a seven-storey block built on the site.[119] 1961 saw the commencement, at Tung Tau, of the first of a new type of seven-storey block, the Mk III – 'cleaner,

Figure 3.11 Mk II Resettlement blocks at Lok Fu and Wang Tau Hom estates: view to north up Junction Road immediately pre-redevelopment in 1983 (MG).

Figure 3.12 (a) Mk III Resettlement blocks at Chai Wan Estate (Blocks 1–12), Chai Wan Road: 1983 photo (MG). (b) Mk III blocks at Kwai Chung, Tsuen Wan: 1983 photo (MG).

more architecturally pleasing', with a 'welcome' central corridor. (Figure 3.11, 3.12a, b) Storey heights rapidly rose: January 1963 saw plans to raise heights from 10 to 17 storeys, and during 1963 the first 16-storey Mk IV Resettlement blocks were built at Chai Wan: three blocks containing 15,400 inhabitants. Overall, 192 Mk I and II blocks in 12 estates had been built in 1954–61, and 14 estates of Mk III and Mk IV would be built in 1962–8, all at the original Resettlement standards of 24 sq ft per adult. In 1963 the PWD explained that the basic plan of the Mk III and GLCH blocks was identical, the latter being distinguished solely by better fittings.[120] (Figure 3.13a–c)

The Architectural Office adopted a strictly incremental approach to enhancing standard types: 'Bramwell did a new "Mark" each time that happened, as standardised predictability was the key. Repeat and repeat! That was the essence!'[121] As the housing programme evolved and expanded later, that principle of standard types would be handed on and developed under different organisational

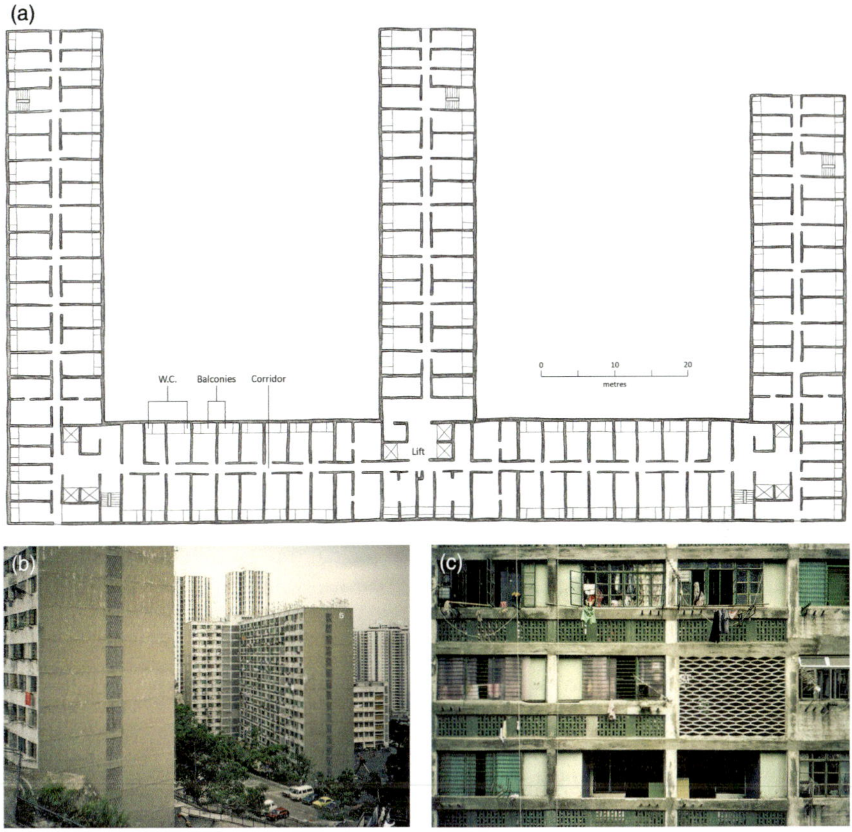

Figure 3.13 (a) 1966 layout plan of Mk IV blocks, showing central corridor plan. Drawing by Joyce Fu, 2023. (b) 16-storey Mk IV blocks at Shek Pai Wan, Aberdeen (1966–8): 1983 photo (MG). (c) Facade detail of Shek Pai Wan Mk IV blocks, showing move to column-and-beam construction: 1983 photo (MG).

arrangements. To offset this regimentation, there were efforts to rectify the low environmental quality of the Resettlement estates: Fung Tung recalled that ‘Bramwell gave me lots of money to improve landscaping in Pak Tin, and we put in lots of bushes around the Mk III and IV Resettlement blocks being built by PWD – we got elderly people to look after the carp ponds’.[122] Those efforts only had a limited impact, however, given the fundamentally utilitarian containment ethos of the Resettlement programme overall.

Planning mass housing: from urban density to New Towns

In all the debates of the late 1950s and early 1960s about greater housing coordination, strong differences of opinion emerged over the effectiveness of the Lands-led system and the desirability of greater state coordination. In these debates, Hong Kong's laissez-faire culture and dramatically variegated built environment ensured that many professionals shared values remote from even the state-controlled development apparatus of Singapore, let alone anything resembling European welfare-state thinking. In March 1960, after Fraser had proposed a Singapore-style Master Plan to remedy supposedly 'haphazard' housing development, J J Robson, AD/D, responded that

> I have had personal experience of the frustration and interference with personal liberties created by the UK Town and Planning Act as well as its abuse for political motives. This, surely, is the last thing we want in Hong Kong where we must do all we can to further encourage the investment of private capital for the development of industry and housing.[123]

Against this, R C Clarke, Assistant Superintendent of Crown Lands (Planning), contested that new or satellite towns such as Kwun Tong or Tsuen Wan, as well as the existing urban areas of Kowloon and Hong Kong Island, must have adequate zoning plans, and he also endorsed the Commissioner for Housing's argument that a 'Regional or Colony Plan' – later renamed the Colony Outline Plan – would be necessary, not least to ensure standards were set for orderly urban development of the New Territories.[124] Wright recalled that Clarke prepared a feasibility report, 'and, rather typical of the Secretariat, they were horrified at the power that this would give the PWD in saying, "OK, we're not just building a low-cost housing estate; we've got to build all those other things as well"'.[125]

All of these cases and debates concerned the main urban area, where the key planning issue affecting housing was that of plot ratio and density. Bedwell noted that Abercrombie had claimed it had 'the highest density in the world'. Reflecting the predominance of fully developed plots and commercial buildings, the emphasis was on regulation of individual built-on sites. Here the 1956 building regulations amended the rules for private developments from the former 'street standard' to 'plot ratio', but with a four-year grace period until 1966 – the resulting building boom making many families homeless.[126] Public housing estates, because they included local areas of open space, were regulated differently, but the highly restrictive system of net and gross densities that applied in London and other cities in Britain was quite impossible here: in April 1960, it was reported that densities of 2,000 ppa were commonplace in new housing, and that the Housing Authority had reluctantly had to accept 1,500. In 1960, Fraser recalled that before he came to Hong Kong, he had believed the SIT maximum of 600 ppa was the highest reasonable density, and was astonished to find 2,500 maxima in Hong Kong: but, in a retreat from the Singapore superiority discourse, he admitted that 'now I believe it is possible to build at up to 2,000 ppa and up to 20 storeys'. In 1962, Firth noted that while Resettlement estates were designed at up to 2,500 and 3,000 ppa net, the HA's Choi Hung was 'only' 1,930 ppa.[127]

The planning position in the New Territories was altogether different – not least because of the prominent role played by the Heung Yee Kuk rural community council. Set up in the 1920s, it had mutated into a communist-infiltrated, disruptive force after 1945, prompting the government to reconstitute it in 1959 into a pro-government, pro-development organisation dominated by rural Hakka elites. Liu Ching Cheung became chairman in 1960 following this upheaval. He recalled that the Kuk gained a new importance with the New Town programme, as it negotiated financial cooperation with the government on villagers' behalf, the district officer acting as land officer and magistrate in the 1950s and 1960s.[128] Glossing over the political differences, Liu argued that it was 'partly because of the poverty and the lack of opportunities for younger people that, in the late 1950s, community leaders and the Heung Yee Kuk were all pressing the government to develop the New Territories by building new towns'. Kwun Tong in the early '50s was 'the first "new town", but lessons were learnt – the planners realised that it was no good just building homes'. 'The government worked hard to consult New Territories villagers about design and layout of the new towns, and many people benefited financially when land was taken over by the government for development'.[129] In October 1962, New Territories Rural Council member S S Lee pointed to the 1902 agreement with China as evidence that the government had no right to ask New Territories residents to move from their original homes.[130]

David Akers-Jones later recalled that

> a way had to be found in which the owners of agricultural land could profit from development without themselves having to be involved in building development. It was estimated that three-fifths of the land acquired for a new town would be needed for infrastructure and official purposes, and two-fifths would be available for private development. Landowners were able to surrender their agricultural land and receive this ratio of building land in exchange, paying the difference between the two. This simple 5:2 formula not only paved the way for eventual urbanisation, but with the sharp rise in land prices, enabled the landowners to sell their rights to building land, and to become rich beyond belief.[131]

Akers-Jones's own work as District Officer for Tsuen Wan in 1959–61 involved 'clearing land, setting out the terms for the removal of villages, finding land for a community centre… .' Following this DO posting at Tsuen Wan, Akers-Jones served as District Officer Islands 1961–2, and District Officer for Yuen Long in 1962–7, later assuming more general oversight over New Territories development, as we will see later.[132]

The 1958 Special Committee report, as in other areas of housing policy, gave the new towns a powerful boost, in their role as a potentially new rehousing strategy: from the beginning, they formed part of a shift from 'containment' to 'welfare' in housing policy. In 1958, economics professor E S Kirby warned that 'Hong Kong may become a huge slum' and argued that although Patrick Abercrombie's 'wonderful plan', being 'too daring', had not been adopted, the government should now urgently consider 'satellite towns' and a 'comprehensive regional planning scheme'.[133] And writing in January 1959, activist Alison Bell, ex-Reform Club committee member, stressed the role New Territories development could play in relief of overcrowding, including building of four satellite towns at Tsuen Wan, Yuen Long, Tai Po and Sha Tin, and electrification and double-tracking of the Kowloon-Canton Railway line. The government response to the Special Committee in 1959 stressed that the building of new towns was desirable, but dependent on successful decentralisation of employment.[134] Donald Liao later claimed, however, that he himself never studied the 1958 Report in detail, and that his own later passionate advocacy of unification of housing and planning just stemmed from 'logical common sense – I didn't refer to the original report, and Jim Fraser hardly referred to it either'.[135]

In 1959, enlarging on plans newly announced by the Governor, Burgess explained the New Territories were to be developed in 10 years, including five new town reclamation schemes.[136] Scott Wilson Kirkpatrick had been appointed in late 1957 following the Special Committee's 1956 First Interim Report, and prepared a report on potential new town sites. Five areas were recommended, totalling 3,000 acres of developable land, but as the government could not afford to proceed simultaneously with all of them, they first decided, in January 1960, to start with a linked scheme for Gin Drinkers Bay/Kwai Chung and Tsuen Wan. This included a 400-acre reclamation and clearances of crops and huts from the beginning of 1962, to release development land.[137] In Tsuen Wan, industrial development was already underway, but, like Kwun Tong, very haphazardly, and adjoining the existing urban area of New Kowloon. In September 1961, a long-term development programme to reshape Tsuen Wan as 'a self-contained satellite town' was promulgated. Its 15-year population target was 640,000, including Kwai Chung and Tsing Yi.[138] In the PWD's 1962 annual report, the Planning Division reported that the Town Planning Board had met several times, and had considered an outline plan for Sha Tin: that future project had been described in April 1960 as 'a large dormitory town for Kowloon', although the existing Sha Tin community was wrecked by Typhoon Wanda in September 1962.[139] At Sheung Shui, a more modestly scaled public housing-led town was proposed, consisting entirely of resettlement housing: 'the town will consist of about fifty seven-storey buildings'.[140] (Figure 3.14a, b)

However, alongside these large-scale state-coordinated new towns, Hong Kong's laissez-faire system also required due consideration to be given to privately led projects. In 1962, and again in early 1963, it was reported that the Town Planning Board was considering a New Town of over 100,000 population in Aberdeen: these years saw a wide variety of sometimes improbable suggestions for private mini-new towns. These included Lamma Island, suggested as 'another satellite town' in December 1961; Junk Bay, suggested as a potentially privately developed new town for shipyard workers in 1960; and the west side of Castle Peak Road, under investigation for development as a private satellite town (November 1962) by the Tai Shing Hing Property Company.[141] In April 1963 it was reported that '"Develop Lantau" is a familiar call… which echoes down the years', but its viability would depend on the building of a bridge – only realised several decades later.[142] In the event, as we will see in Chapter 4, the first private-led development equating in size to a small 'new town' would be built far closer to the urban core – the Mei Foo Sun Chuen project of 1968–78 in Western Kowloon.

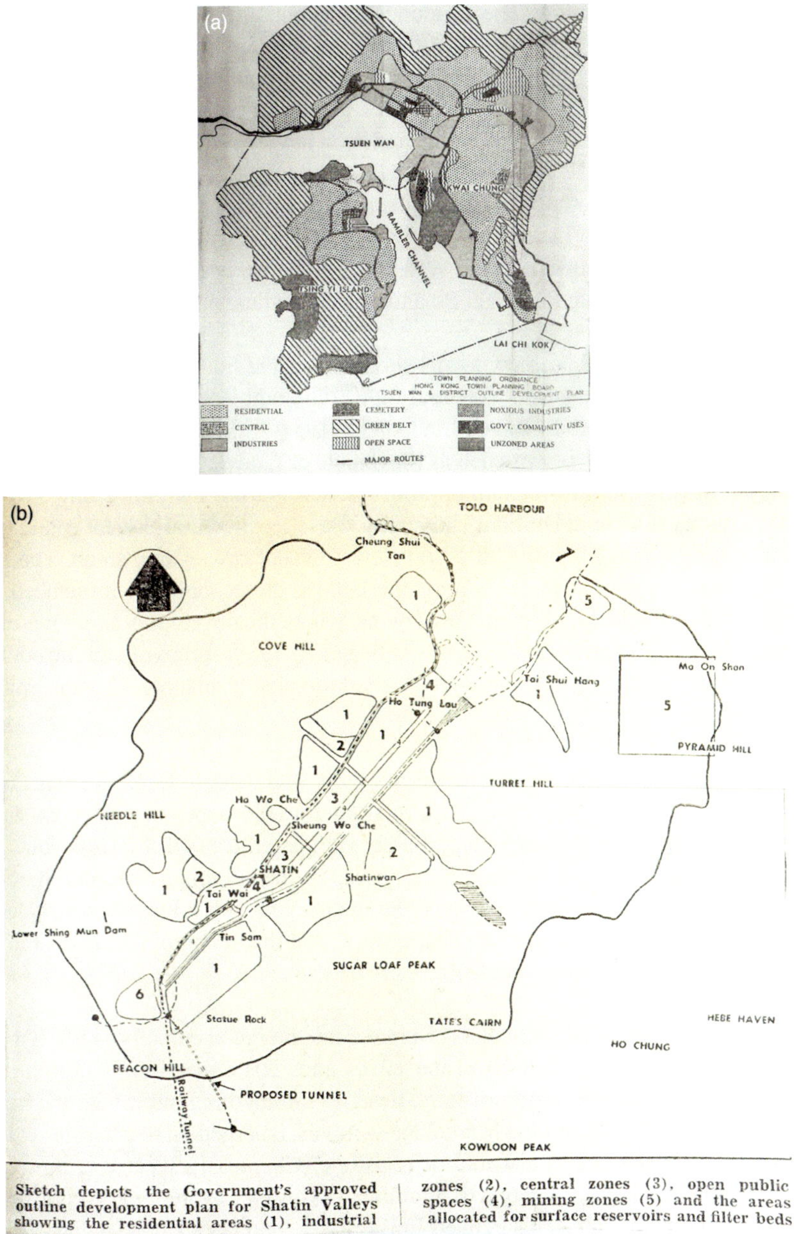

Figure 3.14 (a) Outline Development Plan of September 1961 by Town Planning Board, for 'self-contained satellite town' of Tsuen Wan. (b) Outline Development Plan for Sha Tin 'satellite town', with 360,000 inhabitants, approved March 1962; the dense, strongly linear form was perpetuated in the plan as implemented.

In February 1963, the main, state-led New Towns programme took a step closer to commencement. The announcement that staff would soon be recruited by PWD's Planning Division, operating under the Government Lands & Survey Office, for the colony-wide Outline Development Plan, prompted press comment that 'the planning of these satellite towns is imperative', especially Tsuen Wan/ Kwai Chung, whose target population had been hugely inflated to a city of a million population.[143] A SCMP editorial on satellite towns warned that 'we are making a very late start, but we hope there will be no further unnecessary delay'.[144] And by April 1963, a new PWD section to develop the New Territories satellite towns had been set up, with offices in Tsuen Wan, Yuen Long (to become 'a modern satellite town by 1968'), Castle Peak, Tai Po and Sha Tin, where a new Chinese University was planned.[145]

As to what form these new towns should take, the tide of opinion was sharply turning against the dense residential-industrial jumble of Kwun Tong towards something more ordered. Donald Liao, on his 1957–8 expedition to Britain, visited not just London New Towns such as Stevenage or Crawley, but also the north-east English new towns of Washington and Peterlee, during his Newcastle stay as a postgraduate student at Durham University.[146] He recalled that 'I went round to see as much as I could – visiting all of the New Towns, Crawley and so on. The Hong Kong New Towns concept is certainly the same as these – and also influenced from Scandinavia, by the Stockholm New Towns, where the developers and government started these new towns and built the railway'. In 1958, following an introduction by a friend, he and Cheung Sing-Hoi visited pioneering planner Thomas Sharp in Oxford:

> He was very nice to us. He drove us in his MG saloon, took us from Oxford to the Cotswolds – he said, "You're studying landscape, so you must see the Cotswolds!" He was very kind and showed us all around the Cotswolds, and took us to Stow on the Water. This landscape – the buildings fitted into it, melted into the landscape – what sticks in the memory most is Chipping Campden, its buildings melting into the landscape – it was at that moment that I was initiated into the ideal of "total design".[147]

As we will see in later chapters, what would emerge eventually at Sha Tin, and the other New Towns realised in the 1970s and '80s under Liao's design aegis, was a far more 'urban' vision of 'total design' – if anything, more like the higher-density Cumbernauld and the Mark 2 New Towns, enlarged on to a heroic scale. As Liao's concept for Wah Fu would demonstrate (Chapter 4), what was now emerging in the Housing Authority's programme was a new vision of ultra-high-density housing and landscape. This echoed Fraser's SIT, and post-1959 Singapore, in its close coordination of architecture and planning in integrated schemes of 'planned mass housing', but would rapidly move towards a boldness of scale and verticality that would outstrip Singapore's restrained 'precinct' planning in later decades.[148] For the moment, however, the groundwork for that was still being laid, under Black and his successor, David Trench – as we will see in the next chapter.

Notes

1 Sally Blyth and Ian Wotherspoon, *Hong Kong Remembers*, Oxford UP, Oxford, 1996, 67; *SCMP* 7-11-1999, 12.
2 Holdsworth and Munn, *Dictionary of Hong Kong Biography*, 30–1; Blyth and Wotherspoon, *Hong Kong Remembers*, 67.
3 Tsang, *Governing Hong Kong*, 158.
4 HKRS232-1-12-1 1–1963 cuttings; Lightbody, 2011 interview.
5 Holdsworth and Munn, *Dictionary of Hong Kong Biography*, 31.
6 HKRS232-1-11 6–1962 cutting.
7 HKRS232-1-9 11–1960 cutting, HKRS232-1-12-1 5-1963, 7–1963, 4-10-1963 cuttings (the latter with Black and Wright inspecting water works; HKRS232/1/12/4; HKRS232-1-11 9–1962 SCMP cuttings on Wanda.
8 Holdsworth and Munn, *Dictionary of Hong Kong Biography*, 30–1.
9 Tsang, *Governing Hong Kong*, 94–5; HKMS158-2-9 6–1962 telegram Burgess to Secretary of State for Colonies.
10 Tsang, *Governing Hong Kong*, 81; Lightbody, 2011 interview.
11 Wright, 2011 interview.
12 Wright, 2011 interview.
13 Akers-Jones, 2014 interview.
14 Wright, 1988 Bodleian interview.
15 HKRS394-8-2 correspondence of 21/29-10-1960; HKRS232-1-9 10-1960 cuttings; Grantham, 1968 Bodleian interview.
16 HKRS232-1-11 1962 cuttings; HKRS394-8-2 ministerial visitors from UK, papers of 5-1-1959, 19-12-1959, 21-9-1960, 11-9-1963.
17 Woodhouse later took over when Atkinson retired from BRS: Wright, 2011 interview.
18 HKRS156-1-5264 Firth to CS 6-9-1960; HKMS158-2-9 note on 30-11-1960 Colonial Office visit.
19 HKRS156-1-5264 DCS to CS 13-9-1960.
20 HKRS156-1-5264 CS to DCS 9-1960, and Fraser memo 12-1960.
21 HKRS232-1-9 28-11-1960 Lord Perth to Black.
22 Blyth and Wotherspoon, *Hong Kong Remembers*, 51; 'Sir Ronald: 40 great years', SCMP 30-4-1077, on 1962 trade negotiations.
23 Monnery, *Architect of Prosperity*, 122.
24 Holdsworth and Munn, *Dictionary of Hong Kong Biography*, 30–1; Gavin Ure, *Governors, Politics and the Colonial Office – Public Policy in Hong Kong, 1918–58*, Hong Kong UP, 2012, 191. Edgerton, *The Rise and Fall of the British Nation*, 264–5, 316–7, 378.
25 Monnery, *Architect of Prosperity*, 159–60, 169.
26 Monnery, *Architect of Prosperity*, 161.
27 Ian Scott, *Political Change and the Crisis of Legitimacy in Hong Kong*, Hurst, London, 1999, 75; Holdsworth and Munn, *Dictionary of Hong Kong Biography*, 30–1.
28 Monnery, *Architect of Prosperity*, 195–6.
29 Scott, *Political Change and the Crisis of Legitimacy*, 74; M Castells, L Goh, R Y W Kwok, *The Shek Kip Mei Syndrome – Economic Development and Public Housing in Hong Kong and Singapore*, Pion, London, 1990, 36.
30 HKRS896-1-9 and HKRS232-1-11, 1958 papers.
31 HKRS232-1-8, 27-11-1959 papers; HKRS232-1-9 1-1960 quarterly report of Commissioner for Resettlement. Resettlement costs: W E Collard, 'Housing in

Hong Kong', *Housing Review*, 3–1960, 51–63 (detailed account of the financing of Resettlement Department operations and rent affordability). HKRS232-1-10 3–1961 debate on budget.

32 HKMS158-1-62 financial report tabled to LegCo on 17-12-1958 and papers; HKRS232-1-7 SCMP 18-12-1958, detailed report on Special Committee report and summaries of two interim reports; HKMS158-2-9 9-1961 report by Colonial Secretariat on Special Committee report.

33 HKRS232-1-7 SCMP 18-12-1958; HKRS232-1-7 report for 17-12-1958 LegCo meeting; HKMS158-1-62 telegram from Black to Secretary of State for Colonies 19-5-1959; HKRS890-1-10 3-1959 meeting about proposed merger of HA and Resettlement.

34 HKRS156-1-4809 11-1958, 11-1959 correspondence; Akers-Jones, 2014 correspondence; W E Collard, 'Housing in Hong Kong', *Housing Review*, 3–1960, 51–63.

35 HKRS156-1-4809, 6–1959 and 11–1959 debates.

36 HKRS156-1-4809 11–1958, 11–1959 correspondence; Akers-Jones, 2014 interview.

37 HKMS158-1-62 W Woodhouse note of 3–1959; HKRS156-1-4809, 9–1958 Final Report of Special Committee.

38 Liao, 2010 interview.

39 HKMS158-1-21 19-5-1959 telegram from Sir R Black to Secretary of State for the Colonies.

40 HKRS156-1-4809 and HKMS158-2-10, 19-5-1959 notes by Fraser, and AS (Lands) comments on his observations. HKRS156/1/4809 2–1959 correspondence.

41 HKRS156-1-4809 2–1960 notes by Fraser.

42 J M Fraser, 'Planning and housing at high densities in two crowded tropical cities', *Town and Country Planning Summer School – University of St Andrews*, TPI, London, 1960, 104–116; HKMS158-2-9 1960 correspondence on new towns; F J Carroll 'Looking Back East – a Personal Retrospect' (c. 1981 manuscript, courtesy of Bernard Williams).

43 Summary of history of HA, HKRS156-1-4809 6–59 note by Financial Secretary, and minutes of 7–1959 meeting.

44 HKRS156-1-4809 Nov 1959 correspondence; Akers-Jones, 2014 interview; HKRS156-1-4809 11–1958 correspondence.

45 HKRS156-1-4809; HKMS158-1-62 1959 papers; telegram from Black to Secretary of State for Colonies 5–1959.

46 HKRS156-1-4809 notes of 9–1959 for LegCo on setting-up of GLCH programme. W E Collard, 'Housing in Hong Kong', *Housing Review*, 3/4–1960, 51–63; 'Housing in Hong Kong', *Builder*, 22-4-1960, 795 (Collard on 1956 committee and ten-year plan concept); HKRS232-1-9 2–1960 report on setting up GLCH; HKMS158-2-9 1961 Colonial Secretariat report; HKRS232-1-8 SCMP 22-10-1959 on low cost housing and Resettlement, November 1959 debates in government for and against reduction from 35 to 24 sq ft standard, 9–1959 memos for LegCo on setting up of GLCH to tackle tenements, and 8–1960 SCMP reports on setting up of GLCH.

47 HKMS158-2-10 15-7-1960 note from Trench to Colonial Office.

48 Fung Tung, 2010 interview; HKRS156-1-4809.

49 Wright, 2011 interview; HKRS156-1-4809 notes of 9–1959 for LegCo on setting up of GLCH; HKRS232-1-9 2–1960 report on GLCH; HKRS158-2-9 1961 Colonial Secretariat report; HKRS232-1-9 2–1960 on budget for GLCH.

50 FCO1030-1178 and HKMS158-2-9, on 20-9-1961 by Colonial Secretariat.

51 HKMS158-2-9 1961 Colonial Secretariat report.

52 HKMS158-2-9 Sept 1961 Colonial Secretariat's report; HKRS232-1-9 2-1960 Financial Secretary's budget; HKRS232-1-10 3-1961 report on GLCH.

53 HKRS232-1-10 3–1961 papers for debate on budget.
54 Carroll, 'Looking Back East'.
55 HKRS232-1-10 8-1961 papers; SCMP 26-8-1961; HKRS232-1-10 3-1961 memo on Hung Hom; HKRS232-1-12-3 21-9-1963 papers.
56 SCMP 8-12-1963, including summary of GLC/HA recent estates; HKRS232-1-12-1 1963 papers on Cheung Sha Wan.
57 Fung Tung, 2010 interview; Wright, 2011 interview.
58 Williams, 'Administration of Public Housing'.
59 Cheng, 2014 interview; Wright, 2015 interview; Wright, 2011 interview.
60 J R Firth, 'Housing in Hong Kong', *Builder* 9-2-1962, 298; HKRS232-1-11 11-1962 government announcement on loans to Housing Authority.
61 HKRS232-1-10 3–1961 debate on budget; SCMP 20-12-1963 editorial; HKRS232-1-12-4 12–1963 on opening of Choi Hung; W E Collard, 'Housing in Hong Kong', *Housing Review*, 3–1960, 51–63.
62 Akers-Jones, 2014 interview.
63 HKMS158-1-62 6-2-1959 Rowe sending final report of Special Committee to Colonial Office.
64 158-2-9 11–1960 Black letter to Minister of State.
65 Wright, 2011 interview.
66 Akers-Jones, 2014 interview.
67 Rowe, 1987 Bodleian interview; Wright, 2011 interview.
68 HKRS163-1-781 Collard 4–1960 note on Urban Council.
69 HKRS232-1-12-1 2-1963 HA annual meeting including Fraser report.
70 HKRS232-1-12-4 Urban Council Annual Debate 12–1963; Scott, *Political Change and the Crisis of Legitimacy,* 115.
71 Elsie Tu, *Colonial Hong Kong in the Eyes of Elsie Tu,* Hong Kong UP, 2003.
72 Wright, 2015 interview. Wright also claimed that Alison Bell (Reform Club) had a similar approach.
73 Tu, *Colonial Hong Kong,* 52.
74 HKRS394-21-1 Elliott press conference 9–1963; HKRS232-1-12-4 Elliott at 3-12-1963 Urban Council debate on Resettlement Department.
75 HKRS394-21-1 9-11-1963 J C McDouall to Jack Cater: 'Elsie Elliott has managed to get a letter through to Harold Wilson' and other Labour MPs on the squatter issue, leading to demands from the London Government for a 'full and frank Report'… 'in anticipation of a lively time' in the next session of parliament.
76 HKRS232-1-12-1 Urban Council debate 5–1963; HKRS232-1-12-4 UC Debate 3-12-1963; HKRS232-1-12-4 cutting from *Hong Kong Standard* 9-12-1963.
77 HKRS232-1-12-4, SCMP 29-12-1963 cutting.
78 docomomo.sg/people-and-organisations/james-milner-fraser
79 Akers-Jones, 2014 interview; HKMS158-2-9 St Andrews 1960 lecture. Wright, 2011 lecture.
80 Firth, *Builder* 9-2-1962, 298 (including on Shek Kip Mei H blocks); 11–62 Firth lecture at Reform Club; J R Firth, 'Three new Hong Kong housing projects', *Builder* 6-9-1957, 398–9. Liao, 2010 interview: Rowe 'merely an administrative officer – he didn't make any contribution'; Wright, 2011 interview.
81 Liao, 2010 interview; 'A conversation with Donald Liao', *HKIA Journal,* Issue 72 ('Occupy Housing'), 2016, 30.
82 Liao, 2009 interview.
83 Liao, 2010 interview.

84 *Far East Architect and Builder*, June 1965, 54–5. Liao, 2010 and 2011 interviews.
85 Liao, 2010 interview.
86 Liao, 2010 interview (including on Fraser); Fung Tung, 2010 interview.
87 Liao, 2010 and 2011 interviews.
88 Fung, 2010 interview; Carroll, 'Looking Back East'. HKRS232-1-7 4–1958 extracts on tenants in North Point, and *Housing Review* 12–1958 survey of Hong Kong management systems. HKMS158-2-9 cuttings: *Housing Review* 4–1960 survey of management and rents of Hong Kong housing; J M Fraser, 'Housing in Hong Kong', *Chartered Surveyor*, 2–1964, 391–5: detailed description of HA management system. HKRS231-1-12-2, 5–1963 letter from HA on problems in estates, water supply at Sai Wan. Cadogan Street named Sai Wan 1958, HKRS232-1-7 4-1958 note. HKRS232-1-11 8–1962 note on exemption of HA, HS and HKMHS from the Tenancy (Notification of Termination) Ordinance 1962. Liao, 2010 and 2011 interview. F J Carroll, 'Housing in Hong Kong', *Housing,* 11–1967, 13–17.
89 HKRS232-1-7 2-1958 Rowe papers, and Collard article in SCMP 31-5-1958.
90 'New Housing Project in Hong Kong', *Builder*, 26-5-1961, 985;
91 E Bedwell, 'Low cost housing in Hong Kong, 1958', *Housing Review* 11/12–1958, 181–3; *Town Planning Review*, vol 35, 1964–5, 1; HKRS232-1-10, 3–1961 article. HKMS158-2-9 4-1960 descriptions. J M Fraser, 'Housing in Hong Kong', *Chartered Surveyor*, 2–1964, 391–5; W E Collard, 'Housing in Hong Kong', *Housing Review*, 3/4–1960, 51–63. 'Housing in Hong Kong', *Builder*, 22-4-1960, 795.
92 HKRS156-3-7, 1–1959 detailed report on estate, 3–1960 discussion on block names. Cheng, 2014 interview; HKRS156-1-5264 12-1955 to 2–1956 papers; HKRS156-3-7 1-1959 detailed report on estate. *Hong Kong and Far-Eastern Builder*, vol 13: 5, 1957, 5. HKRS232-1-10, 3–1961 detailed feature on So Uk and Choi Hung.
93 HKRS232-1-9 5–60 description of Choi Hung; *Municipal Journal,* 20-3-1964, 932. SCMP 29-5-1964 (by J A Prescott); *Hong Kong and Far-Eastern Builder*, vol 16:1, 36. 'New Housing Project in Hong Kong', *Builder*, 26-5-1961, 985. 'Housing in Hong Kong', *Builder,* 9-2-1962, 298–9. Choi Hung (central corridor) HKRS232-1-10, 3–1961 article. Demolition of Choi Hung, SCMP 6-11-2023.
94 Fung Tung, interview 2010; Bedwell, 'Low cost housing in Hong Kong, 1958', 181–3. Sanderson, Glover: L C Wong, 2011 interview.
95 Bedwell, 'Low cost housing in Hong Kong, 1958', 181–3; Collard, 'Housing in Hong Kong', 51–63. HKRS232-1-9 cuttings from SCMP 7–1960, 2-8-1960; HKRS232-1-11 10-1962, 12–1962 cuttings on HS; HKRS232-1-12-3 9-1963 on HS rent rises; L C Wong, 2011 interview.
96 *Hong Kong Standard* 13-12-1963; SCMP 5-12-1963; HKRS232-1-12-1 3-1963 cutting on middle-income scheme.
97 HKRS232-1-9, 7-1960 cutting; HKRS232-1-12-4 6-1963 cutting.
98 HKRS232-1-12-4 SCMP 1-10-63 cutting on Lefrak visit.
99 Fluctuation: HKRS896-1-9 1963 review of Resettlement; Williams, 'Public housing and I'; HKRS232-1-12-1 1-1963 by Morrison; HKRS232-1-12-3 9-7-1963 on Resettlement falling short of target.
100 HKRS896-1-9 25-11-1958 note by D J M Mackenzie; HKRS890-1-10 AC Maxwell note.
101 HKRS232-1-12-1 3-1963 cutting.
102 HKRS232-1-10, 3–1961 and 5–1961 cuttings; HKRS163-1-781 note on R C Lee speech of 1961 advocating HA takeover of Resettlement estates (suggestion turned down by CS).

103 Holdsworth and Munn, *Dictionary of Hong Kong Biography*, 30–1, 53; HKRS163-1-781 1960 Burgess speech.
104 HKRS524-3-6 17-4-1963 Sweetman to DCS; HKRS232-1-12-1 5–1963 Paul Tsui in huts dispute.
105 HKRS232-1-12-1 5–1963 Urban Council debate.
106 HKRS232-1-12-4 12–1963 Urban Council debate.
107 Smart, *The Shek Kip Mei Myth*, 159–178 on 1963 Working Party.
108 HKRS934-5-31 12-5-1964 CASCA to SCA, 4-6-64 Secretary of State to Governor, 3-7-64 Teesdale to McDouall, 8-7-64 Barty to Colonial Secretary. Smart, *The Shek Kip Mei Myth,* 159–178; HKRS 394-21-1 1963 papers; Williams, 'Public Housing and I'.
109 HKRS394-21-1 report of 1963 Working Party, map of all Resettlement estates, and 1963 review of Resettlement programme.
110 HKRS232-1-11 11-1962 Urban Council debate.
111 Yeung and Wong, Fifty Years, 210.
112 Public Works Department, *Report for 1961–2.*
113 Wright, 2015 interview.
114 Cheng, 2014 interview.
115 Liao, 2010 interview; Cheng, 2014 interview.
116 HKRS232-1-9, 1960 report on rents.
117 HKRS232-1-10 3-1961 debate on budget.
118 HKRS896-1-9 1960 papers; HKMS158-2-9 9-1961 papers.
119 HKRS232-1-11 1-1962 papers.
120 HKRS232-1-10 1-1961 cutting; 232-1-12-4 5-10-1963 cutting; Cheng, 2014 interview; 232-1-12-1 1-1963 cutting; Hong Kong Housing Authority, *The First Two Million*, Hong Kong, 1980, 46-7. 934-5-31 30-7-63 PWD report, 10-3-64 memo for ExCo.
121 Cheng, 2014 interview; HKRS232-1-12-1 1-1963 on new Resettlement designs.
122 Fung Tung, 2010 interview.
123 Mizuoka, *Contrived Laissez-Faireism;* HKRS896-1-114 21-3-1960 note by Robson.
124 13-2-1960 Commissioner for Housing note, and following notes by Clarke.
125 Wright, 1988 Bodleian interview.
126 Williams, 'Administration of Public Housing in Hong Kong'.
127 Fraser, 'Planning and housing at high densities', 111; lecture also reported in FCO1030-1078, HKMS158-2-9. J R Firth, 'Housing in Hong Kong', *Builder* 9-2-1962, 298–9.
128 Blyth and Wotherspoon, *Hong Kong Remembers*, 37 (Cheung Yan Lung).
129 Blyth and Wotherspoon, *Hong Kong Remembers*, 145.
130 HKRS232-1-11, 10–1962 cutting.
131 David Akers-Jones, *Feeling the Stones – Reminiscences by David Akers-Jones*, Hong Kong UP, 2004, 18.
132 Akers-Jones, *Feeling the Stones*, 23.
133 HKRS232-1-7 9–1958 Kirby note.
134 HKRS232-1-8 25-1-1959 note by Bell; HKMS158-1-1962 response to committee.
135 Liao, 2010 interview.
136 HKRS232-1-8 1959 Burgess memos.
137 HKRS232-1-9 5-1-1960 cutting.
138 D C Y Lai and D J Dwyer, 'Kwun Tong, Hong Kong – a study of industrial planning', *Town Planning Review*, 35, 1964–5, 299–305. HKRS232-1-10, 9–1961 map and development plan; 'Hong Kong's new town experience', *Official Architecture and Planning*, 2–1966, 273–8.

139 Public Works Department, *Report for 1961–2*; HKRS232-1-9 4–1960 cuttings, HKRS 232-1-11 9–1962 cuttings.
140 HKRS232-1-11 11–1962 cuttings.
141 HKRS232-1-11 11–1962 cuttings; Aberdeen proposal, HKRS232-1-11.
142 HKRS232-1-12-1 4–1963 on Lantau.
143 HKRS232-1-12-4, 3–1963, 12–1963 papers.
144 HKRS232-1-12-1 3–1963 editorial.
145 HKRS232-1-12-1 4–1963 editorial.
146 Liao, 2009 interview.
147 Liao 2009, 2010 interviews. Junwei Li, 'Immigration, employment and new town initiatives', 998–1001.
148 Bob Pang, 'Unknown Brutalism in the East 1960s-70s', *C20 – the Magazine of the Twentieth Century Society*, 2023–2, 22.

4 1964–1971

Trench's governorship – pragmatism and tentative reformism

During the late 1960s, Hong Kong's original laissez-faire system, with its assumption of minimum-necessary state involvement, entered an existential crisis. In reaction, a new approach began to coalesce, under which the private sector was still regarded as paramount, but coordinated state interventions in specific, interconnected areas were increasingly seen as essential – not least to re-establish the legitimacy of the British colonial regime after two phases of violent unrest in 1966 and 1967. Responding to these challenges to the sense of collective identity within Hong Kong society, the foundations were laid for a generation of stabilisation – a re-embedding process within which public housing played a central role.

The Governor between 1964 and 1971, David Trench, had previously worked in Hong Kong as Deputy Colonial Secretary in 1959–61, followed by three years as High Commissioner for the British Western Pacific Territories. Trench's outlook was one of realism vis-à-vis the sovereignty issue, an outlook influenced by timing: whereas his successor, Sir Murray MacLehose, felt driven to intervene radically in support of Hong Kong's survival, for Trench, '1997' still seemed somewhat over the horizon. He felt that it was 'inevitable' Hong Kong would be returned to China by 1997, as the ceded territory was 'not really viable on its own', but 'just how it would go back, of course, nobody knew'. In the wake of the 1967 riots, the British government also began planning for another contingency, that of enforced expulsion before 1997, and it was only at the end of Trench's governorship, in a 1971 intervention by premier Zhou Enlai (as we will see in the next chapter), that it became clear that China had no intention of doing this, and would instead wait until 1997.[1] In the meantime, Trench's preference was for a policy of pragmatic management, and opportunistic reformism: 'It didn't matter to us that someone else was almost bound to take over Hong Kong in 1997' – 'we just did the best for Hong Kong'.[2] In the process, policy shifted from 'carrying on as Hong Kong had always carried on' towards greater intervention. Trench's carefully calibrated shift towards reform was not always appreciated externally: although his governorship was twice extended by a year, to 1970 and 1971, Lord Malcolm Shepherd, Labour's junior foreign minister, argued in 1969 against his extension, as likely to perpetuate Hong Kong's 'old ways'.[3]

DOI: 10.1201/9781315563701-5

Reminiscing later, in 1987, Trench recalled that his three overriding aims were, firstly, to 'do anything required' to avoid offending China, short of permitting British authority to be 'usurped', Macau-style; secondly, to defend the currency and the territory's economic reputation, on the grounds that nobody would be interested in Hong Kong if its economy collapsed; and thirdly, to avoid making conditions too pleasant in Hong Kong, which might 'drag in immigrants' – the cynical realpolitik of the latter not being a line of argument that would probably have been supported by MacLehose. The first aim required a careful continuation of the longstanding external low profile of the Hong Kong government, unlike the ideological self-trumpeting of Lee Kuan Yew's PAP government in Singapore – a policy that would continue even under the more activist governorship of MacLehose (Chapter 5).[4]

In reality, many of Trench's policies anticipated MacLehose's reforms, but these were mostly frustrated by traditionalist opponents within the Colonial Secretariat. Michael Wright argued that 'a number of good things started in David Trench's time, but MacLehose got the credit for them'.[5] Trench's own previous relatively junior rank within Hong Kong government was partly responsible for that predicament. As governor, he found himself in an uncertain position vis-à-vis his senior administrators, with Burgess and Barnett both previously senior to him, and Holmes having attended the same Cambridge University colonial scheme.[6] For example, an initial proposal for a City District Officer scheme was blocked by John McDouall, the outgoing 'Secretary for Chinese Affairs', who thought he 'knew the Chinese', and instead argued for cooperation with the established, conservative kaifong associations: Trench recalled that 'initially I got nowhere with it at all'.[7] In 1967, similarly, Cowperthwaite thwarted Trench's attempt to introduce social insurance.[8]

Progress could only be secured incrementally through his patronage role, to bring about gradual, generational changes in senior administrative officers, from traditionalists to progressives. For example, Trench secured McDouall's replacement as Chinese Affairs Secretary (later Home Affairs) by his preferred crisis 'fire-fighter', Ronald Holmes, a success which allowed him to revisit the District Officer issue several years later.[9] The dogged obstruction, by Principal Assistant Colonial Secretary (Lands) Teddy Kidd, of any consolidation of the multiplicity of public housing agencies was only finally cleared in 1969, when Trench secured Kidd's transfer back to London and his replacement by the up-and-coming reformist, David Akers-Jones.[10]

Overall, in these years the administrative class retained the elite, generalist ethos of the cadet system, and its strong sense of autonomy, not answerable to London for orders of any kind, and whose loyalties would if necessary require them to defend Hong Kong against British interests.[11] This team-player ethos insulated the administrative class from low-level corruption and ensured an ability to move from one department to another. 1969 saw a reform of the civil service along less hierarchical lines, but even then Akers-Jones recalled that as newly appointed PACS (L) he was treated as 'a kind of god'.[12] Alongside the generational administrative shift towards progressives, a growing overlap in responsibility developed between administrators and professionals. Earlier, Wright recalled the privileged lines of communication between Kidd, who 'always played everything very close to his chest', and Cowperthwaite. Instead, Trench sought good relations with up-and-coming technocratic leaders: Donald Liao recalled playing golf with the Governor, who then duly opened the Wah Fu Estate.[13]

Balancing the 'tripod of consents' – the 1966/7 riots and their aftermath

What was required was a balancing act between external and internal pressures: in 1971, Denis Bray, then Commissioner for the New Territories, argued that Hong Kong's stability rested on a 'tripod of consents': Britain, China, and the local population.[14]

Relations with Britain during these years mainly meant relations with a Labour government, and here there were growing tensions, with constant pressure by visiting Labour MPs against Hong Kong's supposedly backward social and economic system, together with the implicit or explicit motivations of industrial rivalry as Hong Kong industry boomed following the loss of the Chinese entrepot trade.[15] From Hong Kong's perspective, the most fundamental concern was economic: the constant tension over the sterling currency relationship, especially following the November 1967 devaluation of the pound. Trench recalled that by 1967 the Labour government was increasingly 'panicky' and only concerned with their 'own troubles'.[16] In April 1969, Deputy Financial Secretary Philip Haddon-Cave was involved in a vitriolic clash with two Labour MPs, Walden and Jones, who sternly critiqued 'our "conservative" fiscal policies' with arguments that Haddon Cave privately branded 'quite pathetic': they demanded that 'we *ought* to have higher tax rates and we *ought* to borrow, and we simply *ought* to do this or that'. Relations with visiting Conservatives were uncontentious – including visits by opposition leader Edward Heath, and Duncan Sandys.[17]

Unlike these often furious, but ultimately irrelevant debates with London politicians, relations with mainland China were of more immediate, existential concern, but the central government was in no hurry to raise the sovereignty issue, given its own turmoil.[18] Far more immediate were the short-term pressures stemming from the continuing waves of illegal immigrants, for which a 'touch-base' policy would eventually be agreed in 1974.[19] More indicative of the mainland government's underlying power over Hong Kong was the ongoing crisis over water supply, beginning with the 'terrible drought' (Wright) of 1963. Trench recalled that 'it kept me awake at night, I tell you… water, water, water was on my mind', and there was 'absolutely no solution', despite constant negotiation with the provincial mainland authorities, including regular trips to Canton by the PWD's George Norton and the Deputy Director of the Waterworks.[20] The most immediate expedient was the chartering of tanker ships to fetch water from up the Pearl River estuary, although what was brought back was arguably 'a mixture of water and sewage'.[21] Even in 1968, with tankers 'full of filthy water' still shuttling up- and down-stream, the water supply was confined to only four hours daily between June and September. Although this situation was resolved thereafter by a combination of government investment in a desalination plant, which Wright persuaded

Cowperthwaite was 'not just an expensive toy', and long-term access to reservoir water from the mainland, the sovereignty implication was clear: Hong Kong could not survive in any form without mainland cooperation over resources.[22]

The role of the local population as the third leg of the 'tripod of consents' was uncertain, but growing: a fundamental reorientation in public perceptions was underway. Contrary to the 'borrowed place, borrowed time' world outlook, branded by Liao 'a narrow, English view', a deeper sense of community affiliation was beginning to take hold: in 1969, Prof. Keith Hopkins, recently appointed Professor of Sociology at HKU, argued that the twinkling lights of Hong Kong's new multi-storey blocks provided 'tangible evidence of the government's concern for the poor'.[23] Public housing architect Rosman Wai later recalled that it was in the late 1960s and '70s that 'people started to belong to Hong Kong': 'Hong Kong people are very pragmatic – but people started to say, "We are Hong Kong people". The identity of Hong Kong people started in the 1960s and '70s. You need to have roots here – the reality is that you can't go back to mainland China, and you can't go to Britain. So, this will be your place.'[24] That shift in attitude was not just a gradual, cumulative affair, but was also shaped by two explosive outbursts of unrest: the first, in 1966, concerned with social conditions and the second, in 1967, almost exclusively political in character. These two episodes have been extensively researched and published, in the latter case in Gary Ka-Wai Cheung's authoritative 2009 book.[25]

The 1966 unrest, straightforwardly dubbed a 'social riot' by Akers Jones, is most commonly known as the 'Star Ferry Riots' after the fare increase incident that triggered it: Elsie Elliott played a key supporting role in the unrest. Press coverage was strongly partisan, with many papers favouring Elliott's arguments, and a 'widespread conviction that the police, as a body, are brutal and corrupt'.[26] Some administrators, such as George Rowe, were hostile and contemptuous: the riots were opportunistically stirred up by 'that bloody fool Elsie Elliott, they were her thing, it was simply the lads having a go – in fact, some of these riots were sort of made up on the spot'.[27] And in PWD Director Michael Wright's view, 'I had a lot of time for David Trench but I don't think he had the political sense that MacLehose had. So I think it [the Star Ferry riots] just got out of hand for no real reason.' In Bernard Williams's view, by contrast, the reality was more complex:

> Up until then the bulk of the population, being refugees from China, were quite happy just to go along and do whatever the government said – but the 1966 riots showed that the younger, better-educated people did want to say something. These were students and young people who felt that this increase in the cost of living was unfair.

The authorities, he felt, 'made such a mistake in trying to pin those things on Elsie Elliott'.[28]

The 1967 unrest, by contrast, stemmed from an interaction of external and internal forces. The external force was of course the Cultural Revolution, but the impetus stemmed not from Beijing but from local Guangdong province and Hong

Kong communists, both in urban areas and in rural redoubts of Communist sympathy such as Sai Kung, where the local Heung Yee Kuk had been reorganised as part of the 1958 reform. In Lightbody's view, 'The communists in Hong Kong wanted to show Beijing they were as loyal as anyone else. They wanted to make the maximum noise.'[29] And in Williams's opinion, probably

> the local communist activists in Hong Kong thought they should not be left behind: if everyone else in China were struggling, they should also struggle… So written on the back of the Kowloon Motor Buses you had slogans like "Kill David Trench, Kill Paul Tsui!"

But if Beijing had really wanted 'to get the British out of Hong Kong, they certainly could have done it by closing down all the public utilities, of which the most important, of course, was water'.[30]

Resettlement estates were amongst the fiercest hotbeds of the 1967 uprising, with estates such as Tung Tau becoming running battlegrounds, and Resettlement Department estate offices targeted for attacks, while Housing Authority and Society estates were largely unaffected. (Figure 4.1) The process of pacification negotiated a careful path between Macau-style submissiveness and excessive

YOUTHS DEFY CURFEW

Violence Continues As Demonstrators And Police Clash

Despite an early curfew clamped down on troubled Kowloon districts last night after a day of continuing disturbance youthful demonstrators defied the curfew order and clashed with riot police in a number of incidents during the night.

During the day there were sporadic incidents in Sanpokong and in the vicinity of Tung Tau resettlement area involving demonstrators who were described by a police officer as "people without anything particular to do."

Police were kept busy dealing with these incidents in Sanpokong, where the trouble started on Thursday, the situa-

put the age of most demonstrators at between 18 and 24, on a general basis.

"A lot of children hampered police operations because, naturally, police were reluctant to use any real force against them," Mr Illingworth said.

"Crowds were often gathered when police were not there and I think this is what happened in Tung Tau Tsuen Road," he added. "We deliberately avoided trying to antagonise people in this area."

The curfew, which was to be lifted at 4.30 am, covered the same areas as the curfew on Thursday night — Kowloon Tong, Kowloon Tsai, Kowloon City, Wongtaisin resettlement estate, Sanpokong, Diamond Hill, Choi Hung estate, Ngauchiwan village, Tszwanshan and Wangtauhom.

Car Set On Fire

First reports of the curfew being broken came at 6.20 pm when a crowd in Tung Tau resettlement estate set fire to a car outside Block 10 and also stoned the police party in the vicinity

Figure 4.1 March 1967 SCMP article on rioting at Tung Tau Resettlement estate.

repression, avoiding provocation of the Chinese central government while allowing public indignation against Maoist violence to build up: 'if British troops had been seen firing on Chinese workers, this could have created a very serious situation'. Eventually, the communists' militant stance completely backfired, and permanently delegitimised the radical cause in Hong Kong.[31] A crucial role in pacification was played by Denis Bray, as part of a special duties group during the unrest, and, with Jack Cater, responsible for local liaison and propaganda. Ian Lightbody recalled that

> We treated them harshly, raided them by helicopter, dropped in teams. They didn't get away with it, so it didn't last long. They could see they hadn't any public support. A lot of the refugees came to *avoid* communism, so they didn't want to see that end.[32]

But in the aftermath, while the government avoided any evictions that would further inflame passions, the general condition of Resettlement estates slid into a vicious spiral of neglect and low-level disorder – prompting increasingly tough managerial responses, as we will see below.[33]

The 1967 unrest also had significant local political repercussions, as Trench 'capitalised' on his 'victory' (Steve Tsang) to finally implement the City District Officer (CDO) scheme, previously blocked by John McDouall.[34] It also allowed the unobtrusive abandonment of controversial proposals for local-government reform suggested in 1966 by the 'Dickinson Report', including (inevitably) a British-style local-authority system and a lower tier of local councils below the Urban Council.[35] These were viewed within the Secretariat as a thinly disguised Urban Council 'takeover bid' for central functions, including New Territories governance: Trench argued that 'Hong Kong was so small that you couldn't really have two governments in it – the Urban Council and the ExCo/LegCo system'.[36] The riots enabled this plan to be 'quietly forgotten'. To even reform-minded Secretariat figures such as Akers-Jones, further elective democratisation seemed both undesirable and impracticable – 'it would have been like trying to organise elections on a railway station'.[37] The CDO system, by contrast, established in 1968 a 'first stage of democratic government' (Williams) through somewhat ombudsman-like administrative means, grounded in the existing structure of the New Territories District Officers, and ultimately going back to the 1890s structure established by Lockhart.[38] This arrangement was worked out in detail by Bray, a 'veteran' District Officer himself.

In the urban areas, the CDOs were integrated into the urban fabric, and had physical shopfronts; much of the CDOs' day-to-day work from 1973 onwards would be concerned with organising mutual aid committees (MACs) in public housing estates and other residential areas.[39] In Wright's opinion, this subtly undermined the old traditions of government dirigisme, which had previously blithely disregarded public opinion on development issues:

> Thirty years ago, you could just go in roughshod and build a flyover right in front of their window, and nobody was going to complain. Hong Kong now

is different. The public had to be softened up, and this is where David Trench, I think, did a marvellous job with his District Officer scheme – to explain to people who were affected that they could get compensation and so on.[40]

The development of local pride and civic engagement was the most obvious result. But underlying sovereignty concerns were never far away: Holmes also saw the CDOs as 'political officers' who could bolster the 'legitimacy' of the 'colonial regime' in the build-up to any pre-1997 negotiations.[41]

John Cowperthwaite: intervention without strategy

Trench's measured response to the unrest through limited democratisation and participation was underpinned by a subtler, but arguably more significant development in Hong Kong's economic governance – which had been fronted since 1961 by Financial Secretary John Cowperthwaite.[42] During the later 1960s, Cowperthwaite began to modify the Charles Follows laissez-faire philosophy through a new approach of highly selective government intervention in the economy, involving closely regulated individual spending initiatives. Donald Liao recalled that Cowperthwaite 'always intervened in the workings of policies [such as housing] – he kept a sharp eye on everything'.[43] 'Cowperthwaite controlled everything' (Williams). In housing, this restrained expansionism was encouraged by a growing appreciation for the need of greater social inclusiveness. In Trench's view, Cowperthwaite was 'broad-minded and far-sighted… he fought for the poor', while remaining 'very conscious of the need to preserve the financial strength of Hong Kong and not borrow ourselves into trouble'; and to Akers-Jones, Cowperthwaite was 'quite a humanist – he had his human side'.[44] This approach required not only strong but flexible monitoring of growing government expenditure, but defence of the autonomous 'Hong Kong Way' against any welfare-state reformist pressures from London. In that context, Cowperthwaite unambiguously saw himself as a 'Hong Kong chauvinist', as did other prominent officials concerned with trade and financial matters, such as the 'confrontational' David Jordan of Commerce – in George Rowe's opinion, 'a bloody good officer, but an arrogant bastard' – or Cowperthwaite's successor Haddon-Cave, who had, Akers-Jones recalled, 'an acid tongue'.[45]

Cowperthwaite's most visceral aversion was to the principle of state-led planning. His approach was not unlike that of Robert Moses in New York City, but was carried far further, to include refusal to compile any overall government accounts or data on income, in order to impede any London 'meddling'. His approach was recalled by Michael Wright: 'There was an unwillingness on the part of the Financial Secretary to have a plan that might commit him to spend money'…

'He was very competent, but he felt Hong Kong was in such a state of flux that things had to be dealt with from year to year. For example, in road planning there was a lot of criticism of the ad-hoc planning, and we wanted to develop a long-term road plan, but Cowperthwaite was not prepared to countenance that.

> Every three months, I'd have a meeting with the Governor. He'd raise this, and ask, "What's happened?" I said, "It's come to a dead end on the Financial Secretary's desk". Finally he phoned the Financial Secretary and said, "I have the Chief Architect here – he tells me you have blocked the road plan – can you come up?" A couple of minutes later, Cowperthwaite appeared and explained why he was against it. He [Trench] said, "John, this is a case when it would be very useful to have that long-term road plan."[46]

Overall, government economic strategy continued to rely on revenue surpluses generated by rapid growth to fend off pressures for greater state intervention. These pressures were both external, from Labour Westminster governments pressing for higher taxes and regulation, and, perhaps more significantly, internal, stemming from the social pressures that had culminated in the 1966/7 unrest, and consequent pressure to expand the civil service and finance new social expenditure. Despite Cowperthwaite's 'Gladstonian attitude to public finance' (Steve Tsang), the Hong Kong government was on the brink of a spending boom, which would make it the territory's largest landlord and employer.[47] Here, public housing had a slightly anomalous position, as it already enjoyed high levels of state support. Yet its most dramatic levels of state financial support were still to come, in the 1970s and 1980s.

The distinctiveness of Hong Kong's macroeconomic approach was highlighted by the inevitable comparison with the policies pursued by Lee Kuan Yew in Singapore, which many in Hong Kong's elite regarded as distinctly socialistic in its reliance on state planning and land regulation, including sweeping compulsory-purchase provisions under 1966 legislation – a striking contrast with Hong Kong, where 'money talks, and nobody will touch private land' (Williams).[48] In Hong Kong, by contrast, the territory's more precarious geo-political situation led to a more cautious and more variegated approach, defending the overall laissez-faire system while using the surpluses generated by that system to finance massive, yet curiously low-key, increases in social spending. This approach, which ensured that 'the shape of the state was optimised as far as possible to provide public services in a way that least inhibited economic growth', was dubbed by Trench a 'positive laissez-faire policy'.[49] This expression was later modified by Haddon-Cave, Financial Secretary from 1971, into 'positive non-intervention': Trench recalled, 'he pinched that off me!' Trench himself was as enthusiastic an upholder of the laissez-faire economic status quo as anyone: 'I, like a lot of other people, thought that government had no business, really, in meddling with the affairs of industry and commerce, because it simply wasn't competent to meddle with industry and commerce'.[50]

Ever since 1945, Hong Kong's growing surpluses had been seem primarily as a way of avoiding Treasury control. But by the late-1960s, the safety margin was so comfortable, with a reserve equalling two-thirds of annual government expenditure, that the government could afford to unleash a spending boom, including continuing high support for public housing, while more subtly encouraging a new, more responsive governmental ethos – all without any fundamental change in macroeconomic approach. Indeed, there were potential benefits for the private property sector, which made massive profits from the rise in prosperity through housing purchases by better-off workers. These early phases of state intervention thus provided a foundation for the subsequent dominance of the private real-estate 'tycoons' – as we will see in later chapters.[51] In the early 1960s, the scale of the available surpluses had been limited: Lightbody recalled that 'in the early days, Cowperthwaite only had a limited amount of revenue in his hands!' But despite the 1965 banking crisis, sterling assets rose from £235m to £280m in 1965.[52] And the situation was transformed by the late 1960s: whereas per-capita GDP had been only $582 in 1961, by 1969 it had exceeded $1,000. As a result, budget surpluses soared, from $493m in 1961 and $787m in 1967 to $2,886m in 1971.[53] And between 1968/9 and 1971/2, spending rose by 12% annually, reaching $2.9 bn, but revenue rose by an annual rate of over 14%, to $3.5bn.[54]

The housing implications of this surplus-fuelled spending developed in tandem with the boom in government surpluses in the late 1960s, as favoured by Cowperthwaite. As late as 1965, his budget address was still very cautious. He traced the history of the proliferation of public housing agencies since the Shek Kip Mei fire, praising the Housing Authority and the Housing Society for their role in design and management innovation, but cautioning that the differing standards and criteria of the three main agencies caused confusion. Sternly, he warned against allowing these programmes to develop an institutional life of their own:

> There appears to be a tendency to take the view that their aim should be to build as much housing as it physically can, irrespective of what may be happening at the private field; and that priority must be given to the provision of public funds for this purpose. I do not think I can subscribe to this view myself.

It is unrealistic to think in terms of mass public housing at subsidised rents. We must continue to rely very substantially on new private housing, both because we are most unlikely to have the resources to do otherwise, and because we must not create a situation where a large part of the population has the privilege of having its housing subsidised from public revenue to which the less fortunate minority also contribute. An adequate field must therefore be left open to private-enterprise housing, and government-subsidised housing must not be allowed to depress rents below the level to which, with supply and demand in reasonable equilibrium, commercial rents might fall without inhibiting further private development.[55]

The following year, Cowperthwaite's 1966 budget speech contained a comprehensive denunciation of 'state universalism' as requiring high taxes or cuts in services. By the late 1960s, this spectre was seen in Hong Kong as being vividly embodied in the travails of Labour-controlled Britain. In his 1969 budget address, he warned that 'one only has to look at the serious difficulties Britain has had in reducing the rate of expansion of public spending there'.[56]

Yet in the years of Trench's governorship, government expenditure on housing, as a percentage of social expenditure and public expenditure overall, remained high, varying narrowly between annual minima of $187m and maxima of $224m. Certainly, the housing-related *percentages* of social expenditure and total public expenditure decreased – from 38% of social expenditure in 1963/4 to 19% in 1971/2, and from 15% of total public expenditure to 8%.[57] In effect, during this period, other areas of social spending were catching up with housing. As a result, there were wild fluctuations in the overall production levels of public housing, coupled with shifts in the relative contributions of the three main agencies: Resettlement, Government Low-Cost Housing, and Housing Authority. Most significant was a shift in production emphasis away from Resettlement towards GLCH and HA production. In 1964/5, the year of maximum overall public output under the pre-1973 system (32,595), completions by the three agencies totalled 23,106 (71%) for Resettlement, 4,984 (15%) for GLCH and 4,505 (14%) by the HA. In 1966/7, Resettlement actually recorded its all-time maximum of 25,904 units, the other two accounting for merely 800 and 448 completions (a public total of 27,152). But by the end of Trench's governorship, in 1971/2, with Resettlement production drastically falling off, an overall total of 20,579 was divided very differently: 6,495 Resettlement (31%), 12,612 GLCH (61%) and 1,472 HA (8%).[58]

The Housing Board: coordination without power

This overall shift in the inter-agency distribution of output partly reflected the still-hesitant efforts towards an overall housing strategy, following the reports of the Special Committee on Housing and the 1963 Working Party on Squatting, Resettlement and Government Low-Cost Housing (appointed by Black in June 1963). The coordinating mechanism that stemmed from its recommendations, the Housing Board, was set up in 1965 following the 1964 White Paper on squatting and tenements, and had twelve members appointed by the Governor.[59] It functioned for eight years, until 1973, and had two principal tasks: statistical and policy oversight of all branches of housing, private and public; and active enhancement of co-ordination between housing agencies.

The Housing Board's coordination remit anticipated in many ways the scope of the Housing Branch, under Housing Secretary Dominic Wong, that was set up in the 1990s under Governor Chris Patten. However, Wong's apparatus was armed with more effective powers and proved capable of major policy interventions (Chapter 12). By the late 1960s, the Housing Board was already regarded by administrators such as Bernard Williams as 'toothless' and 'a talking shop': 'There was lots of talk but not much coordination… The poor old Housing Board – they did have a bad time. They should have said, "Unify the structure!" But they were more concerned with rehousing squatters!'[60] Yet the Board did initiate a handful of significant individual innovations, of which two of the most prominent were the 1965 establishment of a new per-person Resettlement space standard of 35 sq ft, instead of 24 sq ft; and the framing of medium-term housing targets in terms of a ten-year programme plan, or 'progressive building programme'.[61] Also of wider significance were a shift in emphasis from Resettlement to GLCH, planned from 1963 and implemented in construction after 1967; and the 1968 transfer of management of Resettlement estates to Housing Authority staff.[62] But 1968/9 also saw attacks by De Sales in a HA meeting on the Board as a 'failure', and claims by others that the shift from GLCH to Housing Authority production was actually a 'miscalculation' by the Board.[63] Liao recalled that 'I thought it [the Board] was a complete waste of money – the wrong thing to do – a hybrid'. In 1970, too, a paper by Bray on the relationship of the Housing Board to GLCH and Resettlement claimed it had 'no overall strategy'.[64]

One feature particularly important for the immediate future was instituted by the Board at Bramwell's instigation in 1965, as an official method of computing housing output for all housing sectors: the 'individual unit' (IU) of dwelling accommodation, a figure corresponding supposedly to the floor-space required by one individual adult. Originating in the earlier Resettlement calculations covered in Chapter 3, this was now based not on 24 sq ft per adult but on the new 35 sq ft per-person Resettlement space standard. All this attempted, as in contemporary Soviet housing, to focus output attention much more precisely on useable living space rather than numbers of dwellings.[65] The IU concept, in its confusing relationship to individual dwellings, was widely criticised from the start, but endured for a surprisingly long time before being finally discarded in 1983 (Chapter 9). Williams recalled that from the mid-1960s 'they did their targets in IUs – 'individual units'. Colin Bramwell was the key person computing it – they did it in IUs, initially 24 square feet, but was changed, and later became 35 square feet. They were going to build a target of so many square feet. But that's not how housing works. The individual unit doesn't mean anything, because you have families! The architects liked it like that, because it was related to buildings. The programme was activated by technical rather than social criteria. So they built seven-person flats, with seven IUs, but the average family size was 4 or 5. So we gaily rehoused people, in families of 4 or 5, into 7-IU flats. Nor did this include the private sector, and no account was taken of income or affordability. Before launching such a target you should do a housing needs assessment – but a lot of this was ad-hoc'.[66]

The Resettlement Department at bay: from flagship to black sheep

The stuttering attempts at inter-agency coordination only threw into sharper relief the growing inadequacies of the Resettlement Department – inadequacies highlighted most dramatically by the focal role of Resettlement estates in the 1967 riots, and which showed how quickly public-authority policy innovation could be left behind by social change and public expectation. On the one hand, landmarks of 'Resettlement progress' were still celebrated, at events coordinated by Bramwell. These included the rehousing of the 'millionth settler' in 1967, at Shek Pai Wan Estate (for which he organised a commemorative plaque), or the completion of the 500th resettlement block, Block 15 at Lam Tin Estate, opened in November 1970. Visiting VIPs such as junior colonial minister Eirene White, in 1966, were still proudly taken to visit the latest estates, alongside all the other disparate housing organisations.[67] (Figures 4.2a–e, 4.3, 4.4)

But at its base at 10 Middle Road, Tsim Sha Tsui, the Resettlement Department was, by the late 1960s, beleaguered on all sides.[68] Partly, this stemmed from the division in responsibility for its operations: the Urban Council's Resettlement

Figure 4.2 (a) Official record of ceremonial opening of the '500th Resettlement Block', Block 15 at Lam Tin (the first completed Mk VI), in November 1970. (b) The Acting Governor, Sir Hugh Norman-Walker, speaks at the ceremony. From left to right: Michael Wright (Commissioner in London); Paul Tsui Ka-cheung (Commissioner for Resettlement); R C Clarke (Acting DPW); Sir Hugh Norman-Walker; David Alexander (Chairman of HA and Urban Council); Henry Hu Hung-lick (Chairman, Resettlement Management Committee). (c) Reception following the Lam Tin event: facing camera on right of Norman-Walker are Freddie Pang, Colin Bramwell and Bernard Williams. (d) Colour view of ceremony, from 1970 *Hong Kong Annual Report*. (e) The same location today: 2023 view (MG) of the redeveloped Lam Tin Estate (Lam Tin Phases 6 and 7), four 41-storey site-specific blocks designed by John Ng's HD team; completed 2009.

Committee, with its strong representation of unofficials, supposedly oversaw policy and production as well as management, through quarterly reports and overviews of construction progress, but the PWD autonomously ran the building programme, including preparation of preliminary planning studies of areas to be developed.[69] Here the good working relationships between PWD officers such as Wright (Deputy Director of Public Works 1959–63, director 1963–9) or Bramwell and Cowperthwaite, ensured relatively smooth progress – despite Wright's more general reservations about the cadets' generalist elitism.[70] Wright recalled that although the Financial Secretary 'had an instinct about people who were over-stating their case', in housing 'we never, ever had a request for money refused for Resettlement; all the money was available to be spent as fast as we could spend

Figure 4.3 Labour MPs Robert Sheldon and Joel Barnett with hawkers during visit to Wong Tai Sin Resettlement Estate in September 1966.

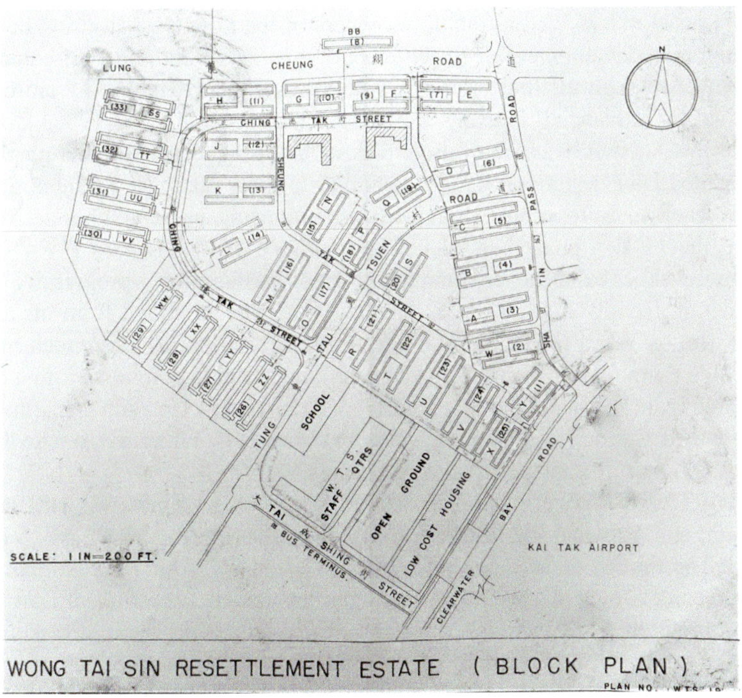

Figure 4.4 Layout plan of Wong Tai Sin Resettlement Estate as at 1967 (cf. Fig. 10.8 as redeveloped).

it – but Cowperthwaite said, "Look, one thing: don't over-estimate!"' A more cautious approach applied to supporting infrastructure:

> the real decisions as to what should go into the public works programme were, in fact, taken first by the Secretariat officers concerned, not the Finance Branch, and then the Public Works Subcommittee – which was chaired by Cowperthwaite – and they would *really* decide.[71]

At its 121st meeting in March 1968, the Resettlement Programme Committee celebrated George Norton's retiral from his post as Deputy Director of Public Works, noting he had served on the committee since its inception 13 years previously.[72] But the real prime mover in Resettlement production matters continued to be Bramwell, whose unambiguously output-orientated values as CA1 were recalled by Akers-Jones: 'He wasn't worried about density, just numbers and getting on – he was a great solver of problems'.[73] Seen variously by administrators as a creatively dynamic character (Akers-Jones) and a domineering, 'feared' tyrant (Fung Tung), Bramwell worked closely with both S T Kidd and the Finance Department, and was responsible for the successive generations of resettlement designs, or 'Mark' blocks (see below), as well as the development of the Low-Cost Housing designs as an upgraded development of Resettlement types with minimum self-contained facilities.[74] Although all these designs would have been regarded as uniformly 'primitive' by 'advanced' housing architects back 'home' in late 1960s Britain, Bramwell was certainly aware of principles such as neighbourhood unit planning. He presented later designs in language similar to early post-war neighbourhood-unit advocacy in Europe and United States, promising in September 1970, for instance, that his first-phase Lek Yuen neighbourhood in Sha Tin New Town would be designed as a 'balanced community'.[75] Most of this more 'progressive' tendency within Bramwell's later work, however, actually stemmed from his architectural deputy, Y L 'Freddie' Pang. He, at this stage, remained very much 'under Bramwell's thumb' and 'frustrated' (Williams), but would soon move into a more autonomous role as a deputy of Donald Liao within the new Housing Department – whereupon, as we shall see, Bramwell simply 'faded out' (Williams), reputedly 'in disgrace' following an unspecified infraction.[76]

During Trench's governorship, however, Bramwell's empire was still in the ascendant, and spawned the last three of the Mark series, the Mk V, Mk VI and Mk VII. The first of those three was designed exclusively for Resettlement use, and the second two were targeted increasingly towards the Government Low-Cost Housing programme as well as, or instead of, Resettlement: the entire sequence from Mk I to Mk VII was summarised in detail in DPW notes of 1970.[77]

The Mk V was designed in 1965 and built between then and 1971, initially at Ngau Tau Kok Resettlement Estate, to facilitate the expansion of the Resettlement programme demanded by the Working Party on Resettlement. It featured a more economical crosswall design of 16-storey blocks, largely omitting the Mk IV's structural beams and columns. (Figures 4.5a, b, 4.6a–c)

While each dwelling-unit had a rudimentary WC and balcony, the yield in habitable space per dwelling (assuming a planning basis of 24 sq ft. IUs) was

Figure 4.5 (a) Ngau Tau Kok Village, Kowloon Bay: 1966 view prior to clearance, from Resettlement Department Annual Report. (b) Mk V Resettlement 16-storey blocks at Lower Ngau Tau Kok estate seen in August 2009 (MG), prior to redevelopment.

considerably higher than in Mk IV blocks: 7,152 IUs from 949 dwellings in a block, as opposed to 5,668 from 875. The greater variety of room sizes allowed less waste in allocation, and an average cost of HK$483 per IU as opposed to the Mk IV's HK$568, while, as Norton told the Resettlement Commissioner in June 1965, avoiding building 'ridiculously small rooms which represent no saving in cost'.[78]

The further shift from Mk V to Mk VI/VII was triggered by ExCo's May 1967 adoption of the 35 sq ft IU space standard – justified by Bramwell at the October 1967 Resettlement Programme Committee on grounds that extra living-space (as opposed to extra facilities) cost relatively little. This meant Resettlement and GLC housing types would, henceforth, be essentially the same.[79] (Figure 4.7a, b)

The '500th Resettlement' block, opened in 1970 (see above), was also the first Mark VI block to be handed over to the Urban Council's management: Henry Hu noted at the ceremony that the UC had been pressing for adoption of the 35 sq ft standard for several years, although even this was seen as 'apparently impossibly small to western eyes'.[80] The Mk VII had by then already been designed, and approved by the PWSC in July 1969, with blocks up to 20 storeys high, based in internal arrangement on the GLCH 'module': the first examples, at Lai King and Kwai Fong, incorporated a Resettlement standard of finishes.[81]

Williams acknowledged that from a production viewpoint, the Resettlement system still seemed attractive:

> the Public Works Department rather liked building Resettlement blocks: they thought it was quite a good thing to churn them out', and 'Finance Branch thought that Resettlement was much cheaper to build than low-cost housing' and that 'unless government maintained direct control over Resettlement, they wouldn't be able to clear land for sale.[82]

But the growing squalor, and the association with the riots, now seemed a far more serious, even existential threat, and prompted ExCo meetings to discuss what

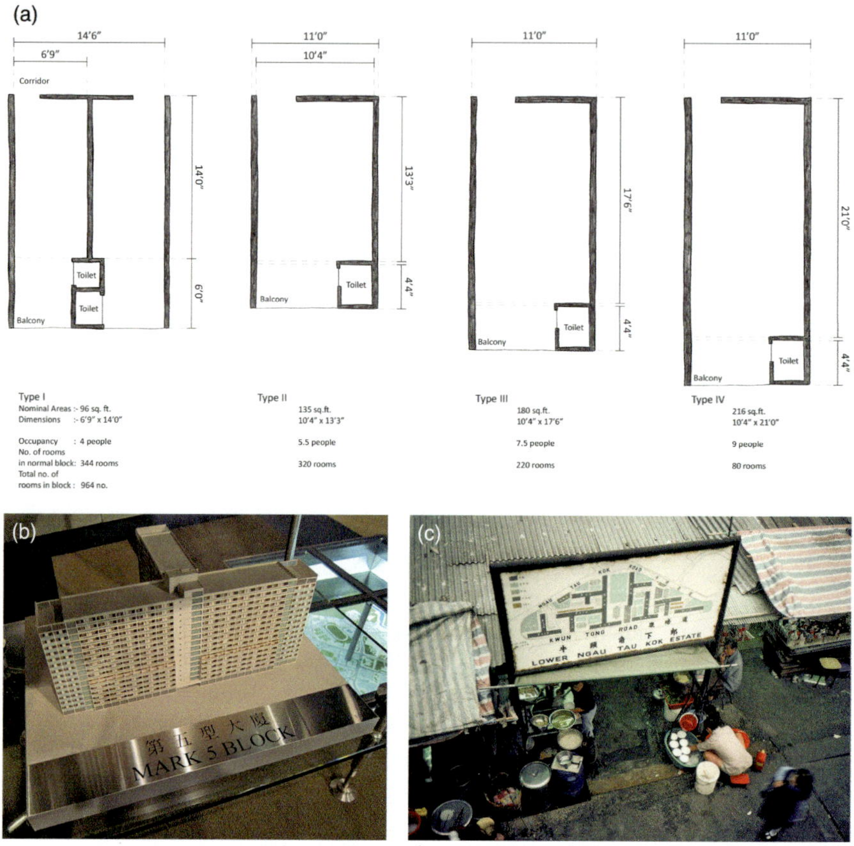

Figure 4.6 (a) Concept layouts of variant unit sizes in Mk V Resettlement room layouts, originally drawn in July 1965 by Colin Bramwell. Drawing by Joyce Fu, 2023. (b) Model of Mk V block in permanent exhibition at HA headquarters, Ho Man Tin, 2011 (MG). (c) Lower Ngau Tau Kok Estate, 1983 view (MG) of hawker market and estate name sign.

to do: in 1969, Denis Bray blasted the 'chaos' of Resettlement estates.[83] As early as 1964, Bramwell had pressed for planting of more trees, but nothing much had been done.[84] The estates were not just visually unsightly, but seen as hotbeds of criminality: the same 'snake-head' triad leaders who organised entry of illegal immigrants into Hong Kong, and provided squatter huts for them, also controlled the provision of hawker stalls within the Resettlement estates, with the collusion of corrupt police and Resettlement officers – as highlighted in particular by Elsie Elliott. There was also significant corruption within their rudimentary management systems – as well as (according to both Liao and Williams) within the building-works system presided over by Bramwell, with numerous allegedly corrupt expatriate British clerks of works.[85]

(a)

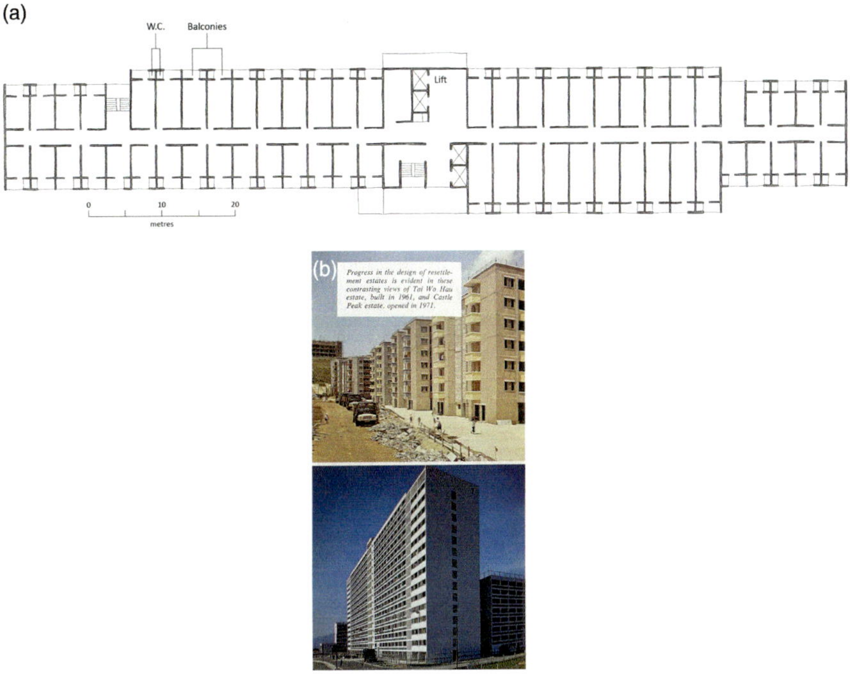

Figure 4.7 (a) 1970 layout plan of Mk VI Resettlement block – with its variegated room sizes, the first Resettlement type to permit allocation at 35 sq ft per adult. Drawing by Joyce Fu, 2023. (b) Image from 1971 *Hong Kong Annual Report* comparing 1961 Mark II Resettlement and 1971 GLCH housing: the now 'outmoded' Mark II blocks at Tai Wo Hau had been showcased a decade previously in the 1961 *Annual Report* as exemplars of 'aesthetically more pleasing' design (with a 'cleaner outline' compared to Mk I).

The crisis of Resettlement became another area in which Trench aspired to progressive reforms, but was frustrated by vested interests within government. Strategic proposals were two-a-penny, beginning with the 1958 Special Committee Report's recommendations of unified housing administration, and continuing throughout the mid-1960s, for example in the 1964 Working Party Report on Squatter Control, Resettlement and Government Low-Cost Housing, which had called for acceleration of building in the New Territories at a strategic level.[86] What did begin to make a rapid impact at the end of the decade, however, was a series of on-the-ground reforms in estate management and squatter control initiated by Bernard Williams, when he joined the Resettlement Department in 1969 as Assistant Commissioner (Estates) under Paul Tsui. Following the 1967 riots, he recalled, 'the place was in a terrible mess, because control over the estates had been withdrawn for two years.'[87] He had been deeply impressed by the Housing Authority's comprehensive management systems and the effective integration of the HA and

Housing Department. Recruited for his experience in the Defence Section during the riots, Williams aimed to break the cycle of triad-driven criminality in shop allocations and hawker structures through interventions by distinctive yellow-helmeted 'tidiness teams', or 'TTs'. These were armed with crowbars and directed by experienced Operations Branch clearance officials such as Hamish MacLeod, Administrative Officer (Estates), and Resettlement Officers Leung Chung Yau and Robert Mok Yiu Kwong.[88]

The TTs applied *within* Resettlement estates, especially against unauthorised hawker structures, the aggressive, summary clearance techniques already developed against squatter outbreaks elsewhere. But they took several years to make a decisive impact. When Ian Lightbody became Commissioner for Resettlement in 1971, and was 'appalled' at the degradation of estates not yet tackled:[89]

> The key problem was the way the open spaces between the blocks had been taken over by hawkers and stallholders. It was a mess. Paul Tsui was the previous Commissioner for Resettlement and he handed it over to me. I remember him taking me up to the top of a Resettlement block to show me. My heart sank – I thought, "Good God, what have I picked up!" It was a shambles at the ground level. A lot of our energies from that point onwards were directed at recovering the open spaces between the blocks from the hawkers. There used to be pitched battles, as our staff began to clear them away. Luckily, the right man appeared for the occasion – Les Pogue, an Irishman, an administrative officer. He set to work with gusto to recover the open spaces, clearing out hawkers – it must have taken a further year or so. He succeeded – he did a wonderful job! He had to be very brave, as there were pitched battles, with axes and so on. He had the police in support. Sometimes I felt he should have the Army too! He did a marvellous job in recovering those spaces for the residents.[90]

These measures, however, met with obstruction on two fronts. Firstly, there was opposition from within the Secretariat prior to 1971, in particular from Paul Tsui and PACS (L) Teddy Kidd, who both felt that Williams's TT initiative was stirring up unnecessary trouble: Tsui, Williams recalled, was 'not happy with the hassle caused by our clearance operations and suggested that we should "let sleeping dogs lie"'.[91] Secondly, Elsie Elliott and other Urban Council members branded the TTs' work harsh and oppressive: on occasion, Elliott and colleagues actively set out to frustrate the Operations Branch's clearance operations, in incidents that often involved violent fighting, for example at Sau Mau Ping in 1970.[92] Williams complained bitterly that 'I was appalled. The Urban Council supplied the hawkers! But they were, rather, the enemy – and I had a method for dealing with them'.[93] Building on this ad-hoc programme, 1970 also saw the establishment of an inter-departmental committee, dubbed 'INTERCEDE', tasked with coordination of the management of external spaces within Resettlement schemes, and especially with hawker control problems. The Social Welfare Department, in 1971, argued that INTERCEDE should adopt a more ambitious approach and 'look beyond hawker suppression' towards a 'social participation' agenda reflecting the Skeffington

Report in England. But in the event the committee proved almost completely ineffective and had faded from view by 1972/3; in July 1972, a memo from Home Affairs administrator J M Rowlands argued that 'the Resettlement Department is floundering from one crisis to another'.[94]

By around 1970, the growth in the GLCH programme had become bound up with pressures for a spread in the scope of resettlement from squatter-related matters to redevelopment in the existing urban areas, including both private-sector tenements and obsolete Mk I and Mk II Resettlement estates. In the former area, the argument was strengthened by the 1971 Chong Hing Mansions scandal, which many argued should fall within the scope of resettlement.[95] A case-study of potential tenement rehabilitation in Sai Ying Pun highlighted the difficulties of urban renewal within the dense existing fabric.[96]

But it was the condition of the original Resettlement estates that seemed more politically urgent: Trench said to Williams and Lightbody, 'You've got to do something about it!' In architectural terms, the first expedient attempted was a policy of gradual conversion of Mk I and Mk II blocks to self-contained units, commencing in 1968–70 with the experimental conversion of Wong Tai Sin Block 25, overseen administratively by Williams. The protracted vicissitudes of this project highlighted the impracticability of easy conversion of the original blocks, as had once been promised in 1953/4.[97] Increasingly, the alternative of redevelopment as opposed to conversion was proposed, beginning with Shek Kip Mei – although this was opposed by agitation by 'do-gooders' against redevelopment.[98] Williams also suggested that the lack of progress stemmed partly from within the Secretariat, who 'tried to stop anything happening, just because they liked the existing system, turning blocks out like a sausage-machine. They got round it and nothing happened until the new Governor arrived'. Eventually, in 1973, Williams himself returned to assume charge of this Mk I/II redevelopment programme, as Assistant Director (Redevelopment).[99]

The Housing Authority in the late 1960s – prelude to power

As we will see in Chapter 5, the revolutionary changes in housing administration and production inaugurated by Governor MacLehose in the 1970s would project the Housing Authority – or more accurately, a successor body with the same English title – into a grand coordinating role within a rapidly accelerating programme of public housing. (Figure 4.8, 4.9)

Yet even on the eve of these changes, in the late 1960s and early '70s, there was no palpable sense of 'imminent destiny', and the politico-organisational division and enfeeblement of the HA became, if anything, even more pronounced. In Williams's opinion, 'The pre-1973 Housing Authority was a sideshow – it wasn't run by the government but by the Urban Council – the Urban Council! – by Elsie Elliott and all that lot!'[100] The difficulties stemming from the Authority's co-dependent relationship to the Urban Council continued, including the general official/unofficial polarisation, the problems of securing decisive policy action, and the difficulty of implementing any decisions – a predicament that would only be

Two members seek form of rent control, Govt help

HOUSING AUTHORITY MEETING

Figure 4.8 January 1970 SCMP article on Housing Authority meeting and debates.

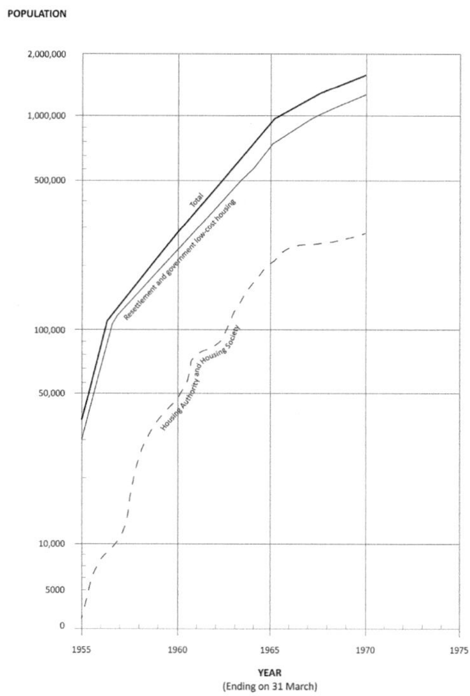

Figure 4.9 Graph of rise in population of public housing estates, 1955–70, based on Housing Authority *Annual Reports*. Drawing by Joyce Fu, 2023.

finally resolved in the 1973 reorganisation, which divorced the Urban Council from both housing and squatter matters.[101] George Rowe, with typical contemptuousness towards the unofficials, recalled that

> the difficulty with the Housing Authority, as a Housing Authority, was not so much getting it to move in a particular direction as getting it to move in *any* direction. [In elections] the Urban Council said, "The housing situation in Hong Kong is bloody awful!" – which was true, anyone could see it – [but] the question was, *what* to do?[102]

The Housing Authority's finances also remained precarious, with development loans procured largely project-by-project.[103]

1967 saw an intriguing attempt to contextualise the HA's work within the wider 'British' public housing world, beyond immediate comparisons with municipal 'council housing'. This took the form of a correspondence, focusing on organisational and financial matters, with two significant regional/national organisations outside the 'council housing' world: the Northern Ireland Housing Trust and the Scottish Special Housing Association. The NIHT's roots in the Ulster world of fiscal conservatism seemed comparable to Hong Kong, but overall the SSHA seemed a closer match, with its large-scale multi-storey programme – although its chief executive, D C Halley, stressed it was 'entirely government-financed, and that its functions are controlled by the Secretary of State for Scotland alone'.[104] Both the SSHA and NIHT, as well as the London GLC, also had a system of dominant professional staff, and strong, Octavia Hill-style housing management. An 'enlightened executive professionalism' was already established in the HA, in Frank Carroll's management system, as perpetuated by younger managers such as Fung Tung. This had been radically expanded into design and planning by J M Fraser, on the model of his integrated structures within the Singapore Improvement Trust – despite the Housing Authority's lack of SIT-style planning powers.[105] Fraser's energetic development of the Housing Department's architectural section was supported by Firth, who attended numerous overseas conferences in the mid-60s, along with Freddie Pang as PWD representative.[106]

The leading 'racehorse' within Fraser's architectural stable, however, was Donald Liao, who rose rapidly within the Authority's structure during the 1960s from a relatively junior architect post to become Commissioner for Housing in 1968, at the age of 39 – in competition for the post with Carroll. Liao recalled of this rapid rise that 'I got promoted to Senior Architect, then Chief Architect. Then Trench appointed me Commissioner for Housing – that was the end of my time as a design architect! I had to choose between being an architect and an administrator.'[107] As a protégé of Fraser, Liao maintained close relations with Fraser's successor in the Singapore HDB, Teh Cheang Wan:

> Cheang Wan would come to Hong Kong and we'd compare notes. He became their Chief Architect, then I became ours. He became head of department, I became Director of Housing. He became Minister, I became Secretary.

> Between him in Singapore and me in Hong Kong, we used to compare notes. They have more land at their disposal, but we made good use of what we had: we built tower blocks from the word go. Cheang Wan would say how well he was doing: "We've housed one million!" I'd reply, "Do you realise we've housed nearly two and a half million people – that's the equivalent of the total population of Singapore!"[108]

Liao combined driving efficiency and architectural innovativeness with personal charm, exploiting the latter to win friends and allies for the Department, in a manner impossible for boorish expatriate traditionalists such as Bramwell. Especially important was the relationship with Urban Council members. At an HA meeting in January 1968 prior to Liao's promotion to Commissioner, Authority chairman David Alexander praised both the design and management inputs of the HA's 'talented and enthusiastic Housing Architect', whose Architectural Section had 'provided virtuosity' in their new multi-storey housing designs – all at the 35 sq ft standard.[109] Liao also tried to anticipate new areas of potential controversy: in September-October 1970, for example, an extensive correspondence with paediatrics professor C Elaine Field of HKU and Queen Mary Hospital concerning lack of fresh air for children in high-density estates, was followed up by Liao with a personal meeting and tour of estates, to demonstrate the steps being taken to provide play-space and cross-ventilation, following which Field enthused, 'I feel you have done a wonderful job'.[110] Small design tweaks also attempted to offset dangers to children from high living. Liao recalled that having personally witnessed injury to a child after falling off a second-floor balcony, he started allowing residents to put grilles across their balconies – despite the fire risk that posed. And a further, more tragic incident of 1968 at Fuk Loi Estate in which a child was killed by a bicycle dropped from a balcony prompted urgent discussions with Carroll over modifications to ground-floor canopies, and infilling of dangerous gaps in upper-floor gallery fronts at Wah Fu.[111]

Overall, Liao's career trajectory from architect to senior administrator symbolised a subtle shift from the heyday of the cadets, with their caste-like elitism, towards a more hybrid, modern policy-making approach, closely integrated with public-sector housing design and city planning. Liao's architectural work for the HA prior to his 1968 promotion also presaged a long-term shift from design by consultant private practices towards in-house architecture and planning – informed by his experience of advanced public-sector housing architecture on his early-1960s European and British tour.

The Housing Authority's aspiration to become a beacon of enlightened design also potentially allowed scope for constructional experimentation. However, although the mid-1960s were the years of maximum European preoccupation with prefabrication and system-building, Hong Kong's low-skilled building industry rendered all this irrelevant, as discovered by Liao on an extensive tour of systems in 1963–4, ranging from Glasgow to Paris.[112] Any industrialised techniques adopted by the Housing Authority would necessarily be limited in character: the only significant early experiment, in 1966–7, was a project for 'tilt-up' concrete-casting using a Japanese system that Pang and Firth had visited in Chiba prefecture in May

1966: it was experimentally tried out at Fuk Loi estate.[113] As we saw in Chapter 3, at the beginning of Trench's governorship the cutting edge of HA architecture was represented by the variegated towers of the newly completed So Uk estate, urbanely coordinated by private practitioner Eric Cumine.[114] By the time the slab blocks of Choi Hung were rising, Hong Kong's land shortages were channelling architects' attention inexorably towards tower-like solutions, which for the first time began creeping higher than multi-storey blocks in Britain.[115] Here, the mid-1960s saw the parallel development of two major projects, Ping Shek and Wah Fu, the first designed by private architects and the second by public architects. They both included as their centrepiece striking 'twin tower blocks' comprising two diagonally attached hollow, galleried towers, and were both opened by Trench, Wah Fu in 1970 and Ping Shek in 1971.

Wah Fu was the HA's eighth development, and the first very large project designed directly by its own architectural staff – namely, Liao and his team, initially under Firth. Still regarded fondly by Liao in the 2020s as 'my baby', it was developed in 1965–70 following his European tour. (Figure 4.10a–c) It consciously echoed a typical London County Council 'mixed development' pattern of towers and low blocks in freely disposed open courtyards, but with a ten-times higher density of just under 2,000 ppa and a design population of 64,000, closer to a small Mk I New Town than an individual London housing estate – and self-contained community/commercial facilities to match, for the first time in Hong Kong.[116] In its final state following extensions, in 1978, it comprised 25 multi-storey blocks of between 8 and 24 storeys, containing 9,259 flats, all planned at the HA standard 35 sq ft per person. The low blocks had conventional centre-corridor plans but the tall blocks were a new design of 'Twin Tower Block', comprising two linked hollow blocks, each with a vast, full-height 50 by 50 ft central courtyard ringed by balconies, giving access to 34 flats on each floor.[117] For simplicity and wind resistance, the blocks were constructed using loadbearing crosswalls rather than the framed construction common in private flats. In a 1971 evaluation of Wah Fu by the international architect-planner Sir Robert Matthew, as part of an International Union of Architects 'Basic Housing Evaluation' study, the estate was hailed as 'a total conception, socially, economically, and architecturally', and Matthew claimed there was 'a dramatic coherence to the whole' – not least owing to the estate's originally uniform field-grey exposed concrete colour.[118] Liao recalled that he had envisaged the hollow Twin-Tower concept above all as a community-building device. (Figure 4.11a–c, 4.12, 4.13a, b)

Ping Shek, by architects Palmer & Turner, employed the same device at a slightly greater height, of 27 storeys, and with a slightly different plan. (Figure 4.14a, b) Its design had previously undergone dramatic transformations, beginning in 1965 with a Choi Hung-style slab concept, then switching to a visionary proposal for 50-storey towers to be built by a 'revolutionary method of construction' to save on casting costs and provide more open space.[119] But in January 1967, this proposal was abandoned by the Housing Authority on grounds of potential cost and delay, and 'a more traditional scheme' of five 27-storey twin-towers and some low blocks, totalling 4,570 flats for 29,000 inhabitants, was substituted and finally built, at a

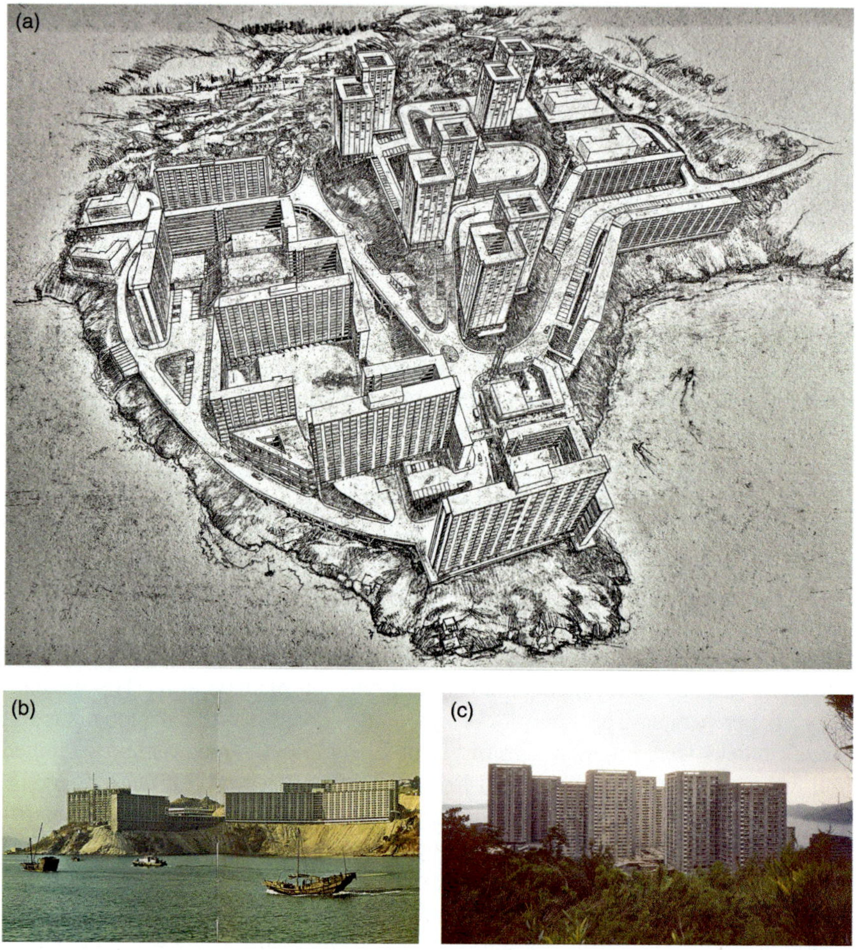

Figure 4.10 (a) Wah Fu Estate (1965–70), 1966 perspective by Donald Liao: containing 9,259 flats, the first large development designed by the HA's own architects. (b) Wah Fu Estate, view of first phase under construction in 1968 *Hong Kong Annual Report*. (c) Wah Fu Estate, distant view in 1983 (MG), before polychromatic repainting.

cost of some $46.3 million (of which $15 million was a loan from the DLF).[120] (Figure 4.15a, b)

At the 1971 opening of Ping Shek, Trench hailed the Housing Authority's role as a pathfinder and leader in housing management, which had resulted in their being entrusted with management of the GLCH programme.[121] However, Wah Fu itself, with its then geographically remote location, initially proved difficult to let, and for a while, in 1970, attracted significant delinquency claims, before settling down as one of the territory's most popular and established estates, and hailed

Figure 4.11 (a) Wah Fu Estate, plaque commemorating 1968 inauguration by Governor Trench. 2019 photo (MG). (b) Wah Fu Estate, 2019 view (MG). (c) Wah Fu Estate, galleried internal courtyard in twin tower block, 2019 view (cf. Fig. 4.15a) (MG).

by Liao as an example of modern public-sector benevolence in action.[122] Overall, Ping Shek and Wah Fu played an architecturally pathfinding role, by exploring the potential of rapidly increasing height and integrated estate design, so different from the utilitarian Resettlement formula, that would prevail in the mature Housing Authority development programme following the 1973 reorganisation.

A HAPPY HOME FOR 54,000

NEARLY 54,000 people will soon be housed in the Wah Fu Estate – the biggest single low-cost housing estate in the Far East.

Covering an area of 29.1 acres of land, this massive estate is attracting families at the average rate of 200 a month.

It will not be finished until August but already the estate has become a little village.

Built on the edge of the sea near Aberdeen, the estate contains most things the average family could want.

Wah Fu Estate is completely self-contained with schools, shops, entertainment areas, a public library, restaurants, and a medical centre.

It will cost the Government $89 million dollars to build Wah Fu Estate. When it's finished it will have 7,788 flats from 210 to 470 square foot.

But not everyone can move into the flats. There is an requirement that says you cannot be earning more than $1,000 to apply.

Reasons

One of the reasons for this is that there is a charge to live in the estate.

The largest flat costs $144 a month. The smallest flat costs about $95 a month.

Comparing these charges with the bloated rents in some of Hongkong's residential areas, the Government is "giving" the flats away.

One resident, Mr Sam Lam, said "It's great" living at Wah Fu.

"The whole estate is surrounded by the sea and you can see beautiful sun sets every day," said Mr Lam.

"It's like living in a holiday camp. Everything is here, the shops, open area for playing and a bowling alley, just to mention a few things.

"And in the morning when you go to work, the number four bus takes you quickly away from the estate to the centre of town.

"I would say it's the nicest place I've ever lived in."

Figure 4.12 Wah Fu Estate, February 1970 article in *Star* marking its impending completion.

However, in the late 1960s and early 1970s the coming ascendancy of a revamped Housing Authority could not have been foreseen, and in these years the Housing Society continued to play an, in many ways, equal role in architectural and management innovation in the social-housing sector. Indeed, from the viewpoint of Michael Wright, as a member of the Housing Society board, it seemed a far more highly integrated organisation than the pre-1973 Housing Authority, with its debilitating polarisation between professionals and unofficials.[123] But by the late 1960s, government funding and land supply for the HS was drying up: one of the last directly financed large schemes, in Tai Hang Road, was appropriately named after the newly retired Wright himself ('Lai Tak Tsuen' – see Chapter 6).[124] The 1968 table of statistics on all Housing Society schemes since 1952 showed this process of atrophy at work, and those years saw increasingly urgent debate within the Society on its most appropriate future policies and orientation.[125] (Figure 4.16)

Towards a grand merger

During Trench's governorship, pressure grew to proceed in some form with the organisational merger, or at least convergence, first advocated in the 1958 Housing Report, while also reinforcing the role of the HA. Trench's own attempts to promote

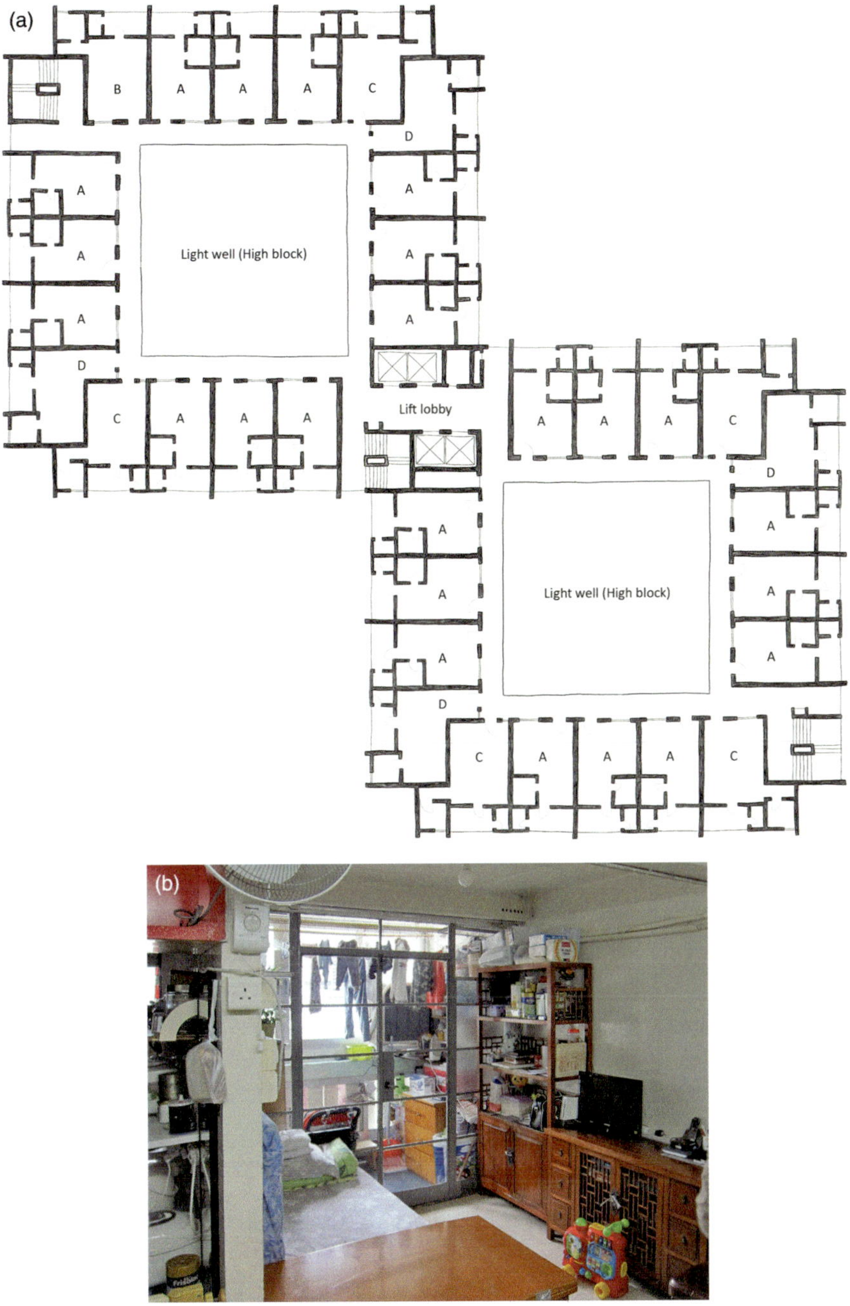

Figure 4.13 (a) Twin Tower block plan. Drawing by Joyce Fu, 2023. (b) Wah Fu Estate Phase 1 (completed 1967), Wah Kin House, Flat 1531, occupied by Mr and Mrs Ngai from new in 1968. 2018 photo (MG).

Figure 4.14 (a) Ping Shek Estate, seen in 1983, prior to external repainting (MG). (b) Ping Shek Estate commercial centre; 1983 photo (MG).

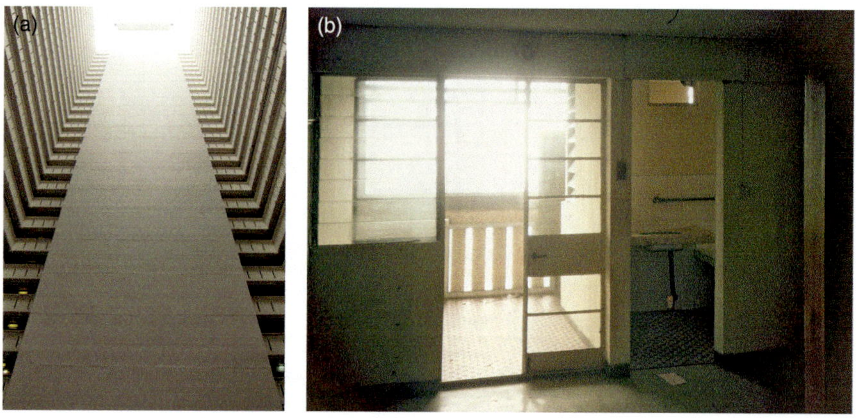

Figure 4.15 (a) Ping Shek Estate, galleried internal courtyard, 2014 photo (cf. Fig. 4.11c) (MG). (b) Ping Shek Estate, Kam Shek House, 1983 view of unoccupied one-room flat (no. 1803) (MG).

Figure 4.16 The Housing Society's Moon Lok Dai Ha estate, built 1964–5: 2011 photo (MG).

merger were, for the time being, resisted within the Secretariat, particularly by Teddy Kidd.[126] Williams recalled that

> One day I happened to be in the Secretariat Lands Branch and managed to read a policy file where the Governor had written a long minute in red ink, [which said] that it was time that the administration of the Resettlement estates should be brought into line with that of the Housing Authority. "There you are", I said triumphantly to Teddy Kidd, the Principal Assistant Colonial Secretary (Lands), "he agrees with what we're doing". "Oh," said Teddy in his soft Irish brogue, "You don't want to worry about that sort of thing." I imagine that the minute was quietly forgotten.

The obstacle was only removed when eventually 'the Governor got rid of Teddy and transferred him to London' – laying the foundations for a firmer line by Trench's successor, MacLehose.[127] The calls within the HA for management integration, and production curtailment, of Resettlement grew louder: the Authority's Chairman, David Alexander, argued it had 'grown like Topsy' and member Gerry Forsgate described it simply as a 'pail of worms' in the 1972 HA Annual Debate.[128]

Pressure was equally growing for a general reform of the Urban Council, not just in relation to its housing and resettlement responsibilities. This was bound up with the more general controversy of the unofficials' role within government. Alexander recalled in 1988 that 'Trench wanted to keep me as a member of the Council and I said,

> There's no point in doing that. All the questions will be directed at me to get government answers. Take all the officials off. Let the members and their chairman ask and deal with the questions in hand, so that you cannot get a government official drawn into the argument.

What I had to do was to stop them talking about things that were not their responsibility, which I tried to do'. And Wright argued more cynically that

> the Urban Council was a bit of a joke. There were two members who were trouble – both were married to Chinese. There was Elsie Elliott – she was convinced everyone was a crook – and there was Alison Bell. They were destructive. There were half a dozen ex-officio members, and the politicians on the Urban Council took every opportunity they could at public meetings of the Urban Council to belittle civil servants and to score debating points. At question-time, the whole object was to try to make the civil servants look stupid. The best thing that ever happened to the Urban Council was in 1969 and 1970, when Ian Lightbody was put on special duties and put up a proposal on the future of the Urban Council, and one of his recommendations was to get all the civil servants off. Now, this has made all the difference, because now they can fight each other.[129]

Underlining the absence of any real culture of public democratic debate within 1950s–60s Hong Kong, even the more restrained unofficials were also treated with some disdain by the administrators, but attitudes were beginning to change. Of Brook Bernacchi, a barrister and former Royal Marines major who had a tea plantation in the hills at Ngong Ping on Lantau and suffered latterly from cancer, Lightbody later recalled that

> I liked him, but, yes, they felt it necessary to become a sort of opposition to the official point of view, which wasn't a bad thing: it was constructive. Elsie said it the way she saw it. At the time, maybe I didn't feel so charitable![130]

In the event, the influence of the unofficials within housing policy was destined to increase rather than diminish in the following decade – a trend grasped rather better by the professionals. Liao, for example, was more pragmatically concerned with securing unofficials' support for the HA building programme: 'These people, if you managed to persuade them, say, that Wah Fu should have tall ceilings, they'd support you. They didn't have their own knowledge, but if you as a professional could explain something to them, they'd support it'.[131]

Towards strategic planning

During the late 1960s, in contrast to Singapore, the cause of strategic planning was still generally frowned upon in laissez-faire Hong Kong, and the 1953 arrangement of the Planning Division within the Crown Lands and Survey Office, originally suggested by Atkinson, continued in force. It was headed by Meyers under R C Clarke, Assistant Superintendent of Crown Lands (Planning).[132] Liao recalled that

> Town Planning was not given a lot of emphasis. The planning department was a subdivision of the Crown Lands Office: there was a little corner called "Planning". In the same way, the Housing Authority was a subdivision of Urban Services: there was a little corner called the "Housing Division".[133]

The multi-headed character of planning in 1960s and early-1970s Hong Kong was further accentuated by the pervasive influence of Cowperthwaite, exerted through a special committee, the Land Development Planning Committee. He had instigated its establishment in 1964/5, not of course as a step towards strategic planning, but to allow the early vetting of major development proposals. This would allow some to be fast-tracked, such as the Kwai Chung container terminal, and in other cases let Cowperthwaite 'shoot it down if he didn't agree'.[134] By 1970, the LDPC's official remit was defined as 'to initiate and deal with all aspects of development and planning policy and to consider all development and planning proposals'. It was restructured in 1974 with a more 'high-powered' membership of heads of all Secretariat branches, and formed part of a somewhat confusing flow-chart for processing proposals at a policy level, beginning with the LDPC and New Territories Development Committee, followed by the Secretary for the Environment, successor to the Crown Lands Office as guardian of the HKOP, and ending with ExCo – to which separate reports by the Town Planning Board would also be submitted.[135]

This multiplicity of 'planning'-related agencies and voices also deterred the establishment of any kind of unified position on specific development control issues, such as the rolling controversy about densities and plot ratios: here, housing issues such as occupancy rates and IU calculations (notably the increase from 24 to 35 sq ft) also impinged on policy. Initially, planning debates on density focused on plot ratios for private development in the existing urban area, within three zones of progressively increased densities (Zone 1 being highest). The four-year grace period following the tougher 1962 building regulations had created a densification free-for-all, leading to some hyper-high-density hotspots, such as one mixed-use block in Tai Kok Tsui Road that was unofficially calculated in 1971 to equate to 9,840 ppa net – 50 times higher than the London County Council maximum.[136] But it was widely accepted that these standards would not apply to public housing – whether Resettlement, GLCH or HA – where calculations not of plot ratios but of net densities in persons per acre, as in British council housing, prevailed. As late as 1966, Kidd was still hopefully proposing that the plot-ratio system could simply be extended to all development in the New Territories, arguing the latter would be largely developed by the private sector. But there had already been fierce public criticism in 1965 of the 'inhuman' high densities of the early stages of Tsuen Wan.[137] And in April 1966, Wright, as Director of Public Works, cautioned against 'this idea that the plot-ratio "free-for-all" which has made such a mess of so much of Hong Kong and Kowloon during the last 10 years should be permitted, or even encouraged, in the New Territories'. In 1968, he and the DCNT argued that densities equivalent to the intermediate 'Zone 2' standard – around 2,000–3,200 ppa – were appropriate for New Territories urban nuclei but that the New Territories as a whole should remain un-zoned.[138] In initial developments within the first three New Towns, confusion stemmed from the application of different standards by different agencies: the first and, in the event, only Resettlement estate in Castle Peak New Town (later renamed Tuen Mun, or 'Fortress Gate') was envisaged in 1966 by the PWD at 2,000 ppa, as opposed to 1,000 proposed by the Housing Division. This estate was equivalent to Sha Tin's Lek Yuen, hailed by Bramwell as a 'balanced community'; but Williams later recalled more candidly that 'we put the barbed wire around it!'[139]

Within the debates about the planning of the new generation of New Towns, the experience of the first 'satellite town' in Kwun Tong was crucial, with professional comment shifting from a positive 1965 characterisation of it as 'Hong Kong's first completely planned new town' to attacks a few years later on the haphazard developments of factories there and in Tsuen Wan: HKU planning professor Gregory branded the two towns 'Disaster Areas' in 1970.[140] The mid-1960s also saw the beginning of the uncoordinated spread of small factories to the Yuen Long area, the eventual response in the 1970s being the designation of it and other rural towns as smaller-scale New Towns themselves.[141] Wright recalled that

> by the time I became DPW, in 1963, we felt we had more or less caught up with housing. Housing was the top priority, but we were running out of sites in the urban and suburban area, and it was a case of looking at Sha Tin and Tuen Mun and Ap Lei Chau, and those involved terrific expense on infrastructure – roads, sewers, water supplies – and with site formation it was going to take a long time – and this is why planning became very, very much more important than it ever had been before.[142]

Yet there was still a strong element of sudden, impulsive improvisation, with attention jumping from one potential site to another. Williams recalled that atmosphere, and the crucial continuing role of Ronald Holmes: in 1964–5

> I was transferred to the New Territories headquarters, where I was dealing with new stuff – local public works, beginning to write reports. I was working with Ronnie Holmes – he had started the Resettlement programme. He was completely reorganising the New Territories, which had to be done, because we were about to start on the New Towns. This doubled and trebled the staff – we had to. Scott & Wilson had produced the first of the reports – for Sha Tin. Where I was, in Junk Bay, was originally going to be a shipbreakers' area – which was very successful – but later it became a New Town. They were doing Tsuen Wan first, because of the factories, which came from Shanghai – they started up their textile factories there. So it was decided that should be a New Town. Then Scott & Wilson did a plan for Sha Tin.[143]

As Wright recollected, the plans for the first three New Towns emerged adventitiously from an interaction between the Scott & Wilson report and the land-planning remit of LDPC and PWD: the latter 'put up a proposal to the Secretariat, possibly by the Director of Public Works himself: when I was DPW, I was chairman of the Town Planning Board'. This contained 'a very broad aspect of a plan, not a detailed plan, but really a zoning plan for both Sha Tin and Tuen Mun.' As to location choices, 'Castle Peak and Sha Tin just seemed to be the two most suitable sites. There wasn't much choice of available land for building new towns'.

> We always thought, when we were discussing the development of the new town of Sha Tin, that it would be predominantly a dormitory town, because it had a good rail connection with Kowloon. Poor Tuen Mun, with its poor links, was planned on the basis that it should be, as far as possible, a self-contained new town; there'd be a lot more industry there than at Sha Tin.[144]

The hybrid, half-developed character of Tsuen Wan, officially designated the third New Town in this group, was recognised: the Town Planning Board outline plan had been issued in 1961 and the target population raised in 1964 to 1.2 million, with the first stages of development proposed for implementation under the aegis of the District Officer. 1965–6 saw the decisive stage in the approvals and Town Planning Board outline zoning plans at both Sha Tin and Castle Peak: the former was estimated to cost double the latter (HK$878m and HK$432m). The PWD produced initial plans for first-stage developments, that at Castle Peak being estimated at HK$14m. At Sha Tin, the LDPC approved in August 1967 the PWD's proposals for first-stage development: an explicit 'dormitory town' of some 30,000 inhabitants.[145]

But when it came to the actual development of the designated New Town locations, the acquisition of land emerged as a formidable problem, as they were far from being *tabula rasa* sites. Donald Liao recalled that 'Sha Tin was such a nice, quiet village when I first went there – it had a little river, and the villagers got on with their fishing'. But all this was about to change, as the emergent Hong Kong 'concept of new towns was either that you don't do it at all, or you *really* do it – it wasn't like the nice little spaced out new towns in Britain – you develop densely, if possible using a railway station as the central point.' Lightbody recalled the procedural obstacles that stood in the way of any all-out approach.

> In the 1960s, I was Principal Assistant Colonial Secretary in charge of land policy. My land remit in the Secretariat, as PACS (L), covered use and disposal of Government land of all types – all leasehold stuff, where we used to give renewable leases of 75 years. A big factor in the housing programme [was land] – but we depended very heavily on the rate at which the District Commissioner of the New Territories could provide us with sites in the New Towns. Getting sites back from the old New Territories residents was like getting blood out of a stone. They felt they were very special people – and they *were.* They were on a lease – they'd been there for years. They were different in every way, and we felt it. We treated them with kid gloves: that's why we had the post of District Commissioner of the New Territories – under him were District Officers. The Commissioner was Denis Bray, a good chap, who had been Secretary for Chinese Affairs – he had been born in Guangdong, spoke fluent Cantonese, and was latterly known as Secretary for Home Affairs.[146]

Reflecting this combination of urgency and sensitivity, one of Trench's first inspection visits as Governor in 1964 was a tour of the New Territories, culminating with a meeting with the Heung Yee Kuk.[147]

Towards a home-ownership scheme?

A housing-policy innovation strongly favoured by Trench, but which remained unrealised and left over for MacLehose to force through a decade later, was the concept of government-aided encouragement of the spread of home ownership to the white-collar lower-middle classes – the groups just above the GLCH income-bracket, earning between HK$900 and HK$2,000 monthly. Underlying this was an urgent desire to reinforce social cohesion by bridging Hong Kong's vast gap between the wealthy and the poor. This challenge had been raised in a discussion within the HA in 1963, in which Fraser and the DPW had suggested HA rental development of higher-value and higher-prestige sites, such as Ho Man Tin, as a stopgap substitute.[148] Efforts also focused on finding ways of assisting private tenants to buy their own flats, initially in December 1963 by a proposal for a Home Finance Scheme funded by the Commonwealth Development Corporation. This proposal was further developed by the CDC in 1964 with support from the Hong Kong Building and Loan Agency and the Hongkong and Shanghai Bank under the aegis of the semi-official 'Gordon Committee' on home-ownership finance, established by Black in January 1964 and published in June.[149] Akers-Jones recalled this was 'an attempt to get the private sector more involved in housing development, and to help home-ownership – to help people to borrow money to buy their tenement flats. The key to home ownership was the grant of *land'*. But at the same time, 1964–5 also saw suggestions that the HA itself could potentially build flats for 'hire-purchase', just as the HDB was about to start doing in Singapore – an idea that both De Sales and Fraser emphasised was in effect ruled out by lack of potential government financial support, as well as shortages of sites.[150]

To some extent, this lower-middle-income housing role was already being played by the massive mixed-use commercial-residential complexes thrown up by the private sector in Density Zone 1 during the mid-1960s grace period in building restrictions – such as the Parker Estate in Quarry Bay, an 18-storey, E-shaped mega-block containing 2,443 flats, designed by architect E Y Wu from 1962 and developed from 1967 by a miscellany of development companies.[151] Their cramped, hyper-dense built form, claustrophobic internal corridors and promiscuous mixing of functions ruled them out as a model for progressive policy-making. But in exactly the same years, a radically different way of responding to this challenge, via a new and explicitly 'modern' style of private development, was set out in the Mei Foo Sun Chuen development, built on a former oil tank farm site in western Kowloon in 1968–78. The developers were unambiguously American: US real-estate firms Turner Construction and Galbreath-Ruffin Corporation worked through the agency of local subsidiary Mei Foo Investments Limited, in a joint venture headed overall by the Mobil Oil Corporation. (Figure 4.17a, b) As documented in detail by Carmen

FOUNDATION STONE OF ESTATE LAID

Governor Stresses Need For More Inexpensive Flats

The need for private developers to build more medium and low-cost houses and provision of a relatively complete system of management for multi-storey buildings or estates was stressed by His Excellency the Governor, Sir David Trench, yesterday when he laid the foundation stone of Mei Foo Sun Chuen — the biggest private housing project in the Colony.

The Governor highly praised the Mobil Oil Corporation, owners of the Sun Chuen, for their efforts towards meeting this need.

The estate, which will eventually provide accommodation for 60,000 to 80,000 people, on Mobil's former site in Laichikok, is aimed at people in the middle-income bracket. Flats ranging from one to four rooms will be sold at prices between $22,000 and $85,000 each, with the option of term purchasing spreading over 12 years.

Piling for the first of 14 20-storey blocks began two months ago, and the building is expected to be completed in 1968.

Laying the foundation stone, Sir David said that there were two aspects of the scheme which he very greatly welcomed.

management of the estate, whether the flats were sold or leased.

"We all know only too well the difficulties, both practical and legal, of providing for an efficient system of management in large buildings whose ownership is sub-divided; just as we are all only too well aware of the extreme ill-effects that can result from the lack of efficient management and control," Sir David said.

It was, therefore, most gratifying to know that Mobil had had the vision to forestall these difficulties and that—as in the Hongkong Land Investment scheme at Taikoo—arrangements would be made to provide the best protection so far devised for prospective tenants or buyers of flats.

His Excellency the Governor, Sir David Trench, and Mr Charles Mortimer examining a model of the first stage of Mei Foo Sun Chuen

Figure 4.17 (a) November 1966 SCMP article on Governor Trench's foundation-stone laying at Mei Foo. (b) 2013 view of Mei Foo (MG).

Figure 4.18 Parkchester, The Bronx, New York City: Metropolitan Life Insurance Company's vast 'city within a city', built 1939–43 and comprising 12,272 flats in highly serviced tower and slab blocks. 2016 aerial photo (MG).

Tsui, Mei Foo was built in 12 separate stages, and comprised an even-height 'carpet' of moderate-height, slender towers of compact cruciform footprint, interlinked in rows, designed by US-trained local architects Wong & Tung and Associates, with J M Fraser as consultant. The self-contained plan generally resembled some US apartment developments of the 1940s and '50s, such as New York's limited-dividend Parkchester (1939–43) or Stuyvesant Town (1943–9) or more recent private projects such as Lefrak City (1962–71), but was more tightly integrated through linking podiums at ground level. (Figure 4.18) The towers contained highly serviced, strictly self-contained family flat units, with four to eight flats on each floor of each tower, and including service cores and internal, artificially ventilated bathrooms and kitchens.[152] The ethos of the project, with its modern, Western-style home-ownership flats, impressed not only the young middle-class Chinese families who flocked to live there, but also many Hong Kong decision-makers, including both David Akers-Jones and Donald Liao: this strong Government support was stressed in the speeches at the Phase 1 foundation-stone laying by Trench in November 1966.[153]

Mei Foo showed private-sector housing could be reconciled with orderly mass modernity – a crucial development within Hong Kong's laissez-faire system. But it also linked to more specifically Eastern Asian models of co-operative or collective living. For example, Liao's upbringing in Taiwan, with its 1950s subdivision of great landowning blocs, had imbued him with Sun Yat-Sen's 'somewhat socialistic' ideal of popular home-ownership, or *zizhijingshen* ('self-government spirit') a concept linked also to the interwar Nationalist government-sponsored movement of 'common people's villages'.[154] In the later 1970s and '80s, Liao would become probably Hong Kong's most effective on-the-ground champion of state-supported home-ownership, a policy increasingly validated by Singapore's progress in putting it into effect – but in Hong Kong all that for the moment lay in the future, like the other reformist policies adumbrated by Trench, which were not yet quite feasible within the territory's laissez-faire world-outlook.

Overall, Trench's administration skilfully exploited the colony's economic growth to allow increases in public social spending while safeguarding Cowperthwaite's 'positive laissez-faire' policy – a policy that would assume a very different and more exuberant form under Trench's successor, MacLehose.[155] Cowperthwaite fortunately retired in 1971, as he and MacLehose would, in Wright's view, probably have clashed.[156] In 1971, the census showed that there still seemed to be a mountain of bad housing conditions to climb, with overcrowding and lack of self-contained dwellings still rampant, not least because of the continuing waves of illegal immigrants. But the next decade, alongside economic vicissitudes, would bring further rampant economic growth, including a fivefold GDP increase to 1981.[157] This would allow MacLehose to force through all Trench's unrealised social agenda, and more, while sidestepping potential criticism from laissez-faire defenders, by remaining within an unchanged framework of fiscal rectitude. The concomitant social spending increases would be financed entirely out of revenue from the territory's growth-generated surpluses, allowing Hong Kong to challenge and, in many ways, outstrip Singapore's achievements without recourse to draconian state dirigisme. In the next four chapters, we will trace the turbulent course of the 'MacLehose Revolution' in Hong Kong housing – while remaining mindful of the unobtrusive but vital foundation provided by Trench's embryonic social reforms. (Figure 4.19a, b)

Figure 4.19 (a) Trench at staff party – 1970 Annual Report. (b) Princess Anne visits Resettlement estate – 1971 Annual Report.

Notes

1 Mark, 'Development without decolonisation?' 316.
2 Trench, 1987 Bodleian interview.
3 Gary Ka-Wai Cheung, *Hong Kong's Watershed – the 1967 Riots*, HKUP, 2009, 138.
4 Trench, 1987 Bodleian interview. Wright, 2011 interview.
5 Wright, 1988 Bodleian interview.
6 Trench, 1987 Bodleian interview.
7 Trench, 1987 Bodleian interview; Tsang, *Governing Hong Kong*, 70.
8 Holdsworth and Munn, *Dictionary of Hong Kong Biography*, 108–9.
9 Tsang, *Governing Hong Kong*, 70; Holmes was previously Director of Commerce 1962–6, SCMP 30-4-1977.
10 Williams, 2012 interview.
11 Tsang, *Governing Hong Kong*, 103, 108, 177.
12 Tsang, *Governing Hong Kong*, 115, 182, 163–5. Scott, *Political Change and the Crisis of Legitimacy,* 120; Akers-Jones, 2014 interview.
13 Wright, 1988 Bodleian interview and 2011 interview; Liao, 2010 interview.
14 Scott, *Political Change and the Crisis of Legitimacy*, 125; Norman Miners, *The Government and Politics of Hong Kong*, OUP, Hong Kong 1975, Preface.
15 HKRS394-8-2 Haddon-Cave 11-4-1969 to Trench; Castells et al., *Shek Kip Mei Syndrome,* 105.
16 Trench, 1987 Bodleian interview. VIP visits, HKRS394-8-2 1958–71; HKRS156-2-3656 1968–70, visit by Fiji HA.
17 HKRS394-8-2, 11-4-69 PHC to Trench.
18 Tsang, *Modern History of Hong Kong*, 154.
19 Liao, 2010 interview.
20 Trench, 1987 Bodleian interview; Wright, 2011 interview.
21 Wright, 1988 Bodleian interview.
22 Wright, 1988 Bodleian interview.
23 Liao, 2010 interview; Castells et al., *Shek Kip Mei Syndrome*, 12. R Hughes, *Borrowed Place, Borrowed Time: Hong Kong and its Many Faces*, Andre Deutsch, London, 1968.
24 Wai, 2010 interview.
25 Cheung, *Hong Kong's Watershed.* Hong Kong Government Information Services, *Events in Hong Kong, 1967: an Official Report*, HKGIS, Hong Kong, 1968.
26 Akers-Jones, 2013 interview; HKRS163-9-427 1967 paper on 1966 disturbances.
27 Rowe, 1987 Bodleian interview.
28 HKRS163-9-427 1967 paper on riots; Williams, 1988 Bodleian interview; Wright, 1988 Bodleian interview.
29 Williams, 1988 Bodleian interview; Hung, *City on the Edge*, 31–3; Lightbody, 2011 interview.
30 Williams, 1988 Bodleian interview.
31 Williams, 1988 Bodleian interview. HKRS394-8-2 memo to ExCo for discussion 2-11-1968.
32 HKRS524-2-15-1 1967 papers; HKRS163-9-427 15-2-1967 Wakefield note; HKRS 869-1-49 10-1967 note; Blyth and Wotherspoon, *Hong Kong Remembers*, 111; Williams, 2012 interview.
33 HKRS163-480-1 7–1967 on evictions; Blyth and Wotherspoon, *Hong Kong Remembers*, 111; Williams, 2012 interview; Lightbody, 2011 interview.

34 Tsang, *Modern History of Hong Kong*, 190; *Scott, Political Change and the Crisis of Legitimacy*, 107.
35 Akers-Jones, *Feeling the Stones*, 57, 66; HKRS163-9-427 1966–7 briefs for Secretary of State visits.
36 Trench, 1987 Bodleian interview.
37 Akers-Jones, *Feeling the Stones*, 57.
38 Tsang, *Governing Hong Kong*, 94.
39 Tsang, *Governing Hong Kong*, 88–94; Janet L Scott, 'Structure and function in an urban organisation': the Mutual Aid Committees', *Journal of the Hong Kong Branch of the Royal Asiatic Society*, vol 22, 1982, 1–30.
40 Wright, 1988 Bodleian interview.
41 HKRS394-8-2 20-3-1968 note by Holmes; HKRS394-8-2 24-6-1968 note by Roy Anson re CDO scheme; Tsang, *Governing Hong Kong*, 70, 94.
42 Monnery, *Architect of Prosperity*, 196–8, 208, 253–266; Wright, 1988 Bodleian interview.
43 Tsang, *Governing Hong Kong*, 182; Liao, 2014 interview.
44 Trench, 1987 Bodleian interview; Akers-Jones, 2014 interviews.
45 Holdsworth and Munn, *Dictionary of Hong Kong Biography*, 108; Rowe, 1987 Bodleian interview. Akers-Jones, *Feeling the Stones*, 121. A close relative of Cowperthwaite's recalled that he himself 'had the most incredibly tactless wife – you could always count on her to put her foot in it!' (interview with family member, 29-1-2023)
46 Wright, 1988 Bodleian interview; Wright, 2011 interview. Robert Moses: Glendinning, *Mass Housing*, 98.
47 Tsang, *Modern History of Hong Kong*, 168.
48 Y C R Wong, *Hong Kong Land for Hong Kong People*, 35–7, 67; Williams, 1988 Bodleian interview.
49 Monnery, *Architect of Prosperity,* 200; Tsang, *Governing Hong Kong*, 80–2.
50 Trench, 1987 Bodleian interview.
51 Tsang, *Modern History of Hong Kong*, 171.
52 Lightbody, 2011 interview; Monnery, *Architect of Prosperity*, 208.
53 Tsang, *Modern History of Hong Kong*, 168; but see Scott *Political Change*, 74, on much lower surpluses, deficit of $137m in 1965–6.
54 Monnery, *Architect of Prosperity*, 256
55 Monnery, *Architect of Prosperity*, 196–8; for subsequent discussion of the speech by Urban Council members see HKRS232-1-14-1 27-2-1965 – P Lee on Cowperthwaite budget speech.
56 Monnery, *Architect of Prosperity*, 259.
57 Castells *Shek Kip Mei Syndrome*, 36.
58 Castells, *Shek Kip Mei Syndrome*, 10.
59 HKRS934-5-31, 11-12-63 Urban Council meeting minutes. Williams, 'Administration of Public Housing'.
60 Williams, 2012 interview; Williams, 1988 Bodleian interview; Williams, 'Administration of Public Housing in Hong Kong', 65.
61 HKRS163-9-390 ExCo 12-9-1967, and 5–1971 report on Mk VI blocks; HKRS310-1-11 Bramwell at Resettlement Programme Committee 9-10-1967.
62 HKRS394-20-9, 26-8-1970 Resettlement Department memo by Williams; HKRS310-1-11 Bramwell at Resettlement Programme Committee 9-10-1967; Williams, 'Administration of Public Housing in Hong Kong'.

63 HKRS523-2-5 23-1-1968 HA meeting; HKRS310-1-11 7-1969 Resettlement Programme Committee.
64 HKRS394-20-9 9-1970 note by Bray; Liao, 2010 interview on Atkinson and Housing Board'; HKRS70-6-789 HA Annual Debates 1970–2, for Liao speeches at Housing Authority annual meetings 1970–2. B Williams, 'Public Housing and I', 1969, on Housing Board, ten-year housing plan, and the various housing organisations; Akers-Jones, *Feeling the Stones*, 67, on financing and effects of rent control.
65 HKRS934-5-31, 3-7-64 Teesdale to MacDouall; HKRS163-9-390 5-2-1965 DCS to Kidd; Glendinning, *Mass Housing*, 311–2.
66 Williams, 2012 interview.
67 HKRS524-2-11 19-11-1970 ceremony: the proposed estate name, Ham Tin, had been vetoed by residents and replaced by Lam Tin. HKRS358-1-3 on 1966 visit; Williams, 2012 interview; Williams, 'Public Housing and I'; 12; HKRS394-8-2 15/27-1-1964 on J D Higham visit.
68 HKRS310-1-11. Resettlement Programme 1964–70, for late-1960s statistics, pictures, facts; HKRS232-1-14-3 13-6-1965 report; HKRS358-1-3 quarterly report 12–1966, list of clearances.
69 For example see HKRS358-1-3 for quarterly reports January-December 1966 and Urban Council meeting 7-2-1967; HKRS1588-9-54 2-11-1970 report; HKRS500-2-1 7–1970 CDO note.
70 Tsang, *Governing Hong Kong*, 169.
71 Wright, 1988 Bodleian interview.
72 HKRS310-1-11 3–1968 Resettlement Programme Committee; HKRS163-9-390; Lightbody, 2011 interview.
73 Akers-Jones, 2013 interview.
74 Liao, 2010 interview; Poon, 2009 interview; Akers-Jones, 2014 interview; Fung Tung, 2010 interview; HKRS163-9-390 5-2-65 DCS to Kidd; HKRS163-9-390, 1965 papers; HKRS232-1-14-3, 1965 papers.
75 HKRS684-1-6 9-1970 Bramwell on Sha Tin; HKRS608-1-40 2-1971 Bramwell on GLC housing.
76 Fung Tung, 2010 interview; Williams, 2012 interview.
77 HKRS524-2-11 19-11-1970 notes on Mk I to Mk VII; HKRS530-1-11 6-7-1969 DPW to CS on new Mk VII; HKRS163-9-390 Barty (Commissioner for Resettlement) to CS 5-1967 on Mk V, and 4-5-1971 notes on new Mk VII; HKRS232-1-14-2 3-5-1965 Wakefield interview. HKHA, *The First Two Million*, HK 1980, 46–9.
78 HKRS163-9-390 Norton to Commissioner for Resettlement 21-6-1965, and discussions with Norton about design of Mk V; HKRS232-1-14-2 'A New Look for Estates' paper 3-5-1965.
79 HKRS530-1-11 6-7-1969 DPW to CS; HKRS163-9-390 Barty to CS 5–1967 and 4-5-71 notes.
80 HKRS524-2-11 19-11-1970 notes, observations by H Hu; *Housing*, 11-1967.
81 HKRS310-1-11 6-7-1969 DPW to CS.
82 Williams, 2012 interview.
83 HKRS686-3-161, Bray 11–1969 memo and 10-8-1969 ExCo meeting on Resettlement policy.
84 HKRS310-10-11 12–1964 Bramwell pressure for more trees.
85 Williams, 'Public Housing in Hong Kong'; Williams, 2012 interview.
86 Yeung and Wong, *Fifty Years*, 210.

87 Blyth and Wotherspoon, *Hong Kong Remembers*, 128–133.
88 Williams, 'Public Housing and I'; Williams, 2012 interview and 1988 Bodleian interview.
89 Williams, 2012 interview, and Lightbody, 2011 interview.
90 Lightbody, 2011 interview and Williams, 'Public Housing and I': both Pogue and MacLean directed the TT operations.
91 Williams, 2012 interview and 'Public Housing and I'.
92 HKRS163-9-480 and HKRS163-9-481 2-6-1970 Elliott dispute; 26-1-1971 special joint meeting of Resettlement Policy/Management Committees of Urban Council about Tung Tau clearances.
93 Williams, 2012 interview.
94 HKRS684-1-6 J M Rowlands to Secretary for Environment 9–1973, quoting 31-7-1972 memo to SHM.
95 HKRS394-20-9 2-1971 on Chong Hing Mansion scandal; HKRS394-20-9, 22-7-1971 Resettlement Department report.
96 Wright, 1988 Bodleian interview.
97 HKRS310-1-11 Resettlement Programme Committee 9-10-1967; Williams, 'Administration of Housing in Hong Kong'; Williams, 'Public Housing and I'; HKRS394-20-9 26-8-1970 Resettlement memo by Williams; HKRS686-3-161 UMELCO visit 17-1-1972; Williams, 2012 interview.
98 Williams, 1988 Bodleian interview; HKRS310-1-11 Bramwell at 9–1969 meeting.
99 Williams, 2012 interview and 1988 Bodleian interview.
100 Williams, 2012 interview.
101 Wright, 2011 interview; Hong Kong Housing Authority, *Annual Report* for 1970–1, list of members; Liao, 2010 interview; HKRS523-2-6 SHA to Commissioner for Housing 12–1969. Forsgate: Holdsworth and Munn, *Dictionary of Hong Kong Biography*, 148. Akers-Jones, 2014 interview; Alexander, 1988 Bodleian interview.
102 Rowe, 1987 Bodleian interview; HKRS232-1-14-1 13-1-1965 on annual debate, and SCMP 27-1-1965 cutting; HKRS232-1-14-3 28-7-1965 HA meeting.
103 HKRS523-2-5 11-1963 HA memo; HKRS232-1-14-3 HA meeting 7–1965. 'Housing in Hong Kong', *Chartered Surveyor*, 2–1964, 391–5.
104 HKRS523-2-5 12–1967 HA exchanges with NIHT and SSHA.
105 Fung Tung, 2010 interview; Akers-Jones, 2014 interview; Liao, 2014 interview; HKRS523-2-7 1–1968 HA meeting. F J Carroll, 'Housing in Hong Kong', *Housing*, 11–1967, 13–17.
106 Liao, 2010 interview; HKRS1588-9-11 Pang and Firth visit to Tokyo May 1966.
107 Liao 2011 and 2009 interviews.
108 Liao, 2009 interview.
109 HKRS523-2-7 Alexander at 1–1968 meeting.
110 HKRS523-2-9 9/10-1970 correspondence; HKRS70-6-837-2 SCMP 20-5-1972 cutting.
111 Liao, 2010 interview. HKRS523-2-7 11-1968 to 4–1969 correspondence.
112 Liao, 2010 interview.
113 *Far East Architect and Builder*, 2–1968, 31–6. HKRS1588-9-11 Firth and others at Tokyo conference 8–1966.
114 HKRS156-3-7; HKRS232-1-14-2 22-5-1965 papers; SCMP 29 and 30-12-1963 cuttings.
115 J H Kinoshita, *From Slocan to Hong Kong*, Trafford, Victoria (British Columbia), 2005, 107–8, on Choi Hung.

116 Liao, 2009 interview and Fung, 2010 interview. *The Surveyor*, 16-11-1963, 1436.
117 *HKIA Journal* 72, 2016, 'Occupy Housing', 34–5; HKHA, *The First Two Million*, 1980, 20. *Far East Architect and Builder*, 2–1966, 47–51; *Far East Builder,* 3–1970, 14–19.
118 R H Matthew, 1-2-1972 letter to UIA, Evaluation of Wah Fu (for UIA/UN Basic Housing Evaluation); 1-6-1968 *Surveyor*, Wah Fu summary.
119 SCMP 20-1-1967 Annual Debate of HA, discussion on abandoned 50-storey proposal; HKRS70-6-823-1 and 2, 26-4-1971 description of Ping Shek; 20-6-1967 memo.
120 HKRS70-6-823-2 Ping Shek 26-4-1971 paper; HKRS394-20-9 26-8-1970 Resettlement memo by Williams; SCMP 20-1-1967. *Far East Architect and Builder*, 8–1967, 45–7.
121 HKRS70-6-823-2 26-4-1971 opening; HKRS394-20-9 26-8-1970 Resettlement memo by Williams.
122 HKRS70-6-837-1; HKRS337-4-3514A correspondence of 2-1971 to 3-1971 on Wah Fu tenancy.
123 Wright, 1988 Bodleian interview.
124 HKRS232-1-14-1 and HKRS896-1-49 on Tai Hang Road site.
125 HKRS896-1-49 HKHS Schemes file 1952-68; HKRS232-1-14-2 SCMP 6-1965 J Glover cutting.
126 Williams, 1988 Bodleian interview.
127 Williams, 2012 interview; Williams, 'Public Housing and I', 1969.
128 HKRS70-6-789 HA Annual Debates 1970–2.
129 Alexander, 1988 Bodleian interview; Wright, 1988 Bodleian interview; Liao, 2010 interview.
130 Lightbody, 2011 interview.
131 Liao, 2010 interview.
132 HKRS896-1-114 18-3-1960 and 11-8-1960 memos by R C Clarke, Assistant Superintendent of Crown Lands (Planning); Commissioner for Housing to CS 13-2-1960.
133 Liao, 2010 interview.
134 Wright, 1988 Bodleian interview; Williams, 2012 interview; HKRS896-1-114 11-12-1964 Colony Outline Plan Procedural Meeting, General Circular 27–1965/Colonial Secretariat 27-8-1965.
135 HKRS500-2-1 7-7-1970 note from C K Wong CDO re LDPC and flow chart of its official relationships, LDPC paper 14/76 for circulation 28-5-1976, and Home Affairs Department paper 5-7-1976.
136 Seng, '*The City in a Building*', 7; Williams, 'Public Housing and I'; Castells, *Shek Kip Mei Syndrome*, 12.
137 HKRS896-1-52 10-1965 note by Aserappa; HKRS896-1-53 Wright note 30-4-1966 and SCMP 6-1-65 cutting of letter on Tsuen Wan.
138 HKRS896-1-53 30-4-1966 Wright DPW to DCS; HKRS896-1-52 2-1968 Wright note.
139 HKRS896-1-53 12-1966 draft zoning plan for Castle Peak; HKRS684-1-6 9-1970 Bramwell note on Lek Yuen; Williams, 2012 interview.
140 *Town Planning Review*, x, 1964–5, 299; HKRS545-1-447-2 10-1970 W G Gregory (HKU) lecture report; Liao, 2010 interview.
141 HKRS394-25-1 1-1966 DPW memo.
142 Wright, 1988 Bodleian interview. Brian J Hadland, 'The planning background to housing in Hong Kong', *Far East Builder*, 1–1970, 28–31.
143 Planning reports and densities of resettlement and HA estates: HKRS896-1-52 2-1968 note by Wright.
144 Wright, 1988 Bodleian interview.

145 HKRS337-4-4337 Sha Tin file; *Official Architecture and Planning*, 2–1966, 273–8.
146 Lightbody, 2011 file.
147 HKRS394-25-1 8-1964 notes arising out of Governor's tour of Tai Po and Yuen Long districts; Liao, 2010 interview.
148 HKRS523-2-5 HA executive committee meeting 21-3-1963.
149 HKRS232-1-12-4 9-12-1963 memo on Home Finance Scheme; HKRS523-2-6 press cuttings on homeownership 1964–5. 934-5-31, 18-6-64 Colonial Secretariat to Government Printer.
150 Akers-Jones, 2014 interview; Liao, 2010 interview; HKRS232-1-14-3 HA meeting 7–1965 minutes.
151 Seng, '*The City in a Building*', 7; Lau Ho Yin, 'The Spirit of the Hong Kong City', MSc, HKU, 2016.
152 Carmen Tsui, 'Housing the nascent middle class: the first high-rise planned community in post-war Hong Kong', *Planning Perspectives*, vol 37:4, 2022, 735–759; HKRS70-3-297, including Mei Foo Phase 1 brochure and 16-9-1966 artist's impression; Wright, 1988 Bodleian interview; Wright, 2011 and 2015 interviews; Liao, 2010 interview. New York developments: Glendinning, *Mass Housing*, 64-6, 102-5 (cf. also Parklabrea, Los Angeles, from 1944, and Castle Village, New York City, 1938–9).
153 HKRS70-3-297, Governor's speech of 17-11-1966.
154 Liao, 2010 interview. Qian Zhu, 'The Production of Everyday Space for Workers', 429.
155 Tsang, *Governing Hong Kong*, 80–4, on Cowperthwaite.
156 Wright, 2011 interview.
157 Castells, *Shek Kip Mei Syndrome*, 12.

Part II

The MacLehose years

5 1971–1973

Building a 'model city'? – The MacLehose Revolution

In Part II, we trace the shift in Hong Kong's public housing paradigm from opportunistic colonial containment to a longer-term, decolonisation-linked strategy of identity-creation, a transition driven by governor Sir Murray MacLehose – Hong Kong's paramount 'Home Builder' – and by growing official anxieties behind the scenes about '1997'.

The early 1970s were the years when China gradually began to re-emerge from the Cultural Revolution and re-engage with the wider world. Following the rapprochement with the USA from 1972, steadily improving relations with Britain were signalled by the visit of opposition leader Edward Heath in 1974.[1] Correspondingly, the 1997 issue was now being discussed within the British government: a 1969 interdepartmental study, and a 1970 Foreign and Commonwealth Office (FCO) report, had concluded that the eventual return of Hong Kong to China in 1997 was inevitable, and the task would be to 'negotiate its return… on the best terms available for its people and for our material interests there'.[2] Following premier Zhou Enlai's 1971 suggestion to a British official that Hong Kong would likely be reclaimed at the end of the New Territories lease in 1997, China's accession to the United Nations the following year was marked by Hong Kong's removal from the list of colonial territories, and the beginning of the claim that it was merely under 'occupation': henceforth Britain would refer to it instead as a 'dependent territory'. Yet residual Cultural Revolution chaos continued to beset China as late as 1973, and, although any return of Hong Kong to China in 1997 was only talked about within the territory in 'secret conclaves' (Akers-Jones), contingency planning within the FCO in London in the early 1970s still (despite Zhou's assurance) contemplated the possibility of the 'doomsday scenario' of a 'humiliating expulsion' from the colony by force ahead of 1997. Domestically, too, it seemed clear that after the upheavals of 1966–7, Hong Kong 'needed a refit' – and that any domestic reform agenda would be inextricably bound up with the external sovereignty issue.[3] In economic policy, these were the years when the emphasis gradually began to shift from manufacturing to finance and property-speculation, a development that would from the 1980s spawn a powerful real-estate oligarchy able to significantly skew public housing policy.[4]

DOI: 10.1201/9781315563701-7

It was in that fast-moving and uncertain context that November 1971 saw the arrival of Sir Murray MacLehose as Hong Kong's 25th governor, as a ruler of an economy and government which, he observed in 1974, equated to that of a small nation-state such as Denmark.[5] MacLehose seemed at first glance a conventional product of the reformist establishment generation that Noel Annan later dubbed 'Our Age', combining progressive liberal views with a more traditional gentlemanly self-assurance, combined in his case with a tall and commanding deportment and an abrupt, sometimes haughty manner.[6] Like so many colonial administrators before him, MacLehose's background was from Scotland – from Ayrshire, in the south-west – followed by education in an English public school. Ayrshire remained the focus of family 'leave' visits, especially around the time of his mother's death in 1974 and a severe horse-riding injury to his daughter in 1975.[7] (Figure 5.1)

Dubbed 'Big Mac' by his civil-service staff, MacLehose was the first career diplomat to hold the governorship. He was initially expected to complete only a conventional five-year tour of duty, and was reputedly seen by London as a potential Trojan horse, who could help foist 'enlightened' metropolitan norms on to the supposedly introverted colonial cadet culture. Instead, the reverse to some extent happened, and MacLehose rapidly mutated into the most intransigent and effective defender of Hong Kong autonomy from London, whether in reaction against Treasury policies or 'pontificating' MPs: several years into his governorship he complained to Denis Bray that he was already being treated by the FCO as 'a cross between Makarios and a bandit chief'.[8] Once in office, MacLehose's dominant personality traits soon rose to the surface, including an unusual 'helicopter view' of the broad spread of public policy affairs, and he rapidly 'took Hong Kong by the neck'.[9] in 1966–8 he had served as principal private secretary to Foreign Secretary George Brown, being seen as 'a person of character' who could 'stand up to Brown if necessary… especially after midday!' (when Brown's alcoholism was at its most pronounced).[10] With this decisive, 'field-marshal' personality went less pleasant traits, including a tendency towards rudeness and

Figure 5.1 Illustration in *China Mail* commenting on the recent change of governorship, December 1971: 'Trench Work Ahead' becomes 'MacLehose Works Ahead'.

intolerant sarcasm to those considered less important. Michael Wright contrasted him with Cowperthwaite, 'who was always the same, always charming – whereas MacLehose was like Little Jemima – when he was nice he was very, very nice, but when he was bad he was horrid!'[11] He cultivated a reputation for no-nonsense dislike of formality, but the reality was a little different, as seen for example in the elaborate instructions for preparation of his tea (made specially luke-warm) at official visits to housing sites.[12]

The MacLehose administration – a 'government in a hurry'

Within contemporary Hong Kong, the dominant perception of MacLehose was as an innovator in the social and economic sphere, imparting to its laissez-faire society a distinctly public-sector-based conception of government's role. Colonial commercial interests and government administrators initially feared that MacLehose might indeed be a mere agent for the importation of British or European welfare-state thinking, until his real role as a defender, rather than subverter, of Hong Kong autonomy emerged.[13] Behind the public debates about matters such as social policy, however, continually swirled more existential pressures and anxieties about sovereignty, and the 1997 deadline in particular, which encouraged a growing concept of housing as an instrument of identity-creation.

MacLehose was well aware of the debates in London about the likely 1997 handover, and the need to avoid a collapse in British rule, or forced expulsion, in the interim. These concerns formed the driving force of all MacLehose's governmental policies – including his mass housing drive – and were presented in a succession of confidential reports in 1973–5 to his FCO contacts. The Hong Kong administration, MacLehose believed, had a window of opportunity of about a decade, while China was emerging from its years of turmoil, to head off any threat of the PRC seizing the colony before 1997. Everyone tacitly accepted China would be likely to move to recover Hong Kong at that point, as already signalled by Zhou, so the aim was to sustain British administration until that end-point. The Hong Kong government could contribute to this by making massive improvements to the territory's social conditions, deficiencies that had underlain the 1966 disturbances in particular: Hong Kong's geopolitical weakness could potentially be counterbalanced by boldness in social policy.[14] In his 1973 Annual Review for the FCO, MacLehose argued that there was only just enough time to do this, and that the Hong Kong government must be a 'government in a hurry', dedicated to enlisting the active support, and sense of collective belonging, of the population.[15] David (Lord) Wilson, then MacLehose's political adviser on mainland relations, argues that his social policies stemmed from purely domestic motives: 'In terms purely of "1997", it wouldn't have mattered if we'd had an appalling housing policy!' But MacLehose does seem to have made a connection between the two. In May 1974 (see Chapter 6), he would argue the aim must be to create breathing space for subsequent political negotiations, and that the government must hurry to make Hong Kong a 'model city'. His 1974 Annual Review, dated January/March 75, returned to this theme, arguing that there was 'so much to be done' and 'so little time to do it'.[16]

Unlike Lee Kuan Yew's social-policy revolution in post-1959 Singapore, the geopolitical delicacy of Hong Kong's position forbade any overtly political framing of the strategy, especially any ideas of 'extension of democracy', which would be certain to inflame Beijing.[17] As we will see, MacLehose had to look towards both China and London, where current government policies often impacted on his initiatives, and where economic protectionism, especially among trade union interests, treated Hong Kong as a competitor.[18] But although ideologically low-key, the new programme was pervaded by a concern with public-relations presentation, to 'catch the public imagination'.[19] In a 1982 valedictory note, he would later acknowledge many of his reforms had been 'little more than extensions of previous trends of government, but they were all deliberately presented and announced over a period of years so as to try to catch and hold the imagination and interest of the population'.[20]

Some measures were largely symbolic, such as renaming of institutions and posts – for instance, in 1973 of the Secretary for Chinese Affairs to Secretary for Home Affairs, or more generally from 'colony' to 'territory'. More important was a sensitivity to the subjects of burning public concern, above all his 'top priority', law and order, where an upsurge in violent crime in the early 1970s prompted clashes with London over the strong public backing for the death penalty.[21] Increasingly more concerning, however, was the more insidious menace of corruption. Here the Independent Commission against Corruption (ICAC), founded 1974 and chaired by Jack Cater, unearthed increasingly alarming evidence of criminality not only within the police, but also in departments linked to public housing, notably the Public Works Department and the Resettlement Department estate management staff. Both the latter had been long lambasted by Elsie Elliott and by the more quirky figure of inveterate complainant Ron Woodcraft, whose corruption accusations continued after the formation of the Housing Department in 1973.[22] Overtones of corruption also underlay other housing controversies of the period, notably the much later '26 Blocks' crisis (see Chapter 9).[23] In housing, the most immediate, life-or-death issues were those of building safety, prompted above all by two mudslides at almost the same location at Sau Mau Ping, the first and more devastating in 1972, and the second in 1976. (Figure 5.2) But the entire spectrum of housing problems rapidly coalesced into MacLehose's greatest challenge of public-service expansion.

For any agenda of boosting public services, the economic position of Hong Kong was a fundamental constraint, and here, the years around 1970 were unexpectedly positive, with sharp increases in government revenues from rising land prices.[24] Throughout the 1970s as a whole, despite recessions, the uncertainty brought by the sterling link, and the huge fluctuations in the land market in 1973 to 1974, GDP growth often averaged around 10% per year, with an annual per-capita increase of 7.5% between 1971 and 1982.[25] Already, under Trench, public spending had been rising sharply by 1970, and the challenge was not what could be afforded, but 'how to boost spending fast enough'. Between 1970 and 1972, government expenditure increased over 50%, and although externally beset by protectionism, the overall trajectory of the economy was inexorably

Figure 5.2 MacLehose seen in 1972 inspecting the aftermath of the Sau Mau Ping mud-slide: at right centre is Housing Secretary Ian Lightbody. Government Information Services photo.

expansionary.[26] That trajectory continued under Cowperthwaite's successor from 1971 as Financial Secretary, Philip Haddon-Cave, whose 'boring speeches' disguised a dramatic underlying reality of soaring spending – all strictly covered by soaring revenues.[27]

MacLehose spent his initial year tentatively, 'fishing… for information' in 'informal' visits to government departments such as Resettlement and GLCH (where he spent two hours talking to local hawkers), or problem areas such as squatter settlements. By his second annual policy address to LegCo, in October 1972, MacLehose was at last ready to set out a broad agenda for reform.[28] His speech listed a bold array of economic and social initiatives, concerning for example law and order and education – programmes that would require a rise of 77% in public service employment, and a 223% rise in public expenditure, by 1982. Spearheading the strategy, however, was the pledge of a revolution in public housing, which MacLehose aimed to convert from an arm of squatter clearance into a fully fledged social service.[29] He argued famously that poor housing 'is one of the major and constant sources of friction and unhappiness between the Government and the population. It offends alike our humanity, our civic pride and our political good sense.' The new housing discourse of identity-creation and welfare provision had now effectively swallowed up the old colonial containment agenda.[30] But despite the previous efforts at reform under Trench, there had still been a distinct lack of urgency, or even enough basic information to allow an overall strategic definition of the problem, for example in accurately estimating squatter numbers. As we saw in Chapter 4, the government did succeed, in 1971, in establishing a unitary system for quantifying housing need and planned output via the 'IU' – but, as we will see, this system proved confusing and controversial in practice.[31] The Housing Board had seemed unable to effectively coordinate housing affairs, and by September 1970 ExCo was still considering its 1968/9 report.[32] Increasingly, the Board focused on pressing for a more unified approach to housing provision, where moves towards a unitary management of resettlement and Housing Authority stocks, as we saw in Chapter 4, had previously been suppressed by Kidd. At the most basic level, output was perceptibly declining, especially in the all-important resettlement programme, and 1971 saw squabbling in the Urban Council over the reasons for this.[33]

To bring about the revolution in housing that he intended, MacLehose exploited a range of existing personalities. His new, unified housing administration (see below) brought together the dynamism of Donald Liao, as Director of Housing, and the more careful and pedantic approach of Ian Lightbody, as Secretary for Housing. MacLehose particularly highly valued civil servants with an unconventional approach, including not just Liao but also the innovative administrator and New Territories specialist David Akers-Jones, whose 'fertile mind' he acknowledged in 1972,[34] and planner/geographer Ted Pryor. The latter, as Assistant Director of Redevelopment and Planning from 1973, played a linchpin role in devising a land strategy, especially for the redevelopment programme, and later authored an overview history of Hong Kong housing. Williams recalled that

> Ted knew how to get hold of land and swap bits around. Bringing in Ted, as a planner, as Assistant Director, we could negotiate about sites. His planning team within the Housing Department did all the planning briefs for new housing estates: then he moved on to drawing up plans for the new estates. He set up a Planning Section, which was then absorbed into the Construction Branch after I left.[35]

The financial aspects of the programme were overseen by Philip Haddon-Cave, who took over in 1971 from Cowperthwaite as Financial Secretary, and projected a somewhat pedantic exterior: Akers-Jones recalled that his annual budget statements

> went on for two hours or more! He just droned on and on, and we all sat there wearily. One hour passed and then another hour passed – nobody understood it very much – it was all fundamental economic theories – he was always talking about the 'GDP deflator' and things like that, which people couldn't understand! Unlike Philip, MacLehose was unorthodox, and couldn't see why things couldn't

be done, and why there wasn't money for this, that and the other. So all kinds of things happened that hadn't happened before. These were all *MacLehose's* doing – and Philip Haddon-Cave had to put up with it.

But Haddon-Cave's liking for 'waffle' concealed an acute awareness of the opportunities and limits of expanded welfare provision within the laissez-faire Hong Kong system, as seen in the key role he played later in establishing the Home Ownership Scheme (Chapter 7).[36] Given MacLehose's consistent opposition to internal political democratisation, as likely to be provocative to China and destabilising to orderly administration, relatively little input stemmed from critical or opposition forces, and were confined to interventions in the Urban Council by figures like Bernacchi, or the indomitable anti-establishment pressure and conspiracy claims by Elsie Elliott.[37]

In Pryor's judgement, MacLehose was responsible for a fresh start in Hong Kong housing, firstly by setting expanded production targets, and secondly by reshaping the organisational landscape around these.[38] His first target was to work out a global estimate of housing need, and to establish what could be reasonably achieved within the ten-year window of opportunity before the likely start of any pre-1997 negotiations. He initially asked Akers-Jones, as PACS (L), to begin working this out.[39] The decisive moment came in July 1972, in a brainstorming boat trip session on the official yacht 'Clementi', attended by key figures including Pryor, Akers-Jones, Liao, and Bernard Williams.[40] Using rough-and-ready methods, a 'crudely derived' estimate of likely housing needs was arrived at, and translated into a ten-year target by Liao.[41] Based on IUs rather than dwelling units, the target depended crucially on calculations of floor space per occupant, and on dwellings' occupancy ratios (discussed in detail below).[42] It was later argued that these potential inconsistencies of definition doomed the IU project to 'failure' from the beginning. But, by comparison with the Housing Board's previous, ineffective recommendations, the Ten-Year Housing Plan at least had the advantage of public-relations immediacy.[43] Financially, the booming early-1970s economy promised lavish resourcing: housing rose from 6% of total government expenditure in 1972/3 to 10–11% in 1974/5.[44] Now, even potentially costly policies such as unification of public housing under a single authority seemed affordable out of current income, and money could be rolled over at the year-end: Akers-Jones recalled that visiting Labour 'MPs from London could never understand how we were doing all this – where the money came from to do it!' In 1972, administrators James Sweetman and Roderick MacLean advocated adoption of a Singapore-style Central Provident Fund, but this unsurprisingly came to nothing.[45]

MacLehose's October 1972 LegCo speech set out his basic strategy, which was rapidly endorsed by ExCo. It had three main elements, which fitted together sequentially, and were all more cautious than the radical reputation of the 'often misquoted' speech suggested.[46] Firstly, the overall output target in IUs – which, despite the 'headline' title of the 'Ten-Year Housing Plan', was actually expressed in conditional terms, as being only achievable under certain conditions. Secondly, organisation, which was addressed through a pledge to unify public housing provision under a single unitary authority – a restructured Housing Authority. And thirdly, land supply, which was dealt with indirectly, through a strategy of building New Towns in the New Territories.[47] In the rest of this chapter, we will deal with these three major elements in turn.

The Ten-Year Housing Plan

The overall target definition, which formed the foundation of the entire strategy, rested on some significant assumptions about household structure and space utilisation. At the root of these, however, was a significant confusion between potential units of definition: individual units, persons, and dwellings. For the public agencies charged with executing it, any housing drive had to be, in practical terms, expressed in numbers of dwelling units, and a target of 40,000 flats a year was envisaged: Pryor highlighted the plan's overwhelming reliance on public low-rental housing, planned private-sector output being only 18,000 flats a year.[48] But the IU was nothing to do with this, being essentially a definition of floor area – although disguised by being broken into artificial units, rather than overtly aggregated as in the Khrushchev 1957 Soviet programme's '*zhilaia ploshchad*'.[49] Its translation into persons housed or flat units depended crucially on occupancy rates. It gradually became clear that the 1.8 million IUs in the Ten-Year Plan equated not to 1.8 million persons but to 1.5 million persons: in October 1972, Denis Bray warned Liao that the Housing Board's target required not 1.8 million but 2.1 million IUs.[50] Other significant assumptions included that 60% of all one- and two-person households would share individual dwellings. The result was confusion in MacLehose's annual report to the FCO, the Ten-Year Plan was highlighted as 'housing for 1.8 million' people.[51] And further developments during the 1970s, including additional household formation and immigration, further worsened the confusion, leading inevitably to later accusations of 'miscalculations' and even, ultimately, of the 'failure' of the plan.[52]

These subtle points of definition emerged only gradually. Far more immediately dominant was the impact of unexpected external economic shocks on the plan's economic foundations, beginning in autumn 1972 when the Chinese government began charging world prices for commodities, followed from October 1973 by the first oil crisis, which raised costs and depressed wages, prompting various 'panaceas'. 1973–4 also saw dramatic fluctuations in the land market.[53] Even in 1973, however, there was a 7.5% increase in GDP, and social expenditure rose from 33% of the budget in 1972–3 to 45% in 1977–8. In his 1974 letter to the FCO, MacLehose claimed these adverse forces had delayed his social programmes by two years overall, and had stalled the 'really dramatic expansion of housing' envisaged in the Ten-Year Plan.[54] The 1974 annual review looked back with nostalgia to the 'boom years' of 1968–73, and predicted the belt-tightening would be further accentuated in 1975, and might even lead to higher taxes or a deficit-financing system.[55] In Chapter 6, we will examine the early-1970s 'crisis economics of housing' in more detail.

Under one umbrella? The new Housing Authority

During autumn 1972, it became clear the organisational foundation of MacLehose's housing reforms, with their overwhelming reliance on public-rental flats, would be a new, unified umbrella entity for all public-sector operations. This would be based on the existing Housing Authority, but separated decisively from the Urban Council, and serviced by the Housing Department, which would become a quasi-government department.[56] By September 1972, prior manoeuvrings were underway between the Resettlement Department, the GLCH Department, and the existing Housing Authority, involving Lightbody, Liao, Bray, Akers-Jones, and Bramwell; many of the existing organisations' employees felt considerable 'unease'. Also to be absorbed within the new organisation was the Housing Board, with its policy-formulation remit.[57] Left outside the new structure, however, was the Housing Society, whose quasi-philanthropic autonomy was preserved and linked to a vaguely defined new role as a 'laboratory' for housing innovation.[58] Liao argued that 'They [the HS] were allowed to get on with it. We didn't interfere – they still got their own land allocations – on a much smaller scale. They were happily going on with their little schemes, with their own application list'.[59] But unlike the HDB in Singapore, with its more unified and homogenised housing patterns, the new system still preserved a fundamental, and in some ways stimulating, split between housing and planning. All design and management of HA estates was concentrated within the Housing Department, but land-use and planning in both New Towns and the urban area were dealt with separately, within the Public Works Department and the Lands Branch.[60]

Precedents abroad for unitary government housing organisations were eagerly examined, beginning with Singapore's Housing and Development Board: December 1972 saw correspondence about Hong Kong's 'upheaval' between Williams and Liu Thai-Ker, and between Lightbody and Teh Cheang Wan.[61] The newly formed Northern Ireland Housing Executive, also rooted in sovereignty issues, was also examined as a potential unitary model, with a visit by Fung Tung.[62] The challenges of integrating the Housing Authority and Resettlement management structures prompted fevered tabulation of letting statistics, and efforts within the Resettlement Department, steered by Williams, to enhance the post-1969 Tidiness Teams system.[63] Public housing estates were henceforth to be organised into 'Group A' estates (former Housing Authority, and Government Low-Cost) and Group B (former Resettlement), with an implicit process of assimilation of the latter into the management practices of the former, as already pioneered in the GLCH system: the perceived 'class distinction' between the two would provoke bitter cultural clashes.[64]

One problem not apparently facing the new organisation initially was that of financial shortages – although by late 1973, as we saw above, the position would seem very different. MacLehose recognised that he was 'lucky' in the coincidence of his reorganisation with the tail-end of the 1968–73 boom, which allowed for a 14% jump in public spending, and a 47% rise in rents, from 1968 to February 1973. He recalled later that 'my problem was not so much money as organisational fragmentation', and that the decision to establish the new HA was taken in principle first, and the finance provided subsequently.[65] In an April '73 address to the first meeting of the new Authority, MacLehose asserted that 'the funds for the programme are available – I believe money will not be your principal problem, but rather how to convert it into well-planned and well-managed estates quickly enough'. However, Lightbody was later accused of over-bidding for extra resources to cover the costs of integration.[66] Initial financial support for the new Authority from 1973 onwards was provided by government loans, coupled with nil-premium land grants. Additional funding was available for tasks such as building of licensed areas. And the HA's ability to construct its own commercial centres, a policy vigorously championed by Liao, promised to significantly raise income, over an extended time.[67] Crucially, the new Housing Authority was not to be a government department, and therefore it was kept at one remove from the central-government control system for financial approval, which allowed Authority members to embark on potentially costly policies, notably the November 1973 decision to raise housing space standards to 50 ft^2, without reference to the Financial Secretary.[68] However, the huge disparity in historic debt levels between Group A and Group B estates was seen from the beginning as a potential long-term threat, with the prudent legacy of the former HA liable to be 'dragged down' by the latter.[69]

The symbolic aspects of merger also received growing attention, including the title of the new Authority, where Liao and the Secretary for Chinese Affairs consulted intensively over the relationship between the Chinese and English alternatives: the outcome was that whereas the English title remained unaltered, the Chinese title was subtly expanded in its scope at Liao's instigation, equating to the English translation 'Housing Authority' rather than, as before, 'Housing Building Development Authority'.[70] Estate names, too, were reorganised and unified, and there was intensive discussion among the members of the new authority about its symbol, or logo, again with input from Liao: an initial proposal was vigorously rejected in favour of the, in the event, long-lasting eventual symbol.[71] (Figure 5.3a, b)

As to the overall status of the new body, there was from the start uncertainty, even tension, concerning the relationship between the Housing Authority, which essentially comprised a relatively small board of governors, and the supporting Housing Department – not unlike the position in some other public housing authority systems, such as the (by then) 40-year-old case of NYCHA in New York City. Even on 1 April 1973, there was still debate as to precisely what powers the new authority had been vested with.[72] In retrospect, Williams argued that people expected too much of it, but nevertheless, June 1973 correspondence between MacLehose and Akers-Jones combined satisfaction that the new organisation was 'settling down well', with calls to 'keep up the momentum'.[73]

The Authority's autonomy, and the place of the unofficials within it, was underpinned by a decisive separation from the Urban Council: MacLehose's aim, clearly enunciated in September 1972, was that the new body's membership must

Figure 5.3 (a) Renaming the Middle Road headquarters from Resettlement to Housing Department, 2 April 1973: April 1973 article. (b) Post-1973 Housing Authority estate name-sign at Ping Shek. 1983 photo. (MG).

be 'harmonious', and decisively separated from the old rancorous politics and Resettlement concerns of the Urban Council.[74] The Urban Council was to lose its policy and management responsibilities, and the new Authority also became financially autonomous. In the process, the role of the unofficials was subtly reinforced, by integrating key figures more firmly into the administrative machinery: eight of the new HA members would be Urban Councillors, appointed personally rather than *ex officio*. MacLehose cleverly included Elliott as well as establishment figures such as Gerald Forsgate, the influential Scottish director of the Hong Kong and Kowloon Wharf and Godown Company, and first chairman of the HA's Building Committee, which oversaw the entire production programme: crucially, the head of the BC would always be an unofficial. While it was agreed, after debate, that the new HA's inaugural chairman should be an official – Lightbody, as secretary for housing – a more general shift to unofficials was clearly underway, depoliticising but also bolstering their contribution.[75]

In its overall hierarchical apportionment of responsibilities between Lightbody, as former Resettlement chief, and Liao, as director of the outgoing Housing Authority, the new organisation reflected the continuing status of the traditional Hong Kong cadet administrative system: Lightbody was assigned the overarching quasi-ministerial post of Secretary for Housing, while Liao the professional became Director of Housing, and head of the Housing Department. Their approaches differed radically, with Lightbody projecting a somewhat more conservative, 'hands-off' approach, unlike Liao's dynamism and personal 'charisma'.[76] The Housing Secretary post formed part of a wider agenda of governmental reform. MacLehose, anxious to avoid 'going native' within the Hong Kong administrative tradition, had commissioned consultants McKinsey to plan a reorganisation and professionalisation of the higher echelons of government. Their report, published in May 1973, recommended a new system of functional quasi-ministries each headed by a permanent Secretary.[77] However, although the Housing Secretary was MacLehose's first point of contact, and Williams recalled that Lightbody was forever being summoned by him at short notice, his more reactive approach increasingly exasperated MacLehose, who, as we will see, 'got rid of' him in a horizontal transfer later in the decade.[78] (Figure 5.4)

Liao, by contrast, was a strongly hands-on figure, not least in his driving project-management style, but he was equally well-attuned to relations with the unofficials, and to public relations in general: this had a much higher profile under MacLehose, who regarded the previous housing structure as 'far too defensive'. A more pro-active approach seemed especially essential after the 1973–4 recession, when the Home Affairs Department's secret 'MOOD' public opinion surveys showed support for the new Housing Authority sharply dropping.[79] Liao was always on hand to escort distinguished visitors, including British luminaries such as Harold Macmillan or visitors from elsewhere: in September 1974, Nigerian leader General Gowon jokingly invited Liao to come to Nigeria to reorganise his own public housing programme.[80] But public relations had other, less celebratory aspects, not least in relation to the 'volatile' (Lightbody) Group B tenants and shopkeepers. (Figure 5.5.) No shirker of public controversy, Liao in 1974 confronted an enraged mob of Group B estate shopkeepers, furious at management and rental reforms, who besieged him in his office. He recalled: 'That caused a hell of a trouble! In the morning, going to my office, I had to walk through this mass of people. At least,

HONGKONG HOUSING AUTHORITY

Secretary for Housing

MR Ian MacDonald Lightbody (53), a "veteran" in the Civic Service, is the Secretary for Housing and the overall head of the Hongkong Housing Authority.

He served on a number of important posts before being appointed to his present job.

Mr Lightbody is also the Chairman of the Housing Authority.

Director of Housing

MR Donald Liao (45) is the Director of Housing. He is also the Vice-Chairman.

AN ESTIMATED 1.8 million people live in public houses in Hongkong and it is a formidable task to keep track of the population growth.

The reconstituted Housing Authority was formally established in April 1973 under the Housing Ordinance of 1973.

Powers

The new Authority has been vested with the powers and functions that were previously fragmented, that is to say, those of the Urban Council, the Resettlement Department, the former Housing Authority and the Housing Board.

The Authority is a statutory body responsible for co-ordinating the many aspect of public housing.

Terms

It has the following terms of references:

(1) To manage existing public housing estates of all kinds, and all future public housing estates as well as Cottage Areas and Licensed Areas.

(2) To plan and build public housing estates "for such kinds or classes of persons as the Authority may, subject to the approval of the Governor, determine."

(3) To be an authority for the clearance of land for development, subject to such directions as the Governor may give.

(4) To be the authority for the prevention and control of squatting, and

(5) To advise the Governor on all housing policy matters.

The Authority comprises of the Secretary for Housing, Unofficials and Officials who are appointed by the Governor.

Business

The Authority meets at bi-monthly intervals but to ensure that business is despatched quickly, effectively and with minimal red-tape, five committees have been set up. These are the Appeals, Building, Finance, Management and Operations Committees.

The executive arm of the new Housing Authority is the Housing Department, which also came into being in April, 1973 as a result of the merger between the former Resettlement Department and the former Housing Division of the Urban Services Department.

THE Squatter Control Section is responsible for the control of illegal structures on Crown Land in the urban areas and Tsuenwan.

While all huts erected on Crown land without permit are unlawful, those recorded in a survey of the urban areas and Tsuenwan in 1964 are tolerated.

Figure 5.4 May 1975 article in *Star* on structure of new Housing Authority and images of Lightbody and Liao.

■ *ONE of the signs resettlement dwellers have put up urging their people not to accep the new Government contracts.*

New rent row looms

By RICHARD YAO

A RENT row on an unprecedented scale is brewing among shop-owner of Hongkong's 25 former resettlement estates.

More than 10,000 shop-owners on the estates received notifications from the Housir Department in the past two weeks 'urging' them to sign a two-year contract with th Government.

According to the Department the move is the first step to unify administration and management methods in the former resettlement and low-cost housing estates.

All separate Government housing sections formerly known as the Resettlement Department, Housing Society and Housing Authority came under the umbrella of the Housing Department in April.

But a spokesman for the Taihangtung Estate's Shop-owners' League told the Mail yesterday the contract was in fact "a cage in which to lock the shop-owners for future Government persecution."

Figure 5.5 September 1973 *China Mail* article on dispute over estate shop rents.

as a Chinese person, speaking Chinese, I wasn't afraid to face them. I said, "Just think – you are the tenants of the government!" – and so forth! And in the end, we won!'[81]

During early 1973, huge office moves were under way, and at its inauguration in April, the new Housing Department had 1,071 staff. Structurally, although the new Housing Authority and Housing Department were strongly distinct from the former HA, at the final meeting of the latter in March 1973 the outgoing chair, David Alexander, could not resist crowing over the 'taking over' of Resettlement, echoing Brook Bernacchi's earlier claim that the Housing Authority was 'taking control'.[82] MacLehose's address to the first meeting of the new Authority, by contrast, looked to the future, reiterating the theme that its main challenge was not shortage of money but how to convert that into high-quality housing as fast as possible, and maximise progress with the Ten-Year Housing Programme: one press conference even suggested that the new Authority might itself only have a time-limited 'ten-year life'.[83]

In both management of existing estates and development of new estates, former HA practices were unapologetically taken as the model, while the squatter clearances formerly overseen by the Resettlement Department were significantly upgraded. In management, the overwhelming challenge was the homogenisation of the unruly

Figure 5.6 November 1974 'before', 'during' and 'after' views in SCMP of Yellow Helmets clearance operations at Sau Mau Ping Estate.

Group B estates into the practices of the well-governed Group A. Already, from 1969, Williams's Tidiness Teams, and Bramwell's hawker control force, had made significant inroads on the problem.[84] (Figure 5.6) However, by 1972–3, despite the higher standards of the new Mk VI blocks, some Resettlement estates were still 'rubbish dump'-like in character, and in 1972, Urban Councillor Gerry Forsgate simply stated, 'That Resettlement is a pail of worms, no-one can deny'. In the same year, Liao suggested potential ways of assimilating Resettlement estates into the GLCH management system. Immediately following the 1973 merger, anti-hawker measures were stepped up, and maintenance backlogs tackled.[85] Significant cultural differences impeded progress, especially the growing tension between Group A and Group B housing managers: in rival letters in early 1974, the former denigrated the latter as crudely amateurish, and the latter attacked the former as 'girlish, baby-faced' and effete.[86] The old accusations of corruption and of triad influence within the Resettlement Department at first continued after the merger, both from Elliott and from Woodcraft.[87] To further the assimilation agenda, a limited programme of Group B rent increases was initiated in mid-1973, both in domestic properties, and, more controversially, within estate shops, with explosive results in the siege of Liao in his office.[88] In 1973, too, a working party report on the housing needs of the elderly recommended they should be housed 'in the community' near relatives and friends, an aspiration that was in practice largely ignored.[89] And in the same year, a more long-lasting management reform was introduced as a development of the 1968 CDO scheme; the Mutual Aid Committees (MACs), intended to provide a direct participatory voice for residents of individual buildings, both in public housing and elsewhere.[90]

The absorption of Resettlement within the new Authority involved significant efforts at reform, reflecting both the difficulties in implementing the 1964 squatter policy, and the new perception that people displaced by public programmes should also be accommodated by Resettlement. An additional built-form challenge stemmed from the fact that the proposed conversion of Mk I and II blocks into larger through-dwellings had met intractable problems of inflexibility and excessive cost, first discovered in the 1968 pilot scheme in a Mk II block at Wong Tai Sin, and then at the start of regeneration of Shek Kip Mei from 1969/70 onwards.[91] Although physical work on Mk I conversion started at Lower Shek Kip Mei in 1972, and in May 1973 the completion of the first stage was celebrated in a visit by the Governor, Shek Kip Mei rapidly became established as mainly a redevelopment rather than improvement project, under the direction of Bernard Williams (who had returned to housing in 1973).[92] (Figures 5.7a–c, 5.8) The new Authority's letting eligibility policies moved away from the income-based criteria of the predecessor bodies, towards broader need-based criteria: between 1973/4 and 1980/1, 34% of HA lettings were for general waiting list applicants, 9% for overcrowding relief in HA estates, 8.5% for emergency rehousing, 21.5% for development clearances (largely corresponding to squatter settlements), 12% for redevelopments of old HA estates, and 15% to other categories. But there were significant shifts over time: emergency rehousing fell from 20% to 5%, and overcrowding and waiting list combined rose from 20% to 50%.[93]

The design and construction practices of the new Authority were also modelled on its predecessor. Here, the role of Liao, as both architect and manager, was crucial, although Fung Tung later expressed scepticism about the HA's 'architect-led' approach. A new Construction Branch was set up, headed by Cheung Sing Hoi, and began a breakneck expansion, from an initial four architects to a target of fifty: in Liao's words, 'We just kept recruiting!'[94] Williams recalls that 'Donald Liao insisted that each architect should manage his own site, whereas Colin Bramwell had delegated everything to clerks of works. This meant huge increases in staff. There was plenty of money. Under MacLehose there was no stinting of money – we could do what we liked! We could create as many posts as we liked in the Housing Authority – we approved our own estimates!'[95] An entire generation of young Chinese architects flooded into the new department, including figures who later exerted great influence on the course of housing design, such as Stephen Poon, or John Ng. Poon recalled that he joined in 1973 'after the announcement of the new Ten-Year Housing Programme, and after Mr Liao took over the helm at the new Housing Authority: I had that hope, of a new mission, and I realised that there were good opportunities for architects'.[96] Old-style expatriate Public Works Department architects, such as Bramwell, were eased out, although allowed to finish off their

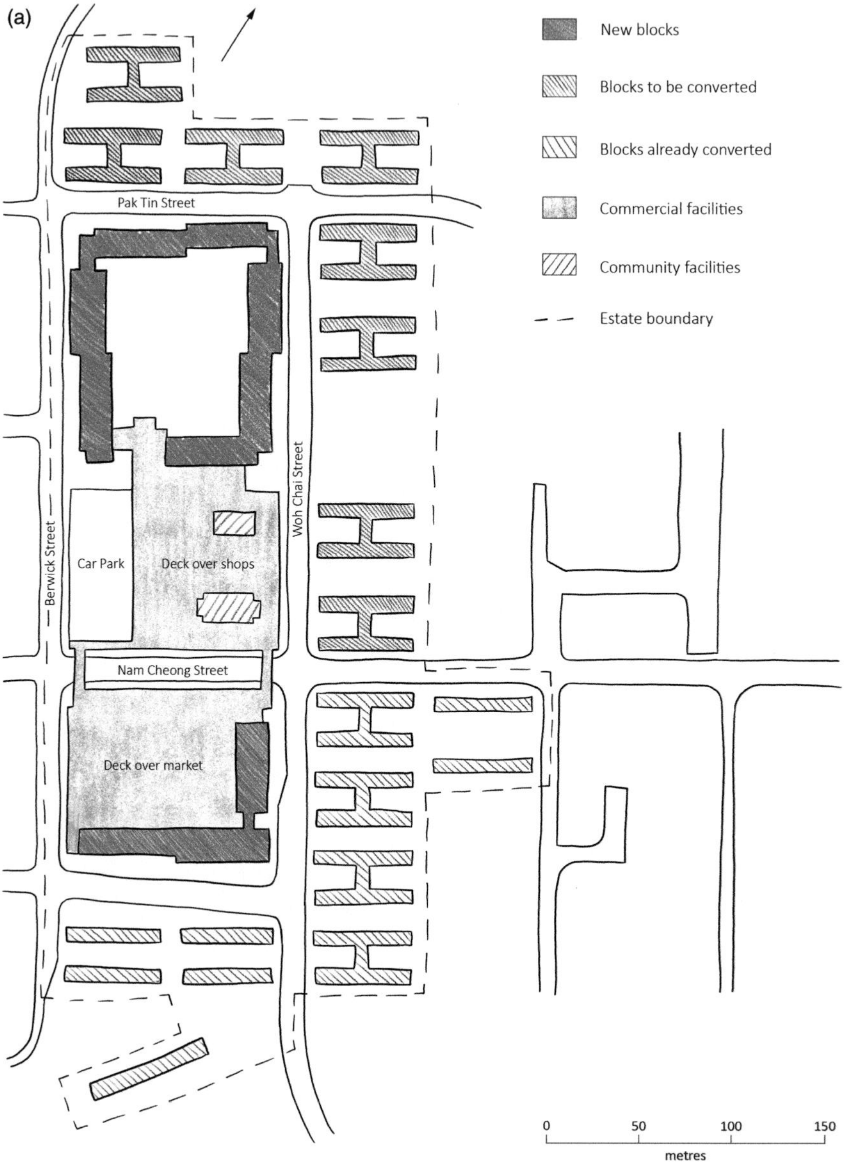

Figure 5.7 (a) Redevelopment plan for Shek Kip Mei, as at 1982. Drawing by Joyce Fu, 2023. (b) Block conversion plan at Shek Kip Mei, as at 1982. Drawing by Joyce Fu, 2023. (c) The Shek Kip Mei redevelopment/conversion operation underway in 1983 (MG).

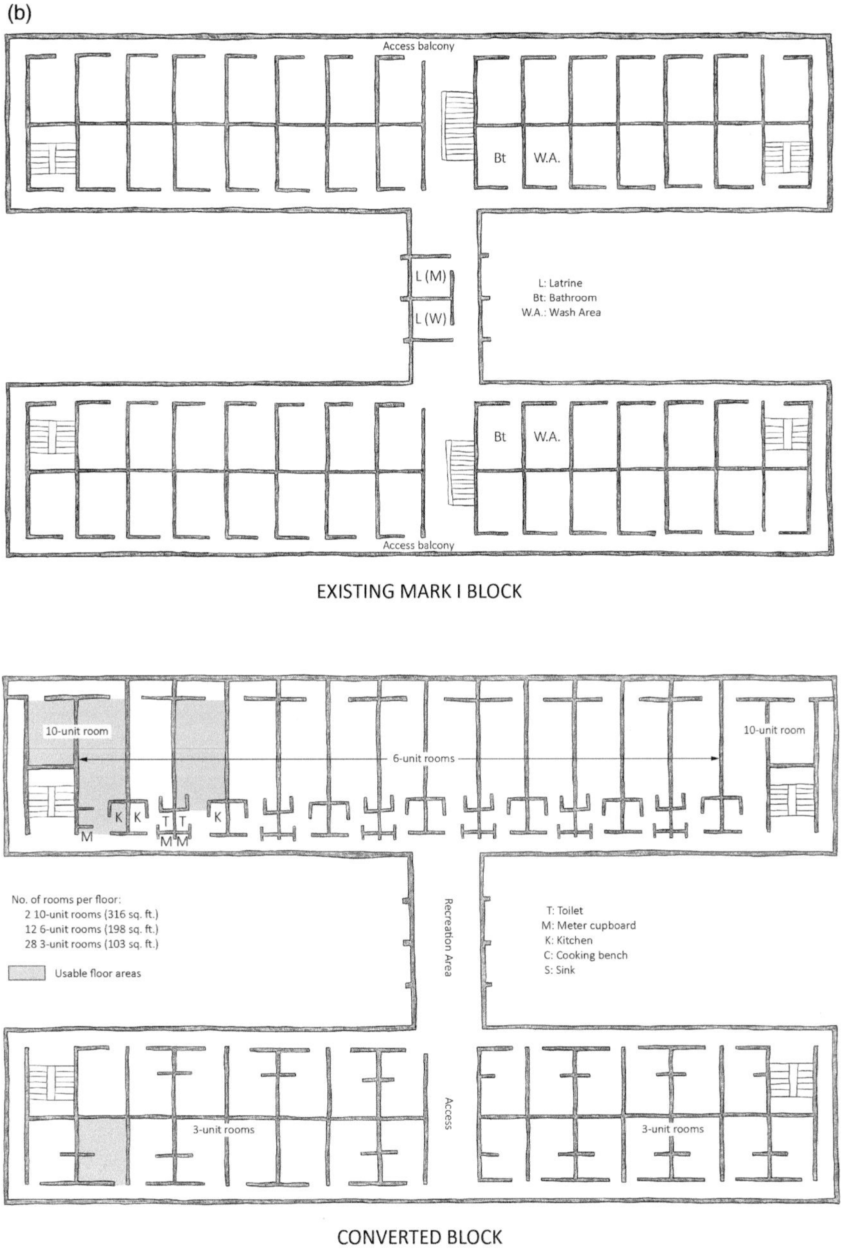

Figure 5.7 (Continued)

Figure 5.7 (Continued)

earlier estates, such as Lek Yuen and Tai Hing (the latter completed 1976). One of Bramwell's team, Freddie Pang, transferred to the new Construction Branch and rapidly assumed a linchpin role. To help bridge the gap between winding down the old system and building up the new, private practices such as Palmer & Turner briefly played a dominant role in some parts of the housing programme in the mid and late 1970s.[97]

Design-wise, the proclaimed ethos of the new programme, enthusiastically endorsed by MacLehose, was that of building for 'community' as opposed to individual 'privacy'. Although 'community' was no more than a common platitude within international modernist discourse, its specific expressions in the ultra-high-density Hong Kong context were in some cases unusual. For example, Liao cited to MacLehose as exemplars of community 'defensible space' the vast, galleried interiors of his twin tower blocks, or of Palmer and Turner's Ping Shek towers.[98] In more practical terms, the design policies of Liao's new department reflected the interaction of the two ideals of minimum space standards and household self-containment, as expressed in IUs. By March 1973, it was assumed that all new housing built by the new Authority would be 'self-contained', but with the important qualification that one- and two-person households would have to share; the first two-bedroom flats were provided shortly afterwards at Oi Man.[99] Prior to April 1973, progress in space standards had been incremental, with discussions in 1971–2 between Lightbody, the Housing Authority and the Public Works Department architects, on possible enhancement of Resettlement standards, and debate about suggestions such as enclosure of balconies.[100] In November 1973, the existing minimum space standard of 35 ft^2, itself a significant expansion of the original Resettlement 24 ft^2, was radically increased to 50 ft^2 for new developments – an autonomous decision by Housing Authority members that caused consternation

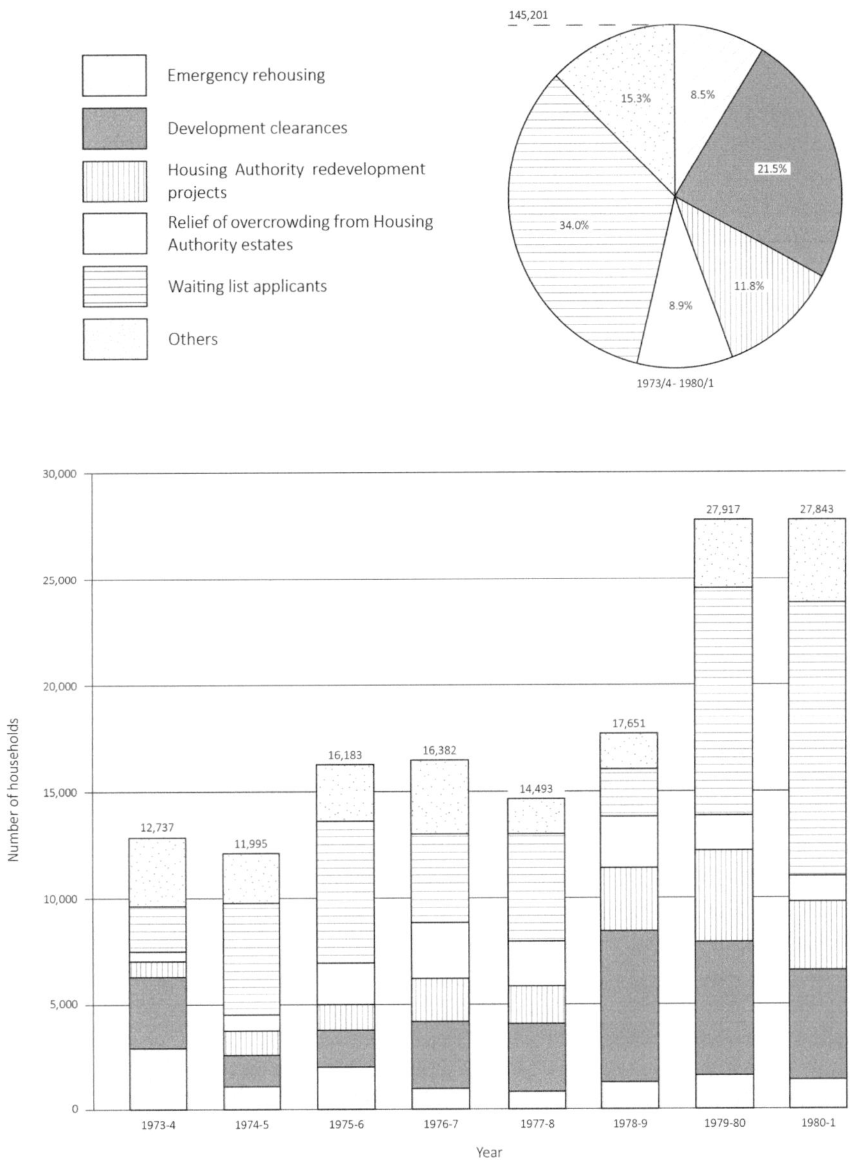

Figure 5.8 Broad categories of households rehoused by HKHA between 1973–4 and 1980–1. Drawing by Joyce Fu, 2023.

in the Finance Department, and prompted awkward questions from MacLehose to Lightbody about the approval process.[101]

Within the new Authority, just as in its predecessors, it was assumed that these radical new demands for mass construction would be answered by continuing the tradition of standard blocks, rather than the flat-based solution that increasingly predominated within Singapore. There was also an implicit opposition between these standard blocks and a more individualistic minority of projects designed for the HA by outside architects in the 1970s. What seemed certain, at any rate, was that any new standard blocks must be very different in approach from the old, utilitarian PWD-designed slabs: Liao cautioned that a Soviet-style 'sausage-machine' approach of ultra-standardisation should be avoided – or, at the least, that any 'sausages' should 'taste good'.[102] 1973 and early 1974 saw intense debate within the Authority, among officials and members, about the advantages and difficulties of the PWD's most recent Mk VI and VII designs, and about whether they could later hypothetically be converted into larger flats. Overall, corridor blocks (as in successive designs from Mk III onwards) were now decisively out of fashion, and HA members were sharply critical of the double-banked corridor planning of recent PWD blocks, because of their supposedly gloomy appearance and the risk of robbery.[103]

What was not, however, challenged by anyone within Hong Kong, was the requirement for ultra-high densities, at least by Western standards. Speaking from the Singapore perspective of strong government land controls, HDB chief architect Liu Thai Ker could smugly deprecate the 'artificially high densities' and land shortages stemming from Hong Kong's laissez-faire property system. But the debates which raged about public housing density within the Housing Authority and the government around 1973–4 pointed further in the other direction, towards a raising rather than lowering of densities – a trend that MacLehose himself strongly endorsed in November 1973.[104] It was seen as vital that any replacement block-types should at least maintain the existing 1,500 ppa standard of 1973, and so the attention of official architects increasingly shifted towards higher, tower-like type-plans. This tendency was anticipated within PWD in the monumental, tapering, cruciform Castle Peak Area 6 (Tai Hing) blocks, but also in the Twin Tower Blocks of Liao's Wah Fu, to which, Poon recalls, all newly joined HA architects were taken as a showpiece in the early 1970s.[105] The same overall layout principles as Wah Fu, including a mixture of Twin Tower and slab blocks, and an integrated commercial centre, were elaborated in the first major estate entirely built by the new Authority, Oi Man ('Love the People'). Fully completed in 1975 and the focus of countless VIP visits, for example from General Gowon or Queen Elizabeth, it was planned for a population of 46,000 and comprised twelve blocks of 7–24 storeys, the latter being Twin Tower Blocks: there were also centre-corridor slabs of 16–18 storeys.[106] Equally important was Lek Yuen, the first housing development in Sha Tin, designed within PWD by Bramwell and Pang with a full range of community facilities. Although its blocks followed more old-fashioned slab configurations, Ted Pryor identified it as Hong Kong's first 'integrated community' estate, and 'the first substantive product of all the efforts' in evolving an integrated, high-density housing development formula: he argued that 'we have not looked back ever since'.[107] As we will see in Chapter 8, by the end of the 1970s the focus would shift to developing standard blocks of much greater heights, above 30 storeys, providing both increased space standards and domestic self-containment – notably the Trident series.[108]

In the construction field, the previous British and Western European experience of industrialised prefabrication in the 1960s and early '70s established it as a potential general aspiration from the outset of the new Authority: MacLehose argued in November 1973 that the labour shortage made it imperative to investigate industrialised building, and in that year Liao visited the UK, followed by a visit by a team of British contractors to Hong Kong, including Wimpey and Taylor Woodrow.[109] However, the territory's overwhelming reliance on traditional construction, and the arguably 'abysmal' standard (at that stage) of much building work, meant that true high-technology or factory-based solutions were not yet remotely feasible.[110] Impetus towards more precise, 'scientific' building methods would only come with the discovery of widespread faults in building construction, culminating later in the so-called '26 Blocks' crisis at Kwai Fong, where serious structural defects found in the mid-1980s in a group of GLCH slab blocks (built 1971–3), led to the eventual demolition of 26 blocks by the HA in 1985–9 (cf. Chapters 6, 9, 10). For now, the focus of innovation was in more restricted fields like semi-mechanised construction or re-usable shattering.[111]

Initially, because of the uncertainties of the reorganisation, and the winding-down of the old Resettlement mass building machine, the quantitative impact of all this seemed uncertain. As early as April 1971, the Urban Council had expressed 'horror' at the plunge in Resettlement building, but this decline subsequently only worsened.[112] From an overall output of 9,434 units in 1973–4, production under the new Authority actually dropped to 5,462 in 1974–5: a 'modest new start', as Prior coyly conceded, although geographer David Drakakis-Smith more bluntly argued that the programme had 'ground to a halt'. Eventually, 220,527 units would be built under the Ten-Year Plan, equating to the housing of 1 million, rather than the 1.8 million individual units proposed.[113]

Revitalising the New Town programme

If the shortage of urban land was the worst constraint on MacLehose's strategy of rapid public-led expansion of mass housing, significant relief of that was promised by his enthusiastic reinvigoration of the New Town programme. Unlike the traditional 'Anglo-Saxon' emphasis on mass slum-clearance of existing urban fabric, MacLehose's Ten-Year Plan was markedly similar in approach to the Continental European *grand-ensemble* formula, with its stress on development at or beyond the urban periphery. In November 1973, Lightbody stressed the government's central policy on housing and land use was to decentralise population to New Towns.[114] From 1973, less than 2% of government housing was let to families displaced by urban renewal; and any suggestion of tackling the intractable problem of the Kowloon Walled City, in particular, was repeatedly deferred.[115] But these New

Towns would need to be approached in a new way, as by the early 1970s a consensus had grown within professional and governmental circles that the 1950s and 1960s satellite townships had degenerated into a haphazard mixture of industrial and residential uses: 1970 saw a vigorous attack on the industrial settlements of Kwun Tong and Tsuen Wan as 'Disaster Areas' by Hong Kong University Prof Gregory, and in 1973 newspapers expressed 'shame' at the 'mess' of Tsuen Wan.[116]

It was widely agreed that a new start was required, one that would incorporate a more planned and coordinated approach, despite the traditional Hong Kong distrust of government planning. That much was stressed by MacLehose, who in December 1971 urged 'proper planning of development in the New Territories'. In his October 1972 speech and an ExCo address, MacLehose stressed that most Ten-Year Plan dwellings must be built in New Towns in the New Territories.[117] During the early 1970s, this shift in emphasis became ever-clearer, not least in papers of November 1973 by Lightbody which argued for an increase in the percentage of the Ten-Year Plan destined for the New Towns, boosting them at the expense of the urban areas.[118] Laid out, in MacLehose's words, as 'integrated New Towns' with their own community and industrial facilities, these would be planned to give every inhabitant 'a full ration of life'. And here, again, there would be no restraint in financial resources: in June 1973, Lightbody explained that $3,000m would be spent on New Town housing and $5,000m on infrastructure, over the Ten-Year Plan period.[119]

However, the ambitious planning aspirations of the New Towns were not, as in Singapore, part of a more homogenising strategic planning framework: in laissez-faire Hong Kong there could be no single unified umbrella body equivalent to the Housing and Development Board (within the Ministry of National Development). Instead, the structure that emerged was multi-headed, with none of the 'heads' exerting any centralised Singapore-style control over land-supply and planning.[120] In July 1972, Public Works Director Robson described the development apparatus in Hong Kong as a 'cluster of tree trunks'.[121] In the view of Liu Thai-Ker, Hong Kong only built 'so-called New Towns'; but it could equally be countered that the results were less homogenous, and more dramatically variegated, as a result. The early 1970s saw incessant debates as to whether government town planning properly belonged to the PWD or the Secretary for the Environment, and a range of official bodies became intermittently involved with it, including the Lands Office, or the Government Central Planning Unit, which also began work in the New Territories.[122] A key coordinating role was played by the LDPC, which in 1973 updated the Colony Outline Development Plan and the following year renamed the latter, in a more post-colonial fashion, the Hong Kong Outline Plan. The proposed reorganisation of the New Territories administration in April 1973 to create new districts, for Tuen Mun, Sha Tin, etc., exempted those from any formal planning by the Crown Lands Office.[123]

However, among all these intersecting agencies, it soon became clear that the key developmental role in the New Towns programme would necessarily be played by the Public Works Department. The PWD, by late 1972, had begun setting up New Town planning teams geared to producing frameworks suitable for the

Ten-Year Housing Programme. Each New Town had a separate multi-disciplinary office and project manager.[124] In November 1974, the PWD Project Manager for Tsuen Wan New Town, Bryan O'Rorke, argued 'good planning' was essential for the New Towns, but made clear this would be a matter of PWD-style engineering coordination, rather than city and regional planning-style coordination.[125] The system was fully ready by March 1973, and in May of that year, a New Towns Progress Committee was set up to manage it, under the oversight of the Colonial Secretariat.[126] The reform was crowned in August 1973 when, following earlier abortive discussions about the setting up of a separate New Towns Department, a New Territories Development Department was created within the PWD, charged principally with preparing and executing the grand strategy of New Town construction in support of the Ten-Year Plan. The New Town planning teams now came under its aegis, as did the management committees for the three initial New Towns.[127]

The new department was headed by Akers-Jones, who was first, in 1973, appointed district commissioner and then, after a few weeks, re-designated Secretary for the New Territories, in a distinct anomaly from the McKinsey formula. He held that post until 1985.[128] Previously, Akers-Jones had become closely involved in the modernisation of New Territories administration. For example, in May 1972, as PACS (Lands), he had chaired a meeting attended by Bramwell, Meyers and others, to discuss the organisation and staffing of Castle Peak (renamed Tuen Mun in 1974) and Sha Tin.[129] Reminiscing in 2014, Akers-Jones recalled the heady atmosphere in the NTDD:

> We were all of us at that time fired up with what we were doing – each town had its own project manager, planners, architects, chartered surveyors. The atmosphere at our meetings was always very positive. It wasn't a case of "Here are some problems, and they're going to stop us!" It was all about how we could overcome the problems. We always went away from the meetings with the feeling, "We're moving on!" And we *did* move on in a huge way – it was wonderful. It was a very happy time, as far as I was concerned. There were a lot of problems, but we were solving those problems, and getting things done![130]

Also crucially involved as New Territories District Commissioner (1971–3) was Denis Bray: in an August 1973 speech he described how New Territories administration had been reorganised around the New Towns, including a new management structure of districts and committees for the three towns. In May 1973, an NTDD sub-committee was instituted under the Public Works Priority Committee to devise development programmes for all public housing, including especially the New Towns.[131]

Within this strategy, unlike the Singapore situation, the formal place of the Housing Department was semi-detached: in some ways it was almost 'client'-like, and it was only loosely subject to planning controls.[132] But in reality, Liao especially was deeply involved in shaping all aspects of the New Towns and their housing-driven development ethos, as were younger HD architects such as Stephen

Poon; the management challenges of such huge tabula-rasa developments were now mainly coordinated by Fung Tung.[133]

A key bridging role was, initially, played by Ted Pryor, who, in his post-1973 role as Assistant Director of Redevelopment and Planning, helped programme the New Towns alongside his own redevelopment work. The development of each New Town was carefully divided by Pryor into 'interrelated but semi-independent packages' of development.[134] In MacLehose's words, the New Towns were designed 'on a "modular" principle, such that the production of schools, police stations, fire stations and public amenities generally kept pace with the development of housing', to ensure they were 'not just dormitories but communities'. The Chief Government Town Planner in February 1974 echoed this theme, hailing the three first New Towns as already being 'balanced, self-sufficient communities' – despite their relative lack of self-contained industry by that date.[135]

In some ways, of course, this programme simply perpetuated, in an updated modern form, the colonial approach of dirigiste surgical remodelling of traditional space.[136] Yet it also made unprecedented concessions to notions of local partnership, reflecting the entrenched and politically controversial traditional land-ownership rights of the New Territories population.[137] Here a vital intermediary role was naturally played by the Heung Yee Kuk, whose reconstitution in the 1958 legislation had transformed it from a disruptive, Communist-infiltrated force to a pro-development organisation dominated by the Hakka rural elites. As early as December 1971, MacLehose pledged to the HYK that it would be fully consulted at every stage in the development strategy for the New Towns and New Territories.[138] In particular, the Kuk would act as the government's chief go-between in negotiations over compensation for land assumptions, and, with the assurance that the financial terms of compensation would be generous, it became an indefatigable supporter of the New Town development and modernisation programme. In a February 1973 speech, the DCNT explained in detail to the Kuk the planned development procedure for the three New Towns, stressing that the explosion of development would need careful planning, and covering resumption procedures in detail.[139]

The core of the procedure was a land-exchange scheme, intended to offset the frustrations of owners of land that was included in the outline zoning plans, and the 1973–6 clearance programme, for the New Towns.[140] The procedure involved the issuing of promissory letters of entitlement to land exchange, known in short as Letters A and B. Although the system had actually existed since 1960, it was only now that it came into its own, and, until its eventual suspension in 1983, largely underpinned the New Town resumption programme.[141] Of the two, it was Letter B (for already-gazetted land) that was far more important, and played a central role in land assembly in all three New Towns. As Pryor noted, the letters of exchange procedure had, by 1981, generated no less than 2,770 serviced hectares of development sites in the New Towns.[142]

As early as 1972, however, challenges to the initial New Towns strategy were emerging, as the LDPC, reviewing the population targets set out in the draft Colony Outline Development Plan, began arguing that cuts in the August 1971 target populations of the New Towns, especially the more distant Tuen Mun and Sha

Tin, might be needed. This might allow some density reductions, although the Kuk pressed for pledges that the New Town programme would continue in some form. In September 1972, it was argued that Tuen Mun could be cut from 1 million to 500,000 total population.[143]

As to the built form of the three initial New Towns, the modular development principle of balanced communities necessitated a systematic approach. Initially, a concept of slightly lower zoned densities than in the urban area was proposed by Pryor and Akers-Jones.[144] But Liao firmly reiterated the need for higher densities, bearing especially in mind the likely pressure on water catchment. In 1974, C Astbury, NTDD chief architect, described the planning of the three New Towns as a game of three-dimensional chess, contrasting their high density, 'full of life', and their reflection of 'the Chinese way of life', with the 'soulless' sprawl of the earlier New Towns in Britain. On his 1973 building-industry tour of Britain and Europe, Liao had also visited key examples of contemporary new town planning, above all Cumbernauld (in July), but also including the privately commissioned, pedestrian-accessible 'Milano Due' residential community in Italy (1971–9).[145]

Of the three initial New Towns, Tsuen Wan was essentially a reformed and enlarged version of one of the earlier, much criticised satellite townships, and had a distinctly higgledy-piggledy industrial and residential core. Its 1973 district outline development plan significantly revised earlier plans of 1967 and 1968, splitting the New Town into three constituent elements. The other two New Towns, Sha Tin and Tuen Mun (originally Castle Peak), were essentially *tabula rasa* foundations, the land being 'carved out' to form their sites.[146] Of the two, the more remote location and poor transport links of Tuen Mun, whose plan was published in July 1972, subtly lowered its status, although Williams emphasised the special dependence of the Ten-Year Plan target on a high rate of building at Tuen Mun.[147]

Unquestionably, the most prestigious of the first three New Towns was Sha Tin, with its combination of a spectacular natural situation, relative closeness to the urban area and good transport links via the Kowloon-Canton Railway, and the unexpected bonus of the construction of a new racecourse complex. Its plan, developed initially between 1965 and 1973, superficially resembled Cumbernauld's in its distinctly linear character. Hailed in January 1970 as a 'huge scheme', and described by PWD director Robson as 'a giant city', progress with the Stage I development, dominated by an accelerated housing programme, was unaffected by the scaling-down of the eventual population target.[148] 1971 saw approval of Sha Tin's first new housing estate, the 'integrated community' of Lek Yuen GLCH estate, planned in Area 8 of the New Town by Bramwell's PWD team: density was 1,000 ppa gross but 1,700 net at the centre of the estate. Phase 1 of Lek Yuen was well underway by 1972, by which stage O'Rorke was significantly involved,[149] and following the formation of the new HA, 1973 saw a renewed declaration of 'full steam ahead' at Lek Yuen. In May, following a report by Akers-Jones that resumption difficulties were delaying the progress of Sha Tin, and a consequent blitz of Letter B designations, the HA Building Committee pressed for Lek Yuen Phase II to be accelerated – which, Liao tactfully pointed out, would mean building blocks of dwellings without any services![150] (Figure 5.9a–c)

Figure 5.9 (a) Acceleration of the Sha Tin project: June 1973 article. (b) March 1973 article on the final phase of GLCH development in the New Territories, and image of Castle Peak Estate (1971; later renamed San Fat Estate). (c) Lek Yuen GLCH Estate, Sha Tin, 1983 view, including commercial centre (MG).

By 1972, Pryor's planning exercises were highlighting the insufficiency of the three original New Towns to support the later years of the Ten-Year Plan, and accordingly, a succession of extensions to the New Town programme began, commencing with the adaptation and expansion into fully fledged New Towns of four smaller market towns, Tai Po, Sheung Shui, Fanling and Yuen Long. Rapidly evaluated in 1972, when the need to preserve the character of Tai Po was emphasised, by 1974 the four proposals were approved, and the first development area plans, including areas 7, 8 and 20 of Fanling, were cleared.[151]

By then, however, the projection of the housing programme forward into the 1980s was highlighting the need to plan beyond even these ad-hoc additions, with potential sites including Junk Bay, for which a first proposal was put forward in 1972, and the north side of Lantau Island. Although as late as June 1972 it was argued that there was no need for building of public housing on Lantau, and that the three original New Towns would be sufficient, by October 1973 MacLehose was openly supporting the investigation of the building of a bridge link to North Lantau.[152] But given the ultimately circular relationship between housing-planning strategy and the sovereignty issue in Hong Kong – the would-be 'model city' – behind all these longer-term issues of New Territories development lurked the ultimate sanction of the ending of the lease in 1997. By the end of the 1970s, this constraint would begin to cast a shadow over not just the New Towns programme but all aspects of the development process – at the same time as the rapid growth of an indigenous Hong Kong real-estate sector presaged future restrictions on the government's freedom of action in land and housing policy.[153] In the next chapter, however, we focus on the way in which MacLehose and his team tackled the more immediate threat from the economic troubles of the early 1970s.

Notes

1 FCO50-547 1973 Annual Review by MacLehose.
2 Mark, 'Development without decolonisation?' 323–4.
3 FCO160-23 Intelligence Reports – Conditions in China, 9.12.1973; Mark, 'Development without decolonisation?' 330–3; J Carroll, *A Concise History of Hong Kong*, HKUP, Hong Kong, 2007, 176; Welsh, *A History of Hong Kong*, 476; FCO40-331 'Long-Term Study of the Future of Hong Kong', 28-6-1971 Wilford to Royle, 27-10-1971 MacLehose to Wilford.
4 Y C Jao, 'The rise of Hong Kong as a financial center', *Asian Survey*, 19 (7), 1979, 674–694. R Y C Tse and S Ganesan, 'Hong Kong', in J Berry and S McGreal (eds), *Cities in the Pacific Rim*, Spon, New York, 1999.
5 FCO40-503 5–1974 MacLehose note.
6 N Annan, *Our Age, Portrait of a Generation*, Weidenfeld & Nicholson, London, 1990, 12.
7 Holdsworth and Munn, *Dictionary of Hong Kong Biography*, 299–302; FCO40-503 8–1974 MacLehose notes.
8 Tsang, *Governing Hong Kong*, 180; FCO40-503 1974 correspondence on MP visits; FCO40-372 5–1972 correspondence on MacLehose visit to London; Akers-Jones, 2014 interview. Makarios – Ray Yep, 'A historical perspective on Hong Kong autonomy', in B C H Fong, T L Lui (eds) *Hong Kong 20 Years after the Handover*, Palgrave Macmillan, London 2018, 246.
9 Lightbody, 2011 interview; Liao, 2010 interview.
10 Lord Wilson, 2023 interview.
11 Little Jemima: Wright, 2011 interview.
12 HKRS1588-2-2 12–1971 first visit to Resettlement and GLCH; HKRS1588-2-5 tea instructions for 22-4-1974 MacLehose visit to Housing Department.
13 Miller, 2014 interview; Liao, 2010 interview; Williams, 2012 interview.
14 FCO40-510 27-5-1974 letter from MacLehose to FCO. Argument that MacLehose and FCO actually believed British rule could be continued after 1997: R Yep and T-L Lui, 'Revisiting the golden era of MacLehose and the dynamics of social reforms', *China Information*, vol 24:3, 2010, 249–272.
15 FCO 40-440 1-1-1973 Annual Review by MacLehose; FCO 40-372, 40–547 Annual Review by MacLehose.
16 Interview with Lord Wilson, 2023. FCO 40-510 27-5-74 MacLehose letter about 'model city' ideal, FCO 40-642 15-3-1975, 1974 Annual Review by Governor; 'Government in a hurry': A Smart and T L Lui, 'Civil disobedience and the rule of law' in R Bickers and R Yep, *May Days in Hong Kong, Riot and Emergency in 1967*, HKUP 2009, 145–159. Chris Patten, *East and West*, Pan, London, 1999, 24–5.
17 Lui Tai-lok, 'Flying MPs and political change in a colonial setting', in Ng and Wong, *Civil Unrest,* 79–80, 86–7. Brown and Foot, *Hong Kong's Transitions, 1842–1997*.
18 Blyth and Wotherspoon, *Hong Kong Remembers*, 122.

19 FCO 40-440 1971 and 1972 Annual Reviews; Holdsworth and Munn, *Dictionary of Hong Kong Biography*, 299–302; Tsang, *Governing Hong Kong*, 140–7.
20 FCO 40–642 MacLehose to Foreign Secretary, 17-4-1982.
21 Williams, 2012 interview; Blyth and Wotherspoon, *Hong Kong Remembers*, 124 (MacLehose on corruption).
22 Blyth and Wotherspoon, *Hong Kong Remembers*, 124–5 (MacLehose) and 148–157 (McGregor); HKRS477-2-4 *China Mail* cutting 12-7-1973, and 9-1973 Woodcraft accusations; HKRS232-1-12-2 *Hong Kong Standard* 14-8-1973 cutting; HKRS530-1-4 2/3-1977 notes: Woodcraft a 'constant critic' of Authority, and advice to ignore him, and *Hong Kong Standard* 23-4-1973 cutting; also Woodcraft vs. corruption, 9/11–1973 and 3–1977.
23 HKRS163-8-113 6–1975 MacLehose on triad shop protection rackets.
24 Blyth and Wotherspoon, *Hong Kong Remembers*, 51.
25 Welsh, *History of Hong Kong*, 463; FCO44-440 Governor's Annual Review for 1972; FCO40-642 MacLehose to Foreign Secretary 17-4-1982.
26 FCO40-292 Trench to Stuart c.1970 on 'not easy to generate public expenditure'; Welsh, *History of Hong Kong*, 478; FCO40-440 Governor's Review for 1972.
27 Akers-Jones, 2014 interview; Welsh, *History of Hong Kong*, 479.
28 FCO40-353 MacLehose 11-9-1971 note.
29 Welsh, *History of Hong Kong*, 479; HKRS 500-6-5 MacLehose 18-10-1972 LegCo address; Williams 1988 Bodleian interview.
30 Pryor, *Housing in Hong Kong*, 67; Kockelkorn, 'Peripheralisation', 620–2; HKRS500-6-5 MacLehose 18-10-1972 at LegCo; HKRS163-8-20; FCO40-642 MacLehose to Foreign Secretary 17-4-1982, FCO40-440 1-1-1973 Annual Review; Akers-Jones, *Feeling the Stones*, 71; HKRS608-1-40 LDPC 26-2-1971, Bramwell on 'integrated community' Government housing estate at Sha Tin, following Governor's September 1970 directive requesting more facilities in housing estates; FCO40-353 1-10-1971 Trench note.
31 HKRS1588-2-2 on original definition 11-1971; HKRS1588-9-3 1972 conversion of Ten-Year Plan to IUs; HKRS163-8-146 memo for ExCo 17-10-1972 on Ten-Year Plan.
32 FCO40-353 25-1-1971 Laird to Wilford and subsequent correspondence.
33 Williams, 2012 interview; FCO40-353 Urban Council minutes 6-4-1971.
34 HKRS163-10-57 MacLehose 9-1972 note.
35 Williams, 2012 interview.
36 Williams, 1988 Bodleian interview; Liao, 2009 and 2010 interviews; Poon, 2009 and 2014 interviews; Akers-Jones, 2014 interview ('droned on'); Miller, 2014 interview; FCO40-1229 evaluation of Haddon-Cave's effectiveness; Blyth and Wotherspoon, *Hong Kong Remembers*, 155, Jimmy MacGregor on Haddon-Cave belittling corruption.
37 Alexander, 1988 Bodleian interview; Williams, 2012 interview; Liao, 2014 interview; HKRS232-1-22-2 SCMP 4-5-1973 and 10-4-1973 cuttings, Elliott letters; Tu, *Colonial Hong Kong*, 62–3.
38 Pryor, *Housing in Hong Kong*, 68.
39 Initially asked: Akers-Jones, *Feeling the Stones*, 72; Pryor, *Housing in Hong Kong*, 68.
40 Pryor, 'Public Housing and I – How Did it All Happen?', undated manuscript recollections, courtesy of Bernard Williams', 1–2; Williams, 2012 interview.
41 Akers-Jones, 2013 and 2014 interviews; Williams, 1988 Bodleian interview; Liao, 2009 and 2014 interview; Lightbody, 2011 interview; Pryor, *Housing in Hong Kong*, 68; Akers-Jones, *Feeling the Stones*, 72.
42 Williams, 2012 interview; Williams, 'Housing in Hong Kong', 12, 19–27.
43 Ten-Year Plan: Williams, *Administration of Public Housing in Hong Kong*.

44 Drakakis-Smith, *High Society*, 108.
45 Williams, 'Housing in Hong Kong'; Williams, 2012 interview; Akers-Jones, 2014 interview; Liao, 2014 interview; Tsang, *Governing Hong Kong*, 117.
46 FCO40-1122 14-5-79 A J Scott to P J Williamson.
47 HKRS600-6-5 MacLehose 18-10-72 Leg Co; HKRS232-1-21-6 11-72 memo; HKRS1588-9-53 1972 papers; HKRS163-8-146 memo for ExCo 17-10-72; HKRS163-10-56 late 1972/early 1973 discussions; FCO46-642 1974 Annual Review report of 15-3-75 by MacLehose.
48 Pryor, *Housing in Hong Kong*, 68.
49 Zhilaia ploshchad: Glendinning, *Mass Housing*, 298, 312.
50 HKRS1588-9-53, HKRS163-8-146; HKRS608-1-40 LDPC 26-2-1971.
51 FCO40-1122 14-5-79 Scott to Williamson on 'HE's often misquoted speech'; Yeung and Wong, *Fifty Years*, 207.
52 Drakakis-Smith, *High Society,* 111–2.
53 FCO160-23; FCO40-547 28-5-1974 letter and report from MacLehose to Foreign Secretary; Nissim, *Land Administration*, 30, on fluctuations in land market.
54 FCO40-547 MacLehose 4-1-1974 note with 1973 Annual Review; FCO40-510 30-5-74 MacLehose to Callaghan; FCO40-642 15-3-1975 note with 1974 Annual Review by MacLehose, and 17-2-1982 letter by MacLehose.
55 FCO40-642 15-3-1975 note with 1974 Annual Review.
56 HKRS500-6-5 2-2-1973 press release; HKRS232-1-22-1 *Hong Kong Standard* 5-2-1973 cutting; HKRS232-1-22-2 3-4-1973 cutting on new HA; HKRS163-10-57 4/5-1973 papers; HKRS177-3-6-1 4-1973 papers on finance, organisation; HKRS1588-2-3 and 1588-2-5; HKRS523-2-2 Liao-Lightbody organisational discussion 23-10-1972, and 2–1973 correspondence between Liao and C Chung, Commissioner for Chinese Language; Mackay, 'Fashion in public administration', 87–9.
57 HKRS895-1-2 1972 correspondence Bray-Akers-Jones; HKRS163-10-56 11-1972 conflicting Robson-Lightbody exchanges, 12–1972 Resettlement-HA staff tension; HKRS1588-9-55 December 1972, Lightbody note to Teh; HKRS1588-4-1, 1588-5-1 10-1971 papers on Resettlement Department structure; HKRS523-2-2 10-1972 organisation chart discussions; HKRS500-6-5 press release 2-2-1973.
58 Fung Tung, 2010 interview, L C Wong, 2011 interview.
59 Liao, 2010 interview.
60 FCO40-510 FCO note of 6-1974 comparing Hong Kong and Singapore.
61 Liu Thai-Ker, 2010 interview; Williams, 2012 interview; HKRS523-2-1/2; HKRS895-1-72 5-1972 correspondence between Bray and Akers-Jones; HKRS1588-9-55 on 'upheaval', MacLehose-Teh correspondence; FCO40-510 FCO note of 6-1974 comparing Hong Kong and Singapore.
62 Fung Tung, 2010 interview; Lightbody, 2011 interview; Williams, 2012 interview; C J Mackay, 'Fashion in Public Administration: The Foundation of the Hong Kong Housing Authority and the Northern Ireland Housing Executive', *International Review of Administrative Sciences*, vol 65 1999, 87–101, on 'technocratic fix' for political crisis.
63 HKRS1588-4-1, 1588-5-1 10-1971 papers on Resettlement Department structure; HKRS523-2-2 10-1972 organisation chart discussions; HKRS232-1-22-1 Hong Kong Standard 5-2-1973 cutting; HKRS232-1-22-2 3-4-1973 cutting on new HA; HKRS163-10-57 4/5-1973 papers; HKRS177-3-6-1; Williams, 2012 and 1988 Bodleian interviews; Williams, 'Administration of Public Housing in Hong Kong', 4.
64 HKRS163-9-1338 2/5-1974 letters; Miller, 2014 interview; Liao, 2014 interview.

65 FCO40-642 MacLehose to Financial Secretary 17-4-1982; Blyth and Wotherspoon, *Hong Kong Remembers*, 122; Williams, 2012 interview.
66 HKRS177-3-6-1 MacLehose 4-1973 speech and papers; HKRS163-10-57 4-1973 note by Scott PAFS.
67 Government loans and nil-premium land: Yeung and Wong, *Fifty Years*, 158; Liao, 2009, 2010, 2014 interviews.
68 HKRS163-7-1 meeting of 14-4-1973 re HA and HD's place in government; HKRS163-8-11 Government House meeting of 11–1973.
69 HKRS177-3-6-1 5-1973 memo, 'The Authority's Finances'; HKRS163-8-2 19-6-1973 Lightbody to Deputy CS.
70 Liao, 2010 interview; HKRS1588-2-3 2–1973 correspondence Liao-C Chung; HKRS1588-2-31 3–1973 papers; Yeung and Wong, *Fifty Years*, 364–7.
71 HKRS177-3-6-1 4-1973 notes on first version of new HA symbol, and 5–1973 papers on estate names; HKRS163-10-57.
72 HKRS177-3-6-1 3-4-1973 memo and 26-4-1973 minutes of first meeting of new HA; HKRS177-3-6-1, 3-4-1973 memo.
73 Williams, 1988 Bodleian interview; HKRS163-10-57 Akers-Jones and MacLehose notes 6–1973.
74 HKRS163-10-57 MacLehose 9–1972 note.
75 Liao, 2010 and 2014 interviews; Akers-Jones, 2014 interview; Tu, *Colonial Hong Kong*, 24; Yeung and Wong, *Fifty Years*, 73.
76 Yeung and Wong, *Fifty Years*, 21–2, 365–7; Williams, 1988 Bodleian interview; Liao, 2009, 2010 and 2011 interviews; Poon, 2014 interview.
77 Tsang, *Governing Hong Kong*, 140–147; HKRS232-1-22-3 5–1973 papers on McKinsey Report; HKRS163-8-10 10-1-1973 MacLehose meetings with each of new policy secretaries.
78 Williams, 2012 interview; Lightbody, 2011 interview; Akers-Jones, 2014 interview (Lightbody was 'quietly moved' away from Housing).
79 HKRS163-10-141; HKRS163-9-1342, 'Movement of Opinion Direction'.
80 Liao, 2011 interview; HKRS545-1-456-1 16-9-1974 Oi Man visit.
81 Liao, 2010 interview; Williams, 2012 interview and 1988 Bodleian interview.
82 HKRS523-2-2, 3–1973 notes; Williams, 'Housing in Hong Kong', 15-16; Williams, 'Administration of Public Housing in Hong Kong', 5-7. HKRS177-3-6-1 3-4-1973 memo; HKRS1548-2-5 22-4-1974 visit to HD; HKRS523-2-2 Alexander, 3-1973 remarks; Lightbody, 2011 interview; HKRS545-1-456-1.
83 HKRS177-3-6-1 26-4-1973 first meeting, MacLehose address and papers HKRS232-1-12-2 3-4-1973 on '10-Year' HA.
84 Williams, 2012 interview and 1988 Bodleian interview; Williams, 'Administration of Public Housing in Hong Kong', 4; HKRS177-3-6-1; Alexander, 1988 Bodleian interview.
85 HKRS523-2-2 4-1973 papers; HKRS523-2-7 2-1972 correspondence Liao-Lightbody; HKRS177-3-6-1 3-4-1973 note on Resettlement estates; HKRS177-3-6-1 3-4-1973 memo. HKRS70-6-789 9-1972 papers, Forsgate on 'pail of worms'.
86 HKRS163-9-1338 2-1974 to 5-1974 letters from Groups A and B managers; Miller, 2014 interview.
87 HKRS163-8-12 Elliott 10-1973 and 8-1975 correspondence; HKRS477-2-4 *China Mail* cuttings of 12-7-1973, and 9-1973 Woodcraft accusations; HKRS232-1-12-2 *Hong Kong Standard* 14-8-1973 cutting; HKRS530-1-4 2-1977, 3-1977 notes (on Woodcraft as a 'constant critic' of HA/HD and advice to ignore him), *Hong Kong Standard* 23-4-1973 article, Woodcraft corruption allegations 9/11-1973, 3-1977.

88 HKRS70-6-88 1973 correspondence; HKRS232-1-23-1 *Hong Kong Standard* 8-2-1974, HKRS232-1-22-3 6-1973 consultation; HKRS477-2-4 2-1974, 8-1974 correspondence; Liao, 2010 interview.
89 HKRS524-3-31 1972-3 papers; Yeung and Wong, *Fifty Years*, 11-3.
90 J L Scott, 'Structure and function in an urban organisation', 1–30.
91 Williams, 2012 interview and 'Administration of Public Housing in Hong Kong' paper; HKRS1588-9-56 late 1972 memo for ExCo; HKRS232-1-20-6, HKRS232-1-21-4, HKRS232-1-22-2, HKRS232-1-22-4, 12-1971 to 7-1973 cuttings; Williams, 2012 interview on vital role of Pryor.
92 HKRS232-1-22-3, HKRS524-2-12 5-1973 report and 7-1973 papers; Williams, 2012 interview; HKRS70-6-789 9-1972 papers; HKRS163-8-20 Secretary for Housing memo of 5-1975 on Pryor redevelopment plan.
93 Pryor, *Housing in Hong Kong*, 94.
94 Fung Tung, 2010 interview; Liao, 2014 interview. HKRS232-1-22-3, *Hong Kong Standard* 12-6-1973 cutting; HKRS545-1-456-1; Lambon, 2012 interview; Liao, 2010 and 2014 interviews; Cheng, 2014 interview.
95 Williams, 2012 interview.
96 Poon, 2009 interview. John Ng, 2012 interview, on aspiration 'to make use of my expertise to serve the maximum number of people'.
97 Williams, 2012 interview; Cheng, 2014 interview; Burns, 2014 interview.
98 Liao, 2014 Interview; Burns, 2014 interview; Ko, 1983 interview.
99 HKRS232-1-22-1 Liao, *Hong Kong Standard* 1-3-1973; HKRS523-2-7 22-3-1972 and 13-3-1973 notes; HKRS177-3-6-1 3-1973 note.
100 HKRS523-2-7 Lightbody to Liao, 2-1972; Lightbody to Principal Government Architect 6-1972, 12-1971 note from Husband, 3-1972 from Cheung.
101 HKRS163-8-11 Government House meeting 11-1973; Fung Tung, 2010 interview.
102 Liao, 2011 interview; Williams, 'Housing in Hong Kong', 23.
103 HKRS523-2-7 13-3-1973 Liao to Cheung; HKRS523-2-7; HKRS1588-9-53 1972 papers; HKRS177-3-6-1 Sept 1973 HA papers.
104 Liu Thai-Ker, 2009 and 2010 interviews; Liao, 2010 interview; Akers-Jones, 2014 interview; Pryor, HKRS163-8-11 11-3-1973 Government House meeting; 163-8-1, Lightbody 11-1973 paper.
105 HKRS523-2-7 13-3-1973 Liao to Cheung; HKRS163-8-1; HKRS232-1-23-1 SCMP 16-1-1974 cutting; HKRS177-3-6-1 9-1973 papers; HKRS232-1-21-5 SCMP 23-5-1973, and *Hong Kong Standard* 22-5-1973 cuttings; 4 HKRS38-4-1 4-1977 papers; Ko, 1983 interview; Poon, 2009 interview (on Wah Fu visits). HKHA, *The First Two Million*, Hong Kong, 1980, 20, 23-4, 28-9.
106 HKRS1588-2-5 4-1975 papers; HKRS70-6-821-2; HKRS70-6-811-2 cuttings; HKRS545-1-456-1 16-9-1974 papers on Gowon visit. HKHA, *The First Two Million*, HK, 1980, 22. *Far East Architect & Builder*, 3-1968, 35.
107 HKRS177-3-6-1 mid 1973 description; HKRS608-1-40 LDPC 26-2-1971 minutes; E Pryor, 'Public Housing and I'. Liu, 2009 interview.
108 Liao, 2011 interview.
109 HKRS232-1-22-22-4 7-1973 Liao-UK correspondence, SCMP 11-7-1973 on UK experts; Liao, 2010 interview.
110 Burns, 2014 interview; 'Abysmal': Ko, 1983 interview and Gabriel, 2009 interview.
111 For example, a specific construction failure was pointed out to Liao in the 1970s, much to his embarrassment, by a group of Italian visitors: Liao, 2014 interview. Tai Hing: Ko, 1983 interview.

112 FCO40-353 6-4-1971 note.
113 'Modest new start', Pryor, *Housing in Hong Kong*, 90; Drakakis-Smith, *High Society*, 112; Yeung and Wong, *Fifty Years*, 22: 'only' 220,527 units built under Ten-Year Plan.
114 HKRS163-8-1 11-1973 Lightbody paper.
115 Drakakis-Smith, *High Society*, 155; HKRS232-1-21-6, SCMP28-12-1972 cutting; HKRS232-1-22-1 SCMP 1-4-1973 cutting.
116 HKRS545-1-447-2 1970 lecture by Gregory; HKRS232-1-22-6 3-9-1973 cuttings; HKRS163-9-931.
117 HKRS232-1-20-6 30-12-1971 MacLehose note; HKRS168-8-146; HKRS232-1-21-1; HKRS163-8-20; HKRS500-6-5.
118 HKRS163-8-1 11-1973 Lightbody paper; HKRS163-8-11 11-1973 meeting.
119 HKRS163-08-11 11-1973 meeting with MacLehose; HKRS232-1-22-2 *Hong Kong Standard* 19-3-1973 cutting, HKRS163-8-1 11-1973 paper; HKRS232-1-22-1 *Hong Kong Standard* 19-3-1973 on 'full ration'; HKRS232-1-22-3 22-6-1973 Lightbody on Ten-Year Plan.
120 HKRS232-1-22-2 *Hong Kong Standard* 16-4-1973 note.
121 HKRS163-8-20 8-7-1972 Robson note.
122 HKRS232-1-22-2 SCMP 29-3-1973 cutting; HKRS232-1-22-4 SCMP 27-8-1973 cutting; HKRS232-1-22-6 SCMP 2-9-1973 cutting; HKRS710-3-3 4-1973 to 2-1974 papers on Central Planning Unit. Liu Thai-Ker, 2012 interview.
123 HKRS895-1-52 12-1973 discussions; HKRS608-1-41 6-1974, Circular 16-74; HKRS163-9-931 LDPC 9-1973 and 4-1973 correspondence from District Commissioner New Territories; FCO40-620 12-75 on discontinuance of term 'colony'.
124 Lightbody, 2011 interview, PWD 'set the pace'. HKRS938-1-12 7-1973 onwards on Pryor; HKRS232-1-21-6 Hong Kong Standard 16-11-1972 cutting; HKRS337-4-6542 11-5-1973 meeting. Project manager and team: Pryor, *Housing in Hong Kong*, 73; Liao, 2010 interview; Poon, 2009 interview, Akers-Jones, 2013 and 2014 interviews.
125 HKRS232-1-23-6 SCMP 8-11-1974 B O'Rorke paper.
126 HKRS232-1-22-2 SCMP29-3-1973; HKRS337-4-6542 seventh meeting of NTPC 11-5-1973.
127 HKRS710-3-3 1973-4 discussions on formation of separate department; HKRS608-1-49 Departmental instruction 17-1973 re NTDD; HKRS163-9-931 DC Bray papers 4/6-1973; Williams Bodleian 1988 interview on NTDD.
128 Akers-Jones, 2014 interview; Fung Tung, 2010 interview; Akers-Jones, *Feeling the Stones*, 92-5, 113-4; HKRS232-1-22-6 SCMP 2-9-1973 cuttings.
129 HKRS337-4-4337 4-5-1972 meeting.
130 Akers-Jones, 2013 and 2014 interviews.
131 HKRS163-9-931 Bray 4-1973, 8-1973 papers; HKRS176-11-18 5-1975, 9-1974 papers on NTDD subcommittee.
132 HKRS163-8-51 7-1975 papers; Williams, Bodleian 1988 interview.
133 Liao, 2009 and 2010 interviews; Fung Tung, 2010 interview.
134 HKRS938-1-12 papers from 7-1973 onwards; Williams, 2012 interview; Pryor, *Housing in Hong Kong*, 73.
135 Blyth and Wotherspoon, *Hong Kong Remembers*, 122 (MacLehose); HKRS545-1-447-2 2-1974 note by Government planner.
136 On the reverse link from colonial discourses to new town planning in the 'post-colonial metropole', see Jesse Meredith, 'Decolonising the New Town: Roy Gazzard and the making of Killingworth Township', *Journal of British Studies*, 57, April 2018, 333-362.
137 Hung, *City on the Edge*, 31-3.

138 Hung, *City on the Edge*, 31-3; SCMP 30-12-1971 MacLehose to Kuk; HKRS163-9-474 DCNT to Kuk 9-2-1973; HKRS232-1-21-1, *Hong Kong Standard* cutting 11-7-1972.
139 Blyth and Wotherspoon, *Hong Kong Remembers*, 145-7; HKRS163-9-474 DCNT to Kuk 9-2-1973.
140 HKRS895-1-24 1973-6 papers on clearance programme.
141 HKRS895-1-52 12-1973 papers on resumptions at Tsuen Wan; HKRS163-9-474 DCNT to Kuk 9-2-1973.
142 Letter B: Nissim, *Land Administration*, 121-6, and Richard Wong, *Hong Kong Land for Hong Kong People*, HKUP, Hong Kong, 2015. HKRS337-4-6542 11-5-1973 New Towns Progress Committee; HKRS232-1-22-4 LDPC 29-6-1973 minutes; Liao, 2010 interview; Akers-Jones, 2013 and 2014 interviews; Fung Tung, 2010 interview, Lightbody, 2011 interview. Pryor, *Housing in Hong Kong*, 81.
143 HKRS608-1-40 LDPC 28-1-1972 minutes and SCMP cuttings 30-6-1972, 29-9-1972.
144 HKRS163-8-20 15-5-1974 Pryor to Liao on possible increase in estate density from 1,000 to 1,120 ppa; Akers-Jones, 2014 interview; Williams, Bodleian 1988 interview.
145 Liao, 2009 interview; HKRS232-1-23-1 Astbury 1974 memo; HKRS232-1-22-4 7-1973 Liao tour. Cumbernauld: Liao, 2010 and 2014 interviews.
146 HKRS176-11-19 4-1973 and 5-1974 papers; Liao, 2010 interview.
147 Liao, 2010 interview on comparison of Sha Tin and more 'scattered' Tuen Mun; Williams, 2012 interview.
148 HKRS232-1-21-1 1-1972 cuttings, *Hong Kong Standard* 4-3-1973 and 5-6-1973 cuttings; HKRS232-1-21-2, *Hong Kong Standard* 28-2-1972, SCMP 21-2-1972 cuttings.
149 HKRS608-1-40 2-1971 papers. Akers-Jones, 2014 interview; Williams, 2012 interview.
150 HKRS163-8-23 22-11-1973 Liao note; HKRS163-9-474; HKRS337-4-4337; Poon, 2009 interview on Sha Tin procedure.
151 Liao, 2010 interview; HKRS608-1-40 LDPC 6-1972 minutes; HKRS176-11-18 9-1974 papers.
152 Junk Bay: HKRS608-1-41 1972 papers; Lantau, SCMP 22-6-1973 and 25-6-1973; HKRS163-8-66 10-1973 papers; HKRS176-11-18 9-1974 papers.
153 Blyth and Wotherspoon, *Hong Kong Remembers* (MacLehose, pp. 299–302).

6 1973–1976

Utopia on hold – from crisis management to programme planning

MacLehose's 'breathing space'

By 1974, although the internal communist threat had dissipated, confining protest disorder to isolated social problems such as rent increases, the overall climate had become gloomier, owing to the mounting economic problems: although the territory's transformation into a global financial metropolis was just over the horizon, it was not yet fully visible. A 30% drop in land prices in the six months to April 1974 was highlighted as a significant 'threat' to government revenue by Haddon-Cave.[1] Where MacLehose in April 1973 had confidently asserted there was 'no shortage of money', now the economic position seemed very different, and MOOD surveys recorded a steep decline in public support for government. Highlighting the sense of crisis, a tanker full of crude oil was anchored off Hong Kong from 1973 onwards.[2] The decolonisation process was becoming perceptible, with the implementation of MacLehose's decision to 'drop colonial language' in the wake of the 1972 United Nations decision, including the terms 'colony' (finally removed in 1975) and 'Colonial Secretary' (changed to 'Chief Secretary' in 1976). And the issue of '1997' was beginning to emerge more clearly, with the end date of individual New Territories leases seen as a particular problem, and the lower middle classes identified as the group most likely to be disadvantaged under any post-1997 'communist form of government'.[3]

MacLehose's reports to the FCO vividly reflected his mounting disappointment and frustration: in mid-1974 he argued that 'much has gone wrong' and that his reforms were meeting 'serious teething problems' just when the social programmes had been 'beginning to bite'. He firmly blamed the programme delays on the combined impact of the 1972 rises in Chinese commodity prices, and the 1973 oil crisis and world slump. The MTR metro project, too, had been severely impacted, when the Japanese company awarded the contract walked away.[4] A confidential May 1974 report to Foreign Secretary James Callaghan summed up the current predicament. While the original plan had been to exploit the booming economy by financing its programmes at constant taxation rates, raised taxes and borrowing now seemed possible – although Hong Kong capitalists' continuing need for quick profits and low-tax solutions to reclaim investment, and reliance on exports, remained undiminished. He stressed that 'Hong Kong continues to exist

DOI: 10.1201/9781315563701-8

because the CPG [Central People's Government] considers it beneficial, the political disadvantages being outweighed for the time being by other considerations'. But as he argued the previous year, the resulting 'breathing space' must be used with urgency.

> Both for these political reasons, and in any case because I'm sure it is what HMG would wish on its merits, we should go for Hong Kong as a model city. But we should do so from a low posture, saying little, and throwing down no overt challenge to China... I think we should also get a move on.

The original draft plans may have been 'attempting to do too much too quickly', and while the enforced re-phasing was 'extremely disappointing', the 'model city' vision would still be achievable if the economy revived as anticipated.[5] (Figure 6.1)

The existential motivation of MacLehose's strategy, and its linkage to both sovereignty and identity, made it surprisingly similar to the position faced by Singapore and Lee Kuan Yew between 1959 and 1965. In both cases, external sovereignty was limited, and housing and social services provided an alternative way, perhaps the only alternative way, to visibly establish power, and even survive as a 'city state' entity. The difference was the stronger position of the PAP government

Figure 6.1 MacLehose inspects progress at the Fu Shan Estate, Diamond Hill, in 1977 (SCMP image).

in Singapore, a strength bolstered by a policy of strident ideological projection that was the opposite of Hong Kong's 'low posture, saying little'.[6]

London tensions with Labour

By mid-1975, MacLehose felt that Hong Kong was past the worst of the crisis, but he now also had severe family problems to deal with, as his daughter's serious illness required a stepped-up frequency of London visits. The visit by Queen Elizabeth in May 1975 was framed as a morale-boosting respite, and included a visit to the Housing Department's new showpiece estate, Oi Man, fully opened in November 1975 – and MacLehose hoped that this might coincide with the crime figures turning the corner.[7]

By then, however, his London interlocutors had significantly changed, following the 1974 installation of a Labour government unsympathetic to Hong Kong's laissez-faire system and inclined to react to its claims of crisis with scepticism: despite his own Labour leanings, he would find pre-1979 Labour a less sympathetic London partner than the post-1979 Tories. During the mid-1970s the FCO dismissed warnings by Haddon-Cave that Hong Kong was 'spending beyond its means', as being excuses to avoid London pressure for higher taxes or public spending: the crisis, they argued in March 1974, reflected an 'uneven road surface' rather than 'imminent collapse of the suspension'.[8] Some Hong Kong–London differences simply continued from before, such as over the death penalty. But for Labour ministers such as Foreign Secretary James Callaghan or junior minister Goronwy Roberts – a working-class socialist and Welsh-language activist – the most keenly felt priority was the enhancement of trade union rights within Hong Kong. (Figure 6.2) They pressed a TUC-supported proposal that trade-unionists should be appointed to LegCo, a suggestion that risked provoking clashes between communist and KMT union groupings and was successfully fended off by MacLehose for over two years. Many in the Hong Kong establishment, whether

Figure 6.2 Goronwy Roberts, Minister of State for Foreign and Commonwealth Affairs and MacLehose's principal mid-1970s FCO 'adversary': 1955 image.

expatriate or Chinese, saw the Labour agenda as stemming not so much from ignorance of Hong Kong's conditions as from a thinly veiled economic-nationalist protectionism dictated by British labour interests: in 1977, MacLehose told an FCO official that he was privately convinced that the National Union of Tailors and Garment Workers (NUTGW) 'would like to see Hong Kong under the sea'.[9]

Behind these specific differences swirled more generalised cultural conflicts, ultimately stemming from a combination of the rise of state-dirigiste economic nationalism in postwar Britain, and laissez-faire Hong Kong's success in securing autonomy within the late-colonial system.[10] Some concerned the tone of communications, with Hong Kong accused in January 1975 of 'small-town stridency', and Haddon-Cave of losing his temper in 1975 with visiting Labour MPs. Others concerned the diametrically opposed attitudes to public spending, with London questioning the Hong Kong government's 'insistence that Hong Kong should pay its way', and Hong Kong insisting that tax rises above an absolute maximum of 20% would destabilise the economy.[11] Even more fundamental were the conflicting superiority complexes of the British social-nationalist and Hong Kong laissez-faire *Weltanschauungen*. Already in 1973, visiting Labour MP Robert Hughes (later notorious in Scotland as one of the MPs who voted in 1979 to overturn the devolution referendum rights) had claimed, without citing any specific examples, that the lack of union rights in Hong Kong had caused general government 'maladministration', and demanded greater compliance with British Labour dogmas. And in 1975, Labour Party officials demanded that the 'repression' in Hong Kong – 'worse than South Africa', in their view – should be replaced by 'democratic, socialist' practices.[12] FCO official Edward Larmour expressed perplexed annoyance that Hong Kong people at all levels had 'no understanding of the social changes taking place in Great Britain and the rationale for them', and thus, infuriatingly, 'regard themselves as a success while they look on the UK as a failure'.[13] Haddon-Cave was a particular bete-noire of London, with his often sardonic, if not confrontational, public pronouncements concerning British welfare-socialist shibboleths: his speeches defending the Hong Kong system were condemned as 'ideological' by Goronwy Roberts, and by Rowlands as being pervaded with 'Victorian attitudes'.[14] By contrast, Elsie Elliott, although essentially a colonial philanthropist rather than a Fabian-style welfare-statist, was favoured by Labour as a kindred spirit, and MacLehose had in December 1976 to fight off Goronwy Roberts's pressure to appoint her to LegCo, as being likely to be 'divisive and disruptive' of the Council's work, and 'unacceptable to many people in Hong Kong'.[15]

In this context, MacLehose's housing drive was a useful distraction, as an area of social spending that the Hong Kong Government actively wanted to expand, and whose successes could help not just to distract attention from Hong Kong's preferred inaction in labour relations, but also to deflect the growing London pressure for introduction of a European-style social security system financed by a 'progressive' system of higher taxes.[16] In mid-1976, MacLehose was faced with mounting pressure from Goronwy Roberts and other FCO ministers and UK trade union leaders for the negotiation of a 'Plan of Action' or 'Planning Paper' – to be kept confidential to conceal its autonomy-diminishing character – that would set a mandatory timetable for this. However, the continued rapid growth of GDP (in 1976, by 16% rather than the 9% anticipated) and his own trumpeting of Hong Kong's housing achievements, repeatedly gave MacLehose an escape route, until in December 1976, the London ministers escalated the dispute by demanding the right to vet Haddon-Cave's budgets – a suggestion that MacLehose greeted with 'horror', as likely to deprive the budget process of any ability to react to short-term economic changes.[17]

The extent to which MacLehose could defensively exploit the achievements of the housing programme was, however, constrained by the chasm in housing-standards expectations between Britain and Hong Kong. The London view of Hong Kong's housing was naturally conditioned by the general 1970s British prejudice against high-rise flats: deputy under-secretary of state Edward (Nick) Larmour argued there was 'a lot to be ashamed of' in Hong Kong's new 'government-subsidised slums'. Continued housing improvements were essential if the defence was to be maintained: in 1976 London conceded that social-security reforms could be deferred so long as housing output was maintained and standards continued to improve.[18] Ultimately, of course, the clashes with London Labour ministers were of only transient significance, as a distraction from the real issues of sovereignty facing Hong Kong. And MacLehose's strategy, no less than like London's, involved social improvements, only of a different kind and for a different purpose – to burnish Hong Kong's international image during the 'window of opportunity' before the likely start of sovereignty negotiations.

The crisis economics of housing

Owing to housing's special role within MacLehose's reform programme, the economic crisis years saw a widening disparity between the recession's wider impact and the strenuous attempts to protect the housing programme from its worst effects. As always, '1997' lay behind this. In March 1975, MacLehose's Annual Review argued that while in 1974 the territory had 'tightened its belt', now in 1975 'the pinch is hurting'. Hong Kong's 'peculiar fiscal limits', he reasoned, reflected the need to maintain investor confidence, which required a more 'attractive' economic environment than rivals such as Singapore and South Korea; yet all the time the window of opportunity was narrowing to 'make good' social deficiencies before the 'shadow' of 1997 would begin to fall in the early 1980s.[19] By January 1975, the FCO was warning that the main problem was 'the financial and budgetary difficulties of completing the Governor's programme in the planned time-scale'. The programmes were predicated on a 7% annual growth rate in real terms, and MacLehose argued that 'I think we can hold our line in 1974'.[20] In August 1975 the FCO warned that the money to keep the social programmes going was under severe threat.

The result was a constant shifting and juggling of housing output figures. Writing several years later, in 1979, the then Secretary for Housing, Alan Scott, argued that the oil recession of 1973–4 had interrupted a climb towards an 'intended target of 40,000' annual completions. And in July 1975, the SCMP argued there would be a housing shortage even if the Ten-Year Plan was fully implemented, as it was only sufficient to house 1.2 million people. The reason, they claimed, was a combination of cuts and delays in New Town infrastructure provisions, and the effect of inflation in reducing the amount that any given allocation could build. Thus, the Ten-Year Plan would become a 12- to 15-year plan, and 'by then, the plan will have become open-ended'.[21]

Alarm bells began ringing at the beginning of 1974, when Haddon-Cave signalled that the social programmes stemming from MacLehose's 'new-look approach to the administration of the colony' might constitute 'spending beyond means', given the reliance of the social programmes on GDP growth.[22] He estimated the rise in GDP from 1974 would taper by half, to 4% – an evaluation seen as optimistic by the FCO. Although the public service overall was 'growing at a rapid, if not alarming, rate', the housing burden seemed particularly acute. T W Aston, the senior British Trade Commissioner, argued in March 1974 that 'it is almost as if the Financial Secretary feels an almost personal resentment at the way the housing programme has mushroomed beyond… the ability to control it', and MacLehose himself conceded in a February 1974 telegram that the new social programmes had 'an indigestible hump' in 1975–8, which was now threatened by the economic crisis.[23] Yet the practical reality was that the housing programme was politically sacrosanct, and Haddon-Cave maintained good working relations with Liao throughout the oil crisis – reflecting MacLehose's May 1974 warning that Hong Kong's 'government in a hurry' must still 'get a move on', to make use of its 'breathing space' by bettering the lives of the Hong Kong 'masses'.[24]

Indeed, the percentage of spending on housing steadily continued climbing, from 6% of total public expenditure in 1972–3 to 10–11% in 1974–5. This stemmed not just from protection from cuts, but from a still favourable underlying macroeconomic reality. As Akers-Jones later emphasised, the economy – short-term fluctuations notwithstanding – was continuing to expand overall: per-capita GDP rose from $35,252 in 1974 to $47,379 in 1975 and $63,500 in 1978.[25] Between 1971 and 1982 the size of the public service would increase by 77%, and public expenditure would mushroom by 223% in real terms.[26]

But that underlying favourable balance was only dimly visible to the actors on the ground, who were preoccupied with the crises immediately confronting them. In July 1974, Liao had suggested using expanded Development Loan Fund loans to support the housing programme,[27] but by December, in the lead-up to the 1975–6 budget, significant cuts were being proposed in ancillary elements within the New Town development packages: at Lek Yuen Estate, for example, only one secondary school would now be provided.[28] The finalised 1975–6 budget envisaged a 7% drop in tax revenue, potentially leading to a $2,238 million deficit – a situation of 'acute financial stringency'. So Haddon-Cave proposed $467 million in new taxes, $489 million in loan finance, and $1,442 million cuts in the Estimates.[29] For the first time, budget deficit and loan financing was envisaged – although 'this path followed too far leads to hell rather than heaven', MacLehose argued, and 'could easily be self-defeating'. He counselled extreme caution in relation to the 'over-bold fiscal policy' being pressed on Hong Kong by the Labour government in London.[30] During the mid-1970s at least, MacLehose conceded, 'the really dramatic expansion in public housing we had hoped for must be re-phased' – deferrals duly reflected in the Public Works estimates for 1975–6, to reduce housing and public works demands on the Development Loan Fund.[31] And in a 1982 valedictory letter he estimated that the 'deep recession' of 1973–5 had delayed his social programmes overall by two years – as had the fresh influx of over 400,000 refugees in 1978–80.[32]

Yet as the budget proposals began to emerge in February 1975, by comparison with other areas of government the outcome seemed surprisingly 'good news' for the Housing Department, which appeared to have been protected by Haddon-Cave. By September, MacLehose was already speculating that Hong Kong had now 'touched bottom', and by November, exports were recovering distinctly from their low point earlier in the year.[33] In February 1976, he was arguing optimistically that while the recession had undoubtedly led to a cut in DLF support for the HA, overall the net impact on housing had been minimised.[34] And by the time of MacLehose's Governor's Speech to LegCo in October 1976, the programme seemed well back on track, and coherently structured by a new 'Housing Programme Plan' framework (HPP – see below). Reasserting his target of self-contained housing 'for all, and within the means of all' – an aim that combined output quantity with careful calibration of rents – MacLehose confidently predicted that 'the back of the problem should be broken by 1984'.[35] With the recession still depressing output, Hong Kong must build for over 200,000 people a year, or risk jeopardising 'social cohesion' – with a vital supplementary role in boosting production to be played, as we will see in Chapter 7, by a new programme of low-cost housing for home-ownership. The rise in the housing share of public spending from 6% in 1972–3 to 11% in 1974–5 would now allow a huge acceleration in production, as the economy recovered from 1976 onwards.[36] While the HA's capital budget for 1975–6 had allowed $96 million in capital expenditure, that for 1976–7 had soared to $235 million, of which $135 million came from DLF loans, $94m from Group A rent surpluses, and $6m from shop rents.[37]

The Housing Authority's finances and management practices – towards consolidation

Public housing in general, then, was protected from the worst of the early 1970s spending cuts. But the financial position of the Housing Authority was at the same time coming into increasing prominence, and 1973–7 saw mounting concern as to how to combat its increasing indebtedness, This, among other outcomes, led to the initiation of a potential Asian Development Bank loan for some housing projects in Sha Tin. At the outset, it was established that both the Housing Authority and the Urban Council had to be accounted for separately from government.[38] 1974–5 had witnessed a succession of attempts to reorganise the HA's financial support. To begin with, rents were raised during 1974 to help cut the huge deficits on the Group B ex-Resettlement estates (where rents would rise by 20–50%) and support the new building programme.[39] In the event, the fear of 'spontaneous outbreaks of disorder' led to a volte-face: what was initially greeted as the first 'real' rent increase since 1954 was eventually deferred until September 1975 under the Landlord and Tenant Ordinance.[40] There were only small increases in Group B and larger increases in Group A, with significant variations within that sector: whereas a seven-person flat at Lek Yuen rose to $200 per month, the equivalent at Oi Man cost $330 – a uniquely high level within the HA's mainstream stock, reflecting Oi Man's prestigious location. Charges of oppressing the poor were promptly levelled at the HA by Elliott and others.[41] More generally, in January 1976, the Chairman's Review for the HA *Annual Report* bemoaned funding shortages as the cause of programme hold-ups, and urged an improvement in the Authority's finances.[42] As we will see in the next chapter, this improvement would soon be put in hand.

To help him decide how best to bolster the financial position of the Authority, MacLehose had briefly visited Singapore on a fact-finding trip in June 1975, staying with Lee Kuan Yew at the Istana, where the two avidly 'swapped notes'.[43] He was all too aware of Singapore's superiority complex vis-a-vis Hong Kong in housing, a comparison which Lightbody's successor as Housing Secretary, Alan Scott, emphasised was 'not new… and usually made in ignorance of the methods of funding public housing in Hong Kong and Singapore'.[44] MacLehose found that the HDB was financed by loans from the government, including the Provident Fund, at 6% over 10 years for home-ownership estates, and 7.75% over 60 years for rental projects. The HDB paid property tax at 36% but in compensation received a direct subsidy which in the previous year amounted to SGD 30m – cancelling out the property tax liability. More generally, he found that Singapore public housing efforts were pitched at a more up-market class of occupant, often straightforwardly middle-class: a low percentage of public housing went to resettlement displacees, and 70% to waiting list cases, and it could be argued that the HDB programme, unlike Hong Kong's, had deliberately distanced itself from the worst housing needs. Rents had only been raised once, by 15%.[45] MacLehose was of course struck by the unified, dirigiste Singaporean approach, inherited ultimately from Fraser's SIT, and by the 'Home-Ownership for the People Scheme' (see Chapter 7). In design terms, as MacLehose freely acknowledged after the trip, Hong Kong's space standards, dictated specifically by the need to keep within rental means, cover management costs, and repay development costs within 40 years (and also constrained more generally by Hong Kong's endemic land-supply shortage), produced far smaller housing units on average – although he stressed that the HA was now building two-bedroom flats for larger families.[46]

Up to March 1976, the Housing Authority had cumulatively drawn HK$300 million in loans from the DLF, and November 1976 saw an initial reform proposal to cancel the large inherited debts from the Group B estates. But in 1977, immediately following the recession, a far more expansive, free-spending reform strategy was implemented. The HA would no longer have to pay land premiums, but land value would be included within its balance sheet.[47] Reflecting the expanded scope of the Authority, its interim head office at 1 Ma Tau Kok Road, inherited from the Resettlement Department, was replaced by 1976 by a purpose-built complex at Princess Margaret Road, Oi Man.[48] As we saw in Chapter 5, its membership reflected the severance of the link with the Urban Council and the selective co-opting of UC unofficials, such as Forsgate and Elliott. Others, correspondingly, were marginalised: Brook Bernacchi, for instance, complained in February 1974 that he had been moved 'sideways' and immediately started to attack the HA's policies – for example in a speech at the Council claiming 'management problems' and 'licensed area space shortages', which prompted a sharp rebuke from Lightbody.[49]

In the process of establishing the Housing Department's operations on a stable basis, a key role was initially played by Lightbody, but MacLehose soon started to become impatient with his distinctly 'hands-off' traditionalist approach. Lightbody, for his part, rapidly showed signs of becoming slightly overwhelmed by the demands of the programme, writing to Liao in February 1974 that 'the Department was too oppressed by day-to-day work' and that a long-term perspective was needed, preferably including planning twelve months ahead.[50] MacLehose kept a close eye on proceedings, with an April 1974 visit to the Ma Tau Kok Road office, along with Yan Oi transit camp and licence area.[51] Liao, by contrast, combined high-profile energy with reliability and political sensitivity: in a 1976 security assessment prior to a visit to his aged mother in Taiwan, Lightbody remarked that 'he can be depended on to avoid any embarrassments'.[52] (Figure 6.3) In 1975, Bernard Williams was promoted to Deputy Director of Housing (Operations), to help reinforce MacLehose's agenda – and November 1976 alone saw creation of nineteen new posts in the Housing Department. Finally, in April 1977 (see Chapter 8), MacLehose secured Lightbody's transfer away from the Secretaryship altogether, and appointed Alan Scott to 'get a grip on' the Department.[53] By the mid-1970s, the new Housing Authority was confronting its inherited management problems in a more concerted way. By March 1974, the total recorded number of squatters was still as much as 320,000.[54] And on his June 1975 Singapore study visit, MacLehose was relieved to hear that Singapore had 'just the same problems' as Hong Kong regarding intimidation and triad shop protection rackets. However, within the 'volatile' Group B estates, the problem was far more acute, and combined crime in general and corruption in particular.[55] Although MacLehose had set up the ICAC in 1973/4, having been shocked by the extent of corruption, the frequent complaints and newspaper allegations of corruption by Ron Woodcraft concerning the HD and PWD (cf. Chapter 5), received short shrift by officials. By 1977, Woodcraft had been stigmatised as 'a constant critic of the Authority and the Department' and officials advised to ignore him.[56] 1975 saw high-profile prosecutions of fraudulent tenants and impostors in fire-affected areas, and the activities of the Tidiness Teams continued to attract opposition, including attacks on the teams by Tsz Wan Shan tenants in May 1974 and by hawkers in September 1974, and a riot by hawkers at Lam Tin in May 1975.[57] In response, new short-tenancy agreements were drawn up to try to curb multiple-tenancy shop rackets – a move that initially triggered the legendary siege of Liao's office in May 1974.[58] (Figure 6.4)

Crime, too, still seemed a major problem in Group B estates, although between June 1973 and January 1975, there was a steady decrease in recorded crimes in HA estates as a whole: roughly 30% of these were robberies and 15% were thefts. However, the Group B estates were also visited by catastrophe,

Figure 6.3 Donald Liao, seen in February 2010 at the Jockey Club Sha Tin Clubhouse, with the mature skyline of Sha Tin visible behind him (MG).

NEAR RIOT AT ESTATE

Angry mob hurls stones at housing office

AN ANGRY mob of 200 stone-throwing villagers today besieged a Housing Estate office in Tszwanshan after four villagers were injured in fights with estate workers.

Police

Figure 6.4 May 1974 report in *Star* on clashes between local 'villagers' and Tidiness Teams at Tsz Wan Shan Estate.

in the form of the two successive mudslide tragedies at Sau Mau Ping in June 1972 and August 1976: in both cases MacLehose took vigorous action to head off further spillages before the onset of the rainy season, establishing a special monitoring organisation, the Review Panel on Hill Slopes, whose report appeared in December 1976 and presaged the systematised slope-monitoring system of recent decades.[59]

There was also a growing fear that 'Group B problems' might start contaminating Group A estates: January 1975 saw an acrimonious dispute about unauthorised hawkers congregating on a designated park area at Wah Fu, with protests by Elliott and a response by MacLehose that 'in the present economic circumstances, we should be careful not to break rice bowls for the sake of building a park'.[60] Even the showpiece of Oi Man, ceremonially visited by the Governor in April 1974, and Queen Elizabeth in April 1975, was in August 1975 identified by the local MAC as a site of many problems, including expensive rents, and rude staff: in November 1975, however, the Oi Man Centre was opened – the successful harbinger of many HA commercial centres to follow.[61] The integration of estate management grades in 1973–4, was, as we saw above, impeded by the continuing divisions between Group A and B managers: it was claimed by the latter in July 1975 that the Resettlement Department had been not amalgamated with the HA but 'conquered' by it. Eventually, in 1976, one of Carroll's last achievements was to reorganise estates into two geographical areas, East and West, to finally bury the A/B distinction.[62]

MacLehose's sensitivity to public relations increasingly shaped government presentation of housing, for example, in a careful correction of 1976 media inaccuracies about numbers of inhabitants in licensed areas, while admitting internally that 'in many respects [the publicity] is a public relations "gain" for the Housing Department'.[63] There were striking differences over publicity between unofficials and HA officials. Elliott in June 1976 pleaded for 'building, not public relations', but Lightbody in September demanded 'a much more aggressive public relations push', arguing the HA had been 'far too defensive'. A MOOD survey of 4,158 respondents in August 1976 on attitudes towards the long-term housing programme pointed to a sharp decline in support since 1973 – a controversy fanned by Elliott, despite her HA membership, with claims that the Authority was a 'greedy, grasping landlord'.[64] The traditional Kaifong associations were ambiguous in affiliation, sometimes attacking government policies but at others proselytising hard-line agendas such as eviction of criminals. In December 1974, for instance, the Wang Tau Hom Kaifong pressured for a law-and-order agenda of cracking down on gangsters, whereas MacLehose ruled eviction of tenants was too harsh.[65]

The Housing Programme Plan

The debates about finance and potential programme cut-backs were echoed within the Housing Authority and Housing Department in an oblique way, with the macro-economic forces and political pressures on the programme being interpreted through a McKinsey-influenced discourse of planning and programming efficiency. Under the McKinsey formula, the heads of all major departments now served on the Governor's Committee, and the relationship of secretaries and departments was closely monitored.[66] In the housing-output extrapolation of this new efficiency ethos into a formal 'Housing Programme Plan', Ted Pryor played a key role, especially after being seconded to the HD in 1975.[67]

The background to this new policy was the growing realisation that the Ten-Year Plan, as originally formulated, would not be achievable, partly owing to the recession, but partly because of the intrinsically makeshift character of the Plan itself. Academics were the first to raise the alarm. In January 1974, Chinese University researchers condemned its calculations, arguing that the planned 1.8 million new IUs should in fact be 2.5 million, and David Drakakis-Smith claimed it had badly underestimated both immigration and household formation. Critics argued that 'inconsistent' Hong Kong could learn from the supposedly more 'consistent' projection of policy in Singapore, with its orderly urban renewal processes.[68] Rapidly, a preferred solution coalesced: a review process for the Ten-Year Plan in the form of a McKinsey-style 'full-scale programme plan for housing'. This would evaluate numerous options (eventually totalling 47, as at July 1975) that would help structure the pace and character of output much more systematically than the 1972 back-of-postcard calculations and targets fixed on the *Clementi*. It was formally launched in September 1974, and in October, the Housing Authority agreed to establish a steering group to review the 1972 target and draw up a formal Housing Programme Plan (HPP).[69]

This new strategy formed part of a wider attempt to boost the coordination of territory development, including elements of town and country planning. The focus of the latter was the Hong Kong Outline Plan (HKOP: before 1974 known as the Outline Ten-Year Colony Development Plan), prepared under LDPC auspices with contributions by the Planning Branch of the Crown Lands and Survey Office, and finally approved in 1979.[70] The OTYCDP/HKOP project was from the beginning entangled with issues of residential density, including a review of standards in November 1974 and review of densities in July 1975. The housing contribution to the Ten-Year Development Plan, including forecasts of demand, was overseen by Ted Pryor, working in coordination with government planner A F Meyers.[71] The Development Plan, spanning from 1973–4 to 1982–3, had been authorised at the March 1974 meeting of the Planning Coordination Committee, chaired by Pryor, at that stage a senior officer in the CLSO Planning Branch, and who in 1974 optimistically argued that Hong Kong might become 'a model to the rest of the world' in high-density urban development.[72] In May 1975, the LPVC was reconstituted to help facilitate the development process, and new procedures were set out at its first meeting in December: the invitation letters for its first meeting were sent out by Pryor, who by now was designated Assistant Director Redevelopment and Planning.[73]

Under the methodical McKinsey framework, the Housing Programme Plan (HPP) would need to be carefully coordinated with the HKOP's land-sourcing procedures. The HPP process would begin by establishing accurate shortfalls and needs – based on the new aspiration of household self-containment – and would proceed to the drawing up of a wide range of options, before fixing on preferred policies to be acted on and incorporated in the definitive HPP. Even the first of these stages, however, generated conflict between MacLehose and the administrators over target definition and public presentation. Based on the presumption of the need to achieve self-containment for all households as soon as possible, in March 1975 Lightbody boldly informed MacLehose that under an initial HPP analysis 'the stated aim of providing all households with self-contained facilities' had revealed an estimated shortfall of 433,000 'living quarters' by 1984/5. This would in turn generate a new 'target' of 250,000 new public and 170,000 private 'living quarters'. MacLehose's initial reaction was one of alarm, urging Lightbody, 'Please keep careful wraps on the conclusion', which 'will need very careful presentation'.[74] In August, responding to MacLehose's puzzlement as to how these targets could be achieved in 10 years, Lightbody stressed that the draft HPP was a 'mathematical model only'. To this MacLehose – always alert to political implications in a way that Lightbody the administrator was not – retorted that any publication should therefore concentrate on what *could* be done, as opposed to what *could not*. Overall, he assured Lightbody, it was

> an excellent bit of planning, as the paper certainly contains a mine of information which should certainly be made available to the public. But you must get away from the presentational technique of showing plans as a shortfall from the ideal standard instead of an advance on present conditions.

Accordingly, by September MacLehose had decreed the initial HPP analysis was 'not suitable for publication'.[75] Instead, the emphasis began shifting instead to standing annual targets: MacLehose argued in October 1976 that Hong Kong would need to build for 200,000 inhabitants a year.[76]

Any direct calculation of HPP output requirements was hugely complicated by the mounting confusion over definition of its basic building block – the individual unit of accommodation, or IU – especially in relation to the flats that were the actual units of *construction*. Throughout 1974–5 there was incessant debate on this between Pryor and the administrators. Pryor pointed out that owing to anomalies in actual occupancy rates of dwellings, achievement of an actual gross density of 1,000 ppa (2,470 ppha) 'on the ground' would require IUs to exceed the design population by some 57%. Pryor argued that 'The present assumption that one IU equates to one "flesh and blood" person will result in a very serious loss of population capacity in the New Towns'.[77] The confusing interplay between IUs and densities was explored in exhaustive detail in correspondence between Liao and Pryor in 1975, and discontent came to a head in late 1976, following a full-scale PWD conference on the IU/density relationship, and an extensive LPVC discussion in September.[78] Following a November 1976 DNTD paper on the relationship between IUs and design population in New Towns, Pryor once again highlighted the contentious relationship between IUs, densities and actual populations, remarking that the PWD was perplexed by this issue: Akers-Jones warned Lightbody, 'Have you seen these pieces of paper? ... Quite a lot of questions need to be answered before this is ready for LDPC'.[79] The next month, Liao briefed Lightbody that inaccurate figures were causing growing mismatches between IUs and design populations: the 'crude estimate' of the Ten-Year Plan target, endorsed in 1972 by ExCo, was being abused by DNTD, which was repeatedly raising densities ad-hoc to circumvent inaccuracies stemming from IU computations. Following this barrage of criticism, the IU was increasingly discredited as a yardstick, especially for its effect in depressing densities.[80]

The waters were further muddied by the effects of the step-by-step upwards shift in the minimum per-person space allowance from the 24 sq ft (2.2 sq m) pre-1972 Resettlement standard, to 35 sq ft (3.25 sq m) for all new dwellings, and the subsequent pressure within the HA for a further improvement to 50 – a proposal deferred in July 1975 and then revived in early 1976.[81] In 1976, a transfer scheme allowed tenants in housing with under 24 sq ft per person to move. This long-running debate was complicated by ambiguities over the minimum size of a household (as one- and two-person households would have to share dwellings), and over the difference within dwellings between 'net' and 'gross' living area (the latter including kitchen, balcony, WC and circulation – recalling the Soviet distinction between 'living space' and 'auxiliary space'). At a HPP Steering Group meeting in November 1974, it was explained that the 50 sq ft proposal was actually a net figure, and that the gross equivalent would be around 70. Responding to administrators' concern at the land implications of this new standard, Liao argued that at the 1,000 ppa density standard adopted for the New Towns, it should be possible to 'fit in' all planned housing.[82]

But by 1976, a rival criterion of accommodation was briefly displacing the IU, namely the 'living quarter' – a concept defined as accommodation for a single household, and thus still not exactly the same as a flat or dwelling. Back in 1974, statistical reports on the *de facto* and *de jure* population of estates already referred to 'living quarters' throughout, and in March 1975, as we saw above, Lightbody's prediction to MacLehose of a 433,000 shortfall by 1984–5 was likewise based on living quarters, as was the shift in the building target from 1.8 million IUs to 170,000 private and 250,000 public living quarters.[83] From there, however, the logical further move was from the confusing halfway-house of the living quarter to the very easily comprehensible concept of the individual flat. 1976 saw growing discussion of flats vis-à-vis units. Already, at a discussion of estate densities in the LPVC in September, Liao argued that, to make a 'significant impact on the HPP, the Housing Department should aim at an increase by 25% in the number of flats, and not IUs, provided'.[84] As Bernard Williams argued later, while an annual building target of 495,000 sq m, based on a multiplication of 3.3 sq m by 150,000 IUs, was clearly 'nonsensical', this could be easily translated into a far more practical annual flat-building target of 30,000, extrapolated from the average household size of five in the 1970s. It took seven years to reach that completions target, later boosted to 35,000 – a figure that soon became established, in Liao's words, as the 'cruising speed' of the permanent public housing programme.[85] (Figure 6.5) Responding to those targets,

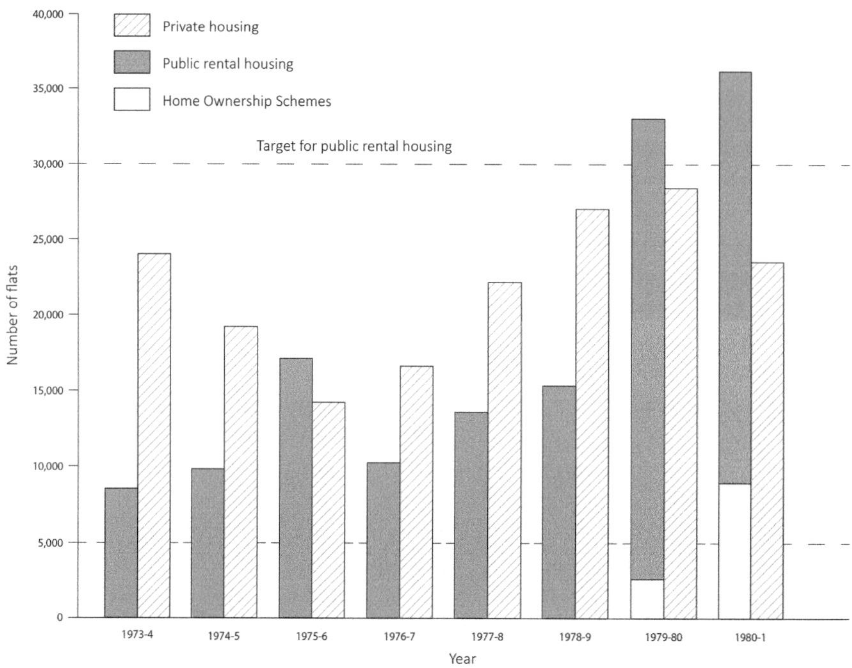

Figure 6.5 Housing production bar chart 1973–81, broken down into different tenures. Drawing by Joyce Fu, 2023.

the actual public housing output figures, including the Housing Society's, gradually stuttered into life, rising from 9,786 completions in 1974–5 to 17,090 the following year, but dropping back to 1,016 and 13,524 in the succeeding years. The percentage of total government social spending accounted for by housing fluctuated just as wildly, rising from 6% in 1972–3 to 10% the following year, but dropping back again to 3% in 1976–7, and 10% in 1977–8.[86]

The Housing Programme Plan process, however, was not just a matter of output. During the development and evaluation of policy options, in mid and late 1975, no less than 47 options were selected for consideration, of which 26 were designated priority A (top), 17 were B, and 4 were C. Stage VI of the standardised McKinsey programme plan process was that of the evaluation of options, under which it rapidly became clear that most fell under the responsibility of the Housing Department.[87,88] The most urgent of these, the options categorised 'A', were almost all concerned with development processes: for example Option 43: to raise site yields via higher densities. Yet that prioritisation was only loosely linked to eventual importance: as we will see in Chapter 7, the highest-profile late-1970s housing policy, the government subsidised Home Ownership Scheme, was only hinted at indirectly, in the low-priority Option 13.[89]

HPP Option 43: increase densities

Although many of the options in the Housing Programme Plan were only of indirect application to the building drive – focusing for example on demographics, finance or rent policy – a number of key options had a direct influence on building and planning policies during the mid and late 1970s.

One of the foundation stones of the HPP was Option 43, which chimed in with the well-established strategy of boosting densities, overseen by Pryor from its beginnings in early 1974, and which generated continuous, often passionate debate. In May 1974, Pryor minuted Liao about how to increase the 'yield' of sites through raising gross and net estate densities, from the current range of 662 to 1,000 ppa up to 1,120 ppa (e.g., at Tuen Mun Area 1 and Sha Tin Areas 1 and 2) or even 1,250 ppa. And in December 1974, as noted above, Pryor pointed out that a gross density of 1,000 ppa/2,470 ppha would require the number of IUs to exceed the design population by around 57%.[90] The review of residential densities was strongly linked with the HKOP Review of Planning Standards – which concluded in November 1974 that 2,470 ppha should remain the standard gross density. On this basis, in July 1975, the theoretical land requirements for 20,000 inhabitants in a public housing estate at 2,470 ppha were calculated, and public and private density zoning requirements were compared in detail. The HKOP planners suggested that in due course, rising housing standards might allow densities to be cut below 2,470 in some situations – for example to 1,730 in market town estates; Wah Fu and Choi Hung were studied in detail as case studies.[91]

In November-December 1975, by contrast, HPP Option 43 raised the possibility of developing at densities *higher* than the current 1,000 ppa/2,470 ppha norm – following 'theoretical' explorations by the Town Planning Office, Housing Department and New Territories Development Department (NTDD). A detailed design evaluation by Chief Housing Architect S H Cheung of sites at Wo Che and Tsing Yi concluded that even if 1,000 ppa were retained as the overall rule, a 'marked environmental improvement' could still result from the selective use of dense hotspots to allow creation of open space.[92] And in a December 1975 debate between Liao and Pryor about public housing plot ratios and densities, Pryor remarked that 'the term "density" can mean different things to different persons', and set out in detail the procedure for estate planning at 1,000 ppa/2,470 ppha.[93] In the event, March 1976 saw LPVC consideration of Housing Department requests for higher density in Yuen Long, and in August the LPVC authorised an increase in the density of Wo Che Phases I and II from 1,000 to 1,250 IUs (not persons) per gross acre, to allow more 'interpenetration' of shops and housing; at the December 1976 LPVC meeting, Freddie Pang presented a revised, denser layout for Phases I(b) and II of Wo Che, including more small flats, as well as a light commercial complex.[94] Other 1976 densification initiatives included insertion of an extra tower block in the Sha Kok estate, and modification to the Ngau Chi Wan estate plan, mainly comprising Twin Tower blocks, to increase the number of flats.[95]

HPP Option 45: augment Mk I/II redevelopment

Although most of the densification pressure focused on tabula-rasa developments, especially in the New Towns, it also influenced the redevelopment programme of existing Mk I and II estates. Here, Option 45 of the HPP proposed sourcing additional land for redevelopment for displacees – higher densities being identified in May 1976 as a potential way of achieving this.[96] Since the failure of the original plans for conversion of blocks by merging single-room units, the programme had shifted decisively towards demolition. In February 1974, the Mk III was also condemned as an 'unsatisfactory design', but whose redevelopment could only come after Mk I and Mk II.[97] In parallel with this, the Housing Society was pursuing its own somewhat small-scale urban improvement scheme, together with new rental estates of significant size (see below) – the latter against the background of fast-disappearing government support.[98]

Shek Kip Mei, of course, was the proving ground for the whole HA redevelopment programme.[99] But when, in May 1975, Pryor produced a proposal for systematic redevelopment of other comparable areas, notably Tung Tau, Wong Tai Sin and Tsz Wan Shan, the stress was not on raising but on *lowering* densities, again to 1,000 ppa/2,470 ppha, but from a higher existing figure, with the idea of creating space for community facilities. The reaction from both Liao and Lightbody was negative. Citing the higher land values in these areas, they agreed that 'we feel Dr Pryor is being too idealistic here'; Liao suggested that the plans should instead specify 'about 1,500 ppa'.[100] However, following an extended re-appraisal of the redevelopment programme in mid and late 1975, the LDPC laid down a density 'of the order of 1,000 ppa' as the norm for Mk I and Mk II redevelopment.[101] A March 1976 LDPC memo argued that, as a result, Mk I/II redevelopment would generate a requirement for 92,000 additional 'living quarters' over 15 years. And in May 1976, an LDPC paper enlarged on this, explaining that at a redevelopment density of 1,000 ppa, only 55–60% of the 490,000 currently living in Mk I and II estates could be rehoused in situ, and that consequently 40–45% of that existing population would have to go to overspill estates both in the urban areas and in the New Towns – posing in a far more acute form the challenge of population 'decanting' that dogged some British cities such as Glasgow in the 1940s–60s.[102]

HPP Options 24–28: the New Towns

These were the years that saw the maturing of the New Towns programme, which MacLehose argued was a demonstration of 'faith in the future of Hong Kong'.[103] Within the Housing Programme Plan framework, the headline target was concerned with encouraging private investment in the New Towns (Option 24) – and eventually, from the 1980s, the New Towns would provide a significant launch-pad for the explosive growth of an indigenous real-estate sector.[104] But for the short term at least, it was clearly recognised in government that the pump-priming spearhead of that great enterprise must largely comprise large-scale public housing development. In March 1975, the difficulty of getting private enterprise to invest in the New Towns, especially at high enough densities, was stressed, as was the likelihood that the target of 30% of the population privately housed would be missed. Overall, private enterprise was showing a distinct lack of interest in the New Territories as a whole. In 1974, for example, an ambitious project by Galbreath-Ruffin to build 'a second Mei Foo' either at Sha Tin or on a tanker-farm site at Tsing Yi, ultimately came to nothing.[105] As early as 1976, it was becoming a matter of distinct concern to the middle classes that security of tenure in individual leases seemed impossible beyond 21 years in the New Territories, raising the spectre of what might happen under communist rule.[106]

The New Towns were the pre-eminent exception within the Hong Kong system of laissez-faire-dominated planning and land use. Their development was regulated at a policy level by the LDPC, in collaboration with the New Towns Development Progress Committee.[107] But unlike the unified Singapore New Towns system, which Pang examined first-hand on a short 1975 study visit (Chapter 7), the Hong Kong system was two-headed. The overarching coordinating role was played by the New Towns Development Progress Committee (NTDPC), set up by the Colonial Secretariat in 1972.[108] Overall, however, the prime movers at this stage were the planning agencies within the PWD/NTDD, to which the Housing Department had a semi-detached relationship: in July 1975 it was claimed that given the HA's autonomy from the PWD/NTDD, town planners 'frequently disagree' with the HD on the proper scale of provision. As at 1975, the NTDD prepared the outline development and layout plans for development areas in the New Territories – in other words the New Towns and market towns – whereas plans for the remainder of the New Territories were prepared by the Town Planning Office: in February 1974 the AD (NT) argued that there was a 'tremendous amount of planning work to be done in the New Territories'.[109] Architectural coordination was the responsibility of PWD architects: in February 1974, H C Astbury, Chief Architect Division I, argued that estate design was 'like playing three-dimensional chess', and anticipated the New Towns will be 'full of life' stemming from 'the Chinese way of life', unlike the 'soulless' low-density British New Towns; Sha Tin, Tuen Mun and Tsuen Wan would be planned as 'self-contained communities'.[110] (Figure 6.6) As to the mechanics of that process, Astbury recorded in September 1974 that in May a sub-committee of the Public Works Priority Committee had been established, to devise development programmes for all public housing and other buildings in the three New Towns and other rural areas.[111] Writing in November 1974, Bryan O'Rorke, the PWD project manager for Tsuen Wan, stressed that the New Towns need 'good planning': Tuen Mun, for instance, would be systematically carried out as a three-stage project (according to David Lam, DO).[112] But from the beginning, stresses appeared within this orderly system: by March 1974, Akers-Jones was warning of New Town 'overload', and by December 1974, the 1975–6 cut-backs on New Town infrastructure were beginning to bite.[113] On the whole, the working of the Crown Lands Resumption Ordinance, and Letters A, B (and later C), took a smooth course, but regular obstruction stemmed from pre-existing communities: in December 1974, the Tai Wai development in Sha Tin was held up by villagers, while in Tsuen Wan, officials spent much effort trying to move a 200-year-old village whose land was needed for a multi-storey car park.[114]

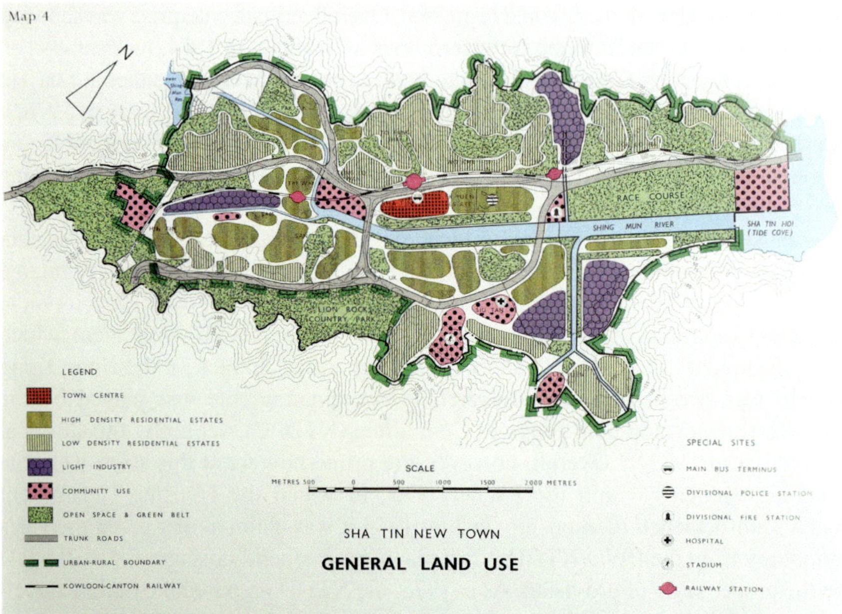

Figure 6.6 Sha Tin general land-use plan, from 1978 GIS/PWD brochure, *Hong Kong's New Towns, Sha Tin*, showing evolutionary development of original linear plan.

As to the specific planning challenges of the New Towns, there was a strong contrast between the first three New Towns and the four additional New Towns. Akers-Jones stressed in 1974 that the four additional towns, approved in 1973, posed 'totally different' challenges: the absence of a *tabula rasa* context meant that there would be more scope for private enterprise, and a lower planned density of 1,730 ppha as opposed to 2,470 in the main urban areas and the three original New Towns.[115] The development report for Yuen Long, for instance, was presented by the ADR/P to the LPVC in May 1976.[116] Outside the New Towns proper, May 1975 saw preparation of a sketch plan for Tai O by the New Territories Development Branch.[117]

Housing design and construction: a new generation of block types

The upgraded planning frameworks linked to the HPP were bound up with development of a fresh generation of standard block types, superintended by a new Layout Plans Vetting Committee (LPVC), established in December 1975.[118] Partly reflecting the London pressure on social provision, and partly reflecting the rivalry with Singapore, a constant, general raising of standards was taken for granted as a guiding principle.[119] But equally inexorable was the continuing shift in design responsibility from the PWD to the new HD architects. In 1976, large numbers of PWD-designed estates were still being finished off, including the last in the Mk VI/VII series, such as Hing Wah, whose first two blocks were completed in

February 1976. At Kwai Shing, 1971–6 saw the building of a multi-stage estate with similar block types, housing 77,000 inhabitants as part of the Ten-Year Plan.[120] Optimistically, the Government Information Bulletin reported in February 1976 that 'a new generation' of 'self-contained' estates was being developed by the PWD as its contribution to the Ten-Year Housing Programme, notably Lek Yuen (Sha Tin) and Tai Hing (Tuen Mun): the latter, a three-stage development designed by Bramwell's PWD architects, achieved an especially high density through slightly tapering cruciform blocks.[121] (Figures 6.7a–d, 6.8, 6.9a, b) The new standard blocks

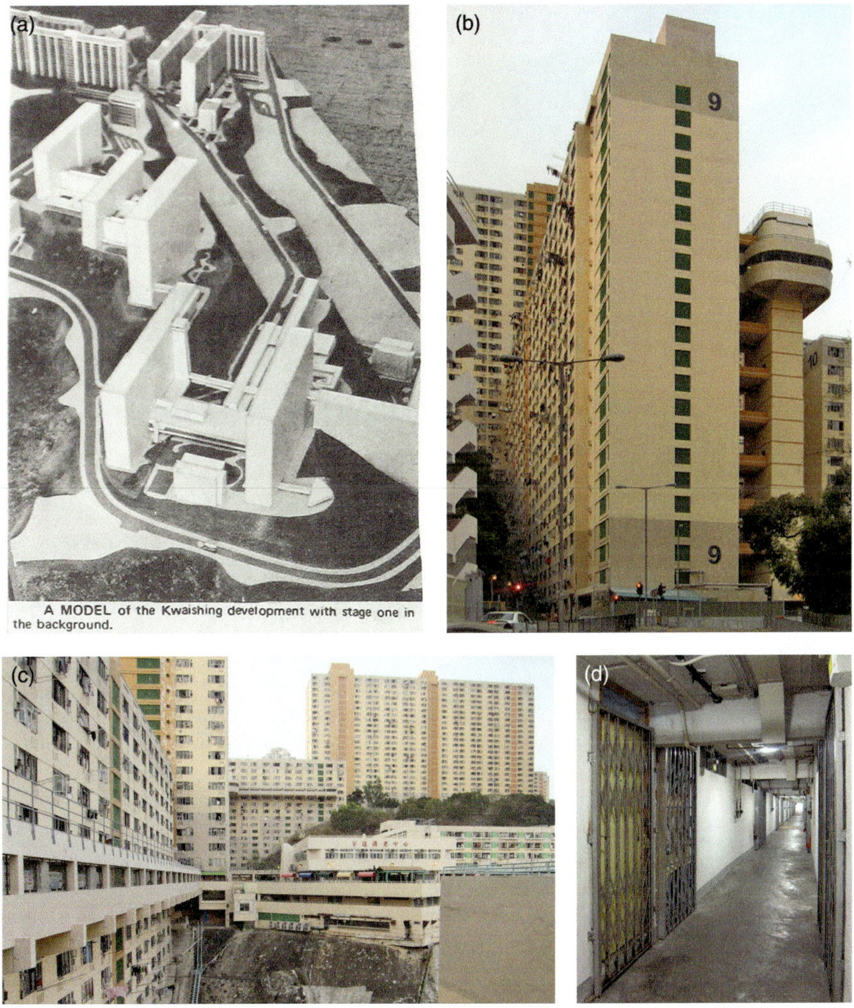

Figure 6.7 (a) Kwai Shing (GLCH) Estate, 1972 *Star* article on Phases 2 and 3, with blocks up to 22 storeys and provision of high-speed lifts on the steeply sloping site. (b) Kwai Shing West Estate, 2013 view (MG) of Block 9 including lift tower. (c) Kwai Shing West, 2013 view (MG) showing multi-level planning. (d) Kwai Shing West, 2013 view (MG) of central corridor.

Figure 6.8 Hing Wah II Estate, Chai Wan (completed from 1976), 2013 view (MG) at upper podium level.

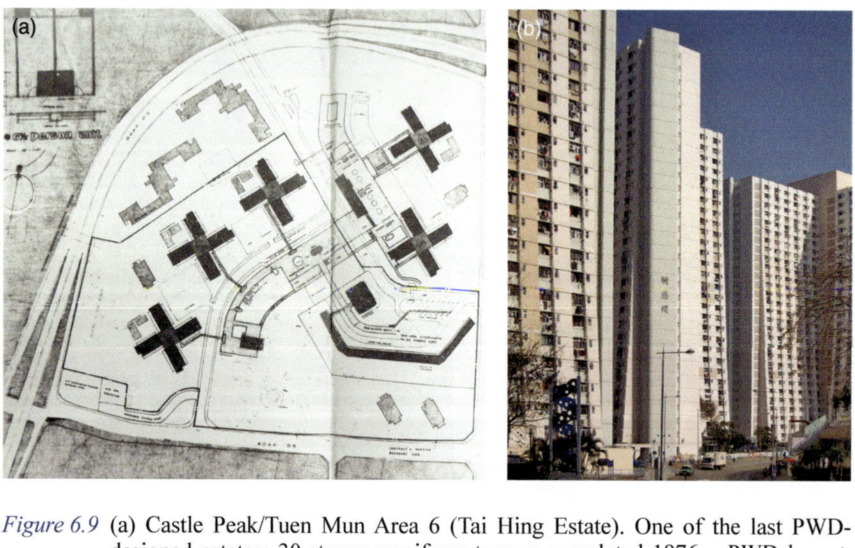

Figure 6.9 (a) Castle Peak/Tuen Mun Area 6 (Tai Hing Estate). One of the last PWD-designed estates: 30-storey cruciform towers completed 1976 – PWD layout. (b) Tai Hing Estate, 2013 photo (MG) showing 'tapered' profile.

designed by Cheung Sing-hoi's HA team included the new 'H-shaped point block', approved in 1976 and normally used in pairs, containing 34 flats per floor (68 in a pair) with services in the cross-bar. (Figure 6.10)

Its linear arrangement, Cheung claimed, could create much more 'privacy' than the twin tower block but also, more nebulously, a better sense of 'community building'. In February 1976, the Ngau Chi Wan estate included a new block design, balcony access with 5-, 7- and 12-person flats.[122] Liao's well-established Twin Tower Block continued to be exploited in order to secure high densities, and in January 1976, in research for the Home-Ownership Scheme (see Chapter 7), the economic and practical aspects of Twin Tower Blocks at Wo Che were compared favourably with private low-cost housing.[123] (Figure 6.11a–c) The mix and layout of these standard blocks was constantly refined by the LPVC in individual projects, as was seen above in the 1976 layout redesigns and density increase from 1,000 IU per gross acre to 1,250 at Wo Che.[124] A mixture of Twin Tower Blocks and slab blocks also characterised the Authority's showpiece project at Oi Man, hailed as the 'model for all [estates] that are now being built'.[125] (Figures 6.12, 6.13a–c) By contrast with the HA's ever-growing stress on new standard designs, the Housing Society's estates remained much more like those of the pre-1973 HA – designed and built on a strictly tailor-made basis, with the additional burden that with the drying up of government subsidies from the mid-1960s, any new estates had to be self-financed. The showpiece HS project of the mid 1970s was Lai Tak Tsuen (1972–6; named appropriately after Michael Wright), designed by architect Wong Cho Tong with three blocks of 27/28 storeys, two of which (Lai Kit Lau and Tak Chuen Lau) featured projecting double circular towers: their full-height internal circular courtyards had continuous balconies with ten flats on each floor. Some later public housing projects in other countries, such as the clover-plan Ang Mo Kio Block 259, Singapore (completed 1982), or Kwangbok Street, Pyongyang (1990), also featured circular towers, but these typically were 'solid' rather than 'hollow' in plan.[126] (Figure 6.14)

In construction, the disruptive effects of excessive fluctuations within the building industry, as well as the growing desirability of greater precision in construction standards, both gradually but inexorably tended towards the adoption of more standardised and mechanised methods. A March 1976 paper by the Economic Analysis Division of the Secretariat highlighted the huge sectoral fluctuations in construction industry output. Fluctuating peaks in private-sector demand up to 1972, and after 1973, a rising public-sector share, were followed by the sustained construction industry downturn of 1974–5. A revival in private enterprise was anticipated in 1976–7, and thus the paper recommended that the government should cut back public output to avoid overload.[127] In such a context, moves towards labour-saving were of obvious potential usefulness. At Tai Hing, for example, semi-mechanised construction, including tower cranes and prefabricated wall and floor components, was incorporated from the outset.[128] At Kwai Chung Phase II, Twin Tower Blocks in December 1974 included semi-mechanised shuttering. And in November 1975, Pang visited Singapore to research mechanised construction there, noting with interest the HDB's 'Merit

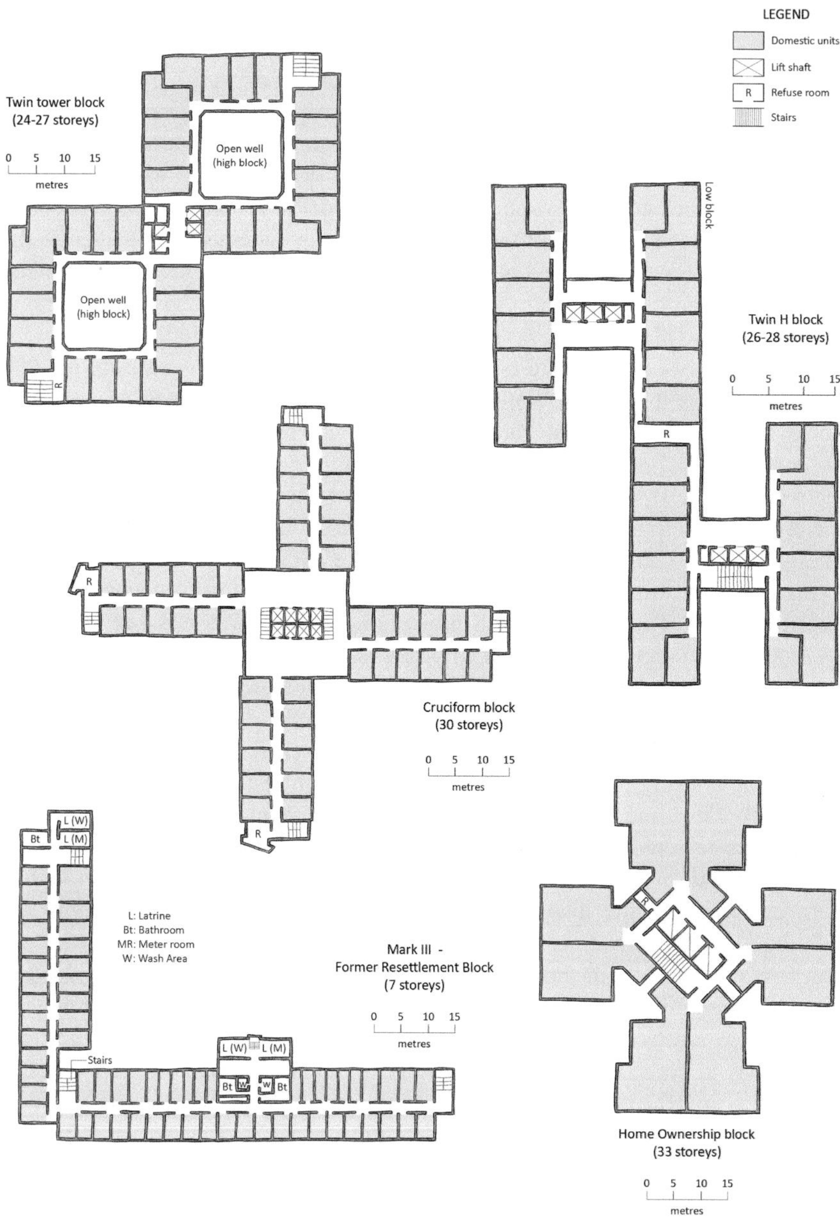

Figure 6.10 Schematic upper-floor plans of various 1960s–70s block types, including Twin Tower, Twin H, Mk III Resettlement, PWD Cruciform and HOS cruciform. Drawing by Joyce Fu, 2023.

Figure 6.11 (a) Plan of Wo Che Estate from the 1980 Density Study (cf. 8.17). (b) Wo Che Estate seen in 1983 (MG). (c) Wo Che, seen from Sui Wo Court in 1985, with Sui Wo Commercial Centre in foreground (MG).

Start' scheme of approved contractors, and scanning with admiration the HDB's 1975 propaganda book on the housing programme. The outcome was a consultancy study by Mitchell McFarlane, who singled out 35 systems and methods as of potential interest to Hong Kong, and advised a focus on rationalised-traditional rather than fully prefabricated systems.[129]

For the moment, this flurry of investigation and experimentation was premature, owing to the relatively basic character of the building industry in the 1970s. But the design and organisational professionalism of Liao's staff in the rejuvenated Housing Authority was meanwhile laying a solid foundation for more revolutionary changes in the mid and later 1980s, including fully fledged prefabrication: this would be seen in Hong Kong as a means of enhancing building quality rather than (as in 1960s Europe) circumventing labour shortages. As we will see in Chapter 9, a decisive tipping-point would be reached after 1980, in the so-called '26 Blocks'

OI MAN ESTATE

A SHOWPIECE OF PUBLIC HOUSING IN HONGKONG

Oi Man Housing Estate – the showpiece of public housing in Hongkong – which will be officially opened by the Acting Governor, Sir Denys Roberts, today, stands on the main Princess Margaret Road in Kowloon, ideally situated for cross harbour travel by bus through the tunnel or for the Kowloon urban area.

Built at a cost of $186 million, Oi Man, with its modern facilities and futuristic planning, is one of the Housing Authority's most popular estates, and was visited by the Queen during her visit to Hongkong in May this year.

Sited on 21 acres of what was once the former Homantin Cottage area, the estate comprises 12 blocks between seven and 24 storeys designed by the Housing Department's own architects.

These blocks include the twin tower blocks with inner balcony access facing Princess Margaret Road and some 16 and 18 storey blocks with central corridors as well as several low blocks to lend variety and contrast.

At Oi Man which fits the description of a little town within a city, some 46,000 people can live and work in a clean, healthy and amiable environment at rentals only a small fraction of private housing in that area.

The estate has been so designed and planned as to provide every convenience for its residents from banks, markets to barbershops.

It provides about 6,200 flats which allocated on the basis of the Housing Authority's current allocation standards, that is, 35 square feet of net living area per person, will house up to 46,000, giving a density of around 2,200 per acre.

All flats at Oi Man have a living / dining room with a kitchen, toilet and private balcony which can be used as an extra room. Total floor areas of the flats range from 357 square feet to 591 square feet. Of those flats with the larger areas, about 200 have been designed as two bedroom flats for larger families.

The majority of the tenants of Oi Man are selected from the Housing Authority's waiting list and the remainder allocated to other categories of applicants.

One of the criteria for eligibility as a tenant of Oi Man is based on the number of people in a family and total family income. The minimum number of persons per flat is four and maximum total income around $1,500 per month. For families of ten the maximum total income is about $2,250.

The first blocks of the estate were completed and occupied around April last year and the remainder was completed and fully occupied in September this year.

The Housing Department's architects paid particular attention to providing plentiful commercial facilities both to meet the tenants' needs and to provide a shopping centre for the Homantin district.

A three-storey air-conditioned commercial complex has shopping arcades on each of its three floors with space for a total of 90 shops, two banks, two large restaurants, a supermarket, a department store, a cafe and the Estate Office.

In addition there are 25 ground floor shops in the estate blocks. These shops sell a wide range of commodities so that almost every item necessary in the day to day running of a household is available on their shelves to the tenants.

All these commercial premises are let on a public tender system and the tenancy normally goes to the person bidding the highest premium for the tenancy, which is on a fixed monthly rental basis.

Banks, restaurants and other larger premises, because of the heavy investment required in fixtures, are let on a five year tenancy agreement with the tenderers competing on the basis of monthly rent offered rather than a premium. The tenancy agreements provide for regular rent reviews and options for renewal for further periods.

Oi Man Estate is one where no hawkers are permitted to ply their trade. Instead the estate provides a covered market stall area for the sale of fresh fruit and vegetables as well as three modular structures for 12 cooked food stalls.

Edited and produced by the Publications Division, South China Morning Post Ltd.

The stalls are let by tender, initially restricted to hawkers of long standing operating in other public housing estates.

The Chartered Bank and the [illegible] have branches operating on the ground floor of one of the estate blocks and the Hongkong and Shanghai Bank has space reserved for a branch in the commercial complex.

Other shops on the ground floor of the estate blocks range from provision stores, groceries, medicine shops selling both western and herbal medicines, a stationer, photo studio, haberdashery and a toy shop.

Although the commercial complex, at the time of writing, is still not fully occupied, it is fully let. Workmen were actively engaged on all three floors of the complex in various tasks of making the many shops ready for business.

On the ground floor to the left of the entrance is the Ritz Restaurant, serving mainly European style food and quite well patronised at the time of this writer's passing visit.

An escalator leads to the floors above. On the first floor is the space reserved for the Shanghai and Hongkong Bank's branch and the Man Yee Restaurant where a large number of workmen were putting the finishing touches to the interior fittings and decor of the large estate Chinese cuisine restaurant.

On the top floor is the Swing Superstore where everything from cosmetics, clothing to kitchen utensils are available.

The commercial complex, located conveniently near the main road, is intended to serve the general public in the Homantin area as well as the tenants of Oi Man Estate.

Amenities in the estate include five kindergartens as well as a large area as open, covered and roof top playgrounds. In addition, the roofs of the commercial complex and one of the two multi-storey carparks have been designed as play areas.

The car parks have total space for about 940 cars and an additional 160 spaces for shoppers.

All buildings on the level areas are linked by covered walks and the shopping precinct is connected to the five twin tower blocks by a pedestrian subway.

Fronting the estate itself is a large sitting out plaza with shade giving trees and flower beds.

A bus terminus adjacent to the estate ensures that transport is available for Oi Man tenants at regular intervals to almost every part of the Colony.

Two schools are also under construction and these when operational will provide educational facilities for the estate's children.

Much thought and planning designed to give its tenants the best possible in relation to the money spent has gone into the building of Oi Man.

Planning started in 1960 to turn the Homantin Hill Cottage Area from an isolated maze of wooden huts into what it is today – a showpiece and model of what public housing will be like in the near future.

Oi Man was built at a total cost of $3,998 for each of its 46,000 tenants and an average total cost of $27,986 per 357 sq.ft flat.

– C. D. SUNG.

Oi Man Estate has car parking facilities for 1,000 vehicles. Pictured is one of the two car park blocks.

official opening

Tun Man House, one of the twin tower blocks in the estate. In the foreground is part of the large sitting out area.

At the Oi Man Commercial Complex we have incorporated the latest technical innovation in fire prevention system

Davie, Boag (Engineering) Ltd.

WITH THE COMPLIMENTS OF

OI MAN RESTAURANT LTD

Oi Man Commercial Complex
Oi Man Estate
Kowloon
Tel: 3-039472

The Chartered Bank plenty of help for the people of Oi Man Estate.

The Chartered Bank's Oi Man Estate branch is situated in the commercial complex within the Oi Man Government Housing Estate. It offers a comprehensive range of banking services including safe deposit boxes – all amounting to plenty of help and service for residents and businesses in Oi Man.
Come in and see our branch manager Mr. Wong Chi-wai (Tel. No. 3-039231/2)

The Chartered Bank

Figure 6.12 Full-page SCMP feature in November 1975 commemorating the opening of Oi Man Estate.

Figure 6.13 (a) November 1983 view of Oi Man Estate, prior to external painting (MG). (b) Oi Man, balcony view inside Block L, Wai Man House (a Twin Tower Block), including the door of Flat 805, visited by MacLehose on an April 1974 official tour: 2017 photo (MG). (c) Oi Man, estate map: 2017 photo (MG), showing central position of commercial centre.

scandal, in which revelations of the shoddy construction of pre-1973 GLC and Resettlement blocks would draw a dramatic demarcation line between the old, ad-hoc building practices, and potential new approaches, merging rationalised, high-precision design and construction into a unified ethos of professionalised modernity.

Figure 6.14 The Housing Society's showpiece Lai Tak Tsuen development, Tai Hang, 1972–6; named after Michael Wright, and designed by Wong Cho Tong: two of its blocks featured projecting double circular towers. 1983 photo (MG).

Notes

1 HKRS163-8-81 Internal Security Assessment of 6-1974; HKRS232-1-23-1, Hong Kong Standard cutting of 8-2-1974; HKRS232-1-23-2 1-4-1974 SCMP cutting.

2 HKRS177-3-6-1 26-4-1973 first meeting, MacLehose address and papers; HKRS232-1-12-2 3-4-1973 on '10-Year' HA; HKRS163-9-1342 8-1976 papers; HKRS394-27-9 8-1976 papers; Akers-Jones, 2014 interview.

3 FCO40-620 12-1975 and HKRS189-2-40 1975 on discontinuing term 'colony'; FCO40-711 2-7-1976 MacLehose to Cortazzi; HKRS835-1-171 8-1976 note.

4 FCO40-547 early 1974 papers; FCO40-617 4-1975 papers; MacLehose in Blyth and Wotherspoon, *Hong Kong Remembers*, 299-302; FCO40-510 6-1974 MacLehose note; FCO40-547 27-5-1974 MacLehose to Callaghan on 'Hong Kong objectives'; Miller, 2014 interview.

5 HKRS40-547 27-5-1974 MacLehose to Callaghan on 'Hong Kong objectives' (and 28-5-1974 covering letter).

6 M Glendinning, 'From European welfare state to Asian capitalism: the transformation of "British public housing" in Hong Kong and Singapore', in M Swenarton, T Avermaete and D van den Heuvel (eds), *Architecture and the Welfare State*, Routledge, London, 2015, 299-320.

7 HKRS1588-9-38 11-5-1976 note; HKRS1588-2-5 4-1974 MacLehose visit to Oi Man; HKRS70-6-821-2; FCO40-642 May 1975, FCO40-616 1975 papers; HKRS545-1-456-1 11-1975 on opening of Oi Man; HKRS189-2-40 9-1975 on daughter's illness.
8 FCO40-510 21-3-1974 FCO memo; FCO40-518 27-2-1974 MacLehose telegram, Aston 1-3-1974 note, Goodfellow 13-3-1974 note, Haddon-Cave address 19-7-1974.
9 FCO40-678 8-1975 note; FCO40-708 3-5-1976 note, 13-5-1976 Lipsey to O'keeffe; FCO40-711 7-7-1976 MacLehose to FCO, 19-7-1976 Lipsey to Cortazzi, 13-7-1976 discussion Goronwy Roberts-MacLehose, 22-7-1976 Crosland on 'symbolic importance' of appointment. 'Under the sea': FCO40-799 7-10-1977 MacLehose to John Stewart. Edgerton, *The Rise and Fall of the British Nation*, 379-410.
10 Background to autonomy: L Goodstadt, *Uneasy Partners – the Conflict between Public Interest and Private Profit in Hong Kong*, HKUP 2005; L Goodstadt, 'Fiscal freedom and the making of Hong Kong's capitalist society', *China Information* 24 (3), 2010, 273-294. Edgerton, *The Rise and Fall of the British Nation*, 382–420.
11 FCO40-621 Larmour to Cortazzi 12-1975; FCO40-616 1-1975 memo; FCO40-498 8-5-1974; FCO40-711 21-7-1976 meeting MacLehose-Ted Rowlands.
12 FCO40-617 4-1975 criticisms by Callaghan, 12-1975 correspondence with Labour Party officials.
13 HKRS189-2-40 12-1975 discussions at FCO; FCO40-621 Larmour to Cortazzi 12-1975.
14 FCO40-711 7-1976 meetings; 21-7-1976 meeting with Rowlands, claim of Hong Kong 'Victorian attitudes'.
15 FCO40-711 40-712 MacLehose visit to London 7-12-1976; 9-12-1976 Goronwy Roberts meeting with MacLehose and Haddon-Cave.
16 FCO40-711 21-7-1976 MacLehose meeting with Rowlands.
17 FCO40-712, 2-12-1976 briefing paper by FCO; FCO40-712 9-12-1976 Goronwy Roberts-MacLehose meeting at FCO. Contrary argument that MacLehose actually agreed with the reforms imposed by London in 1976: Yep and Lui, 'Revisiting the golden era of MacLehose', 257.
18 HKRS189-2-40 12-1975 papers; HKRS163-8-124 1976 papers.
19 FCO40-642 15-3-1975 note from MacLehose; Governor's Annual Review for 1974.
20 FCO40-616 1-1975 note; FCO40-547, 1-1974 note.
21 Castells et al., *Shek Kip Mei Syndrome*, 10-11, Table 2.13; Pryor, *Housing in Hong Kong*, 91; SCMP 1-7-1975; FCO40-620.
22 FCO40-518 Aston note, 1-3-1974, Goodfellow note, 13-3-1974, and Haddon-Cave address 19-7-1974.
23 FCO40-518 Aston note, 1-3-1974; FCO40-518 MacLehose telegram 27-2-1974.
24 Liao, 2010 interview; FCO40-510 6-1974 MacLehose paper; FCO40-440 1972 Governor's Annual Review.
25 Drakakis-Smith, *High Society,* 108; Castells et al., *Shek Kip Mei Syndrome*, 10-11, Table 2.13; Pryor, *Housing in Hong Kong*, 91; FCO40-617 4-1975 note on re-phasing of Plan; FCO40-1012 1975 papers; Akers-Jones, 2013 interview.
26 FCO40-642 17-4-1982 MacLehose letter.
27 FCO40-619 9-1975 MacLehose 'now touched bottom'; FCO40-620 1-1975 papers; HKRS163-8-29 7-1974 Liao report. July 1975 Lightbody argument to CS that the HA must reduce its dependence on Government by raising rent income: HKRS163-8-21 7-1975 IML note to CS.
28 HKRS163-9-1331 12-1974 papers.
29 HKRS1588-9-22 MacLehose at special LegCo budget debate 2-4-1975.
30 HKRS40-617 4-1975 MacLehose note; HKRS189-2-40 4-1975 papers.

31 HKRS163-8-113 MacLehose notes on Singapore visit 6-1975, including detailed financial basis of Singapore programme; HKRS163-8-29 Public Works estimates 1975-6.
32 FCO40-642 17-4-1982 MacLehose letter.
33 FCO40-619 9-1975 MacLehose 'now touched bottom'; FCO40-620 1-1975 papers; HKRS163-8-29 7-1974 Liao report. July 1975 Lightbody argument to CS that the HA must reduce its dependence on Government by raising rent income: HKRS163-8-21 7-1975 IML note to CS.
34 HKRS163-9-1331 27-2-1975 note; HKRS163-8-29; HKRS1588-9-35 MacLehose to Housing Authority 4-2-1976.
35 HKRS177-3-6-2 10-1976 speech.
36 HKRS545-1-459-1 and FCO40-712, 6-10-76 MacLehose to LegCo concerning HOS; Drakakis-Smith, *High Society*, 108.
37 HKRS177-3-6-1 11-1975 HA memo on capital budget.
38 HKRS 163-7-1 4-1973 notes; FCO40-518 27-8-1974 F Carter note.
39 SCMP 9-8-1974; HKRS163-8-29; HKRS 477-2-4 1974 papers; HKRS163-8-81 6-1974 papers.
40 HKRS163-8-81 6-1974 papers; SCMP 1-7-1975; HKRS163-8-88 Quarterly Housing Report 7/9-1975.
41 SCMP 1-7-1975; HKRS477-2-4 2-1974 dispute; Drakakis-Smith, *High Society*, 108, 117.
42 HKRS1588-9-33, HKRS1588-9-34 12-1975 draft; 13-1-1976 Annual Review discussion.
43 HKRS163-7-3 11-1974, 10-1975 correspondence; HKRS163-7-3, HKMS189-2-40 4-1975 papers. 'Swapped notes': Miller, 2014 interview. HKRS163-8-113 6-1975, MacLehose notes on Singapore
44 FCO40-1122 Scott to Williamson, 1979 correspondence.
45 HKRS163-8-113 6-1975; MacLehose notes on Singapore.
46 HKRS163-8-113 6-1975 brief for MacLehose.
47 HKRS163-7-1 4-1973 Lightbody to Deputy Financial Secretary and 11-1976 report on Group B estates; HKRS1588-2-5 22-4-1974 papers on loans and capital funding; Drakakis-Smith, *High Society*, 117.
48 HKRS1588-2-5 27-4-1974 visit to Housing Department.
49 HKRS1693-1-1 12-2-7194 Bernacchi Urban Council speech; 8-3-1974 Lightbody to Bernacchi; HKRS177-3-6-1 papers on July, August HA members' tour to Wong Tai Sin, Tung Tau, Shek Kip Mei.
50 HKRS163-8-31 Lightbody to Liao, 2-1974; HKRS163-8-53; Liao, 2010 interview re 'hands-off' Lightbody, and MacLehose asking Liao, not Lightbody, to show Queen round Oi Man in 1975.
51 HKRS1588-2-5 MacLehose visit to HQ 27-4-1974.
52 HKRS163-8-149 1-1976 Lightbody note. HKRS545-1-456-1: Liao masterminded the Department's external liaisons, including membership of EAROPH, in November 1974; also notes on 16-9-1974 Gowon visit. HKRS163-8-86 19-11-1974 Liao to Lightbody.
53 HKRS163-8-78 11-1976 note; Akers-Jones, 2014 interview; Hong Kong Gazette 1/2-1974; HKRS163-8-78 4-1974 Lightbody note; HKRS163-8-78 6-1976 papers, HKRS1588-2-3 7-1976 papers; HKRS163-8-26 on organisational structure of the Housing Authority in July 1976.
54 HKRS232-1-23-2 SCMP 31-3-1974 cutting; HKRS163-8-88 3-1975 papers; HKRS530-1-4 6-1976 papers; HKRS545-1-456-2 2-1976 papers.
55 HKRS163-8-113 6-1975 papers, MacLehose notes on Singapore; 'volatile' HKRS163-8-82 29-5-1974 IML note.

56 FCO40-420 8-1973 papers; HKRS530-1-4 2-1977 papers.
57 HKRS489-7-27 6-1975 papers; HKRS70-6-788 9-1974 and 5-1975 papers.
58 HKRS477-2-4 2-1974 papers; HKRS163-8-82 30-5-1974 note.
59 *Hong Kong Standard* 8-1-72; HKRS177-3-6-2; HKRS163-8-26 Review Panel on Hill Slopes 1976.
60 HKRS163-8-102 MacLehose 29-1-1975 note.
61 HKRS1588-2-5 4-74; *Hong Kong Standard* 19-4-1974; HKRS70-6-811-2 4-1974 and 10-1974 papers; FCO40-642 5-1975 royal visit; HKRS1588-9-34 11-5-1976 note; HKRS70-6-821-2; HKRS545-1-456-1 9-1974 papers; HKRS1588-2-10 9-8-1975 papers; SCMP 1-7-1975; HKRS70-6-811-2 11-1975 papers.
62 HKRS163-9-1338 1973-4 papers; SCMP 1-7-1975; Pryor, '*Housing and I*'.
63 HKRS530-3-4 1/2-1986 papers.
64 HKRS163-10-141 5-6-1976 E Elliott note; Lightbody 9-1976 note; HKRS163-9-1342 MOOD 9-1976 survey; HKRS163-9-1342 8-1976 papers; HKRS394-27-9.
65 HKRS177-3-6-1 12-1974 correspondence with Wang Tau Hom Kaifong; HKRS177-3-6-1 12-1974 papers; HKRS163-8-117 8-1974 correspondence.
66 HKRS163-9-930 13-8-1974 note; HKRS163-8-115 23-6-1975 note.
67 HKRS232-1-23-2 3-1974 cutting; HKRS1693-5-6 HPP papers 1974-6; HKRS608-1-44 1-1974 report by Planning Branch.
68 HKRS477-2-4 *Hong Kong Standard* 8-1-1974 cutting; Drakakis-Smith, *High Society*, 108; HKRS163-8-20.
69 HKRS163-8-20, 9-1974 note; HKRS163-8-21 10-1974 note; HKRS594-1-1 9-7-1975 Lightbody memo and table of options 1–47; HKRS163-8-157; HKRS163-8-23 23-10-1974 and 17-10-1974 notes; HKRS1588-9-33 late 1975 draft of Chairman's Review for Annual Report, comments on progress of Ten-Year Plan; HKRS1693-5-6, HPP papers 1974-6.
70 HKRS608-1-41 circular of 1-6-1974.
71 HKRS163-8-51 11-1974, 7-1975 papers; HKRS608-1-41 circular of 6-1974; HKRS608-1-44; HKRS163-8-90 12-76 papers; HKRS232-1-23-6 SCMP 6-11-1974 cutting.
72 HKRS608-1-44 1-1974 papers; HKRS232-1-23-2 3-1974 cutting, on Pryor book and CV information.
73 HKRS1882-1-3 5-12-1975 – LPVC's first meeting.
74 HKRS163-8-20 4-3-76 Lightbody to MacLehose. HKRS163-8-20 12-5-1975 MacLehose to Lightbody.
75 HKRS163-8-23 MacLehose on HPP 6-8-1975; HKRS163-8-21 MacLehose discussion with Lightbody 6-8-1975; HKRS163-8-88 9-1975 Quarterly Housing Report.
76 HKRS545-1-459-1 MacLehose to LegCo on HOS 10-1976.
77 HKRS163-8-20 28-12-1974 Pryor note.
78 HKRS1588-3-22 1975 Liao-Pryor correspondence; HKRS163-8-159 1976 PWD Conference; HKRS1882-1-2; HKRS1882-1-3 LPVC 24-9-1976; HKRS1588-3-22 Pryor 11-1976 note, 15-11-1976 Akers-Jones note to Lightbody. HKRS163-8-146 12-1976 papers.
79 HKRS1588-3-22 15-11-1976 Akers-Jones to Lightbody.
80 HKRS163-8-146 Liao to Lightbody 12-1976; HKRS163-8-20 15-5-1974 Pryor to Liao.
81 Castells et al., *Shek Kip Mei Syndrome*, 12-13; HKRS489-7-27 12-4 1976 paper; SCMP 1-7-1975.
82 HKRS1693-5-6 HPP Steering Group 22-11-1974 and 2-5-1975 meetings. Glendinning, *Mass Housing*, 313.

83 HKRS1588-3-21 1974; HKRS163-8-20 4-3-75 Lightbody to MacLehose, 12-5-1975 MacLehose to Lightbody, and Lightbody, HPP Team update; Williams, 'Housing Demand in Hong Kong', 3-4.
84 HKRS1882-1-3, LPVC 24-9-1976 meeting; HKRS1588-3-21 1974 statistical reports on estates.
85 Liao, 2010 interview, Williams 'Housing in Hong Kong', c. 1987.
86 Castells et al., *Shek Kip Mei Syndrome*, 10-11, Table 2.13; Pryor, *Housing in Hong Kong*, 91.
87 HKRS177-3-6-1 18-8-1975 note.
88 HKRS163-9-991; HKRS163-8-20 5-1974, 28-12-1974 notes.
89 HKRS594-1-1 9-7-1975 Lightbody memo and table of options 1–47 (including 13).
90 HKRS163-8-20 15-5-1974 Pryor to Liao; HKRS163-8-20 5-1974 papers; HKRS1588-3-22; HKRS1882-1-3 8-1976 LPVC papers; HKRS163-8-20 5-1974, 28-12-1974 Pryor notes.
91 HKRS163-8-51 11-1974, 7-1975 papers.
92 HKRS1588-3-22 HPP option 43 papers; HKRS1588-3-22 28-11-1975 SH Cheung note.
93 HKRS1588-3-22 12-1975 papers.
94 HKRS1882-1-3 LPVC 9-1-1976, 8-1976, 3-12-1976 (Pang).
95 HKRS1882-1-3 8-1976 papers; HKRS1882-1-3 LPVC 9-4-1976 minutes; HKRS1882-1-3 5-1976 note on Luen Long. HKRS1882-1-3 LPVC 13-2-1976 on Ngau Chi Wan, 12-11-1976 on Sha Kok; HKRS1882-1-3 9-1-1976 on Wo Che.
96 HKRS163-9-991; HKRS163-8-146; HKRS163-8-159, 1976 papers; HKRS163-9-991 LDPC paper for committee 28-5-1976.
97 HKRS1588-3-25 2-1974 discussion; HKRS177-3-6-1 5-1974 papers; HKRS177-3-6-2 1974-5 papers; HKRS1588-3-25 2-1974 papers.
98 Hong Kong Housing Society, *Annual Report 1978*, Hong Kong, 1978, 24-5; LC Wong, 2011 interview. HKRS163-8-89 1-1980 papers; Akers-Jones, 2014 interview; HKRS545-1-456-2 SCMP 9-3-1979 cutting; 163-8-1989 2-1979 correspondence.
99 HKRS177-3-6-1 22-5-1974 Shek Kip Mei brochure, Lower Wong Tai Sin and Tung Tau; HKRS1588-2-7 6-1975 on Tsz Wan Shan; HKRS177-3-6-1 22-5-1974 and 21-8-1974 notes on Wong Tai Sin, Tung Tau.
100 HKRS163-8-20 7-5-1975 Lightbody memo; HKRS177-3-6-2 12-3-1976 memo; HKRS163-9-991 5-1976 LDPC paper; HKRS163-8-88 Quarterly Report for July-September 1975.
101 HKRS163-9-991 5-1976 notes; HKRS177-3-6-2 12-3-1976 paper.
102 M Glendinning and S Muthesius, *Tower Block*, Yale UP, London, 1994, 220-235; Glendinning, *Mass Housing*, 147-164; HKRS177-3-6-2 3-1976 memo. HKRS163-9-991 5-7196 LDPC paper.
103 HKRS189-2-40 1975 papers.
104 HKRS594-1-1 9-7-1975 Lightbody memo and table of options 1–47.
105 HKRS594-1-1 3-1975 HPP evaluation; HKRS163-8-43 2-1974.
106 HKRS835-1-171 8-1976 papers.
107 HKRS163-8-51 8-1974 and 5-1975 LDPC minutes; Ian Scott, 'Administering the New Towns of Hong Kong', *Asian Survey*, Vol. 22, No. 7 (July 1982), 659-675.
108 HKRS1588-9-55 11-1975 papers; HKRS337-4-6542 NTDPC 7th meeting 11-5-1973, and press cuttings on town planning and New Towns 1970-9.
109 HKRS710-3-3 2-1974 papers; HKRS710-3-3 4-1973 to 2-1974 papers.
110 HKRS232-1-23-1, and HKRS545-1-447-2 cutting of 21-2-1974 quote by Astbury.
111 HKRS176-11-18 4-9-1974 Astbury memo.

112 HKRS545-1-447-2 8-11-74 O'Rorke HKRS232-123-6 8-11-1974 and 30-11-1974.
113 HKRS163-9-1331 12-1974 papers; HKRS545-1-447-2 30-3-1974 cutting.
114 HKRS895-1-52 5-1975 papers; HKRS232-1-23-6 14-12-1974 on Tsuen Wan.
115 HKRS545-1-447-2 23-12-1974 Akers-Jones cutting; 176-11-18 9-1974 papers; HKRS163-8-51 7-1975 papers; HKRS232-1-23-6 13-12-1974 Akers-Jones on market towns.
116 HKRS1882-1-3 LPVC 14-5-1976 minutes.
117 HKRS176-11-20 5-1975 papers.
118 HKRS1882-1-3 11-1975 papers.
119 HKRS163-8-13 6-1975 brief for MacLehose on Singapore.
120 HKRS545-1-456-2 2-1976 and *HKIA Journal* 72, 2016, 49, on Hing Wah; HKRS70-6-811-1 1976 papers on Kwai Shing.
121 HKRS232-1-23-1 SCMP 16-1-1974 cutting; HKRS545-1-447-2 16-1-1974 cutting; HKRS500-6-5 1-2-1976 press bulletin.
122 HKRS545-1-456-2; HKRS1882-1-3 LPVC 9-1-1976, 13-2-1976 minutes. HKHA, *The First Two Million*, HK, 1980, 30-1.
123 HKRS163-8-146 1-1976; HKRS163-8-148, 1976 comparison of public rental housing with Li Ka-shing's middle-income scheme.
124 HKRS1882-1-3 LPVC 9-1-1976, 8-1976, 3-12-1976 (Pang/Wo Che general).
125 HKRS70-8-811-2 4-1975 paper; HKRS70-6-811-2 4-1974 papers; HKRS1588-2-5; FCO40-642; FCO40-616 on 'model'; Liao, 2010 interview.
126 HKHS, *The Hong Kong Housing Society Annual Report 1978*, Hong Kong, 1978, 4-6, 41; LC Wong, 2011 interview. HKRS163-8-89 1-1980 papers; Akers-Jones, 2014 interview; HKRS545-1-456-2 SCMP 9-3-1979 cutting; HKRS163-8-1989 2-1979 correspondence. HKRS232-1-14-1 and HKRS896-1-49 on Tai Hang Road site.
127 HKRS163-8-123 3-1976 by Economic Analysis Division.
128 HKRS500-6-5 1-2-1976 press bulletin.
129 HKRS1588-9-55; HKRS232-1-23-6 SCMP 23-2-1974 cutting.

7 MacLehose's 'brainchild'

The Home Ownership Scheme

Introduction: prelude to a revolution

Of the main strands of MacLehose's new, 'identity'-orientated housing drive, the one that most vividly bore the imprint of his driving, progress-chasing *modus operandi* was the Home Ownership Scheme (HOS). This programme was 'entirely the brainchild' of MacLehose (Bernard Williams) and was rushed into operation in the late 1970s with astonishing speed.[1]

The discussions in 1963–5 concerning potential ways to expand home-ownership with government help (Chapter 4) had proved abortive, largely because no precedents for modern mass home-ownership yet existed in Hong Kong. However, interest continued growing in the later 1960s, especially reflecting the HDB's new home-ownership scheme in Singapore. The first significant exemplar was the initial portion of Mei Foo Sun Chuen, completed in 1971, which firmly established a new linkage between middle-income home-ownership and modern, compact blocks of flats.[2] As Mei Foo rose out of the ground in its successive stages, the former Public Works chief, Michael Wright, now a consultant to the developers Galbreath-Ruffin, repeatedly impressed on Hong Kong's building elites the potential attractiveness of European-style flats to middle-class Chinese occupants. One key government convert was Akers-Jones, who recalled that Mei Foo 'sold me on the idea of home-ownership, and what it could do for a community, their psychology, and their support for the government.' It 'proved that good management could keep an estate going'.[3] An early step in the direct policy chain leading to the HOS was made in the early 1970s by Liao, in his capacity as Commissioner for Housing, in a speech at the Rotary Club. (Figures 7.1, 7.2)

To all this was added MacLehose's new pressure for output, and the idea of directly harnessing the private sector to help boost this strategy. The unleashing of the Ten-Year Programme in his October 1972 speech raised the possibility of home-ownership construction as a way of supporting the programme, possibly by selling leases – but the initial overwhelming emphasis on public rental production dwarfed all else.[4] Only once that began to run into output problems did government-promoted home-ownership re-emerge as a potential help. Following an April 1973 comparison with the Singaporean CPF, Lightbody raised in June the possibility of selling existing or new public rental housing leases to tenants to offset

DOI: 10.1201/9781315563701-9

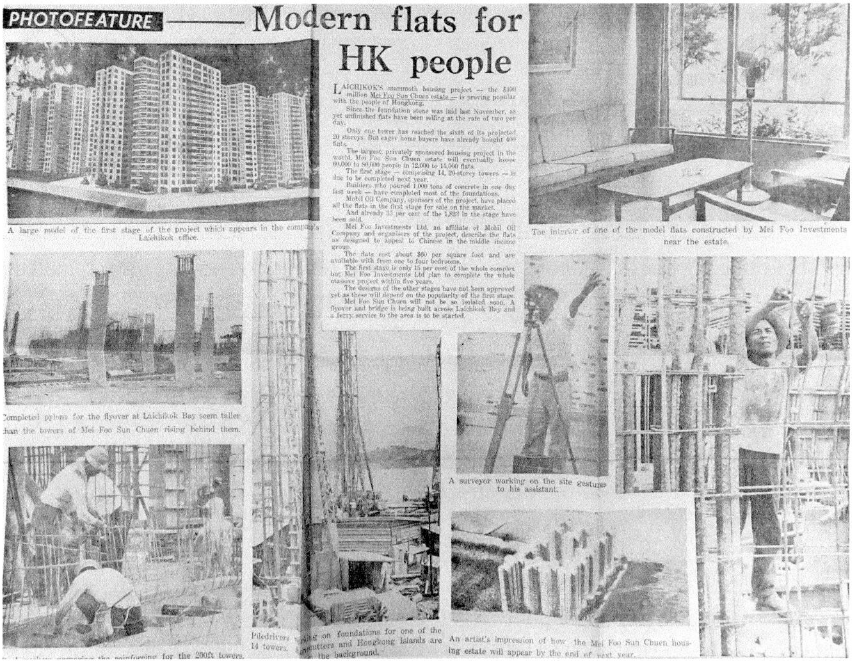

PHOTOFEATURE

Modern flats for HK people

LAICHIKOK'S mammoth housing project — the $400 million Mei Foo Sun Chuen estate — is proving popular with the people of Hongkong.

Since the foundation stone was laid last November, as yet unfinished flats have been selling at the rate of two per day.

Only one tower has reached the sixth of its projected 20 storeys. But eager home buyers have already bought 400 flats.

The largest privately sponsored housing project in the world, Mei Foo Sun Chuen estate will eventually house 60,000 to 80,000 people in 12,000 to 15,000 flats.

The first stage — comprising 14, 20-storey towers — is due to be completed next year.

Builders who poured 1,000 tons of concrete in one day last week — have completed most of the foundations.

Mobil Oil Company, sponsors of the project, have placed all the flats in the first stage for sale on the market.

And already 35 per cent of the 1,827 in the stage have been sold.

Mei Foo Investments Ltd, an affiliate of Mobil Oil Company and organisers of the project, describe the flats as designed to appeal to Chinese in the middle income group.

The flats cost about $60 per square foot and are available with from one to four bedrooms.

The first stage is only 15 per cent of the whole complex but Mei Foo Investments Ltd plan to complete the whole massive project within five years.

The designs of the other stages have not been approved yet as these will depend on the popularity of the first stage.

Mei Foo Sun Chuen will not be so isolated soon. A flyover and bridge is being built across Laichikok Bay and a ferry service to the area is to be started.

A large model of the first stage of the project which appears in the company's Laichikok office.

The interior of one of the model flats constructed by Mei Foo Investments near the estate.

Completed pylons for the flyover at Laichikok Bay seem taller than the towers of Mei Foo Sun Chuen rising behind them.

A surveyor working on the site gestures to his assistant.

... for the 200ft towers.

Piledrivers ...ing on foundations for one of the 14 towers. ...cutters and Hongkong Islands are ... the background.

An artist's impression of how the Mei Foo Sun Chuen housing estate will appear by the end of next year.

Figure 7.1 Double-page *China Mail* feature of June 1967 on the first stage of Mei Foo Sun Chuen, then under construction.

Mr. R.R. Kendall (left), managing director of Mei Foo Investments Limited, and Mr. Edwin Martin, the American Consul-General, inspecting the Mei Foo Sun Chuen yesterday.

GIANT ESTATE OPENS ITS FIRST TOWERS

THE first five 20-storey towers of the first stage of the giant Mei Foo Sun Chuen housing project at Lai Chi Kok were opened recently.

Figure 7.2 Feature in *Star* on opening of first five blocks at Mei Foo, November 1968.

the cost of the Ten-Year Programme, under the heading, 'Flats-for-Sale Scheme', but his conclusion in 1973 was that the time was 'not yet ripe'.[5] The following year, in November 1974, with public rental output dropping, Lightbody reversed that judgement, and argued that the 'time is probably ripe' for a flats-for-sale scheme, to help revitalise output; and in that same month his staff began examining the financial and budgetary aspects of a potential home-ownership building programme.[6]

'Option 13': Flats-for-Sale and the Housing Programme Plan

By this stage, discussions about any flats-for-sale scheme were integrally bound up with the new Housing Programme Plan, following its launch in September 1974.[7] Although, in late 1975, Liao and Haddon-Cave were still discussing acquisition of flats built by the private sector as a potential way forward,[8] by now a very different approach, direct government building of home-ownership flats, was emerging from the proliferation of HPP options as the favoured way forward – although only behind-the-scenes, given MacLehose's August 1975 directive to keep the HPP's 'negative' strategic recommendations under wraps.[9]

An immediate source of inspiration for any flats-for-sale scheme was naturally Singapore, and so on his June 1975 visit, hosted by Lee Kuan Yew, MacLehose made sure he obtained as much information as possible from the 'horse's mouth', by investigating the CPF and the linked Home-Ownership for the People Scheme (HOPS). MacLehose focused on the potential lessons of both schemes for Hong Kong, as well as their limitations if adapted for its less dirigiste society.[10] (Figure 7.3) In very full annotated notes, he concluded that while the CPF had massively boosted funds available for housing and new town development in Singapore, he was 'not sure Hong Kong citizens would generally welcome such a scheme' [as the CPF] and that Singaporean public housing was essentially in competition with the private sector, rather than targeted at the poor.[11] When MacLehose later floated

Figure 7.3 Commonwealth Estate, Blocks 81–3, Queenstown Neighbourhood 3: Singapore's first Home Ownership for the People project, designed and built by the HDB in 1962–4, and comprising three 16-storey gallery-access slabs of three-room flats. 2012 photo (MG).

the idea of adopting a mandatory CPF-style scheme, it was vetoed by both unions and employers as 'not relevant to us'.[12] Correspondingly, Liu Thai-Ker, Deputy Chief Architect of the HDB, later acknowledged the greater significance of the private sector in Hong Kong, where it provided the 'life-sustaining force' of housing.[13] Nevertheless, several follow-up visits by officials to Singapore followed, including an investigation of the HOPS by Freddie Pang; a paper by Harry Fong for LegCo about the Singapore experience in home-ownership duly followed.[14] The HD also consulted the Greater London Council, but the very different cultural prejudices and density constraints in England made their experience irrelevant: Bernard Williams recalled that 'they said, "You can sell houses, not flats!" '[15]

The HPP heading under which the flats-for-sale scheme began to coalesce was tucked away unobtrusively among the draft options. This was Option 13, a lesser, Priority B option, which proposed to 'increase the cash flow by selling blocks of flats in new housing estates to existing or potential tenants'.[16] As late as December 1975, Lightbody freely admitted no work had yet been done within HD on investigating Option 13, yet MacLehose was clearly determined to use the Option as a cover not so much for selling existing flats as for building new ones: as the Accountant-General was already examining the financial implications of potential government guarantees for any flats-for-sale scheme.[17] The eventual evaluation of Option 13 at the February 1976 HPP steering group was obviously just a formality, as MacLehose then immediately approached the Housing Authority to propose a 5,000 unit annual programme – officially known until November 1976 as the Flats-for-Sale Scheme, only changing after that to the Home Ownership Scheme.[18]

This additional new programme was one of many social enhancements allowed by the mounting surpluses generated by increased growth, but its funding support was not unlimited. The January 1976 research into the comparative costs of public and private enterprise development had found the twin-tower blocks at Wo Che compared favourably with private developments, while a September 1976 paper also examined selected private developments potentially relevant to any flats-for-sale scheme.[19] However, it was clear from the start that the scheme's financial implications were of secondary rather than primary significance. MacLehose emphasised in January and March 1976 that the fundamental motive was to boost output, as existing funds would only support 24,000 new units per annum. Assuming building at high densities, it could significantly compensate for 'construction lost during the recession' and 'make up for lost time'. The driving constraint was emphatically output, not money: whereas under Cowperthwaite, cost had always been the ultimate deciding factor, the growth he had helped generate now allowed a very different approach to public spending, with programmes such as this the beneficiaries.[20]

Immediately, MacLehose took the key organisational decision to entrust the entire construction process for the new programme to the Housing Authority, rather than private developers, and he wrote formally to the HA in February 1976, stressing the programme's overriding purpose was to minimise recession-driven output shortfalls.[21] After lengthy discussion by HA unofficial members, and criticisms from Elliott, Huang and Cheong-Leen, the Authority reluctantly accepted the plan, ultimately voting for it on February 12 by 12:1.[22] Equally worrying to MacLehose was potential administrative procrastination: in February he warned Lightbody, 'I do hope you will not let this get bogged down in detail', and suggested shortcut devices, such as to 'farm out' design to the PWD or (as eventually transpired) to private architects for the first 5,000 units to get construction moving quickly.[23] Driven on by MacLehose, the Flats-for-Sale Scheme pushed forward on all fronts of government, featuring strongly in Haddon-Cave's budget speech in March, and in LegCo speeches by MacLehose in April and July.[24] Within the HA, Liao rapidly emerged as the central driving actor, confirming in July to MacLehose that he aimed 'to make up for lost time' from the recession, and to meet the housing target earlier.[25]

From July 1976 onwards, however, the scheme's strategic aim was cautiously extended beyond mere output to embrace a broader social agenda: in a July minute, MacLehose argued that 'I have for some time felt that the absence of such a scheme is a serious social deficit in Hong Kong'.[26] In an October LegCo speech, MacLehose heralded the broadening of the scheme from its original restriction to public rental tenants, to include lower-middle-income applicants from outside the public housing system: home-ownership, he argued, was 'such a desirable social objective in its own right' that it was 'too important' to be left to private enterprise.[27]

In parallel with this, attention rapidly focused on site-selection for Phase I, with March meetings at Government House and in LDPC.[28] For sites provisionally identified, any competing uses were peremptorily suppressed, especially public-sector ones: at Oi Man North for example, Urban Council and DUS plans for a swimming pool were swatted aside in October/November 1976 by the Housing Department, which cited MacLehose's personal interest in the case, and the 'urgency' attributed it by the Governor. Furthermore, in a distinct aberration from 'Hong Kong tradition', both before and after, the private sector was given an explicitly lower priority: throughout 1976 MacLehose repeatedly insisted on prioritising the Flats-for-Sale Scheme over private enterprise for site acquisition. Pryor played a key role in identifying a shortlist of 25 potential sites in September, rapidly evaluating candidates in depth.[29] In the event, sites for the first 5,000 units were split between the urban core and the New Territories, despite secret warnings by MOOD in August 1976 that the threat of post-1997 communist rule might disincentivise home-ownership in the New Territories.[30]

Laying the ground-rules: the Home-Ownership Steering Group

In November, matters seemed sufficiently advanced for Lightbody to write formally to the Housing Authority, inviting it to undertake what was now officially re-titled the Home Ownership Scheme (HOS). In an echo of the politicised pre-1973 UC housing debates, the Authority remained lukewarm towards the proposal in initial discussions, a significant minority being either reluctant to take on the HOS at all, or only willing to do so if explicitly 'outside' the public rental housing programme.[31] Elliott trenchantly opposed the HOS, as it 'made all promises impossible to keep and only swelled the long list of low-income families in drastic need

Homes scheme may start next year

Prospective home buyers may be able to apply for flats under the Government's home ownership scheme early next year.

The Housing Authority will design, build, sell and manage the flats, as was reported exclusively by the S.C.M. Post on Wednesday.

The Financial Secretary, Mr Philip Haddon-Cave, said at a press conference yesterday the basic framework of the scheme has been worked out.

Mr Haddon-Cave, who chairs the scheme working party, said the intention is to help the lower middle income group buy their own homes on terms they can afford.

The first five sites have been chosen at Aberdeen, fronting Yue Kwong Road; Chaiwan, near a road junction on Chaiwan Road; Laichikok Headland, facing Lai King Hill Road; Hungshin, near Oi Man Estate, and Shatin, next to the railway overlooking Tide Cove.

The Housing Authority has produced development proposals, along with cost estimates, of phase one of the programme, which calls for about 7,200 flats by 1979/80.

The authority has commissioned several architectural firms to produce development proposals.

Each flat will have a kitchen, toilet facilities, and a balcony. The smaller flats are likely to be open plan and the larger ones should have at least two bedrooms.

Mr Haddon-Cave said the cost of these flats will not be known until contracts have been let. But he said that based on present estimates the flats may be sold at a price range of $80,000 to $140,000.

The flats will range in size from about 400 sq ft to about 600 sq ft of lettable floor area.

As to eligibility, Mr Haddon-Cave said the flats are intended for families with a total monthly income of below $3,500 and who have been living in Hongkong for at least five years.

Tenants of public housing flats will not have to satisfy the normal criteria and will be treated as a special category with some priority.

It is expected that about 360,000 households will be eligible.

On the subject of mortgage finance, Mr Haddon-Cave said the working party has envisaged that funds will be provided mainly by commercial and financial institutions lending directly to the Government's nominated flat-buyers.

He said terms with banking and finance houses have yet to be negotiated, adding that the mortgages will cover some Government guarantee.

The working party is also planning a mortgage institution, to be wholly owned by the Government. The institution will raise funds for on-lending to supplement funds of commercial banks.

However, the institution may not need to be introduced, and even if brought into operation, will not compete with the banks for funds.

The basic mortgage terms the working party has in mind are:

- Down payment – a minimum of $10,000 or 10 per cent of the sale price, whichever is the higher.
- Maturity – 15 years.
- Interest – [illegible] be set initially between eight and nine per cent a year, for fixed periods of three, five or seven years, subject to periodic review and to any arrangements which will minimise the risk to the mortgagor of fluctuations in monthly payments.

Referring to the possible situation where the open market values of these flats will be considerably higher than the sale price, Mr Haddon-Cave said the Government will have to introduce certain restrictions on resale.

Details have yet to be completed, he said, but the

(Cont'd on Page 20, Col. 7)

Figure 7.4 Report in SCMP on March 1977 news conference by Haddon-Cave on progress in setting up the HOS, and a perspective of Sui Wo Court.

of affordable housing'. Hong Kong, she felt, should 'house its most needy citizens first'.[32] In 1977, the SCMP publicised the scheme, predicting it would start the following year; eventually, Haddon-Cave finalised the terms of agreement with the HA in March 1978.[33] (Figure 7.4)

The Authority's initial reluctance made it necessary for the government to establish its own executive mechanisms for forcing through the HOS, and behind the scenes, Haddon-Cave played a crucial role, not just financially but more generally as a broker in 1976–8.[34] His main vehicle was a Working Party on Home-Ownership, established by MacLehose in July/August 1976, and converted immediately into a steering group under Haddon-Cave's chairmanship. Its terms of reference were, firstly, to offset shortages in public housing production indirectly by securing the vacating of public rental flats, and secondly, to pursue the 'social objective' of encouraging home-ownership by low-income groups. A May 1977 letter by Haddon-Cave stressed the paramountcy of the second objective, and of the HOS concept as a 'social measure'.[35]

To avoid any ambiguity, MacLehose stressed to the Chief Secretary in late 1976 why the private sector was excluded from the terms of reference of the steering group: the programme was *not* to be delegated to the private sector, as the Housing Department machinery was already in being. MacLehose explained that 'I have tried to make clear from the start that it is the Housing Authority which should build the 5,000 flats'.[36] In September 1976, he wrote to the Chief Secretary in response to warnings of site shortages, pointing out that as sites were not to be delegated to private enterprise, this should not happen: 'since I have directed that, if necessary, sites for that could be withdrawn from land earmarked for the private sector, it follows that sites *will* be available'. So delegation to private enterprise 'should be ruled out of the working party's terms of reference. This is because, now that the Housing Authority has geared up to build these flats, any kind of alternative arrangements will merely result in delay': he suggested that Akers-Jones should investigate whether land reclamation could be used to provide compensation for the private sector.[37] In a paper on the management of slippage, MacLehose agreed that if both the Authority and the private sector could be satisfied, that was an ideal position. But if not, the HA must have priority, 'in case there is any doubt in anyone's mind on the matter'.[38] This was new territory indeed for laissez-faire

Hong Kong – even if, for very good reasons stemming from Hong Kong's 'caretaker' governmental system, it sedulously avoided anything resembling the draconian character of Singaporean home-ownership, financed by a state-enforced savings system.

On the whole, the executive role of the steering group worked effectively, even although there were sometimes misunderstandings between it and the Housing Department: a March 1977 exchange of letters between Liao and Haddon-Cave alluded to a 'muddle' on several issues.[39] Eventually, following full commencement of the HOS in 1978, executive responsibility passed from the steering group to the Housing Branch, and to a new Home Ownership Committee set up by the Housing Authority in May 1977. The final steering group meeting occurred in April 1978.[40]

By the mid-1970s, a powerful speculative real-estate sector was emerging, complete with controlling 'tycoon' families: it would ultimately exercise a decisive veto power over government housing policy by the 1990s, as well as providing much of the impetus for the growth of the Hong Kong stock market and the general 'financialisation' of the Hong Kong economy.[41] The dominant developers were all founded in the 1970s, many based around earlier family firms – New World Development in 1970, Cheung Kong in 1971, Sun Hung Kai in 1972 and Henderson Land in 1976 – and were soon afterwards listed in the Hong Kong stock market. And within this already-powerful private property sector, the unexpectedly rapid emergence of the HOS as a potential interloper immediately provoked unease, as reported by Haddon-Cave at the Governor's Committee in March 1976.[42] Likewise, the April 1976 LDPC reported significant private-sector opposition to Flats-for-Sale Scheme proposals.[43] In March 1976, key private developer Henry Fok, President of the Real-Estate Developers of Hong Kong, wrote to Lightbody that developers were 'worried', protesting that 'only in a socialist state like Singapore would government take part directly in property development', whereas in the Hong Kong context, government intervention would 'inhibit property development'; Liao later recalled 'the complaints from the private sector that we were taking their "rice bowl"'. In reply, Lightbody assured Fok in June that the HOS would not compete with the private sector. And there was also a feeling within government about the HOS that 'if you push the envelope, the private sector will get better still'.[44] This qualified rebuff highlighted that the property 'tycoons' had not yet attained the crushing dominance within housing policy that they would establish by the 1990s.

Although the HOS was not intended chiefly as a financial device, but rather as a two-pronged production and social strategy, the laying of the financial groundwork was of vital importance for its success, and it was here that both Haddon-Cave and, more surprisingly, Liao, played linchpin roles. MacLehose preferred to entrust unconventional policy initiatives to officials with an entrepreneurial, interdisciplinary versatility, rather than orthodox administrators such as Lightbody, and the founding of the HOS allowed people such as Liao, Haddon-Cave or Akers-Jones to range some distance from their strict areas of responsibility. From the outset, it was accepted as desirable that the HOS should be based on a revolving-fund formula, possibly linked with the Hong Kong Building and Loan Agency.[45] After his researches on Singapore, and the vetoing by workers and employees themselves of anything resembling Singapore's compulsory CPF system, MacLehose instead opted for a subsidised system with deferred repayment of premium. In an April 1979 briefing, it was emphasised that the fundamental principle of the HOS was that it was self-financed.[46] It was predicted to provide 16% of total public housing output over the eight years to 1986/7, contributing a potential total of 44,292 flats. If there were wider problems in output, for example if funds for the rental programme stayed tight, the government could potentially convert a further 10% of public rental housing to HOS. In their financial organisation, HOS flats involved 10% equity contribution by the borrower, repayment over 15 years, and a limited interest rate of 7.9/9% over five years; ordinary private housing required 30%, 10 years, and 10%.[47]

Straying some distance from his original architectural focus of gravity, Liao was tasked with carrying out initial negotiations with four leading banks about potential mortgage provisions. Haddon-Cave also encouraged the HA to open discussions with Rothschilds.[48] In December 1976, it was reported that financial arrangements for the HOS were 'not yet clear', but the following month, a Home Ownership Fund was established by LegCo resolution, and Haddon-Cave wrote to the general manager of the Hong Kong and Shanghai Bank that it was essential to avoid 'giving the buyer a hidden subsidy'.[49] In February, Phase I of the HOS, comprising 8,373 flats in six developments, was offered for sale: it had been decided that in contrast to public rental housing schemes ('chuen' in Cantonese, translated as 'Estate' in English), HOS developments would be titled 'yuen' (a word with garden-like connotations, and translated as 'Court' in English). And by 1979/80, a complex network of banking and mortgage provisions had been established.[50]

In terms of eligibility, Liao recalled that from the start there was a two-pronged approach, encouraging people to move 'up' from public rental housing and 'in' from outside – using a dual system of green and white forms. In public housing, the aim was to 'encourage people to move forward', through a system that was like 'a revolving door'.[51] According to Bernard Williams, the financial equation underpinning the supply side of the HOS was a combination of free land and self-financed building costs, so that 'the Housing Department part of the housing programme is self-financing' – the eventual aim being that home-ownership should account for 25% of the programme. Akers-Jones recalled that while the Housing Department did not have to pay for land, there was 'an element of profit' for the HD in construction.[52] Haddon-Cave emphasised that buyers must not receive any hidden subsidy, and that their contributions, including a substantial 20% down-payment, were central to the scheme's viability.[53] Complex rules of eligibility for both green and white form applicants were drawn up, but in 1978 it was reported that there was no time for extensive checking of eligibility and potential fraud.[54]

Designing for home-ownership: private architects and the expansion of the Housing Department

The HOS programme represented a sharp departure not only from previous organisational practice within Hong Kong public housing, but also from its previous architectural norms. It was shaped physically by a combination of the far larger and better-equipped flats that were required for home-ownership – always allowing for Hong Kong's small average dwelling size by international standards – and the higher site densities necessitated by the programme-supplement character of the HOS, together with the specific typological precedent of the Mei Foo towers.[55]

MacLehose's February 1976 suggestion to Lightbody to use both private architects and the PWD to get the first 5,000 Flats-for-Sale Scheme flats moving quickly had been speedily implemented by Liao, with assistance from Fung Tung.[56] Liao invited several experienced, housing-specialised Hong Kong private architectural practices to a lunch, at which

> I just dished out the contracts [for the Phase I HOS sites] and said "Get on with it!!"'... 'I didn't want to interfere with these firms – I just said, "Here's the brief, we want a shopping centre and so on, the basic requirements..." – without tying their hands. All we wanted was something that the owner would be proud to keep.' Liao's policy-entrepreneurial approach to setting up the HOS, he recalled, enjoyed the 'greatest support from the Governor, and so it got off the ground very quickly. This was the challenge of getting things moving – that was my approach: "Don't interfere with me – let me get on with it – if I make a mess, you can always sack me!"[57]

Most of the Phase I projects generically resembled Mei Foo in their relatively small, plain towers with central service-cores, as for example at Oi Man North (1978), designed by Jackson Wong's group. (Figure 7.5) The major exception to this – an exception that pointed the way towards the future dominance of ever taller and slimmer towers in the mainstream housing programme – was the contribution of Palmer & Turner, in developing a series of projects for high, clustered towers, with collective sky lobbies linking multiple floors in a spatially inventive manner.

Figure 7.5 Oi Man North (Chun Man Court, 1978), one of the first-phase developments of the HOS. 2011 photo (MG).

Figure 7.6 Sha Tin Area 42A HOS (Sui Wo Court), November 1983 general view (MG).

Their seminal development within HOS Phase I, headed by project architect James Kinoshita with Nicholas Burns and other colleagues, was Sha Tin Area 42A (Sui Wo Court; 1978–82). It comprised an array of clustered blocks up to 37 storeys high. Each of these clustered blocks was made up of four pairs of towers each arranged in the shape of a 'T', the four 'Ts' forming a windmill shape on plan, and with the two elements of each T being separated by half a floor's level. Multi-level 'sky lobbies' every three floors at the centre were intended, according to Kinoshita, to 'create community'. Burns, too, recalled that 'the aim was to try to break up public housing into smaller communities'.[58] (Figures 7.6, 7.7)

After robust clashes between contractor Hsin Chong and job architect Burns, who insisted on the replacement of sub-standard reinforced concrete finish and windows, Sui Wo Court was opened in May 1981 by MacLehose, who used the opportunity to trumpet the 'unqualified success' of the HOS to date, stressing that the 5,000 flats had not been achieved 'at the expense of' rental output.[59] For Liao, too, Sui Wo Court was one of the new programme's proudest achievements: 'It's the best of the bunch, and got the HKIA Silver Medal: the site and the view from there are absolutely phenomenal, and it has an integrated shopping centre'.[60] (Figures 7.8, 7.9) Palmer & Turner went on to design a smaller-scale repeat block for the HA at Tsui Yiu Court in Lai King, along with slightly different variations on the same sky lobby/atrium tower theme for the Housing Society, at Cho Yiu Chuen, Kwai Chung (a 39-storey centrepiece block, 1975–81 – cf. Chapter 8)

Figure 7.7 Sui Wo Court: close-up in 2010 (MG).

Figure 7.8 Plaque commemorating MacLehose's official opening of Sui Wo Court on 21 May 1981: 2010 photo (MG).

and Clague Garden, Tsuen Wan (1988). Much larger in scale, but similar in general principle, was Palmer & Turner's Hing Man Estate, Chai Wan, an unusual prototype rental development which anticipated the extension of the sky-lobby clustered-tower principle above 40 storeys – the first in the programme (see Chapter 8).[61]

Despite this frenetic private-sector activity, the ultimate preferred solution was to gradually take HOS design in-house, and the result, in June 1977, was the expansion of the Division to include two architectural branches rather than the previous one, and the authorisation of a massive recruitment drive.[62] As to how the HOS would be administratively and organisationally supported within the Housing Department, the 1977/8 establishment of the Home Ownership Committee was paralleled by massive change and expansion on the design and construction side of the Department.[63] To head the new HOS architectural branch, a new chief architect post was to be recruited: in March 1977, Williams wrote informally to an ex-president of the Institute of Housing in London, that Lightbody was moving away in April to be replaced by the much younger Alan Scott, who 'knows nothing about housing', and that 'we are thinking of recruiting a really high-powered Chief Architect from England' at a monthly salary of HK$9,650: 'If you happen to know anybody suitable who would like two-and-a-half or three years in Hong Kong perhaps you could let us know'.[64]

The eventual choice for the post, Derek Messling, was a housing specialist previously employed in the London Borough of Islington since 1973, as Assistant Borough Architect (Housing) under Borough Architect Alf Head. Paradoxically, the London public housing programme was, during the 1970s, experiencing a sharp downturn both in numbers and, following the 1968 Ronan Point disaster, in building height. In Islington, however, the typical 1970s London trend towards complex, 3–4 storey and (by English standards) high-density redevelopments was accompanied by an Indian summer of housing production, and in both 1973 and 1975, Islington seized the top spot in the London housing output league table, with 3,491 and 2,972 dwellings under construction, respectively, in its dozens of 'HDAs' ('Housing Development Areas').[65] Messling was concerned not with design issues but above all with problem-solving within the increasingly complicated and fragmented land-assembly and organisational processes of inner-London redevelopment, where – just as he would in the Hong Kong HOS – he coordinated the projects of in-house teams and external consultants such as Darbourne & Darke, and ran the contract administration. One of his Islington group leaders, Philip Boyle, recalls,

> He was laid-back, rather smooth, listened to you and took things on board, never expressed any views on architecture, and left people to get on with stuff – but didn't avoid making the decisions that were necessary. He was clearly ambitious, and was somebody who wanted to run something big – I remember him as this chap who appeared from somewhere, I'm not sure where, was quite benign and nice and managed things for a bit, and was here one year and the next was gone![66]

Figure 7.9 Visit by Lord Privy Seal Humphrey Atkins (bending over) with MacLehose to Sui Wo Court in 1982: image from 1981–2 Housing Authority *Annual Report*.

Arriving in Hong Kong in December 1977, Messling exchanged the avuncular and low-key oversight of Alf Head for the distinctly more forceful leadership of Donald Liao, and soon proved himself more than prepared for the pursuit of public housing as a more uninhibited 'numbers game', and to deal with even more challenging contractual problems and delays: eventually he stayed in Hong Kong not for two or three years but for over fifteen, latterly as executive head of the entire design and construction programme.[67]

Messling's new team in the HOS design branch pioneered a range of architectural policies, shaped not by any specific British public housing precedents but instead more by the local precedent set by Mei Foo, as well as by the HOS designs of the external consultants. That was only to be expected, given his lack of strong architectural preferences, which meant that the jump from Islington low-rise to Hong Kong high-rise towers was less incongruous than it appeared. At any rate, at an April 1978 discussion at ExCo, it was agreed that each HOS unit should be self-contained and feature two bedrooms, a combined living/dining room, bathroom, and perhaps a balcony.[68] Within that overall framework, considerable flexibility in sizes and plans was possible, but it was taken for granted that, as with the rental programme, standard block types would predominate, here overwhelmingly of a tall tower-like form – although on special sites the HOS programme also occasionally allowed for non-standard in-house designs, such as Po On Market (1982).[69] In designing successive standard types, however, the architects had a major problem: the time-lag of several years between design and completion, which left them always racing to keep up with the sharp rises and falls of Hong Kong's housing market.

Almost exclusively, the first generation of in-house-designed HOS towers were relatively slender, cruciform blocks, sometimes arranged in linked groups. (Figure 7.10a, b) These were informed by the 1976 comparison of the cost of a standard twin-tower block at Wo Che with normal private-enterprise blocks.[70] The first standard HOS block was the 'Old Cruciform' block, as seen, for example, in the ten linked 17-storey blocks of Siu On Court in Tuen Mun (part of HOS Phase IIIa, 1981). These were strikingly similar in general configuration to private blocks at Mei Foo and slightly later schemes: Williams argued that 'they are so well-designed and well-appointed that they are comparable to high quality private sector flats'.[71] They were designed from the mid-'70s by Stephen Poon and his team, working under S H Cheung prior to his retiral and Messling's arrival:

> I didn't get any specific brief from him [Cheung], except that they were not to have enclosed lightwells as you have in the private sector, as they cause maintenance and management problems. So I designed something with 'left-overs' – the staircases have natural ventilation.[72]

The mainstay of the first HOS generation was the Flexi Block, which also incorporated generously sized flats: the largest Flexi development would be the enormous, brown-clad Tuen Mun Area 51, Siu Hong Court, whose 4,676 flats would be occupied between August 1982 and December 1984.[73]

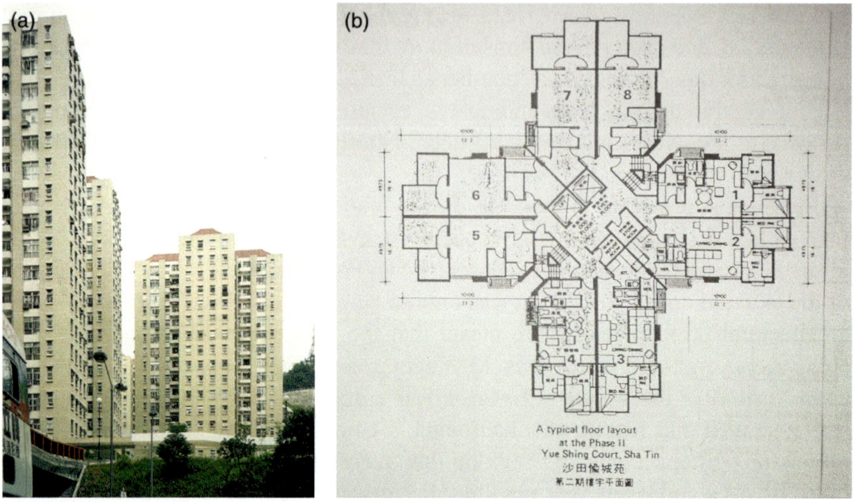

Figure 7.10 (a) Shun Chi Court, the first HOS estate completed: the first of its 17-storey Old Cruciform towers was opened in December 1979. 1983 photo (MG). (b) Specimen upper-floor plan of Old Cruciform blocks, for example at Yue Shing Court, Sha Tin, completed from 1980: displayed at exhibition on Hong Kong in Edinburgh City Art Centre, 1996 (MG).

However, the general escalation in land and construction prices soon left Messling's branch struggling to keep up. At a September 1979 LPVC meeting to discuss HOS flat sizes and layouts – including whether Cruciform or Flexi blocks were the optimum in planning and economic terms for use at Tuen Mun 51 – it was generally agreed the current Phase I and Phase II HOS point blocks had been too expensive and no longer affordable, and that the Flexi block would need to be 'shrunk' to allow smaller flats, although not less than 40 m^2 gross.[74] Various ways of achieving this were discussed, including adapting the rental H block for up to 50% of future HOS output – an option not proceeded with. In December 1981, however, a new block type, the 36-storey Windmill, designed by Stephen Poon's team, was introduced to HOS, with the aim of cutting costs by 12%, and containing 16 flats of 40–52 sq m on each upper floor (in some cases without normal bedroom partitions, to allow buyers to divide them up themselves). The first Windmill was built from 1982 at Mei Lam, and others followed at, for example, Lung Poon Court (Diamond Hill) and Tin Ma Court (Wong Tai Sin).[75] But almost immediately the easing of the economic situation (see Chapter 8) switched the spotlight back towards cruciform blocks of larger flats, the result being the New Cruciform Block. Poon recalled that the latter 'was in some ways not a very nice building', with 'strange planning and drainage problems'.[76] (Figure 7.11a, b)

Interviewed in 1983, senior architect Denis Ko summed up this rapid evolution of HOS type-plans during the first five years.

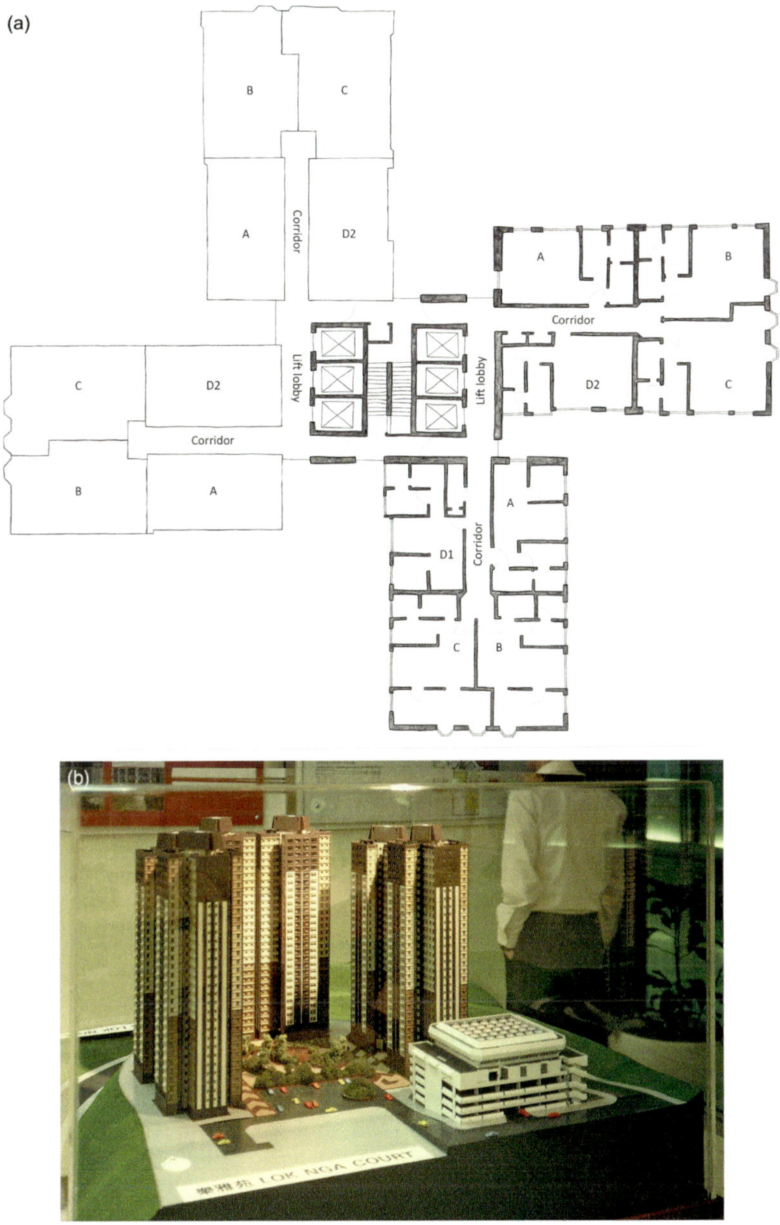

Figure 7.11 (a) 1981 floor plan of the Windmill block, showing both open-plan and pre-partitioned variants. Drawing by Joyce Fu, 2023. (b) 1983 detail from the Home Ownership Centre at the HA headquarters, Princess Margaret Drive, Kowloon, showing model of Lok Nga Court, Kwun Tong – six Flexi 2 blocks completed 1984, and featuring somewhat 'postmodern' colouring scheme (MG) (cf. Fig. 8.7a).

> At the start of the HOS, Shun Chi was designed in-house – the Old Cruciform block – but a number of other jobs were done by private architects at first. Then we brought it in-house, and the block types were these: first came the Flexi, with flats averaging 50 sq m, built in a boom market and which then became too big, and people couldn't afford them. Then came the Windmill, which crammed in more flats, slightly reducing the area of the individual unit. Then that's become out of date since 1981 as the land cost is now exempted, and people can afford the Flexi again, so we've got a development of that, the New Cruciform, as is being built for instance at Tuen Mun Area 44, to the north of Butterfly Estate.[77]

'Come and join us!' The PSPS and MIHS

While the mainstream HOS was powering ahead, MacLehose and Liao were considering potential ways of responding to the disquiet of the private housing developers, and by December 1976, a proposal by property tycoon Li Ka-shing for a joint-venture proposal was beginning to coalesce, under the title 'Private Sector Participation Scheme' (PSPS). It was conceived as a more private-friendly back-up to the main programme, resembling some of the original flats-for-sale concepts.[78] According to Liao, it was a reaction to the developer's previous complaints that 'we were taking their rice bowl', by devising another way to involve the private sector: 'I said, "Why don't you join in?" '[79] Liao devoted much effort as Director of Housing, and then in 1980 as Secretary for Housing, to wooing the private sector under the slogan, 'if you can't fight them then join them!' Miller recalled that 'there was the usual predictable reaction from the private sector, "They're stealing our business!" ' to which 'we said, "Come and join us!" '[80]

Eventually introduced in October 1977, the PSPS put out to tender what were seen as otherwise undevelopable pieces of land, specifying only the selling price of the flats, and allowing the private sector to keep the profitable commercial parts of the resulting development. Architecturally, Liao felt, the results were 'not much to write home about', while Yeung and Wong later argued the PSPS was a failure because developers skimped on costs.[81] A far more credible candidate as a 'failure', however, was a further linked programme, the Middle-Income Housing Scheme (MIHS), introduced in 1980 on the model of Singapore's Housing and Urban Development Company with the intention of catering for the lower-middle class, but ultimately undermined by a general drop in mortgage interest rates, as we will see in Chapter 9. In May 1981, the first MIHP scheme was approved, at a developer premium of $303m, on a site at Tuen Mun previously offered unsuccessfully to Letter A and B holders.[82] (Figure 7.12) The MIHS and the PSPS together were expected to spike at 60,000 completions in 1987–8, with the MIHS starting at 5,000 or 10,000 completions in 1980–2, but instead the latter scheme was destined to be abandoned altogether in 1983.[83] Also briefly evaluated at MacLehose's instigation in 1979, as a more literal version of HPP Option 13, was the possibility of selling existing public rental housing flats to their occupiers, so as to secure, in Secretary for Housing Alan Scott's words, a 'quick return to the DLF'. This option was not proceeded with – not least as the pressure for recovery of costs was relatively low

Figure 7.12 1983 view of display in the Home Ownership Centre on the abortive Middle-Income Housing Project (MIHP) and the Melody Garden scheme (MG).

in view of the buoyant economy – but, as we will see in later chapters, the concept would keep bobbing back to the surface over the following two decades.[84]

HOS in the early 1980s – crisis and revival

The first years of the HOS saw wild variations in output up to 1982, but far greater consistency thereafter, with HOS consistently accounting for around 20% of total public housing output, compared to 16% as predicted in a 1979 paper.[85] (Figure 7.13) HOS output rose from 2,439 completions in 1979/82 and 8,674 in 1980/1, falling back to 4,399 in 1981/2 but thereafter hovering around 6,500–7,500 completions annually. By 1981, a 5,000 annual target was firmly established. Given the need to plan ahead, the greatest perceived output crisis of HOS Phase I in fact occurred in 1980–1, and was countered by a boost in expenditure on rental construction. The July 1981 LDPC, for example, reported a clash between the land-exchange rights of Letter B holders, who were being treated as lesser priority, and site-allocation requirements for HOS/PSPS.[86]

A more fundamental HOS problem in those years, however, was the increasing buyer unaffordability of the early phases of developments on their original funding terms, owing to escalating land costs. From the outset, MacLehose followed the determination of the sale price of each phase of HOS flats with particular interest.[87] In 1981, with prices rapidly increasing, the Working Party on Home Ownership was

A mother and her children look at a model of the new flats, where they hope t
home... if they're lucky!
— Picture by P. Y. T

Big rush for new homes

By TOM ASHBROOK

More than 200,000 applications for 1,917 new flats being offered under the Home Ownership Scheme were snatched up in the first day of distribution.

Crowds gathered at City District Offices throughout Hongkong yesterday to queue for the forms that will give them a chance to buy one of the new flats coming up for sale in Aberdeen and Shatin.

ernment first offered the flats two years ago.

With the scheme's special interest rates on a 15-year loan, buyers will face a monthly repayment bill of about $1,500 for one of the cheaper flats.

To qualify for a flat, buyers must be current residents of a Housing Authority flat or have a combined family income of less than $5,000.

At the Home Ownership Centre in the Oi Man Com-

Figure 7.13 SCMP feature of February 1980 showing would-be HOS buyers inspecting a model of a Flexi block planned for Hong Tin Court, Lam Tin, including cutaway of Flexi plan.

reconvened. And in September-October of that year, MacLehose determined on a bold response: to remove the element of land cost altogether from the price of new HOS flats. Addressing a LegCo debate, MacLehose predicted this would reduce HOS prices to roughly half the private level, and was praised by one member for this 'gallant move by the government'. To compensate, however, a premium was from now onwards charged if initial buyers sold on their flats at a profit.[88] Writing two years later, in 1983, Pryor firmly attributed the move to the soaring land prices, and emphasised the linkage between this relaxation of prices and the compensating new resale and premium restriction. The pricing regimes for Phase IIIb onwards – on sale from February 1982 – were thus quite different from those of the 28,000 units built under Phases I to IIIa. As at 1983, Pryor summarised the targeting of the HOS: 50% of new units were for external applicants with incomes of less than or equal to HK$3,500 per month, while 50% were for public-rental tenants with no income limits, and flat prices were generally about 50% of private-enterprise levels.[89]

By the end of MacLehose's governorship, the HOS had rapidly established itself as a key element in the HA's financial regime. Fung Tung recalled it was gradually realised one could use the HOS to make a 15% surplus to plough back into public rental building, and say to the government, 'Don't give us funds, you give us the land!'[90] Williams recalled,

> We insisted on a significant down-payment, to make sure people *could* afford it. So what would happen was that people would get all their family and friends to raise the deposit. A tremendous effort went on getting that deposit. It meant we would have no deficits at all. The 20% deposit was a jolly good idea. People living in public housing had first choice. There was no income limit, because they were vacating a rental flat.[91]

In his 1982 retrospective, MacLehose emphasised the social rather than profit-orientated ethos of the HOS, and Liao argued in retrospect that the secondary market was not a key concern – 'It was not meant for people to "speculate"'. More important was to create a 'revolving door' within public housing, and hence avoid an 'over-luxurious' approach.[92] Recent historians have been divided in their evaluation of the success of the HOS, particularly following its 1981/2 reform. In the view of Richard Wong, the HOS, unlike its Singapore equivalent, acted as a barrier to citizens upgrading their housing conditions, by impeding secondary-market formation through the premium charge – although it should be remembered that, in contrast to Singapore, its funding was not supported by compulsory confiscation of people's savings. Ngai Ming Yip, by contrast, argued that its shared-equity organisation, as a 'property-based welfare pillar within Hong Kong's productivist regime', played a beneficially redistributive role, by restraining upgrades to private enterprise, which were largely confined to early HOS buyers: only 20% of HOS buyers, he claimed, had been able to trade up onwards as at 2010.[93] Likewise, Yeung and Wong argued in 2003 that the only partly decommodified character of HOS was socially beneficial overall, as the shared equity allowed the government to reinvest the profits in future developments: the HOS was a 'stakeholding' rather than a speculative vehicle.[94]

In its early years, then, the HOS could potentially be viewed as an appropriately limited social intervention, commensurate with the limited role of Hong Kong's caretaker-state. But as we will see in later chapters, from the 1980s its operations were increasingly seen in relation to an arguably less beneficial development within the Hong Kong economy – the ever-expanding power of the private-sector property 'tycoons', and their demand for an effective veto over perceived state intrusions into their fiefdoms. Eventually, the economic crisis following the 1997 takeover would prompt the tycoons to turn their fire directly on the HOS; but for the remainder of MacLehose's office, and for that of his immediate successors, it would play an ever-greater role in consolidating his new, social identity-based housing paradigm.

Notes

1 Williams, 1988 Bodleian interview.

2 HKRS232-1-23-1 7-1971 cutting; Carmen Tsui, 'Housing the nascent middle class: the first high-rise planned community in post-war Hong Kong', *Planning Perspectives*, vol 37, no 4, 2022, 735-759.

3 Akers-Jones, 2013 interview; Wright, 2011 interview; Liao, 2014 interview.
4 HKRS500-6-5; HKRS163-8-20 MacLehose 10-1972 policy speech; HKRS163-8-11, HKRS163-7-3 on previous flats-for-sale proposals; Pryor, *Housing in Hong Kong*, 69.
5 HKRS232-1-22-1 *Hong Kong Standard* 16-4-1973 cutting, comparison with Singapore CPF; HKRS 545-1-456-1 Lightbody 3-1973 note; HKRS477-2-4 Lightbody on possible flats-for-sale; HKRS232-1-22-3 *Hong Kong Standard* 26-6-1973 Lightbody cutting; HKRS70-6-788 9-1973 Lightbody note.
6 HKRS545-1-456-1 13-11-1974 Lightbody note; HKRS163-7-3 11-1974 papers on possible flats-for-sale scheme, and opposition from Elliott; HKRS1588-9-35 1979 papers.
7 HKRS163-8-20, 9-1974 note; HKRS163-8-21 10-1974 note.
8 HKRS163-9-1342 12-1976 note; HKRS 163-8-148.
9 HKRS163-8-21 7-1975, 8-1975 MacLehose-Lightbody; HKRS163-8-20 8-1975 note.
10 HKRS163-7-3 11-1974, 10-1975 correspondence; HKRS163-8-113, HKRS163-7-3, HKMS189-2-40 4-1975 papers. 'Swapped notes': Miller, 2014 interview.
11 HKRS163-8-113, HKRS163-7-3, HKRS1588-9-55; HKMS189-2-40; Miller, 2014 interview; Akers-Jones, 2013 interview.
12 Miller, 2014 interview.
13 Fung Tung, 2010 interview; Liu Thai-Ker, 2010 and 2012 interviews.
14 HKRS545-1-456-1, conference paper of 23-10-1975.
15 Williams, 2012 interview.
16 HKRS1693-5-6 HPP Steering Group 5-2-1976; HKRS163-8-147 1-1976 papers.
17 HKRS163-8-44 11-1975 correspondence; HKRS 163-8-96 20-12-1975 Lightbody memo.
18 HKRS163-8-147 MacLehose to HA 4-2-1976.
19 HKRS163-8-148, HKRS163-9-1342.
20 HKRS163-8-147 4-2-1976 MacLehose to HA, 15-7-1976 Liao to MacLehose, 7-1976 notes from MacLehose.
21 HKRS163-8-147 4-2-1976 MacLehose to HA.
22 HKRS163-8-143 1-1976 to 5-1976 correspondence.
23 HKRS163-8-143 4-2-1976 MacLehose to Lightbody; HKRS163-9-1342; HKRS545-1-459-1.
24 HKRS545-1-459-1 16-3-1976 Haddon-Cave budget speech to LegCol HKRS545-1-459-1 and HKRS1588-9-22 MacLehose at LegCo 4-1976, 10-1976; HKRS163-8-124
25 HKRS163-8-147 15-7-76 Liao to MacLehose.
26 HKRS163-8-147 MacLehose 7-1976 note.
27 HKRS163-8-96; HKRS1588-9-35; HKRS835-1-171; HKRS 545-1-459-1 MacLehose speech 6-10-1976; HKRS163-9-3; HKRS1588-9-35; HKRS163-8-124 MacLehose 3-1976 note; HKRS545-1-45 MacLehose LegCo speech 10-1976; HKRS163-7-83 5-1977 Home-Ownership Committee; HKRS163-8-78 on staff implications; HKRS163-9-134 9-1976 MacLehose correspondence.
28 HKRS608-1-40 3-1976 LDPC meeting; HKRS163-8-44 late 1975 papers; HKRS163-8-143 1-1976 to 5-1976 papers.
29 HKRS608-1-40 4-1976 LDPC meeting; HKRS163-8-147, 15-4-1976 Henry Fok to Lightbody; HKRS163-9-1342 7-1976 papers. Oi Man North: HKRS835-1-171 10-1976 and 11-1976 papers, and HKRS 483-4-1 4-1977 MacLehose note on 'urgency'; HKRS 163-9-1342 Lightbody 1-9-1976 note, HKRS835-1-171 Pryor 9-1976 note.
30 HKRS835-1-171, HKRS163-9-1342 8-1976 papers.
31 HKRS163-8-78 Lightbody to HA 11-1976; HKRS163-8-44; HKRS163-8-78; HKRS163-9-1342 9-1976 papers.
32 Tu, *Colonial Hong Kong*, 46.

33 HKRS163-7-84 Steering Group 1977-8; HKRS835-1-171 2-1977 to 4-1978 meetings; HKRS163-7-1981 3-1978 Haddon-Cave and HA.
34 HKRS163-7-84 Steering Group 1977-8.
35 HKRS835-1-171 8-1976 on terms of reference; HKRS163-7-83 Haddon-Cave 5-1977 note.
36 HKRS163-9-1342 9-1976 MacLehose to CS.
37 HKRS163-8-147 MacLehose to CS 1-9-1976; HKRS163-9-13.
38 HKRS163-9-1342 7-1976 and 1-9-1976 MacLehose note.
39 HKRS163-7-83 3-1977, 5-1977 papers.
40 HKRS163-8-78 1978 papers; HKRS835-1-171 4-1978 meeting; HKRS163-7-83 March 1978 summary of political aims of HOS.
41 Tang, 'Hong Kong under Chinese sovereignty'; Tse and Ganesan, 'Hong Kong'; A Smart and J Lee, 'Financialisation and the role of real-estate in Hong Kong's regime of accumulation', *Economic Geography* 79 (2), 2003, 153–171.
42 HKRS163-8-147 3-1976 Haddon-Cave at Governor's Committee; HKRS163-7-3.
43 HKRS608-1-40 LDPC 4-1976.
44 HKRS163-9-1342; HKRS163-8-147 15-4-1976 Henry Fok to Lightbody and 30-6-1976 reply; Liao, 2014 interview; Miller, 2014 interview; Pryor, *Housing in Hong Kong*, 69–72.
45 HKRS163-9-1342; HKRS163-8-44; HKRS163-7-3; HKRS545-1-459-1 1976 revolving fund; HKRS163-7-84 1977 papers on HOS financial arrangements.
46 Miller, 2014 interview; FCO40-1012 paper for ExCo discussion 11-4-1978.
47 FCO40-1122 briefing for MacLehose on 19-4-1979 meeting; Drakakis-Smith, *High Society*, 125-7.
48 HKRS163-9-1342; Liao, 2010 interview; HKRS163-7-84 3-1978 papers; HKRS163-7-83 5-1978 papers.
49 HKRS835-1-171 12-1976, HKRS163-8-147 18-1-1977 Haddon-Cave to General Manager HSBC.
50 Liao, 2010 interview; HKRS163-7-83 3-1978 on Phase II HOS names; HKRS545-1-456-2 5-1979 Phase II HOS names.
51 Liao, 2009, 2010 interviews; Lau, 2009 interview.
52 Williams, 1988 Bodleian interview; Akers-Jones, 2014 interview.
53 HKRS163-8-147 18-1-1977 Haddon-Cave to General Manager, HSBC.
54 Williams, 2012 interview; Pryor, *Housing in Hong Kong,* 69-72; HKRS500-6-5; HKRS163-7-83; HKRS483-1-1 9-1977 applications and selection; HKRS163-7-83 1978 on 'no time'.
55 HKRS163-7-83 1978 HOS Phase I progress report, and Phase II proposed projects; HKRS163-7-84 Phases I–VII production figures.
56 HKRS163-7-3, HKRS545-1-459-1 3-1977 articles.
57 Liao, 2009, 2010, 2011 interviews.
58 HKRS1882-1-3, 1977; Liao, 2011 interview; Gu Daqing, 'Affordability as the inspiration of design for public housing', in *HKIA Journal 72, Occupy Housing*, 2016, 48–52; 'A Conversation with James Kinoshita', *HKIA Journal* 72, 2016, 37–41.
59 Burns, 2014 interview; HKRS667-2-4, MacLehose at 21-5-1981 opening; HKRS545-1-459-1.
60 Liao, 2011 interview.
61 Burns, 2014 interview; Gu Daqing, 'Affordability', 48-52.
62 HKRS163-8-141 15-6-1977; HKRS163-8-78, HKRS163-7-83.
63 HKRS163-7-83 5-1977 papers.

64 HKRS1588-2-30, 3-1977 letter from Williams; Williams, 2012 interview. A Watts (ed), *Directory of Official Architecture and Planning*, Godwin, London, 1975, 95.
65 Islington LBC Housing Committee minutes, 22-11-1973.
66 Interview with Philip Boyle, 2023.
67 Messling, 'Public housing – a numbers game!'
68 FCO40-1-12 11-4-1978 ExCo discussion.
69 HKRS 461-1-12-5.
70 HKRS163-8-148; HKRS 163-9-1342 9-1976 papers.
71 Williams, 2012 interview; HKRS545-1-459-1.
72 Poon, 2010 interview.
73 HKRS696-3-165; Hong Kong 1983 (yearbook), 108; HKRS461-1-12-5 on tenders.
74 HKRS1882-1-3 BC 13-9-79 and 12-1979.
75 HKRS545-1-459-1 press release 26-12-1981; Gabriel, 2009 interview; Tin Ma Court, HKRS696-3-165 1981 papers.
76 Poon, 2010 interview.
77 Ko, 1983 interview: Tuen Mun 44, HKRS461-1-12-8, HKRS461-1-12-5 11-1982 tender at BC, standard HOS tower blocks, HO 24. Tuen Mun HOS 22-5-1981 545-1-459-1.
78 HKRS163-8-148, HKRS163-9-1342, 12-1976
79 Liao, 2014 interview; Yeung and Wong, *Fifty Years*, 267–9.
80 Miller, 2014 interview.
81 Pryor, *Housing in Hong Kong,* 70-1; Liao 2010 interview; Yeung and Wong, *Fifty Years*, 267–9.
82 Liao, 2010 interview; HKRS545-1-459-1, 22-5-1981 cutting.
83 HKRS696-3-7, 22-3-90 HA paper on sandwich class housing. Pryor, *Housing in Hong Kong*, 70–1.
84 HKRS163-8-143 24-8-1979 Scott memo.
85 FCO40-122 briefing for MacLehose on housing 19-4-1979.
86 Pryor, *Housing in Hong Kong,* 69-72; HKRS163-8-131 2-1980 on Phase I output; HKRS667-2-4 LDPC 11-7-1981.
87 HKRS163-7-84 1-1978 memo.
88 Pryor *Housing in Hong Kong,* 69-72; HKRS545-1-459-1 10-1981 papers; HKRS696-3-165, SCMP 9-10-1981 on MacLehose speech and Fung-Ho Ip praise; Liao, 2010 interview.
89 Pryor, *Housing in Hong Kong*, 69–72.
90 Fung Tung, 2010 interview.
91 Williams, 2012 interview.
92 FCO40-642 17-4-1882 MacLehose report to FCO; Liao, 2009, 2010, 2014 interviews; Fung Tung, 2010 interview.
93 Tsui, 'Housing the nascent middle class', 753-7; Ngai Ming Yip, 'Housing, crises and interventions in Hong Kong', in J Doling and R Ronald, *Housing East Asia – Socioeconomic and Demographic Challenges*, Palgrave Macmillan, London, 2014, 73.
94 Yeung and Wong, *Fifty Years*, 267–9; Fung Tung, 2010 interview.

8 1977–1982

Consolidating the revolution

MacLehose versus London – tension and relief

Just as MacLehose had predicted earlier in the decade, a slow but inexorable transition was now underway from internal to external preoccupations, focusing initially on tensions with the Labour government in London, and then, after MacLehose's March 1979 visit to Beijing, rapidly shifting to the existential issue of 1997. This was a time when the inevitability of sovereignty transfer in 1997 was becoming tacitly accepted within Hong Kong, but, as Akers-Jones recalled, 'you didn't talk about it openly', to protect public confidence.[1]

Perhaps anticipating this wider shift, Hong Kong's own well-established policy detachment from London became ever stronger throughout 1977 and early 1978. Both sides reacted negatively to each other's manner and world-outlook.[2] While visiting MPs and civil servants argued that Hong Kong was cut off from the 'mainstream' of British political and social thinking, and that MacLehose's 'achievements… seem so remarkable *only* because so little had been done before', Hong Kong elite public opinion was firmly on the Governor's side – with a SCMP leader in February 1977, for example, arguing Hong Kong should be judged by 'contemporary Asian, rather than Western European' criteria.[3] In the 'eyeball confrontations' of MacLehose's London visits, his interlocutors invariably assumed the inferiority of Hong Kong's standards of social provision, housing included.[4] In a November 1977 exchange with MacLehose at the FCO, for example, Goronwy Roberts argued Hong Kong's 'housing expectations are too low' and that Liao's articulate defence of post-1973 Housing Authority achievements was invalidated by myopia:

> When Donald Liao said he had all the money he could spend, this was conditioned by his knowledge of limited objectives: the present programme involved poor-quality housing with increasing overcrowding. It was the objectives that should be reassessed to the higher level. Having reassessed objectives, then only should revenue be considered.

DOI: 10.1201/9781315563701-10

To which MacLehose riposted that extra money would not affect the production reality that 'to attempt to redraw housing plans now' would massively retard production, given the long lead-time of housing developments.[5]

On his periodic visits to London, Goronwy Roberts and his colleagues tried to nudge MacLehose towards accepting tax increases and a social security scheme, and to give London ministers a preview of the Hong Kong budget.[6] More generally, they pressed the principle of identifying objectives first and securing budgets second, rather than the reverse. Trade union rights continued to be a sore point, not just because of Hong Kong's perception of the British garment unions' hostility, but also because of the politically destabilising implication of bolstering union representation.[7] After the distraction caused by a November 1977 police riot and subsequent amnesty over corruption, London pressure for social-economic convergence resumed.[8] Goronwy Roberts tried to drive the government into a corner by arguing that Haddon-Cave and Jeaffreson were 'constantly crying wolf' about likely deficits, while the economy continued to boom, and revenues to flow in.[9] In April 1978, MacLehose was forced to accept an outline planning paper on convergence with British Labour policies drafted by the FCO, and presented to ExCo under the pretence of its having been 'developed in Hong Kong'.[10]

The Conservative victory in June 1979 removed these tensions at a stroke. At a personal level, Hong Kong–London relations radically improved overnight, with junior FCO minister Peter Blaker on first-name terms with MacLehose, and Foreign Secretary Lord Carrington's initial visit to Hong Kong the following month hailed as a 'tour de force' that had 'made the best impression… for a long time'.[11] In October, building on the newly positive climate, MacLehose stressed London's relations with Hong Kong must henceforth 'be a two-way affair, based on a commercial as well as a political relationship which is felt to be both welcome and mutually beneficial'.[12] London rhetoric switched abruptly from a superiority to inferiority complex, expressing much admiration for the Hong Kong laissez-faire economy and contrasting it with Britain's 'serious industrial problems'.[13] (Figure 8.1)

Now the emphasis in Hong Kong–London relations shifted to external matters, beginning in 1980 with the sudden spike in illegal immigrants from China, which threatened to cancel out the effects of MacLehose's social policies, and for which a 'touch-base' policy was suggested as a remedy; and continuing with the Vietnamese boat-people crisis, which MacLehose saw as 'almost insoluble'.[14] Overall, the transition from Labour to Conservative in London had the effect, for a few years, of further bolstering the autonomy of the Hong Kong government and of MacLehose in particular. The old leftist internal threat, although fading, could not simply be brushed aside, and leftist schools were progressively closed from the late 1970s. And more generally, low-income areas were still looked on with suspicion, with one residents' association subjected to Special Branch surveillance as a 'front' organisation in 1977.[15]

Reflecting his increasing indispensability as governments in London changed and those in Beijing evolved, MacLehose was persuaded to accept a succession

Figure 8.1 Inspection of model of Wo Che Estate in June 1979 (SCMP view): from left to right, New Territories Secretary David Akers-Jones, Foreign Secretary Lord Carrington, Director of Housing Donald Liao Poon-huai, and MacLehose.

of extensions to his post. As early as December 1976 an extension was being considered owing to likely changes within the Chinese leadership. In the event, there were three further extensions, to August 1979, April 1980, and finally May 1982.[16] The extension to 1980 was pushed through by the new Labour Foreign secretary, David Owen, on grounds that this was an especially sensitive time, with growing worries about the New Territories leases. MacLehose's extensions had to be balanced against the negative impact of two hip operations, in November 1979 and in mid-1981, followed by an extended recuperative break, and to persuade him to stay, he was largely 'left a free hand'.[17] By this stage of his governorship, MacLehose's policies and characteristics were well known among the Hong Kong population, and in December 1978, a detailed evaluation of his 'achievements and failures' was published by journalist Wong Po Lo in the pro-Kuomintang *Kung Sheung Daily News*. MacLehose himself read the article in detail and commented on its mainly favourable conclusions, which hailed housing policy as 'one of his most successful and far-sighted improvements, second only to the establishment of the ICAC'.[18] Similarly, correspondence with the Maryknoll Sisters charity produced mainly favourable evaluations, including fulsome praise of his 'sincere concern for the common man'.[19]

Internal and external policy-making: a modern Confucianism?

By the end of his governorship, MacLehose's governmental ethos was equated by one commentator with a Confucian-style ideal of 'as good government as practicable'.[20] Stressing an Asian rather than European context, he publicised his social interventions systematically, highlighting his differences with London over social-service provision by setting out to equal the best in Eastern Asia (other than Japan).[21] This aim, as we have seen, he pursued by combining firm central direction with diversity of agencies and structures: in a December 1981 overview of Hong Kong's governmental structures, Haddon-Cave highlighted numerous different 'seats' of government. Overall, MacLehose's governorship saw a significant increase in state intervention, and a rise in the number of ordinances.[22]

MacLehose ruled out on principle anything suggesting significant 'democratic' reforms, to avoid provoking Beijing.[23] But he equally stood up for collective Hong Kong autonomy from London pressures, arguing the proposed labour reforms were a thinly disguised plot to make the territory uncompetitive.[24] To Hongkongers, the most urgent social problems seemed very different, with crime at the top of the list: MacLehose reported to Labour ministers in 1975 that London's suspension of the death penalty was 'bitterly resented in the Colony'.[25] The assault on corruption through Jack Cater's ICAC, culminating in the police riot of 1977, also impinged significantly on housing, not just in estate management and shop tenancy, but also in building contract management, as at the Hin Keng estate in Sha Tin, where the contractor emptied his bank accounts and fled to Taiwan.[26] Corruption and government abuses of power continued to be a principal concern of Elsie Elliott: much involved in following-up the Inspector MacLennan police suicide scandal in 1981, she devoted much effort to combating sweat-shop working conditions, while remaining generally faithful to pre-welfare-state traditionalist values of philanthropy and self-help: in 1977 she even protested Housing Authority staff should study at night to improve their skills, rather than being allowed time off. MacLehose's attitude to her was ambiguous: in 1978, at her CBE award ceremony, he reputedly whispered to her to 'keep up the good work' (despite his previous behind-the-scenes veto of her appointment to ExCo only two years previously), while Chris Patten later highlighted her conflicted values, describing her in 1992 as 'a real, old-style lefty' who was 'in many respects a rather admirable creation of the British Empire'.[27]

MacLehose's usefulness to London in domestic affairs seemed self-evident. But he also seemed a potentially invaluable interlocutor with mainland China, as concerns were growing of a confidence and investment 'crunch' in the late 1980s, possibly precipitated by the non-extensibility of individual New Territories leases beyond 1997. Given Zhou Enlai's 1971 statement of China's intention to reclaim Hong Kong in its entirety in 1997, it already seemed clear to MacLehose that there was no realistic question of extension of British control and that negotiations could only be about the terms of transition.[28] During MacLehose's March 1979 ice-breaking visit to Beijing at the end of the Labour administration, Deng Xiaoping indicated that China was determined to reclaim sovereignty but would grant Hong Kong, like Taiwan, a special status which would allow 'investors in

Hong Kong to put their hearts at ease'. He refused to enter into detailed discussion about the issue, raised by MacLehose, of the renewal of individual New Territories leases: the Chinese government subsequently indicated that this stemmed from a wish to avoid discussion about any aspects of the 1997 issue at the moment, until it had worked out its own preferred plan.[29] This was partly, it was thought in London, because of concern about the implications for China's disputes with the USSR, but also because the Chinese government also feared that the individual lease issue might be used as a Trojan horse towards extension of British involvement in Hong Kong after 1997 – an issue that (as we will see below) also impacted on MacLehose's 1981 decision to approve a joint development with a Chinese mainland company at Tin Shui Wai in the north-western New Territories.[30] MacLehose commented in his April 1979 report to the FCO on his Beijing visit that 'Deng did not seem aware that any such assurances would give no confidence [in Hong Kong] unless China's political life had settled down for many years, or there was a satisfactory example of how a special status worked out in practice, e.g. in Taiwan… . Memories about what happened in Tibet, with its particular form of special status, are long'.[31] By July 1980, MacLehose and his FCO counterparts gradually became aware that while any continuing British involvement post-1997 was 'almost certainly out', the 1997 issue could not be 'postponed much beyond 1982', and that the Chinese were well advanced in developing their own plan for Hong Kong. This would involve (MacLehose sceptically speculated) 'an intermediate stage in which they would run Hong Kong as a separate, capitalist part of China outside the Renminbi currency area. This was crazy!'[32]

Gradually, in early 1981, it became realised that like the leases problem, the impending Nationality Bill, by suggesting a lessening of UK commitment to Hong Kong, might set off a confidence crisis.[33] With an impending visit by Mrs Thatcher to China and Hong Kong, already pencilled in for mid-1981, secret briefing papers started to explore 'grim scenarios' of disorderly British withdrawal in the event of a collapse in confidence, and warned that the Hong Kong population would now expect to be consulted about the outcome; on the positive side, the negotiating hurdle that separated Beijing and London was 'very low'.[34]

Economic volatility and the 'second crisis' of the Ten-Year Housing Plan

If the growing rumblings over sovereignty formed the dominant external geopolitical frame for MacLehose's continuing housing boom, its main internal context was the continuing volatility of Hong Kong's economy. Overall, the period 1972–1982 saw incessant fluctuations, including a sharp GDP rise from 1974 to 1978, but a significant setback in 1979 – all serving to obscure a significant overall GDP increase, and the beginnings of an underlying structural shift from a manufacturing to a financial and services-based economy. The short-term economic fluctuations impacted indirectly on housing output, requiring Haddon-Cave to seek support from the Development Loan Fund and Home-Ownership Fund to maintain production.[35] A further rise to 1981 was followed by a levelling-off in growth to 2.9% in 1982. Overall, between 1980 and 2010, the ratio of housing capital to 'national' income rose from 122% to 209%, rather less than most advanced countries (e.g. from 134 to 300 in UK, 134 to 236 in Germany and 122 to 371 in France).[36] Although housing production was, as always, protected from the direct effects of recession, the legacy of the previous cuts in Public Works Department infrastructural works now began to impinge on output, as we will see below.[37]

Haddon-Cave's role remained central in coping with these economic vicissitudes.[38] Unlike his bête-noire status with some London politicians and civil servants, within Hong Kong his reputation was that of a mildly reformist heir to the Cowperthwaite legacy. He institutionalised the latter under the slogan of 'positive non-intervention', and disguised his considerable economic competence behind a renowned tendency to waffle in budget speeches.[39] His personality combined a private love of the luxuries of the bon-viveur with a tendency towards flippantly provocative (towards London) public pronouncements over matters such as tax and the budget.[40] On his promotion to Chief Secretary in 1981, MacLehose candidly evaluated Haddon-Cave's personality, suggesting his real 'forte' was administration rather than finance, and highlighting the way in which the experience of office had moderated his tendency towards public gaffes.[41]

During the late 1970s, a growing confidence at last began to prevail concerning the Ten-Year Housing Strategy. There was, in MacLehose's words, a 'steady acceleration' now underway towards the anticipated 1981 targets; after 1975 it was increasingly accepted that the housing programme was in effect open-ended.[42] MacLehose maintained his close questioning of progress, and in discussions in February 1977 stressed that he was 'disturbed' at 'slippages' in production – to which the Secretary for Housing assured him that these could all be made up in 1979/80.[43] Key individual schemes, such as the megastructural development above Lok Fu MTR station, he chased up in detail: it was obligatory that the quarterly production reports of Housing Branch 'must be on HE's desk ten days after the expiring period'.[44] In August 1978, MacLehose argued that, to maintain output, the government would need to proceed with Junk Bay, the Sha Tin extension, possibly North Lantau, and other New Territories developments: it was calculated that, with their contribution, by 1986 the 'back' of the housing problem would be 'broken'.[45] At the same time, there was a growing consensus that the targets of the Ten-Year Plan itself had been unrealistic and hasty, and John Walden argued that the Plan 'has failed'. Much later, it was calculated that a total of 'only' 220,527 dwellings had eventually been built under the direct provisions of the Plan.[46]

At a more detailed level, there was intensive discussion of the precise calculation mechanisms used to correlate both the Ten-Year Plan, and the 1974 HKOP, with housing demand and supply.[47] The shift from IU-based (1.5 million) to dwelling-based (35,000) annual targets from 1980 was acknowledged as inevitable, on the basis that 'you can't build people'.[48] Pryor highlighted the discrepancies within current housing computations, especially between units and dwellings, and a 1977 discussion stressed the tension between the 1.8 million IUs and the HPP. By 1982, the real-world effect of the shift from IUs to dwellings could be evaluated, potentially including a 10% rise in living space in rental flats.[49] In 1980, Liao argued that with the rise in output from 14,000 in 1978–9 to 33,000 in 1979–80, the 'housing target' had almost been reached: 35,000 would be a plateau, or a 'cruising speed', as 'we can't go on indefinitely at this vertical take-off production rate', but could maintain 35,000 without fuelling inflation. Yet even this would not be enough to 'solve the housing problem' – that was 'a long way off'.[50]

All this was cut short in 1979 and early 1980 in the 'second crisis' of housing in the MacLehose years – as highlighted in those years' progress reports to him. Partly, these resulted indirectly from cuts to the Public Works Department budget during the first crisis, a crisis within which direct housing expenditure had, of course, been protected.[51] The 1979 budget attempted to relieve pressure on the building industry by cuts in the public works programme. It was left to Scott to defend housing's corner and 'face down' the Financial Secretary in this new crisis – a crisis in which again, however, 'housing was cut less than anything else'.[52] In August 1979, Scott confirmed that land availability would allow combined public rental and HOS production to be maintained at 35,000, and indeed re-accelerated following any budget delays, through a working group on housing demand; to which MacLehose riposted that he hoped output could be increased beyond 35,000, perhaps even to 45,000.[53]

Whereas the 1974–5 recession was said in 1977 by Lightbody to have set back the programme by 18–24 months, the 1979–80 budget had a lesser effect.[54] However, by December 1979, MacLehose was chafing to Jack Cater at a 'deplorable discrepancy' in figures for planned output in 1980–4, which appeared to suggest that the 35,000 pledged at LegCo in October might be in jeopardy: MacLehose stressed, and 'Philip [Haddon-Cave] agreed', that 'on no account could we admit to planning for less than 35,000'.[55] In the panic countermeasures that followed, already-approved sites were rearranged in February 1980 to fit in extra tower blocks, leading to vehement protests from Graham Barnes, Deputy Secretary for the Environment, who argued it would be 'unforgivable' to prejudice planning standards, especially in the New Towns, by piecemeal outbreaks of higher densities. A special finance committee met several times in 1981 to discuss the wider macroeconomic context of the housing programme.[56]

As the programme recovered from this fresh dip, ambitions began to soar once again: the aim was now to build 200,000 units by 1983, and by 1984–5 to exceed 35,000 annual completions.[57] In the March 1980 LDPC meeting, a target level of no less than 47,000 per annum after 1986 was posited, with the caveat that fresh land supply would be needed. In 1981, the LDPC duly adjusted planning standards towards higher densities, with the aim of exceeding 35,000.[58] By that year, the population in public housing estates had reached 2 million. And the following year, 35,745 were completed – a new annual record, as Freddie Pang stressed to the HA Building Committee.[59] The HOS played a crucial role in this further expansion of the programme, as MacLehose had intended when it was first set up – hence the emphasis given to the 1980 countermeasures against phase I HOS lateness, including switching land allocations to raise densities. In 1979 it was argued that HOS could be boosted if needed to take over a further 10% of the programme – although in 1981 Liao rebutted claims from Denny Huang of the Hong Kong People's Council that this HOS expansion was at the expense of ordinary output, a line strongly held also by Elliott.[60] (Figures 8.2, 8.3)

Figure 8.2 Shun Lee Estate, plaque commemorating March 1979 visit by MacLehose: 1983 photo (MG): in the background is Shun Chi Court (cf. Fig. 7.10a).

New Towns and redevelopment – towards an open-ended strategy

For all this production, both mainstream rental and HOS, a steady stream of land production was vital, not least because of the huge fluctuations in the land market in 1981–2 – the lead-in to one of the most significant collapses in property prices in Hong Kong, which would endure until 1985. In July 1977, the LDPC was told that all sites would be used up by 1986.[61] In 1978, MacLehose was demanding 'something solid' in land production, and although additional ad-hoc areas were released each year, the need for a 'contingency reserve' was increasingly stressed, especially by Pryor. By 1980 it was being argued that a land reserve for 47,000 completions per annum would be needed by 1986.[62] Every year, in the early 1980s, land releases for public housing were set by a Land Disposal Sub-Committee of the Special Committee on Land Supply: land was free of charge for HA rental developments.[63] The New Towns were crucial here: Williams recalled that 'We were going to build our 35,000 flats, which we did. OK, the fact that 10,000 of these were in Tuen Mun, that's just bad luck. That was our target and we were going to reach it. Now a lot of people said, "Well, why the hell are you building all these out at Tuen Mun?" The

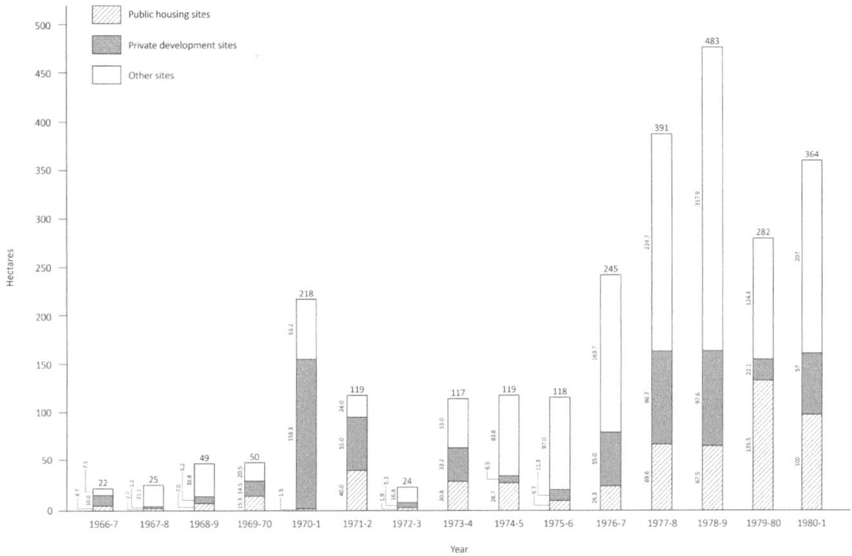

Figure 8.3 Bar chart of land cleared annually by Housing Department Clearance Division, 1966–81. Drawing by Joyce Fu, 2023.

answer was, "Well, that where the land is – so that's where we're going." Should we not have met our target, should we have said, "No, sorry, we're not going to build in Tuen Mun", and then we can't produce our 25,000 flats?'[64] In 1978 it began to be argued that a fixed link to Lantau was required, to allow development there as well as at Junk Bay.[65]

In building up a more strategic approach to land supply, the most straightforward mechanism was that of enhanced planning powers – an approach that, as in the Abercrombie years, still aroused wide suspicions in laissez-faire Hong Kong. In pursuit of that, 1978 saw a visit by the Deputy Director of Public Works, W C Bell, and Graham Barnes, to study town planning and the Ministry of National Development in Singapore (and a follow-up visit in 1981, in which planning standards were compared). They concluded unsurprisingly that the planning system there was far more draconian, far more closely coordinated by the MND, and, indeed, that 'unlike in Hong Kong, the planning permission is the major hurdle for any developer' in Singapore. Any such system, they argued, was unattainable in the Hong Kong context.[66] Instead of this unified system, Hong Kong had a two-headed system, with two planning branches, the Town Planning Board and the LDPC; some planning standards applied to public housing, but not all.[67] Nominally overarching everything was the Hong Kong Outline Plan, endorsed by the LDPC in 1979, together with a miscellany of individual initiatives, for example by Pryor in 1978 in relation to the Ten-Year Plan.[68] (Figure 8.4)

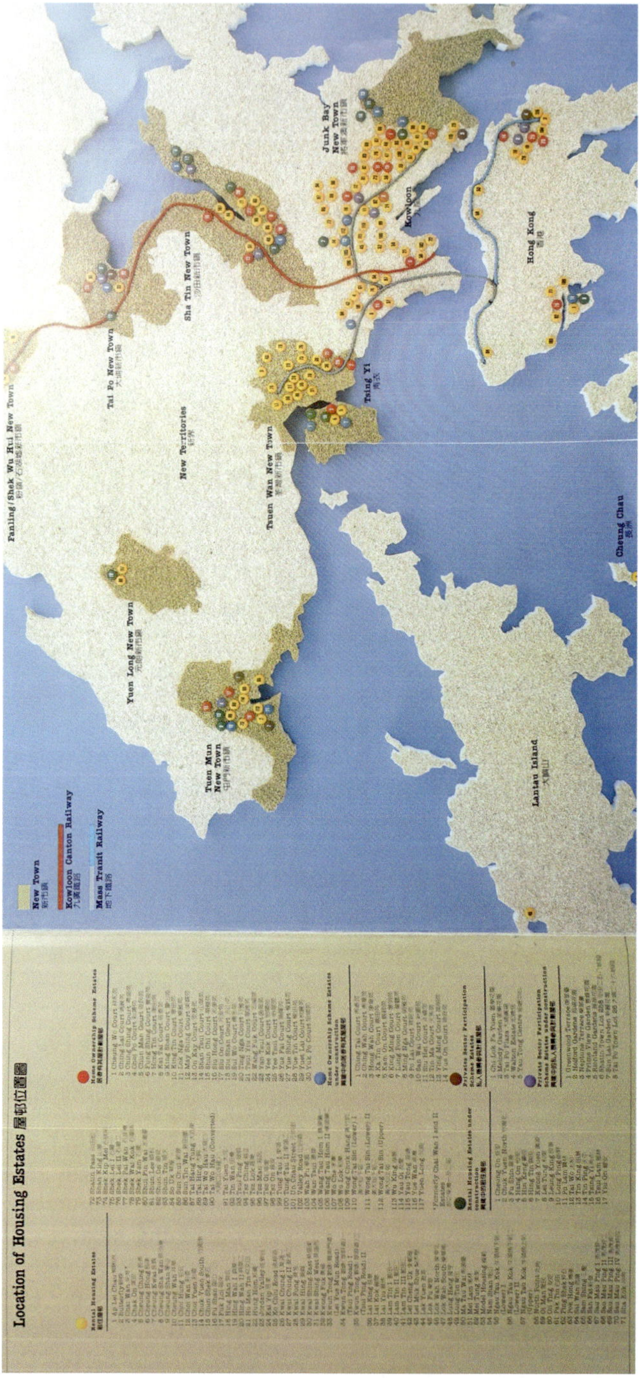

Figure 8.4 Fold-out map in Housing Authority 1984/5 *Annual Report*, showing all developments completed and under construction by 1984, colour-coded by category.

In the absence of a central planning system, the nearest approximation available was the development system devised for the New Towns – although this avoided the hyper-coordination seen within Singapore's New Town development structure, coordinated by HDB.[69] A reasonably coordinated approach in Hong Kong's New Towns was unavoidable, given the huge resources devoted to them, with a 21-fold rise in expenditure from 1973 to 1981, and, in 1977 alone, $348 million spent on the first three New Towns. Yet even here, despite the McKinsey recommendations, there was a distinctly two-headed approach, with development split between the PWD proper and the NTDD, presided over by Akers-Jones as New Territories Secretary.[70] Overall, despite the recession-prompted cutbacks in the programme in 1977, the emphasis was now shifting beyond development of the first three New Towns, of which Sha Tin in particular was assuming its mature form, under the direction of the planner-staffed Sha Tin Development Office.[71] Later administrators, such as Fung Tung, had to grapple with this tremendous built legacy: 'we had to work out how to make the New Towns work!' This was especially challenging given the general lack of coercive powers in Hong Kong, and the lack of any 'deliberate policy of decentralisation' or of 'active' population or industrial decanting.[72] Between 1977 and 1979, Ted Pryor continued to play a prominent role in determining future strategy, and New Town planning, especially within the LDPC: by 1979 he had moved from Assistant Director Redevelopment and Planning to Assistant Director (Planning and Research).[73] (Figure 8.5) To try to overcome the gulf between planning and housing, Tai Po Area 24 was developed according to a joint HD/NTDD brief of 1979–80.[74] It was noted at a 1978 LDPC meeting that new production involved long lead times in comparison with Singapore, where, predictably, more dirigiste project-management prevailed.[75]

But even this was not enough: by the late 1970s, Liao recalled, 'we suddenly realised that the three New Towns were not supplying enough land for public housing!'[76] The outcome of that realisation was a broad range of short-term and long-term land-production expedients. These were not helped by the abolition of the Letter B system in 1982, following an LDPC debate about its effectiveness in 1981 and a sharp decline in its use after that.[77] But by 1978, work was proceeding on a western extension to Tuen Mun, albeit hampered by the lack of a dedicated Project Manager. And in 1979, the four market towns already targeted for expansion – Tai Po, Yuen Long, Fanling, and Sheung Shui – were officially designated New Towns.[78]

Beyond that, a fresh generation of full-scale New Towns, combined with extensions, was in view, beginning with the much discussed Junk Bay site, centrepiece of an extension strategy of 1979–80 and a full-scale development study of 1981 – along with a north-east extension to Sha Tin, 'Sha Tin B'.[79] A LDPC 1978–9 debate on strategy for future housing and the New Towns identified a long-term potential total of 430 ha and recommended that development of Junk Bay and Sha Tin B should be immediately commenced.[80] Also suddenly in contention, as a supplement, or rival, to this, was a large site at Tin Shui Wai in the northwestern New Territories. This was originally acquired from 1978 by a consortium, 'Mightycity', in which Li Ka-shing's Cheung Kong teamed up with a mainland

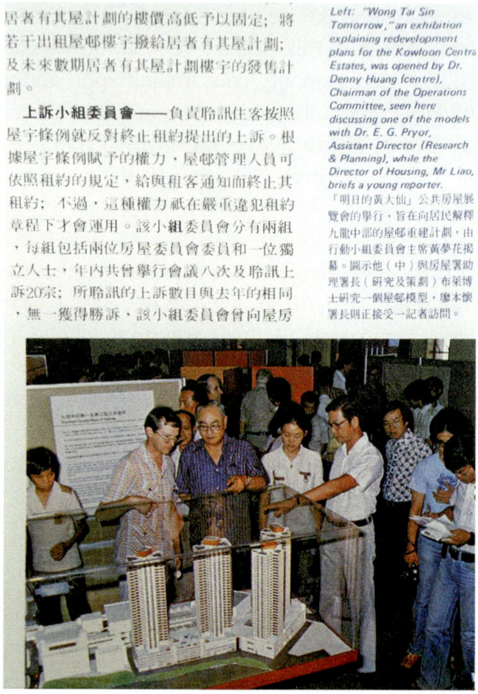

居者有其屋計劃的樓價高低予以固定；將若干出租屋邨樓宇撥給居者有其屋計劃；及未來數期居者有其屋計劃樓宇的發售計劃。

上訴小組委員會——負責聆訊住客按照屋宇條例就反對終止租約提出的上訴。根據屋宇條例賦予的權力，屋邨管理人員可依照租約的規定，給與租客通知而終止其租約；不過，這種權力祇在嚴重違犯租約章程下才會運用。該小組委員會分有兩組，每組包括兩位房屋委員會委員和一位獨立人士，年內共曾舉行會議八次及聆訊上訴20宗；所聆訊的上訴數目與去年的相同，無一獲得勝訴，該小組委員會曾向屋房

Left: "Wong Tai Sin Tomorrow," an exhibition explaining redevelopment plans for the Kowloon Centra Estates, was opened by Dr. Denny Huang (centre), Chairman of the Operations Committee, seen here discussing one of the models with Dr. E. G. Pryor, Assistant Director (Research & Planning), while the Director of Housing, Mr Liao, briefs a young reporter.

「明日的黃大仙」公共房屋展覽會的舉行，旨在向居民解釋九龍中部的屋邨重建計劃，由行動小組委員會主席黃夢花揭幕。圖示他（中）與房屋署助理署長（研究及策劃）布萊博士研究一個屋邨模型，廖本懷署長則正接受一記者訪問。

Figure 8.5 Illustration from 1979/80 *Annual Report*, showing Ted Pryor, Denny Huang, a journalist and Donald Liao discussing an initial proposal for an integrated HOS housing and commercial centre.

Chinese corporation, China Resources Capital, to circumvent the growing uncertainty about individual post-1997 leases. Maurice Yip's comprehensive account explains how, in 1981, MacLehose attempted to assert government control over the Tin Shui Wai project, with its awkward sovereignty implications, through a buy-back of the land (in 1982), which was then partly leased back to the consortium, with provision for public housing to be built on the remainder.[81] (Figure 8.6)

Unlike these straightforward new-development areas in the New Territories, the problems of redevelopment and squatter clearance in the main urban area seemed likely to generate additional housing liability rather than net housing gain. During the late 1970s and early 1980s, the programme for redevelopment of Mk I and Mk II estates was creaking into action. In 1978, the Sham Shui Po redevelopment was said to be imminent, and in 1977–8 the Tai Hang Tung redevelopment likewise.[82] (Figure 8.7a–c)

In November 1980, MacLehose received an invitation (complete with 40,000-signature petition) from some Mk I and Mk II residents to spend the night in their estate, to sample their 'insanitary, crowded and crime-ridden conditions'; his staff politely declined, on grounds that he would be in London at the time.[83]

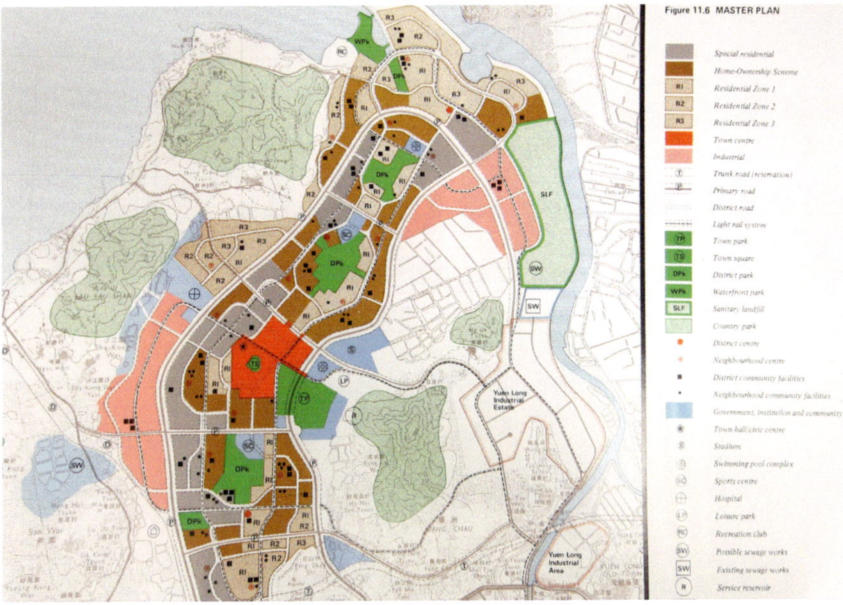

Figure 8.6 February 1981 proposal for Tin Shui Wai by Mightycity Ltd, showing public rental housing in light brown, HOS in dark brown, and private housing in grey. The development as realised corresponded roughly to the southern half shown on the map.

Squatter clearance, likewise, was still surrounded by a climate of negativity and stress. Attacks by hut residents against the control teams (successors to Williams's tidiness teams of 1970–4) were recorded in 1977 and 1979; 'ruthless and dangerous' racketeers were involved in building huts in 1978; and squatter control teams were still experiencing many stresses and tribulations in 1981.[84] (Figure 8.8) On the opposing side, Elsie Elliott made it her business to defend squatters against excesses during clearances, for example in 1977 at Lai Chi Kok; and both she and Ron Woodcraft raised issues about corruption in hut-building, for instance in the Pak Tin temporary housing area, and at Tsuen Wan.[85] (Figure 8.9a, b) MacLehose insisted on frequent update briefings on the squatter situation, and in 1980 was given an approximate estimate of 750,000 squatters overall; 1981–2 saw significant progress in the clearance programme.[86] Especially controversial was the area immediately beside the Kowloon Walled City, where squatter clearance, as if by association, was felt to be almost impossible. However, the processes of rehousing fire victims in temporary housing areas, or village renewals, were now becoming more settled.[87] In the 1980s, redevelopment of Resettlement estates (including the aided self-help cottage developments that still continued to proliferate in the New Territories) would eventually coalesce into a long-term programme, effectively paralleling the New Town strategy – but that point had not yet been reached.

Figure 8.7 (a) Jordan Valley Estate, showing rehabilitated Mk I blocks, with Lok Nga Court HOS under construction behind: 1983 photo (MG). (b) Kwun Tong Estate in 1983, showing Mk I blocks under conversion in foreground, and in the background, Kui On House, a 19-storey Old Slab Block built in 1965–6 at the HA's Wo Lok Estate (designed by Liao's team) (MG). (c) 1983 view of Mk I blocks at Kwun Tong Estate being converted from back-to-back units to through flats (MG).

A 'New Deal' for the Housing Authority

Overall, the late 1970s consolidation of the Housing Department formed part of the post-1972 McKinsey Report shift towards a more corporate organisation of government, and away from the generalist cadet tradition that had prevailed in the days of Resettlement.[88] In 1977, the Housing Authority received a new financial deal from the government: the requirement to pay land premiums was abolished, the accumulated deficit for Group B estates was removed, and rent pooling was introduced across the entire estate stock – followed by a rent increase in 1978. The HA could now carry over funds at the financial year-end.[89] Additional ad-hoc finance came from a loan from the Asian Development Bank in 1977, which financed the building of Sun Chui estate, completed 1981, and also Wo Che and Sha Kok, from 1977 – all in Sha Tin.[90] Shopping centres also contributed growing financial support to the HA.[91] In 1978, there was debate as to whether cash surpluses should continue to be used to finance both new estates and redevelopment, or just the latter; and in the same year, the HA protested against any move to privatise the management of the Lok Fu Commercial Centre, on grounds of potential loss of income.[92]

Figure 8.8 Illustration in 1982–3 Housing Authority *Annual Report* of Yellow Helmets at work demolishing illegal structures at Wong Tai Sin.

Figure 8.9 (a) Elsie Elliott inaugurating a hut-building scheme for the rehousing of victims of a fire at Ma Tsai Hang: extract from October 1979 SCMP article. (b) View from south-west of Hammer Hill squatter area in 1983, with the towers of King Shan Court HOS and the slabs of Fu Shan Estate rearing up in the background (MG).

Management-wise, a succession of moves followed the eventual squeezing-out of Lightbody from the Housing Secretaryship, in April 1977. He was replaced initially by Liao as acting Secretary, and then (by January 1978) by Alan Scott, 'a much younger man' who (Williams reported) 'knows nothing about housing', but brought a highly combative, at times incendiary attitude to bear on fighting the Authority's corner. Clashes included a blazing row with Elliott on TV and a behind-the-scenes feud with the Director of Broadcasting at Radio Television Hong Kong, over alleged 'bias' against the HA.[93] Liao then in 1979 became acting Chairman of the HA, and succeeded Scott as Secretary in 1980. Gradually, he became sucked further into administrative roles, but he emphasised that 'I still poked my nose periodically into Freddie Pang's office'.[94] (Figures 8.10, 8.11)

During Liao's latter years as Director and Acting Secretary, his fearsome reputation as a progress-chaser generated a host of stories concerning his legendary inspection visits, especially the annual end-of-production-year tours. These comprised, as Derek Messling recollected in 1993,

> an all-day drive around the territory, each chief in turn biting his or her nails as we approached their own sites. Such were the political pressures to achieve the set targets that even the Director stretched the meaning of "Practical Completion" to unprecedented lengths. I well remember one project where, on arrival, the responsible Chief was open-mouthed to find there was no glass in any of the windows, contrary to all the assurances he had received from the contractor. The Director [Liao] coolly observed that he was sure the windows would be glazed by the end of the day and in any event it would take Housing Management Branch several months to fill the blocks with new tenants.[95]

Other visits by Liao were more impromptu, but no less potentially explosive. Derek Messling recalled that, in the late 1970s,

> a site visit was arranged for him to inspect the new Ap Lei Chau estate which was nearing completion (and opened in 1980). The new road connecting the estate to the new bridge was scheduled to be completed that week. On arrival at the island end of the bridge our Clerk of Works diffidently advised the Director that the road was still incomplete and very muddy in places and offered Donald some Wellington boots to put on. The Director glared at the proffered boots and proclaimed to the assembled party that the road should be complete, dismissed the boots, and strode off confidently in his elegant suede shoes. On reaching the other end, plastered in mud up to his shins, he went to the nearest phone and gave the Highways Department Engineer a roasting he will probably remember to this day. The rest of us never again doubted that Donald took programmes seriously.[96]

Stephen Poon added that 'we purposely trod on the muddy grass so the reporters could take good photos, the message being that we couldn't allow this to happen to our public housing tenants – we must have that bridge link! Donald Liao has

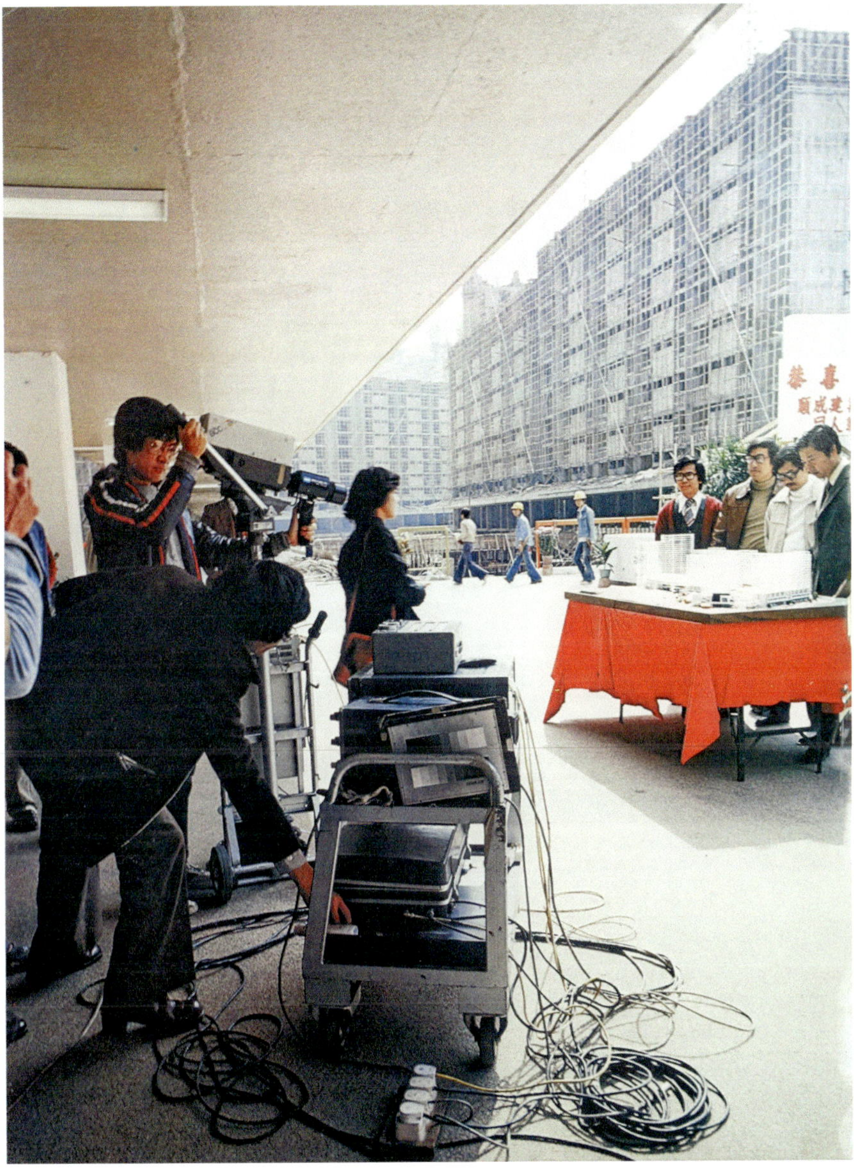

Figure 8.10 Illustration from 1978/9 HA *Annual Report* showing filming of housing feature for RTHK, at Tak Hau Street, Wo Che Estate, Sha Tin. Standing behind the table on the right are (right-left) Donald Liao, Stephen Poon, S T Chow and an unidentified architect.

Housing Authority Members
房屋委員會委員名表

Chairman
Hon D.P.H. Liao *CBE JP*
Secretary for Housing

Vice-Chairman
Mr B.V. Williams *ED JP*
Director of Housing

Members
Mr Hilton Cheong-Leen *OBE JP*
Company Director; Chairman, Urban Council; Wan Chai District Board Member

Mrs E. Elliott *CBE*
School Supervisor; Urban Councillor; Kwun Tong District Board Member

Hon R.H. Lobo *CBE JP*
Company Director; Executive and Legislative Councillor

Dr the Hon Henry H.L. Hu *CBE JP* (to 9.9.82)
Barrister; Legislative Councillor

Mr H.M.G. Forsgate *OBE JP*
Business Consultant; Vice-Chairman, Urban Council; Central & Western District Board Member

Mr Kenneth T.C. Lo *OBE JP*
Solicitor; Urban Councillor; Southern District Board Member

Dr Denny M.H. Huang *JP*
Medical Practitioner; Urban Councillor; Yau Ma Tei District Board Member

Hon Cheung Yan-lung *MBE JP*
Company Director; Legislative Councillor; Member, Heung Yee Kuk & North District Board

Mr Charles C.C. Sin
Solicitor

Hon F.K. Hu *JP*
Company Director; Legislative and Urban Councillor; Wan Chai District Board Member

Mrs Lee Lo Yuk-sim *JP*
Housewife/Housing Authority estate tenant; Wong Tai Sin District Board Member

Mr Lawrence H.L. Fung *JP*
Company Director; Urban Councillor; Wong Tai Sin District Board Member

Dr Philip C.K. Kwok *JP*
Company Director; Urban Councillor; Yau Ma Tei District Board Member

Hon Maria W.C. Tam *JP*
Barrister; Legislative Councillor; Eastern District Board Member

Hon D. Akers-Jones *CMG JP*
Secretary for District Administration

Hon S.E. Alleyne *JP* (to 28.2.83)
Hon J.W. Chambers *JP* (from 1.3.83)
Director of Social Welfare

Mr A.N. Savage *JP*
Principal Assistant Financial Secretary (1)

Hon D.W. McDonald *CMG JP*
Secretary for Lands and Works

Hon A.J. Scott *CBE JP*
Secretary for Transport

2

Back Row
Dr Kwok, Mr Chambers, Mr Hu, Mr Williams, Mr Cheong-Leen, Mr Savage.

Middle Row
Dr Huang, Mr Scott, Mrs Lee Lo, Mr McDonald, Mr Cheung, Mr Sin.

Front Row
Mrs Elliott, Mr Lo, Mr Liao, Mr Forsgate, Miss Tam.

Absent
Mr Lobo, Mr Fung, Mr Akers-Jones.

Figure 8.11 Group photo of HA members from 1982/3 *Annual Report*: (back) Kwok, Chambers, Hu, Williams, Cheong-Leen, Savage; (middle) Huang, Scott, Lee Lo, McDonald, Cheung, Sin; (front) Elliott, Lo, Liao, Forsgate, Tam. Absent: Lobo, Fung, Akers-Jones.

that charisma!'[97] At Lai Yiu Estate, Kwai Chung, faced with drainage delays by the Highways Department in the late 1970s, Liao simply told Poon to barge in and chair their site meetings: 'That wouldn't have been allowed after the MacLehose years!'[98]

With the massive expansion of the Housing Department, all rival power sources were eclipsed. The Urban Council, seen as too incompetent to manage housing, had already been sidelined in 1973.[99] The Housing Society, by contrast, was seen not as inefficient, but as a distraction from MacLehose's drive for numbers. The government had 'never really liked the Housing Society – it was seen as complicating the picture' – and even set out to 'run them out of business' (Akers-Jones) during the 1970s. By 1979, the Housing Society felt great uncertainty, as its need to pay one-third site premium contrasted starkly with the HA's nil-premium arrangement: several large-scale projects of the 1970s were seen as likely to mark the end of its regular general-needs rental programme.[100]

The two culminating projects of this 'Indian summer' of HS rental construction were Cho Yiu Chuen, Kwai Chung (1975–81), and Jat Min Chuen, Sha Tin (1979–82) – both named after early luminaries of the Society. (Figure 8.12) The multi-phase Cho Yiu Chuen, designed by Palmer & Turner around the centrepiece of a 592-flat, 39-storey tower block with 'sky lobbies' somewhat recalling Sui Wo Court, comprised 2,532 dwellings, all modelled in a somewhat 'brutalist' exposed concrete style. (Figure 8.13a–c) Jat Min Chuen, financed directly by a bank loan rather than government grant and completed in 1981/2, was a more straightforward design on a level site, comprising 3,725 flats in three 33-storey stepped-plan slab blocks, with nine-storey wings, including 100 elderly flats. (Figure 8.14a, b) The government strategy seemed to be to progressively nudge the Society towards the specialist roles of urban improvement and rural and elderly housing: under the Urban Improvement Scheme of 1977, the HS directly took over an initiative it had begun in 1974 through a consultancy,[101] focusing especially on the Western District of Hong Kong Island. Significant numbers of tenements were demolished by 1979, and the largest of the replacement schemes, Western Garden (432 dwellings), was completed in 1982: architecturally, these UIS schemes were designed piecemeal by private practices and were indistinguishable from small private-sector projects.[102] In 1982, an update for MacLehose's successor, Edward Youde, summarised the work of all these niche organisations, including the Housing Society, the Model Society (eventually taken over by the HA) and the Hong Kong Settlers' Housing Corporation, with its single estate at Tai Hang Sai (1965–77) – emphasising their peripheral status vis-à-vis what was now the mainstream housing drive, that of the HA.[103] (Figures 8.15, 8.16)

Within the Hong Kong Government in general, the late 1970s and '80s moves towards self-decolonisation included a comprehensive so-called 'localisation' of the civil service. In 1961 half of all administrative officers were expatriate, whereas the shift following the 1985 agreement with China reduced the percentage almost to nil. However, among the professionals of the Construction Branch this process was significantly obstructed from 1980 by the pressure from 1976/7 on the construction sector, and consequent losses of architects and engineers to the private

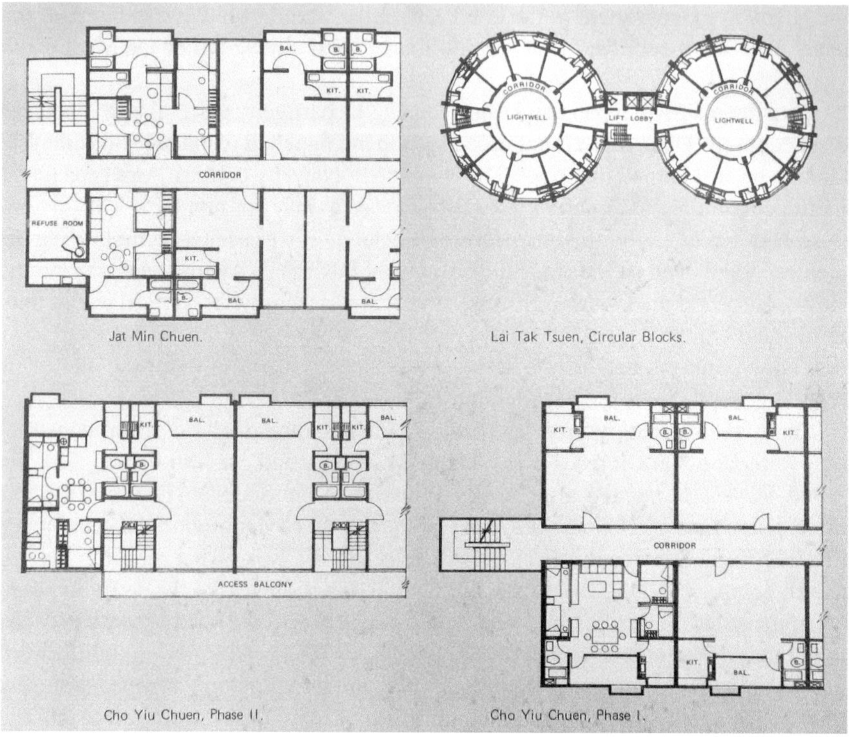

Figure 8.12 Floor plans of key Housing Society estates of the 1970s and early '80s, from 1978 Housing Society *Annual Report*.

sector.[104] As a consequence, 1977 actually saw a significant step *away* from 'localisation' in housing architecture, with Messling's appointment to the new HOS Chief Architect post, as part of the massive architectural staff expansion within Construction Branch in 1977, in the course of which the branch head became a Deputy Director.[105] But although Messling's appointment may have gone against the flow of decolonisation, as we will see, he soon showed himself to be an effective heir to Donald Liao, for example as the coordinator of numerous standard tower block series.[106] Lower down the scale, other young expatriate architects flooded in. For example, Chris Gabriel arrived in November 1980 from the London Borough of Camden, where the once lavishly funded housing drive was petering out:

> Cook had just left, Maiden Lane, Alexandra Road, the low-rise high-density projects of Neave Brown and Benson & Forsyth – were still going on. Cook's successor, Alfred Rigby, left around then, and took his lieutenants with him. Thatcher had come to power, and was targeting the left-wing boroughs. Our funding had been cut, so only renovations and conversions could proceed. Every project I worked on was eventually put in the drawer, and not progressed.[107]

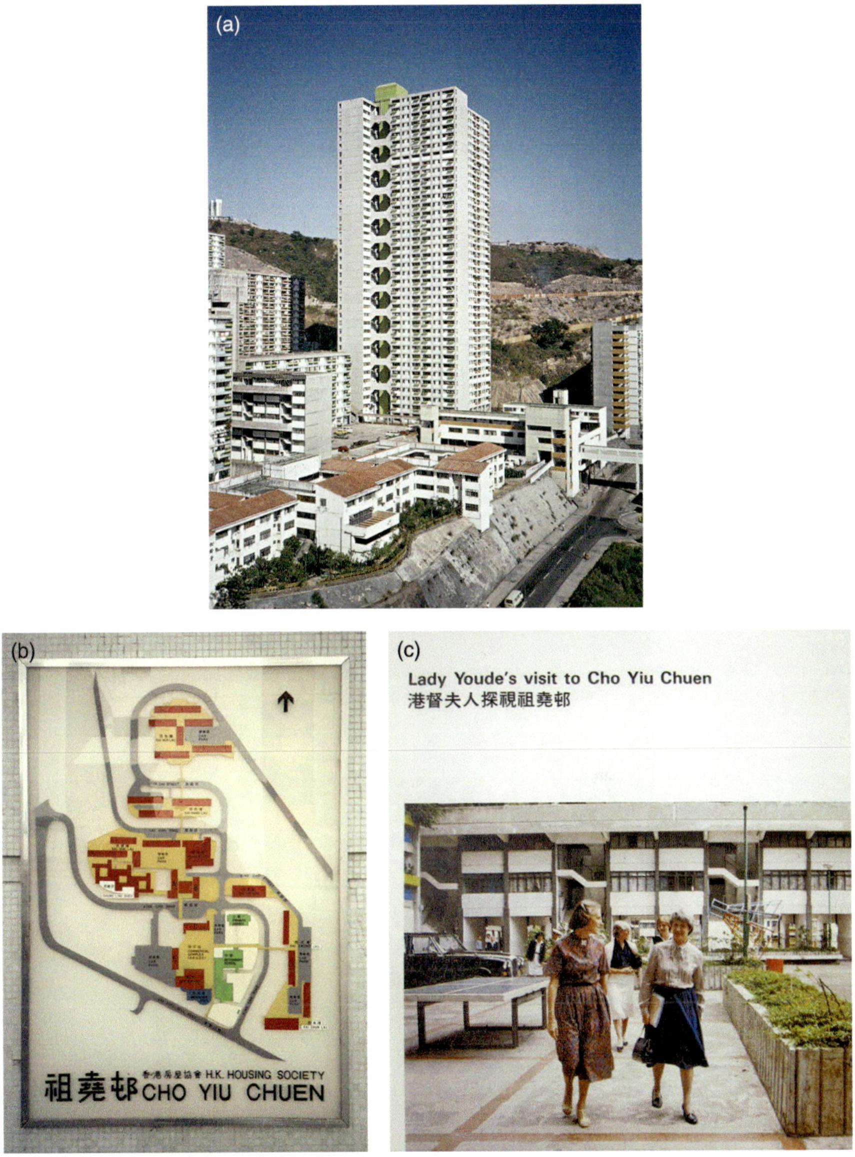

Figure 8.13 (a) The HKHS's Cho Yiu Chuen, 1983 view (MG) of Kai King Lau (Block 19, 39 storeys). (b) Cho Yiu Chuen, estate map, 1983 photo (MG). (c) Illustration of 1983 visit by Lady Youde (on left; the wife of Governor Youde) to the Hong Kong Housing Society's Cho Yiu Chuen, with the Society's chief Housing Manager, Sheila Sersale: from the Housing Society's 1984–6 *Annual Report*.

Figure 8.14 (a) Jat Min Chuen (HKHS, 1979–82), general view from north-west in 2013 (MG). (b) Jat Min Chuen, 1983 detail (MG) including original estate sign.

Figure 8.15 The front cover of the Housing Society's 1984–6 *Annual Report*, featuring a selection of current estates (Cho Yiu Chuen top left).

Figure 8.16 Tai Hang Sai, Shek Kip Mei, 2011 photo (MG) of the only completed large development by the Hong Kong Settlers' Corporation, founded 1952. Seven blocks were initially completed in 1965 and the eighth in 1977. (MG).

To him, the frenetic pace of activity in Hong Kong could not have been more different from the stagnation in London.

Within the HA, the late 1970s saw a shift towards a more participatory style of management, and a more critical housing discourse departing from the old traditions of 'benevolent paternalism'. This localised 'housing democracy' arguably served as a partial substitute for the 'political democracy' avoided by successive governors as potentially provocative to China. The new City District Officers were busy establishing MACs, 1974 had seen the launching of a 'Community Involvement Plan', and 1977–8 saw increasing numbers of 'meet the tenants' visits by Housing Authority members.[108] The number and variety of critical voices also grew. Elliott and other established critics continued to denounce poor management, 'bad housing' and evictions, and in 1977, Scott responded cautiously to letters of complaint from the Maryknoll Sisters, a longstanding Catholic missionary organisation, about housing conditions and rent levels.[109]

Far more significant for the future politicisation of housing debates, however, was the foundation of a new and more militant body in the early 1980s, the Hong Kong People's Council on Public Housing Policy (HKPCPHP). This fronted a growing chorus of criticism of government housing policies in general and the Housing Authority in particular.[110] Two largely incompatible critical discourses were now emerging in parallel: on the one hand, a higher-profile championing by groups such as the HKPCPHP of the interests of the poorest against shifts in focus to middle-income groups (e.g. the HOS) and higher rents; and on the other hand, a growing public discontent at the consequences of the rising incomes of many public rental tenants, as symbolised by the increasingly repeated trope of the 'Mercedes parked in the housing estate', and leading to calls for a differential rent policy. Indeed, in some ways access to rental housing was widening, not narrowing: between 1979 and 1981, residency requirements were reduced first to 15 and then to 10 years.[111]

Planning standards and block-types: towards higher densities and improved construction

With Hong Kong's fierce land constraints, and the further complication of the government's allegedly 'expensive land' policy, the question of density arguably loomed larger and more urgently than anywhere else – even Singapore, whose planning standards directly reflected its more dirigiste planning system, and subordinated private-sector real-estate interests to government policy. Around 1980, public housing density discussions in Hong Kong reached a new level of complexity and intensity – a level that would be maintained for the foreseeable future.[112]

The chief vehicle for those debates, especially from 1978, was the LDPC. Previously, during 1977 in particular, discussions had focused on the relationship between IUs, occupancy and density. The shift from IUs (now dismissed by Williams in 1977 as 'purely theoretical') to flats as the chief unit of computation had, it was claimed, led to a 10% increase in the living space within flats.[113] The relationship between internal and external density continued to be a focus, for example in an 'extensive discussion' in 1979 about the relationship between household size, occupancy policy, plot ratios and density at Tai Po Area 24, and a 1981 discussion about the relationship between IUs, assumed to equate to 3.3 m^2, and higher densities.[114] The IU still continued in notional use, however, and in 1982, internal space standards were increased to both 4 m^2 per IU, begging the question about the uneasy relationship between the two: Messling briefed the BC on the 'advantages' of the improved 4 m^2 standard.[115]

Within LDPC, however, the emphasis was naturally on external density, and in 1978, extensive investigation focused on the relationship between densities in housing areas and zoning regulation, for both HOS and public rental housing, including very full tables of densities.[116] Previous precedents were assessed. In 1980, an in-depth investigation led by Pryor, in relation especially to the Chuk Yuen site in Wong Tai Sin, evaluated the concept of density 'pump-priming': this involved development of initial phases of Resettlement estates at higher density to generate cycles of internal decanting.[117] This debate linked naturally to the 1980 pressure for urgent add-ons to sites, generated by the housing shortfall, which had prompted protests from Barnes.[118] In Britain and the USA, 1940s–1960s public housing redevelopments had generated similar expedients, albeit at much lower density and storey-height levels, as recalled by Enfield London Borough Council's 1965–8 Housing Chairman, Eric Smythe: 'It was because you had no land. So firstly you had to create the holes to put a tower block up – which you did by pulling a couple of streets down. You could then put a tower block in and commence pulling the rest of the area down. You can house, at the same density, or gain [extra density]'.[119] In redeveloping Hong Kong Resettlement estates, with their existing densities of up to 3,862 ppa or 9,543 ppha, there could be no question of density gain, but even to yield the current new-development density standard of 2,470 ppha, far higher blocks than in London would of course be essential. Individual cases of pump-priming in 1980 included insertion of tower blocks at Mui Wo, Chuk Yuen and Kwun Tong.[120]

Figure 8.17 Front cover of pilot 'Density Study' issued by HKOP Working Group, 1981. The Study showed 3,000 ppha/1,215 ppa was achievable on 'unencumbered flat sites' using various block permutations, including Trident and New Cruciform (HOS) in the front-cover variant. Area 17 was actually built slightly differently (Fu Shin Estate, Ming Nga Court and Yee Nga Court HOS).

The following year, in 1981, a more general re-evaluation of public housing densities by LDPC, in relation to the HKOP standards under development since 1973, was underway. (Figure 8.17) Its aim, forcefully advocated beforehand by Pryor, was to move from the current 2,470/2,500 ppha density standard for public rental housing, up to 3,000 ppha. It included a pilot 'Density Study' by an ad-hoc HKOP Working Group on Population Densities in Public Rental Housing Estates, using Tai Po Area 17 as a pilot, and showing the effects of different combinations of towers.[121] This burst of activity was prompted especially in relation to the imminent availability of the new Trident and New Cruciform blocks (see below). Eventually, the Working Group recommended that 3,000 ppha (1,215 ppa) should become the new net density standard for public rental housing in the second-generation New Towns, and 2,500–3,000 in the urban areas and first-generation New Towns.[122]

These debates were separate from, and parallel to, considerations of plot ratios and densities for private housing developments, although open-space provisions were an area of overlap: private developments were claimed to benefit from the higher open-space provisions within adjacent public housing. Other miscellaneous measures included a recommendation to use THAs as intensively as possible.[123] However, perhaps surprisingly, the pressure for output was by no means inexorable, and sometimes the process worked in the other direction, as in a revised plan for the Diamond Hill HOS development, from which one tower was eventually omitted in 1982, the original development having been judged to be too cramped. Likewise, in 1982, at Tuen Mun Area 44 (HOS), a 10% cut was agreed to 'avoid monotony'.[124]

By 1980, complaints were also being levelled at the HA's reliance on standard block types, a policy that would continue for decades into the future, as for example in the 'Harmony' series of the 1990s.[125] Unlike the vast numbers of standardised blocks used at relatively low densities in Soviet cities, the number of Hong Kong blocks, in absolute terms, was quite limited, but Liao still faced criticisms of monotony: 'People would say to me, "You're producing sausage-machine housing!" I'd say back, "Yes, but I like them to be sausages that taste good!"'[126] The 'over-standardised' planning of two estates in Tuen Mun, Areas 13 and 15, On Ting and Yau Oi (by a team led by senior architect Denis Ko) as virtual mirror images of each other, provoked criticism from senior estate manager H R Husband; but as Ko pointed out in 1983, the issue of 'monotony' was just as much concerned with the standard block mixes laid down by the HA as with the details of block design and non-standard elements under the individual architect's control. On Ting was hailed in 1980 as the hundredth HA housing estate completed.[127] (Figure 8.18)

Ko also emphasised in 1983 the severe constraint imposed by low building skills on construction standards and thus on any attempts at a more precise design approach: with the 'appalling' finishes that were prevalent, even tentative attempts at industrialisation or systematisation of the building process were very problematic.[128] In response to arguments in favour of labour-saving techniques, owing to the shortage of skilled labour, 1981 saw an abortive visit by UK contractors with

Figure 8.18 1983 view of specimen one-room flat in slab block at Yau Oi Estate: along with On Ting, one of a pair of high-density (2,833 ppha) Tuen Mun estates, completed in 1979–81 (MG).

Figure 8.19 (a) Sun Chui Estate Phase II, Sha Tin, seen under construction in November 1983, using sliding formwork (MG). (b) Sun Chui Estate Phase II, contract noticeboard: contractor Hsin Chong Construction. 1983 photo (MG). (c) Sun Chui, 2023 view from the same location as 8.19b (MG). (cf. Fig. 11.10c).

system-building experience, as well as attempted reforms to tendering methods.[129] But nothing remotely resembling the package deals of 1960s system-building in Britain, let alone industrialised construction in the Soviet Union, was contemplated, and the principal outcome was a modest degree of rationalised traditional construction, for example involving sliding formwork, as at the Sun Chui (Sha Tin) and Kwong Fuk (Tai Po) projects, both tendered in 1982. (Figure 8.19a–c) For these, the Building Committee minutes record intensive debates about costs and tenders – in the case of Kwong Fuk, Chun Shek (also 1982) and Fu Shin (Tai Po Area 17) (1981), all involving the new Trident blocks.[130] 1982 also saw the tendering for the giant Tuen Mun Area 51 HOS project (Siu Hong Court), built in traditional in situ construction.[131]

To be sure, any worries about building defects in housing in the 1970s had been dwarfed by the far more catastrophic issue of slope failure, and its public housing impacts in the Sau Mau Ping mudslides of 1972 and 1976 (aside from other cases involving private housing, such as the Kotewall Road collapse of 1972). Yet the discourse of problematic public housing construction in Hong Kong continued to gradually gather pace throughout the late 1970s, most embarrassingly for Liao in late 1978 when a visiting delegation from Italy spotted a 'serious structural fault' during a guided tour of estates.[132] Ron Woodcraft alleged 'appalling construction defects' in 1977 at Lek Yuen, and defects were also under investigation in 1978 at Nam Shan Estate.[133] The climax, however, came in the 1980s (Chapter 9): the so-called '26 Blocks Scandal', involving construction defects and cracking stemming from use of salt-water in building.[134]

Of the standard blocks in use in the late 1970s, the PWD's standard series were now rapidly being discontinued. One of the last PWD-designed schemes to be finished was the non-standard Tai Hing (in 1980); the slightly earlier PWD-designed Yue Wan estate in Chai Wan, completed 1977, featured the same Mk VII plans as at Hing Wah II but with 'rather superior' finishes.[135] The Twin-Tower Block had by now become ubiquitous, including extensive use in the New Territories, for example at Sha Tin's 6,075-flat Wo Che.[136] And new rental types followed, such as a new I-shaped domestic block of five-person and seven-person flats designed by Stephen Poon's team in 1977. John Ng recalls: 'In my early days, we always used the most current standard domestic block, which in those days was the 'I' block. That was Stephen Poon's baby – I can still recall once, after 5 pm, seeing him still at work preparing the I-block drawings – Cheung Sing-Hoi was in hospital and Stephen was going to pay him a visit later. Trying to get schematic drawings available and get them together – we were always in a rush!'[137]

The introduction of the HOS gave a substantial boost to slimmer, tower-like standard blocks, as we saw in Chapter 7.[138] HOS block design processes were, as with rental blocks, greatly preoccupied with flat sizes. The shift towards smaller flats within the HOS from 1979 onwards prompted a range of proposals, including modification to standard H-blocks to create small flats, and provision for open-plan units suitable for partitioning by the owners themselves.[139] The Windmill, designed by architect S K Lo (SA/6) in 1981, was a 36-storey development of previous proposals for a 41-storey HOS 'Cross Block' or 'HOS Mk III', with a plan presaged by the pinwheel layout of Sui Wo Court, and staggered wing-heights to 'avoid monotony on the skyline', especially on flat sites. It was intended, as Pang and Messling explained to the Home Ownership Committee in April 1981, to answer the requirement for reduced costs, affordability and smaller flats (with a 20% reduction in building costs compared to the earlier Flexi blocks), and allow open-plan options.[140] In general, the early 1980s saw a decisive move away from universal use of standard blocks below 30 storeys, such as the Twin Tower or the H block, motivated by a new conviction that the optimum height was 35–36 storeys. However, that did not remain the limit for long. The colossal Hing Man project at Chai Wan, also designed by Palmer & Turner and featuring a similar clustered form and grouped sky-lobbies to Sui Wo Court, pioneered a further jump above

Figure 8.20 (a) Hing Man Estate, Chai Wan, 1979–82: three towers up to 44 storeys high, designed by Palmer & Turner with similar clustering and sky lobbies to Sui Wo Court: 1983 view (MG) of estate-office model. (b) 1983 general view of Hing Man from south-east (MG). (c) 1983 view of sky lobby on the 39th floor of one of the Hing Man towers (MG).

40 storeys (to 44 storeys), partly motivated here by the exceptionally steep and difficult site: it was officially visited by Liao in September 1981.[141] (Figures 8.20a–c) Two significant new block-types were developed together: the New Cruciform Block for HOS use, designed largely by Stephen Poon's team, and the Trident, a much more massive, Y-shaped structure of multi-room flats designed either for public rental or HOS use, and first approved in 1982: both are covered in detail in Chapter 9.[142]

New and more specialist types were also suggested, such as hostels for the able-bodied (proposed in 1981) or hostels for the elderly (including 'cage men'), suggested by Pryor in 1977 following a 1973 working-party report on elderly housing.[143] (Figure 8.21) Decisively rejected, however, was a 1981–2 suggestion to respond to the growing demand for temporary housing areas by building emergency flatted blocks of three storeys – a plan that recalled the earlier build-up from

10,000, mostly the elderly, still living in wired-in world of misery, working party survey shows

Report blames Govt for plight of cage men

by Sa Ni Harte

OVERNMENT housing olicy has led to the ontinued existence of Hongkong's "caged en", it was claimed esterday.

More than 10,000 eople are still living in he "cages," whose xistence caused a public utcry when they were evealed several years go.

A new study, compiled y Chinese University udents, says that 41 per ent of the caged men are ed 61 or over.

The old men, about 68 r cent of whom have no latives in Hongkong, live in series of three-decker unks which are wired-in for curity reasons.

Their conditions are scribed in the students' port as "Miserable, with credibly inadequate oking and fire prevention ilities. People living there ffer from overcrowded, darkness, damp, bad

seek refuge in the "cages."

About 74 per cent of these elderly men are either retired, unable to work or unemployed, the report says.

Those employed or receiving Public Assistance have monthly incomes ranging from about $100 to $800. The report says about 69 per cent are between the $201 and $400 income bracket. Only 1.1 per cent earn slightly more than $800, it adds.

Not only confronted with poor living conditions, about 46 per cent of the "caged men" are also reported to be in poor health. The report says some of the common illnesses are serious stomach disease, TB, arthritis, mental disease and industrial accident injuries.

About 40 per cent of these "caged men" have been living in this environment for more than 11 years, whereas about 35

"there is a need to implement a contributory pension scheme to protect the work force from reduced income in old age."

As a considerable number of residents in boarding houses are elderly job losers, they should be helped to make better use of the placement service of the Hongkong Council of Social Service Employment Service or the Labour Department, the report says.

"For those who cannot compete in the open market, sheltered employment might be a viable solution," it says.

The report says two experimental projects will be launched to provide handicraft work in social centres and multi-service centres for the elderly.

The working party has also recommended that emergency accommodation for old men with declining self care ability should be expanded to 20 places.

It says that in Hongkong emergency placement for this group was limited to

Figure 8.21 August 1981 *Star* article on the plight of the 'cage men'.

Bowring Bungalows to Mk I (and which was in turn echoed, in modified form, some 40 years later during the Carrie Lam administration). Also ruled out absolutely by the LDPC was the somewhat more radical proposal, also briefly floated in 1981–2, for an updated version of the Mk I/II block for temporary use ('multi-storey temporary housing') – although a visiting delegation from Bombay in these years had actually expressed interest in Mk V blocks, with their similarity to Indian 'chawl' blocks, as an ideal formula for new housing there.[144] All the time, however, modification work continued to the existing Mk I and II blocks, for example by conversion of some penthouses into flats in 1978.[145] And among the ancillary buildings of housing developments, the evolution of new variants also proceeded apace, such as a new 15-storey flatted factory type.[146]

MacLehose's final lap

By 1981–2, with MacLehose's final extension coming rapidly towards its end, and discussions about a replacement underway, fresh clouds appeared on the economic horizon, with the onset of the 1981–5 'Volcker shock'. This triggered a collapse in property prices: 1981–2 saw huge fluctuations in land value, not unlike 1973–4.[147] In the sceptical opinion of Leo Goodstadt, MacLehose bequeathed an economy in a precarious condition, with the excessive speculation of the 1970s having led to an artificial spike, a property bubble, from 1978.[148] As we will see in Chapter 9, between the end of 1981 and the end of 1983 the stock market and property values would fall sharply (by 38% and 31%, respectively), and a credit squeeze would follow in 1983: the gloom would not lift, overall, until 1985. Coinciding with the onset of this fresh phase of uncertainty, a government reorganisation in November 1981 also included the move of Haddon-Cave from Financial Secretary to Chief Secretary.[149]

What was still just over the horizon was the impending 1980s shift from an export-based manufacturing to a 'financialised' economy, but just as in previous recessions, the effect of this economic turmoil on the public housing programme was indirect.[150] Instead, output continued at around Liao's preferred 'cruising speed' of 35,000 completions per annum: 1982 saw 35,745 completions, and the allocation of 35,100 flats, and in July of that year, Bernard Williams signed five contracts covering no less than 11,252 dwellings, the largest ever single contract-signing to date.[151] By the beginning of 1982, memos to MacLehose were focusing in detail on forecast production until 1986, and it began to be argued that the first Ten-Year Plan would now in effect terminate in 1986, and should be succeeded by another, for 1,150,000 flats.[152]

The public lead-up to the end of MacLehose's governorship, however, gave few hints of crises bubbling below the surface, and was marked in the housing field by some self-celebration, for example in MacLehose's opening of Sui Wo Court in May 1981, or later of Mei Lam in November 1982 by Liao as Secretary for Housing. In September 1982, Crosby claimed Hong Kong was a 'world leader in planning, development and management of housing'. But in contrast to Singapore, such a claim had no overt ideological or nationalistic overtones – for obvious reasons.[153]

In his final valedictory message to the FCO, MacLehose expressed regret that he was leaving just when 'the curtain is about to go up' on the sovereignty negotiations, and the hoped-for geopolitical ramifications of his efforts at building a 'model city' would begin to unfold: 'The count-down period has now started and all that we have worked for will shortly be put to the test'. In retrospect, he conceded, his reforms had been 'little more than extensions of previous trends of government, but they were all deliberately presented and announced over a period of years so as to try to catch and hold the imagination and interest of the population'. 'We were favoured by an annual growth rate… of 10% per year and an annual per capita increase of 7.5%. But a government which couldn't make something out of such prolonged growth would be contemptible. So we were lucky.' As to the immediate future, Hong Kong should 'stick to its present course with every appearance of normality', as 'confidence cannot be stretched for more than two or three years more, and it could break sooner if something triggered disinvestment. Confidence is largely maintained now because everyone assumes all will be well'. Perhaps ominously, as a harbinger of thunder-clouds ahead, MacLehose's last night before departure was marred by illness.[154]

Notes

1 Akers-Jones, *Feeling the Stones*, 134; Akers-Jones, 2013 interview.

2 FCO40-617 4-1975 to 12-1975 MacLehose-FCO correspondence; FCO40-628 18-8-1975 MacLehose to Duncan Watson and reply; FCO40-761 4-3-1977 Stewart to Milton; uncertainty, Akers-Jones, 2013 interview. Background to autonomy: Goodstadt, *Uneasy Partners*; Goodstadt, 'Fiscal freedom', 273–294.

3 FCO40-954 19-4-1978 Sir Paul Bryan note and Quantrill background briefing; FCO40-761 21-11-1977 briefing by Stewart; FCO40-799 SCMP cuttings 1976-7.

4 FCO40-761 4-3-1977 Stewart to Milton.

5 FCO40-761 notes of 22-11-1977 Goronwy Roberts/MacLehose meeting.

6 FCO40-761 1-7-1977 Goronwy Roberts to Secretary of State; 28-9-1977 Stewart memo; FCO40-799 Goronwy Roberts meeting with MacLehose 22-11-1977.

7 FCO40-799 7-10-1977 MacLehose to John Stewart; FCO40-1156 1-1977 background note on Turner.
8 FCO40-761 22-11-1977 talking points by Stewart; 22-11-77 notes of meeting Goronwy Roberts/Maclehose.
9 FCO40-965 20-2-1978 telegram of congratulations by Goronwy Roberts.
10 FCO40-954 brief for MacLehose/Goronwy Roberts meeting.
11 FCO40-1057 8-6-1979 notes for discussion with Thatcher and 4-7-1979 MacLehose to Blaker.
12 *Hong Kong Hansard*, 10-10-1979, 34.
13 FCO40-1281 1-3-1881 MacLehose meeting with Sir Keith Joseph. Thatcherite revitalisation of 'declinist' theory: Edgerton, *The Rise and Fall of the British Nation*, 450–1.
14 Gabriel, 2009 interview; Scott, *Political Change and the Crisis of Legitimacy*, 157; Blyth and Wotherspoon, *Hong Kong Remembers*, 122–4
15 HKRS163-8-159 7-1977 papers; HKRS530-1-4 1-1977; Scott, *Political Change and the Crisis of Legitimacy*, 129, 163; Drakakis-Smith, *High Society*, 133; Blyth and Wotherspoon, *Hong Kong Remembers*, 99.
16 SCMP 16-12-76; FCO20-954 24-4-1978 John Stewart note; FCO40-1038 14-3-1979 Owen to MacLehose; 19-9-1879 Shawcross to Secretary of State.
17 FCO40-1038 MacLehose to Youde, 29-8-1979 and 22-11-1979 Quantrill to MacLehose; FCO40-1281 21-8-1981 memo to Ridley; FCO40-1057 15-5-1979 phone call by Lady MacLehose; FCO40-1038 Reuter press release 20-3-1979.
18 HKRS684-2-16 'Achievements and Failures – A Critical Review of Sir Murray MacLehose's Governorship'; 'Big Mac': Holdsworth and Munn, *Dictionary of Hong Kong Biography* (on MacLehose).
19 HKRS1693-4-11 1977 correspondence.
20 Tsang, *Governing Hong Kong*, 191, 197.
21 FCO40-1057 14-6-1979 MacLehose meeting with Blaker; FCO40-642 MacLehose to Secretary of State, 17-4-1982.
22 Scott, *Political Change and the Crisis of Legitimacy*, 258; FCO40-1259 17-12-1981 lecture by Haddon-Cave, 'The Government of Hong Kong'.
23 FCO40-1259 17-12-81 lecture by Haddon-Cave; avoidance of 'democracy', Ng and Wong, *Civil Unrest*, 79–80, 86–7.
24 FCO40-617 11-4-1975 Callaghan/MacLehose discussion, 10-4-1975 Goronwy-Roberts to Secretary of State, and 3-12-1975 MacLehose meeting with Callaghan and TUC; FCO40-628 18-8-1973 MacLehose to Watson and reply.
25 FCO40-617 2-12-1975 Goronwy-Roberts-MacLehose meeting.
26 HKRS477-2-4 *China Mail* 12-7-1972; HKRS163-8-35 1974 on Tsz Wan Shan triads; HKRS1588-2-9, *Hong Kong Standard* 26-1-77. Hin Keng: Lambon 2012; HKRS461-1-12-8 October 1982 BC minutes.
27 FCO40-1258, notes on Elliott; FCO40-1281, minutes of 22-6-1981 meeting; HKRS483-4-1 7-1977 Operations Committee minutes; HKRS530-1-4, *Hong Kong Standard* cutting 22-4-1978. Tu, *Colonial Hong Kong*, 62-3. Chris Patten, *The Hong Kong Diaries,* Allen Lane, London, 2022, 130.
28 J Dimbleby, *The Last Governor – Chris Patten and the Handover of Hong Kong*, Little Brown & Co., London, 1997, 37; FCO40-1156 Cortazzi memo 8-1-1980.
29 Ng and Wong, *Civil Unrest*, 366–371; Blyth and Wotherspoon, *Hong Kong Remembers*, 122–4; Akers-Jones, *Feeling the Stones*, 134.
30 HKRS160-63 11-4-79 report on visit by MacLehose. M Yip, 'New town planning as diplomatic planning: scalar politics, British-Chinese relations, and Hong Kong', *Journal of Urban History*, 48:2, March 2022, 361–380.

31 HKRS160-63 report of 11-4-1979.
32 FCO40-1156 5-11-1980 minutes of meeting Carrington-Youde-MacLehose.
33 FCO40-1281 1-3-1981 meeting MacLehose with Sir K Joseph.
34 FCO40-1282 SCMP 29-11-1981 cutting.
35 Scott, *Political Change and the Crisis of Legitimacy*, 128; FCO40-1012 ExCo 17-10-1978 meeting; FCO40-1122 14-5-1979 A J Scott to Williamson and briefing for MacLehose on housing 19-4-1979.
36 R Wong, *Hong Kong Land for Hong Kong People*, 216.
37 Liao, 2010 interview; HKRS163-8-113 Liao memo for MacLehose 8-2-1980; HKRS163-8-130 11-2-1977 briefing; HKRS608-1-41 LDPC 3-1980; HKRS163-8-176 Scott memo 24-8-1979 and MacLehose reply.
38 FCO40-954 24-4-1978 J Stewart to MacLehose
39 Holdsworth and Munn, *Dictionary of Hong Kong Biography* (Goodstadt on Haddon-Cave); Tsang, *Governing Hong Kong*, 80; Scott, *Political Change and the Crisis of Legitimacy*, 257.
40 Akers-Jones, *Feeling the Stones*, 121; FCO40-1258 'Reports on Leading Personalities'.
41 FCO40-1229, 1981 evaluation.
42 1HKRS63-8-176 24-8-1979 Scott meeting with MacLehose and SCMP 1-7-1975.
43 HKRS163-8-130 11-2-1977 briefing.
44 Williams, 2012 interview; HKRS1693-4-4 3-1978 on Lok Fu; HKRS163-8-89 Operations Branch 3-1980.
45 HKRS183-8-58 22-8-1978 MacLehose note; HKRS163-8-131 6-3-1980 exchange with MacLehose. FCO40-1012 Parliamentary written answer 14-4-1978.
46 P Geddes, *In the Mouth of the Dragon, Hong Kong, Past, Present and Future*, Century, London, 1982, 88; Yeung and Wong, *Fifty Years*, 22.
47 HKRS608-1-41 LDPC 4-1978 and 5-1978 minutes.
48 Williams, 2012 minutes; Scott, *Political Change and the Crisis of Legitimacy*, 154.
49 Pryor, *Housing in Hong Kong*, 70-1; HKRS1588-3-27 1977 discussion; HKRS461-1-12-8 9-1982 BC minutes.
50 Liao, 2010 interview; HKRS545-1-459-3, Liao 3-1980.
51 HKRS168-8-131; HKRS608-1-41; Miller, 2012 interview.
52 FCO40-1156, 3-1-1980 R D Clift memo; HKRS545-1-456-2, SCMP 5-4-1979 cutting.
53 HKRS163-8-176 Scott memo 24-8-1979 and MacLehose reply; HKRS545-1-456-2, MacLehose 10-10-1979 to LegCo.
54 HKRS163-8-157, 3-1977 memo by Lightbody; HKRS163-8-176 Scott memo 24-8-1979.
55 HKRS545-1-456-2 MacLehose to J Cater.
56 HKRS163-8-13 Liao memo 8-2-1980; HKRS163-8-131 2-1980 Barnes note; HKRS1075-4-133 1-1980 joint Tai Po Area 24 planning NTDD and HD housing brief; HKRS163-11-20 2-1981 Special Financial Committee meeting.
57 *Hong Kong 1983* (yearbook).
58 HKRS608-1-41 LDPC 3-1980 minutes; HKRS163-8-65 27-3-81 LDPC minutes; HKRS461-1-12-2 BC 4-1982 minutes.
59 Yeung and Wong, *Fifty Years*, 433; HKRS461-1-12-2 BC 4-1982 minutes.
60 HKRS 163-7-84 memo with HA on HOS 3-1978; HKRS163-8-130 1-2-77 HD briefing and 4-1977 MacLehose note; FCO40-1122 briefing for MacLehose 19-4-1979; HKRS545-1-456-3 10-1981 Liao and Huang; HKRS163-8-132 8-2-1980 Liao memo.
61 R Wong, Hong Kong Land, 109; HKRS163-8-55 7-1977 LDPC minutes.
62 HKRS163-8-58 MacLehose note on 'something solid', 22-8-1978; FCO40-823 6-1977 papers; HKRS163-8-57 LDPC 7-1978, HKRS163-8-58 Pryor 8-1978 LDPC minutes; HKRS608-1-41 LDPC 3-1980 minutes.

63 FCO40-1122 14-5-1979 AJ Scott to Williamson. Pryor, *Housing in Hong Kong*, 80.
64 Williams, 1988 Bodleian interview.
65 HKRS163-8-58 11-10-1978 memo.
66 HKRS1588-3-22 7-1978 Mary Sneddon note and 7-1981 comparison; HKRS163-8-57 6-1978 report on visit; HKRS608-1-41 report on visit to LDPC 6-1978.
67 Liao, 2010 interview; HKRS938-1-2 Planning Area System, 3-1977 detailed list of New Towns zoning and development plans; HKRS1588-3-22 18-11-1981 Arrick report.
68 HKRS608-1-41 LDPC meetings of 15-4-1978 and 8-1979 to endorse HKOP; HKRS163-8-64 3-1981 on HKOP analysis of Tai Po schemes.
69 Williams, 2012 interview.
70 HKRS545-1-447-2 1-3-1977 cutting.HKRS608-1-49; Scott, *Political Change and the Crisis of Legitimacy*, 154–6; Akers-Jones, *Feeling the Stones*, 92–3; Liao, 2010 interview.
71 HKRS163-8-157 3-1977 memo for ExCo; Akers-Jones, *Feeling the Stones*, 94-5; HKRS163-8-90 Pryor table; HKRS608-1-49 25-8-1980 on Development Office.
72 Fung Tung, 2010 interview; Yeung and Wong, *Fifty Years*, 96–7; HKRS608-1-41; *Built Environment*, 9: 3/4, 1983, 266–77.
73 HKRS608-1-49 memo of 3-1978; HKRS938-1-12, 10-1977 and 9-1979 notes; Williams, 2012 interview.
74 HKRS1075-4-133, 1-1980 note; HKRS163-8-131 8-2-1980 Liao memo.
75 HKRS1589-1-4; HKRS608-1-41, 18-8-76 LDPC minutes.
76 Liao, 2010 interview.
77 Pryor, *Housing in Hong Kong*, 76–7; Liao, 2010 interview; R Nissim, *Land Administration and Practice in Hong Kong*, HKUP 2016 (4th edition), 121–3.
78 HKRS1004-1-1 5/6-1978 letter from J Todd SNT and Peter Ng District Officer Tuen Mun; HKRS545-1-447-2 1-1979 memo; HKRS608-1-141 LDPC 8-1979 on Yuen Long; HKRS1075-4-133 14-1-1980 New Territories Development Progress Committee on Tai Po, Fanling.
79 HKRS163-8-65 8-1981 Interim Report; HKRS163-8-59 8-1979 LDPC; HKRS163-8-58 1-1979; HKRS163-8-68 and 163-8-69 on LDPC 7-1982; HKRS163-8-68 LDPC 25-9-1981; HKRS608-1-49, 27-9-1980 memo; HKRS608-1-41 4-1979 and 1-1980 LDPC.
80 HKRS608-1-411 LDPC 2-1979 to 6-1979; HKRS163-8-57 8-1979 N Lantau discussion; HKRS163-8-131 DPHL 18-7-1979; HKRS163-8-58 8-1978 pressure from MacLehose; HKRS163-8-59 LDPC 7-1979 paper, 8-1979 meeting; HKRS163-8-131 20-5-1980 Liao note and 5-6-1980 from Chief Secretary.
81 Yip, 'New town planning as diplomatic planning', 361-380. HKRS163-8-61 22-2-1980 meeting on Tin Shui Wai with MacLehose; Akers-Jones, *Feeling the Stones*, 106–9; HKRS163-8-64 LDPC 2-1981. HKRS163-8-57 LDPC 'confidential' 8-1979 discussion about leases and 1997.
82 HKRS500-6-5, 1-4-1978 note; HKRS163-8-59, 7-1977 to 1-1978 correspondence; HKRS1588-3-22, 17-4-1980 note about programming of redevelopment schemes; Pryor, *Housing in Hong Kong*, 82.
83 HKRS545-1-456-3, SCMP 5-11-1980 cutting; HKRS163-8-11 6-1982 brief for Housing Secretary.
84 HKRS545-1-456-4, 1-1983 cutting of Williams in SCMP; HKRS483-4-1 HA Operations Committee memo 12-10-1978; HKRS163-8-89 Progress Report 9-1981; HKRS545-1-456-3 7-1981 interview with Asprey DDH (Operations).
85 HKRS483-4-1 Operations Committee 4-1977; FCO40-1122 18-7-1979 Williamson note; HKRS530-1-4 3-77, 10-1977 correspondence.

86 HKRS163-8-130 2-1977 briefing for MacLehose; HKRS530-1-5, copious press articles about illegal immigrants and squatters.
87 Tsui, 'Minimum government assistance', 1270-4; HKRS163-8-89 9-1981 report; *Hong Kong 1983* (Yearbook), 107, 112; HKRS163-8-55 LDPC 25-3-77; HKRS163-8-67 3-1982 papers; HKRS163-8-11; HKRS1589-1-4 1974-8 papers.
88 Scott, *Political Change and the Crisis of Legitimacy*, 140.
89 HKRS696-3-163 5-1977 ExCo memo and review; HKRS163-8-88 4-1977 housing progress report; *Hong Kong 1983* (Yearbook), 111, on new HA finance arrangements; HKRS1693-4-11 'Maryknoll' correspondence;; Drakakis-Smith, *High Society*, 117; HKRS483-4-1 4-1977 papers; FCO40-1012 ExCo meeting 17-10-1978.
90 HKRS163-8-26 papers of 3-1977; HKRS696-3-165 BC 9-11-1981; HKRS461-1-12-2 4-1982 BC meeting.
91 Liao, 2010 interview; Williams, 2012 interview.
92 HKRS1588-9-34 4-9-1978 papers; HKRS1693-4-4 1-1978 note from Scott (Secretary for Housing).
93 HKRS1588-9-22, 4-1977 note; Akers-Jones, 2014 interview; HKRS1588-2-30 Williams note 3-1977; HKRS163-8-87 3-1979 correspondence.
94 HKRS1588-9-35 7-1979; HKRS 1588-9-22 11-1980 and 4-1981 Liao speeches to LegCo; Williams, 1988 Bodleian interview; Liao, 2010 and 2014 interviews.
95 Messling, 'Public housing – a numbers game', typescript recollections, 1993, courtesy of Bernard Williams.
96 Messling, 'Public housing – a numbers game'; HKRS545-1-456-3 7-1981 on Liao visit to part-completed Hing Man.
97 Poon, 2014 interview.
98 Poon, 2014 interview; HKRS1588-9-35 1979 Walden and Liao correspondence over completions.
99 FCO40-1156 R D Clift brief 3-1-1980.
100 HKRS163-8-89 1-1980 papers; Akers-Jones, 2014 interview; HKRS545-1-456-2 SCMP 9-3-1979 cutting; 163-8-1989 2-1979 correspondence.
101 L C Wong, 2011 interview; HKRS163-8-89 1-1980 note; HKRS524-3-32 5-1977 Sersale to Williams. HKHS, *The Hong Kong Housing Society Annual Report 1978*, Hong Kong, 1978, 4–6, 41; HKHS, *The Hong Kong Housing Society Annual Report 1982*, Hong Kong, 1982, 20.
102 Drakakis-Smith, *High Society*, 1979 on Western District tenement demolitions; HKRS163-8-72 LDPC 2-12-1983. HKHS, *The HKHS Annual Report 1982*, HK 1982, 6.
103 HKRS163-8-11 6-1982.
104 Williams, 1988 Bodleian interview.
105 Messling, 'Public housing – a numbers game', 2; Williams, 2012 interview; Lambon, 2012 interview; HKRS483-4-1 7-1977 note.
106 HKRS461-1-12-8 BC 11-1982; Personalities, FCO40-1258. Liao, 2010 interview: Forsgate 'supportive, very knowledgeable'.
107 Gabriel, 2009 interview; Mark Swenarton, *Cook's Camden, The Making of Modern Housing*, Lund Humphries, London, 2017, 265.
108 HKRS483-4-1 2-1978 to 10-1978 papers; Scott, *Political Change and the Crisis of Legitimacy*, 141 on Community Involvement Plan.
109 HKRS1693-4-11 24-6-1977; HKRS530-1-4 SCMP 6-12-1977 Elliott letter; SCMP 483-4-1 3-1977 to 7-1977 correspondence.
110 Yeung and Wong, *Fifty Years*, 217-8; HKRS 545-1-456-2 19-11-1979 SCMP cutting on housing plight of poor.

111 HKRS545-1-456-4 15-7-1983 Williams note.

112 Compare the similarly acrimonious density controversies between 'housers' and 'planners' over 1960s Glasgow council housing: M Glendinning and S Muthesius, *Tower Block*, Yale UP, London, 1994, 220–42.

113 HKRS163-8-55; HKRS163-8-157 3-1977 Lightbody memo; HKRS1588-3-22 1977 paper by Pryor; HKRS483-4-1 11-10-1977; HKRS461-1-12-8 9-1982 BC minutes; HKRS163-8-30 4-1977; Williams to Secretary for Housing.

114 HKRS1075-4-133 Tai Po/Fanling Works Progress Committee 4-10-1979; HKRS461-1-12-8 1-1980 planning brief; HKRS163-8-55 2-1977 Lightbody to Liao; HKRS1882-1-2 3-1977 LPVC minutes; HKRS1588-3-22 12-1976 to 1-1977 papers; Richard Wong, *Hong Kong Land*, 46.

115 HKRS461-1-12-8, BC 10-1982 and 11-1982 minutes.

116 HKRS608-1-41 LDPC 4-1978; HKRS163-8-57 LDPC 2-1978, 3-1978; HKRS163-8-58 24-11-1978 correspondence; HKRS163-8-59 1979 papers; HKRS1588-3-22 2-1978 on plot ratios and HOS; SCMP 28-9-1982 piece by S K Tse on North Point as too spacious.

117 HKRS1588-3-22 17-4-1980 Pryor note.

118 HKRS 163-8-131 21-2-1980 Barnes protests.

119 Smythe interview 1988; Glendinning, *Mass Housing*, 151–2.

120 HKRS1882-1-3 1979 LPVC meetings re Mui Wo, Kwun Tong redevelopment; HKRS1588-3-22 17-4-1980 Pryor note on pump-priming.

121 HKRS163-8-65 4-1981 paper; HKRS1588-3-22; HKRS163-8-64 Report of Working Group, especially p.6, and LDPC 3-1981 minutes.

122 HKRS163-8-65 LDPC 7-4-1981 minutes; HKRS163-8-64 LDPC 27-3-1981 minutes.

123 Poon, 2009 minutes; HKRS696-3-165 BC 11-1981.

124 HKRS461-1-12-5 BC 7-1982 minutes; Liao, 2010 interview on landscape architecture consultants, Sha Tin; HKRS461-1-12-5 7-1982 on Tuen Mun Area 44.

125 HKRS1588-3-22 comparison with Singapore.

126 Liao, 2011 interview; Glendinning, *Mass Housing*, Chapter 10; Poon, 2009 interview on effects of small design decisions.

127 Ko, 1983 interview; HKRS1882-1-3 Husband at 4-3-1977 LPVC; Cheung, 2012 interview; Yeung and Wong, *Fifty Years*, 82–3.

128 Ko, 1983; Gabriel, 2009.

129 Cheng, 2014 interview; HKRS483-4-1 9-9-1978 note; HKRS696-3-165 6-1981 BC memo; HKRS696-3-165 10-1981 BC minutes.

130 Ko, 1983 interview; HKRS461-1-12-2 BC 4-1982 and 5-1982; HKRS461-1-12-3 minutes of 6-1982 BC and 461-1-12-8 BC of 21-10-1982; HKRS696-3-165 memo for BC 12-1981 on Kwong Fuk, Chun Shek, Tai Po.

131 HKRS461-1-12-3; HKRS461-1-12-5 BC minutes for 7-1982; HKRS461-1-12-8 12-1982 minutes.

132 HKRS163-8-145 6-1977 report by A J Scott; HKRS601-1-2 Public Housing Development Review Committee 22-1-1979.

133 HKRS163-9-1392 26-1-1977 Woodcraft letter; HKRS163-8-159 13-1-1978 HD memo on defects.

134 HKRS461-1-12-6 BC 8-1982 Messling memo on Kwai Fong Block 6; HKRS594-1-3, 2-1978 Pryor memo on 1975-8 costs of housing types, materials, and cost pressures, specifically at Wo Che.

135 HKRS483-4-1 4-1977 papers; HKRS545-1-456-3 1980 cutting.

136 HKRS483-4-1 4-1977; Yeung and Wong, *Fifty Years*, 141–2; Lambon, 2012 interview; Liao, 2014 interview.

137 Ng, 2012 interview.

138 HKRS545-1-456-1, press release 26-11-1981 on 12% cut in costs; Ko, 1983 interview; HKRS696-3-165 11-1981 on Ma Chai Hang HO32; HKRS461-1-12-8 BC 11-1982 on 'standard HOS TBs'; HKRS667-2-4 7-5-1981 papers; Burns, 2014 interview.

139 HKRS1882-1-3 LPVC 13-9-1979, BC 9-1979; HKRS545-1-456-1 5-6-1980 papers.

140 Windmill: HKRS1881-3-2, 7-1-81 S K Lo to CA/4, 30-4-81 Messling presentation to H O Committee; LPVC 26-3-82.

141 Akers-Jones, 2013 interview; HKRS1882-1-3 LPVC 26-8-1977, presentation by Kinoshita; HKRS545-1-456-3 8-1981 visit by Liao; Liao, 2014 interview. According to the late Denis Ko, Hing Man was originally envisaged as HOS, and was then changed to rental, but Stephen Poon was doubtful about that: Ko, 1983 interview and Poon, 2014 interview.

142 HKRS163-8-64 LDPC 3-1981 minutes; Poon, 2009 interview. HKRS545-1-456-3; 461-1-12-5 BC 7-1982, 461-1-12-8 BC 11-1982, 461-1-12-3 BC 6-1982, 461-1-12-2 BC 4-1982; HKRS545-1-456-3 14-6-1981 article; Lambon, Pritchard and Hall, 2012 interview; Ko, 1983 interview; Ng, 2012 interview; HKRS461-1-12-3 8-1982 minutes.

143 HKRS 524-3-32 3-1977 Pryor memo.

144 HKRS163-8-65 9-1981 report, and LDPC minutes of 7-4-1981,11-7-1981, 2-1982; HKRS163-8-65 25-9-1981 LDPC Temporary Housing Sub-Committee; HKRS163-8-64 3-1981 report to LDPC of Working Party on Temporary Housing; Williams, 2012 interview; Glendinning, *Mass Housing,* Chapters 1 and 2 (on Bombay chawls).

145 HKRS483-4-1 8-6-1978 on penthouse conversions; HKRS1882-1-3 LPVC 2-1978 Husband report.

146 HKRS483-4-1 25-9-1978 report for Operations Committee; HKRS696-3-165 BC 10-1981; HKRS483-4-1 25-9-1978, potted history of flatted-factory programme.

147 FCO40-1259 Bremridge 3-1981, 6-4-1981 and 13-4-1981 meetings in London; Richard Wong, Hong Kong Land, 109; Nissim, *Land Administration*, 30.

148 Holdsworth and Munn, *Dictionary of Hong Kong Biography*, 5-6 (Goodstadt on MacLehose); Lord Wilson, 2023 interview (Wilson disagreed with Goodstadt's criticism).

149 FCO40-1259 17-12-1981 lecture by Haddon-Cave.

150 *Hong Kong 1983* (Yearbook), 111, on follow-on to 1977 new HA financial arrangements.

151 HKRS545-1-456-3 7-1982 and HKRS545-1-456-4 7-1983 contract signings.

152 HKRS163-8-11 early 1982 memo to MacLehose; HKRS545-1-456-4 7-1983 evaluation of Ten-Year Plan by Williams.

153 FCO40-1258 on personalities; Tsang, *Governing Hong Kong*, 191; HKRS667-2-4 21-5-1981 opening; HKRS1588-9-22 9-4-1981, Liao LegCo speech; HKRS545-1-459-3 9-1982 Crosby note; HKRS163-7-70 1983 Williams valedictory letter from public housing.

154 FCO40-642 MacLehose to Foreign Secretary, 17-4-1982.

Part III

Countdown to the handover

9 1982–1986

Youde's governorship – from sovereignty to stabilisation

So far, the impending transition of sovereignty from Britain to China had been implicit, and the interventionism legitimised by MacLehose had been correspondingly low key in its ideological projection: MacLehose himself recalled in a December 1982 speech that he ensured the political 'status quo had been maintained because that was the policy of the Chinese government'.[1] But as we will see in Part III, from 1982 the increasingly urgent timetable of decolonisation burst into the open, confronting the British colonial elite, and especially the administrative class, with the limited time that they had left 'to leave their final trace in history'. The political constraints of 'caretaker' government forbade any overt propagandising or efforts to depart in a public 'blaze of glory': but the Anglo-Saxon tradition of exerting social control by spatial manipulation ensured that the built environment, and housing in particular, would help give this interstitial space a sharply defined character, within a policy framework that was, from 1987, strongly defined by a new and enduring mechanism – the Long-Term Housing Strategy (LTHS).[2] At the same time, the eventual agreement over '1997', coupled with the opening-up of China, would revolutionise the Hong Kong economy, with export manufacturing moved across the border to Shenzhen and the internal economy rapidly 'financialised': the local real-estate sector would provide 40–50% of the Hong Kong stock market's capitalisation.[3]

Edward Youde and the sovereignty negotiations

Where governors up to and including MacLehose had enjoyed policy autonomy, externally constrained only by London's weak demands, from now on the dominant external relationship would be that with Beijing. To carry forward this decolonisation agenda, the British government appointed from May 1982 a low-profile successor to MacLehose, from within the FCO apparatus: Edward Youde, a quietly spoken Chinese scholar who had previously served as British Ambassador in Beijing and, in 1967–8, as private secretary to Harold Wilson, but who suffered within the FCO's snobbery-ridden ruling circles from 'an unflattering reputation as an able but uninspiring administrator' or even as 'a grammar school boy without an Oxbridge degree who never lost his Welsh accent'.[4] (Figure 9.1) Unlike

DOI: 10.1201/9781315563701-12

Figure 9.1 Governor Youde and Donald Liao tour a show flat at the Housing Authority Headquarters permanent exhibition in November 1984: SCMP article.

MacLehose, however, Youde's relationship with his senior officials was less domineering: Akers-Jones recalled that he 'administered calmly and quietly, reading his papers and files, talking to many people and visiting widely to see for himself the housing estates, squatter villages, and factories'; he displayed no deference towards wealth or status (Goodstadt).[5] He had an uneasy relationship with Haddon-Cave, recently promoted to Chief Secretary in 1981, who felt 'overshadowed' by Youde and abruptly left in June 1985, to be succeeded by Akers-Jones (1985–7).[6] Haddon-Cave's successor as Financial Secretary (1981–6), Sir John Bremridge, was a more combative character, unpopular with the media and civil servants owing to his abrasive and patronising manner. Unlike his predecessors, Bremridge was brought in straight from the private sector, where he had been chairman of Swire Pacific: his laissez-faire preferences left him relatively ill-equipped to deal with the economic rollercoaster of the early 1980s, including protectionism, rising labour and land costs, inflation and a vulnerable banking system.[7] To succeed him in 1986, Youde secured the appointment of Sir Piers Jacobs, counselling him not to emulate the 'great and ebullient' Bremridge.[8]

Although widely liked within Hong Kong for his accessibility and 'warm friendliness', Youde was also generally preoccupied with negotiations with

Beijing – a worry that culminated in a sudden, fatal heart attack in December 1986 in Beijing, in the course of a round of negotiations.[9] Just like MacLehose, Youde transformed himself from a career diplomat to a champion of Hong Kong autonomy vis-à-vis London, but as a result of the dominance of constitutional affairs, during his governorship to some extent 'housing and planning was left to run itself'.[10]

At first, everything seemed to be going smoothly, with initial visits by Youde to the Housing Authority and meetings with the Secretary for Housing in mid-1982: the most urgent external pressure seemed to be the growing flood of Vietnamese boat people refugees, especially following the growing repression of ethnic Chinese in Vietnam from 1979.[11] But the 1997 question now could not be avoided. At his inaugural oath-taking in City Hall in May 1982, Youde optimistically argued that 'the omens are good' for a continuation of prosperity post-1997, and already, both sides had begun to float potential solutions.[12] In September 1981, the concept of a special administrative region of the PRC was proposed by the president, Marshal Ye. And in May and June 1982, Deng Xiaoping and Zhao Zhiyang met Li Ka-Shing, trade union leaders and local politicians to sound out their opinions, following which, in July, Deng announced that China intended to recover Hong Kong as a 'Special Administrative Region' of the PRC, and advised Hong Kong citizens to study the concept carefully.[13]

En route to Beijing in September 1982, Mrs Thatcher stopped off in Hong Kong.[14] During her visit, she refused to meet a delegation from the Urban Council and from the unofficials, on the grounds of their supposedly leftist, disruptive character, despite civil servants' warnings that public opinion now expected 'Hong Kong should have a direct say in its own future'.[15] She toured housing estates with Liao, including Shek Wai Kok in Tsuen Wan – in its typically monumental compactness, a strong contrast to the higgledy-piggledy, low-rise built-form associated with her own right-to-buy and privatisation policy in England.[16]

At the end of the Beijing negotiations with Thatcher, Deng indicated that the Chinese side would allow a year or two to obtain agreement, but would then announce their own solution.[17] During the 1982–4 British–Chinese negotiations, Youde attempted to ensure ExCo was consulted, while initially excluding any commitment to elections or democracy: Akers-Jones recalled that

> there was a grumbling in Whitehall – we were slow to get on with "democracy". It was very difficult for people to understand the reality of the fact that we couldn't do anything like that without incurring the wrath of China, and no-one knew what direction that wrath would take. It was just as well we resisted that Whitehall pressure!

In 1985, however, Youde conceded indirect elections of some seats in ExCo, to China's displeasure.[18] In May 1983, the Territorial Development Strategy noted private-enterprise involvement was precarious owing to 'political uncertainty', and in August Beijing declared flatly that it would take over Hong Kong in 1997 regardless of the outcome of negotiations with the UK government.[19] The reality of the sovereignty situation was summed up by Ian Lightbody, who argued that although negotiations had been

> held back until the last possible moment… the return of the whole colony to China was completely inevitable, regardless of what we said or did. China would never have agreed to an extension. It was a great source of unhappiness in China that Britain had ever forced China to hand over Hong Kong in the 19th century. As sure as night follows day, and people recognised that in their heart of hearts at the time, China was likely to get Hong Kong back – although of course the final target was Taiwan.

The ramifications of this were 'micro' as well as 'macro' – Wilson noted that 'as things were, on July 1st 1997 no policeman in the New Territories would have been able to issue a speeding ticket – so some agreement was clearly needed!'[20]

At the end of the process, the September 1984 Joint Declaration unleashed a wave of optimism in Hong Kong.[21] Following the Declaration, transition machinery was set up in parallel with the drafting by the National People's Congress of the Basic Law of the Hong Kong special administrative region of the PRC.[22] On her way back from signing the Joint Declaration in December 1984, Mrs Thatcher made a second visit to public housing estates, on this occasion in Ap Lei Chau, and Liao showed her a model of Lei Tung Estate: 'I was "selling" them to her, explaining that it was by necessity rather than choice that we had to build high blocks, that there was no other way. She was very polite, she accepted this. I said, "We must provide space for housewives to chat."'[23] (Figure 9.2)

In parallel with the growing high-level constitutional contacts, more everyday contacts with mainland officials expanded too, but with Hong Kong increasingly seeing itself in the position of teacher or exemplar rather than suppliant.[24] Within the field of housing, although Hong Kong's programme was more diversified than Singapore's, it seemed like a paragon of unified coordination in comparison with the mainland's anarchic 'danwei' system of housing provision by individual work-units. In June 1983 alone, the vice-president of the People's Construction Bank of China toured low-rental housing, and a group of Shanghai planners inspected the Wong Tai Sin and Shek Kip Mei upgrade, hailing Hong Kong as an example for Shanghai to follow.[25] Liao recalled that

> in the 1980s I talked to the Chinese Foreign Minister, an elderly gentleman, when he came here. I was explaining about public housing, and saying, "In many ways, Hong Kong is probably more socialistic than China!" They didn't like to hear that! In the early days, when visiting China, you buckled your seatbelt – and breathed a sigh of relief on returning.[26]

December 1982 saw HD experts on an exchange trip to China, led by Messling, who emphasised the importance of imaginative estate landscaping and facilities in talks with the Ministry of Urban and Rural Construction.[27] Correspondingly, the role of visiting British VIPs was now rapidly diminishing. In 1986, Queen

Figure 9.2 Donald Liao, Mrs Thatcher and Chan Nai-keong (Secretary for Lands and Works), inspect models of Lei Tung Estate, Ap Lei Chau, during Thatcher's 1984 stopover in Hong Kong after signing the Sino-British Agreement: the smaller model shows the whole development and the larger one the two Trident towers and commercial centre of Phase 1. Image included in the HA's 1984–5 *Annual Report*.

Elizabeth and Prince Philip were hosted for lunch at the Sha Tin Jockey Club by Liao: 'Youde asked me to show them the housing from up there – it's rather like a Geddes Outlook Tower!'[28]

Overall, between 1979 and 1985 Hong Kong accounted for two-thirds of foreign investment in China.[29] And in reverse, anticipating the eventual flood of mainland investment in construction and land in the 2010s, PRC building enterprises eagerly leapt on the bandwagon of housing projects, beginning with main-contractor bids, as for example in a 'very competitive' March 1983 winning bid by the Guangdong Water Conservancy and Hydro Power Engineering Development Corporation for construction of the Tuen Mun Area 7 Phase 1 HOS scheme.[30] Stephen Poon recalled that the earliest and most effective was China State Construction, which first became involved from the late 1970s, and made a unique input

> because the guy who ran the company decided to do it the Hong Kong way. They followed the Hong Kong tradition of local construction companies relying on local subcontractors to support them; they got the labour locally, doing things the local way. All the traditions were the same as those here. For example here, when construction work starts on a site, usually there's a ceremony, making offerings to the gods, all local contractors do that. But [in CSC] Lo Pan, the patron saint of construction workers here and on the mainland, was celebrated every day in the same way – that was really unusual for communists in those days![31]

And in February 1986, a thirteen-member delegation from China headed by Lu Ping, secretary of the Hong Kong and Macau Affairs Office, hailed Hong Kong public housing as having 'achieved impressive results in the bid to solve the needs of lower income groups'.[32]

For the public housing drive, the most immediate impact of the Joint Declaration was in the provision, in Annex iii, Clause 4 of the Agreement, to establish a joint Sino-British Land Commission to regulate land disposals for private-sector housing from June 1985 until 1997, working to a maximum figure of 50 ha per year – 'an arbitrary figure plucked out of the air' (Akers-Jones) – from which public rental housing, but not HOS and PSPS, was excluded.[33] The revenue from land disposal during that period would be shared equally between the (British) government of Hong Kong and the future government of the Hong Kong SAR. The motivation for this provision was openly acknowledged within Hong Kong: 'a fairly visceral feeling north of the border that the colonial government would cut and run, ransack the Treasury and run off with the crown jewels'. Lord Wilson argued that

> Chinese officials felt that we, the British, being the kind of people we were, capitalists and imperialists and so on, would try to drain Hong Kong dry. They didn't realise that that wasn't at all how the Hong Kong Government behaved!

This worry was sharpened by the relatively recent memory of the Soviet plundering of Manchuria during the 1945 war with Japan.[34]

But what was less clear was the Land Commission's actual impact on the housing programme. Akers-Jones argued in detail that it fuelled house-price inflation: to the private sector, 50 ha 'seemed enough at the time but was not, and by the time government's plans and policies had been met, there was never sufficient land to meet the appetite of private development or for a balanced housing programme. Because of the short supply and because of an accelerating economy, land increased in value to astronomical levels. Additional land could not be sold to try to bring the price down and home buyers were forced to pay absurd prices for their apartments. The concomitant was that, through wise investment by a Joint Land Commission set up to supervise this part of the agreement, taking a half-share of land sale proceeds, the incoming government in 1997 gained a dowry of billions'.[35] But from the perspective of the public housing programme, its effects seemed less onerous. Of the 1980s, Stephen Poon recalled that 'our [rental] housing wasn't affected, but it affected the Home Ownership Scheme, as our housing programme was driven by demand'. Later in the 1990s, however, with land supply beginning to recover, incoming Director of Housing Tony Miller found that 'it didn't affect the HOS, it didn't affect me, as I had a huge land bank, it didn't affect me at all. The price spike leading up to 1997 was nothing to do with the 50 ha restriction on land sale'.[36]

During the mid-1980s, complex negotiations continued, to fine-tune the implementation of the Commission's work: A R Crosby, responsible for planning liaison within HD, stressed in November 1985 that all sites proposed for disposal should be 'strictly net building land', to make maximum use of the quota. An April 1986 report argued that redevelopment would also need to be expanded, as being exempt from the disposal restriction, and that some recalibration of the proportions of rental and HOS might be needed; in March 1986 the Commission agreed to increase disposals from 50 to 55 ha.[37] The following month Crosby argued that the Joint Declaration and the Land Commission would force up densities for HOS and PSPS, and in July the Chinese side on the Land Commission, moving outside its strict brief, demanded that rental housing, too, should be developed at no less than 2,700 ppha in all cases.[38] In contrast to this thorny issue, collaboration with Beijing also promised to positively unlock other intractable problems, above all the perennial running sore of the Kowloon Walled City: as late as August 1985, Akers-Jones, newly installed as Chief Secretary, reiterated the 'sensitive nature' of this case and the 'need for great caution', and suggested that an appeal might be made to China to allow clearance during the 1990s.[39] As we will see in Chapter 10, China preferred Britain to solve the problem, and initial suggestions put to officials of the new China News agency and sounded out quietly by them with local kaifongs would bear fruit with surprising speed.[40]

During Youde's governorship, the tension between laissez-faire entrepreneurialism and growing administrative consolidation became more accentuated. To some extent, Hong Kongers in the '80s were still arguably to some extent a transient people, not convinced that the state was fundamentally responsible for their welfare, and concerned in housing above all with family social advancement and speculative profit.[41] In many respects, the most powerful housing actors in Hong

Kong from the 1980s and '90s onwards were not the government agencies but the oligarchic grouping of leading property developers, above all Li Ka-Shing, head of Cheung Kong Holdings and Hutchison Whampoa, but also the Kwok family, owners of Sun Hung Kai. As we will see in the next four chapters, the dominance of these 'tycoons' in housing and land policy would only strengthen during the following two decades – a position very different from Singapore.[42] But on the other hand, the numbers of government ordinances passed each year rose from an average of 69 between 1965 and 1974, to 81 in 1974–84, and numbers of administrative officers and civil servants had already risen from 116 and 85,000, respectively, in 1972, to 383 and 154,000 by 1982.[43] (Figure 9.3) This expansion of bureaucracy was combined with ever-increasing administrative 'localisation'[44] But as we saw in Chapter 8, in professional areas such as architecture or engineering, staff shortages meant that the trajectory of decolonisation was more complex: expatriate architect John Lambon argued that 'our work, was, in a way, a colonial imposition. We came from England and said that bedrooms should have a window and that there should be a bathroom for every family. Now these ideas have been internalised'.[45]

Within the political life of Hong Kong, Youde mainly maintained MacLehose's suspicion of direct democratisation, and the old CCP-versus-KMT conflict faded from view in the 1970s–90s following the failure of the 1967 riots.[46] It was replaced by the beginnings of a locally embedded discourse of community engagement, encouraged by the government through its late-1980s establishment of district boards: increasingly, housing projects now had to negotiate a complex procedure of consultation. Youde's 1985 reform extended this process by establishing a system of functional constituencies, under which 56 LegCo seats were filled by twenty-two government appointees, ten government officials, twelve functional electees, and twelve appointed by electoral college. In 1991, the system was adjusted to provide a total of 60, made up of eighteen, three, twenty-one and eighteen members. However, further proposals of 1987 for limited direct elections, backed especially by ExCo Senior Member Lydia Dunn, were watered down following Chinese government opposition, partly through a manipulated public consultation survey in 1988, and the 1990 Basic Law would enshrine a colonial style 'executive-led' system.[47]

More significantly, these years also saw an explosion of general public participatory initiatives within social policy. The 1970s and, especially, '80s witnessed a proliferation of single-issue mobilisation movements, especially following the 1971 foundation of SoCO: these roughly quadrupled in number between 1971 and 1978.[48] Reflecting this shift, the role of the unofficials within housing, only recently entrenched under the aegis of UMELCO and traditional radicals such as Elliott, began to fragment again as new organisations entered on the scene.[49] The Hong Kong People's Council on Public Housing Policy (HKPCPHP) was founded in 1979 and began fully operating in 1982, its first major campaign focusing on the '26 Blocks' scandal of 1985–6.[50] In March 1985 the Housing Authority was restructured to accommodate HKPCPHP and SoCO members, with Elliott, Forsgate and Lo being removed and replaced by Fung of the HKPCPHP.[51] Some of the old-style unofficials protested at this, but Denny Huang, retained on the Authority in

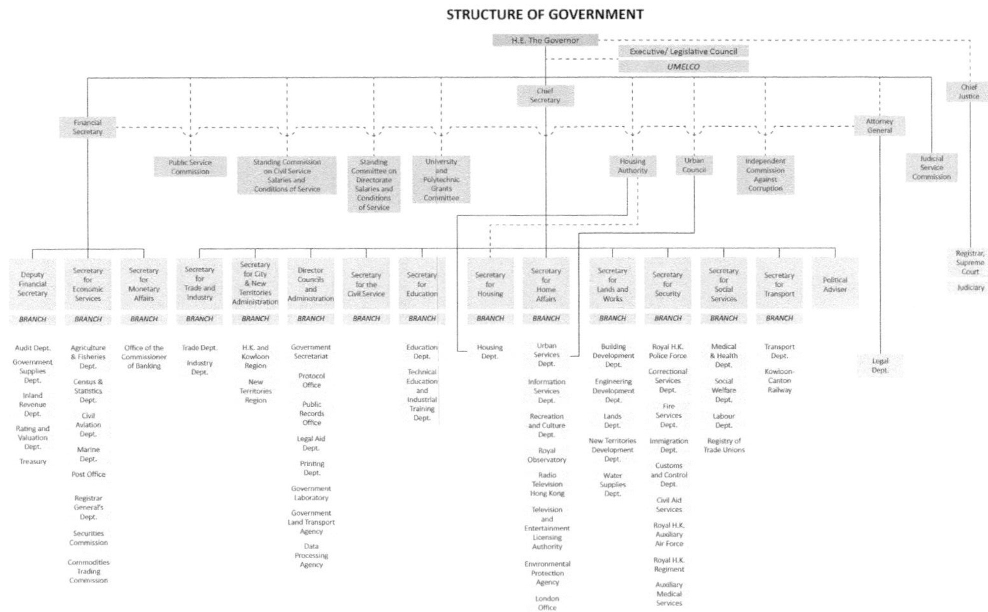

Figure 9.3 Structural diagram of the Hong Kong Government in April 1982, just prior to Youde's arrival, showing the anomalously complicated relationship between Housing Secretary, Authority and Department. In this diagram, solid lines denote hierarchical relationships and dotted lines refer to indirect links. Drawing by Joyce Fu, 2023.

1985, argued that they 'only represent themselves'.[52] Further community support and praise from the HKPCPHP, in 1984, was garnered by official consultation with New Territories village elders, local district boards and local inhabitants on street and estate (re)naming (for example in Tuen Mun in 1983).[53]

Now the government was increasingly caught in a dynamic of rising expectations, which at first worked to the advantage of the HA and public housing, only turning negative later: a 1984 Home Affairs Department public-opinion survey found that satisfaction with the Housing Department's efforts had risen from 43% in 1982 to 48% in 1984, while an August 1986 public attitude survey suggested most people agreed with the Authority's policies. More specifically, a 1984 survey about the HOS showed that most respondents supported increases in output of both HOS and public rental housing, and regarded Sha Tin as the 'best' New Town.[54]

Economic vicissitudes of the mid-1980s

During Youde's first years, the growing uncertainties of the sovereignty issue were compounded by harsh economic headwinds: he arguably inherited an economy in 'dire straits' (Leo Goodstadt), with out-of-control money supply, a precarious currency (declining 20% in 1978–82), soaring inflation (6% in 1978, 15% in 1980–1), a stock-market boom from 1978 that was turning to bust, and a property bubble about to burst. Inflation made manufacturing exports uncompetitive in 1979/81, while financial and property speculation triggered inflation and destabilised the Hong Kong dollar. Under the impact of the 'Volcker Shock', the property boom indeed turned to bust and prices fell by 44% between 1981 and 1985. Growth was erratic, varying from 1.4% in 1982 and 0.5% in 1985 to 7% in 1981 and 8% in 1984. The three interconnected economic crises in the early 1980s – financial, fiscal, currency – interacted with the sovereignty uncertainties. The consequence, combined with the growing constitutional uncertainty, was a mounting 'brain drain': during the early 1980s 100,000 households, mostly managerial and professional, left Hong Kong, a problem which in housing seemed to underline the urgency of boosting the HOS to support the incipient 'financialisation' of the economy.[55]

To some extent, the crisis stemmed not just from the impact of the sovereignty uncertainty of 1982–4, but from core Hong Kong values such as the addiction to speculation. However, during the early 1980s, it gradually became clear that weak regulation of the banking sector was a specific, and crucial, factor in exacerbating that instability, coupled with the effects of the growing global shift from fixed to fluctuating exchange rates – neither of which were foreseen by the relatively economically inexperienced Haddon-Cave either as Financial Secretary or Chief Secretary, or by laissez-faire Bremridge, who responded to the corporate banking crises of 1983–5 with 'near-panic'.[56] Instead, it was largely Youde's close supervision of radical financial reforms, including adoption of a fixed exchange rate against the USD in 1983, the rescue of seven failing banks in 1982–6 at a massive, undisclosed cost to the reserves held with the Exchange Fund, and the passage of a Banking Ordinance in 1986, that steered Hong Kong through to a system that would bring long-term financial stability. John Bremridge struggled to keep budget deficits as small as possible: the only two years in which Hong Kong had a deficit were FY 1982 and 1983, and the bank failures from 1983 caused near-panic in Hong Kong financial circles, and significant capital flight. A further vital bulwark stemmed from the MacLehose years: the prudence of the government in the 1970s in setting aside part of its surpluses to build a reserve of non-fixed assets for an Exchange Fund to stabilise the economy.[57]

Industry in the 1980s responded by new machinery orders, foreign investment, decentralisation of production to China and revival of Hong Kong's entrepot role (now in finance rather than manufacturing) – as in the case of Tin Shui Wai, with the Hong Kong Government's desire to promote investment for the PRC-led consortium formed to build it. Government spending also rose sharply in absolute terms, from $31,000 million in 1981–2 to $48,000 million in 1986–7, but dropped as a proportion of GDP, reflecting Hong Kong's overall laissez-faire allegiance: the percentage of GDP accounted for by government expense, having risen from 8% in 1949–50 to 23% in 1981–2, now dropped back to 16% over the 1980s – even though the percentage of social services expenditure (including public housing) in total government expenditure was continuing to rise, to 45% in 1987.[58] Government social and infrastructure investment was based on land sales plus accumulated reserves in the Exchange Fund, used in support during the 1982–5 troubles. With the wild fluctuations in property and land prices, the percentage of government revenue accounted for by land sale revenue fluctuated equally dramatically, from a maximum of 44.8% in 1980–1 to 19.1% in 1983–4 and 22.5% in 1984–5. Except in 1983, land and building revenues always accounted for more than 20% of government revenue. Thus the indirectly redistributive role played by land revenue, from businesses and middle-class home owners to lower-income groups, was always an unstable one. During the late 1970s and early 1980s, the property boom led to a land-revenue glut, whereas in the mid-1980s and early 1990s property values and land revenues both slumped. The 1983 Governor's Address optimistically claimed an export-led recovery was underway, but the property market remained depressed.[59] However, the July 1985 government *Review of the Property Market* suggested confidence had fully returned, with more transactions in the first quarter of 1985 than in the whole of 1984. And in 1986 Hong Kong once more became the world's most dynamic economy, with 11% real GDP growth in 1986 and 12% projected for 1987.[60]

The role of public housing within this wider economic landscape was distinctly declining, relatively as well as absolutely. Whereas in 1981/2 it represented 27.5% of total government social expenditure, by 1985/6 it had fallen to 10.8%. Overall housing-related government capital expenditure decreased from $808m in 1982/3 to $674m in 1984/5.[61] Public housing's role, as before, was partly as a safety-net for workers and small enterprises, giving social and civic stability and turning a rebellious labour-dominated city into a growth engine. Housing expenditure was not a systematic, deliberate contribution to an economic development strategy, but instead was shaped ad-hoc by local conditions.[62] Within that overall position, the need for government financial support for the Housing Authority was a source of growing problems. Funding mainly comprised 40-year loans, with interest, from the DLF.[63] There had been a steep build-up in capital injections to the HA from nil in 1973–4 to over $10,000m in 1980, and $40,000m in 1988: total government 'funding' for the HA comprised only $181m in 1965, but $27,179m in 1985.[64] In 1983–5, a capital expenditure table for HA activities explained that the government's $21,600m subsidy to public rental housing over that period was largely made up of $18,500m in free land, $1,500m to support construction costs of public rental estates, and $1,400m for interest on government loans to finance rental housing since 1 April 1976.[65]

Changing the guard within the Housing Department: the founding of 'D & S'

During Youde's governorship, the HA continued the McKinsey-style management and administration principles established under MacLehose.[66] The HA still set policy, with the HD as its executive arm, both for the time being under the aegis of the Secretary for Housing.[67]

Within the HD's developmental arm, these years saw a transition of power within the department, as the dominant figure of Liao gradually receded towards more general governmental responsibilities. He had succeeded Alan Scott as Secretary for Housing (May 1980 to February 1985) and was himself followed by David Ford in 1985 and John Todd in 1986. He recalled that 'I must have been a fearsome boss in my department – that's why I got on well'.[68] But now a more dispersed pattern prevailed. Liao's 1980 move away from the HD triggered a two-stage promotion sequence with musical-chairs overtones: he was first succeeded as Director by Bernard Williams, with Pang moving into the Deputy Director of Construction role (following Cheung Sing-hoi) and Messling becoming Housing Architect. On Williams's departure in 1983, Ford became interim Director, until a further rearrangement in February 1985, following Liao's departure from Housing, saw Ford as Secretary, Pang as Director, and Messling promoted to Deputy Director. The progress of the 'localisation' agenda was offset by the constraints of the mushrooming demands for professional staff numbers, leading to engagement of numerous younger expatriate architects in the 1980s: in February 1986, for example, Derek Messling was complaining that delays to the redevelopment of the defective '26 Blocks' (see below) were caused by recruitment 'inflexibility'.[69]

Of the 1980–3 period, Williams recalled in 2012 that 'the Vietnamese [boat people] were the main challenge. Otherwise everything else was working very smoothly by then. We had a good organisation, we had all the staff we needed, it was a good period – things were working well. Freddie [Pang] was in charge of construction, Tony [Fung Tung] in charge of management. John Heywood oversaw the operations with the refugees. Then Derek Messling was recruited from Islington, just before my time as Director – he was an architect, and strongly supported the drive for numbers in Hong Kong.'[70]

During his last two years as Housing Secretary, Liao increasingly sought to consolidate his legacy of high output, and combine this with environmental improvement. In a March 1984 speech at the opening of the Po Leung Kuk Kindergarten, for example, he announced that the annual target for 1985–6 was to be 40,000 flats, and that an all-time maximum of 38,680 had been completed in 1983/4. In 1984, too, he argued that the redeveloped Wong Tai Sin 'will take on a new look as an ideal district for living in East Kowloon'.[71] His interventions in individual projects tended now to be more intermittent, often in committee meetings which he attended *ex officio* – for example, in a 1983 Building Committee meeting, when Messling parried a criticism from Liao that the layout plan for the Long Ping estate in Yuen Long was 'too crowded', arguing that this was necessitated by the detailed planning brief for new estates.[72] At Liao's February 1985 farewell dinner, his successor, Ford, spoke of 'Mr Housing, who has forsaken his first love, and moved to pastures new', while Forsgate reminisced that in 1965 he had been 'a slim, energetic architect, a nice wee laddie, who impressed us all with his enthusiasm and professional ability and everything else, to the extent that, 20 years later, public housing is synonymous with his name'.[73]

After his accession to the Directorship in 1985, Pang's emollient reputation as 'Friendly Freddie' meant he was 'best able to unite and enthuse the Department', while the department's developmental expansion allowed previous Liao protégés such as Stephen Poon to carve out significant areas of autonomy on the back of the large increases in staff numbers.[74] Representative of the new generation of expatriate architects, John Lambon and Bob Pritchard both joined in 1981, and Pritchard became involved in the development of the 'Trident' block type, while Lambon soon joined a new research and development group (see below). Alongside them, large numbers of Hong Kong-trained architects were recruited, such as Rosman Wai or Ken Cheung, both of whom joined the HD in 1984 and were promoted to Senior Architect grade in 1990.[75]

The chief inheritor of Liao's previous role within the HD as an 'architect-cum-production-enforcer-cum publicist' was undoubtedly Derek Messling. Although, as an expatriate who only worked in Hong Kong for sixteen years, between 1977 and 1993, he lacked Liao's density of connections within Hong Kong society – or his general breadth of vision – Messling nevertheless built up a formidable reputation during the early 1980s, not least because his partner and colleague, ex-GLC architect Penny Ward, was an equally capable organiser. Showing how the memory of Liao's earlier dominance was beginning to fade, John Lambon in 2012 recalled Messling as 'the biggest power in the history of the Department – very sharp, efficient and supportive, forceful but never nasty'… 'a real mover, a real figurehead'.[76] The decisive episode in establishing Messling's reputation as not only a key organiser but also the public face of the Department was the so-called '26 Blocks Crisis' – a crisis of 'concrete cancer' defective construction from 1980, which will be dealt with in detail later in this chapter. From the early 1980s onwards, Messling also became the chief public front of the Housing Department's commitment to continued high output, providing explanations for any setbacks – for example arguing in March 1983 that the likely completion of only 35,387 units for 1982/3 rather than the planned 36,181 was due to 'exceptionally bad weather', and that problems on the Ma Chai Hang HOS site were due to an unreliable contractor.[77]

In the work of the Architectural Division and the Construction Branch, this period saw a transition towards a new governing philosophy of higher output combined with higher standards, initially charted by Liao. Naturally, higher output was still the core task, and 1984/5 saw a new record annual total of 36,522 completions, with 65 contracts in hand by mid-1985 and enough land to support programme production targets for eight more years.[78] Unlike the previous decade, now it was taken as read that the housing teams would design entire areas, including both housing and commercial elements.[79] 1983 also saw the establishment of a landscape section within Construction Branch, following the appointment of several individual posts in the 1970s, in an area where demand had 'increased tremendously'.[80] And the same 1983 staffing boost allowed the establishment of a Development and Standards (D & S) Group, hailed by Messling in March 1983 as a 'think-tank' that would allow Hong Kong to begin 'challenging Singapore's leading role in public housing'.[81] Headed by Tim Nutt as a Senior Architect, its core staff initially included John Lambon, Dave Hall and Colin Chan-Pensley, but it rapidly expanded and after Nutt was promoted to Chief Architect in 1985, other architects such as John Ng and Stephen Tong were included.[82] (Figure 9.4)

Figure 9.4 An unlikely visitor to the Housing Department in 1984: English anti-flat polemicist Alice Coleman. She is seen on the right of this view (in an HA press release), inspecting a model of the Kowloon Central Area Redevelopment with Assistant Director of Housing (Housing Architect), Stephen Poon; her travelling companion, Mrs Margaret Nicholls; and Deputy Director of Housing (Construction) Derek Messling.

Figure 9.5 Shilhay housing scheme, Exeter, England: modular low-rise mid-1970s council scheme by Marshman Warren & Taylor, on which John Lambon worked prior to his 1981 move to Hong Kong. 2013 photo (MG).

This new research and development unit drew in often unexpected ways on the previous experiences of the younger expatriates 'at home'. For example, in the late 1970s John Lambon had worked with Devon architects Marshman Warren & Taylor on two low-rise Exeter council housing schemes at Shilhay and Exe Street, whose modular, metric-coordinated design approach, using a 300-mm grid, was combined with a neo-vernacular style influenced by the Essex Design Guide.[83] (Figure 9.5) In Hong Kong, that rationalism, including dimensional coordination and the 300-mm grid, would be channelled by him and others towards radically different built forms, by facilitating standard components while also allowing 'flexibility' in flat mix. Stephen Poon recalled that 'the job of the research and development [i.e. D & S] group was to assess what the demand was, both in quantity and quality, for example via density control, the size of units to be built and what we put into them'. Under that 'demand-led approach', the 1980s saw a final rejection of the 'IU' area-based system of square metres per person (last discussed in 1983 as a potential cost yardstick) for the simpler criteria of bedrooms per unit.[84]

The agenda of precision and standardisation, via grids and dimensional coordination, was carried forward via a CAD system developed by Hall and introduced in November 1985. He recalled that

> we were awash with fairly poorly trained technicians and a few highly trained architects. We needed CAD for coordination rather than draughting purposes, for coordination between the disciplines, but in the event we also ended up with a ruthlessly efficient draughting machine for standard designs and components, using an IBM-based CADAM system – a predecessor to Autocad.[85]

All this flurry of innovation took place within the walls of the HD, out of public view, whereas for the average citizen, the highest-profile policy issue in housing during the mid-1980s was nothing directly to do with development: namely, the mounting pressure for reform of rents and tenancies, responding to the perceived problem of the 'well-off tenant'. 1984 saw the first attempt to highlight the problem, in the setting up of an ad-hoc Committee on Subsidy to Tenants of Public Housing, reporting in 1985.[86] In a chatty July 1984 letter to Liao, Forsgate remarked that pressure groups were already 'working up a head of steam' against tenancy reforms or means-testing; in a September speech Liao argued it was 'unreasonable that subsidised public housing should become a perpetual hereditary privilege of the tenants and their children'.[87] Fung Tung later recalled the conflicting pressures:

> The HA had never stipulated anything about kicking people out when they got better off, but in the '80s, the pressure got very big – people were in public housing with a Maserati or a Porsche, and that was not acceptable. I was pressured to kick these tenants out. But how do you define "rich"? After all, we'd accepted a basic principle of "no means test".[88]

Eventually, Fung, Pang and Liao devised a principle of graduated but non-means-tested rents, set out in a 1985 Green Paper on Housing Subsidy to Public Housing Tenants, with double rents to be charged to longstanding tenants with significant savings.[89] Paradoxically, despite her reputation as champion of the 'poor', Elliott led opposition to the measure, arguing it was punitive and unfair, and the double-rent proposal was scaled back and only finally implemented in 1987.[90] Overall, however, PRH rents rose steadily from 1984/5 to 1998/9.

Towards a strategic vision: from PHDP to LTHS

The years 1982–6 were a decisive time of transition from the provisional, unstable concept of a rolling ten-year programme, established in the MacLehose years and compromised by immediate political expediency, towards a settled, longer-term strategy that could continue from one administration to the next – and ultimately outlast the transition of sovereignty in 1997. Discussions had begun in earnest in 1982 following MacLehose's departure, prompted partly by changes in the way housing demand was calculated: the trend to smaller households led the HA Management Committee to raise the space allocation per person from 3.25 to 4.00 sq m, alongside the continuing shift from IUs to households as the basis for housing-space calculations. But they also reflected the growing shortfall of sites and the delays in handing them over for housing use: Pang reported to the BC in September 1982 that maintaining current construction levels would require significantly improved long-term land supply, while Forsgate argued in 1983 that post-1989 land shortages, rather than post-1997 leases, were the most urgent land issue requiring discussion.[91]

During the early 1980s, a bridge towards a longer-term vision was provided by a more sophisticated ten-year framework, and quarterly review system: the Public Housing Development Programme (PHDP). This was a central framework for monitoring 'committed' sites and projects approved by ExCo, LDPC or DPC (within a development plan or individually) on a rolling ten-year basis, to which all other government departments and development programmes had to cross-refer – especially the annual New Towns Development Programme, the urban redevelopment programme, and the overall Public Works Programme.[92] Liaison with government planners, led from the HD side by the AD Research and Planning (Ted Pryor up to 1982, thereafter the New Zealand-trained A R Crosby) allowed strategic evaluation of the potential impact on the PHDP of the emerging Territorial Development Strategy. This was a computer-generated plan overseen by Pryor after his move from HD, which identified future New Town sites and specified future ratios of urban/New Territories and tenure mixes.[93] Crosby fed in updates on site availability and future production levels to the PHDP: in October 1983, for example, he reported HOS would provide 20% of future production, but Messling added that while the current PHDP was 'in very good shape for the first seven years', the last three years were threatened by a 'severe shortage' of rental and HOS sites: units under construction (HOS and PSPS as well as PRH) had increased from 124,000 units in September 1982 to 133,000 a year later.[94] Land supply was everything: typically, PHDP updates tended to predict adequate land supply for the first five years, but apocalyptic shortages in the final 2–3 years. A September 1984 update by Crosby on the current ten-year PHDP to 1993 painted just such a picture, warning of a major fall-off in production from 1990 because of lack of sites from 1987: additional infill sites could provide a stop-gap until 1991 but thereafter the programme would depend on major sites generated by the TDS.[95] Then, in August 1986, the Building Committee learned the TDS had so far failed to provide the necessary sites to cover the final years of the current PHDP, and a shortfall of more than 61,000 completions was predicted for the last two years (1994/5 and 1995/6).[96] (Figure 9.6)

In January 1984, despite these uncertainties, Liao nevertheless argued that 'we have adopted a steady approach to production rather than exploiting the slumping market, which offers competitive tender prices'. The aim was to avoid a 'sudden surge' and to carry on with the rolling ten-year programme.[97] In contrast to the violent peaks and troughs that would later characterise the programme in the 1990s and 2000s, here the aim was to iron out excessive fluctuations and maintain the overall target rate. However, that target was gradually increasing: following the achievement of an all-time maximum of 38,680 completions in FY 1983/4, the rising output of HOS and PSPS allowed a raising of the target from 35,000 to 40,000 as from 1985/6, a rate Liao pledged in late 1984 would be maintained 'for the foreseeable future'.[98]

Progress with current contracts within the PHDP was fine-tuned each month, via monthly production situation reports to the DDH by the Assistant Director, the contracts being grouped by supervising Chief Architect, and highlighting contractor delays. In a typical report of March 1986, Stephen Poon noted that four problem contracts (Long Ping Phase 1, Kwun Tong TPR Phase 3, Tsing Yi Phase 2 and Cheung Hong Phase 5) could partly be counterbalanced by one that was running early (Ma Chai Hang HOS Phase 1). This could, 'for production purposes,

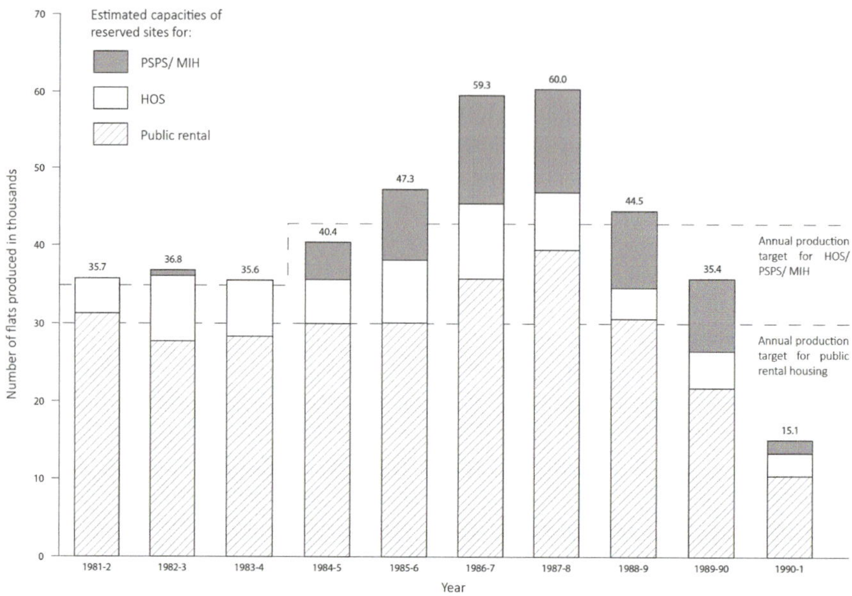

Figure 9.6 The rolling Public Housing Development Programme (PHDP) as at March 1982, showing targets and estimated capacities of reserved sites. Drawing by Joyce Fu, 2023.

be brought forward to maintain the balance'.[99] Tsing Yi 2, one of several contracts awarded to Hyundai in 1984, allegedly fell foul of union problems and site lockouts, while Cheung Hong Phase 5 was delayed by cash-flow problems of contractor On Lee Siu. Other monitoring mechanisms such as the Building Progress Review Committee, or the New Towns and Public Housing Sub-committee of the Public Works Priorities Committee, came and went as required.[100]

By mid-1986 the elements that would soon converge in the Long-Term Housing Strategy (LTHS) were taking shape. A Housing Mix Study looked beyond the ten-year horizon and anticipated a demand breakdown until 2001 of 34% PRH, 24% HOS/PSPS, and 41% private-sector – a two-thirds home-ownership prediction that was later enshrined by Governor Chris Patten in 1992 as a key policy pledge – while additional papers forecast demand and supply of public and private housing sites over that time-frame, alongside the continuing review of site availability for the PHDP.[101] And by September/December 1986 both Pang and Housing Secretary Todd confirmed that, despite the growing disruption from the '26 Blocks' scandal (see below), the LTHS was now about to be formalised, and would specially emphasise demand and supply constraints for PRH and HOS, and a wider redevelopment strategy for earlier estates.[102]

As the Housing Mix Study emphasised, the HOS and other subsidised-ownership programmes were playing an ever more prominent role within the government's housing strategy, and would expand further under the LTHS. Just as with HOS in 1976, output concerns were still paramount, with Liao announcing in July 1983 that production could be boosted by 5,000 additional HOS units, all Trident-2 – fuelling the subsequent target rise from 35,000 to 40,000.[103] However, whereas expenditure constraints initially constrained HOS expansion, after 1985 the average 7.6% annual economic growth meant that the expansion of the HOS was increasingly targeted at meeting home-ownership demand in its own right. The proportion of household spending devoted to housing rose from 20% to 30% between 1981 and 1996.[104] However, there would be no wholesale switch-over to a Singapore-style near-compulsory home-ownership strategy, despite Hilton Cheong-Leen's 1982 claim that the HOS had 'put real meaning into the term, "Hong Kong belonger" '.[105] Whereas for PAP-dominated Singapore, the high-pressure fostering of a new sense of national identity was the paramount motive of the home-ownership drive, such a strategy was undesirable and impracticable in Hong Kong, with its laissez-faire caretaker government and lower-key identity discourse.[106]

The HOS programme had certainly been revitalised by MacLehose's October 1981 decision to remove land cost from sale prices (outlined in Chapter 7) – a reform perhaps aided by the departure from the Financial Secretaryship of Haddon-Cave, who had criticised it as a misuse of public assets to subsidise asset acquisition by private individuals.[107] The policy was announced by Liao at the February 1982 opening, three months early, of the first phase of the largest single HOS project, Siu Hong Court in Tuen Mun Area 51 (project architect Allan McDonald – awarded the HKIA Silver Medal). He argued it would help 'achieve the most dearly cherished hope of most people in Hong Kong – namely ownership of their own houses'.[108] Reflecting the fact that owners were now only allowed to sell on their flats if they paid a premium equal to their gain in value, many owners bought HOS flats as a collective extended-family investment and a 'ladder' out of PRH, retaining ownership for lengthy periods rather than selling on quickly.[109]

HOS prices continued to rise, however, and thus higher densities were required, not least in response to the Land Commission 50 ha limit, after abortive 1985 suggestions to pressurise the Commission to exempt HOS from it.[110] This provoked a succession of controversies about HOS projects' density and appearance. For example, in early 1983, the 3,900-unit Diamond Hill HO 27 development (Lung Poon Court: project architects Peter Chattrabhuti and Ada Fung), with a layout of seven 35-storey 'Windmill' HOS towers, at a density of 1546 ppa/3824 ppha, was criticised at a Building Committee meeting by both Liao and Akers-Jones for its 'massive appearance'. One block was eventually removed from the project, and the remaining six towers, a car park and commercial centre were completed in late 1986 in a $329m contract.[111] By 1985 the new generation of HOS point blocks was in prospect, including the New Cruciform Block and the Flexi III, first used at Yue On Court, Ap Lei Chau, and Ka Tin Court, Sha Tin.[112]

Already, by the end of 1983, Fung Tung was highlighting sharply increased HOS sales, and the 1984 Sino-British Agreement boosted the long-term prospects of the HOS further still, with the possibility of mortgages extended beyond 1997, and flats commanding a 25% discount over private ones. It was only now that

Figure 9.7 (a) Siu Hong Court, Tuen Mun Area 51, 1981–4: 4,676 flats in Flexi point-blocks, designed by HD Construction Branch: Phase II finishing-work and mosaic-cladding in 1983 (MG) (cf. Fig. 11.10c). (b) Siu Hong, landscaped central court, 2013 (MG).

mortgages for longer periods than three years became common.[113] 1984/5 saw HOS completions exceed 10,000 for the first time, and exceed one-third of PRH completions for several years running. By now, over forty banks and deposit-taking companies were providing mortgages for HOS and PSPS, with loans of up to 90% and up to 15 years.[114] In celebration, the entire 4,676-unit Siu Hong development, including the '40,000th HOS flat', was opened in March 1985 by Haddon-Cave: having chaired the original Working Party on Home-Ownership a decade before, he now hailed the gathering recovery in the property market following the Sino-British Agreement.[115] (Figures 9.7a,b, 9.8, 9.9)

The 'black sheep' of the supported-home-ownership sector was the Middle Income Housing Programme, targeted at a lower-middle-class income group above median HOS levels, popularly dubbed the 'sandwich class'. The MIHP had been hard hit by the soaring prices of the late 1970s, and was abruptly scrapped in March 1983 after mortgage interest rates dropped from 21% to 12% in a year – leaving the only scheme built, the 2,240-unit Melody Gardens at Tuen Mun Area 28B, as a 'great headache' (Liao) with many flats empty.[116] The ensuing decade would see a succession of proposals for subsidised housing for this 'sandwich class' – with no significant outcome.[117]

Planning, zoning, land supply: towards expanded urban redevelopment

Public housing's most important external relationship within government was with the apparatus of planning in general, and the New Towns programme in particular. In both cases, the all-consuming quest for land was immensely complicated by the multi-headed government developmental structure and the powerful private sector – unlike PAP Singapore. Akers-Jones recalled sardonically of the latter that 'we always had one eye over our shoulder, looking at Singapore, and were still rather envious of Singapore, and still are! But they are a socialist state with an

Figure 9.8 Chief Secretary Sir Philip Haddon-Cave officially opens Siu Hong Court, and hands the keys of the '40,000th HOS flat' to its new owners, Mr and Mrs Yip Ho-kay, in March 1985: image in 1984–5 HA *Annual Report*.

Figure 9.9 Plaque commemorating the Siu Hong Court opening ceremony: 2023 photo (MG) in its now mature landscaped setting.

elected dictatorship in charge – so they could plan things "properly!" '[118] Besides the government's overall laissez-faire orientation, its dependency on land revenue obliged it to safeguard private-sector land supply – a constraint that even MacLehose was unable to challenge.[119] As a result, as Messling recalled in 1993, 'forward planning… .. was always a cliff-hanging affair, due to Government's apparent difficulty in releasing in good time sufficient land for our building programme. Clearly Government had its own numbers game in attempting to balance the needs of the private sector, our requirements, and the value of land sale receipts'.[120] Arguably, public housing found it easier to secure land in periods of real-estate depression: for example, a May 1983 briefing for LDPC on the TDS stressed that enhancement of the role of the private sector was 'unrealistic' given the political uncertainties over sovereignty.[121]

In 1977, MacLehose had set up a Special Committee on Land Supply to comprehensively investigate the problem. In its eventual 1983 report to Youde, it argued that land for public rental housing (PRH) would run out after 1986, unless the proposed New Towns at Junk Bay and Ma On Shan (see below) were approved. The report stressed that the average gross density of 'about' 2,700 ppha laid down by LDPC – reflecting the Hong Kong Planning Standards and Guidelines of 1982, and not compulsory for public housing but generally respected by HD – must be observed to maximise use of what remained.[122] Within HD, during the mid-1980s the Planning Division headed by Pryor (followed by A R Crosby) aimed to coordinate the 'community' planning of estates in accordance with these density levels, to coordinate with other agencies and to monitor the ongoing ten-year PHDP.[123] Reassessment of density levels in rental estates was aided by the final discontinuation of the much-criticised IU system in May 1983, allowing greater precision in correlating design and occupation densities: in 1983 an interdepartmental working group had recommended that new block types could allow densities to be raised to 3,000 ppha, but the HD, at Pryor's instigation, insisted that the 2,700 average should be retained to allow for constraints in practice.[124]

Confusingly, PSPS and HOS densities were not measured using this traditional 'housing' criterion but via the more 'commercial' gauge of plot ratio. The introduction of the Land Commission's 50 ha limit on annual private housing land release in June 1985 complicated the position significantly, and according to Crosby in 1986, had the effect of forcing up densities of HOS and PSPS in New Towns, by requiring the 'optimising' of sites and making it more difficult to fit in community and recreational facilities: most PSPS schemes were now rising from a plot ratio of 5 to 8, and HOS schemes to around 5 in first-generation New Towns; 7 in second-generation New Towns and the main urban area. Many infill sites were also being rezoned for public housing.[125] (Figure 9.10) The PRH programme was not subject to these controls, and by 1986 it was being suggested that a 30,000 annual PRH programme until 2001 could be achieved with average densities of only 2,600 or even 2,400 ppha, owing to declining household sizes.[126] In response to queries from the Chinese side in the Land Commission about the densities of PRH sites to be made available between May 1985 and March 1986, the government planners riposted that while the average density for public rental estates laid down in the HKPSG was 'about' 2,700 ppha, with a maximum of 3,000, site-specific constraints such as slopes, school sites or works areas often 'drastically' restricted this.[127]

Housing density to rise in new towns

By CHIU KIT-YING

The Government is seeking ways to increase the density of housing in new towns.

This follows the implementation of the 50-hectare annual land production limit stipulated under the Sino-British Joint Declaration.

In effect, less land will be allocated for the construction of higher density flats built under the Home Ownership Scheme and Private Sector Participation Scheme.

Senior housing planning officer Mr Alan Crosby revealed that the Housing Authority will ask for 3.8 hectares of land for Home Ownership Scheme projects in the years 1991 to 1996.

Mr Crosby

tion despite the falling household sizes."

He said Private Sector Participation Scheme projects could be built using higher densities as they are not required to include schools and other community facilities.

The Housing Authority is asking for 5.3 hectares for the Private Sector Participation Scheme per annum from the period between 1990 [illegible] 1996. This compares to [illegible] 6.1 hectares it recommen[illegible] last year.

The authority rec[illegible] submitted a report on lan[illegible] quirements for the pr[illegible] and public sectors to the [illegible] and Building Advisory [illegible] mittee.

The authority has [illegible]

Figure 9.10 May 1986 SCMP article on plea for higher-density development of New Towns by Senior Housing Planning Officer Alan Crosby.

Within the New Territories, the first generation of New Towns was now in the full flow of development – a boom that had previously been enabled by the Letters A and B system: this by 1981 encompassed 36 million sq ft of exchange commitments, but was significantly curbed by the recession, with consequent calls for intervention: in March 1983, for example, the government pledged $16m of extra investment in Tuen Mun to counter the sluggish economy. Unsurprisingly, the Letter B market plunged catastrophically in the 1982 property crash, and so in 1984, to regularise the position, the government allowed it to be monetised, valuing the earliest certificates (1960) at over fifteen times the level of the 1983 certificates.[128] The system had allowed the New Towns programme to be undertaken at low up-front cost, but most certificates were now acquired by the four largest private property companies. Thus under the 1984 Joint Declaration it was agreed that all outstanding commitments would be settled by June 1997, a process which generated huge profit margins of between 77% and 364% for the owners, and further bolstered the power of the 'tycoons'.[129]

Repeatedly, however, the government made it clear that the New Towns programme must carry on at full speed – as emphasised by Akers-Jones in key LegCo speeches of March 1983 and November 1984, and in a statement by NTDD Director Don.[130] In a 1983 overview of the New Towns programme from Abercrombie until the 1973 establishment of the NTDD within the PWD, Akers-Jones highlighted the integrated character of their plans, complete with social and community facilities – in implicit contrast to the dominant laissez-faire development model in the urban area.[131] In October 1983 NTDD Director Bryan O'Rorke boasted that the scale and pace of New Territories development was 'unrivalled' in the world.[132] And in April 1986, the NTDD was merged with the Urban Area Development Office into a new Territory Development Department, still within PWD but now including the urban areas too.[133] Already, the Market Towns expansion programme was well underway, based on the original 1975 proposals by Maunsell Consultants.[134] The Market Towns were generally much slower to show the impact of the public housing programme: although the proportion of public tenants in the population of the New Towns averaged 65% overall in 1986, but, within this, varying from 83% in Tuen Mun to only 24% in still semi-rural Yuen Long.[135] In a July 1984 opinion survey of all New Towns, Sha Tin was seen as the most desirable New Town, with Tai Po and Yuen Long the runners-up.[136] In 1986, the Housing Mix Study reported regarding a potential adjustment of the existing 40%–30%–30% mix of PRH–HOS–private in the New Territories.[137] Strategic planning had now been transformed from Cowperthwaite's bete-noire into a radical territorial-reconstruction tool supporting economic transformation – even though its dirigisme was far more restrained than Singapore's – and facilitated significant population displacements of (mainly) lower-income citizens: the New Towns now unambiguously became dormitory towns rather than industrial centres.[138]

The most vital of all the proposed New Towns to the future progress of the public housing drive was Junk Bay. It was steered within NTDD by a development office headed by Norman Tucker.[139] (Figure 9.11a, b) After repeated threats of curtailment, it had finally been authorised in principle as a New Town by

Figure 9.11 (a) Junk Bay, view from east in November 1983 (MG) prior to start of development. (b) Junk Bay Development Study (Maunsell Consultants Asia, Shankland Cox Partnership, and Brian Clouston and Partners), 1981, front-cover perspective.

ExCo in September 1982 but without specific approval of Maunsell Consultants' development masterplan. This led to claims within LDPC that 'positive decisions on Junk Bay' were being put off, resulting in programming becoming 'very tight', and necessitating repeated minor adjustments. Commencing with Area 14, Junk Bay by that stage was already hard-wired into planned public housing output from 1986 onwards.[140] Crosby stressed to LDPC in August 1983 that to maintain the programme from the late 1980s onwards, rapid progress with Junk Bay was imperative, as 'it is already a central and basic element in the current public housing programme', and would yield 2,500 units as early as FY 1986/7. To help speed progress on that first phase (Area 14), at the April 1983 BC, Crosby and Poon successfully proposed it should be changed from a HOS/PSPS to a HOS/PRH development, containing 6,656 flats at 2,673 ppha.[141] However, by mid-1985, with the first development on track for completion in 1986, a significant phasing problem reared its head: the noxious presence of the Chiaphua steel mill/alloy works. This complex had originated ironically in a government industrial relocation policy of two decades previously, but its polluting fumes now required it to be relocated before any flats could be occupied in the first three public housing estates, scheduled for completion in 1988.[142] By November 1985 a relocation package costed at $300 million was being discussed between Akers-Jones and the Chief Secretary, to avoid Junk Bay starting life as a 'ghost town'.[143]

Within the urban area, the focus was shifting from squatter clearance to systematic redevelopment of early public housing estates, especially given their potential exemption from the Land Commission limits. Partly, the squatter crisis had been replaced by the Vietnamese boat-people, who had taken over the role of 'disruptive incomers' without any rehousing liability.[144] There was also a shift in emphasis away from squatter demolition to improvement in the New Territories: a separate

Improvements Division was set up in 1982, although the main squatter control unit still had 3,000 staff. The most recent squatter-clearance programme, initiated in 1981, yielded 487 ha of redevelopment land and displaced 53,000 people. Half of these went to permanent housing and half to THAs, which totalled 44 in 1981, with 118,000 inhabitants: from 1981, squatters with 15 years' residency could obtain a public housing flat.[145] Although a 1984/5 survey indicated there were still 477,000 squatters, 9% of the total population, the urban squatter proportion was fast shrinking, especially with the increasing diversion of THAs to New Territories sites. The programme continued to provoke protests, including 1982 criticism by HKPCPHP of a lack of fire precautions in squatter areas. In 1983, clearances at Hang On Street, Kwun Tong, led to scuffles, while the clearance of the Kowloon Bay transit centre and decanting of inhabitants to a new THA in Tai Po provoked a sit-in protest by inhabitants around the Secretariat and the HA headquarters.[146] However, the government was unmoved, arguing that Hong Kong 'is a free society where people can make their choice' whether to take up a THA place or not. By 1987, the total number of squatters had fallen to 427,000.[147]

As squatter clearance receded from view, the urban redevelopment programme correspondingly increased in prominence and scale. (Figure 9.12a, b) By 1984, the existing clearance of Mk I and II blocks was being accelerated, and a likely extension to include Mk III and IV blocks was signalled in January 1985 by David Ford, the newly appointed Housing Director, despite protests from traditionalists such as Elliott: they argued that it would lead to 'queue-jumping' by displacees at the expense of regular waiting-list applicants.[148] The undisputed centrepiece of this expanding programme was the Kowloon Central Estates Redevelopment, an all-encompassing regeneration of the Mark I and II estates (mostly built from 1958) in the Wong Tai Sin, Tung Tau and Lok Fu districts. This had been originally authorised in 1979 on the basis of Shek Kip Mei-style block conversions, but after limited progress was revitalised from 1984 as a replanned scheme of 27,000 new flats for 136,000 inhabitants. Designed by multi-disciplinary teams, this vast project was to be implemented in a complex sequence of phases, including construction of 'pump-priming' blocks on existing USD playgrounds, followed by demolition and

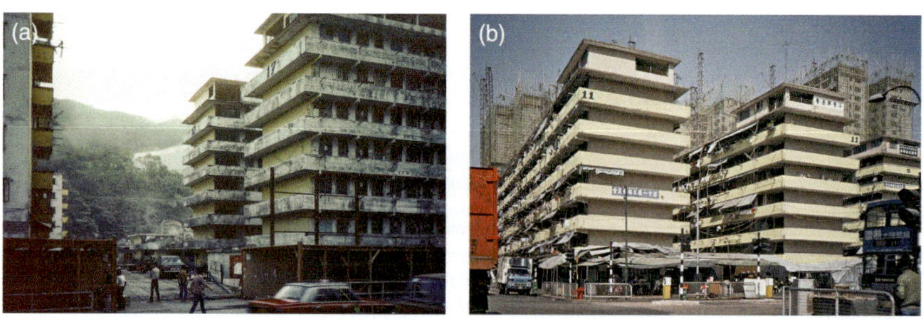

Figure 9.12 (a) Chai Wan Estate, Blocks 16–20: Mark I blocks under demolition, 1983 (MG). (b) Lei Cheng Uk, Mk I blocks under redevelopment, 1983 (MG) (cf. Fig. 2.6a).

'build-back' construction, with some 10–20% of the new development envisaged as being HOS.[149] To gain initial momentum, a special decanting operation would be mounted for Lok Fu, Wang Tau Hom, Wong Tai Sin and Tung Tau inhabitants, to Sun Chiu Estate in Sha Tin.[150] In 1985, Assistant Director (Housing Architect) Cheung Wing-kun claimed that Kowloon Central was 'the largest redevelopment project in South-East Asia' but that its construction needed to 'speed up', to ensure it was completed in eight years, as only 20% of the existing Mk I and II housing had so far been redeveloped.[151]

The beginning of rapid action in Kowloon Central only threw into sharper relief the impasse over the immediately adjacent Kowloon Walled City. Finally, in September 1985, a special meeting convened by the HA advocated approaching the Chinese authorities for support – on the grounds, as Akers-Jones recalled, that relations were now good, and that there were 'persuasive reasons' for allowing Britain to clear up 'this disgraceful blemish on Kowloon' rather than bequeathing the problem to China to deal with. Following initial feelers to the New China News Agency, and sounding-out of local kaifongs by the Chinese government, it was finally agreed clearance could go ahead – with dramatic effects, as we will see in the next chapter.[152]

Housing design: linking type-standardisation and construction quality

During the MacLehose years, the built form of Hong Kong housing remained polarised by income group, with the lower and/or more massive forms of public rental housing contrasting with the new HOS pattern of slender towers. Some individual cases were challenging that polarity, notably the Hing Man project, and by the early 1980s it began to break down under the general pressure for higher densities and higher blocks, stemming partly from the Land Commission's work and partly from the more general shortage of sites. The old types of centre-corridor or inner-courtyard blocks were phased out in favour of taller towers and slabs. At the same time, again with HOS leading the way, spartan estate environments were replaced by complex schemes of landscaping and aesthetic harmonisation. And the structural defects bequeathed by the old rough-and-ready building techniques, above all in the '26 Blocks' scandal of 1980–6, were tackled by increasingly precise constructional methods involving both standardisation and mechanisation.

The idea of estate 'image' had originated two decades earlier, in Liao's conception of Wah Fu as an architecturally modelled unity on a dramatically landscaped site. With the rise in block heights during the early 1980s, it became common to consider the visual 'profile' of a housing project in the context of nearby mountains. At the October 1982 Building Committee, for instance, Messling argued the tall Trident blocks of the Hin Keng and Ha Keng Hau developments (Sha Tin 31B and 31A) would help give visual continuity between the wooded Lion Rock and the landscape within the estate, and that their massing had been 'carefully considered' to avoid overshadowing existing villages. Likewise, the stepped wing heights of the 1981 HOS Windmill tower design had been intended to 'avoid monotony on the skyline'.[153] In January 1983, there were claims that the planned Shek Wu Hui Area 8 would be 'overshadowed by a "wall" of public housing', and an argument by Liao that Tsing Yi Area 1 layout seemed 'to lack cohesiveness'. At the same BC meeting, in a more complex sequence of argumentation which highlighted the hierarchy of esteem within public housing, Akers-Jones asserted that the serried, brown brick-clad 30-store HOS Flexi-Blocks at Tai Po Area 44 (Wang Fuk Court), immediately overlooking his own official 'home' at Island House, had a 'gloomy' outward appearance that made them look like rental blocks, while the point blocks were also more crowded together than rental blocks usually were: he warned that 'the designer should watch out for such factors'.[154] And between February and December 1983, there were wide-ranging discussions between Messling, Pang and Liao about the layout of Long Ping estate in Yuen Long, with a 'better grouping' of blocks proposed, including increased numbers of Trident-2 blocks in Phase 2; Messling justified the predominant use of the new standard slab blocks at Long Ping as a way of maximising numbers of smaller flats and improved space standards within a ceiling of 2,855 ppha, but Liao argued that more HOS towers should be included for 'variety'.[155]

During the mid-1980s, coordinated external colour schemes started to be used for the purposes of image and identity-creation – building on earlier precedents, such as the lift and service core towers, differently coloured in each block, at Hing Man, Lung Poon Court or the Housing Society's Cho Yiu Chuen, or the brown mosaic-clad Flexi towers of Siu Hong Court, Tuen Mun. As we will see in Chapter 11, a decisive role in this agenda would later be played by French designers Michel and France Cler, who were engaged to create individual estate identities through chromatic schemes – although the initial means of doing this through mosaic tiles (a method prefigured in earlier French projects by Emile Aillaud – see Chapter 11) would be later replaced by painted schemes in cases when the tiles began to fall off.[156] (Figure 9.13)

The move to higher block-types formed an essential part of the new HD design agenda. Stephen Poon played a decisive role here. He later recalled the process in chiefly practical terms: 'The move to higher blocks came about because of pressure, including political pressure, to optimise the use of land. Our engineers were asked to make things possible. Our density yardstick remained more or less constant: a lot of low-rise buildings like schools and commercial centres formed part of housing projects, so if you take the whole piece of land, the number of persons per hectare remained the same. But the fitting in of housing units is not so easy to do, so we needed to optimise the land. We needed to make adjustments, firstly, in the structure which was needed to build something that would stand up to the height; then, the lifts, to raise lift speed and capacity. These were overcome by the engineers: they used further lifts, which kept the waiting time down.' Later in the 1980s, those site-optimisation challenges would increasingly guide Poon towards a concentration on cruciform block-plans, giving rise to the 'Harmony' series (or, more specifically, the 'Harmony 1' sub-type: see Chapter 11).[157] For the moment, however, the cruciform tower configuration was still largely confined to HOS, as part of the ongoing legacy of the Mei Foo compact tower tradition.

Figure 9.13 Mei Lam Estate, Sha Tin, completed 1982, job architect John Ng: 2010 view (MG) showing mature landscaping and mainly green colour scheme ('Mei Lam' translating as 'Beautiful Forest').

Whichever configuration was in favour, however, one principle remained constant: the continuing reliance on Modernist standard block designs, an approach strongly divergent from Singapore's 1980s shift towards designs of increasingly ornamental, even Postmodernist character. Messling argued in 1983 that Hong Kong was 'challenging Singapore's leading role in public housing'.[158] At first, however, the shift to taller standard towers within the mainstream rental programme took a distinctively massive turn, in the Trident series of standard blocks, designed within the group of CA/1 S T Chow and planned on a 'Y' layout – a pattern pioneered in the early post-war years, especially in US or Australian public rental housing. Poon freely conceded later that the Tridents were not only awkward in practical terms, as having quite a large footprint and thus being difficult to fit into infill sites, but also potentially looked oppressive.[159] But administrator Tony Miller, later Director of Housing at the turn of century, highlighted the disjunction between exterior massiveness and interior flexibility: 'They don't look great from the outside, but if you're a resident it's different: the Tridents were one of the first short-armed blocks, and whereas in previous types, with lifts at either end, you were faced with a bloody great corridor stretching before you, a bit like a prison block, with forty or fifty flats per floor, the Tridents broke up that up, and you come out of the lift and turn into a much smaller, more sociable corridor: it's easier to feel secure in such a setting'. The main initial variants were the 35-storey Trident 1, containing 1,224 two-room Type A flats, and the 35-storey Trident 2, a mixture of 612 Type B and 204 Type C units.[160] (Figure 9.14a, b)

The key forum for consideration of new block types was the LPVC (Layout Plans Vetting Committee). Here Pang and Messling in March 1982 presented the Trident, together with the Windmill for HOS use, as 'additions to the stock of standard designs' that were 'in no way meant to make the existing stock obsolete'.[161] The pace of evolution of the standard types was shown by the way the massive Windmill type was already being rejected in the later 1980s, as containing too many flats on each floor.[162] By January 1983, progress with the Trident series was so far advanced that the Building Committee annual tour visited both Trident 1s and Trident 2s under construction in Sha Tin, hailing the Trident as a 'New Design Concept' of 'multi-room' planning. Project architect Bob Pritchard escorted the committee round the bottom two floors of a Trident 2 block at Phase 2 of Chun Shek Estate. Although the Trident was initially conceived as a chiefly PRH block, potential HOS adaptation was also kept in mind: at the January 1983 Building Committee, Messling went along with Liao's suggestion for a re-phasing of Tsing Yi Area 1 to include two Trident-2 towers for HOS, agreeing with Liao that Trident-2 flats could be 'potentially saleable' at this location.[163] Initially, the Trident was also used along with H blocks, for example at Shan King, or at the Kwun Tong Mk I redevelopment, where the balance of the two types was debated in the Building Committee.[164]

Alongside these, slab blocks were also still prominent. In February 1983, a 19-storey 'New Standard Slab Block' devised by Nutt's D & S Group was approved, based on a single-room concept for small households. Nutt highlighted its 'better light penetration', and 12% larger 'small flats' of 30 sq m area.[165] Lambon and Hall recalled its genesis within D & S:

> The New Slab Block was based on a room concept – basically, it was all one big room, you have toilets in the room, and tenants could subdivide it, using gratings to get light and ventilation into the internal rooms from the corridors – it was a hang-over from the Twin Tower blocks. The New Slab Block tested the concept of multi-disciplinary working – we were all working in one room, our team in D & S was multi-disciplinary – including Rick So, the only structural engineer, and building services specialists. We were given a brief to design the block, when Tim Nutt was on holiday, and we'd got it designed by the time he came back – it took 12 weeks. We'd talked the thing through amongst ourselves: he wasn't very happy when he came back![166]

February 1984 saw extended discussion, led by Pang and Poon, with management input from Fung Tung, of two new types, the Trident 3 and New Linear Block, for use with immediate effect: both allowed partitioning of flats into separate rooms with their own windows.[167] (Figures 9.15a,b, 9.16a–c)

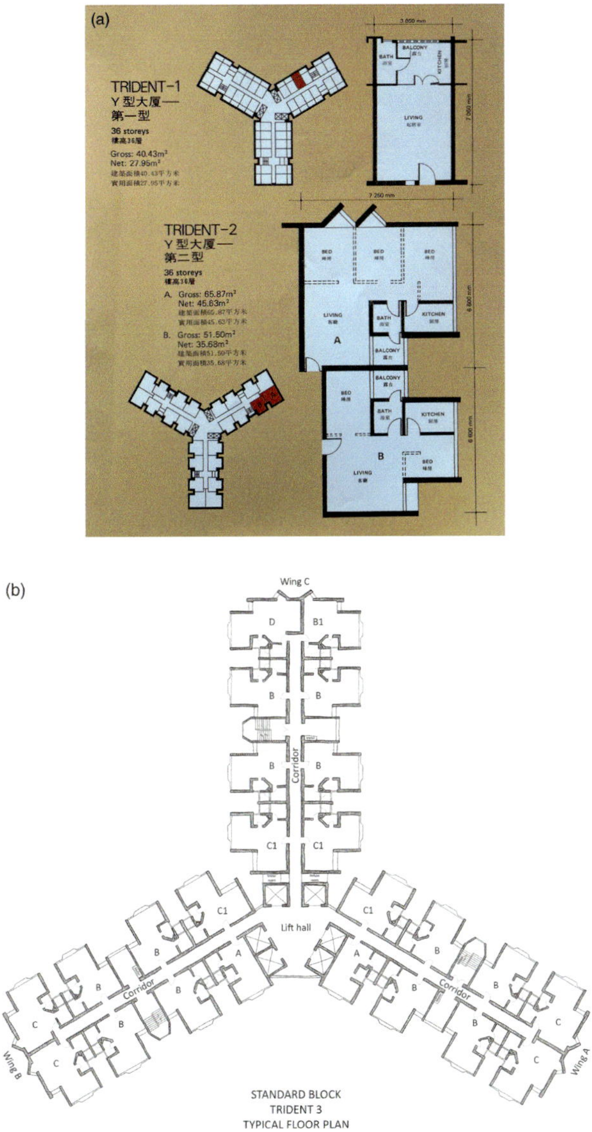

Figure 9.14 (a) Plans of Trident-1 (one-roomed flats) and Trident-2 (two and three bedrooms) standard Y-plan towers, included in Hong Kong Government 1996 exhibition in Edinburgh: 1996 photo (MG). (b) Plan of Trident-3 block. Drawing by Joyce Fu, 2023.

Figure 9.15 (a) Hin Keng Estate, Sha Tin Area 31B (eight Trident-2, -3, -4 blocks, opened 1986): model of 36-storey Trident-2 block, originally part of overall estate model, presented to author by job architect Bob Pritchard. 2012 photo (MG). (b) Hin Keng, 2013 view of Trident-2 block (MG).

The Trident 3 formed part of an agenda of flexible sizes, to allow multi-room flats for all: in March 1984 Messling argued the Trident-3's 'multi-room concept' heralded 'the end of the one-room flat design', as did the Linear Block, which avoided dark central corridors.[168] And in November 1984 the Governor and officials inspected a mock-up of a Trident IV flat of 40.8 sq m outside City Hall, to be built first at Hin Keng in 1986.[169] By 1985, too, the new generation of HOS point blocks was also in prospect, replacing the Windmill, including the New Cruciform Block and the Flexi III, first used at Yue On Court, Ap Lei Chau, and Ka Tin Court, Sha Tin.[170]

All these developments in type-plans went hand-in-hand with a growing drive to improve construction standards, especially through limited prefabrication linked to the shift to mainland factories. As the 1980s continued, and the build-up to the LTHS gathered pace, the stress was increasingly on 'quality as well as quality', as emphasised by Messling in a 1986 introduction to an HD 'Portfolio' of current types.[171] Nutt's group developed further this tandem evolution of type-plans and prefabrication, into an R & D-led concept of 'Housing for the 90s', culminating in the immensely important Harmony initiative – as we will see in Chapter 11.[172]

The close interlinking of pursuit of quality in design and quality of construction owed much to the eruption in just those years of the '26 Blocks Scandal', a

Figure 9.16 (a) Tsui Ping North Estate, Tsui To House (Old Slab, 23 storeys), under construction in 1985 (MG) – among the last built examples of this type, first designed by Liao for Wah Fu. (b) The same block as in 9.16a, seen in 2023 (MG). (c) Tsui Ping North, Tsui Yung House (Trident-2) under construction in 1985 (MG).

construction-standards crisis concerning early-1970s PWD blocks, already hinted at in preceding chapters. Sloppy site supervision had overlooked the use of salt water in the concrete mix, leading to rampant tie-beam corrosion, crumbling concrete and water leakages from public toilets and elsewhere.[173] The problem was first detected in three blocks of 1971–3 at Kwai Fong Estate, and investigations began in 1980. In 1985, the three blocks were condemned to demolition, and a wider survey of all 1,032 blocks over five years old was begun, headed by HD engineer Peter Ainsworth: it reported a few months later that a number of pre-1973 blocks were seriously affected, and 26 would need to be demolished – requiring rehousing of 17,000 families at a cost of over $800 million.[174] As all the blocks concerned were of crosswall rather than RC frame construction, at least these haphazard corrosion patterns did not threaten their overall stability – a lesson taken to heart in design of later tall towers such as Harmony, which almost exclusively used shear-wall construction.[175]

All the blocks involved in the scandal were former Government Low-Cost units inherited by the Housing Department in 1973, and thus there was no question of formal institutional liability. Nevertheless – given the ICAC's involvement in checking for any illegality – there was some potential political danger to the HA. In response, Pang and Messling took decisive ownership of the HD's investigation and public-relations presentation of the case. Messling's forceful argumentation won a general public acceptance that the case was a historic one, not involving current officers, and whose lessons would be vigorously exploited through setting up a HA testing lab and quality-assurance regime, and regular monitoring of all blocks of over five years' remaining life.[176] This converted the crisis from a public-relations liability to an asset for the HD. Messling later claimed that 'the great professionalism that was applied led to the Branch being acknowledged as world leaders in the diagnosis, analysis and cure of what was to be later recognised universally as "concrete cancer"'; and the task of 'handling all the media attention that was focused on this construction and human drama' created 'a good rapport with the media which stood me in good stead for the rest of my time in Hong Kong.' The far rarer incidence of structural problems in HOS blocks was dealt with through similar investigations, as in the case of crumbling concrete at Shan Tsui Court, Chai Wan, in 1986, caused by insufficient cover of reinforcing bars.[177]

As part of the HA's emergent quality-assurance regime – perfected two decades later under the construction deputy-directorship of Ada Fung – the early 1980s had seen significant steps towards greater use of mechanised construction, with the first mechanised contracts approved in 1982 at Tai Po Area 24 Phase III (Kwong Fuk Estate) and Area 17 Phase 1 (Fu Shin Estate). (Figure 9.17) The winning (lowest) tenderer at Kwong Fuk III, which comprised two 35-storey Trident-2s and one 19-storey slab, was the long-established French system-building firm Coignet, whose engineers completely redesigned both block types in a mechanised system of in situ shear walls and precast concrete floor-slabs.[178] The original project architect, Dave Hall, recalled that at Kwong Fuk

Figure 9.17 Newly completed Trident-2 towers at Kwong Fuk Estate, Tai Po, November 1985 (MG).

> they reclaimed 15 hectares of land, we developed the land, and the whole place was occupied in 6 years, with 48,000 people – a complete town, with car parks, commercial centre, 2,000 Home Ownership flats. That was why high-rise housing was successful in Hong Kong, where it failed in Britain. That saw one of the first experiments in three-wing blocks – the Trident. There were also Twin Tower Blocks at Kwong Fuk – I felt the old Twin Tower had a lot of merit. I originally planned out virtually the whole estate with either the Slab Block or the Twin Tower. I did the whole layout with consideration for feng shui: every dwelling had a view, but looking *past* other ones. Later, they took out two of the Twin Tower Blocks and plonked in two Tridents, without asking me at all! They wanted to give this French firm, Coignet, a try. But they couldn't make the numbers work for precasting – they needed a large off-site area.[179] (Figure 9.18)

Shorter construction time (26 months rather than 34 as normal) was an additional claimed benefit of mechanisation, but doubts still persisted and at the January 1983 Building Committee there were heated exchanges between doubters, such as Kwok ('no advantage') and advocates such as Messling ('should stick with it' in anticipation of 'efficiency savings') and Pang ('gives contractors an incentive to improve').[180] By mid-1984 the momentum had begun to build, with Pang reporting many contractors were voluntarily adopting mechanisation.[181] Cost-saving was not,

Figure 9.18 Blocks of experimental stepped design at Butterfly Estate (project architect Denis Ko), Tuen Mun Area 28, seen newly completed in November 1983 (MG).

in itself, an aim of mechanisation, especially as Director of Housing Ford also reported many mainland Chinese firms were showing a sudden interest in Hong Kong housing, with 'very competitive tendering' the result.[182] At Lung Poon Court Phases I and II (Diamond Hill HO 27), for example, the $329 million contract for 3,340 flats in six 34/38-storey stepped Windmill towers, built from 1984–6, used 'advanced mechanised construction technology' including wall and table-steel-formwork, and precasting of some non-structural elements; construction at Fu Shin Estate in Tai Po was similar.[183] (Figures 9.19, 9.20a, b)

Regularisation of construction went hand-in-hand with closer monitoring of contract progress. In a 1986 lecture to the Building Contractors Association, Messling even ventured a 'naming and shaming' exercise to emphasise the Department's seriousness about programme monitoring: he revealed the HD had served notice on Cheung Kee Ltd, principal contractor for Hin Keng Phases 2 and 3, and for Yiu On Phase 1 (both scheduled for completion in late 1987): the company had not paid subcontractors since the previous month and work had ground to a halt. In its warning notice, the Department stated it expected both estates to be finished by March 1988 to avoid any adverse effect on overall housing production, including the extended redevelopment programme.[184]

Twenty years later, Stephen Poon recalled in detail the rationale for the construction shift.

> Our move to semi-mechanised construction aimed *both* to improve quality *and* to get round shortages. The decision was not based on an aim of speeding up

Figure 9.19 Lung Poon Court, Diamond Hill HO 27 development, six 34/38-storey Windmill towers, built in 1984–7: 2015 view (MG).

Figure 9.20 (a) Lam Tin Extension Phase 1 HOS development (Hong Wah Court). Three 38-storey Windmills under construction in November 1985 (MG). (b) The same three Windmill blocks seen in 2023 (MG) (cf. Fig. 11.10c).

> building – it didn't speed up the work. Even if you mechanised, construction would go faster, but the finishing work on services would not move at the same pace – it was always left behind. You ended up having the same amount of time. The issue was *quality*, and how that related to labour. When we first started mechanisation, we demanded that construction should use large panel formwork: because of economy and building structure, you go for a lot of structural walls in high-rise buildings. Before then, we used traditional timber formwork. Contractors, being what they are, don't care too much about what the surface of the wall looks like. So, when we were building high-rise structures at two weeks per floor, contractors would need to use two sets of formwork. Before they could put down the formwork for one floor, they were already there on the upper floor. But by the time the concrete had cured and they were ready to remove the formwork, you could get a lot of surprises – curves and so on. In those situations, you couldn't ask the contractor to take the whole thing down! Mechanisation removed uncertainty. We still use bamboo scaffolding even today, though, for finishing work.

Likewise, Gabriel recalled, 'it was an issue of *quality* at that time. There had been an even production level through the '80s. Then capacity became an issue in Hong Kong – and it eventually led to our downfall in the early 2000s!' However,

> there was a problem with some semi-mechanised schemes, because it was not a straightforward process to introduce precasting into blocks which had not been designed for it. I took over one building contract which had been built by the French contractor SOGEA, where the junction of PC and in situ works had not been properly thought out – which led to some problems where water leaks from flats were difficult to trace through the various construction joints.[185]

Conclusion

Following Youde's sudden death in Beijing in December 1986, Akers-Jones was appointed interim Governor until the arrival of Sir David Wilson the following April. Within the housing programme, the imminent publication of the Housing Strategy, following the economic stabilisation steered through by Youde, and the ongoing transformation of Hong Kong's economy, promised to bring a new stability and momentum. Despite a fresh upsurge in external political instability in 1989, that momentum would be significantly carried forward in the following five years, not least by David Akers-Jones, as the unexpected new head of a reorganised and far more autonomous Housing Authority.

Notes

1 Castells, *Shek Kip Mei Syndrome*, 154; HKRS70-8-1698, MacLehose 12-1982 speech.
2 Castells, *Shek Kip Mei Syndrome*, 154, 332.
3 Kockelkorn, 'Peripheralisation', 622–3; Tse and Ganesan, *Hong Kong*.

4 Holdsworth and Munn, *Dictionary of Hong Kong Biography*, 483 (Goodstadt); B C H Fong, T L Lui (eds) *Hong Kong 20 Years after the Handover*, Palgrave Macmillan, London 2018, 248.
5 Akers-Jones, *Feeling the Stones*, 137; Holdsworth and Munn, *Dictionary of Hong Kong Biography*, 483 (Goodstadt). L Goodstadt, 'Fiscal freedom and the making of Hong Kong's capitalist society', *China Information* 24 (3), 2010, 273–94.
6 Akers-Jones, *Feeling the Stones*, 161–3.
7 Holdsworth and Munn, *Dictionary of Hong Kong Biography*, 147.
8 Blyth and Wotherspoon, *Hong Kong Remembers*, 220.
9 Akers-Jones, *Feeling the Stones*, 134–7.
10 Liao, 2010 interview; HKRS696-3-168, 5-1982 note.
11 HKRS696-3-163, 1982 visit; HKRS163-8-11, 6-1982 brief.
12 Akers-Jones, *Feeling the Stones*, 137.
13 SCMP, 11-4-1982; Scott, *Political Change and the Crisis of Legitimacy*, 168–9.
14 HKRS394-29-191, 1982 briefing for Thatcher; FCO40-1440, 25-5-1982 Hall to 10 Downing St and briefing to PM mid-1982.
15 Elsie Tu p129; Dimbleby.
16 FCO40-1440 25-8-1982 M M Hall to 10 Downing Street, and briefing to Prime Minister; FCO40-1441 Jeremy Bray to Thatcher 31-8-1982.
17 Mark, 'Development without decolonisation?' 335; Goodstadt, *Biographical Dictionary*, 196.
18 Akers-Jones, 2013 interview; Holdsworth and Munn, *Dictionary of Hong Kong Biography*, 483; Patten, *East and West*, 26–7.
19 HKRS163-8-70, 5-1983 papers.
20 Lightbody, 2011 interview; Wilson, 2023 interview.
21 Tsang, *Governing Hong Kong*, 222-232; Akers-Jones, *Feeling the Stones*, 162.
22 Akers-Jones, *Feeling the Stones*, 162; Housing Authority, *Annual Report*, 1994/5, 9.
23 Liao, 2010 interview.
24 Williams, 2012 interview.
25 70-3-3670 5, 6-83 visits; Glendinning, *Mass Housing*, 383-393 on danwei system.
26 Liao, 2010 interview.
27 SCMP 21-12-1992, 22, on Messling and Ministry of Urban and Rural Construction.
28 Liao, 2010 interview.
29 Castells, *Shek Kip Mei Syndrome*, 103.
30 HKRS461-1-12-11, 3-1983 BC minutes; HKRS70-11-169, cutting from SCMP 11-1984.
31 Poon, 2010 interview.
32 HKRS1693-1-3, SCMP cutting 2-2-1986.
33 HKRS545-1-456-1, 11-84 Chung on public housing maintaining social stability; Akers-Jones, *Feeling the Stones*, 162.
34 Miller, 2014 interview; Wilson, 2023 interview. Later claims that the private housing 'tycoons' had pressured Beijing to restrict land supply in order to drive up prices: S M Shaw, 'Homing in on reality', SCMP 24-6-1990, 16.
35 Akers-Jones, *Feeling the Stones*, 162.
36 Poon, 2010 interview; Miller, 2014 interview.
37 HKRS1693-1-3, 11-85 note by Crosby, and 4-86 report.
38 HKRS545-1-456-6, 5-86 cutting; 1693-4-8 correspondence of 7, 8-1986.
39 HKRS 394-29-208, 8-1985, 9-1985 papers.
40 Akers-Jones, *Feeling the Stones*, 187-8.

41 James Lee, *Housing, Home-Ownership and Social Change in Hong Kong*, Ashgate, Aldershot, 1999, 173–9.
42 SCMP 30-3-1988, 35; Alice Poon, *Land and the Ruling Class in Hong Kong*, Enrich, Singapore, 2011, 29–30.
43 I Scott, *Political Change and the Crisis of Legitimacy*, 258; Castells, *Shek Kip Mei Syndrome*, 124–5.
44 Tsang, *Governing Hong Kong*, 194; Lambon, 2012 interview. Organisation chart of entire Hong Kong Government as at March 1982: HKRS394-20-191.
45 Lambon, 2012 interview.
46 Chung-kin Tsang, *Home Ownership in Hong Kong*, Routledge, Abingdon, 2021, Chapter 3.
47 Tu, *Colonial Hong Kong*, 135; Dimbleby, *The Last Governor*, 105–6; Patten, *Hong Kong Diaries,* 231–6, 290.
48 Castells, *Shek Kip Mei Syndrome*, 141–3, 154.
49 HKRS545-1-456-5, 1-1985 on UMELCO.
50 Castells, *Shek Kip Mei Syndrome*, 149; HKRS545-1-456-5, 3-1985 on HKPCPHP.
51 HKRS 70-8-2052 and 545-1-456-5, both papers of 3-1985.
52 HKRS 70-8-3665, 8-1983 Huang.
53 The proposed estate name, Ham Tin, was vetoed by residents and replaced by Lam Tin in 1970: HKRS524-2-11, 19-11-1970 ceremony; HKRS70-11-169, 1-1984 Fung Tung note.
54 HKRS394-29-196, 4-1984 note; HKRS545-1-456-6, 8-1986 survey. HKRS70-11-168, 7-84 survey by Survey Research (HK) Ltd. Another paper of October 1981 argued new towns 'breed hatred rather than community spirit': HKRS 545-1-447-3, paper of 10-1981.
55 Holdsworth and Munn, *Dictionary of Hong Kong Biography*, 483 (Goodstadt). Richard Wong, *Hong Kong Land for Hong Kong People*, 109; Castells, *Shek Kip Mei Syndrome*, 102-3; Lee, *Housing, Home-Ownership and Social Change*, 13.
56 Castells, *Shek Kip Mei Syndrome*, 99; Holdsworth and Munn, *Dictionary of Hong Kong Biography*, 196.
57 Sir John Bremridge, *Hong Kong Hansard,* 15 January 1986, 479; T K Ghose, *The Banking System of Hong Kong*, Butterworths, Singapore, 1987, 96; Goodstadt, 'Fiscal freedom', 2010, 284; Holdsworth and Munn, *Dictionary of Hong Kong Biography*, 483; Castells et al, *Shek Kip Mei Syndrome*, 83-4, 101-3; SCMP 7-8-1988, 33; 19-2-1989, 44; HKRS1693-1-3, 7-1985, 'Review of Property Market'.
58 Castells, *Shek Kip Mei Syndrome*, 84, 106.
59 Castells, *Shek Kip Mei Syndrome*, 95, 106. Lee, *Housing, Home-Ownership and Social Change*, 128, 135; 1983 Governor's Annual Address.
60 HKRS1693-1-3, 7-1985, Review of Property Market; Castells, *Shek Kip Mei Syndrome*, 103.
61 Housing Authority, *Annual Report*, 1982-3, Appendices J, K, N; *Annual Report*, 1984-5, 122.
62 Castells, *Shek Kip Mei Syndrome*, 49.
63 Lee, *Housing, Home-Ownership and Social Change,* 128, 135.
64 Yeung and Wong, *Fifty Years*, 163–4.
65 Housing Authority, *Annual Report*, 1984/5, 121. Ka Fu Wah, 'An analysis of the organisational structure of the Housing Department in Hong Kong', HKU 2002 Master's thesis.

66 HKRS394-29-192, 11-1982 paper.
67 Yeung and Wong, *Fifty Years*, 26.
68 Liao, 2011 interview.
69 Burns, 2014 interview; Lambon, 2012 interview; HKRS70-8-2052, 2-86 Messling note.
70 Williams, 2012 interview.
71 HKRS70-8-2048, Liao 3-1984 speech; HKRS70-11-68, 4-1984 Liao speech; HKRS545-1-456-4 Liao 1984 on Wong Tai Sin. Liao to LegCo November 1984: 'old names such as Shek Kip Mei, Li Cheng Uk and Chai Wan are no longer symbols of drab housing in dull surroundings': HKRS70-11-68, 11-1984 note.
72 HKRS461-1-12-10, BC minutes 2-1983 on Long Ping; HKRS461-1-12-11, 3-1983 Messling on Long Ping.
73 HKRS70-8-2044 2-1985 farewell.
74 Messling, 'Public Housing – A Numbers Game', 1; HKRS70-8-2052 10-1985 on 'Friendly Freddie'; HKRS70-8-2044, 1-1986 press release.
75 Lambon, 2012 interview; Cheung, 2012 interview. Project architects for individual HOS schemes included Allan McDonald (Siu Hong Court), John Lambon at (Yue Tin Court); Peter Chattraborti and Ada Fung (Lung Poon Court).
76 Lambon, 2012 interview.
77 HKRS461-1-12-11, 3-1983 BC minutes, Messling interventions.
78 Housing Authority, *Annual Report*, 1984/5, 37.
79 Poon, 2010 interview.
80 HKRS461-1-12-10, BC 2-1983 minutes.
81 Housing Authority, *Annual Report*, 1982/3, 34; HKRS545-1-456-4, Messling at 3-1983 meeting.
82 Tim Nutt and Chris Bale, *Hong Kong – a Moment in Time*, Chinese UP 1997; Cheung, 2012 interview; Lambon, 2012 interview. D & S: HKRS1881-1-9.
83 Lambon, 2012 interview.
84 Poon, 2009 interview; HKRS461-1-12-11, 4-1983 discussion.
85 HKRS70-8-2048, 5-1984 papers on CADD; Lambon, 2012 interview.
86 Housing Authority, *Annual Report*, 1984/5, 60.
87 HKRS696-3-120, Forsgate to Liao, 7-1984; HKRS545-1-456-4 9-1984 Liao speech.
88 Fung Tung, 2010 interview.
89 HKRS545-1-456-5 and 456-6, 8-1985 and 11-1985 articles; Lee, *Housing, Home-Ownership and Social Change*, 44; Yeung & Wong, *Fifty Years*, 182.
90 HKRS545-1-456-5, 11-1985 Elsie Tu article; HKRS545-1-456-6 10-1986 Liao address to LegCo.
91 HKRS461-1-2-7, BC 9-1982 minutes; HKRS1881-1-2, 9-1982 papers; HKRS70-8-3670.
92 HKRS1693/4/8, Crosby memo 21-6-1985. PHDP: HKRS1882-3-19, BC paper 93/86; HKRS 1881-2-19 P Ward to P K Chiu 5-8-1992 on PHDP.
93 SCMP 21-12-1997, 11; HKRS163-8-70, 5-1983 papers.
94 HKRS601-1-5 10-1983 PHDP review; HKRS545-1-456-1, 8-1983 memo.
95 HKRS163-8-77, 9-1984 memo by Crosby; HKRS1693-4-8 6-1985 explanation of PHDP.
96 HKRS1693-4-8, 7-8-1986 paper for BC. HKRS1882-3-19, BC paper 93/86, appendix by Planning Division 18-7-1986.
97 HKRS545-1-456-4, Liao 1-1984 note.
98 HKRS1693/5/3 press release by Pang DDH/C 28-9-1984; HKRS70-8-2048 Liao 9-1984 note; HKRS545-1-456-4 Liao 11-1984 note.
99 HKRS1693/5/3 S Poon to DDH/C Messling, 10-3-1986.

100 Problem contracts: information from Chris Gabriel, 2023. HKRS601-1-5 BPC 9-1983; HKRS276-8-639 4-1986 discussion of programme.
101 HKRS394-25-5 7-1986 housing mix study; HKRS1693-1-3 4-1986 paper.
102 HKRS70-8-2052 9-1986 Pang paper; HKRS545-1-456-6 26-12-1986 Todd paper.
103 HKRS545-1-456-4 7-1983 Liao memo.
104 Yeung and Wong, *Fifty Years*, 245; C K Tsang, *Homeownership in Hong Kong*, Routledge, London, 2021, 58.
105 HKRS545-1-456-4, 2-1982 Cheong-Leen note.
106 Lee, *Housing, Home-Ownership and Social Change*, 210–12.
107 HKRS70-8-2060, 10-1981 cutting.
108 HKRS545-1-456-4, 2-1982 Liao note.
109 Richard Wong, *Hong Kong Land for Hong Kong People*, 29–33; Lee, *Housing, Home-Ownership and Social Change*, 136–40, 266; C K Tsang, *Homeownership in Hong Kong*, 30.
110 HKRS1693-1-3, 11-1985 note; HKRS1881-1-2 5-1983 Arrick note.
111 HKRS461-1-12-12, 8-1983 BC minutes. Lung Poon: HKRS545-1-456-4 11-1984, HKRS461-1-12-2 BC 5-1983 minutes.
112 Housing Authority, *Annual Report*, 1984/5, 55.
113 CK Tsang, *Home Ownership*, 58–9.
114 Castells, *Shek Kip Mei Syndrome*, 10; Housing Authority, *Annual Report*, 1984/5, 75.
115 HKRS545-1-456-5, 21-3-1985 opening of Siu Hong Court by Haddon-Cave.
116 HKRS70-8-3635, 11-1983 Liao speech; HKRS70-8-3670, 11-1983 Liao speech; HKRS545-1-456-4 3-1983 note on MIHP; HKRS163-10-164 12-1982 to 3-1983 correspondence; Special Committee on Land Supply, *Report*, Hong Kong, March 1983, 14.
117 HKRS70-8-2052, 6-1986 Todd quotation.HKRS696-3-7, 22-3-1990 paper on sandwich class.
118 Akers-Jones, 2013 interview.
119 Lee, *Housing, Home-Ownership and Social Change*, 43.
120 Messling, 'Public Housing – A Numbers Game', 3.
121 HKRS163-8-70 5-1983 briefing for LDPC.
122 Special Committee on Land Supply, *Report*, Hong Kong, March 1983, 12.
123 Housing Authority, *Annual Report*, 1984/5, 40.
124 HKRS1882-1-4 LPVC minutes of 7-1982; HKRS163-8-70 LDPC minutes of 3-1983, Planning Standards Sub-Committee; HKRS461-1-12-11, BC 4-1983 on Diamond Hill HO27.
125 Housing Authority, *Annual Report*, 1984/5, 41; HKRS545-1-456-6 5-1986 Crosby on higher densities; HKRS394-25-5 7-1986 housing mix study. 1882-3-19 20-11-1986 Cooper to Department of Territory Development.
126 HKRS1693-1-3, 4-1986 papers.
127 HKRS1693-1-3, 6-6-86 note from Crosby to Housing Secretary; Rosanna Wong, 2014 interview.
128 HKRS1588-9-19, 11-1984 papers.
129 Alice Poon, *Land and the Ruling Class*, 73-6; Castells, *Shek Kip Mei Syndrome*, 45–7; HKRS1004-1-12, 7-1982 paper on rural housing; HKRS1588-2-14, 11-1984 Secretary for Housing letter.
130 HKRS545-1-447-3 11-1984, 12-1984 cuttings on New Towns and 3-1983 key Akers-Jones speech.
131 HKRS545-1-447-3, 24-3-1983 Akers-Jones speech, 'Planning for social and community facilities in the New Towns – a historical perspective'.

132 O'Rorke previously started work on Junk Bay/Tin Shui Wai, and left 1984: HKRS705-2-1 10-1983 O'Rorke note; HKRS70-8-2048 and 545-1-447-3 11-1984 and 12-1984 papers on New Towns.
133 HKRS276-8-639, mid-1986 papers of New Towns and Public Housing Sub-Committee of Public Works Priorities Committee.
134 HKRS597-1-1, 10-1982 papers; HKRS163-8-71, 8-1983 LDPC papers.
135 Castells, *Shek Kip Mei Syndrome*, 29.
136 HKRS70-11-168 7-1984 opinion survey; HKRS 545-1-456-6 8-1986 papers; HKRS 1004-1-13, papers of NW Development Investigation Working Group. HKRS545-1-447-3 8-1984, 10-1984, much information on Tin Shui Wai project history. HKRS454-1-456-6, 5-1986 Ma On Shan progress report (60% to be PRH-HOS-PSPS).
137 HKRS394-25-5 7-1986 Housing Mix Study.
138 Kockelkorn, 'Peripheralisation', 622-3; P-Y Ho, *Making Hong Kong*, Elgar, Cheltenham, 2018.
139 HKRS163-8-69 11-1982 papers; HKRS705-2-1 4-1982 papers.
140 HKRS163-8-71, LDPC 8-1983 papers.
141 HKRS163-8-71, memo of 8-1983; HKRS461-1-12-12 BC minutes of 4-1983.
142 HKRS394-29-208 papers of 7/8-1985.
143 HKRS705-2-2 11/12-1985; HKRS394-25-4, LDPC 31-1-1986, Phase 1 Outline Plan.
144 Lord Wilson, 2023 interview.
145 Castells, *Shek Kip Mei Syndrome*, 34; HKRS394-29-196 4-1984 papers; Lee, *Housing, Home-Ownership and Social Change*, 188; Yeung and Wong, *Fifty Years*, 34–5.
146 Castells, *Shek Kip Mei Syndrome*, 34; Yeung and Wong, *Fifty Years*, 34-5; HKRS545-1-456-4 12-1984 papers.
147 HKRS70-8-4535 1/5-1983 papers; HKRS70-8-2052 1-1986 papers.
148 HKRS70-8-2052 1-1985 papers; HKRS545-1-456-6, 10-1986 Elliott note.
149 HKRS1882-1-4 5-1982 LPVC discussion; Housing Authority, *Annual Report*, 1984/5, 42; HKRS1878-1-4.
150 HKRS70-11-168 6-1984 papers.
151 HKRS70-11-169 12-1984, W K Cheung.
152 HKRS394-29-208 9-1985 on Walled City problem; Akers-Jones, *Feeling the Stones*, 187–8. HKRS1881-3-2 LPVC minutes 26-3-1982.
153 HKRS461-1-2-7, BC minutes 10-1982.
154 HKRS461-1-12-10, BC 2-1983 minutes; HKRS461-1-12-9 BC 20-1-1983; HKRS461-1-2-10 BC 1-1983.
155 HKRS461-1-12-9 24-2-1983 note for BC; HKRS461-1-12-10 2-1983 papers; HKRS461-1-12-11 BC 4-1983 papers.
156 Poon, 2009, 2010 and 2014 interviews; Lambon, 2012 interview.
157 Poon, 2010 interview; Lambon, 2012 interview.
158 Cheung, 2012 interview; Gabriel, 2009 interview; Lambon, 2012 interview.HKRS545-1-456-4, 3-1983 papers; HKRS70-8-3665 5-1983 papers.
159 Lambon, 2012 interview; Poon, 2014 interview.
160 Miller, 2014 interview; Housing Authority, *Annual Report*, 1984/5, 95–8.
161 Trident: HKRS1882-1-4 LPVC 3-1982 minutes; HKRS1881-3-2 10-1981 papers and D Messling to CA/1 12-3-1981; HKRS163-8-64 LDPC 3-1981 minutes; Poon, 2009 interview. Detailed Information on Trident, HKRS545-1-456-3; 461-1-12-5 BC 7-1982, 461-1-12-3 BC 6-1982, 461-1-12-2 BC 4-1982; HKRS545-1-456-3 14-6-1981 article; Lambon, Pritchard and Hall, 2012 interview (including small model of Hing Keng Trident block); Ko, 1983 interview; Ng, 2012 interview; Fung, 2010 interview;

Gabriel, 2009 interview. HKRS461-1-12-8 BC 11-1982 and HKRS461-1-12-3 8-1982 minutes, on comparatively high cost of Trident blocks, mainly in frame costs, also with efficiency rate of lettable to gross floor area of only 69% for Trident 1 and 2 compared with 72.5% for slab blocks. 'Avoid monotony', HKRS1881-3-2 CA/4 at LPVC 26-3-1982, 7-1-81 S K Lo to CA/4.

162 Lambon, 2012 interview.

163 HKRS461-1-12-9 BC minutes of 1-1983.

164 HKRS461-1-12-6 BC 8-1982 minutes; Siu Hong 'giant' scheme', HKRS545-1-456-3.

165 HKRS 1882-1-3 LPVC 26-9-77; Ng, 2012 interview; Lambon, 2012 interview.

166 Dave Hall and John Lambon, 2012 interview.

167 HKRS70-8-3665 BC 2-1983 minutes; HKRS70-11-168 2-1984 papers.

168 SCMP 11-3-1984, 10; HKRS 545-1-456-4 Messling note of 3-1984.

169 HKRS545-1-456-4, SCMP 11-1984 cutting.

170 Housing Authority, *Annual Report*, 1984/5, 55.

171 HD Construction Branch, *Portfolio of Works*, 1986, Messling introduction.

172 Lambon, 2012 interview.

173 Lambon, 2012 interview; Castells, *Shek Kip Mei Syndrome*, 53–4.

174 Castells, *Shek Kip Mei Syndrome*, 53-4; HKRS461-1-12-10, BC 2-1983 minutes.

175 Castells, *Shek Kip Mei Syndrome*, 53-4; Lambon, 2012 interview; Gabriel, 2009 interview.

176 HKRS461-1-12-10, 2-1983 BC minutes; HKRS545-1-456-5 3/4-1985 articles; HKRS70-8-2052 6-1985 D Ford note, 10-1985 papers; SCMP 2-2-86.

177 Messling, 'Public Housing – A Numbers Game', 3; HKRS545-1-456-5, 4-1985 Messling article rebutting criticisms of 26 blocks crisis to Association for Promotion of Public Justice, and 1986 Messling briefing for HA members of progress of Kwai Hing estate redevelopment. Lambon, 2012 interview. HKRS545-1-456-6, 1986 cutting on Shan Tsui. HKRS545-3-369, 13-8-1988 cutting (Messling).

178 HKRS461-1-12-7, BC 7-82 tenders; Housing Authority, *Annual Report*, 1982/3, 34; Dave Hall, 2012 interview.

179 Dave Hall, 2012 interview.

180 HKRS461-1-12-9 BC 1-1983 minutes.

181 HKRS696-3-120 Pang at 7-1984 BC.

182 HKRS70-11-69 11-1984 report by Ford.

183 HKRS70-11-168, 7-1984 BC papers.

184 SCMP 16-3-1986, 12, Messling speech.

185 Poon, 2009 interview; Gabriel, 2009 interview and 2023 information.

10 1987–1992

The Wilson years – accelerated decolonisation and the Housing Strategy

Introduction: a low-key decolonisation?

By the late 1980s, the Sino-British settlement on the future of Hong Kong seemed to have brought a new stability, allowing government policies and strategies stretching beyond 1997, and exploiting the economic opening-up of China, to be developed in areas such as housing – as exemplified in the 1987 Long-Term Housing Strategy. The shocking impact of the 4 June 1989 Beijing crackdown, however, threw this progress up in the air, and the remaining decade of British rule would see an uneasy mixture of continued practical decolonisation and intermittent political tension. Yet throughout this period, the housing drive continued to unfold, steadily, as an autonomous cultural and socio-economic phenomenon within the 'interstitial space' of Hong Kong between two sovereignties. (Figure 10.1)

In the first five years of that decade, during the governorship of Sir David Wilson, the emphasis throughout was on continuity and avoidance of confrontation with China. Wilson, a professional Foreign Office diplomat and China specialist, born and educated in Central Scotland, had spent six years in 1968–74 editing the journal *China Quarterly*, and then, significantly, served as MacLehose's political adviser on relations with the mainland in 1977–81. He echoed Youde in his relatively low-key and modest approach, as opposed to (according to one journalist in 1988) 'the… moral certitude that Lord MacLehose once wore like a crown'. However, with his journalistic experience, Wilson departed from his predecessors in emphasising 'open government' through press conferences and public engagement, believing that 'gone are the days when the government could make difficult and controversial decisions without holding public opinion firmly in mind'.[1]

Concerning sovereignty, Wilson shared with both his predecessors, and with key Whitehall sinologists such as Sir Percy Cradock, a pragmatic appreciation of the colonial regime's declining power, and believed that in the wake of the Agreement, the most that could now be achieved would be to 'insulate' Hong Kong against the uncertainties of 1997 rather than aspire to 'determine Hong Kong's destiny' in any way. However, the three major policy initiatives announced in his 1989 annual address, in response to Tiananmen – the building of a new airport at Chek Lap Kok, the passing of the bill of rights to protect Hongkongers' freedoms post-1997, and the granting of British passports to members of the elite – became immediately

DOI: 10.1201/9781315563701-13

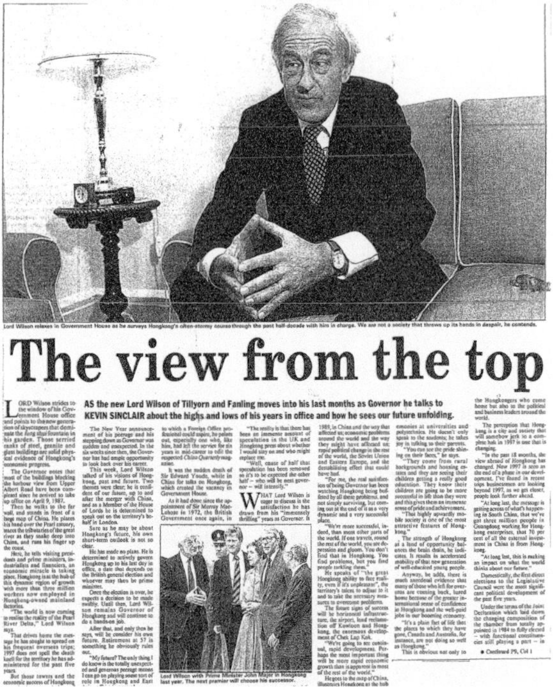

Lord Wilson relaxes in Government House as he surveys Hongkong's often-stormy course through the past half-decade with him in charge. We are not a society that throws up its hands in despair, he contends.

The view from the top

AS the new Lord Wilson of Tillyorn and Fanling moves into his last months as Governor he talks to KEVIN SINCLAIR about the highs and lows of his years in office and how he sees our future unfolding.

Lord Wilson with Prime Minister John Major in Hongkong last year. The next premier will choose his successor.

Figure 10.1 Retrospective SCMP article in February 1992, at the end of Lord Wilson's governorship – in which he set out a personal vision of Hong Kong's future, as the cornerstone of the coming 'economic miracle' of the Pearl River Delta.

mired in controversy both with China and Britain. Within domestic policy, Wilson argued that China meanwhile had no 'veto over decisions', and that 'this will be the decade of greater freedom of choice politically… now is the time for Hong Kong to develop its own leaders, to find Hong Kong solutions to Hong Kong problems'. In 2023, he recalled that in its relations with London concerning domestic policy, the Hong Kong government had now achieved a position of 'almost complete autonomy – what on earth would we have wanted or needed authority for from London? And that impacted on housing, because issues like that were entirely Hong Kong Government ones, not London at all!'[2]

On the key social-economic issues facing the community, however, Wilson emphasised continuity with his predecessors, arguing in his 1990 annual address that while Hong Kong had already created a thriving, well-equipped urban community after the 'sacrifices' of the early postwar decades, the challenge now was to further 'improve our social services without creating the sort of dependency culture found in some Western welfare states' – with a further enhancement of housing, and a shift towards home-ownership and private enterprise, leading the way. He recalled that 'Cowperthwaite had been hugely influential earlier on, and a

"Cowperthwaitian" attitude persisted throughout my time in Hong Kong'.[3] During this period the process of 'localisation' within government gathered pace, although in July 1988 Sir David Ford, Akers-Jones's successor as Chief Secretary (1987–93), predicted that a third of department heads would still be expatriates after 1997. Financial Secretary (1986–91), Sir Piers Jacobs was succeeded by Sir Hamish Macleod (1991–5): Chris Patten later recalled the combination of 'Ford, politically shrewd and subtle; Macleod, clear-headed and direct'.[4]

Although for much of Wilson's governorship, the most high-profile external pressure was still the continuing influx of Vietnamese 'boat people', the relationship with China was naturally always dominant in the background.[5] Chief Secretary Ford spelt out the historical reality of the relationship for the first time in January 1988, noting that 'to move towards independence has never been an option for Hong Kong. This a very important limitation: it has always been well understood by the people of Hong Kong', as has the fact that Beijing 'has always had the power to change substantially the way of life for Hong Kong but has never done it'. For example, although the spring 1962 influx had provided 'a graphic warning' of what would happen 'if China chooses to open the floodgates of emigration', in practice, in 1982 it had agreed to limit emigrants to 27,500 each year.[6]

The Joint Liaison Group continued to meet for 13 years in Beijing and London.[7] As early as 1987, however, signs of instability in China, including student demonstrations and the sacking of CCP chief Hu Yaobang and other officials, began to provoke unease in Hong Kong. In the immediate wake of the June 1989 violence, however, the potential post-1997 fate of Hong Kong provoked conflicted reactions even within professional spheres such as the 'housing community'. For example, in a public advertisement, the staff of the HD Architects Department condemned 'the brutal suppression of the peaceful struggle for freedom and democracy in China' but stressed more pragmatically that

> we will continue to stand firm in our commitment to the public housing development programme and would like to appeal to the people of Hong Kong to join us in making every effort to contribute to the stability of Hong Kong and the future of China.[8]

More pragmatically still, Donald Liao's valedictory in November 1989 on his final retirement from government after 29 years' service, latterly as the most senior Chinese civil servant, expressed a fervent hope that on 1 July 1997 'things will still be the same and it will just be another day': whereas his retirement only affected a small circle of people, 1997 'affects everybody', but his experience as a member of the Joint Liaison Group led him to hope that Beijing would honour the promise of 'one country, two systems', and that in that case 'I see a very bright future in Hong Kong'.[9] In contrast to Murray MacLehose's adoption of a 'low profile' externally, Wilson's task now was a slightly different one, namely to actively persuade external opinion that Hong Kong would 'continue as it was' after 1997 – 'so I made all sorts of visits, to the US, to France, Germany, Singapore and so forth'.[10]

Adjusting the political system: paternalism to participation

Internally, according to Steve Tsang, the Basic Law of the Hong Kong SAR, whose first draft was published in April 1988 and which was promulgated in April 1990, committed China to 'a Chinese version of the British crown colony system of government'.[11] The reining-in of the tentative 1987 democratisation proposals in 1988 chimed in with that position.[12] However, that late-colonial system was now significantly evolving. In an October 1988 speech at CUHK, Akers-Jones argued that as Hong Kong's sovereignty constraints had prevented it from developing along 'normal' decolonised lines, an alternative system had had to be developed during the 20th century, including negligible taxation, consensus government, and no elections – a formula which had 'contributed greatly to our progress and prosperity'. Seen in hindsight, he claimed, the 'most beneficial bequest of colonialism' would not be 'political stereotypes of the West' like parliamentary democracy, but the 'peace and stability' conferred by Hong Kong's unique administrative and legal system, including district administration, public and semi-public organisations and privately supported social provision for a 'caring society'. Under this system, the 'government supports, subvents and subsidises but stays in the background and tries not to interfere'. He concluded that 'it would be a sad day for Hong Kong should these organisations be allowed to wither away, to be replaced by armies of civil servants and a multitude of public-sector institutions'.[13] Under this view, the colonial government's posture of staying neutral and above sectional interests helped give it some legitimacy, despite its lack of an elected mandate.

In 1988, the first territory-wide District Board elections were held, for 264 out of 462 seats, that would in turn return 10 members to LegCo, and the 4,295 MACs also a growing force – divided roughly 2:1 between urban areas and the New Territories. Turnout was only 30%, which, journalist Bernard Fong argued, reflected the fact that the government was now 'powerless to effect serious change' pending the finalisation of the Basic Law in Beijing.[14] But a new kind of restricted representative politics was now developing, the old 'CCP versus KMT' politics having now disappeared. Among the new parties such as the pro-Beijing Liberals, June 1989 brought a period of confusion.[15] But some of the old politicians were still around. In March 1989 Brook Bernacchi won Shaukeiwan ward, pledging to clear hawkers: he was branded 'a benevolent patron… not particularly big on democracy, but charitable and with a sense of duty', seeing local politics as 'a wealthy man's duty', and hoping that the Basic Law could be improved, not challenged. He stayed on the Urban Council until 1994, and Forsgate chaired the Council from 1986 to 1991.[16] From the perspective of professionals in the Housing Department, the main impact of growing public participation was in estate participation, with most comments from district boards, MACs, etc. relating to management issues rather than design. There was a growing shift, as earlier in Western countries, away from contentment at paternalist provision to growing discontent: 'Whatever we did was wrong – rising expectations, steered by political motives – it was a problem of success!'[17]

Alongside all the new domestic political excitement, however, commercial and industrial involvements with China were soaring, with 14% of Housing Authority building contracts between January 1987 and June 1988 awarded to mainland firms, and general trade with China growing by 15% in 1990 and an astonishing 27% in the first seven months of 1991 alone.[18] Eventually, two decades later, the flow would reverse course, with a torrent of mainland capital into Hong Kong, but for the moment the influence was all in the outward direction: Bernard Williams recalled consultancies at World Bank summer-schools in Shanghai around 1987, in which '"learning from Hong Kong" was the cry'.[19]

Correspondingly, the old links with Britain now became more intermittent and unpredictable. In January 1987, for example, Poon and Messling welcomed a highly incongruous visitor, in the form of the rabidly anti-modernist geographer Alice Coleman, arch-critic of tower blocks in England for their alleged encouragement of vandalism and crime, and author of the 1985 book *Utopia on Trial*. Pictured in a Housing Authority press release inspecting a model of the towers of Shun Lee Estate, following a tour of Tsui Ping and Lok Wah estates, and Lok Nga Court HOS, Coleman professed herself 'deeply impressed by the security in Hong Kong's public housing estates', arguing that 'the people have the chance to make their homes individual'. Poon recalled optimistically that 'after the visit, she was converted – she came to be educated by us!'[20] (cf. Figure 9.4).

The economy: return to expansion

As the end of British rule came in sight, and the 'financialisation' of the Hong Kong economy kicked into high gear, fiscal autonomy and the low-tax, budget-surplus regime (which kept public-spending rises strictly proportionate to growing GDP), continued to be the basis of the territory's economic policies. By 1997 the government had achieved surpluses in 45 of its budgets since 1945, despite the monetary mismanagement that had required the bailing-out of the ailing financial sector in the 1980s.[21]

A new resilience in the face of the recurrent market cycles was demonstrated in late 1987/early 1988. On 19 October 1987, following a Wall Street slump, the Hong Kong stock market lost $65 billion and the Hang Seng dropped by over 10%. As Jacobs noted in his March 1988 budget speech, Hong Kong was now embroiled in another boom–slump cycle, but this downturn would prove short-lived: overall, between 1987 and 1997, the average growth rate was 4.2%, allowing public spending as a percentage of GDP in 1997 to fall back below its level in the early 1980s.[22] The surge in government revenue which began in 1986/7 had continued in 1987/8, with two years of double-digit growth: GDP growth was 8.5% in 1986 and 6% in 1987, despite the October 1987 stock market slump. A much higher surplus in the General Revenue Account, of $7.6 billion, was now expected. Two years of renewed growth had allowed further increases in services and tax cuts at the same time, and expenditure on the Consolidated Account had been at 7% in real terms (1.5% above budget). Of this, the redevelopment of Kowloon Walled City (see below) had accounted for 1.2% of growth in the CA.[23]

This relatively favourable picture only bolstered the prestige of the principles of fiscal autonomy among the late-colonial elite, which was beginning to look to its post-1997 reputation. Reviewing Jacobs's August 1988 mid-year budget reassessment, the SCMP argued that thanks to the Joint Declaration he would have to be 'even more conservative than his predecessors', and that 'if Britain is to walk away from Hong Kong with honour, Mr Jacobs (and successors) will have to produce some masterful fine-tuning of the economy'. The underlying resilience of the economy was stressed: although in the early 1980s, boom had turned to bust and Bremridge had been 'scrambling to keep his budget deficits as small as possible… by 1986 business confidence had returned'.[24] Wilson recalled that 'on one visit from a senior Chinese official, the governor of Guangxi province I think, I was trying to get across the fact that we were highly autonomous, and I gave him this example: "We're coming up to a new budget. The Financial Secretary consults me about it, and I can make changes if I want, but it only becomes known to the Executive Council the day before it is introduced at the LegCo – and a copy of the budget is sent down to London, but it isn't *opened* until the Financial Secretary is on his feet making the statement in LegCo". The official looked at me pityingly, as if to say, "Do you really expect me to believe this is true?" But it was!'

In his March 1989 budget speech, Jacobs highlighted a rise in inflation (to 7.5% in 1988), and accumulating budget surpluses ($15 billion in 1988/9 as opposed to $5.5 billion budgeted) being covered by three years of 'exceptional' economic performance, with 6% expected in 1989 (7.5% in 1988). Hong Kong had survived the October 1987 stock market crash largely unscathed, and its entrepot role had now revived. Consolidated government reserves were $60 billion in 1988/9, and would be $71 billion the following year. Jacobs argued that the surpluses now needed to be invested in a major infrastructure programme. The expenditure of $14.5 billion was 12% above budget, largely due to the new financial arrangements for the HA, including the handing-over to the Authority of the Home Ownership Fund: the hiving-off of the Housing Authority was not an 'abdication of responsibility'. For now, expenditure on housing would only rise by 5% (social services 13%, transport and environment 10%).[25]

A year later, the picture was surprisingly similar, despite the new need to restore confidence in the wake of June 1989: commentators argued it was 'essential that Hong Kong Incorporated puts on the bravest of faces'.[26] In his March 1990 budget, Jacobs recorded that GDP had only grown at 2.5% in 1989 (sharply down from 14% in 1987) and argued the need was for consolidation, with a budget surplus for 1988/9 of 'only' 9.3 billion as opposed to the estimated 11.3 billion. Yet consolidated public-sector expenditure would rise sharply as part of confidence-rebuilding, and would be 29% above the actual figure for 1988: the 1990/1 estimates envisaged the housing programme would account for around one-eighth of total expenditure, including clearance of Kowloon Walled City, while overall public expenditure would rise to 19% of GDP (compared to 17% in 1989–90).[27]

The revenue from land sales played an important and ambiguous role in this expansion of spending. Revenue from land sales alone produced an average of 10% to 13% of total government revenue between 1970 and 1998, but with wild fluctuations (1970–1, 7%; 1980–1, 35%; 1983–4, 6%; 1992–3, 7%): the late '70s, early '80s and late '80s saw booms in property value and land revenue, the mid '80s and early '90s saw slumps in both. But as Akers-Jones argued, the dependency spread far wider: in the late 1980s, for example, the revenue from land sales, property taxes, stamp duty, bank profits and taxes on property company income amounted to as much as 50% of government income and 'played an unreliable and unhealthily dominant role in the economy'. The property price slumps during recessions would thus trigger wider falls in government revenue. However, Wilson denied that there was any deliberate government policy to restrict land supply and keep prices high: 'That wasn't a deliberate policy, that would have been too Machiavellian, and the Hong Kong Government wasn't a particularly Machiavellian set-up!'[28] But at any rate, by the early '90s, the land shortage, along with inadequate competition, and supply cartels between the large developers, of whom only six built 75% of flats, was certainly leading to high house prices and declining affordability, and starting to slow home-ownership growth.[29]

Housing and the economy: from slump to boom

In the housing sector, despite all the economic vicissitudes, the wider context of the 1980s and early '90s was of sharp expansion: between 1981 and 1996, the percentage of household spending on housing rose from 20% to 30%. On the back of this, a formidable private speculative housing sector had now mushroomed at the heart of Hong Kong's new financial and service economy, creating a new elite of property 'tycoons', such as Li Ka-shing or the Kwok brothers, who exerted an increasingly inordinate, cartel-like influence on government housing and land policy, not least by themselves building up massive New Territories land-banks.[30]

Within the public housing sector, this expansion coincided with renewed growth in public expenditure (by 15.7% on Consolidated Account in cash terms), but also with a relative shift in emphasis away from housing towards transport and other spending areas such as medical and social services.[31] But it also coincided with soaring costs stemming partly from rampant labour shortages, and partly from rising standards, with the new Harmony blocks (see Chapter 11) costing an estimated 30% more than existing ones. The extra costs were predicted in November 1989 to add $770 million to the housing bill: rising HA expenditure had helped raise government estimates from $1.4 to $2.2 billion in 1989/90 and from $2.9 to $4 billion in 1990–1 (a 70% jump). The Deputy Director of Housing (Administration and Policy), Nigel French, noted that the average cost of a Housing Authority unit had increased by 19% from June 1988 to June 1989, but the Housing Authority still forecast a $1.8 billion surplus for 1990/1.[32] These years also witnessed a significant devolution of power to the Housing Authority, or 'corporatisation' (see below). In October 1987 Treasury Chief Accountant Hassan Faruqi gave the Asian Pacific Housing Conference a detailed account of the HA's existing financial settlement of 1 April 1976, and set out the new and hopefully more 'flexible' system.[33] Yet in January 1991 Messling reported that the HA's continued cash flow problems would leave it 20,000 units short of its 228,000 construction target for 1991–6, and suggested in compensation that it would need to build 170,000 rather than 125,000 units in the following five years; the Authority had not yet decided whether to borrow money from the private sector to meet the 1991/2 FY deficit.[34]

The end of the 1987–92 period was marked by a sharp upturn in economic optimism, but also the first warnings of future overheating in the housing sector. In early 1992, Hamish Macleod's budget speech predicted GDP growth of 5% for 1992, as opposed to 4% and 3% in 1991 and 1990, respectively, and a budget surplus of $14 billion as opposed to the $13 billion previously estimated. On that basis he proposed a $14 billion boost in government spending, to $115 billion, allowing social spending to rise, including in 'our traditional areas of strength which we often take for granted', such as housing, with 39,000 more flats to be built in the current year.[35] 1992/3 government expenditure was predicted as 19% of estimated GDP (18% the previous year). In April 1992 the 'first signs of life' in the property market following the October bank lending restrictions were detected, with warnings by Brooke Hillier Parker that prices could increase by 15% over the year, heading back beyond first-time-buyer affordability.[36] As we will see in Chapter 12, during the term of office of Wilson's successor, Chris Patten, this revival would develop into a full-blown housing bubble, with unexpected long-term consequences for the viability of public housing production.

Inaugurating the Long-Term Housing Strategy

The immediate housing response to this improvement in the macro-economic environment, and the gathering transformation in Hong Kong's economy, was the Long-Term Housing Strategy, announced in April 1987 and subsequently proselytised extensively at a professional, academic and public level, not least by special meetings of all District Boards.[37] It was an elaboration and extension of the existing PHDP framework, rather than a revolutionary change from it: the existing programme absorbed a third of the government's capital works spending, and the Strategy was costed at $20 billion over the years to 2001. Liao stressed on 8 April 1987 that this was not a 'change in housing policy'.[38] Fung Tung recalled that 'I was terribly involved in developing it, along with Freddie Pang, who was Director before me, and John Todd, then Secretary for Housing. It was a refinement by the Governor of the earlier ten-year framework, which extended further the ten-year housing programme. It accepted that a ten-year 'solution' couldn't be achieved, so we moved to a Long-Term Housing Programme, as the standard was constantly rising'.[39]

The Housing Strategy addressed a range of short- and longer-term problems, and shifted towards a demand-led rather than supply-led approach intended to promote social stability and a sense of belonging to Hong Kong, while reconfiguring the entire territory in the interests of capitalist modernisation.[40] It built on existing policy trends, including the perceived shift in demand from rental to home-ownership, and the boosting of the standard of rental housing, especially by redevelopment of Resettlement estates. Now, the redevelopment programme was extended to include all pre-1973 Group B (Resettlement and GLCH) estates, contributing to a new target of 1,085,000 new flats needed by 2001, rather than the existing 980,000 target. A new system of subsidised home-ownership, the Home Purchase Loan Scheme (HPLS), beginning with a modest initial tranche of 2,000 loans, was intended to supplement the HOS and increase home-ownership opportunities for public rental tenants.[41] The reorganisation of the Housing Authority and its financial support (see below) would underpin this, Todd argued in November 1987. A revised PHDP in March 1987 included the new redevelopment programme, complete with bar charts and safety margins. The LTHS's emphatic shift towards promotion of home-ownership unsurprisingly provoked controversy, including a major LegCo debate in July 1987, as well as some criticisms from housing academics on grounds of lack of coherence.[42]

In his public-relations capacity, Messling riposted in a September 1987 speech that the government had been 'putting off the long-term solution for far too long', and that an annual output of around 70,000 would be required for the foreseeable future, split 30,000/40,000 between private and public sectors. This open avowal of the open-endedness of the public housing drive was a decisive turning-point in administrative and political mentality, pointing forward into the post-1997 years: Messling argued that 'no-one should think for one minute that the year 2001 will see by some act of magic the end, or even the running-down, of the housing programme. It simply does not happen like that. It's rather like the popular sign hanging over the public bar, "Free beer tomorrow!" – but tomorrow never comes!'[43] And in December 1987 Todd reported that while a 'record' 56,000 public-housing flats would be built in 1988, continued maintenance of the standing 40,000 annual target, which included a 10,000–15,000 safety margin, depended vitally on the Territorial Development Strategy producing sites in the near future.[44] In August 1988, too, Stephen Poon argued that the 'demand-led' character of the Strategy made it inevitable it would carry on beyond 2001, with an increasing percentage of post-1993 output coming from urban redevelopment; three new block types were under development for this programme.[45]

In practice, the first period of the Housing Strategy, up to 1991, was dominated by the ups and downs of the globally driven private property market (increasing by 332% in 1989–97), which ensured that the LTHS aspiration of 60% home-ownership by 1997 would be substantially under-achieved: the home-ownership level would reach only 35% in 1986, 44% 1996, and a maximum of 53% in 2006.[46] Other competing construction demands impacted on progress. In October 1988, Edward Ho warned LTHS targets would have to be revised following the decision to ban foreign building workers, and the consequent labour shortages; although 150,000 flats were under construction, it was unclear if 60,000 could be completed in 1989.[47] In March 1990, three years after the Housing Strategy's launch, the Housing Authority announced it was to be extended from 2001 to 2011, including an extra 131,000 units, on top of the currently anticipated total of 900,000 new completions by 2001. HA chairman David Akers-Jones explained that potential sites for post-2001 construction were being identified, but that reclamations in West Kowloon and Lantau would be crucial.[48] And in July 1991 Edward Ho claimed the

Strategy was 'on course', with sites identified for over 90% of the 410,000 public flats now planned to be built between then and the turn of the century, of which 55% would be HOS: use of the new, higher-standard 'Harmony' blocks (see below) would ensure rental and HOS occupiers all enjoyed larger kitchens.[49]

Housing supply, according to a Knight Frank report, was now growing at twice the rate of demand, with only 158,000 needing better accommodation but the stock expanding by 79,500 a year, with more than half of new flats (46,000) publicly built: housing supply would be more than ample by 1994 and so the government, they argued, must rein in public housing production or risk oversupply by 1995 and weakening residential prices.[50] But as we will see in Chapter 12, that warning of a housing glut by the mid-1990s would prove wildly off the mark, owing above all to the pervasive problems of land supply.

The 'corporatisation' of the Housing Authority

The planning and implementation of the Housing Strategy was intimately bound up with a radical change in its organisational position. During these, the Housing Authority's first completely 'post-Liao' years, the HA underwent its most significant transformation, in the form of a so-called 'corporatisation' (conversion of a government organisation into an autonomous entity). This reform was intended to increase its flexibility and responsiveness, as part of the Housing Strategy's philosophy of demand-led activity – and was celebrated in the commissioning of a grand new headquarters in Fat Kwong Street, Ho Man Tin, in 1987.[51]

The key to the new arrangement, approved by ExCo in September 1987, was the abolition of the government Housing Branch and the post of Secretary for Housing, and transfer of their responsibilities to an expanded HA, chaired preferably by an unofficial ExCo member, reporting direct to the Governor. In some ways this would return the Housing Authority to its pre-1973 status but on a vastly larger scale – although the Housing Authority had always retained a policymaking role even during the 1973–88 period. Without doubt, this represented the high point of the influence of the unofficials within public housing – following which the trajectory would be one of steady administrative aggrandisement, as we will see in Chapters 12 and 13.[52] This 1988 reorganisation was facilitated by the imminent retiral of Housing Secretary Todd, who stayed on for six months to oversee the transition. The HA's specific functions would stay largely the same, although some design responsibilities would pass to Lands and Works Branch, and the Planning, Environment and Lands Secretary, Tony Eason, would eventually act as an intermediary with government on some housing issues.[53]

Todd stressed in November 1987 that the new Housing Authority would be the 'cornerstone' of the Housing Strategy, and – vitally – would enjoy a financial autonomy commensurate with its new organisational autonomy. This would be conferred through a massive dowry in the form of a $13,251 million loan from the DLF, supplemented by the transfer of the $377 million Home Ownership Fund (the Housing Authority previously having been merely the government's agent for HOS) and the promise of a further $10,000 million reserve that could be drawn down at will between 1989 and 1994.[54] This continued the existing trend of steeply growing government capital injections to the Housing Authority – from nil in 1973 to $10,000 million in 1980, $40,000 million in 1988/9 and over $150,000 million in 1993/4.[55] In compensation, the Authority's commercial properties would now be treated as the government's 'non-domestic equity' in the organisation: this commercial contribution to HA income rose from 13% in 1976 to 32% in 1989.[56] Rosanna Wong (HA Chairman from 1993) argued the corporatisation had occurred because 'people believed that it would allow for more independence from government bureaucracy, thus making room for greater efficiency and flexibility'.[57]

The Housing Strategy envisaged allocating nearly HK$700,000 million more funds to the HA over the period 1991–2001. As of 1991/2, the Housing Authority had a 'healthy income' of 1.3 billion from its commercial properties as in previous years, and shared the net surplus with government: the total inflow of cash from HOS/PSPS was $4.1 billion.[58] And the following year's Annual Review related that the last $1.23 billion balance of the $10 billion Government capital injection pledged after 1988 had now been drawn down, raising the government's permanent capital in the Authority to $26.3 billion: the HA received $2.9 billion from commercial projects and shared the $1.6 billion net surplus equally with the government.[59]

A key step in corporatisation was the appointment of the new Housing Authority Chairman. This was bundled together with those for the Land Development Corporation and the Housing Society, with Akers-Jones, conservative LegCo councillor Hu Fa-Kuang and former MTR chairman Norman Thompson initially seen as being in contention. The HS was increasingly retrenching into a specialist role, focusing on the Urban Improvement Scheme and (by 1992) housing for the elderly, with one large-scale development in these years at Clague Garden, Tsuen Wan – an array of three towers, one for rental and two for sale, designed by Palmer & Turner on similar cluster lines to Sui Wo Court.[60]

In the event, February 1988 brought the 'surprise move' of the appointment of Akers-Jones as chairman of the 'newly independent Housing Authority, now freed from Government chains'. (Figure 10.2) Although older than the others, Akers-Jones was Hong Kong-domiciled rather than expatriate, and with a strong track-record in administrative affairs – he conceded that he had not been interviewed for the post, as 'the Government knows me enough'. Wilson recalled that 'he was an extremely knowledgeable and competent person and the idea was, how can we use his talent? The poor chap – he'd been Chief Secretary, then Acting Governor following Teddy Youde's death, so he couldn't go back to what he was doing, but here his talent could be used – it was ideal for him!'[61] Given their affinity at a working and personal level, the direct reporting line to the Governor here made very good sense. And once established as Chairman, as a fluent Cantonese speaker Akers-Jones established a 'godfather-like' relationship (as Fung Tung put it) vis-a-vis tenants. His stated policy aim was to 'make sure that "the machine" continues to work smoothly towards building as many flats as possible' while shifting emphasis towards home-ownership.[62] By 1991, 40% of new public-housing units should be for sale, rising to 65% in 2001. He argued it was chiefly land shortages

Sir David Akers-Jones helps with the balloting for phase 10A of the Home Ownership Scheme.

Figure 10.2 Sir David Akers-Jones, in his role as Housing Authority Chairman, officiates at the ballot for Phase 10a of the Home Ownership Scheme: 1989 SCM P article.

that prevented the Housing Authority from boosting annual public production above 40,000–45,000, but that overall production, public and private, must be maintained at around 80,000 to achieve the Strategy aims, in 'one global attack on housing problems in Hong Kong' – not language that Cowperthwaite would ever have used.[63] Reflecting this approach, Akers-Jones led a visit in April 1989 (his fifth since 1978) to see Singapore's 'integrated and comprehensive' programme, including the HOPS, of which 441,000 units had so far been sold, and hosted a reciprocal HDB visit to Hong Kong in 1990.[64]

Akers-Jones also involved himself in detail in a range of Housing Authority policies: for example, in building and architecture, as we will see in Chapter 11, he intervened significantly in 1988 in the planning of a new 'family' of Housing Authority tower block types, as well as instigating its name – the 'Harmony'. There was also a measured 'democratisation' of the processes of public housing, reflecting his recognition, like Wilson, of the limits of political innovation now feasible for the Hong Kong Government. The membership of the Authority was extended to include critics in decision-making: former HKPCPHP head Fung Kin Lee had already been appointed in 1985, with LegCo councillor and former Ho Man Tin squatter resident Ms Leung Wai-Tung; activist Lee Wing-Tat was added in 1990, and others followed. In December 1987 the PHCPHP argued that under the 1988 reform the government would be reducing rather than increasing HA funding.[65] Akers-Jones conceded public access to only selected Authority meetings, and tried to prevent these from being 'hijacked' by protest groups, as happened in September 1991 when HKPCPHP demonstrators unfurled banners and punched security guards at the first publicly open meeting.[66] The continued strength of public-rental housing in Hong Kong increased the potential for bottom-up protest and public input, in comparison to government-dominated Singapore: in Stephen Poon's opinion (2009), whereas the Singaporean government kept firmly in charge by 'locking people into mortgages', in Hong Kong 'the government has much less

Figure 10.3 Sir David Akers-Jones, seen in 2014 at his office in the Hopewell Centre (MG).

power', and with growing public participation, 'the people who rent can demand everything and not pay anything – they are telling the Housing Authority what to do. Half of our population is controlling the Housing Authority'.[67] Eventually, as Fung Tung recalled, 'too many social pressures piled up' on Akers-Jones.[68] And as we will see in Chapter 12, the final straw was the departure of Wilson in 1992 and his replacement as governor by Chris Patten, whose ideas and plans were very different in character. (Figure 10.3)

The corporatisation process naturally had a significant impact on HD staff, including the architects. Following the reorganisation, the HD pay structure was reshaped in April 1988, with a plan to upgrade some directorate posts in line with the Ross Committee on directorate salaries. Following the abolition of the Housing Secretaryship, Freddie Pang was upgraded to D6 (Secretary) level, although his official title remained 'Director', as HA chief executive. Various Deputy Directors were upgraded, including Messling, to reflect additional responsibilities.[69] The progress of 'localisation' among the architects remained patchy. On the one hand, it was strongly encouraged in personnel policy by the late 1980s and 1990s, and the organisation of expatriate contracts into discrete 'tours of duty' was arguably a deterrent to continuity and efficiency.[70] Young Hong Kong-trained architects were now rising to senior positions within the production system originally established by MacLehose and Liao. Stephen Poon, for example, rose from a junior architect in 1973 to Senior Architect in 1977, Chief Architect in 1980, Assistant Director in 1986, Senior Assistant Director in 1994, and Deputy Director of Housing in 1997. He recalled that 'I went to the Housing Department at the right time', but that promotion brought an inexorable shift away from active design involvement: as a Chief Architect, 'I was like director in a private firm', heading projects; but as Assistant Director he was 'mainly working on policy'.

Yet even in the late 1980s, more attractive private-sector pay continued impacting negatively on this agenda. Within housing architecture, recruitment problems compelled a continued reliance on expatriate staff. Here the prime example was the ascendancy of Derek Messling as the 'driving force' (Poon) within the Construction Branch, retiring eventually in 1993.[71] John Lambon argued that

> when you had someone like Derek Messling at the helm, in the early '90s, you had a powerhouse representative at the Building Committee. He and Penny, every night, would leave with an empty desk at 5PM, whereas there were some other colleagues, in later years, who would have stuff piled high, and would stay until 10PM! When outside political pressure started, questions in the committees became tough, but they could handle it: Derek was a figurehead, and Penny was a figurehead too – the expat Chief Architects in these years were Bob Storey, Tim Nutt and Penny Ward.[72]

Alongside his efficiency reputation, Messling also cultivated some more quirkish characteristics, including a passion, common to many expatriates, for entering competitions. In February 1991, for example, he won a British Airways/ *Sunday Morning Post* 'Concorde Connection' competition, his name having been drawn from over 6,000 entries by BA chairman Lord King in London: the prize included two first-class return tickets to London and Concorde flights to and from New York (accompanied by Penny Ward); and the following April, he won a champagne dinner for four at the Mandarin Oriental Hotel in *Sunday Money*'s 'Luxury Index' contest, by correctly guessing that 273,000 bottles of champagne were consumed in Hong Kong the previous year.[73] Despite the increasingly massive scale of Hong Kong's public-housing apparatus, its leading figures were emphatically not 'faceless state-socialist bureaucrats' by any definition! (Figure 10.4)

During this period, Messling's principal strategic contribution, building on Liao's legacy, was to put the Housing Strategy into effect, while turning unexpected crises and challenges to advantage in boosting the Construction Branch's prestige, exploiting the media rapport established during the '26 Blocks' crisis.[74] (Figure 10.5) In September 1987, he argued against the proposition that resources should be focused on short-term housing need: 'Nonsense! We have been putting off the long-term solution for far too long, and at this rate, there will never be a long-term solution, only an ever-present short-term problem'.[75] But despite Messling's efforts, the combination of democratisation and rising expectations were fundamentally changing public attitudes to the Housing Department's architects. Beforehand, one recalled, 'we were heroes to the Hong Kong community, you got praised for what you did, because we didn't have a representative LegCo: there was no need to fear when the Housing Authority did anything wrong' – whereas now a far more sceptical attitude began to prevail.[76]

Land policy and the Housing Strategy

To implement the Housing Strategy properly, Messling argued, the most pressing constraint was land supply. Here, the corporatisation process had left a significant gap in responsibilities, with the new Housing Authority further removed from government land-planning than it had been previously. As early as April 1990, senior

BA boss Lord King drawing the contest winner last week.

Lucky winner Derek Messling yesterday, a man looking to mix business with pleasure when he flies the Concorde from London to New York.

Winner claims his seats

ARCHITECT Mr Derek Messling hopes to mix business with pleasure when he wings his way from London to New York on the Concorde later this year.

Mr Messling, Deputy Director (Construction) at the Housing Authority, is the winner of the British Airways/*Sunday Morning Post* Concorde Connection travel competition which finished earlier this month.

Mr Messling's name was drawn from over 6,000 entries by British Airways Chairman, Lord King, in London last week. He was thrilled at his good fortune, but said it was not the first time he had won a competition.

"I suppose I enter a reasonable amount of competitions," said Mr Messling. "With all the lucky draws and the Mark Six it has become a way of Hongkong life."

The 58-year-old Briton, who has lived in Hongkong for 14 years, said he had always wanted to travel on the Concorde. "Although it is now getting mature, it is still a technical breakthrough," he said.

He said he hoped to do some research while he is in the US.

Mr Messling's prize includes two first class return tickets with British Airways to London, three nights' accommodation at the London Hilton Hotel on Park Lane, two return tickets on the Concorde to New York and three nights' accommodation at the Hilton's New York Vista hotel. The total package is worth over $200,000.

The Concorde Competition asked readers to identify four cities British Airways flew the Concorde to. They are New York, London, Miami and Washington.

Mr Messling is planning to take his partner, Ms Penny Ward, with him on the trip, but he intends to delay it for a while.

"Because of the war I would like to go later than sooner," he said. "I think I'd go around Christmas time."

Figure 10.4 Derek Messling, HD Deputy Director of Construction, seen in a 1991 SCMP article following his British Airways 'Concorde' competition win.

Mr Edward Ho, right, chairman of the Housing Authority's Building Committee, at yesterday's press conference. On his left is Mr Derek Messling, deputy director of the authority's Construction Branch.

Figure 10.5 Messling seen with Edward Ho (HA Building Committee Chairman) at a press conference about the 26 Blocks scandal: *Star* feature, September 1987.

officials within government and the HD were highlighting the risk posed by the lack of a policy Secretary to represent the housing interest in government, especially in securing forward land supply. After his retirement in 1993 Messling recalled that 'Forward planning, even with the excellent LTHS, was always a cliffhanging affair due to government's apparent difficulty in releasing, in good time, sufficient land for the building programme. Clearly, government had its own numbers game in attempting to balance the needs of the private sector with our requirements and the value of land sale receipts' – but the overriding reality was that there could be 'no end to the public housing numbers game'.[77] Eventually, Tony Miller later argued, it was the negative consequences of this post-1988 'disconnect in the forward planning of land' that would lead to the partial reversal of corporatisation in 1994 and the resurrection of the Housing Secretary post.[78] And looking back in retrospect at the early years of the Housing Strategy, Akers-Jones's successor as Chairman from 1993, Rosanna Wong, argued that while the policy of housing-led 'pump-priming' development in locations such as Junk Bay/Tseung Kwan O 'was very clever, because the government had to give us land instead of cash,' in reality this strategy was constantly undermined by the deficiencies in land supply, where the government 'talked about it but didn't do it', although 'we chased them up day and night once the Housing Authority became independent'. That process of 'chasing-up' was directed personally by Akers-Jones, who bombarded Director of Territory Development Kenny Kwok with suggestions of potential New Territories sites, especially on derelict agricultural land – his own personal bete-noire. He argued in September 1988, for instance, that 'I personally think that the area between Tuen Mun and Yuen Long is a disgrace to the administration', and that in areas such as Hung Shui Kiu, 'anything would be better than the present awful mess'.[79]

The Hong Kong system of land-use, inherited from the British colonial system, involved separation of state ownership rights and land use rights; a low direct tax environment; and careful management of the land supply to balance land's use-value and its revenue value for government.[80] By the late 1980s, the land problem was increasingly bound up with the question of affordability, rather than that of squatters and the need for land for industry. Here the Beijing government was now an active participant, through its role in the Land Commission. The 50 ha land restriction was fully in force for the whole of this period, and Akers-Jones recalled that 'it was a constraint, but we were able, within those constraints, to build a respectable amount of housing each year. Although it was a bit hampering, it allowed us to get on with land formation and reclamation.' Overall, 274 ha was vested in the HA for public rental housing over the five years 1987/8 to 1991/2.[81] In 1989, the Metroplan (masterplan) was announced, and specified maximum populations and densities for all areas. The 50 ha restriction, because of the short supply, increased urban land values to 'astronomical levels', and removed 'a valuable element of flexibility' from planners: a decade and a half was 'a long period to be hamstrung'. In parallel with this, November 1991 saw a new Town Planning Ordinance – the first comprehensive review of town planning since 1939. It imposed new planning controls, and tackled problems such as building of residential developments in industrial areas, but was attacked by architects and others as 'inflationary and harmful to investor confidence'.[82]

Reflecting the growing pressure for more dense development, and specifically the difficulty of accommodating new block-types like the massive Trident within the old rule-of-thumb gross density of 2700 ppha, 1990–1 saw the approval by LDPC, in co-operation with the HKPSG, of a new system of density calculation for public housing (PRH and HOS): the 'Development Ratio', or DR, a concept similar to commercial plot-ratios that related floor area directly to site area. A DR range of between 5 and 7 was recommended for public housing developments, the higher figure for large sites and the lower for difficult infill sites. However, many public housing developments actually exceeded DR 7, and after 1997, the latter became a general rule, even a minimum.[83]

New Towns: towards the third generation

The implementation of the Housing Strategy involved, in land supply terms, a significant shift from New Town virgin sites to urban area redevelopments, but the former remained vital to progress. (Figure 10.6) In December 1990, the Housing Authority took all the urban areas off the general waiting list, which was from then on to be solely catered for by the seven existing New Towns: urban output would be reserved for squatters and redevelopment decanting, reflecting increased use of more desirable urban sites for HOS projects, and pointing to a partial 'peripheralisation' of lower-income housing location. The PCPHP argued that in response to this shift in the waiting list, the Housing Authority should 'greatly reduce' New Town rents to attract tenants.[84]

During the Wilson years, the third phase of the New Towns programme got underway, and was celebrated in a succession of TDD publications. The NTDD, originally created in 1973, with three New Town development offices, had been merged with the Urban Area Development Office into the TDD in 1986: the formation of an autonomous Planning Department in 1990 had involved transfer of New Town layout planning from TDD.[85] It was clear by 1988 that the original ideal of 'self-containment' was unrealistic: Sha Tin, especially, had 'become a dormitory town', with 450,000 inhabitants so far, rather than the planned 700,000, and 60% in public housing.[86] Higher densities would also be essential in the New Towns,

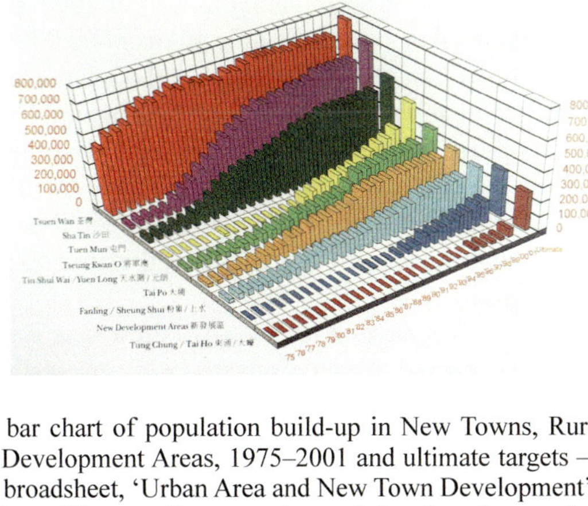

Figure 10.6 1993 bar chart of population build-up in New Towns, Rural Townships and New Development Areas, 1975–2001 and ultimate targets – included in TDD 1993 broadsheet, 'Urban Area and New Town Development'. The chart shows how Tsuen Wan was far more advanced than the others early on, while Sha Tin and Tuen Mun caught up from the 1980s.

in reaction to the 50 ha limit: as we saw in Chapter 9, in May 1986, Alan Crosby, Senior Housing Planning Officer, argued that much more attention would have to be paid to 'optimising' land, defining PSPS and HOS densities in private-sector 'plot ratio' terms, with PSPS schemes rising from 1.5 to 1.8 plot ratio and HOS remaining around 1.5, due to the need for community and recreation facilities: the adoption of the DR in 1990–1 clearly expanded on this agenda.[87]

Of the third-phase New Towns, the most firmly embedded into the mainstream housing programme was Junk Bay/Tseung Kwan O, of which Phase 1 (including Po Lam) was now underway, overseen by Stephen Poon's team: in his September 1987 overview lecture on the LTHS, Messling stressed Phase 2 of Junk Bay was vital as a decanting outlet to unlock the redevelopment programme, especially of the estates in central and eastern Kowloon. With the progress of development, Tseung Kwan O became a visitor showpiece: a 1991 article on the 'Mini-City' by the HA's public relations section predicted 200,000 inhabitants would be in residence by the late 1990s: the road tunnel from Kowloon would open in late 1990.[88]

Also envisaged as a showpiece, but one dictated by the very tight timetable of the airport project, was Tung Chung New Town, planning for which was taking shape by the end of Wilson's governorship. In January 1992, for example, Tom Armour, Project Manager in the South Western Development Office, reported that site formation tenders were due imminently for the first estates, which would by 1997 total 15,000 inhabitants, plus another 5,000 in private blocks.[89] And in March 1992 it was stressed that this, 'possibly the most ambitious mass housing development ever attempted in Hong Kong', faced a 'race against time', as detailed planning could only start in early 1994 and the first flats had to be ready three years later. Messling predicted that although it was not possible to predict exactly the proportions of public housing and HOS, the public housing blocks were unlikely to be as high as 38 storeys. An illustration showed 20-storey towers: 'I am happy the area will not be as dense as a normal housing development.' The first 14,700 public tenants would have to be rehoused 'at the last minute', and high-class low-density private housing would be built on surrounding hills after 2000: Sun Hung Kai and one other firm were 'believed to' have accumulated over 600,000 sq ft on the island of Ma Wan on the NE tip of Lantau.[90] In the event, although the first public housing development at Tung Chung actually comprised full-height 41-storey blocks, it still retained its location-derived prestige: John Lambon, the group leader, recalled that 'people could see the public housing when landing at the airport, and originally there was nothing between it and the water. That could be our visitors' first impression of Hong Kong: it is a very special design, including its colour scheme by Michel Cler' (on which see below).[91]

At the opposite end of the spectrum from both of these was Tin Shui Wai, whose problematic character stamped it from the outset as a lower-prestige development – despite the prominent role played by Li Ka-shing and Cheung Kong in realising the project, following the 1982 buy-out of the land by the Hong Kong government. In view of its potentially controversial sovereignty implications, the project only proceeded in earnest after the drafting of the Basic Law. In December 1988, Li announced a plan for a $5 billion 'new city' for 390,000 inhabitants, including 10.2

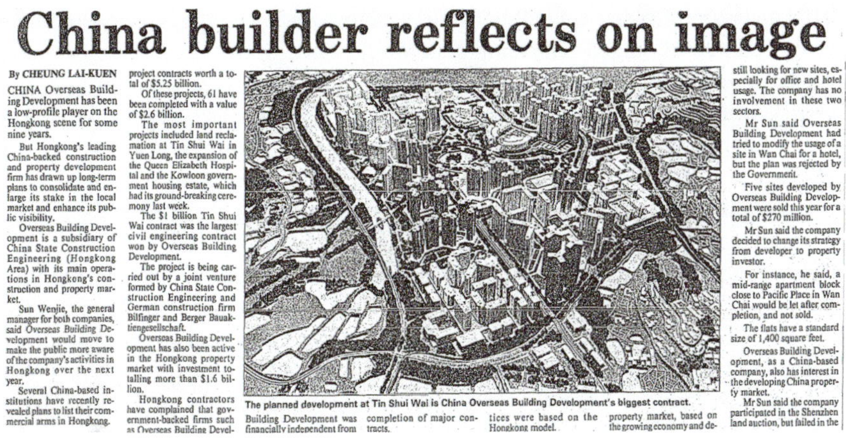

China builder reflects on image

By CHEUNG LAI-KUEN

CHINA Overseas Building Development has been a low-profile player on the Hongkong scene for some nine years.

But Hongkong's leading China-backed construction and property development firm has drawn up long-term plans to consolidate and enlarge its stake in the local market and enhance its public visibility.

Overseas Building Development is a subsidiary of China State Construction Engineering (Hongkong Area) with its main operations in Hongkong's construction and property market.

Sun Wenjie, the general manager for both companies, said Overseas Building Development would move to make the public more aware of the company's activities in Hongkong over the next year.

Several China-based institutions have recently revealed plans to list their commercial arms in Hongkong.

project contracts worth a total of $5.25 billion.

Of these projects, 61 have been completed with a value of $2.6 billion.

The most important projects included land reclamation at Tin Shui Wai in Yuen Long, the expansion of the Queen Elizabeth Hospital and the Kowloon government housing estate, which had its ground-breaking ceremony last week.

The $1 billion Tin Shui Wai contract was the largest civil engineering contract won by Overseas Building Development.

The project is being carried out by a joint venture formed by China State Construction Engineering and German construction firm Bilfinger and Berger Bauaktiengesellschaft.

Overseas Building Development has also been active in the Hongkong property market with investment totalling more than $1.6 billion.

Hongkong contractors have complained that government-backed firms such as Overseas Building Devel-

The planned development at Tin Shui Wai is China Overseas Building Development's biggest contract.

Building Development was financially independent from

completion of major contracts.

tices were based on the Hongkong model.

property market, based on the growing economy and de-

still looking for new sites, especially for office and hotel usage. The company has no involvement in these two sectors.

Mr Sun said Overseas Building Development had tried to modify the usage of a site in Wan Chai for a hotel, but the plan was rejected by the Government.

Five sites developed by Overseas Building Development were sold this year for a total of $270 million.

Mr Sun said the company decided to change its strategy from developer to property investor.

For instance, he said, a mid-range apartment block close to Pacific Place in Wan Chai would be let after completion, and not sold.

The flats have a standard size of 1,400 square feet.

Overseas Building Development, as a China-based company, also has interest in the developing China property market.

Mr Sun said the company participated in the Shenzhen land auction, but failed in the

Figure 10.7 1988 SCMP article on the involvement of China Overseas Building Development at Tin Shui Wai.

sq m of housing – half private and half public – developed jointly between Cheung Kong and mainland developer China Resources Capital: the latter was guaranteed a minimum profit of $750m, and Cheung Kong would receive the rest. Developed rapidly after that and eventually 'opened' by Governor Chris Patten in 1993, Tin Shui Wai would soon acquire a distinctly negative reputation.[92] (Figure 10.7)

The Comprehensive Redevelopment Programme – and the Walled City Clearance

In land-use terms, the most significant innovation of the Housing Strategy was its significant shift in emphasis towards urban redevelopment, by extending the latter's scope to include Mk IV–VI and GLC housing, in the Comprehensive Redevelopment Programme (CRP) inaugurated in 1988: a previous iteration in 1986 had been dubbed the 'Extended Redevelopment Programme'. Eventually completed in 2010, this hugely added to the decanting burden, as well as the complexity of the housing development process.[93] Unlike squatter settlements, which because of their often precarious locations were rarely redeveloped in situ, this redevelopment of permanent dwellings was constrained by complex requirements of staged decanting and replacement, previously pioneered in the Anglophone countries that were addicted to slum clearance, including Britain and the United States, but now using new terminology: 'pump-priming' denoted initial construction of blocks on vacant sites to allow a cycle of decanting and demolition to begin, and 'build-back' referred to replacement blocks built on the cleared sites. For such a process, very tall towers with a small footprint were ideal, as already seen especially in London's LCC point blocks and New York's NYCHA 'alphabet towers' in the 1940s–60s.[94] Although Messling's previous work in Islington (and Ward's in the GLC) had largely focused on the low-rise developments typical of the later, 1970s phases of London council housing, for any London public housing architect the procedures of staged redevelopment would have been 'in the bloodstream'. The same applied to the largely unrealised Camden projects worked on by Chris Gabriel, who recalled that unlike the complex and abortive negotiations for pocket sites in London, in Hong Kong 'once named, a project proceeded very rapidly and in the case of redevelopment projects, we would build a reception estate first, then move people from the first phase, then knock down the first phase – we'd do 2,500 flats at a time!'[95]

However, a significant reduction of density was always involved in the programme, with a 50% population drop predicted in August 1988 for Kowloon Central Estates.[96] (Figure 10.8) Thus it was also vital to have large external sites available for decanting, as argued by Messling in September 1987 in relation to Junk Bay Phase II and Kowloon Central: it was obviously easier to decant people on a large scale than 'moving people around within the estate'.[97] For the latter approach, individual clearance cases were critical to wider progress: for example in a November 1987 LPVC discussion on the Tai Wo Hau redevelopment and planning briefs, Penny Ward wrote that the demolition of Block 19 was critical, but that in turn depended on the availability of flats in Phase 4. In a further illustration of the

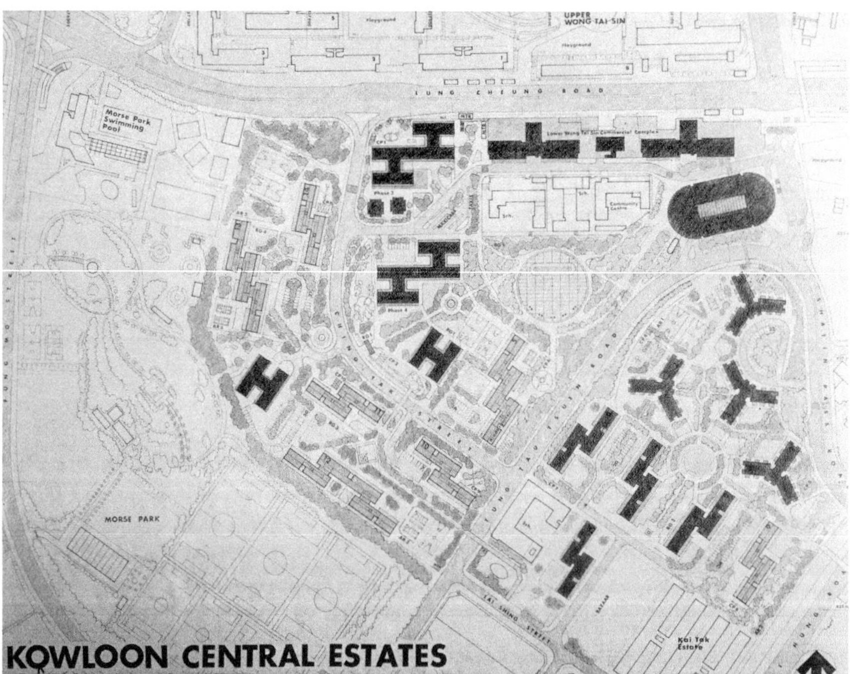

Figure 10.8 1988 PWD layout plan of Lower Wong Tai Sin redevelopment (cf. Fig. 4.4 pre-redevelopment).

problems of decanting, it was argued in May 1987 that the semi-empty Kwai Hing had become a 'haven for criminals' since tenants started moving out in 1986: three of the five blocks were to be demolished as unsafe by 1989.[98]

With the expansion of the redevelopment of early permanent housing, the old fight against the squatters no longer seemed a paramount problem, having been displaced in public perceptions by the Vietnamese boat people. By the later 1980s, although squatter numbers were still high, they were no longer an obtrusive presence in the urban areas: in July 1987 Liao reported almost two-thirds of the 430,000 remaining squatters (280,000) were in the New Territories: it was now hoped to rehouse all squatters from dangerous slopes by 1992 and all in urban areas by 1994.[99]

Gradually, the marginal place occupied by squatter settlements was replaced by the Temporary Housing Areas, with corresponding efforts to reduce the latter. In 1988, there were furious complaints by Beacon Heights condominium residents in Kowloon against plans to build a THA nearby, with 26 duplex blocks housing 2,000 inhabitants. The Housing Department riposted that the need for temporary housing overrode amenity considerations, but predicted that the shortfall in temporary housing would start easing in 1991.[100] Later that year, the HD pledged to phase out not just urban squatters but also Temporary Housing Areas by the mid-1990s: as the squatter problem came under control, Operations Branch would be absorbed into Estates Management Branch and subdivided between urban areas and New Territories.[101] And the following month it was speculated that the Lantau THA, at Mui Wo, could be used to rehouse previously arrived Vietnamese refugees.[102] By April 1989, following protests at Kai Fuk THA in Kowloon Bay, THA and cottage dwellers even began moving ahead of squatters in rehousing priority: they could now move to permanent public housing after seven rather than ten years, a concession subsequently denied to squatters.[103]

Situated at one remove from the mainstream CRP, but nonetheless placing it under severe stress in output terms, was the spectacular, stand-alone project for the redevelopment of the 2.7 ha Kowloon Walled City. (Figure 10.9) Here the preparatory work of the mid-'80s suddenly reached fruition in 1987. The operation was organised during Akers-Jones's stand-in governorship following Youde's death, and 'solved the problem' before Wilson's arrival. In full agreement with the Chinese Foreign Ministry, an ingenious, low-controversy compromise of demolishing the complex for a public park was devised: 'an extremely good solution, that didn't involve the Hong Kong British government building on the land' (Wilson).[104] Prepared in great confidentiality and approved by ExCo in December 1986, the clearance itself was coordinated, as 'the best-kept secret in HK's administrative history', by Lui Hau-Tuen, Deputy Secretary for Home Affairs (Special Duties) of the City and New Territories Administration: Lui was seen as an able troubleshooter due to his 1978 experience in the Sai Lau Kok clearance in Tsuen Wan for the MTR. An advance team worked under the guise of a rooftop structures team, and on 14 January 1987, a surprise site-survey of the entire Walled City was carried out by a force of 360 Housing Department clearance and squatter-control staff, organised in sixty teams of six, each accompanied by a plain clothes police

Walled City's year of change

TWELVE months ago the Government announced its plan to turn the Kowloon Walled City – Hongkong's most infamous slum – into a park. JIMMY LEUNG looks back on a year of progress.

A YEAR ago today, the Government unveiled one of its best-kept secrets – the plan to clear Kowloon Walled City and turn it into a park after 1990.

For 31,000 residents of the squalid slum, the news was a shock as both landlords and tenants were worried about rehousing and compensation.

For the Government it was a relief. The Walled City, so long a social and political embarrassment, was no longer a problem.

Many observers saw the park idea as a clever compromise. The eyesore was to be removed with no loss of face to either Britain or China.

Those same observers noted

were encouraged to stay away.

The result was the spread of brothels, pornographic cinemas, abortion clinics and unregistered hospitals. Unlicensed doctors and dentists are still a problem.

It was the signing of the Sino-British Joint Declaration that provided the impetus to resolve the issue.

A Government spokesman admitted the Chinese and British governments had discussed the matter in the months prior to the January announcement. He would not give any details but said as far as he knew, there had been no formal exchange of documents.

The same spokesman did not give a direct answer when pressed on the legal status of the

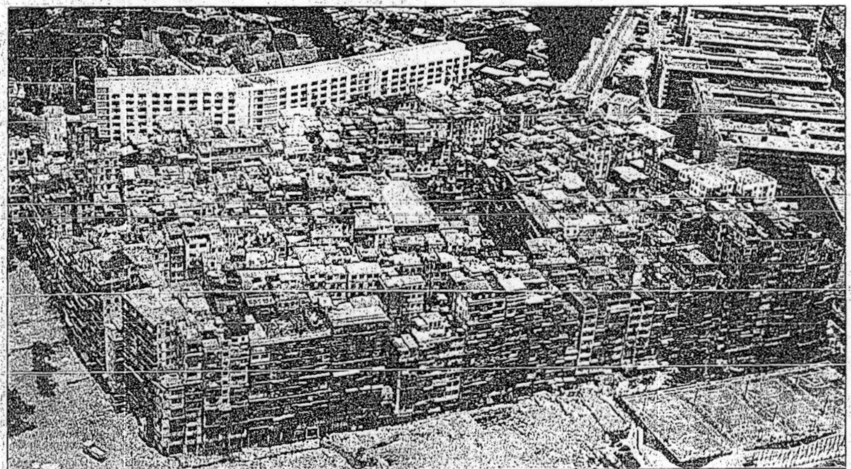

The Kowloon Walled City . . . a problem "left over from history" that will now be turned into a park after 1990.

been a significant drop in the number of cases last year compared with the previous year. Police records show that only 297 crimes were reported against 401 in 1986.

District Commander Chief Supt Felicia Wong Leung Kam-shan said part of the city would be boarded up to prevent it from becoming a ghost town when the first batch of residents began to move out in March.

The special committee finally announced the compensation and rehousing package early last month – 11 months after the clearance announcement.

At the news conference, Mr Hu said they considered that owner-occupiers should be assisted, where possible, to re-establish their ownership status after the clearance.

"However, given the low values of Walled City properties, any financial assistance to them to acquire properties in the private sector will inevitably involve a substantial sum of money which may be considered over-generous and therefore not appropriate," he said.

Rates of payment based on the Government-subsidised Home Ownership Scheme (HOS) prices will be applied to all premises as there is no distinction on the use of the premises, whether they are do-

Figure 10.9 Extract from January SCMP 1988 article on clearance of Kowloon Walled City.

officer. Lau Po-Chi, HD Assistant Director for Clearance, recalled in November 1989 that the HD 'had been told in early January that there was a very special assignment coming up'. Of the staff 'only a select few knew where and what' – hence, according to Lui, 'the surprise on their faces and the "waah" that went up when they first heard it'. By 11 pm on the 14th, this 'freezing survey' had been completed, most documentation had been done, and notices posted.[105]

Following the survey, the HA immediately established a Special Committee on Clearance of Kowloon Walled City, chaired by Hu Fa-kuang, to settle compensation. Owner-occupiers were assisted to re-establish their ownership status post-clearance, with priority given in applications to HOS or the new HPLS. John Corrigal, Government Land Agent (Special Duties), oversaw this negotiation work. A suggestion by Housing Secretary Todd to make HOS flats available to Walled City displacees was enthusiastically embraced.[106] The survey unexpectedly found that, despite the complex's chaotic appearance, most flats had actually been built by the same group of developers to a uniform size – which was used to calculate a 'unit rate' formula of compensation that would allow dwellers to afford the smallest HOS flat, or alternatively to move into a public rental unit with a HK$20,000 cash offer for an average flat: there was a 95–98% acceptance rate for these offers. Although a decanted population of 40,000 had been anticipated, by November 1989, the anticipated final figure was 33,000 inhabitants. By that stage a full-scale 'exodus' was underway, placing a severe and unexpected strain on the housing and redevelopment programmes more generally, and making the search for additional sites 'ever more critical' (Messling). More than 10,000 ex-residents were initially dispersed to as far away as Junk Bay and even Tuen Mun. By November 1992, the total number actually decanted, in four phases, was even lower: 28,220. Of these, 11,160 accepted public-rental units, and 13,320 HOS and PSPS.[107] Although the Walled City had not itself been replaced by new dwellings in situ, its clearance was undoubtedly the single most dramatic 'housing' episode of the late 1980s.

Rebalancing home-ownership and public rental

Alongside the CRP, the other key developmental thrust of the Housing Strategy was the growing drive towards home ownership, partly reflecting the belief in owner-occupation, and housing individualism in general, as a collective-identity anchor, and partly reflecting public housing's shift from a social resource to an integrated element within economic modernisation. Freddie Pang, at the opening of an IKEA store in Wo Che Shopping Centre in October 1987, argued that the home-improvement ethos it expressed, demonstrated the 'sense of attachment' to Hong Kong 'as a permanent home and not as a transient place'.[108]

Here the driving motor was partly the ongoing success of the HOS, but also the ever-increasing impact, on both the public consciousness and the 'financialised' economy, of the parallel, considerably larger, private-sector developments that had followed the 1978 completion of Mei Foo Sun Chuen: Taikoo Shing and Kornhill were hailed in 1989 as 'complete towns of new tower blocks' with town centres – 'more than just a dormitory town'.[109] The growing prestige and power of Li Ka-shing and the other property 'tycoons' only accentuated the phenomenon further. In contrast to the more egalitarian, state-enforced cohesiveness of home-ownership in Singapore, this reflected and bolstered the further growth of social inequality in Hong Kong in the decade 1986–1996: the Gini coefficient increased from 0.45 to 0.475 in 1986–91 alone. Housing policy from the late 1980s encouraged richer tenants to rely more on their own resources, even though the 'housing ladder' of housing aspiration and self-improvement still survived during the 1990s.[110]

But although in Hong Kong the HOS unambiguously enjoyed a lesser status vis-à-vis the private sector, it still continued making great strides: the ratio of HOS to PRH completions increased from 1:6 in 1986/7 to nearly 1:2 in 1992/3, and annual HOS completions from 3,370 to 10,652.[111] A July 1987 public-opinion consultation suggested a consensus that both rental and HOS construction should be maintained, and the LTHS report predicted a growing shift in demand towards HOS from around 1996 onwards.[112] Some new HOS owners who moved straight from overcrowded early public housing experienced disillusioning feelings of isolation and alienation in their new, domestically self-contained home-ownership units – for example the family of one longstanding Lok Fu Resettlement tenant Yuen Kong Ming, who moved out on its demolition in 1989 to an HOS flat in Tseung Kwan O, where they found that 'the atmosphere was not the same, as everyone lived behind shut doors', and they were far from their friends back at Lok Fu.[113] But although these displacement problems were widely shared, and although the resale premium stipulation continued to prevent the development of a Singapore-style secondary resale market, neither factor significantly diminished the public appeal of the HOS – or its contribution to the development of a sense of Hong Kong identity in those years.

Architecturally, the affinity with the private-sector formula of arrays of slender towers was already unmistakeable in the massive Siu Hong HOS project (Tuen Mun Area 51), completed in 1985, straightforwardly evoking a Corbusier-style vision of towers in communal parkland, in its array of 20 slim point blocks,[114] but the increased use of chromatic design concepts (see below) allowed more complex effects to be created, for example at Lung Poon Court, where an 'earth tone' was used externally 'to enhance the feeling of a warm and inviting atmosphere', with two-tone brown wings, and coloured cores.[115] For HA architects, the need to visually demarcate private and public posed challenges in balancing status, economy and practicality: Stephen Poon argued that while private blocks were 'more decorative', with 'lavish' clubhouses, 'people believe they are better but the flats inside are the same, or smaller'.[116] The HD architects also felt that the PSPS was particularly susceptible to a different 'private' tendency, that of cramming in the maximum saleable floor-space: in 1987 Messling argued that the previous twelve months had seen a 'disturbing trend' in PSPS design, with many blocks achieving 92% efficiency through floor-plans 'being tortured into incredible shapes', with bedroom windows looking directly into each other – whereas fully private-sector developments with 85% efficiency had 'sensible, regular-shaped flats'.[117]

Alongside the reinforcement of the HOS went a new purchase policy, the Home Purchase Loan Scheme (HPLS), which was destined to fall foul of Hong Kong's soaring property prices, with discounts that proved insufficiently high.[118] Akers-Jones pushed through the scheme despite warnings from Liao at LegCo that it was 'not viable' to sell flats to existing tenants within Hong Kong's volatile market. In June 1988, applications opened for an initial tranche of 2,500 interest-free loans of $70,000, but in March 1989 the Authority announced it was to raise these to $100,000, as flat prices had risen by 30% from January 1987 to January 1989.[119] In April 1990, residents of Pok Hong Estate at Sha Tin backed a Housing Authority proposal to sell 862 PRH flats in three blocks, but there were concerns that even 70% of the normal HOS price might be too high.[120] And in June 1991, Sun Yan Leng, the Chinese lead on the Land Commission, said the proposed sale of PRH flats might need to be approved by the Commission, as, like HOS, it involved the issue of government leases to private owners. Akers-Jones still expressed 'confidence' that the programme would see the first 4,000 flats privatised in the autumn, and by August of that year, a repackaged variant of the scheme was launched as the 'Sale of Flats to Sitting Tenants Scheme' (SFSTS), with a sale price scaled down to only 55% of market value, and with any block only offered for sale if over 50% of its tenants had agreed. But by December Akers-Jones admitted continuing 'difficulty' with the HPLS, partly due to distortion by massive HOS production, along with excessively high prices, which he conceded had made the sale a flop.[121]

By 1992, a further permutation of the state-sponsored home-ownership discourse had emerged, spurred by renewed house-price inflation. Discussions within LegCo now focused increasingly on the concept of the 'sandwich class' – the 'squeezed' lower-middle-class previously addressed by the abortive MIHP. Stephen Cheung of the Cooperative Resources Centre proposed a government-subsidised scheme for 100,000 individual sales to buyers of $18,000–30,000 per month income, at 30% below market price. In March 1992, Edward Ho urged the government to increase land supply to cater for the 'sandwich class', either by extending the scope of the HOS, or by increasing plot ratios in the New Towns and in the proposed redevelopment of Kai Tak Airport. And in May 1992, LegCo voted to press the government to address the housing needs of the 'sandwich class' – in response to which Planning Secretary Tony Eason promised that an interdepartmental working group was developing a scheme for them, with a report expected in September. By 1992, the battle-lines between advocacy of low-income public-rental and middle-income home-ownership had set into a zero-sum relationship: Frederick Fung, a Housing Authority member, blasted the LTHS as 'outdated' in its 'inappropriate' reliance on private flats often bought for investment, which 'nobody could control'; and Lee Wing-Tat criticised the government for 'siding with' private developers, and the LTHS for failing to help the lower-income group.[122]

Within the public rental sector, alongside the LTHS's massive developmental commitments, its shift away from indiscriminate producer subsidies for low-income rental housing led to an ever-growing stress on management reforms, especially more differentiated rent policies, heralded in the 1985 Green Paper on Housing Subsidy. In 1987, Fung Tung, as Deputy Director of Housing, introduced a fully fledged Housing Subsidy Policy (HSP) providing for the charging of double rents to high-income tenants, with the intention of dislodging the latter rather than – as actually transpired – sharply increasing rent revenue.[123] Over two decades later, Fung freely admitted that

> I made a miscalculation – I expected 60% or 70% of [eligible] tenants would not pay double rent. Instead, 90% of them willingly paid double rent! That immediately increased our rental receipt by 25–30% overnight, coupled with HOS and commercial tenancies, and the Housing Authority became very well-off. We could go to government and say, "Don't worry about giving me a budget, just give us the land!" We were the only public housing authority in the world that could say that![124]

By 1992, 11% of all Housing Authority households were paying double rent, but that total gradually fell by 90% following the introduction of a '1.5 times rental' intermediate policy in 1993. Overall, between 1988 and 2003, when it was abolished, the HSP higher-rent policy generated a grand total of $3.4 billion in additional rent.[125]

Despite the willingness of 'wealthy tenants' to pay higher rents, the policy was persistently criticised by pressure groups such as the HKPCPHP, which claimed in 1988 that only 5% of PRH rentals were ploughed back into support of public housing, and argued in December 1989 that given the anticipated cash surplus, the Housing Authority should not increase rents.[126] In November of that year, however, Freddie Pang proposed – without immediate effect – that overall rents should rise from 15% to 20% of median income, partly because the larger and better-equipped 'Harmony' blocks now standard in public housing (see below) would prevent the HA from maintaining a 15% median rent/income ratio.[127]

Complaints about differentiated rents were bound up with growing complaints about poor conditions and triad activity in many estates, with the legacy of the Group A/B polarisation still perceptible. In 1988, for example, it was reported that Lam Tin Block 15, so proudly opened as the 500th Resettlement block in 1970, was now severely degraded, with areas round refuse containers 'filthy'.[128] Likewise, among single elderly people forced to share small flats with strangers, outbreaks of violence caused concern, and prompted LegCo protests from Elsie Tu (Elliott): for example, one old man jumped to his death at Lam Tin in 1989 after hacking another elderly man he shared with, following a dispute.[129] Although HA representatives argued crime was actually decreasing in places like Tuen Mun, pressure was now rapidly building to extend private/HOS-style security entrances to at least the newer public-rental blocks, a campaign that would eventually bear fruit in 1994 with a comprehensive security programme.[130]

Conclusion

The publication of the Long-Term Housing Strategy in 1987 stimulated a radical shift in tenurial and land-use policies, and in the organisation of the Housing Authority. Its permanent, open-ended character seemed to symbolise public housing's institutionalised role in creating a new and settled sense of cultural identity within Hong Kong, and in supporting its economic transformation into a 'capitalist metropolis'. However, its impact in built form was equally far-reaching, as it stimulated the emergence of a bold new departure in the *design* conception of Hong Kong's public housing towers. In Chapter 11, we conclude our account of the Wilson years by focusing, with the aid of extensive recollections by key actors, on this architectural achievement, whose drive for 'Harmony' in housing design made a ubiquitously monumental impact on the Hong Kong skyline.

Notes

1 SCMP 20-4-1988, 2; 16-10-1988, 10.
2 Lord Wilson, 2023 interview. J Dimbleby, *The Last Governor: Chris Patten and the Handover of Hong Kong*. Warner, New York, 2002, 13; SCMP 10-10-1991, 11; SCMP 11-10-1990, 13–15.
3 Lord Wilson, 2023 interview. SCMP 11-10-1990, 13–15.
4 SCMP 9-7-1988, 1; Patten, East and West, 46.
5 R Y C Wong, J Y S Cheng (eds.), *The Other Hong Kong Report 1990*, Chinese University Press, Hong Kong, 1990, 159–74.
6 SCMP 27-1-1988, 1; 10-10-1989, 6.
7 *Building Journal,* 8-1988, 82.
8 SCMP 11-6-1989, 7.
9 Lord Wilson, 2023 interview. SCMP 30-11-1989, 25.
10 Lord Wilson, 2023 interview.
11 Tsang, *Modern History of Hong Kong*, 244.
12 Patten, *Hong Kong Diaries,* 231–6, 290.
13 SCMP 7-10-1988, 25.
14 SCMP 9-1-1988, 13; 19-3-1988, 33.
15 SCMP 25-11-1989, 40.
16 SCMP 12-3-1989, 12.
17 Poon, 2009 interview.
18 BJ 8-1988, 47; Poon, 2010 interview; SCMP 10-10-1991, 12–13.
19 Williams, 2012 interview; H-F Hung, *City on the Edge*, Cambridge UP, Cambridge, 2022, 78–84.
20 HKRS70-8-2044, PR release 1-1-1987; Poon, 2099/2014 interviews; SCMP 5-10-1989, 2.
21 Leo Goodstadt, 'Fiscal freedom and the making of Hong Kong's capitalist society', *China Information*, 24 (3), 2010, 273-294.
22 Patten, *East and West*, 195.
23 SCMP 3-3-1988, 10.
24 SCMP 7-8-1988.
25 SCMP 2-3-1989, 22; 19-2-1989, 44; 1-1-1989, 34.
26 SCMP 14-7-1989, 30.
27 SCMP 8-3-1990, 15; 11-10-1990, 13–15; 10-10-1991, 12–13.
28 Lord Wilson, 2023 interview. Akers-Jones, *Feeling the Stones*, 161. P-Y Ho, *Challenges for an Evolving City*, Commercial Press, Hong Kong, 2004.
29 Ngai Ming Yip, in Doling, *Housing East Asia*, 73.

30 Chung-kin Tsang, *Home-Ownership in Hong Kong*, 2021, 58; A Smart and J Lee, 'Financialisation and the role of real-estate in Hong Kong's regime of accumulation', *Economic Geography* 79 (2), 2003, 153–71.
31 SCMP 3-3-1988, 10.
32 SCMP 10-11-1989, 3.
33 HKRS70-8-2044, SCMP 16-10-1987 cutting. HKRS545-2-320, note of 4-1987; HKRS1693-1-1, 12-1987 cutting from *HK Standard.*
34 SCMP 28-1-1991, 2.
35 SCMP 5-3-1992, 12.
36 SCMP 26-4-1992, 39.
37 HKRS2106-2-10, extracts from District Boards' meetings, April-June 1987. HKRS2298-1-87, 13-4-1989 note from Akers-Jones to Director of Housing. R Chiu and P Fong, 'Urban development in Hong Kong in the 1980s – the implications of the Long-Term Housing Strategy', lecture of 27-2-1989 at Extramural Studies Department, HKU; Y-M Yeung, 'Fifty years of public housing in Hong Kong, retrospect and prospect', CUHK Geography Department occasional paper 97, 2-1989.
38 HKRS70-8-2044, text of Liao 8-4-1987 speech.
39 Fung Tung, 2010 interview.
40 Lee, *Housing, Home-Ownership and Social Change*, 267.
41 Yeung and Wong, *Fifty Years,* 2003, 10; HKRS2145-1-1 paper, HKHA, Long-Term Housing Strategy, A Policy Statement, 4-1987, 1-5. HKRS2106-2-10, D B Gould at WTSDB meeting 5-5-1987.
42 HKRS70-8-2045. Todd speech 5-10-1987; HKRS276-8-412, note of 9-1987; HKRS2145-1-1, April 1987 papers; HKRS276-8-639, papers of 4-1987, 7-1987.
43 HKRS70-8-2044, 30-9-1987 speech to Conference on Bidding for Construction Projects organised by Institute of International Research, 'The Long-Term Housing Strategy: a flexible policy to meet changing needs'.
44 HKRS1693-1-1, Todd note of 12-1987.
45 *Building Journal*, 8-1988, 13.
46 Richard Wong, *Hong Kong Land for Hong Kong People*, 13–15.
47 SCMP 22-8-1988; 14-10-88, 8.
48 SCMP 23-3-1990, 5.
49 SCMP 1-7-1991, 6.
50 SCMP 19-3-1991, 42.
51 New HQ: BJ 8-1988; HKRS 70-8-2044 17-3-1987.
52 Yeung and Wong, *Fifty Years,* 2003, 26.
53 HKRS70-8-2052, note of 9-1987.
54 SCMP 27-11-1987; HKRS70-8-2044, PR release of 26-11-1987; HKRS70-8-2045 Todd note of 26-11-1987.
55 Yeung and Wong, *Fifty Years*, 163–4.
56 Yeung and Wong, *Fifty Years*, 116. Financial aspects of Housing Authority: HKRS70-8-2044 16-10-1987 Faruqi note; SCMP 10-11-1989, 3; 28-1-199, 2.
57 Rosanna Wong, 2014 interview.
58 Housing Authority, *Annual Report*, 1991/2, 6.
59 Housing Authority, *Annual Report*, 1992/3, 6.
60 Lord Wilson, 2023 interview. HKRS276-8-639 9-87; HKRS1588-2-14 1-87. SCMP 16-5-1992, 26; SCMP 11-12-1991, 32; LC Wong, 2011 interview; Burns, 2014 interview.
61 Lord Wilson, 2023 interview.
62 Akers-Jones, *Fifty Years*, 203; SCMP 23-2-1988, 3; Fung Tung, 2010 interview.

63 SCMP 7-4-1988, 3.
64 HKRS696-3-8, 27-10-1990 HA Secretary to SHA re HDB. SCMP 10-10-1988, 5.
65 SCMP 9-7-1988, 1.
66 SCMP 29-6-1990, 5; 27-9-1991, 3.
67 Poon, 2009 interview.
68 Fung Tung, 2010 interview.
69 HKRS696-3-7, 25-4-1990 Bowen Leung memo and 1988 report by Civil Service Branch on staff structure. SCMP 27-4-1988, 5; April 1990 HK/GB-trained architectural graduate vacancies in those departments: SCMP 8-4-1990, 43.
70 Poon, 2009 interview; Lambon, 2012 interview.
71 SCMP 9-7-1988, 1; 2-10-1989, 19; 12-6-1989, 8; 3-1-1990, 4; Lambon, 2012 interview; Poon, 2009 and 2010 interviews.
72 Lambon, 2012 interview.
73 SCMP 24-2-1991, 2; 5-4-1992, 33.
74 Messling, 'Public housing – a numbers game'.
75 HKRS70-8-2044, report of Messling speech of 30-9-1987; HKRS1882-3-19 Messling to Elizabeth Wong on Ho Man Tin site.
76 Gabriel, 2009 interview.
77 HKRS696-3-7, 25-4-1990 memo by Bowen Leung; Messling, 'Public housing – a numbers game'.
78 Miller, 2014 interview.
79 HKRS 1882-3-19, Akers-Jones-Kwok correspondence. Rosanna Wong, 2014 interview.
80 C K Tsang, Home-Ownership in Hong Kong, 51-3; SCMP 2-12-1991, 13 (on plans for 426-unit Pat Sin Leng Country Park development)
81 HKRS545-7-352 LegCo 14-10-1992 proceedings. *Building Journal*, 8-1988, 82.
82 *Building Journal*, 8-1988 on Metroplan; Akers-Jones, *Fifty Years*, 163; SCMP 6-11-1991, 3.
83 HKHA, Memorandum for Building Committee, BC 93/99, 18-5-1999, 'Current density guidelines for public housing development'.
84 SCMP 14-12-1990, 3; Kockelkorn, 'Peripheralisation', 623.
85 Territory Development Department (TDD), 'New Towns in HK', 1992 film; TDD, 20 Years of New Town Development, 1993; Fung, 2010 interview.
86 SCMP 25-5-1988, 45.
87 HKRS545-1-456-6, 5-1986 cutting.
88 Gabriel, 2011 interview; Poon, 2014 interview; HA Public Relations Section, *Tseung Kwan O, Mini City in the Making,* 1991. And in October 1993 the visiting Secretary of the Royal Fine Art Commission for Scotland, Charles Prosser, was taken to King Lam Estate (JB02) at Tseung Kwan O after a briefing from Fung Tung and others.
89 SCMP 24-1-1992, 62.
90 SCMP 25-3-1992, 43.
91 Poon, 2014 interview.
92 Yip, 'New town planning as diplomatic planning', 361–80.
93 HKRS1882-3-19, BC paper 93-86; HKRS2145-1-1, 11-1987 note; HKRS276-8-639, 4-1987 note; Gabriel, 2009 interview; *Building Journal*, 8-1988, 63; HKRS1693-2-3, 3-1987 note; HKRS70-8-2045, Messling 30-9-1987 speech.
94 Poon, 2014 interview, on Harmony as vital to CRP. Use of high blocks for 'pump-priming' in 1960s London and 'sectional construction' in 1940s New York: Glendinning, *Mass Housing*, 151–2.
95 Gabriel, 2009 interview.

96 *Building Journal*, 8-1988, 63.
97 HKRS70-8-2044, Messling 30-9-1987 speech.
98 HKRS1881-2-33, Nov 1987 note; SCMP 17-5-1987, 2; HKRS276-8-639, 9-1987 note.
99 SCMP 1-1-1990, 4; HKRS70-8-2052, 4-1987 note; HKRS70-8-2044, 1-7-1987 Liao speech.
100 HKRS1881-2-5, notes of 1-1986 to 10-1987.
101 SCMP 24-10-1988, 5.
102 SCMP 7-11-1988, 5.
103 SCMP 26-6-1989, 3.
104 Wilson, 2023 interview. Housing Authority, *Annual Report*, 1992/3, 12. Akers-Jones, *Feeling the Stones,* 185–6; SCMP 11-11-1989, 1–2.
105 HKRS1078-1-2-4, 25-8-1987 minutes of HA special committee on clearance of Kowloon Walled City; progress report on KWC clearance as at 1-9-1987. SCMP 14-1-1988, 17; 11-11-1989, 1-2; 8-10-1991, 7.
106 HKRS1078-1-24 memos and progress reports on KWC 8/10-1987; SCMP 29-2-1988, 12; 14-1-1988, 17; 11-11-1989, 1-2; 8-10-1991, 7.
107 1882-3-19, Messling to Peter Pun, 16-1-87, and Messling to Elizabeth Wong 16-2-1987. Housing Authority, *Annual Report*, 1991/2.
108 HKRS70-8-2044, 10-1987 note; Yeung and Wong, *Fifty Years*, 333; Kockelkorn, 'Peripheralisation', 623.
109 SCMP 11-1-1989, 32; Carmen Tsui, 'Housing the nascent middle class', 755.
110 CK Tsang, *Home-Ownership in Hong Kong*, 65–7.
111 Lee, *Housing, Home-Ownership and Social Change,* 266.
112 Yeung and Wong, *Fifty Years,* 245; HKRS2145-1-1, LTHS draft, 3. HKRS70-8-2052, notes of 7-1987, 8-1987 on opening of Tin Ma Court by Todd. Yeung and Wong, *Fifty Years*, 245.
113 Blyth and Wotherspoon, *Hong Kong Remembers*, 128–33.
114 *Building Journal*, 8-1988, 94–6.
115 *Building Journal*, 8-1988, 108.
116 Poon, 2009 interview.
117 HKRS70-8-44, Messling 30-9-1987 speech.
118 HKRS2016-2-10 5-5-1987 WTSDB minutes; HKRS2298-1-87 Akers-Jones to Director of Housing 13-4-1989; Lee, *Housing, Home-Ownership and Social Change,* 266; Ngai Ming Yip, in Doling, *Housing East Asia*, 76.
119 HKRS70-8-2044, Liao 8-4-1987 speech; HKRS70-8-2052, 5-1987 note; SCMP 16-6-1988, 3; 14-3-1989, 3.
120 SCMP 13-4-1990, 2.
121 HKRS394-29-216 26-11-1990 meeting of Lands and Works Policy Group. SCMP 19-8-1991, 14; 21-12-1991, 4; Yeung and Wong, *Fifty Years*, 208. HKRS696-3-8 3-1990 (Report of Ad-Hoc Committee on Sale of Flats to Sitting Tenants); HKRS696-3-9 2-4-1991 memo for ExCo, 'Sale of Flats to Sitting Tenants' (also on 50% minimum tenant agreement rule).
122 HKRS696-3-7, 22-3-1990, HA report, 'A Study of the Housing Needs of the Sandwich Class'; SCMP 26-3-1992, 6; 7-5-1992, 7.
123 Yeung and Wong, *Fifty Years*, 333.
124 Fung Tung, 2010 interview.
125 Yeung and Wong, *Fifty Years*, 183.

126 SCMP 29-2-1988, 12.
127 SCMP 27-12-1989, 4.
128 SCMP 16-1-1988, 12; HKRS70-8-2052, 4-1987 note.
129 SCMP 1-1-1990, 7; 5-2-1988, 6; 6-11-1990, 7 (Elsie Tu).
130 SCMP 29-2-1988, 12.

11 Living in ‘Harmony’

A revolution in Hong Kong housing design

In this chapter, we focus exclusively on the built form of housing in the Wilson years. Previously, we traced a succession of radical design innovations and pivotal projects, from Shek Kip Mei and Wah Fu through to the HOS, which helped shift housing design towards a philosophy of slim, standardised towers. In this chapter, we witness the climax of this evolution process: a veritable design revolution whose outcomes continue to shape Hong Kong housing right up to the present. In tracing that story, an especially vivid testimony is provided by the recollections of the key design staff involved – evidence that slightly counterbalances the dominance of administrative governmental sources in most of this book.

This was a revolution which marked a decisive divergence from the HA’s perennial ‘sibling rival’, Singapore’s HDB. In Singapore, HDB estates up to the ’80s had incorporated large flats and individually designed, medium-height blocks in an austere external environment.[1] But from the 1990s, a new, somewhat Postmodernist tendency began, using exotically decorative features to help reflect Singapore’s ethnic diversity through accentuated individual estate ‘identity’.[2] Hong Kong headed in a very different direction, combining new standard Modernist blocks of radically increased height – the ‘Harmony’ series – with lavish communal landscaping and a new concept of external colour harmonisation to create a more abstract estate identity. (Figure 11.1) Stephen Poon played a key role in formulating this ethos within the HD: commenting on Singaporean attempts to use Postmodernist decoration as an identity-creation device, he recalled, ‘Here in Hong Kong, in my time, there were architects in my department who had some of these strange ideas: I’d find them trying to do something funny with our standard blocks. I always used to stop them straight away – I always maintained the view that we’re designing for the general public, not our own private residences!’[3]

This was not a straightforward Modernist egalitarian ethos, as it also reflected a hierarchy of decorum, subtly ranking public ‘below’ private: Ken Cheung recalled that ‘in the design of public housing, Stephen Poon’s key rule was consistency: the golden rule was that if you build housing of varied spatial configuration, people would claim it was unfair, so you go for a standard block’.[4] There were also strong overtones of land-use efficiency: in Rosanna Wong’s view,

DOI: 10.1201/9781315563701-14

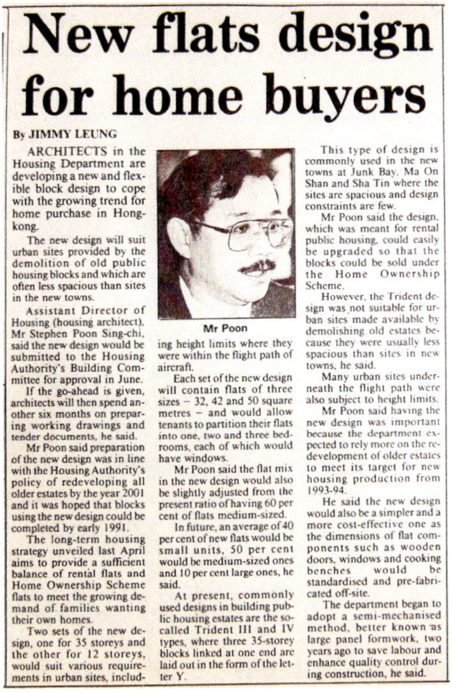

New flats design for home buyers

By JIMMY LEUNG

ARCHITECTS in the Housing Department are developing a new and flexible block design to cope with the growing trend for home purchase in Hongkong.

The new design will suit urban sites provided by the demolition of old public housing blocks and which are often less spacious than sites in the new towns.

Assistant Director of Housing (housing architect), Mr Stephen Poon Sing-chi, said the new design would be submitted to the Housing Authority's Building Committee for approval in June.

If the go-ahead is given, architects will then spend another six months on preparing working drawings and tender documents, he said.

Mr Poon said preparation of the new design was in line with the Housing Authority's policy of redeveloping all older estates by the year 2001 and it was hoped that blocks using the new design could be completed by early 1991.

The long-term housing strategy unveiled last April aims to provide a sufficient balance of rental flats and Home Ownership Scheme flats to meet the growing demand of families wanting their own homes.

Two sets of the new design, one for 35 storeys and the other for 12 storeys, would suit various requirements in urban sites, including height limits where they were within the flight path of aircraft.

Mr Poon

Each set of the new design will contain flats of three sizes – 32, 42 and 50 square metres – and would allow tenants to partition their flats into one, two and three bedrooms, each of which would have windows.

Mr Poon said the flat mix in the new design would also be slightly adjusted from the present ratio of having 60 per cent of flats medium-sized.

In future, an average of 40 per cent of new flats would be small units, 50 per cent would be medium-sized ones and 10 per cent large ones, he said.

At present, commonly used designs in building public housing estates are the so-called Trident III and IV types, where three 35-storey blocks linked at one end are laid out in the form of the letter Y.

This type of design is commonly used in the new towns at Junk Bay, Ma On Shan and Sha Tin where the sites are spacious and design constraints are few.

Mr Poon said the design, which was meant for rental public housing, could easily be upgraded so that the blocks could be sold under the Home Ownership Scheme.

However, the Trident design was not suitable for urban sites made available by demolishing old estates because they were usually less spacious than sites in new towns, he said.

Many urban sites underneath the flight path were also subject to height limits.

Mr Poon said having the new design was important because the department expected to rely more on the redevelopment of older estates to meet its target for new housing production from 1993-94.

He said the new design would also be a simpler and a more cost-effective one as the dimensions of flat components such as wooden doors, windows and cooking benches would be standardised and pre-fabricated off-site.

The department began to adopt a semi-mechanised method, better known as large panel formwork, two years ago to save labour and enhance quality control during construction, he said.

Figure 11.1 February 1988 SCMP article reporting an initial briefing by Stephen Poon on the new standard block types – soon to become the Harmony range – and the rationale behind the project.

> Customised design uses more land… with small land packages, you must do development efficiently. The people have been lining up waiting for so long, they don't care whether it's in a standard block or not. You can't allow too many choices, as this would delay things.[5]

However, it was well-established throughout the 1980s that there could sometimes be practical reasons for non-standardisation: Chris Gabriel recalled that

> modifying standard blocks was sometimes the only solution, though not to satisfy the architect's own creative needs. When I started my first large project on Tsing Yi Island in 1981, it was on a recently formed hillside site where the platforms were small and the supporting slopes could not be built on without an extended design programme and greater costs. The brief required in the order of 3,000 flats, a car-park and a sports hall. My solution was to use Trident blocks, which had a large footprint, because the higher 35-storey blocks would achieve the numbers required, and then to modify the lower floors for car-parking linked to a further free-standing car-park building with the sports above and access to

> the blocks and the sports facility at podium level. Standard blocks on that site would simply not have met the brief. The same approach was adopted on the following phase simply to achieve the numbers required.[6]

What chiefly concerned the inhabitants themselves, however, was internal accommodation. Messling's September 1987 speech on the LTHS highlighted the crucial role of rising expectations in the Strategy: 'By 2001, estates like Wah Fu and Oi Man, hailed as showpiece estates when completed in the early '70s, will then be 30 years old and will only offer single-room flats with balcony kitchen areas'.[7] The next generation of blocks, such as the Trident and New Cruciform Block, had been designed on the basis of feedback,[8] and the introduction of each standard type would be followed by three/four years of initial building projects, then further feedback: 'You make a change then, after the limitations and constraints or imperfections emerge. Around seven years on, you start thinking that maybe we need to go for a new block'.[9] From the late 1980s, the criteria of size in HA flats changed from square metres per person to the more practical, project-related definition of one, two or three bedrooms per flat,[10] coupled to a slight increase in overall flat sizes, especially in the one-bedroom unit. Kitchens also became larger, leaving room for a standard washing machine and refrigerator: bedrooms better planned, and three-bedroom flats had a separate WC.[11]

Chromatic harmonisation and estate identity

The new Housing Authority design ethos was bound up with an overarching aesthetic concept, that of external colour harmonisation. This was integrally linked to block standardisation, even in the name of the 'Harmony' blocks, and was conceived as a way of offsetting it with 'estate identity'. Poon recalled that 'because of all these standard designs, we were very careful to make sure every estate should have its own identity, by way of different colour schemes'.[12] Although already tried out at projects such as Lung Poon Court or Hing Man, or at Mei Lam – whose name ('Beautiful Forest') was reflected in John Ng's variegated palette of green mosaics and paintwork, the breakthrough came in the late-1980s with the engagement of French chromatic consultants Michel and France Cler, advocates of 'colour as the basis of harmony'.[13] They had previously worked in French new towns in the 1970s and '80s, and were initially commissioned to colour-coordinate footbridges in Central by the Highways Department, before being 'discovered' and brought into public housing by Messling. He recalled that 'the colouring of buildings will never be the same after we met Michel Cler and dared to appoint that French genius'.[14] Poon recalled: 'one day, he just appeared – he was in the office, talking about colours'; and John Lambon: 'we went to Paris to his studio, and then he and his creative wife would come and digest the colours in the built environment in Hong Kong'.[15] Thereafter they were engaged by Messling to produce preliminary chromatic studies of numerous housing projects on sites of contrasting character, published in a 1993 booklet, 'Harmony Chromatic Chart'. In this booklet, the Clers defined the chromatic *genius loci* of Hong Kong as stemming from 'a high percentage of atmospheric humidity. The climate results in misty, diaphanous effects that dissolve any vivid hues and create a field of depth through a diffused perspective'. Michel Cler later explained the specific techniques required.

> The closer the high-rise buildings were situated next to each other, the lighter the colours that were used on the first levels, in order to reflect natural light into the public space areas. The material applied to the building surface was a mixture of paint and mosaic pieces called *pâte de verre* (glass paste). Reproducing a specific colour uniformly posed technical problems. This led us to create an aggregation of 3–4 nuances of the same colour that was then applied to the building surface – we called this approach a "jumble".[16]

In fact, chromatic harmonisation using pâte de verre already had a considerable history in France, especially in the projects of Emile Aillaud, working with his artist son-in-law Fabio Rieti, to create a multi-colour effect on his 'tours nuages' ('cloud towers') at the Pablo Picasso municipal housing project at Nanterre, 1973–82, including Hong Kong-scale blocks of up to 39 storeys.[17] (Figure 11.2a, b)

The new concept was first employed on a large scale in Hong Kong housing at Tin Shui Wai New Town, probably the location where the challenge of creating 'identity' and combating social 'alienation' seemed most acute: the first projects modified to receive the new Harmony blocks (Tin Yiu I and II, completed 1992/3, and Tin Shui I and II, 1993 – see below) were also among the first developments to receive the new chromatic treatment – although, Ng explained, the Clers' palette was not prescriptive in detail, but could be adapted by each project architect at will. In 1993, Chief Architect 1 Joseph Kong Churk-fan argued that the preoccupation

Figure 11.2 (a) Emile Aillaud's chromatic, mosaic-clad 'tours nuages' at the Cité Pablo Picasso municipal HLM project, Nanterre, 1973–82: 2023 photo by Jess Hindle. (b) Expatriate architects involved in the Harmony and/or Trident programmes, seen in 2012 in Surrey: (left–right) John Lambon; Bob Pritchard; Dave Hall (MG).

with 'harmony' derived from the HA's determination to create a 'fully integrated New Town': 'In seeking Harmony', the Housing Authority had called on

> the well-known French creative consultant, Mr Michel Cler, to design an external colour scheme that would simultaneously provide links to past, present and future. Drawing inspiration from both Tin Shui Wai's name, which meant, "City of Fire and Water", and its coastal location looking towards the setting sun, Mr Cler's proposals combined the two. Working on a grand scale, he suggested using a range of blues and purples in a soft, loose pattern… across several consecutive buildings to represent a seascape. Linking with this, he planned a series of equally flowing highlights in sunset colours of orange and pink, yellow and gold, overlaid on the blue and purple background.

This concept was linked to enhanced landscaping: Poon argued that 'We were leading the way, especially in the HOS' over the private sector in landscaping.[18]

A 'perfect storm' – birth of the Harmony

In practice, chromatic harmonisation was hardly likely to make a significant impact on Tin Shui Wai's problematic social-economic structure, but the concept of 'harmony' played a far more tangible and impactful role as part of the new, coordinated ethos of standardised housing-block design for the LTHS. 1987–9 saw a radical shift in the HD's standard block concept, through the replacement of an entire generation of somewhat disparate block types by a new and closely integrated family of modular towers: the 'Harmony' series. The significance of this generational shift lay not only in its comprehensiveness but also in its longevity, as it directly dominated HD housing design for nearly two decades, and was also then indirectly perpetrated in the modular elements of a later phase of 'site-specific' designs, continuing essentially to the present.

In cultural terms, the Harmony project was a particularly vivid example of the hybrid, interstitial character of Hong Kong public housing, and stemmed from a strong partnership between Chinese and expatriate architects and decision-makers: it was emphatically *not* any kind of 'colonial spin-off from British high-rise council housing', but instead a vivid demonstration of the autonomy and, at times, defiance of 'British' norms by Hong Kong policymakers, here in the architectural and construction fields.[19] Chris Gabriel recalled that

> when I arrived in Hong Kong in 1980 it was immediately clear to me that HKHA estates were very comprehensive and included all of the essential elements required for housing to be a success. Certainly the flats were a long way from being perfect, but everything else that had often been left out in high-rise estates in UK, was there; transport facilities, shopping, fresh food markets, schools, sport and leisure and a full range of social welfare support services.[20]

As we saw in earlier chapters, as early as the 1950s the ultra-high-density character of HA schemes such as Cadogan Street had prompted protests from George Atkinson in London, and the attacks on Hong Kong housing as 'inferior' in the 1970s by Goronwy Roberts had continued the same theme. Disregarding these, heights and densities had continued soaring, with net densities in the '70s and '80s over five times higher than the 200 ppa that was deemed the absolutely maximum tolerable level for new housing by the LCC and the GLC.[21] And by the time that the generation of expatriates involved in the Harmony project arrived in Hong Kong, in the 1970s, the disjunction from any kind of 'British high-rise public housing precedent' was total, as British public housing had been almost entirely low-rise and traditionally built since the mid-'70s – as exemplified in Messling's work for Islington Borough Council, or Lambon's in Exeter – and many of these programmes were in any case shrivelling to virtually nothing, as experienced by Gabriel in the last years of 'Cook's Camden'. The only British project on a comparable scale to Harmony – the City of London Corporation's lavish Barbican development (1964–76), with its three towers up to 43 storeys – was so far removed from orthodox 'public housing' as to be an irrelevance. Only a few expatriate HD architects had had any British high-rise experience, and then in a very junior role – for example Dave Hall in 1960s/70s Birmingham, with its (by Hong Kong standards) midget-scale standard 11-storey towers. The sheer scale and boldness of the Hong Kong programme forbade any meaningful connection: asked if they had looked at previous tower blocks in the UK, the USA or elsewhere, when working on the Harmony, Lambon simply replied, 'No, I don't think any of us knew anything about these, or cared in the slightest! We had a breath-taking programme, and we responded to the constraints that faced us. Any 'historic' references came purely from within Hong Kong' – and, one might perhaps also suggest, occasionally from Singapore.[22]

The origins of Harmony lay in the coming-together within Tim Nutt's Development and Standards (D & S) Group, in the late 1980s, of a range of pressures, both organisational and architectural. Nutt was unambiguously the Chief Architect initially responsible for the initiative, but other designers such as John Ng and John Lambon were involved from the start, partly working autonomously from Nutt; in the early 1990s the latter was caught up in the localisation process and left the HD. Lambon recalled that 'Tim Nutt had a concept of "Housing for the 90s" – we were all sent away one year when he was on leave, and brainstormed it.' 'It was the perfect storm, things coming together at a particular time. The issues that Harmony answered were these: the "26 blocks" problem of stability of construction; vertical servicing; new standards; flat mix; and room concepts. Harmony addressed all of these.'[23] (Figure 11.3)

> Already, the previous generation of block types, as set out in the HD's 1986 *Portfolio of Works*, had placed great emphasis on 'quality as well as quantity'.[24] Significantly, however, there was still a strong contrast between rental and HOS types – all now called into question by the Housing Strategy. The latter started the process that made these existing standard blocks redundant, and initiated the development of 'a new generation of flat designs… for the 1990s', reflecting

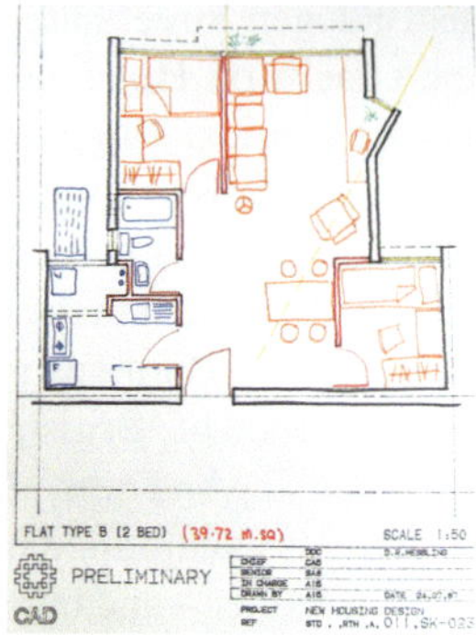

Figure 11.3 Preliminary drawing of July 1987 by John Lambon of a ‘Type B’ two-bedroom flat of the ‘New Housing Designs’ project, showing the flexible room planning possible within the overall planning concept.

not least the fact that families were getting smaller.[25] The Strategy’s emphasis on demand-led ‘flexibility’, especially in the ratio of public rental to HOS, made ‘greater interchangeability’ between PRH and HOS essential.[26] Poon recalled in 2009, There were two basic reasons for the move from Trident to Harmony. Firstly, there was people’s demand, and expectation, for something better. So in terms of the size of flats, Harmony ones were similar to Trident ones. But, that’s where the *other* reason came in, because in the late ’80s a decision was made by the Authority to encourage public housing tenants to own rather than rent. In those days, we were asked to design rental buildings to a higher standard, which would allow these buildings to be transferred from rental to ownership with minimal upgrading, in a short period. We already had the Home Ownership Scheme, starting from the early 1980s, but when it was first started, it was a distinct category. Buildings were distinctively rental, or distinctively HOS. But the later types of Trident started to become more flexible, and the Harmony was a further step to make that transfer more feasible.

Lambon argued that ‘Harmony was the salvation for all issues of housing, including change of tenure to Home Ownership halfway through’.[27]

Reconciling flexibility and standardisation

The concept of the Harmony emerged from out of a series of complex debates within the HD in 1987–8, following publication of the Housing Strategy, about what were initially simply referred to as the ‘New Standard Blocks’ (or sometimes the ‘Housing for the ’90s’ project). An August 1987 memo from Peter Ainsworth set out a rationale for such a project, and a late 1987 note from Nutt to Messling reported on brainstorming work.[28] As always with Hong Kong public housing, there was overriding concern to avoid infringing on the private sector. In November

1987 Messling argued, it was 'not considered advisable' to build flats with a larger IFA (internal floor area) than 50 sq m, as 'we shouldn't appear to be overtaking the private sector', and these IFAs were 'already at HOS/PSPS level'.[29]

The new blocks also responded to the land-supply consequences of the Housing Strategy's shift towards an expanded urban redevelopment programme, whose requirement for complex sequences of pump-priming, decanting and build-back required blocks of smaller footprint than the massively expansive Tridents. Here, the year the slim tower formula pioneered at Mei Foo, and then appropriated by the HOS, seemed the obvious solution. Poon recalled that

> Ultimately, the Harmony was modelled after our first Home Ownership block – the one we designed ourselves, not the ones designed by consultants. I did that, actually! [the HOS design] Before, we had rental flats, and most of them were small and had a very narrow frontage. Then later, immediately before we had the Harmony, we had the Trident. It had quite a lot of flats in one block, rather a large footprint compared to the Harmony. There was a shortage of suitable sites around that time, and sometimes we had to clear relatively small sites – so we wanted a block with a small footprint. That's how we came to get the Harmony. In the design, there was this consideration of the efficiency ratio as well. This has to be very important – you can't be too generous with public areas, lift lobbies and so on.[30]

Dislike of the oppressive bulk of the Tridents was a factor too: John Ng argued that one of the main drivers was 'contextual: the site, in the 70s, in New Town developments, the whole urbanisation pattern was moving out, with big blocks, Trident blocks, really big – or ziggurat blocks as at Butterfly Estate, because of the vast sites. Then in the 90s we came back to the urban areas for redevelopment, and the sites became small, so the Trident couldn't survive – we said, "We can't use it, it has to go!"'[31] The same applied to the HOS-only Windmill, which was now felt to be 'too big for Home Ownership: it had too many flats on each floor, whereas with the Harmony block, you could get up to 960 flats in a block'.[32] As at December 1987, the average gross density normally achieved in normal estates was 2600 ppha (1050 ppa), with school sites excluded, at an average occupancy rate of 3.8 persons per flat, but the new urban redevelopment sites could potentially be far smaller, making point blocks the optimum solution.[33]

The Trident was now seen as not only too massive overall, but also awkward in specific planning details:

> The Harmony also had to solve some problems of lighting and ventilation. Previously, for instance in the Trident, we'd liked to provide a deep recess in the building, where we concentrated the kitchen and bathroom windows: in that way, they didn't eat up the more valuable external facades of the building. But that kind of configuration didn't any longer satisfy the minimum standards in the building regulations, and in public housing, in these deep recesses, funny things can happen: you can't see from the outside. So one of the basic design

> parameters we fixed on before we designed the Harmony was not to have these deep recesses: we instead turned them sideways and diagonally instead, and at the core, we used the diagonal windows at the core to light it.' (Poon)[34]

From the outset, debates within the Housing Department about the New Standard Blocks were torn between the Hong Kong preference for repetition, and a new discourse of flexibility and adaptability. In a detailed August 1987 memo, accompanying initial concept drawings for 'a new, or new, "blocks"' prepared by CADD in 'under 40 hours', Lambon argued that there was a consensus within D & S that, the LTHS having rendered previous standard types redundant, any new designs should not be 'standard "blocks" in the rigid sense of the word – that of repetitive blocks at repetitive heights', but instead a 'total environment' based on a grid plan of shear walls, that would allow up to 50 variations at 10, 20 and 30 storeys: 'One concept can fulfil our entire needs with well-rationalised design standards' without negating 'human' design. Echoing his previous dimensionally coordinated work in Exeter, he stressed that 'as an Architect, naturally I am also seduced by the potential in both section and elevation [to create] identity and individual site design, within a very controlled concept' – controlled especially through the 'cores and their configurations'. In the Asian context, he noted that 'in the principles of good Japanese design, such "order" does not preclude "interruption" and variations … within pre-determined rules'.[35] In July 1987, initial CAD concept drawings of the New Standard Blocks, initialled by Messling, had shown a very different approach from the eventual Harmony: a rather ungainly pattern of stepped 20- and 30-storey blocks tapering off at the top, with Type C flats at the bottom and Types A and B (two- and three-bedroom) above. The growing emphasis on CADD design created a new staffing constraint: for example in November 1988 Ada Fung, then A/20 and project architect for Fung Tak Estate Phases 2 and 3 (eight Trident and New Slab blocks), wrote to CA/4 that 'I desperately need' a CADD-trained technician to help prepare construction drawings.[36]

However, the 'flexibility' side of the debate was unexpectedly bolstered in October 1987 in a lecture to HD by Delft University professor and low-rise high-density advocate Professor Age van Randen on the 'Open Building' principle of N J Habraken's Stichting Architecten Research (SAR). This concept of dimensionally coordinated grids and variegated infill, influenced by megastructural thinking, aimed to maximise 'the potential of every individual system'[37] – a somewhat libertarian philosophy that seemed an unlikely potential inspiration for the increasingly gigantic blocks of Hong Kong, yet exerted a distinct impact on the flexible-layout strand of the New Standard Blocks project within D & S. Lambon recalled that

> We started playing magic tricks: we had a talk from a Dutch university researcher about flexibility in housing: they thought they could subdivide flats at a later stage, in a fixed column and beam structure. They (the Dutch people) didn't work with us, but what we *could* do – and this was the root of the *whole* Harmony range, was to work in variations within the shear wall system, with its spine walls going through, and crosswalls giving stability.[38]

The Harmony 'family': flat mix, variants and modifications

Potential variations within the New Standard Blocks were not just an architectural abstraction but a vital way of securing PRH-HOS 'interchangeability', as stressed in a November 1987 memo from Y G Lim about flat mix in the new blocks.[39] A December 1987 *Design Brief for New Rental Domestic Blocks* argued that 'if the spirit of the LTHS is to be achieved, this need for flexibility encourages a new generation of flat designs to be prepared for the 1990s'.[40] Accordingly, after several D & S iterations of potential alternatives, a new flat-mix was authorised by LPVC in October 1987. From now on, rather than 60% medium-sized flats, instead the mix would be 40% small (32 sq m), 50% medium (42 sq m), 10% large (50 sq m): each block would contain flats of all three sizes in four different permutations (Options 1–4) and, as with the Windmill, would allow tenants to partition-off bedrooms within their flats.[41] (Figures 11.4, 11.5a–c) Lambon recalled that 'the magic of the Harmony range was that if you go out from the one-person flat in the middle, you can then get 1B–1P–1B, 2B–2B, or 1B–3B. You could change your mind on the mix, without affecting *anything* about the structure. We'd be given a brief of the required percentages of 1P, 1B, 2B, 3B, and the block could answer these percentages by this trickery: we could also add in an end bedroom.[42]

The need to fit both urban infill sites and large virgin sites caused a significant divergence within the overall configuration of the new series, into three completely different configurations. In 1988, Poon wrote that the (still unnamed) 'new flexible block design', designed using CADD, would be submitted to the Building Committee for approval in June. For small urban sites freed as part of the CRP policy of clearing all older estates by 2001, two variants were designed: the 39-storey Tower Block I, a relatively slender cruciform point-block, optimal for small urban redevelopment sites (designed by SA/15 John Ng and project architect A/51 Stephen Yeung); and the 27-storey 'Low Block', intended for 'restricted' long, narrow urban sites, with an elongated T-plan and swivel wings (designed by SA/8 P S Chan and project architects A/15 John Lambon and A/25 Colin Chan-Pensley). Lastly, the 37-storey Tower Block II (with 97% efficiency) was Y-shaped and directly replaced Tridents (designed by Ng and project architect A/32 Stephen Tong). Later, these became the Harmony 1, 2 and 3, and Harmony 1 was rapidly heightened to a standard 41 storeys, including 40 residential floors and up to 800 flats per block (depending on mix). Ada Fung recalled that 'at the time of Hing Man in the 80s, there was no regulation saying we couldn't build that high – it was just a matter of lift capacity and the economics of building at that height'.[43] (Figures 11.6, 11.7a, b)

Recollecting the evolution by D & S of the New Standard Blocks into the Harmony, the principal designers each projected a distinctive 'angle' on the project. John Ng set the story in its longer-term context, leading on towards the 'site-specific' modular towers of recent years:

> Of the three versions, the Harmony 1, which I worked on, is the typical cruciform version; it fits in the city fabric; cruciform is the most compact way you can fit blocks in. It maximises the allowable travel distance, too. The Harmony

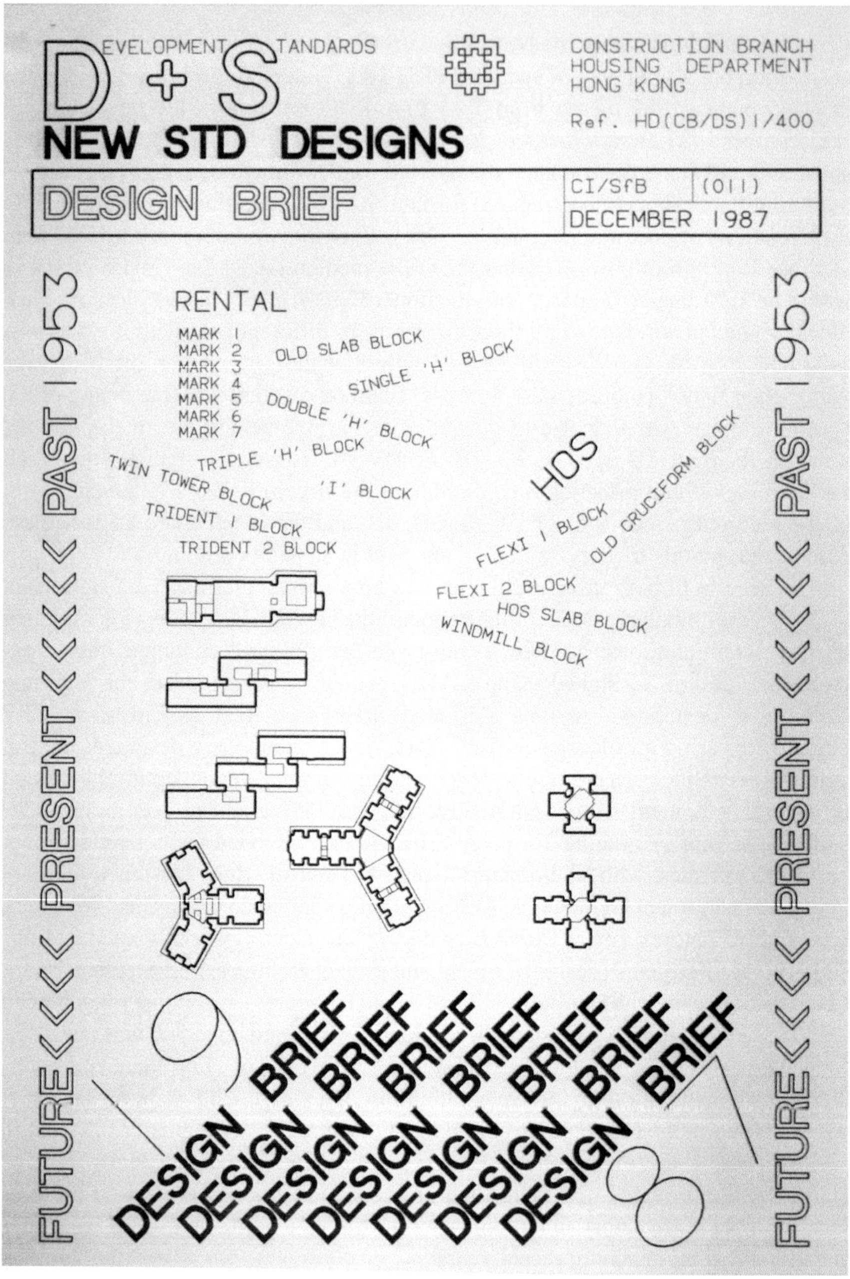

Figure 11.4 Front cover of December 1987 Design Brief by D & S for 'New Standard Designs' – featuring outlines of previous standard blocks.

(a)

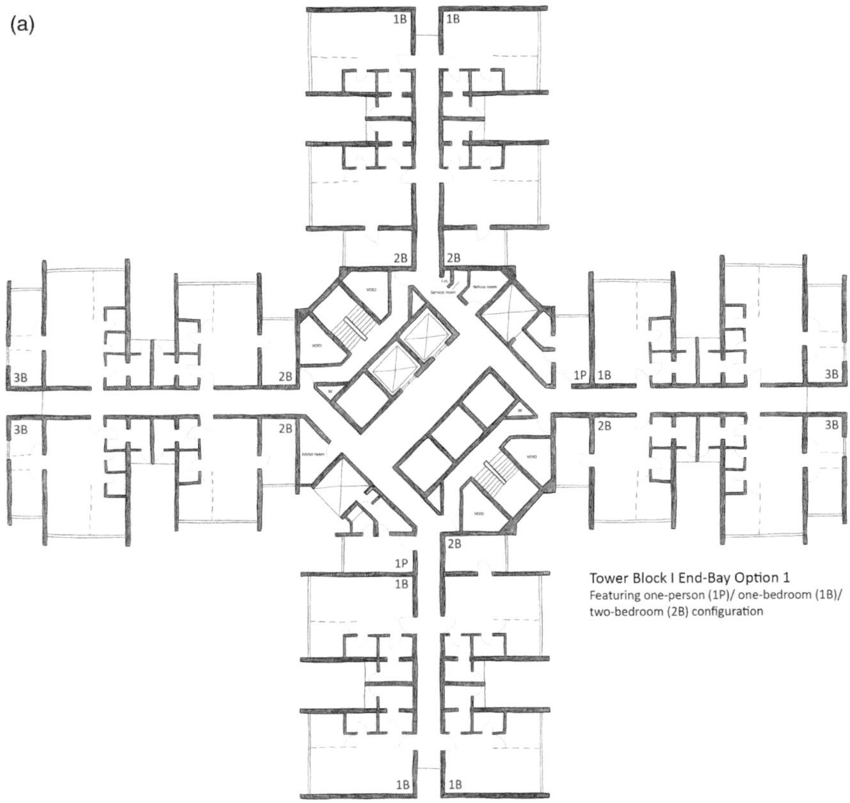

Figure 11.5 (a) and (b) Concept plans of 'Tower Block 1' and 'Tower Block 2' (i.e. the later Harmony 1 and 2) as at August 1988, with explanations of upper-floor layouts: Tower Block 1 has not yet been adjusted to reflect Akers-Jones's kitchen enlargement, whereas Tower Block 2 shows the 'definitive' façade protrusions. Drawing by Joyce Fu, 2023. (c) Concept plans as at August 1988 of standard upper floor of Low Block (Harmony 3 – originally also termed 'Unity Block'), showing alternative diagonal and right-angled variants of rotatable wings. Drawing by Joyce Fu, 2023.

2, designed by Stephen Tong, is in a Trident shape: we wanted to replace the Trident blocks, and on sites where a Trident had been planned, we could easily replace it with a Harmony 2. Once those projects were done, the Harmony 2 was finished. The Harmony 3 was a slab block, which could be used instead of the old Slab Blocks – again, a limited use. Of the three, the Harmony 1 was the one which was always going to survive the longest. It's the most popular block for use in the city, on the mostly small sites, for obvious reasons, as it's cruciform. And even now, with the new [site-specific] modular [approach], there are a lot of cruciform-shaped blocks, as one tower crane can handle the whole thing.

(b)

Figure 11.5 (Continued)

Now there's 300 blocks, built everywhere – but if we were starting the whole thing today, most likely it would be the same. If, after twenty years, a block has still retained its shape, there must be a good reason for it![44]

Likewise, John Lambon recalled in 2012,

The "Housing for the '90s" project eventually became the Harmony – the idea was to have high-rise blocks of around 35 storeys, and low-rise up to 20 storeys for the urban areas. It developed into one key flat plan, in variants of 30, 40, 50 square metres, and 1, 2 or 3 bedrooms – and three types of blocks to house them. We developed, in the team, a family of three blocks, using computers to assist

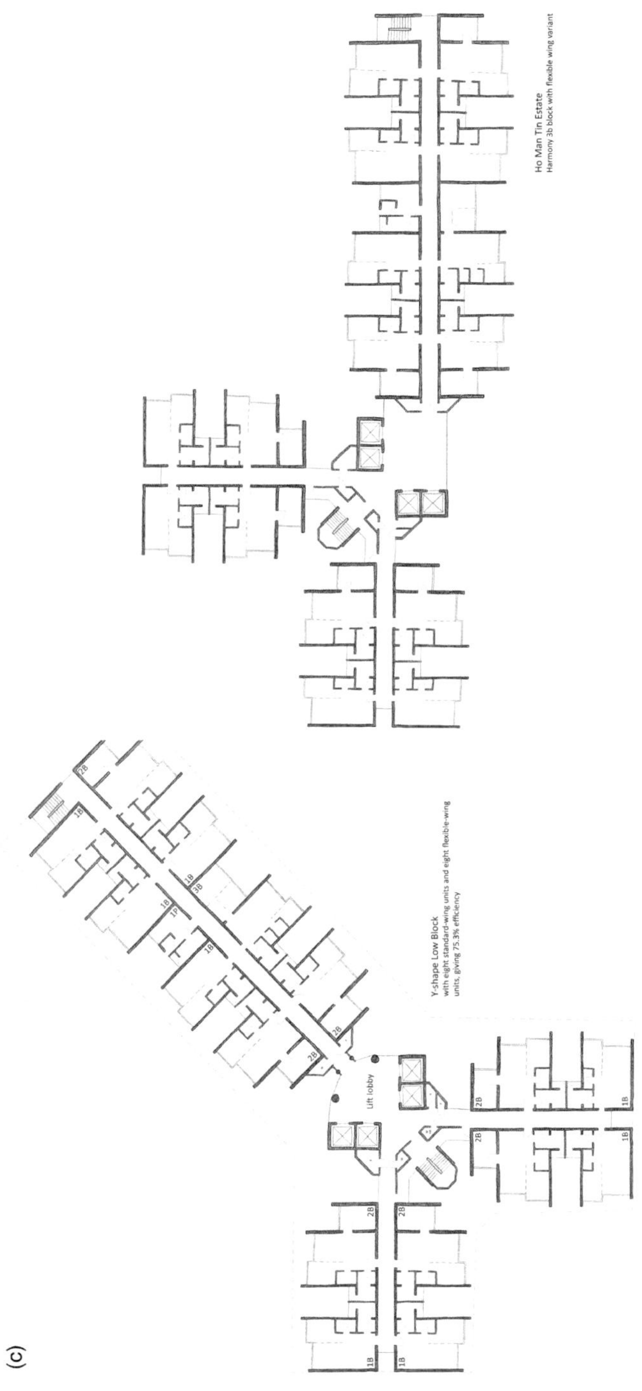

Figure 11.5 (Continued)

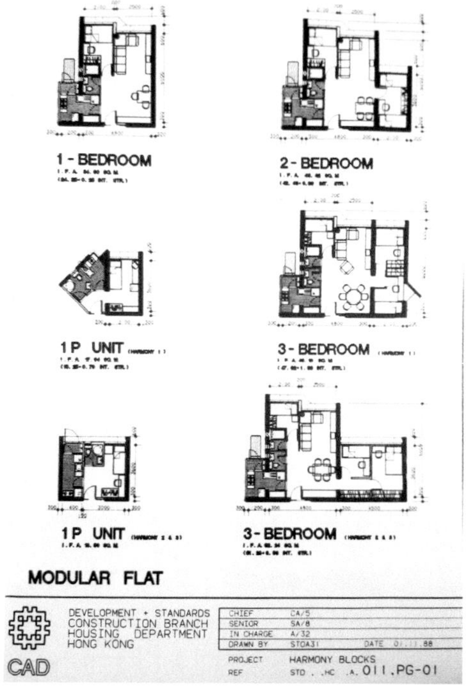

Figure 11.6 November 1988 diagram of Harmony modular flat permutations, after the kitchen enlargement (cf. Fig. 11.11c).

> us. [For the design] there was a family of interfaces between us, with individual contributors for the different blocks. The Harmony 1 and 2 group, which was headed by John Ng, developed two standard blocks: Stephen Yeung was behind the cruciform block, as being the *only* efficient block to get the numbers. The Harmony 2, by Stephen Tong, developed as a three wing block: that design was a bit adventurous! And finally there was Harmony 3, where Colin Chan-Pensley and I developed the lower-rise version. The Harmony 3 was flexible – you could spin its wings round at 90 degrees. The family of flats was the same – all three of these blocks, wherever they were, used the same flats. There were the same crosswalls, the same variations at the end bay – A or B type and so on – and the variations in the central core, where you could introduce one-person flats.[45]

In the structural design of the Harmony, given the 39 (later 41) storey heights that would now predominate, and Hong Kong's frequent typhoons, wind forces were a uniquely important constraint: overall, 'we never entertained column and beam construction'.[46] In early notes of June 1987, Ainsworth argued shear walls were best:

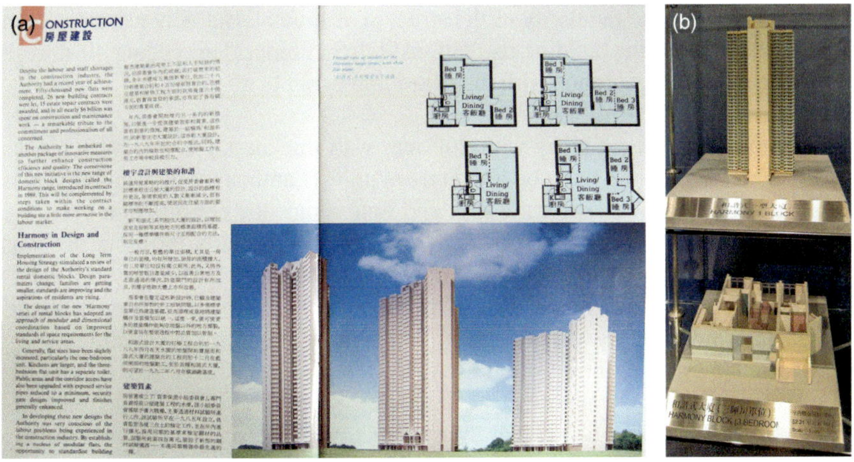

Figure 11.7 (a) Two-page spread from HD brochure, *Living in Harmony*, 1989, illustrating the three Harmony types, and the standard flat plans in their finalised form. Harmony 1, 2 and 3 are shown at the initial 39-, 37- and 27-storey heights. (b) Model of standard production Harmony 1 (in 41-storey form), and three-bedroom flat, in the permanent HA headquarters exhibition: 2011 photo (MG).

> Structural system must match resource capabilities – i.e. shear walls are good (if not essential), but this does not preclude a frame. Flexibility can be assured with less frequent shear walls. But for stiffness, shear walls at least at core and possibly ends are really essential. Point blocks are better than linear (being stiff in two, not one, directions).

Additionally, this approach was also cheaper than frame construction.[47] A January 1988 paper by Lambon discussed wind-loading in relation to torsional effects: any change in overall layout would need a new wind-coefficient, and so the optimum would be a monolithic RC structure of shear walls interconnected with flat slabs, stabilised by a central core. The paper argued that frames were sufficient for up to 20 storeys, shear walls to 35 storeys, and a combination of frame and shear wall to 50 storeys. In Hong Kong the controlling factors on building height were wind effects, plot ratio, aviation restrictions, and travel distance on each floor, and the optimum structure on Hong Kong's small sites would be a relatively slender tower with a height-to-width ratio between 5 and 7, avoiding both slab-like elongation or pencil-like slimness. Indeed, to eliminate torsional forces, Lambon suggested a symmetrical layout in both dimensions was desirable, as eventually exemplified in the Harmony 1.[48] Greater formalisation of means-of-escape regulations later codified the 41-storey limit: Ng explained that the Harmony 1

> is 40 storeys [above ground floor] – basically a vertical cantilever, a very expensive structure. The regularity of the structure is crucial. But why not more than that? Because of the building regulations! [Higher blocks] exceeding 40 storeys now needed refuge floors, with the next jump being to 50 storeys.[49]

'We were able to get away with 200 mm wall thickness for 41-storey blocks by transferring the load three or four storeys up'[50] (Lambon). A typical floor was constructed in five phases, for the core and four wings: the construction cycle for a standard Harmony 1 required eight days per floor in the early '90s, but this was gradually cut to six and then four in prototype projects.[51]

The most emphatic demonstration of the modular flexibility of the New Standard Block/Harmony concept was the ease with which its plan-form accommodated an unexpected but radical intervention by Akers-Jones, at the mid-1988 HA Building Committee meeting that approved the detailed block plans. In the course of discussion, he remarked off-the-cuff that the kitchens were too small for contemporary expectations, and suggested a modest enlargement: he recalled later that

> I was very worried about the housewives, because they had to spend so much time in the kitchen. Little things like that are vital. I also tried without success to get shower cabinets introduced in all blocks rather than baths, which were taking up so much space and were unpopular in Hong Kong owing to people's dislike of sitting in dirty water![52]

Lambon recalled the intervention at length: 'Sir David Akers-Jones, at that Building Committee meeting, changed the whole course of public housing in Hong Kong with one remark: he said he thought the kitchens weren't big enough. This kitchen enlargement shunted everything outwards, and we then had to extend the bedroom outwards, putting a kink in the façade, otherwise the bed wouldn't have fitted in! He was recognising that we shouldn't just stick to the brief, but should bump up the area. But that, in turn, would have a phenomenal effect on the space we constructed. Adding two square metres to, say, 40,000 flats a year – that would be millions of square metres over decades! It pushed out the bedroom by 600 mm, and in turn made every third wall longer by 1200 mm across the whole width of the block, which did of course add to stability. Now you can feel the structure, the crosswalls, coming into the lift lobby. Sir David was a nice old soul, gentle, genuine, colonial, polite, and he said the kitchen should be bigger. People said, "Does he know how much this is going to cost?!" – but we went ahead and did it!' New CAD drawings by D & S in November 1988 showed the enlarged 'modular' plan, with the two-bedroom flat, for instance, now 48 sq m in area. Finalised 'modular' flat drawings were eventually produced in November 1988 by D & S.[53]

Akers-Jones also suggested, and secured Wilson's agreement to, the name 'Harmony', for the project, with its Chinese translation, 和諧(Cantonese pronunciation 'wo hai'). 'I suggested Harmony because it translates very nicely into Chinese, as does Concord too. It stood for social harmony, which we were talking a lot about at the time'. Poon recalled that 'There were some discussions before we decided on that name, but not much! And eventually, it was Akers-Jones who said, "This is it!"' Wilson recalled, 'We needed to find a nice name for it, and Harmony was rather good, I thought! That's exactly why David was such a good person on occasions like that – he'd think of a good name right away. He's the archetype of the sort of person you wanted as a public servant in Hong Kong – deeply imbued with an understanding of Chinese culture'.[54]

From that point, the detailed implementation of the three designs was carried forward by weekly meetings of all the Senior Architects with Nutt, and in December 1988, it was announced that the first Harmony contracts would be awarded in mid-1989. Messling argued that this would encourage Hong Kong's manufacturers to start new production lines to prefabricate standard components such as doors, windows and cooking-benches; as flat-sizes, unlike Trident and Linear, were standardised, this would 'require the same construction components'.[55] In the same month Akers-Jones contended that Harmony prefabrication would help continue high output, by counterbalancing the shortage of building workers: in the meantime, because of slippage from last year, the Housing Authority would build a record 60,000 units in 1988–9 and the private sector 38,000, making this 'another bumper year' for housing production, with the first 8,000 inhabitants being moved out of the Walled City.[56] (Figure 11.8)

In a further output boost, the new blocks' more compact plans allowed appreciable density gains, and a higher proportion of HOS. This began emerging as early as July 1988, when some of the first estates to host the new blocks, chiefly at Tin

Welcome mat for Harmony housing plan

HONGKONG families are becoming smaller, but the Government flats they occupy will be bigger, reports JIMMY LEUNG.

HONGKONG families will have a lot more space when they move into "production-line" government flats which will be completed between mid-1992 and 1993.

The 10,000 to 15,000 Harmony flats will not only be 10 per cent larger than the average Government high-rise accommodation, they will have fewer bedrooms and concentrate instead on larger living areas.

The floor area of a single-bedroom flat will be 34 square metres while the two and three-bedroom units will be 43 and 50 square metres respectively.

The switch to flats with only one or two bedrooms has been made because Hongkong couples are having fewer children. At present, many Government flats have three bedrooms.

Harmony flats, which will house up to 57,000, also overcome the shortage of labour in the building industry, and are more cost-effective to build than a conventional design.

Many of the fittings are mass-produced in factories, whereas in the past they were made on-site.

Housing Department chief architect Tim Nutt said existing designs were considered unsuitable for the 90s.

"The existing flat designs, which call for larger three-bedroom flats, will not meet future demands as Hongkong families are getting smaller. Therefore, the latest flat mix concentrates mainly on one or two bedrooms."

The severe shortage of labour in 1988 prompted Mr Nutt's team of housing architects to study ways of reducing on-site labour.

"Labour shortage encouraged us to look at mechanised methods of construction," he said.

At present, only the Trident IV blocks are considered suitable for upgrading from rental to Home Ownership Scheme (HOS) housing. But the Harmony blocks will be built close to HOS standards in order to achieve flexibility in switching from rental to HOS.

"The use of modular designs to create housing is a very interesting and exciting concept. It is a different form of architecture which retains total dimensional co-ordination," said Mr Nutt.

The new designs standardise building components and fittings. These include doors, windows, sinks, cooking benches, concrete staircases and iron railings.

"This enables more of the building elements to be fabricated off-site, thus facilitating quality management throughout the whole process," said Mr Nutt.

The Housing Authority has insisted that concrete manufacturers comply with standards at source.

A separate list of approved building contractors will be drawn up. A new points scheme has also been approved. The aim is to weed out builders with poor workmanship.

So what do the customers get? A Harmony show flat opposite Lok Fu estate in Wang Tau Hom has a bigger utility area and kitchen than the average flat. The kitchen has enough room for a refrigerator and a washing machine.

Electric wiring and television circuits are concealed above the ceiling.

The ledge supporting the window has been pre-cast and reinforced to avoid the common problem of leaks.

Housing Authority consultants are studying an appropriate colour scheme for the Harmony flats.

The new design was approved by the authority's building committee in October 1988. The first piling contract was awarded in December that year for an estate in Tin Shui Wai, northwest New Territories.

The first building contract was awarded in September last year to build the Hau Tak estate in Junk Bay, which is scheduled for completion in early 1993.

Inside a new two-bedroom Harmony home.

Figure 11.8 March 1990 SCMP article on finalised Harmony plans, with commentary on the project by Tim Nutt.

Figure 11.9 Tin Shui Estate, HD model of revised August 1988 layout, including ten 39-storey Harmony 1s and four 37-storey Harmony 2s, complete with indicative Michel Cler colour scheme, and flat interior with original square-paned metal windows – pictured in 1991–2 HA *Annual Report.*

Shui Wai, were rapidly replanned. At TSW Area 5 (Tin Yiu Estate: PHDP code YL03), a 2,728 ppha net layout of March 1988 for fifteen Trident 3 and 4 blocks, with 9,384 rental and 1,224 HOS units, was replaced in July by seven Tridents, in Phases 1 and 2, and a combination of five 35-storey 'Tower 2' blocks in Phase 3 and three 39-storey 'Tower 1' in Phase 4 – yielding a new net density of 2,962 ppha (2400 gross), and providing 8,990 rental and 1,824 HOS flats. At TSW Area 16 (Tin Shui Estate/YL04), whose planning was less well-advanced, twelve Tridents were completely replaced by ten 39-storey 'Tower 1' and four 37-storey 'Tower 2' blocks, nudging up density from 2,400 to 2,474 ppha and flat units from 9,044 to 9,248.[57] In March 1989, Nutt and Messling explained detailed design drawings were nearing completion, and the first piling contract for the new design had been let in December 1988 at Phase 4 of Tin Yiu for three Harmony 1s containing 1,824 flats.[58] (Figures 11.9, 11.10a–c)

John Ng recalled the irony that '1989 was the year of Tienanmen – a very difficult year for Hong Kong – and it was the birth year of the Harmony'.[59] But there was a significant down-side: by late 1989 it was becoming appreciated that Harmony blocks would be 30% more expensive than existing blocks, for an equivalent numbers of flats – although DDH Administration and Policy Nigel French stressed this would not affect the HA's $1.8bn forecast cash surplus for 1990–1.[60]

In a March 1990 interview, Tim Nutt made a virtue of these costly higher standards, highlighting the 10% overall increase in size and lower proportion of large flats, reflecting the fact families were having fewer children: he argued the 1988 labour shortage had accelerated the drive towards greater prefabrication and stressed that while the only Trident convertible to HOS was the Trident 4, all Harmony variants could easily change to HOS: the Harmony's modular design was 'a very interesting and exciting concept'.[61] By May 1992, IKEA's Hong Kong franchise-holder Dantas was fitting up show-flats in Tin Yiu Estate – the first time

Figure 11.10 (a) Tin Shui Wai Area 5 Phase 4, Tin Yau Court, using 39-storey Harmony 1 for HOS, with original square-paned windows; in background, Tin Yiu Estate Phase 3, 35-storey Harmony 2. In this 2019 photo (MG), the original mosaic scheme has been replaced by differently coloured paint on the concrete. (b) Phase 1 of Tin Shui Wai Area 5 was completed slightly earlier (February 1992) and featured Trident 3s whose original mosaic scheme, in horizontal bands, still survives: 2023 external view (MG). (c) Mosaic specimens (fallen tiles) from 1980s–90s developments, each comprising one row. From top: Sun Chui Estate Phase II, Sun Kit House (Twin Tower Block); Tin Yiu Estate, Yiu Foo House (Trident-3); Hong Wah Court HOS (38-storey Windmill); Siu Hong Court HOS (Flexi). 2023 photo (MG).

an outside firm had assisted in this way. Dantas's marketing director Stella Kwan argued 'the flexibility and diversity of our furnishings are ideal for the limited space… of a government flat'.[62] In March 1993 the SCMP highlighted the colour-coordination of the newly opened Harmony developments at Tin Shui Wai, 'to reflect the sky and water themes of sea and sunsets': these contrasted with adjacent private developments that were, 'by deliberate and complementary design, in a neutral off-white for balance'. Kong Churk-fan, chief architect, said of the modular principle that: 'Each room becomes a giant piece of Lego', and claimed that the name Harmony expressed the HA's 'determination to create a fully integrated New Town in harmony with its surroundings'.[63]

By then, however, the series was already evolving year-by-year, not least in the Harmony 1's heightening to 41 storeys: Ng recalled that by comparison with its predecessors, 'The Harmony has a much longer lifespan, with various versions to meet changing needs. Every year, we would have new versions – like Mercedes or Toyota, each year they have a slightly different version!' (Ng).[64] (Figure 11.11a–c) Lambon highlighted one adaptation tailor-made for a specific urban site:

> We were having more and more private architects working on our schemes, and they were obliged to use Harmony blocks. One of the schemes, at Sham Shui Po Camp, became a truncated Harmony: the Harmony 1a. One of the blocks there was a Harmony 3: the Harmony 3 was mostly patterned to fit into sites where older blocks were being demolished. The Sham Shui Po Camp site was under the flight-path, and the private architect there wanted to use a Harmony 1, so we worked out a truncated Harmony 1, coming down to about 14–19 storeys. That was when we'd gone through the CAD stages, and were a dab hand at knocking out a block quickly. So we could knock down the block to a reduced-height standard cruciform block.

The end wings in the Harmony 3 could already be rotated at any angle to help fit into awkward small sites. The most significant of all Harmony modifications, the 'Harmony Annex', approved in 1994, and a more economical 'New Harmony' series in 1999, will be dealt with in later chapters.[65] (Figures 11.12, 11.13)

During that evolution process, certain elements of the Harmony configuration – such as the central core, the flat sizes and maximum block height, remained as unchangeable core elements. Ng argued in 2012 that 'only one thing doesn't really change – the size of flat! The standard flat, even today, dates back to the early days of the Harmony: we developed a typical flat module, dictated by functional requirements: a kitchen with sink, cooking bench, fridge, washing machine, and circulation space, designed around a minimum. Any smaller than that, and you couldn't get in! Likewise the bedrooms. Not much changes in size – if you compare with the Harmony from the early '90s, flats haven't changed too much in size.'[66] Also fiercely defended was the 40 (upper-floor) storey height, as Gabriel recalled:

> In Design and Standards, around 1993–4, I was in an industry-wide working group looking at the Means of Escape Ordinance, many of whose members

Figure 11.11 (a) Ho Man Tin Estate, 2011 photo of upper-floor plan of a standard 41-storey Harmony 1, completed in 1998, included in an exhibition flat display (MG). (b) External view in 2011 of Yat Man House, Ho Man Tin, a standard Harmony 1 41-storey block (MG). (c) Yat Man House, Ho Man Tin: 2011 detail view of kitchen in Flat 3103 (MG).

Figure 11.12 Tsui Ping South Estate, Kwun Tong, four 37-storey Harmony 2 blocks completed 1995. 2015 photo (MG).

Figure 11.13 Ho Man Tin, Fat Kwong St, Tim Man House: low-rise Harmony 3b (completed 2000) with right-angled wing configuration, seen in 2010 (MG) from adjoining 41-storey Harmony 1 (Yat Man House) (cf. Fig. 11.5b, 11.5c).

> wanted to put refuge floors in any building above 25 storeys. We were only two years into the Harmony programme, and I said to them we just couldn't support this. Harmony established a benchmark, so as a result, a refuge floor has to go in above 40 floors. We got away with the refuge areas, but after the review we had to completely redesign all staircases in Harmony blocks.[67]

Ma Hang: individualising Harmony

Although the main stress within the Harmony programme was exploitation of small sites through standardisation of small-footprint towers, the Harmony concept had equally been, since its Habraken-influenced origins, potentially attuned towards individualised solutions. That alternative slant was vividly highlighted in the late 1980s/early 1990s in a project energetically promoted by Ward and Messling themselves – the protracted Ma Hang redevelopment project in Stanley. Although unusually low in gross density (634 pph/257 ppa), it proved to be the first harbinger of a new, 'site-specific' approach that would eventually dominate Hong Kong housing design from the 2000s. (Figure 11.14a, b)

Originally, the Ma Hang valley was a squatter area, incorporating also a local pig-farming community, and in the mid-1980s, renewal plans were begun by Penny Ward. In 1986, plans drawn up under the LTHS banner envisaged almost all the 8,000 existing inhabitants would be rehoused in 'village' groupings of 12-storey blocks, but this was opposed by influential local residents, and by Friends of the Earth, who blasted it as 'very oppressive' and 'not rural by anyone's standards'.[68] Gabriel recalled that despite the noxiousness of the pig farms, the plans provoked 'a lot of objections from the neighbouring private enclave of Chung Hom Kok, as we were going to build public housing next to it – the campaign was mainly led by articulate expatriates, and resident High Court judges'. The Town Planning Office also objected (1986/7) to Ward's proposal for 12-storey in situ redevelopment.[69] 'In the end, it was decided we would build something more acceptable, and this became the first of our site-specific designs. It used modular flats, but some arranged in single aspect [to avoid] any overlooking houses'. John Lambon, as Senior Architect (SA/13) under Penny Ward (CA/3), put together the concept plans in the late 1980s, and Rosman Wai developed and turned them into reality in Phase 1 (1989–94). Ma Hang was a mixture of rental and home-ownership, but targeting former residents of the squatter area.[70] Lambon recalled that

> the special Harmony at Ma Hang was all interconnected with the concept of a "rural Harmony". Stephen Poon was never behind the low-rise concept – he was the man who liked cruciform blocks, as that way you could fit more in, and he never favoured this long, winding configuration of "special Harmony", but Penny was such a power in her own right, and had collared the best sites, and the project was her and Derek's "baby", that it got built, and it turned out to be the Department's prestige scheme.[71]

Figure 11.14 (a) Ma Hang Estate, Stanley, 'Harmony Rural' low-rise blocks of up to 12 storeys, completed between 1993 and 2000: distant view showing stepping-up profile, 2010 (Chief Architect Penny Ward, project architects Rosman Wai, Phase 1, and C K Yeung, Phase 2) (MG). (b) Derek Messling and Penny Ward, seen at the 2004 reunion of the Hong Kong Housing Authority Golfing Society (UK Branch) at the Springs Hotel, Wallingford: Messling founded HAGS-UK, for retired expatriate staff, on his own retiral in 1993.

Rosman Wai later recalled her own pioneering work on Phase 1 in detail:

Phase 1 was completed in 1994, Phase 2 in 1997, and the non-residential Phase 3 later, including relocation of the Murray Building. In Phase 1, we used truncated Harmony blocks with pitched roofs – a sustainable, low-rise plan with the trees conserved. I was working under Stephen Poon, who insisted on consistency, with variation only between standard designs. But we were able to get some variations in this special case. In Phase 1, I established the design language of the domestic blocks and the external work, which was followed in Phase 2 with variations. On

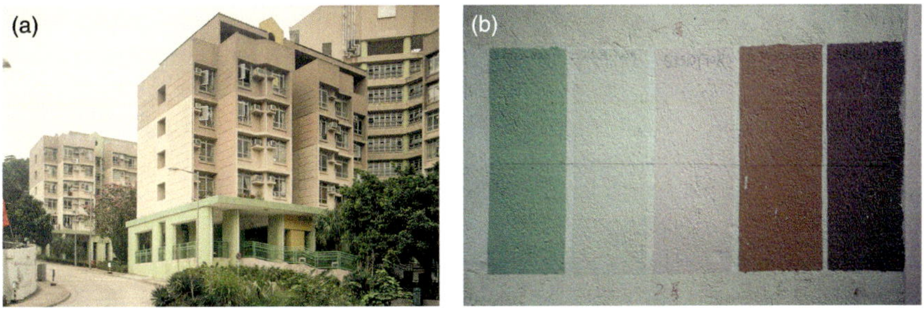

Figure 11.15 (a) Ma Hang Estate Phase 2, detail view of low-rise Harmony Rural blocks, 2010 – showing green mosaic base and acrylic paintwork above. The scheme was initially specified by Michel Cler, emphasising the structure of the blocks (MG). (b) Ma Hang Phase 2, detail of paint colour-match patches for maintenance staff: scheme originally supplied by Cler, and adapted by the project architects. 2010 photo. (MG).

> the blocks, I put in colour externally, and changed the outside balcony, giving it round corners. I thought it would be good if people could extend their home outwards, and play mah-jong there – but in the event I've never seen people using them to extend their homes. On the colour, we worked with Michel and France Cler. He drew on paper, but it was so difficult to transfer that colour on to the building materials, to give that subtlety there. Even for this more site-specific design, it had to be within the tight budget. We didn't spend money on decoration, but we did, and still do, spend a lot on external works, which is what most people can enjoy. We have a tight budget – even at Ma Hang – so there we focused more on the bottom of the blocks, at the pedestrian level. Ma Hang only cost 5% more, for all the site works, etc., than the standard cost per square metre.[72] (Figure 11.15a, b)

The layout concepts of the three phases were rather different, with the courtyards of Phase 1 aiming 'to recreate the form of the squatter community' but Phase 2 adopting a 'village street' configuration. Overall, the building heights stepped up the hillside, to twelve storeys maximum.[73]

In the design work of Wai and later colleagues at Ma Hang, the Hong Kong stress on high-quality external works and landscaping, as against Singapore-style (or private-sector) embellishment of the blocks themselves, took a decisive leap forward:

> It was good to be able to work with landscape architects on the whole design, not just trees or hard landscape. When I first went to Ma Hang, I assumed from the name there must be a stream there. The Engineer said, "Oh, no – there was, but I've already diverted them into a manhole." So we created an artificial stream, like a bathtub, in fibreglass, with a drain-hole, using stream water, replenished with tap water. Later on I saw lots of beautiful granite stones here.

> The Engineer said, "Oh no, you're not going to preserve these stones, are you?" I said, "Yes!" So we managed to find a place to store them, and put them back, mixed with other stones. We also preserved or transplanted over three hundred trees alone. First we put them on the outside of the road, then we put them back. Then we designed around the old trees in laying out the courtyard. After the project, I began to realise that the trees were all different – the trees have different characters themselves, they complement the design.[74]

Building contracts – quantity *and* quality?

Paralleling the new design trends and the emergence of Harmony, was a growing trend in construction towards 'quality'. As Poon recalled, the key problems were now both of capacity and of quality: 'There had been an even production level through the 1980s, but by the late '80s capacity became an issue – the same issue that would later lead to our downfall in the early 2000s'.[75]

In August 1988, Messling reported labour shortages were impacting on half of the 150,000 units under construction: the proportion of delayed projects had jumped from 8% in 1985–6 to 37.5% in 1987–8. For example, at Tai Wo Phase 1, 9,360 flats scheduled for completion in March 1988, were now delayed until October. In that month a speech by Wilson framed the Harmony as a response to this 'acute labour shortage'. And in April 1989, the developers Shui On reported labour shortages had pushed up prices and depressed starts: the HA had to increase its capital budget from $4.5 billion for 1989–90 to $4.9 billion.[76] In a January 1989 update, Messling advocated greater mechanisation and better conditions for building workers as 'vital' to help tackle the shortages, whose first signs had appeared eighteen months previously. Possibly because the building industry's bad working conditions were unattractive to young school-leavers, it was now 10,000 workers short, out of an optimum 70,000 workforce, and the problem had 'eaten deep into the housing programme': tender prices had soared by 10–12%, and 55% of the 85 building contracts started at the end of October 1988 were now late. In 1987–8, exceptionally, the HA would not achieve its 40,000 target; only 24,000 would be completed. Of the 225,145 public-sector flats planned for 1990–5, if construction times lengthened by 10%, only 214,236 would actually be realised.[77] However, Messling predicted, the shortages would ease during 1989 as the economy slowed, and mechanisation would help the HD prepare for the 'next property boom'; and a year later, in January 1990, he reported the labour shortage had stabilised, possibly because of the 'Tiananmen effect'.[78]

In parallel to this quantitative challenge, the issue of quality control was also rearing its head, an issue exacerbated at times of industry overload by the competitive-tendering system – an unchallenged shibboleth in laissez-faire Hong Kong. Assistant Housing Director (Construction Branch) Tom Blair reported in January 1990 that there were still workmanship problems even following the '26 Blocks' scandal, rehousing for which (16,644 families) had been only recently completed; 1987 had seen the charging of ten individuals by the ICAC, but Blair emphasised the 26 blocks' crosswall construction precluded any structural failure.

Site safety in general was still poor, with one in three workers in the construction industry injured the previous year – a situation that only further deterred new entrants.[79]

The first response, in 1989, was to bolster the system of preferred contractors: in January 1990, it was reported that 190 applicants were to join the HA's 'elite list', who would have to implement quality management schemes by March 1993. This was reinforced in 1990 by the introduction, initially on five pilot sites, of a new and more sophisticated Performance Assessment Scoring System (PASS) for contractors.[80] The coincidence of labour shortages and this drive for contractual quality massively reinforced the shift towards prefabrication – a trend linked to the migration of factories to the mainland and the more general 'de-industrialisation' of Hong Kong. In August 1987 Todd reported that 75% of current contracts were using large-panel formwork, which hugely reduced the amount of carpentry needed. In 1988 Poon explained all tenders from July would require use of large-panel system elements, largely for quality-control purposes, as this would not save any time.[81] He later recalled, 'Our move to semi-mechanised construction was *both* to improve quality and to get round shortages'. But even in the early 1990s, 'for the main structure, we still did these in situ. For non-structural elements, we used precast only – we only precast the facades, not the bathrooms, etc., whereas they do precast the bathrooms nowadays'.[82] Gabriel recalled that during the early 1990s,

> we made it mandatory for contractors to provide precast concrete facades, staircases and so forth. We introduced factory production of all internal components – windows, doors. Our requirement for this led to the development of lots of factories across the border in China to make doors, cooking-benches and so on. This exercise led to the development of a precast concrete business in Hong Kong, with ten companies, firstly on some construction sites and separate sites in Hong Kong, but later with factories across the border in Guangdong.[83]

This drive for higher building quality culminated, as we will see in the next chapter, in the HD Construction Branch becoming, in 1993, the first design office in Hong Kong to adopt ISO 9000, linked to a drive for contractor accreditation.[84]

More generally, the building shortages of around 1989 provided a first opportunity for Chinese mainland enterprises to launch large-scale involvements in Hong Kong – a phenomenon that would culminate a quarter-century later (Chapter 14).[85] Both contractors and property enterprises were involved, with housing providing particular opportunities for skilled workers in short supply in Hong Kong, such as formwork assemblers.[86] An August 1988 article on China Overseas Building Development, a subsidiary of China State Construction Engineering, highlighted the unprecedented scale of the $16 billion civil engineering contract at Tin Shui Wai, being carried out jointly by CSCE and Bilfiger & Berger (Germany). COBD, which already had an annual turnover of $600–700 million in 1984–7, had invested $1.66 billion in Hong Kong property, while local contractors complained of undercutting by it and other Chinese government-backed building enterprises, which could afford a smaller profit margin. General Manager Wenjie openly argued that profit was 'a secondary consideration' for COBD.[87] For the moment, the potential 'mainlandisation' of the Hong Kong construction sector was a small cloud on the horizon. At the other end of the spectrum were Japanese contractors, 'awash with cash, and selling mechanisation'.[88]

Conclusion

1992–3 saw the First Review of the Housing Strategy, published in October 1993 as the *Report on the Mid-Term Review*, at the end of its first 6-year period.[89] This highlighted that good progress had been made on output: between 1985/6 and 1992/3, 612,000 new flats had been built by private and public sectors (against a target of 605,000), of which 355,000 were public. Two major problems, however, were highlighted. The first was in organisation of the housing programme, with a decline anticipated in annual public-sector supply from 44,000 currently to 34,000 after 1994/5, partly owing to land shortages, with sites for only 29,000 flats annual output identified up to 1998. Secondly, there was the mobility of public housing tenants, with urgent corrective action needed to get the target of 60% home-ownership back on track: too few of those displaced by redevelopment (4–9%) opted for HOS, while 13% of public rental tenants owned other flats, many as extension space for large families. Thirdly, there was the failure of the HPLS, which the original LTHS had assumed would cover 102,500 private flats from 1988/9 to 2000/1: rising prices over the previous two years meant only 15% of the original target was likely to be achieved. This left the newly financially autonomous HA now facing (in Tony Eason's words) a potentially 'huge deficit'.[90]

Probably the most important problem addressed in the October 1993 Review, however, was land supply (Chapter 3). Ongoing problems weighing down on the PHDP were highlighted, especially at Tiu Keng Leng/Tseung Kwan O Town Centre (where 19,100 completions were at risk from lack of sites), and Tung Chung Areas 30 and 31, which might slip 'outside the LTHS period'. The previous PHDP review, in June 1993, had set a target of 63,000 units to be realised from 'problem' sites such as these by 2000–1, but this was now halved, to only 31,600. This shortfall would be combated by devices such as cutting the lead time on development sites, raising densities on existing sites, and government acceleration of clearances and land supply – all expedients that would be repeatedly revived over the following three decades, both before and after 1997, as we will see in the next three chapters.[91]

However, the potential trajectory of the remaining five years until 1997 had now begun to look potentially more confrontational, as London, in one of its now rare interventions in Hong Kong governance, moved to end Wilson's governorship despite ExCo objections in 1992: Prime Minister John Major and Foreign Secretary Douglas Hurd both allegedly wished to see a politician rather than diplomat in charge for the final five years. (Figure 11.16) Senior ExCo member Lydia Dunn, the highest-ranking Chinese member of government, warned that this would create a 'prolonged period of speculation and uncertainty'. According to journalist Jonathan Dimbleby, Hurd and Major both regarded Wilson as 'one of the principal advocates of the "appeasement" of China, an approach which they believed could

Figure 11.16 Visit by Prime Minister John Major to Heng On Estate, Ma On Shan, in 1991 – as pictured in the 1991–2 HA *Annual Report*. Left to right: Sir David Akers-Jones; Sir David Wilson; Mrs Norma Major; John Major; a prime-ministerial aide; Fung Tung; and Sir Percy Cradock.

no longer be sustained after the atrocity in Tienanmen Square in June 1989'.[92] There were also claims that London had attempted to override the open public tendering system in favour of British firms, but that Wilson had successfully defended Hong Kong's autonomy, for example concerning award of a patrol-boat contract to Australia. On 27 December 1991 Hurd wrote to Dunn that he and Major had agreed a 'political personality' should take over. Dunn was 'clearly surprised and unhappy', as Wilson had been seen as an 'old China hand' who could secure cooperation with Beijing on sovereignty matters.[93]

In his final annual address two months earlier, Wilson had acknowledged the modest but unmistakeable shift towards elected membership of LegCo – now including over half its members for the first time – but continued to place greatest emphasis on the transformation of society by government social programmes, with education and housing leading the way. In final reflections in February 1992, Wilson wrote in glowing terms of the government's achievement in raising the social conditions of poorer immigrants, with public housing a key foundation:

> You can see the pride shining in their faces. They come from manual backgrounds and housing estates and they are seeing their children getting a really good education... That highly upwardly mobile society is one of the most attractive features of Hong Kong.

1997, he predicted, would not be 'the death knell for the territory'. But as we will see in the next chapter, the ride towards that point would be an increasingly bumpy one, and the trajectory of public housing in those five years would become correspondingly erratic and unpredictable.[94]

Notes

1 Lambon, 2012 interview.
2 Gabriel, 2009 interview. Singapore: Glendinning, *Mass Housing*, 516–17.
3 Poon, 2009 interview; Lambon, 2012 interview. Compare with 'housers vs. planners' debates in 1960s Britain, Glendinning, *Mass Housing*, 158–64.
4 Cheung, 2012 interview; HKRS 276-8-639 8-1987 cutting.
5 Rosanna Wong, 2014 interview; Cheung, 2012 interview.
6 Information from Chris Gabriel, 2023.
7 HKRS70-8-2044 Messling paper 30-9-1987.
8 HKRS2298-1-35 11-8-1988 note to CA/5; Poon, in *BJ* 8-1988, 43. HKRS70-8-2044, papers of 10/11-1987.
9 Cheung, 2012 interview.
10 Yeung and Wong, *Fifty Years,* 2003, 57.
11 *Tseung Kwan O, Mini City in the Making*, 1991, 20; HKRS276-8-639 13-11-1987 memo to LPVC; *BJ* 8-88 on Lei Tung, Ap Lei Chau and Kowloon Walled City.
12 Ng, 2023 interview; Poon, 2010 interview; Lambon, 2012 interview.
13 Ng, 2023 interview.
14 Messling, 'Public housing – a numbers game', 4; V M Schindler, 'Polychrome Environments at the Centre Pompidou in Paris'; 1993 booklet, 'Harmony Chromatic Chart'; SCMP 26-3-1993, 46.
15 Poon, 2014 interview; Lambon, 2012 interview.
16 'Housing Chromatic Chart', 1993; Ng, 2023 interview; SCMP 26-3-1993, 46.
17 Franck Gintrand, 'Emile Aillaud et la théorie des grands ensembles', *Chroniques d'architecture*, 12-6-2018.
18 SCMP 26-3-1993, 46; Poon, 2009 interview.
19 Goodstadt, 'Fiscal freedom', 2010, 273-294.
20 Information from Chris Gabriel, 2023.
21 Hong Kong housing as a micro-ecology: cf. *The Corrupting Sea.*
22 Lambon, Pritchard and Hall, interview 2012.
23 SCMP 20-10-1988, 2: Wilson on Nutt's role; Lambon, 2012 interview; Poon, 2009 interview; SCMP 22-3-1990, Nutt on Harmony; SCMP 22-3-1990, Jimmy Leung; Gabriel, 2011 interview.
24 Construction Branch, Housing Department, *Portfolio of Works*, 1986 (John Lambon collection): includes HD organisation chart: Director of Housing Y L Pang, DD(C) D Messling, AD (Housing Architect) S C Poon.
25 HD, *Living in Harmony*, 1989 (John Lambon collection).
26 HD, *Design Brief for New Rental Domestic Blocks*, 30-12-1987 (John Lambon collection).
27 Poon, 2009 interview; Lambon, 2012 interview.
28 8-1987 memo from P Ainsworth (John Lambon collection).
29 13-11-1987 memo by Messling (John Lambon collection).

30 Poon, 2009, 2014 interviews.
31 Ng, 2012 interview.
32 Lambon, 2012 interview.
33 30-12-1987 paper, 'Design Brief for New Rental Domestic Blocks' (John Lambon collection).
34 Poon, 2014 interview.
35 3-8-1987 memo from A/15 (Lambon) to CA/5, SA/8, SA/15, A/25, A/32, A/46, A/51, 'Development & Standards – New Standard Design' (John Lambon collection).
36 HKRS1881-1-9 17-11-1988 memo from Fung A/20 to CA/4; CADD 'macros', CA5 memos of 17-11-1989, 15-8-1989. 24-7-1987 and 29-7-1987 CAD drawings, 'New Housing Design' (initialled by DDC D R Messling, CA5, SA5, and A/15 Lambon. (John Lambon collection).
37 23-10-1987 memo from SC Poon AD/Housing Architect, to all professionals in Architectural Division (John Lambon collection).
38 Lambon, 2012 interview, and John Lambon collection.
39 Memo of 11-3-1987 from Y G Lim about flat mix (John Lambon collection).
40 30-12-1987 paper, 'Design Brief for New Rental Domestic Blocks' (John Lambon collection)
41 Options 1-4: 1881-1-9 4-8-1988 PS Chan memo, 29-7-1989 project table. SCMP 8-2-1988, 4 (Poon).
42 Lambon, 2012 interview; 20-8-1987 Lambon to CA/5 D & S, 'New Standard Design' (John Lambon collection).
43 HKRS1881-1-9, 4-8-1988 and 10-8-1988 from P Chan. Ada Fung, 2023 interview; Ng, 2023 interview. Chan and Chan, 'Public housing construction in Hong Kong: a review of its design and construction innovations', *Architectural Science Review*, vol 45, 2002, 349–59. Differences between Harmony 1, 2, 3: Poon, 2009 interview; Lambon, 2012 interview; Ng, 2012 interview.
44 Ng, 2012 interview. Harmony 3: 11-1-1988 papers, 'New Standard Designs – Low Block' (John Lambon collection).
45 Lambon and Pritchard, 2012 interview.
46 Lambon, 2012 interview.
47 18-6-1987 memo and debate, J Lambon and P Ainsworth (John Lambon collection).
48 11-1-1988, 'Standard Low Block', proposal by SA/8, A/15 (John Lambon collection).
49 Coupled shear walls: Ng, 2012 interview; Gabriel, 2011 interview; Poon, *BJ* 8-1988, 85–9. Flexibility with less frequent shear walls: 3-8-1987 memo from J Lambon A/15 to distribution list (John Lambon collection). Poon on new generation of housing blocks likely to be 36 storeys maximum, including 27-storey 'Low Rise' blocks 'to fit into long, narrow sites': *BJ* 8-1988, 46–9.
50 Lambon, 2012 interview.
51 Ng, 2023 interview. Chan and Chan, 'Public housing construction', 351–5: each extra floor below 40 cost 3% extra, above 40 10% extra; construction periods as at 1996, Harmony 1, 41-storey, 35 months; Harmony 2, 41-storey, 35 months; Harmony 3, 30-storey, 31 months; New Cruciform Block, 38-storey, 34 months; precast facades first introduced in contracts from 1989, and covered 25% of blocks by 1991. Lambon, 2012 interview. HD, *Living in Harmony*, 1989 (John Lambon collection).
52 Akers-Jones, 2013 interview.
53 Lambon, 2012 interview; 1-11-1988 CAD drawings, 'Harmony Blocks', by CA/5, D & S, Construction Branch (John Lambon collection).

54 Lord Wilson, 2023 interview; Akers-Jones, 2013 interview; Poon, 2014 interview.
55 HKRS1881-1-9, 12-9-1988 D & S meeting 8, minutes; SCMP 12-12-1988, 6.
56 SCMP 26-12-1988, 2.
57 HKRS307-5-15, 8-1988 redrawn plans of Tin Yiu, Tin Shui; HKRS1881-1-9 28-7-1989 table of Harmony projects, 3-5-1990 CA/5 memo. See also Edward Ho in SCMP 25-3-1989, 4; Housing Authority, *Annual Report*, 1992/3, 16-19; SCMP 22-3-1990 (Nutt); SCMP 3-1-1989, 3.
58 SCMP 25-3-199, 4 (Edward Ho).
59 Ng, 2012 interview.
60 DDH Administration and Policy Nigel French, in SCMP 10-11-1989, 3.
61 SCMP 22-3-1990 ('welcome mat').
62 SCMP 13-5-1992, 41.
63 SCMP 26-6-1993, 10–16.
64 Ng, 2012 interview; Lambon, 2012 interview. HKRS1881-2-33 minutes of LPVC 10/11-1987 (e.g. on Tai Wo Hau – flexi vs. NCB blocks); Gabriel, 2009 interview.
65 Lambon, 2012 interview. General evolution of block-types and 'Hong Kong housing database': see www.teoalida.com.
66 Ng, 2012 interview.
67 Gabriel, 2011 interview.
68 HKRS1881-2-19 papers of 2-1990 to 8-1992; SCMP 30-11-1988, 28 (on Ma Hang).
69 HKRS1881-2-5 on Ma Hang preliminary negotiations, dominant role of Penny Ward, and also 7-1987 note, Mary Sneddon.
70 Gabriel, 2011 interview; SCMP 17-7-1992 (K Sinclair); Lambon, 2012 interview.
71 Lambon, 2012 interview.
72 Wai, 2010 interview.
73 HKRS1881-2-25 notes for SDB 6-9-1993 meeting.
74 Wai, 2010 interview.
75 Poon, 2010 interview.
76 Tai Wo, SCMP 22-8-1988. Acute labour shortage, SCMP 13-10-1988, 9. Shui On, SCMP 11-6-1989, 45. Hsin Chong, SCMP 5-1-1989, 25.
77 Ada Fung, 2023 interview. SCMP 18-1-1989, 10.
78 Elite list, SCMP 2-1-1990, 6.
79 HKRS 545-2-318, 2-1987 and 11-1987 papers; HKRS70-8-2052, 4-1987 papers; Lambon, 2012 interview; SCMP 5-10-1988, 3. Fung Tung, 2010 interview; Poon, 2010 interview.
80 The PASS system was developed from Singapore's CONQUAS system: SCMP 2-1-1990, 6.
81 HKRS70-8-2044, Todd note, 1-8-1987; Poon, *BJ* 8-1988, 48–9.
82 Poon, 2009 and 2010 interviews.
83 Gabriel, 2009 interview.
84 Messling, 'Public housing – a numbers game', 3.
85 See Hung, *City on the Edge*, 78–81.
86 Ng, 2012 interview.
87 SCMP 24-8-1988, 34.
88 SCMP 11-6-1989, 45; Lambon, 2012 interview.
89 *LTHS – A Report on the Mid Term Review*, October 1993.
90 HKRS545-7-352: Eason in SCMP 3-4-1992.

91 *LTHS – A Report on the Mid Term Review*, 1993, 6–14.
92 Dimbleby, *The Last Governor*, 10–11. Lord Wilson, 2023 interview.
93 SCMP 2-1-2019: an account based on newly declassified files in National Archives, London. Lord Wilson, 2023 interview. See also SCMP 8-9-1991, 10; 31-12-1991, 15; 5-1-1992, 9; 6-1-1992, 16.
94 SCMP 15-2-1992, 19.

12 1992–1997

The last Governor – from constitutional impasse to housing boom

Introduction

Britain's last governor in Hong Kong, Chris Patten, a leading Conservative politician and close ally of Prime Minister Major, departed sharply from his predecessors in adopting a deliberately assertive role vis-à-vis Beijing, in the process setting up a more unpredictable dynamic for public housing. It is beyond the scope of this book to investigate why the Major government embarked on a course likely to antagonise China only a few years before the handover. As indicated in Patten's own diaries, the impact of Tiananmen was clearly fundamental in spurring a desire to entrench democratic reforms, as was a desire to bolster Hong Kong's growing middle class and 'middle-class values', but motives of national prestige were also in play: Patten wrote of the need to 'show the world that we can handle this last imperial responsibility in a decent way and which doesn't betray the people of Hong Kong', as a last flourish of 'British sovereignty, British honour and British competence in governing this great city'.[1] Undeniably, a post-Tiananmen vicious circle of misunderstandings and suspicions came to a head in these years, with roots stretching back to the debacle of the 1987–8 'public consultation' on democratisation. However, our more limited concern in this chapter is the impact of that 'vicious circle' on public housing, which was distinctly mixed.[2] Initially somewhat neglected in favour of Patten's political reforms, the housing programme was later seized on with furious energy, partly in reaction to setbacks in the constitutional field and partly in reaction to increasing public perceptions of a housing affordability crisis. Ironically, that belated drive for numbers would then provide the foundation for the identity-building housing strategy of Patten's post-1997 successor, C H Tung, including a much-trumpeted 85,000 annual completions target.[3] All this unfolded against the background of Hong Kong's transformation into a financialised global metropolis, and the ever-greater power of the property tycoons and their special interests.

It should be emphasised that the researching and writing of this chapter, and Chapters 13 and 14, was more challenging than Chapters 1–11, owing to the 30-year government archive rule which, in combination with the author's lack of Chinese reading ability, compelled an inordinate reliance on English-language newspapers, above all the establishment SCMP – alongside other published sources

DOI: 10.1201/9781315563701-15

and interviews with key actors, each with their own personal perspective. Every effort has, however, been taken to minimise bias or partiality in coverage!

Politicising the governorship: 'people's champion' or 'lame-duck'?

Immediately following the announcement of his appointment, in May 1992, Patten struck a bullish note, signalling his intention to 'mix it politically' and arguing that 'there is no difference [in Hong Kong] with the politics of the UK… There are people who think they are big shots, whether pundits or tycoons,' but in reality, 'as Governor, you are on top of the mountain'. The political aim internally would be 'open and accessible government', and externally, 'courteous but firm' dealings with Beijing.[4] Patten's inaugural policy speech in October focused mainly on the constitutional issue, and took a forceful line, with a 'go-for-it' proposal to extend the franchise to the whole working population (2.7 million people) via an extension of the functional constituency system in order to secure 'the widest democratic participation by the people of Hong Kong in the running of their own affairs': a political agenda branded by most commentators as 'certain to bring him into conflict with China'.[5]

In line with a new emphasis on 'accountability', Patten simplified and dramatised his domestic policy into a series of bullet-point 'pledges' which could then later be reported on in public 'report cards'. In the social-policy section of his address, where Patten later recalled that 'it did seem to me that Hong Kong had a first world economy, but pretty Third World social and community services', the pledges promised radical improvements, but with relatively little practical change from the ethos of restrained interventionism financed out of the annual surpluses.[6] The focal spending increases planned before 1997 were health (22%) and education (16%), whereas housing commitments were more vague, focusing chiefly on a pledge of 60% homeownership by 1997 and two-thirds by 2001, a small-scale programme of 'sandwich class' housing of 13,000 flats by 1997, and a pledge to rehouse all existing urban squatters by 1996 (on all of which see below). Patten promised that the government would spend twice as much on public housing as on the new airport.[7]

The result was criticism from both sides: from business and 'united front' interests, on grounds of unnecessary provocation of China, and of the 'unrealistic' homeownership plans; and from social activists such as Lee Wing-tat, who argued the government should 'feel shame' for the territory's social deficiencies, including the 'inadequacy' of public housing.[8] Unprecedentedly, former governors, including even MacLehose, joined in the attacks on the constitutional proposals, and within the Hong Kong establishment, where much resentment lingered at the manner of Wilson's departure, arguments bubbled up that Patten was 'fiddling precariously' with the Joint Declaration and Basic Law. Akers-Jones, for example, questioned the shift to a 'penalty shoot-out over elections'.[9]

The Chinese response, to what Beijing viewed as British bad faith and backpedalling, was not long in coming, and gathered pace inexorably during 1993: talks collapsed in December, and six months later a Xinhua spokesman said that no

Patten: a one-issue Governor?

This week sees the first anniversary of Chris Patten's governorship of Hongkong. But apart from a very public battle with Beijing over constitutional reform, has he achieved anything else? Political Editor DANNY GITTINGS and QUINTON CHAN assess the first 12 months of the Patten administration.

EVEN before Governor Chris Patten's plane touched down at London's Heathrow Airport last week, the British public was ready for his arrival.

Spectator editor Dominic Lawson had been despatched to write a friendly profile explaining the dilemmas of a crusader for democracy. And London *Sunday Times* political columnist Michael Jones had been treated to a trip aboard the Lady Maurine before he, too, filed a column on the subject.

There were radio and television appearances before the ritualistic photo call with Foreign Secretary Douglas Hurd and his team.

This week, Hongkong will see another publicity blitz – celebrating Mr Patten's one-year tenure at Upper Albert Road. There will be the usual round of interviews in

thing else off the administration's agenda.

The Governor's team claim this is unfair; that the media only pays attention when he bashes Beijing, while calls to clean up the harbour pass almost unnoticed.

Yet, while political groups wanting to discuss the 1995 polls are still welcomed with open arms at Government House, other del-

Figure 12.1 Extract from July 1993 SCMP article on public perceptions of Governor Chris Patten in Hong Kong.

discussion on 'substantial issues' was possible with Patten, while Hong Kong and Macao Affairs Office director Lu Ping attacked him in May 1994 as being concerned only with staging 'a political show'. The rupture of negotiations the following month triggered a decisive shift from the previous 'through train' transition model to a sharp break in 1997, referred to in a contrasting metaphor, as 'building a new kitchen'. Negotiations on the massive airport project also stalled, only to be finally resolved in 1995.[10] A partial Chinese boycott of joint mechanisms such as the Land Commission, largely deadlocked the government's housing plans, including the sandwich class scheme – for which Planning, Environment and Lands Secretary Tony Eason was left to fend off criticisms.[11] (Figure 12.1) A July 1993 opinion poll in the SCMP on the question, 'Who has done the most good for Hong Kong?', returned 52% for Wilson, 29% for democratic politician Martin Lee, 27% for Patten, and 10% for Lu Ping – arguably reflecting some public boredom with the 'non-stop discussion' about the political reforms.[12] By the time of Patten's second policy address in October, some commentators unkindly argued that 'the crucial question this year is not so much what Mr Patten will say, but how many people will really bother to listen', and a *Sunday Morning Post* poll in June 1994 found that a majority (52 to 32%) believe that 'his job here is now done'. In his defence, John Walden, former Secretary for Home Affairs (1976–80), argued that he was 'the first Governor ever to have his predecessors and other protégés publicly oppose his efforts and lend their support to the Beijing government in its efforts to undermine his activity'.[13]

By December 1993, when Patten buried a 'time capsule' celebrating the 40th anniversary of the public housing programme in a new extension of Lei Cheng Uk estate,[14] many critics were already branding him a 'lame duck governor'. However, by then, housing – and more precisely soaring house prices – was re-emerging as an alternative domestic agenda issue, one whose public 'heat' contrasted with the apathy surrounding constitutional matters, and around which he could attempt to re-launch his governorship, as a 'people's champion'.[15] Underlining the character of housing as an 'alternative identity discourse', this tension or even opposition between the housing and constitutional-reform agendas was one that would persist and re-emerge, for example in the wake of the 2019 unrest. (Figure 12.2a, b)

Like previous governors, Patten had launched straight away into a programme of fact-finding tours, in which housing naturally featured prominently, for example at Ma Hang in September 1992.[16] On one of these tours, in March 1994, on an evening visit to Tin Shui Wai, now unexpectedly the scene of some of the 'hottest property speculation' in Hong Kong, with prices rising 40% in three months, Patten was 'struck by the stark contrast' between dark and largely empty private blocks and brightly lit and fully occupied public blocks next door. In reaction, as we will see later, he established an 'Interdepartmental Task Force on Land Supply and Property Prices', whose recommendations, by the time of his third policy address in October 1994, signalled a significantly boosted housing output of 505,000 public and private units by 2001, supervised by a new Policy Branch and Housing Secretary.[17]

Figure 12.2 (a) Chris Patten seen in mid-1992, visiting a resettlement block scheduled for redevelopment in Upper Wong Tai Sin Estate. (b) Chris Patten seen in December 1993, burying a 'time capsule' commemorating the 40th anniversary of the housing programme, in an extension to Lei Cheng Uk Estate.

We will trace the response to the affordability crisis in greater detail later, along with other emotive housing issues of more restricted scope, notably the rumbling issue of whether high-income tenants should be charged higher rents, or the controversy over Patten's October 1993 pledge to offer rehousing to all temporary housing area residents by 1997.[18] First, however, we need to note the housing-specific repercussions of Patten's clashes with Beijing. Professional and technical collaboration continued unabated, with numerous fact-finding visits in both directions.[19] But at a policy level there was mounting confusion, especially over land supply, where the boycott of the Land Commission was compounded by conflicting statements from mainland representatives. In July 1994 Lu Ping, Deputy Chairman of the Preliminary Working Committee, warned sternly, and in the event rather presciently, that 'housing supply would overtake demand if China yielded to all the [Hong Kong] government requests', and that the resulting glut could, after 1997, 'lead to the collapse of the property market due to over-supply'. Yet only four months later the Chinese PWC's social and security sub-group chair robustly lambasted the Hong Kong government for starving the public housing sector of land, on grounds that this created a risk of serious shortage in 1997 and after, and May 1995 PWC co-convener Wang Shuwen stressed public housing must be stepped up 'to satisfy the massive demand from residents'.[20]

Clearly, in contrast to the MacLehose-Liao era, the days of decisive unitary direction of the housing drive were now gone, and there was instead a situation of multiple competing drivers at the wheel, not forgetting of course the long-entrenched real-estate lobby – a situation which, as we will see, would be further compounded by growing divisions within the Hong Kong Government housing apparatus itself during the mid/late-1990s.[21]

Political debate and administrative reforms

Patten's task in re-establishing 'ownership' of the housing issue was also complicated by the politically polarising effects of his constitutional reform proposals. The new political front-line between pro-Beijing 'Liberals' and pro-autonomy 'Democrats' cut through the existing jungle of issue-based protesters and interest groups: for instance the well-established United Democrats, led by Martin Lee, had established strong pro-autonomy credentials in their battles both with Beijing and with Wilson immediately post-Tienanmen, but were now partly eclipsed by Patten.[22]

Some housing-issue lobbyists came down on Beijing's side: Elsie Tu (Elliott) branded Patten 'a phoney' dedicated to whipping up 'mass hysteria', and was appointed a Beijing adviser in 1994, only to be unseated from the Urban Council the following year by Szeto Wah of the Democratic Party: her continuing 'Victorian-philanthropic' attitudes towards 'the poor' were seen in her claim that overcrowding was to be deplored as an encouragement to incest by placing 'men and women… in close proximity', or that high house prices undermined 'the competitiveness enjoyed… by Hong Kong'.[23] Conversely, Lee Wing-Tat of the HKPCPHP (and OMELCO housing convener) became a United Democrats legislator while remaining highly critical of Patten's housing record, threatening in 1994 to sue the

Government in the International Court in The Hague for housing shortcomings, and singling out Housing Secretary Dominic Wong in 1996 for its 'annual award for the worst performance in housing'.[24] SoCO, now led by the charismatic Ho Hei-Wah, pursued a more neutral path: Ho criticised communist totalitarianism while harassing the government on housing matters, for example organising an annual protest march by cage-men to the Governor's house, or pointing out that a 1994 pledge by Patten to build 140,000 more public rental flats by 2001 merely recycled an existing plan.[25] Both HKPCPHP and SoCO, in their exclusive championing of rental housing, were now increasingly at odds with the wider political and societal pressures towards home-ownership.[26] On the pro-Beijing side, key establishment figures became involved as advisers, including Akers-Jones, Liao, and the architect and HA member Edward Ho, chairman from 1994 of a recently founded pro-Beijing business group, the Business and Professionals Federation (BPF). Handpicked by Wilson in 1987 to join LegCo and then (in 1991) ExCo, Ho resigned from the latter shortly after Patten took office, protesting that 'You can't be an adviser to someone who does not want your advice'.[27]

A 1994 study by Agnes Allcock of residents' associations both city-wide and locally (focusing on Kwai Tsing district) found that the new proliferation of pressure groups had created a lot of noise and activity, but their policy impact was uncertain, not least owing to the shared institutional consensus between Hong Kong and Chinese governments (in the latter case enshrined in Article 65 of the Basic Law) in favour of 'a very strong executive-led government'. Her case study of the redevelopment of Kwai Shing East Estate found that the agitation by local MACs for particular phasing or rehousing strategies usually ended up frustrated.[28] However, an executive-led system did not necessarily mean a well-coordinated system, as became abundantly clear in public housing during the 1990s, in a textbook example of bureaucratic change for change's sake. In these years, which saw Sir David Ford replaced as Chief Secretary in 1993 by Anson Chan, arguing in his retirement speech that the modern Hong Kong system 'isn't socialism, it's a society of compassion', the government service was publicly dominated by the imperative of localisation.[29] But alongside this, attempts at organisational reform continued apace – including in housing administration.

'Landlady for three million' – from Akers-Jones to Rosanna Wong

Patten's arrival catalysed a growing discontent within government administrators at the complete devolution to the post-1988 Housing Authority of not just executive but also policy responsibilities: calls began for it to lose some of its autonomy. Patten was disturbed by the public criticisms of the Authority, and senior officials argued it had 'failed to justify' its autonomy, especially given the low current output and ballooning waiting list (of 180,000) – although those stemmed largely from government failure to provide an adequate land-supply. There was also public unease at the rumoured low attendance records of some HA members, especially members of the Building Committee, and when the data were eventually released in 1995, the HKPCPHP demanded the sacking of all the 'lazy-bones'.[30]

But there were also personal animosities at play, as Akers-Jones's outspoken advocacy of the 'through train' principle, and his frequent visits to Chinese cities to 'break down barriers', brought him into direct conflict with Patten: he found his views were 'not welcome to the government, and I now had little or no contact with the Governor or Chief Secretary'. In this context, the post-1988 direct reporting line to the Governor had now changed from an asset to a liability.[31] The failure of Akers-Jones's 1990 Sale of Flats to Sitting Tenants Scheme (abandoned by ExCo in 1993) also undermined his status with the new administration, and Patten decided to allocate his new Sandwich Class Scheme to the Housing Society rather than the Authority (see below). Although his term as Chairman had been extended for two more years in April 1992, Akers-Jones had already decided that 'the time had come for a Chinese chairman to take over… an organisation responsible for housing half the people of Hong Kong'.[32] And the crisis, combined with stress from acrimonious attacks by tenant protest-groups, completed a 'process of outing' on his part. In March 1993, acknowledging the rift with Patten, and following calls to quit from two Democratic Party LegCo members, he resigned as HA Chairman on the spot, and shortly afterwards accepted nomination to Beijing's advisory body, electing to 'join my friends, knowing that this would expose me to criticism from the "stand up to China" hardliners who were spoiling for a fight' – although political opponents claimed there were also conflicts of interest with his business activities. A three-month interregnum brought to the surface the administrators' agenda, including demands from Tony Eason that the HA should henceforth report to him rather than directly to the Governor, and that its ideas must go through the 'discipline' of vetting by a 'policy branch' before going to Patten.[33]

Fung Tung, however, successfully fended off any change to the HA's governing ordinance, and then exploited Messling's retirement in September to defensively reorganise housing production, absorbing Construction within the Housing Management and Works directorate, while creating a new layer of assistant directors to shield top staff from the burgeoning pressure groups.[34] A new post of Deputy Director Works was created, which was filled by AD/Maintenance, Raymond Bates. Stephen Poon eventually succeeded Bates as DDW in 1996 when he retired.[35] As part of a systematic clear-out or demotion of senior expatriate staff before 1997 – facilitated by the fact that expatriate architects were employed on contract rather than incorporated in the permanent establishment – Tim Nutt left to work with contractor Paul Y to manage their precast-concrete component production for Harmony blocks (and later moved to a teaching post in CUHK), Bob Storey (also Chief Architect) left for Shun Shing Construction. Penny Ward retired at the same time as Messling: following clashes with Fung Tung over the planning of Ma Hang and Tung Chung, she was denied either extension of her post as a Chief Architect or even the conventional 'cruise ship' passage back home. However, after Miller took over from Fung as Director of Housing, Ward and Messling were invited back for the opening of Murray House in Stanley, which 'reconciled everything'.[36] Non-senior expatriate professionals domiciled in Hong Kong, however, were generally able to stay on – in John Lambon's case by engineering his own demotion from Senior Architect to Architect grade, after pressure on his behalf by the Association of Expatriate Civil Servants of Hong Kong.[37]

In place of Akers-Jones, Patten in 1993 appointed Rosanna Wong as HA chair. She was a member of his 'inner cabinet' of advisers, an Executive Councillor (the youngest-ever, on her 1988 appointment, and subsequently Convenor in 1996) and CEO of the Hong Kong Federation of Youth Groups. Initially, perhaps, he saw her as a more amenable figure who might also cope better with the stresses of grassroots participation. Her appointment initially provoked a storm of protest, on grounds of alleged inexperience, but in practice Wong proved a feisty and determined defender of the HA's powers and interests. Dubbed successively by the press the 'Iron Lady', 'Landlady for three million' and 'Home builder in a hurry', she developed further the emphasis on 'accountability' and consultation – for example expanding the EMAC network, or putting a full-scale interior model of the newly designed 'Concord' HOS standard flat on show on a site near the HA's Ho Man Tin headquarters (coordinated by Theresa Yim, Ken Cheung and Chris Gabriel) for public comments.[38] (Figure 12.3)

Wong's policy was to focus on only a few key issues at a time, and so she was quite happy, for instance, that Akers-Jones's tenant purchase scheme (which she thought risked creating 'ghettoes') had been scrapped. (Figure 12.4) She maintained an intense focus on land supply, and on cutting the waiting list – suspecting that of the 149,000 on the list, only about 60% might genuinely be eligible.[39] For her the 'number one issue' was land supply. 'I fought with the government – I said, "You must give me a stable supply of land!" They always owed me land. You had to form the land, which took five or six years to complete. So if they supplied me with land in 1994, I could only start building on it in 1996, and if they ceased supplying, it would have an impact in 1998! Before 1993, when Sir David Akers-Jones was chairman, they had the same problem – ever since the Housing Authority became independent, we had chased the government up day and night over the land supply. Fighting with the government, negotiating with the government. But finally we got our supply, in 1997–8, and we were building well over a hundred flats a day,

Figure 12.3 Rosanna Wong, seen in 2014 (MG).

Sheltering the needy

Rich tenants are to be encouraged to move out of public housing, writes **Ng Kang-chung**

HOUSING Authority chairman Rosanna Wong Yick-ming has set a new target for her subsidised housing reforms – ensuring resources and subsidies go to those who are really in need.

Authority members meet today to discuss a new scheme, which, if endorsed, will allow poorer public tenants to have their rents cut by half.

While about 150,000 families living in squalid huts or dilapidated blocks are waiting for public rental units, some subsidised flats are being occupied by wealthy tenants who own private apartments elsewhere.

A household on the waiting list has to wait about seven years before they are given a public unit.

At the same time, the authority is subsidising its rented homes to the tune of $1.5 billion this financial year.

It is against this backdrop that Ms Wong, also the convenor of Governor Chris Patten's Executive Council, is talking about "re-distribution of subsidies".

It will be a very sensitive task, demanding "a good deal of political courage", said the softly-spoken chairman, clenching her fists as she spoke to show her determination to deal with the difficult problem.

"The question is – are we subsidising those in need the most?

"We must address the question very carefully.

"Some may suggest using strict and harsh measures. It is easier said than done.

Social reformer . . . chairman Rosanna Wong on a visit to one of the Housing Authority's temporary flats. Photograph: Martin Chan

Figure 12.4 Rosanna Wong pictured visiting a temporary housing area in 1995, in a SCMP article on targeting of housing resources.

which led to the monitoring problems and short piling scandal that followed. But that was the number one agenda item on my plate – the land supply.'[40] A few other high-profile issues were also prioritised, such as the 'wealthy tenants' issue: North Point was identified as the worst culprit, 18% of its tenants owning private flats in the urban area. As an inducement to move, loan limits for private-sector flat purchase under the poorly performing HPLS were doubled in May 1995, as proposed by Akers-Jones at his last HA meeting in March 1993.[41]

Another underlying concern behind Patten's pressure on the HA was financial: a suspicion that, despite the failure of the HPLS and the claims of imminent income shortfalls, the Authority might in fact be sitting on billions of dollars of unused reserves, steadily accruing despite its obligatory annual transfer to government of 50% of its non-domestic surplus, amounting to $125 million in the 1992–3 financial year. Rosanna Wong recalled that

> when I was there, the government did not have to give me cash in hand. Because the most expensive thing in Hong Kong is land, so what was preferred was that the government gave the Housing Authority land free for rental, and charged 30% for the HOS land cost. And every year we gave them money back – we split our commercial earnings 50%–50% with them.[42]

During late 1993, the focus on the financial relationship with government sharpened: Patten insisted that the Authority should use its reserve rather than simply hoarding it, or risk confiscation by the government.[43] Rosanna Wong began doing just that, for example on a gated security project for PRH estates (see below). In May 1994, a deal between Treasury and the Authority was unveiled, under which the latter would siphon off almost all of its remaining $9.5 billion reserves to speed up public housing. That figure was later scaled down to $7.5 billion, which would be used to establish a development fund to allow building of an extra 10,000 public flats annually: it would finance site-enabling works, squatter rehousing, infrastructure works and urban renewal. Financial arguments also supported the drive to maximise HOS output, on grounds that the sale of one HOS flat paid for the construction of 3½ public rental flats.[44]

Dominic Wong – field-marshal without an army?

In his organisational reforms to the housing apparatus, Patten reacted against the devolved organisational model devised by Wilson and Akers-Jones, and in particular against the perceived failure of Akers-Jones's policy of rental flat sales. Instead, he returned almost, but not quite, full circle to MacLehose's post-1973 McKinsey reforms, by resurrecting the post of Housing Secretary, which was now charged with across-the-board coordination of all housing tenures, and serviced by a revived Housing Branch within central government – a plan initially suggested by Chief Secretary Anson Chan and Financial Secretary Macleod, and 'warmly endorsed' by Patten.[45] And contrary to 'new kitchen' rhetoric, these attempts at a more dirigiste approach in housing would continue, and would even be reinforced, post-1997 (Chapter 13). This bolstering of administrative power correspondingly implied a diminution of the unofficials' well-established involvement in public housing decision-making, but it was not yet a full-scale reversal: that would only come a decade later in the wake of economic crisis.

The new department had been initially conceived in October 1993 as a 'Housing Policy Division' under the aegis of Tony Eason, to be headed by his deputy, Leo Kwan Wong-Wah. However, by 1994 a fully fledged Secretary and Branch (established in November 1994) had been authorised, their principal task being a comprehensive update of the Long-Term Housing Strategy for the next thirty years – especially the coordination of land supply. The HA and the recently appointed Rosanna Wong were assured the new structure would not impinge on 'the current functions of the HA', including its direct reporting line to the Governor.[46] Rosanna Wong recalled the uneasy balance that followed:

> After a few years [from 1988] the government changed the team round again. They asked, "Who's looking after *policy*?" After the Housing Authority became independent, they did it all. But the government suddenly thought, "OK – the Housing Authority can still continue, but we want a Secretary for Housing, who'll take care of land supply". The Housing Branch was formed in 1994, but my relations with government were okay. The Housing Authority was

independent: the Branch "is over there". Sometimes I needed to talk to the Housing Secretary, but I had a certain degree of freedom.

On the whole, she recalled, the HA was left a relatively free hand by Patten in implementation, and the Housing Secretary's 'main concern was in developing the Long-Term Housing Strategy'.[47]

In June 1994, John Walden grumbled that 'it does not always follow that a post that looks essential in theory will, in practice, help achieve the prescribed objectives', and recalled the claims of ineffectiveness made against the Housing Secretary post during Lightbody's tenure in the 1970s – although the pre-1988 Secretary only had responsibility for *public* housing.[48] Nor was the feeble Housing Bureau of the 1960s a reassuring precedent: confusingly, the new Housing Branch was renamed 'Bureau' after 1997. Although a number of 'heavyweight' candidates were touted for the new Secretary post, such as Home Affairs Secretary Michael Suen and Culture Secretary James So,[49] the official eventually appointed, on 15 December 1994, Dominic Wong Shing-wah, was a controversial choice: in his previous role as Director of Education, he had unsuccessfully attempted to remove mention of the Tiananmen Square crackdown in school history textbooks and to lower admission standards to colleges of education. Wong immediately stirred up further controversy at the first Housing Authority meeting he attended, in January 1995, by proposing across-the-board rent rises – an off-the-cuff intervention that provoked outrage and derision from Authority members, with HKPCPHP chief executive Virginia Ip denouncing him as an 'incompetent' who 'knows nothing about housing'.[50] Eventually, as we will see later, Dominic Wong succeeded in drawing up a range of quite well-balanced policy reform proposals, while maintaining a good working relationship with Rosanna Wong and the Director of Housing, although some commentators saw the Branch–Authority relationship as one of intrinsic 'policy rivalry and disagreement'.[51] Tony Miller recalled that

> previously, there had been a disconnect in the forward planning of land. The reorganisation brought in Dominic. This was designed to ensure that at policy level in central government there was a clear voice to ensure the forward supply of serviced sites – which went back to the problems we had in the 1970s.[52]

Overall, however, the two-headed structure set up in 1994 prevented either Dominic Wong or the Housing Branch from establishing any decisive executive authority – especially with the behind-the-scenes power of the real-estate lobby.[53] He was like a newly promoted field-marshal with no direct power of command over his chief 'general' – or her 'army'. Against this background, quite radical policies could potentially snowball without anyone taking real ownership of them, with unforeseen circumstances – as we will see later in the egregious case of the 85,000 annual housing target that later came to haunt the HKSAR's first Chief Executive, Tung Chee-hwa, after 1997.

Upping the stakes: the mid-1990s house-price boom

The economic background of Patten's plans to boost public spending by $8 billion by 1997 – plans that were, ironically, denounced by some Beijing sympathisers as 'a kitty-draining attempt to turn Hong Kong into a socialist society' – remained firmly within the Hong Kong tradition of spending increases financed out of growth, albeit with the airport project now looming behind all spending discussions. Financial Secretary Hamish Macleod, and his successor from 1995, Donald Tsang, adapted their public profile to Patten's 'accessibility' mantra, submitting to LegCo 'grilling' in a way 'unthinkable' under Bremridge. January 1994 saw predictions that, yet again, an anticipated deficit would turn out to be a massive surplus ($20 billion surplus for 1993/4 rather than $3.3 billion deficit), only $2 billion less than in 1992/3.[54]

Land sales continued to provide a significant proportion of this government revenue, averaging by one calculation 17% between 1983 and 1995. Of this, half had to be immediately set aside in the HKSAR Land Fund, which reached a maximum of $85 billion in 1995, before being largely drawn down for approved purposes; however, stamp duty made up much of that shortfall. The corresponding figure in 2010–11 was still 17% (plus 7% stamp duty).[55] Thus the government's continuing prosperity – and, indeed, that of government personnel who might later move into consultancies with the major firms – remained interdependent with the real-estate industry and the time-honoured 'speculative landscape', and tied into the longstanding ideology of Hong Kong the 'land of opportunity and market freedom' that lay at 'the core of its coloniality' (Chu).[56]

The monopolistic, cartel-like structure of private housing production, and the dangers of collusion in bidding and price-fixing, were widely highlighted in this period, for example by the Consumer Council in 1996: in 1991–4 70% of all new units were built by seven developers, 50% by three (Sun Hung Kai, Cheung Kong and Henderson Land) and 25% by Sun Hung Kai alone – a position that would remain largely unchanged in 2012. The big firms had by now accumulated huge land banks, mainly agricultural, in the New Territories, with Sun Hung Kai alone holding 15 million sq ft, plus $1.5 billion in Letter B entitlements.[57] Yet public housing still had a vital supporting function, in its pump-priming role: Rosanna Wong recalled that

> because land was – and remains – so expensive, the plots that were suggested to the HA were in Tseung Kwan O and Tin Shui Wai, on reclaimed land. No one was going to go in and form that land first. So the government asks the Housing Authority, "You go in first!" I would need to form the land, build the roads, so that what used to be reclaimed land became formed land with infrastructure. Land prices go up from $1 to $100: you're using public housing to put up the value of land a hundredfold, and then the government sells the land to the private sector. It's pump-priming using public housing. That's how the government worked so cleverly: without any cash output, they were still able to be the winner by later selling the land!'[58]

The house-price spike of the early Patten years formed the culmination of Hong Kong's longest housing boom to date: there was an eightfold increase in prices between 1986 and 1997, when the average price of a 500 sq ft flat was fifteen times the 1980 figure. Between 1986 and 1996, the price index for private housing rose by 20% annually, far outstripping inflation (under 10% annually); and between 1991 and 1996 the Gini coefficient of inequality in Hong Kong society rose by 11%. Nobody could anticipate that a 57% crash in house prices lay ahead, between 1998 and 2003.[59] Rather, people were mesmerised by the seemingly unstoppable rises: in September 1993 a Hang Seng Bank report claimed an average 400 sq ft flat now cost $1.7 million, fifteen times the annual salary of a graduate and well beyond first-time buyers' means.[60]

In many ways, the trouble stretched back to 1983, when the banks relaxed mortgage lending restrictions, allowing loans of up to 90%, and home-ownership purchases steadily climbed. However, price rises soon outstripped salary growth, and the mortgage affordability index, having dropped from a baseline of 100 in 1981 to around 25% in 1985–7, steadily climbed back up again to between 43 and 54 during 1994 (coinciding with five successive interest-rate rises within a year): increasingly the price-rise impetus was being maintained not by home-buyers but by speculators. Following the shock of the 30,000 registrations for 1,700 flats at Cheung Kong's Kingswood Villas development in Tin Shui Wai, the Wilson administration had tinkered ineffectually with maximum mortgage levels, bringing them back down to around 70%, but these were circumvented by separate bank top-ups.[61]

Eventually, in March 1994, Patten acted decisively, with prices having risen by 200% in three years: the role of speculators was highlighted by his night-time visit to Tin Shui Wai (see above), and by estate agents' estimates that over 70% of new flats were speculator-owned, and that the 'doomsday scenario' of a property bubble burst was possible. Accordingly, Macleod's budget statement announced a task-force to examine how to cool the 'fevered market', including land-bank expansion as well as market curbs.[62] The cooling package eventually implemented in June 1994, whose most effective surprise measure was a ban on resale of pre-sale units before completion, provoked a 40% decline in prices by late 1995, but also a drop in the stock market – highlighting the centrality of the 'speculative spirit' in Hong Kong's economic ethos.[63] (Figure 12.5) Despite harsh 'nanny state' accusations from realtors, such as Centaline Property MD Shih Wing-ching, who rhetorically asked, 'Is this a socialist country or a capitalist country?', the 1994 reforms bought temporary relief to buyers, and some political kudos for Patten, whom the SCMP argued was more generally shifting Hong Kong away from the laissez-faire ethos. But the curbs, which also brought a disquieting drop in government land revenue for 1994–5 to around $30 billion, had only a relatively short-lived effect on prices: early 1997 saw the beginnings of another price bubble, with speculators' renewed 'bullish sentiment' helping push prices up by 38% in 1996, prompting calls for Housing Secretary Dominic Wong to 'produce a strategy for a soft landing', including renewed pre-sale restrictions.[64]

'Some may see our measures as not tough enough, others will see them as too interventionist'

Property package bans resale of unfinished flats

By BARRY PORTER and Staff Reporters

THE Government yesterday released its far-reaching but watered-down review on property price stabilisation, pledging to provide enough extra land supply to cater for an additional 45,000 to 60,000 flats over the next six years.

It also announced a string of anti-speculation measures, springing just one surprise – a ban on resale of unfinished flats before assignment, normally about three months after the occupation permit is issued.

Real Estate Developers Association of Hong Kong spokesman Leung Chi-kin described this as the "killer weapon" that would kick the majority of speculators out the market.

However, the Government refrained from introducing a controversial punitive increased stamp duty or capital gains tax on transactions, at least for now.

The Government said it did not want to do anything that might make property prices crash and noted that average home prices had come down between 10 and 15 per cent since the review began two months ago.

Kong Island, Kowloon and the New Territories for residential development.

It hopes to allocate some 15 hectares of this land this year and next, subject to agreement by the Land Commission.

Mr Eason said the administration would continue to monitor demand and supply, and seek the allocation of the remaining 55 hectares over the next two years as and when appropriate, again subject to Land Commission approval.

The taskforce noted that

As part of its widely expected action package to dampen property speculation, the Government has struck out at lucrative internal trading by developers, slashing the quota for private sales of uncompleted flats from 50 per cent to just 10 per cent.

This would release up to 10,000 more private domestic flats directly to homebuyers each year.

Mr Eason said maintaining a residual 10 per cent was considered a reasonable balance between the interests of the buyers and developers.

He also moved to restrict forward sales to not more than nine months before the date of assignment, thus limiting the time available for speculation.

Martin Chan

On the streets . . . Tam Fu-kuen and his wife Melissa Tam Wu May-sau were left window-shopping outside a Chai Wan estate agency.

Figure 12.5 June 1994 SCMP article on Patten's anti-speculation package.

Recalling the episode subsequently, Patten argued that the problem was 'insuperable', as

> any convincing attack on the monopoly effectively enjoyed by a few extremely rich property developers in Hong Kong, making grotesquely large profits, could have had a serious effect on market confidence at a sensitive time. The stock market could have plummeted and the property market collapsed. While property prices rising too quickly cause political problems… falling prices, which leave many mortgaged homeowners with negative equity, cause a great deal more trouble.[65]

Land supply and the Sino-British Commission

In the 'affordability crisis' that culminated in 1994, a great number of factors combined to hamper any straightforward solution, including not just property economics and relations with China but also land supply, development density and the organisation of housing production. Here, Hong Kong's dependence on real-estate speculation, and the territory's endemic land-supply shortages, both now part of its genetic make-up, acted in Scylla and Charybdis fashion to make impossible any Singapore-style state-dictated coordination (even if Hongkongers had actually desired that), and instead encouraged dramatically convulsive extremes in policy-making. Akers-Jones's later summary of the period highlighted one of the major themes of this chapter and the next: the way in which the government's 1994–6 policy initiatives unwittingly created an unstable, if undeniably exciting, legacy for its post-1997 successor. He argued that while the Land Commission 50 ha restriction had left planners 'hamstrung' and depressed land-supply and housing production by removing 'a valuable element of flexibility', after 1994

> the planners and engineers had a rush of blood to the head and produced land in such quantities in 1995–6 that, after the three years that it takes to build, public housing production in 2000 and 2001 reached about 60,000 or 70,000 units a year… At the same time, private property developers also recovered their confidence and began to build. This resulted in a gross oversupply of apartments for sale just when prices had plummeted.[66]

In fact, the role of the Land Commission, prior to the 1993 schism with Patten, had been generally constructive: Eason reported to LegCo in 1994 that through negotiation, it had released more land than the 50 ha limit in every year since its 1985 establishment.[67] In early 1997, the Chinese office of the Land Commission even claimed, slightly disingenuously, that land releases since 1985 had averaged 240 ha rather than 50 ha annually, without making it clear that almost half of that was for the new airport – but the 'real' figures for housing land releases were still impressive, averaging 148 ha a year between 1991/2 and 1995/6.[68] Undoubtedly, the overall increases in private residential plot layouts – from 3.35 in 1975–85 to 4.27 in 1985–94 – reflected government attempts to maximise revenue from the sites available, but the impact on even HOS was limited.[69] Tony Miller, who succeeded Fung Tung as Director of Housing (and HA vice-chairman) in July 1996, recalled that the 50 ha restriction 'didn't affect the HOS, it didn't affect me, as I had a huge land bank – it didn't affect me at all. The [second] price spike leading up to 1997 was nothing to do with the 50 ha restriction on land sale.'[70] Rosanna Wong was less certain on this point, arguing that the extra bidding for any available land, and the general densification, had impeded HA land acquisition, and Poon also recalled some restrictive effect on HOS land supply.[71] (Figure 12.6) The response to this restrictive environment was twofold: firstly, negotiation with the Land Commission to build up a land-bank for medium-term output; and secondly, short-term internal densification of public housing estates.

In the first area, the building-up of a land bank, although a giant site of over 200 ha at Tin Shui Wai (requiring $2bn to develop, for completion in 2000) was lurking in the background, initial progress in 1994 was limited and incremental. In April the Land Commission released 57 ha for both private and public construction;[72] and in May Rosanna Wong pledged to build 10,000 additional flats on top of the existing 35,000–40,000 annual production, to be paid for out of the $7.5 billion development fund drawn from the HA's large surplus – provided a further 58 ha could be secured immediately. The following month she pleaded for the establishment of a permanent land bank to guarantee 50 ha steady supply each year, and permit a reliable 40,000 programme to be maintained.[73] In June 1994, advance notice was given

Tony Aw

Step forward . . . Chinese team leader Chen Rongchun and the territory's lands chief Tony Eason after the deal.

Land body to release 10.9 hectares for flats

By CHRIS YEUNG and MICHELLE CHIN

THE Sino-British Land Commission yesterday agreed to provide an extra 10.94 hectares of land this year to add another 10,500 residential flats to help ease the strain on housing supply.

In another major step forward for the new airport and rail link, the land body

Category	Total area (ha)	Number of flats
Home Ownership Scheme	4.39	4,500
Sandwich class	3.55	2,923
Tung Chung new town	3	2,384
Public rental	1.48	724
Total	12.42	10,541

How the new housing land will be divided.

The premiums for each site will be assessed not earlier than nine months before development proceeds.

It was also agreed that the average cost of land production for 1993/94 would be $4,428 per square metre, and that for 1994/95 it would be $4,754 per square metre.

Among the 59.8-hectare rail link land, 7.52 hectares will go to two projects in

Figure 12.6 Tony Eason, Secretary for Planning, Environment and Lands, and Chen Rongchun, Chinese team leader on the Land Commission, following a November 1994 agreement to increase short-term housing land supply.

of the release of 25 redundant defence sites (potentially accommodating 15,000 flats) and 60 ha adjoining the airport railway, partly earmarked by Hamish Macleod as a subsidy for the airport project itself, while the Interdepartmental Task Force's report claimed to have identified 120 ha of developable land across the territory.[74] Limited progress had been made on Wong's demands by November, with 11 ha released by the Land Commission (mainly for HOS and sandwich-class flats), but the HA protesting that a remaining 38 ha land shortfall risked cutting 23,513 units off the 141,000 completions planned by 2001: the HA's argument that more land was needed immediately was flatly contradicted by the Housing Branch, in an ominous sign of a growing split over housing strategy between the two.[75]

In the second area – the pursuit of short-term output gain – an emergency estate densification programme was authorised in April 1994, and drawn up by Stephen Poon, as HD Senior Assistant Director (New Development). It proposed to scrap 26 schools in various locations and squeeze tower blocks (mostly Harmonys) into the small sites released, in a programme totalling 9,900 flats split half-and-half between rental and HOS. Following fierce criticism from district boards and the wider public, these were reduced to 9,500 on 21 sites, some scaled-down in height, in November 1994. Rosanna Wong argued that 'I need land today for estates that will open in five years' and that although she hated using open space in an estate for infills, here 'there is no option'. In November 1995, for example, a planned public park at Sham Shui Po on a THA site was shelved, to allow 500 rental units to be built on the first part of the site. Other densification expedients included plans to build low blocks of aged persons' flats on top of car parks and community buildings in the urban area.[76] Miller recalled that 'those silly infill schemes, all of which were underway by the time I got there in 1996, were emergency work while the programme cranked up.'[77] But Ted Pryor, now government Principal Town Planner and shortly due to retire, insisted that 'high density living is not a thing to be feared', but instead had a 'wonderful' effect of enabling lavish infrastructure.[78] From the perspective of those working at the development pit-face, such as HA project architects, 1996 seemed the worst point of the land shortage, while the effects of the planning 'rush of blood to the head' were still working their way through the earlier stages of the development process.[79]

Towards 85,000: the inflation of the Housing Strategy

The process through which these financial and organisational strategies were converted into completed dwelling units was none other than the Long-Term Housing Strategy, as refined in the early 1990s and entrenched following the 1994 crisis. Reacting partly against the makeshift character of MacLehose's Ten-Year Plan, a process of methodical, staged review was built into the post-1987 LTHS process, including a 1993–4 Mid-Term Review whose finalisation in June 1994 coincided with the report of the interdepartmental task force on land supply and house prices – yet again underlining how Hong Kong's housing apparatus, even if not formally and imposingly unified like Singapore's, was still significantly interconnected behind the scenes.

The first iteration of the LTHS Mid-Term Review in 1993 identified several key problems in realising the original objectives of 1,085,000 new flats by 2001, including increases in demand (partly stemming from redevelopment decanting), and shortfalls in rental output: land-supply problems were causing production bottlenecks within the PHDP at Tseung Kwan O and Tiu Keng Leng in particular.[80] It now seemed, contrary to Patten's 'pledge', that overall homeownership would reach only 51% by 1997, of which only 13% would be public sector. Suggested remedies to the production shortfalls, endorsed in the June 1994 Final Report of the Review, and incorporated in the PHDP, included cutting project lead-times from 6 to 5 years, maximising densities and sourcing more land (especially through the school-site programme). All of these together would generate 20,700 more units, while leaving the redevelopment programme intact.[81] While low output until 1995 was seen as unavoidable, Chapter 4 of the Final Report, responding to a rise in estimated 2000/1 demand to 606,000 rather than the 1993/4 estimate of 527,000, demanded enough additional land to allow not just a 20,700 but a 50,000 overall boost to production over the following six years.[82] It argued that

> we need to raise our production targets to meet the increasing demand. According to past experience, we believe that the Housing Department and the construction industry have the capacity to produce up to 50,000–60,000 flats a year. Allowing for the lead time, the Housing Authority proposes to government to increase its production by 50,000 flats, to be spread out over a five-year period 1997/8 to 2001/2, in order to meet the rising demand for assisted home purchase, and, to have a direct impact on property prices, a larger proportion of the additional production should be HOS and PSPS flats.[83]

Several smaller new commitments were also made by Patten in late 1993, including a programme of 4,000 elderly persons' units, which generated the 'Harmony Annex' design (see below), and the rehousing of all current THA residents by 1997: the THA settlements would then be re-purposed for new mainland immigrants.[84]

An unobtrusive but crucial shift in the Final Report was a new emphasis on the undesirability of fixed annual production targets, and an insistence that low-income housing was intrinsically demand-led – potentially begging the question of the relationship to construction-industry capacity. This was the first building-block in what would, within just over a year, turn out to be a significant and open-ended expansion in the housing drive. It was conceived strictly in tandem with the institution of the new Secretary post and the June 1994 measures to dampen prices. Patten declared that 'I hope we've got the balance right', stressing that most of the measures were long term and would only affect the market from 1997–8 onwards.[85] The complete package met with a guarded welcome: Lee Wing-tat, for example, argued for the United Democrats that while the measures were somewhat 'weak', owing to the importance of land revenue to the government, nevertheless the latter had 'done a very good job' in adverse circumstances.[86]

But the demographic and land constraints facing the public housing programme did not stay still. During the mid-1990s, not only did the site shortage continue unabated, but the medium-term demographic pressures of demand were unexpectedly exacerbated in 1996 when Pryor admitted that the government had underestimated likely population growth in its analysis of the 1991 census. But by then, in 1995–6, the quantitative impetus of the entire programme had been subtly but significantly boosted by Dominic Wong, in response to the unremitting pressure from Patten for higher output. Miller recalled that Patten 'was able to be firm, like MacLehose. Praise him or criticise him, he pushed very hard for more numbers!'[87] In February 1995, just after his appointment, Wong announced both medium-term and short-term measures to increase output, especially in the public sector. (Figure 12.7) In the medium term, a new LTHS update for the period after 2001 would be prepared by a 6-month task-force review of housing demand chaired by Pryor. In the short term, to speed up the 1995–2001 phase, an interdepartmental 'Housing Action Team' would be established to fast-track big projects that would yield 32,300 units, and speed up the 1988 Comprehensive Redevelopment Programme of all non-self-contained flats (totalling 500 blocks): this was to be completed by 2001, 286 having already been redeveloped.[88] An extra $8 billion

Housing body to fast-track development to meet growing demand

Branch to provide affordable homes

Dominic Wong Shing-wah, the new Secretary for Housing, reports on the work, strategies and objectives, and challenges facing the Government's recently-created Housing Branch during its first four months of operation in one of the world's most expensive housing markets.

THE Housing Branch has taken over responsibility for developing policies and strategies for the provision of both public and private housing, and for co-ordinating the implementation of the Government's housing policies and programmes.

Its principal aim is to provide an adequate supply of housing at affordable prices or rents to meet demand in both the public and private sectors.

To achieve this, the Housing Branch is taking a number of initiatives.

Infrastructure development will be accelerated so as to bring forward the development of land for residential purposes and information on land supply will be improved.

The processing of development projects will be hastened, with the objective of providing 504,000 flats by April 2001.

Property prices in January were on average 14 per cent down from the peak prices in April last year, but were still about 37 per cent higher than those of January 1993.

As a result, we have no intention of introducing further measures to influence the market.

The branch will continue to provide more land for housing, increase the supply of flats, and let the property market find its own price level.

It will monitor developments in the property market closely, and will take note of views that individuals or organisations wish to express on this subject.

32,300 flats on 61 hectares.

Another 19 sites totalling 84 hectares for 61,300 flats are being monitored to ensure not only the land is availability in time for development, but that the required infrastructure will be

> 'The most effective way of stabilising residential property prices in the long run is to increase the supply of land for housing.'

to finance land formation, water supply, road improvement and building projects.

Good planning is essential in housing production because it takes a relatively long lead time to produce flats to meet demand.

We need to establish how much land is required for the different categories of housing and at what time it should be disposed of.

We also need a better grasp of the timing when flats will be built on the land.

To answer these questions, we have taken various initiatives to strengthen the planning process of housing production.

Firstly, a systematic and

private housing, subject to the agreement of the Sino-British Land Commission.

Secondly, apart from new land, redevelopment is also a major source of flats supply in the private sector.

The Planning Department has just commissioned a study of the redevelopment potential of the entire territory for housing development, starting with the metropolitan area.

The study is expected to be completed by March next year.

Thirdly, five other stud*ies will also be undertaken to* explore the feasibility and assess the housing development potential of about 170 hectares of land.

The sites covered by these studies are in both the urban areas and the New Territories.

Fourthly, action is being taken to computerise the work of the Lands Department in order to streamline the processing of land ex-

Figure 12.7 March 1996 SCMP article by Dominic Wong explaining the government's expanded housing drive, whose annual completions target of 84,000 closely anticipated C H Tung's post-1997 strategy.

would also be spent on infrastructure projects to expedite approved housing developments. Pressure would also be put on the HA to speed up ejection of better-off rental tenants through 'more forceful' measures. All the time, Patten's aim of raising the proportion of home-ownership was publicly trumpeted, despite criticisms from Ho Hei-wah and others. The public housing programme would increasingly be dominated by HOS/PSPS – the ownership percentage in the 102,918 flats in current production in December 1995 being 49%.[89]

By late March 1995, Dominic Wong's proposals had been further fleshed out into a 'comprehensive housing blueprint to encourage home ownership, boost stability and give people a greater sense of belonging'.[90] Based on the composite demand made up of the 150,000 waiting list, redevelopment displacees and current THA residents, a planned 6-year output was pledged of 141,000 public rental, 175,000 HOS/PSPS and 195,000 private flats – making up a grand total of 511,000 new flats of all tenures. This, Dominic Wong significantly emphasised, averaged 85,000 each year, far higher than the 1994/5 total of 55,907, but slightly below the 1989/90 figure of 86,179 completions.[91] Miller recalled that

> Rosanna Wong regarded this programme with concern and wrote to Patten expressing that concern: she supported the idea of cranking up production, but not on that scale. She had concerns about the ability of the industry and the Housing Department to deliver.[92]

Dominic Wong reiterated his plan in December 1995, adding that he hoped to see it to its completion over the next seven years before his retirement – his post-1997 continuation being likely, owing to his good links with China. The new target was duly enshrined in the 1996 Governor's Policy Address, and repeated by Wong in an address at a celebratory 1996 housing exhibition at the Edinburgh City Art Centre in Scotland, at which he accompanied Patten, and which re-used the mock-up Concord flat interior previously displayed at Ho Man Tin.[93] Stephen Poon recalled the output-inflationary effect of the 'demand-led' principle: 'Around 1996, what we had was a demand-led programme. Some planners worked out the projected demand for those years, they counted up the demand for both private and public housing, and they cooked up from this the 85,000-a-year figure'.[94]

Subsequently, Miller recalled at some length the outcome of these policy shifts, and his unease at its open-ended character: 'I took over [as Director of Housing] at the end of 1996. Dominic Wong, the Secretary for Housing, had pulled together a comprehensive housing policy, which, if you connected all the dots, was pretty radical, and long overdue. It built on the idea that ownership was better in the long term than rental. It studied a range of measures to speed up the process of moving over from rental to home-ownership. The document was notable for not connecting the dots, though. When I arrived and quizzed Dominic about it, he said, "If I'd connected the dots, we'd never have got it through!" There was no central strategic focus that talked about the financial arrangements for moving from rental to home ownership or allowing tenants to purchase their homes. The second prong of public housing policy [in 1996] was slightly bizarre, as it was moving in the opposite direction. It was a knee-jerk reaction to a spike in private housing prices because of the approach of 1997: there was a certain amount of speculative involvement. Chris Patten, the Governor, reacted to this price spike by instructing the Secretary for Housing and the Chairman of the Housing Authority to crank up a huge new production programme. And even before I'd arrived in 1996, the Housing Authority and the Works Department had injected significant quantities of new land, and had initiated measures of putting infill blocks on small sites. They went into overdrive on the new housing programme – which, frankly, from my earlier knowledge of the MacLehose era, I knew would stretch the construction industry beyond capacity. I recall mentioning it, briefing the ExCo members that once the combined public and private sector output gets much beyond 70,000, it ends with liquidated damages and tears! There was a slightly counterintuitive coincidence of, on the one hand, a well-intentioned policy Secretary crafting a policy to move the machine away from radically direct government intervention in steel and concrete towards financial subsidies and ownership incentives, while the new Governor was busy cracking the whip and saying, "We must build faster!" and not really worrying about whether it was home-ownership or rental'. In fact, despite all the rhetoric of home-ownership, 'Patten's programme was disproportionately public rental housing'.[95] Patten himself privately bemoaned that owing to the impracticability of anything more than 'marginal adjustments to policy', to avoid pre-1997 instability, 'we are now locked into a socialist housing policy which doesn't meet our needs', combined 'exotically' with the tycoons' dominance of private housing.[96]

Although the overall trend of completions during the Patten years was relatively level – with both HOS and PRH only seriously plunging in 1998/9, to a combined total of 13,000 – eventually, after that, combined public–private output would soar far above 85,000, let alone 70,000, briefly peaking in 2001 at 100,000, with grave consequences for the HOS in particular.[97] Within overall public housing output, there was a significant redistribution from PRH to HOS, from 41%/4% of all dwellings in 1986 to 35%/12% in 1998, but almost no HOS inroads on the private sector.[98] Reflecting Patten's 1992 pledge of two-thirds home-ownership by 2001, the HOS remained the ideological bedrock of government housing policy, and the financial bedrock of the HA: in April 1994, $3.5 billion net profit ($5.2 billion gross, minus $1.7 billion building costs) was anticipated from selling 4,600 flats in four projects in Kwai Chung, Fanling and Chai Wan, and in 1995 the total revenues from HOS sales generated $17 billion income.[99] During the mid-1990s, the HA tinkered with HOS eligibility criteria to expand the proportion of 'green form' (existing PRH) to 'white form' (external) applicants: white form applicants were encouraged to apply for HPLS instead. The HOS was also exploited to help with market cooling in July 1994, with a phase of 8,168 units put on sale six months early (i.e., 2 years rather than 18 months pre-completion), generating some $6 billion for the HA, priced at 52% of market value and with two-thirds allocated to green form applicants.[100]

By comparison, the $2 billion Sandwich Class Scheme heralded in Patten's October 1992 policy speech proved very slow to take effect.[101] Take-up of the initial 10,000-flat tranche, allocated to the Housing Society as executive agent (with a

50% reduction in land premiums), was impeded by tough, anti-speculation application criteria and mortgage regulations, with only 1,557 applicants (4% of those eligible) by September 1993. By January 1994, 15 months after the scheme opened, only 168 flats had been sold in the first project, Tivoli Garden, Tsing Yi (as against 1,000 planned). In late 1995 Patten proposed to enlarge the scheme by a further 10,000 units, supported by a $7 billion loan to cover their land premiums, against warnings from some market analysts that this could damage the private market: the Housing Society, which had recently discontinued rental production, also planned 22,000 further home-ownership units of its own by 2001. By 1996 proposals were bubbling up again within LegCo to revive Akers-Jones's scheme to sell flats to existing tenants: Rosanna Wong argued the 'timing' was not yet right, but that the proposal would be included in an LTHS review in 1997: eventually, a new Tenants Purchase Scheme covering 250,000 units, drawn up by Stephen Poon from late 1996, was announced by the HA in December 1997.[102]

Towards greater focus in the rental stock

Alongside the ideological foregrounding of home-ownership, attempts continued to re-focus the rental stock on low-income groups, and to enhance the PRH environment. Here the new EMAC (Estate Management Advisory Committee) system vigorously promoted from 1994 by Rosanna Wong, in a development of the 1973 MAC network, was a powerful vehicle for decentralisation. The social level of PRH tenants was gradually rising, from 4% professional in 1980 to 14% in 2001.[103] The relative ineffectiveness of the 1987 double-rent policy in dislodging higher-income tenants was now clear. By 1992, 11% of tenants were paying double rents, but this dropped steeply after the 1993 introduction of a new and supposedly fairer 1.5 category; in 1996, under a new 'Safeguarding Rational Allocation of Public Housing Resources' (SRA) initiative, market-level rents based on regular means-testing were introduced. Higher rents seemed especially attractive as the HA, alongside its multi-billion-dollar reserves, was now running significant current deficits – $1.8 billion in the mid-1990s. Cost-cutting as well as efficiency also lay behind Wong's 1995 proposal to devolve the running of all estates to private firms by 1997–8.[104]

The government ruled out punitive measures against the soaring number of tenants who owned other flats (85,000 as at May 1994 – 13% of all tenants, some owning up to five flats), given the potential unfairness of singling out property assets as against stocks or jewellery: Virginia Ip of the HKPCPHP argued, 'Being a rich public tenant is not a sin – why should they be punished?' A proposal to encourage neighbours to inform on flat-owning tenants, focusing on North Point, Fuk Loi and Choi Hung, met with widespread derision.[105]

At the same time, concern sharpened about the condition of some estates. The campaign since 1992 to exclude pets had successfully banished some 2,000 dogs by 1994, although complaints about droppings and mess continued in places such as Ngau Tau Kok, and the annual 'Keep Estates Clean' campaign continued. The danger posed by broken upper-floor railings or tenants tossing objects out of upper flats (Tai Hing being particularly afflicted by the latter, despite its outward-sloping

Can we make these estates safe?

It's not only in Hong Kong that housing blocks have been hit by rising crime. **Sue Green, Eleanor Yeung, Jake Niall** in Los Angeles and **Sheel Kohli** in London look at what is being done here and elsewhere to counter the problem

THE residents of Tuen Mun's 10 giant housing estates want their homes made safe from murderers and sex criminals, who stalk young women in deserted, gloomy corridors and empty lifts. And they want it done now.

But work on the Housing Authority's plan to install security doors, guards and closed-circuit television in just 280 of Hong Kong's 1,200 housing blocks will not even begin until early next year.

There's no policy covering the rest yet, and many are so old and difficult to secure they may not be included at all. Last year's murders and sex attacks did not prompt the authority to bring its plans forward – in fact, it had no plans at that stage, and began by trying to persuade residents they should pay for better security.

Danger area . . . the empty hallways of a typical block in Tuen Mun spell danger for women late at night, and it's likely to get worse

Figure 12.8 Illustration of lift hallway in 'a typical block in Tuen Mun' from a July 1994 article decrying allegedly high crime in housing schemes, immediately following the murder of Ip Wing-sze.

facades) was also addressed by management teams.[106] Far more serious, however, was a perceived upsurge in violent crime on many PRH estates – a trend no longer linked to former Group B status but instead associated with estates of all types in specific hot-spot locations. Tuen Mun became a particular lightning-rod of discontent, with recently completed and originally 'pleasant, friendly' estates such as Yau Oi or Butterfly plagued especially by the Sun Yee On triad, as well as by juvenile crime and violence. There were even complaints about triad intimidation of tenants concerning decoration of newly completed Harmony flats in Tin Yiu Estate.[107] (Figure 12.8) Akers-Jones vainly pleaded in February 1993 that Tuen Mun did not deserve its bad reputation, but the only decisive long-term remedy would be to homogenise the rental stock with the concierge security systems that prevailed within HOS and PSPS. Nine months later Rosanna Wong did just that, boldly drawing on the HA's reserves to authorise a $1.5 billion programme of gated security measures in its 1,200 PRH blocks, starting in the interests of speed with the 280 newest and simplest blocks (the cruciform and Y-shaped Tridents and Harmonys), with two Harmonys at Tin Yiu and Siu Sai Wan Estates acting as pilot blocks. $250 million was voted by the HA in July 1994 for this initial 280-block phase, to last four years.[108]

But events outpaced even this massive initiative, with the gruesome and highly publicised murder, the very day after the $250 million vote, of 19-year old clerk Ip Wing-sze in a six-year-old block on Leung King Estate. This immediately projected attention back on Tuen Mun: some commentators argued its remoteness had prevented it from ever developing into a traditional 'community', and residents highlighted the ubiquitous 'incense burners outside many flats and… messages designed to appease the spirits of the dead', and demanding that their homes should be 'made safe from murderers and sex criminals, who stalk young women in deserted, gloomy corridors and empty lifts. And they want it done now!' In response, Assistant Housing Director Isaac Siu Che-wong promised that Tuen

Mun would get priority in the 280-block upgrade, which would now take only two and a half years.[109] Exclusion of undesirable outsiders was, however, only a partial solution, as recalled by Chris Gabriel, one of the architects for the security upgrade: 'By the mid-1990s, we were building 41-storey buildings, which could hold 600–1,200 flats, or up to 4,000 people – a village in one building. There were cases reported of women being assaulted, so we went to the Royal Hong Kong Police with proposals for improving security: we made recommendations to provide the same security in public rental housing as in the HOS, with entrance doors, concierges, entryphones etc., all agreed with the Estate Management Division. I went along and explained it all to the police, and they said, "Very good – now the only problem is the community who live *inside* the building!"'[110] Reviewing the Tuen Mun crime scandal as a whole, outgoing TDD director Chow Che-king openly conceded that 'the Government got it wrong when it planned the New Towns as self-contained satellites which could offer work, living and leisure facilities': given Tuen Mun's transport isolation, its facilities now must be upgraded to the standard of the urban areas, where some recent estates, such as for example Lok Wah in Ngau Tau Kok, were now even hosting 'meet-the-people' tourist guided tours.[111]

But the baton of 'worst new town' was by now being passed on to Tin Shui Wai, officially inaugurated by Patten in March 1993, the project having to date cost $10 billion, of which the government had covered two-thirds. Here, despite the carefully planned chromatic harmonies masterminded by the Clers, and the respect paid by the planners to a traditional feng shui sight-line bisecting the town, a combination of location, transport inaccessibility and letting policy almost immediately prompted a reputation for alienation and deprivation, as 'Sad City' – 'a dumping area for new immigrants, from China, broken families, on very low incomes'. The hierarchy of New Town esteem was transmitted on to the next generation – with TDD statistics showing that Tseung Kwan O and Tung Chung cost far more to build and from the start established a higher public reputation.[112] In June 1995, Standard Chartered chief economist Kwok Kwok Chuen argued that house prices aside, the crude housing shortage was now a thing of the past, with households and dwellings now roughly equal, and that this allowed more complex patterns of demand to emerge, not just concerning dwelling size (with too many small flats being built) but also location, with 'far-flung places' associated with disproportionately high private vacancy-rates – including 19% in the outer New Towns.[113] (Figure 12.9)

Seen in that light, the relative stigmatisation of Tuen Mun and Tin Shui Wai, and the popularity of relatively well-connected Sha Tin, Tung Chung and Tseung Kwan O (but less so the well-located but industrial Tsuen Wan), seem relatively self-explanatory. By the mid-1990s the big developers had accumulated significant land-banks in Tseung Kwan O in particular, whose housing in 1996 was still 90% public, in line with the 'public housing-led' strategy. There was also progress with a private-sector-led proposal of 1992 by Sun Hung Kai for a joint public–private housing extension of Sha Tin north-eastwards to Ma On Shan, complete with MTR extension.[114] However, it was Tung Chung that took on the greatest urgency during Patten's governorship, owing to its vital role in the airport project. Its first

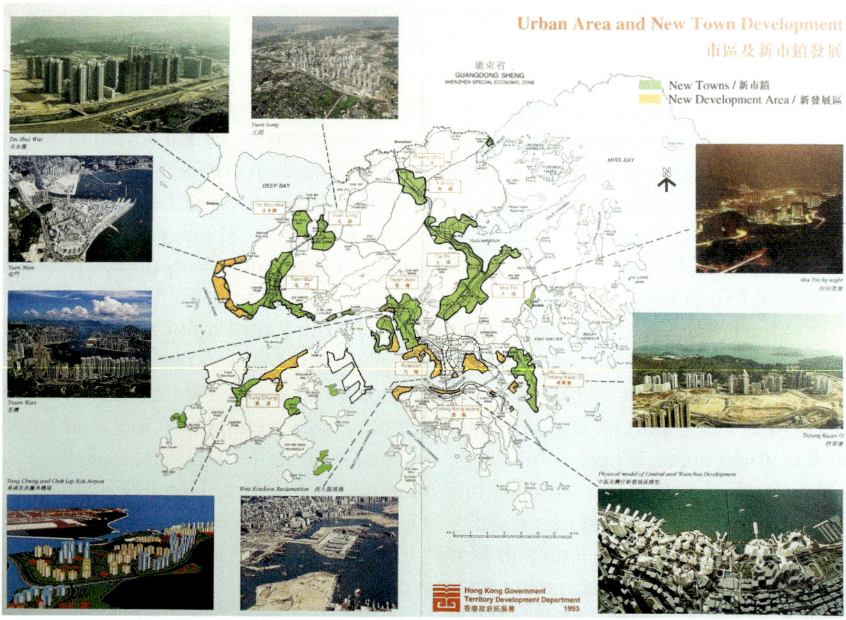

Figure 12.9 Map of New Towns and development areas as at 1993, included in a Territory Development Department broadsheet, 'Urban Area and New Town Development'.

two schemes (opened 1997), Fu Tung Estate (PRH) and Yu Tung Court (HOS), designed chiefly by John Lambon and colleagues with Harmonys, were populated mainly by airport staff from July 1997 onwards.[115] The 345-ha Tung Chung site, its clearance delayed by the displacement problems of Ma Wan Chung village, faced initial reluctance by tenants to move there, but the opening of a high-speed MTR link in 1998 and the low cost of the HOS units (only $1,050 a square foot, much less than in the urban area) soon counteracted that. Its chief planner, Au Pak Man, predicted in 1997 that it would avoid 'new town troubles', whereas 'fighting crime and chronic social problems are facts of life in places such as Tuen Mun, Tsuen Wan and Tin Shui Wai'.[116]

Fung Tung recalled the post-1994 coordination process between housing and planning in the New Towns:

> In a New Town, development is mostly led by public housing. But the Secretary for Housing works very closely with the Secretary for Lands and Planning (Public Works). Each time land is allocated to the Authority… we also make sure the Welfare Department, the Education Department and Transport all have to look at the New Town plan, to make sure it provides enough facilities. We would not complete an estate until transport was provided. The departments are

supposed to be connected by the Chief Secretaries' Committee: all the other Secretaries would provide their services to feed in, or otherwise raise at the Chief Secretaries' Committee.[117]

The progress of this renewed eruption of development under Patten won him unexpected acclaim from none other than Murray MacLehose. On a 1996 visit, he returned from a helicopter tour of housing and New Towns bubbling with enthusiasm about 'all those things we dreamed about, all those things we were told were impossible, [now] rising from the ground', and conceded that, contrary to his earlier misgivings, here at least Patten had 'managed to get things done'.[118]

Recalibrating redevelopment

As Kwok suggested in his analysis of locational demand, one potential remedy for the relative unpopularity of some 'far-flung' new towns was to refocus on redevelopment in the urban area. Here the Comprehensive Redevelopment Programme was already making relentless progress with its rolling 5-year phases: 240 blocks in 12 areas already redeveloped by 1991, including all unconverted Mk I and II: according to Deputy Director Estate Management Lim Yew-Guan, another 400 resettlement/GLCH blocks would be cleared by 2000. In May 1995, following re-calibration of the programme and deferral of some elements in the 1994 LTHS Interim Review, a fresh iteration of the plan was approved by the HA.[119] This envisaged a $20 billion five-year redevelopment (1995/6 to 1999/2000) of 185 blocks in 29 estates, replacing 76,600 existing units with 63,500 new PRH and HOS units by 2000, but hugely expanding the overall gross floor area by 72%; further demolitions in other areas would by then have begun. By 1996 286 blocks, containing 93,000 families, had been redeveloped. The Kowloon Walled City project was by now well advanced: 14,020 claimants had been paid a total of $2.1 billion by late 1992 in a 'secretive' negotiation process, with payments based on HOS or market value even if the applicant was moving to public rental housing.[120] (Figure 12.10)

Outside the CRP programme, the urban renewal activities of the Land Development Corporation were meeting with rather less success. As its chairman Lau Wah-sum admitted in 1997, its obligation to provide new housing for displacees while making a profit impeded the scaling up of its operations, and so it was 'fighting a losing battle'… 'all we can do is tackle one quarter every ten years'. In 1995 LegCo debates, it was also claimed that the LDC built to an unrealistically high standard, which private developers could not match.[121]

Also uneven in their progress were smaller redevelopments of traditional rural villages, which posed awkward clearance problems, While the redevelopment of the notorious Rennie's Mill area in Tseung Kwan O, a KMT stronghold since 1949, raised complex political issues, with 'all sorts of stories about "the Hong Kong government doing the Mainland's job for them"', other developments sometimes had intangible-heritage complications.[122] For example, in 1994, a 304-unit HA redevelopment on Cheung Chau, rehousing some 1,500 residents, was held

Figure 12.10 Tsui Ping North Estate, 2012 photo (MG) showing 22-storey New Slab Block on left and 28-storey Linear Block on right, both completed 1990 under the CRP, on a site formerly occupied by Mk I blocks (cf. Figs. 3.10b and 9.16a): job architect was Rosman Wai.

up by villagers' objections to removal of a tree with good feng shui. Likewise, in August 1994, a 550-unit project completing the redevelopment of the depopulated Tai O fishing village on Lantau was complicated by inter-departmental debates about the township's touristic potential.[123] And in July 1995, the Antiquities Board having given up on earlier proposals for preservation of Nga Tsin Wai, the last remaining urban village in the Kai Tak/San Po Kong area, and one of the last urban settlements still served by night-soil collectors, the residents abandoned their protests and focused on maximising compensation and accelerated decanting.[124] Especially complex was the ongoing redevelopment of Ma Hang, clearance of whose 4,500 remaining inhabitants was underway by the mid-1990s. As we saw in Chapter 11, the design of the stepped-down courtyard groups of modified Harmonys was overseen by Rosman Wai, John Lambon and C K Yeung. The entire development culminated in the reconstruction of Murray House, a former Victorian military building dismantled by the Architectural Services Department from its site in Central to allow for the construction of the new Bank of China, and stored for several years in a temporary site in Tai Tam. The re-erected Murray House became the centrepiece of a 'Covent Garden'-style multi-purpose complex on the Stanley waterfront.[125]

The progress of Ma Hang highlighted that the squatter issue was at last losing its perceived urgency, and fading from the urban area. Following Patten's 1992 pledge to clear all urban squatters on public land by 1996, in December 1993 the number of urban squatters had fallen from 160,000 in 1983 to 42,000, and in June 1994 to 38,000. By February 1995 it was admitted the pledge target would be missed by 25% – to which LegCo Housing Panel chairman Lee Wing-tat responded that 'It seems as if the Governor just likes to make pledges, but doesn't care whether they can be fulfilled or not'. Dominic Wong later ingeniously argued, in 1997, that the pledge had only covered rehousing *offers* rather than actually achieved rehousing. Some of the remaining hard-core settlements were on landslide-threatened sites, for example at Lei Yue Mun or Tai Wan Tung, Pokfulam, and some were also experiencing triad-syndicate infiltration, especially in Kwai Tsing and Tsuen Wan.[126]

Increasingly, however, the mantle of controversy was assumed by the 32 Temporary Housing Areas, of which fourteen were under clearance by 1995: in October 1993, following an earlier inspection visit to Ping Shek THA, Patten had pledged to rehouse all existing inhabitants by 1997.[127] That did not, however, necessarily equate to physical clearance of the sites. Here an unobtrusive policy shift by Patten, to boost mainland immigration to avoid a 1997 'flood', caused increasing misunderstanding and claims of another broken pledge, as the government admitted fourteen further THAs would remain open until at least 1999, to house new immigrants. The squalid condition of many of the areas, despite the very low density (by Hong Kong standards) of their rows of back-to-back huts, was the subject of lurid exposes.[128] Exploiting the ambiguity over the mainland immigrants, protesters started claiming that the October 1993 pledge had promised physical clearance of the sites, rather than (as in reality) rehousing of existing inhabitants. The result was Patten's embroilment in a near-riot during a 'very unpleasant' September 1995 visit to Kai Cheung THA in Kowloon Bay: he was surrounded by over a thousand enraged protesters chanting, 'The Governor tells lies!' and a caged rat was thrust in his face before the police hustled him away.[129] (Figure 12.11) The cancellation of further THA visits led to claims that he was 'hiding' from controversy, but within the mainstream housing stock he attempted to maintain some degree of 'accessibility', including fortnightly 'unannounced visits to problem housing areas', to 'shake hands, peer in the rubbish bins, and poke around some resident's flat', and more generally to 'knock on doors' of 'ordinary families' within public housing estates, such as Tung Tau in January 1996, where one tenant tactfully remarked that Patten 'seems like an honest man. He is very kind and doesn't put on the airs of a high government official.' Confusingly, other protests outside the THAs were often *opposed* to redevelopment, such as a 1995 demonstration by Tsuen Wan roof-dwellers.[130]

Following the Kowloon Bay debacle, in November 1995 a physical rebranding of the THA programme was announced. Of the 20,000 residents in the 13 THAs now scheduled for demolition, urban displacees would be rehoused in conventional towers in the New Territories, while New Territories inhabitants would be

Menacing mob blames Patten for breaking promise of better housing

Governor runs the gauntlet

By EMMA BATHA

AN angry mob greeted Chris Patten yesterday as he visited three of the temporary housing areas he once pledged to close down.

More than 1,000 residents and demonstrators – many of whom were involved in fights with the Governor's police escort – accused him of going back on promises to move them out of the grim slums.

Chanting, "The Governor tells lies!" and, "You should be ashamed of yourself!", the crowd jostled Mr Patten as he walked through the rat-infested sites.

They hurled abuse through loud-hailers, waved banners and blocked his way with sit-down protests. Then three men produced a caged rat which they tried to put on the Governor's Daimler. They were pulled away by police.

One 73-year-old man, Mr Cheung, had to be taken to hospital after fainting in the crush. Nine policemen were also injured.

Wan Kam-yan

A demonstrator brandishes a caged rat near the Governor during yesterday's protest.

Mr Patten, who was accompanied by housing chairman Rosanna Wong Yick-ming, looked hot and flustered after emerging from one particularly bad scrum, but quickly regained his composure.

Housing chiefs had originally said they would bulldoze all but four temporary housing areas by 1997.

Yesterday's demonstration was sparked by the announcement that nine additional areas would be kept on – condemning an estimated 13,500 people to the homes until after 1997.

Mr Patten's first stop was at Fortune Street Temporary Housing Area.

One woman, Pin Kin-ying, 32, said she had been living in a 116-square-foot room with her husband and two children for 10 years.

"It's a disgrace we haven't been rehoused. We have rats and ants. The ceiling is collapsing and the water pipes are broken," she said.

"It's really bad, especially in the typhoon season when all the rain comes in."

Mr Patten also visited construction worker Yeung Fat-fai, 44, in the 220-square-foot flat he shares with his family of seven.

But the demonstration turned nasty when Mr Patten arrived at the second site, Kai Cheung in Kowloon Bay.

Moments after emerging from his car, he was caught up in a stampede and badly jostled by the surging throng.

(Cont'd on Page 2, Col 6)

Figure 12.11 The scuffle at Kai Cheung Temporary Housing Area in Kowloon Bay during Patten's visit on 28 September 1995, in which a caged rat was thrust in his face: SCMP September 1995 article.

rehoused in 12,000 units on two new sites totalling 49 ha (in Tin Shui Wai and Tuen Mun) in so-called 'interim housing'. These comprised 'modern' four-storey blocks, each containing 48 self-contained four-person flats (with WCs and kitchens) constructed of prefabricated panels – rather than the THAs' 'rotten timber' – and costing $100,000 each. The first two pilot blocks were built in 1996 at Sha Kok Mei, Sai Kung, followed by another site at Long Bin, and similar blocks were built by Sun Shing Construction for airport workers at Chek Lap Kok. To this initiative, HKPCPHP chairman Lo Chau responded acidly that the HA was 'conspiring' to keep needy families in makeshift housing.[131]

Housing design: consolidating the Harmony revolution

In the Patten years, housing design was mainly a matter of consolidation of the 'Harmony revolution' – with a few significant enhancements. Initially, Stephen Poon predicted that the series' mainstay role would last for a decade. By the time the first block was completed at Tin Shui Wai in November 1992, it was already clear that the cruciform Harmony 1 would be the dominant variant, both in the urban areas and equally in Tung Chung.[132] As envisaged from the outset, a constant process of feedback from contractors and tenants began, and senior architect

Chris Gabriel reported in December 1993 that outcomes had included an upgraded kitchen with larger sink, replacement of the bathroom with a shower, and simplified front door locks: as John Ng recalled (Chapter 11), 'only one thing hasn't changed since then – the size of flat!' Over the ensuing years, the proportion of precast façade elements would rise from 60% to as near to 100% as possible, and thermal efficiency would be incrementally pursued, for example by replacing the large metal-framed windows with smaller openings.[133]

Regarding the Clers' much-trumpeted harmonic colour schemes, Poon saw their main benefit as their educational effect on HD staff, as part of the agenda of giving estates greater individual identity: 'It is very subjective, but it works. Our architects are now paying much more attention to colour', which is 'now to be decided at the outset of a scheme.' Colour was yet another way in which public housing architects could produce 'good design' within the tight budgets that continued to condition their approach, reflecting Poon's ethos that 'quality buildings in the context are not pretty or expensive buildings, but those which meet the demands of the users – VW standards rather than Rolls Royce ones!'. Cost limits averaged only 65% of the most basic private developments: for example, 'we could easily have used some space as a balcony, but the policy was not to'.[134] The design of Tung Chung by Lambon and others reflected the new colour-sensitive landscape ethos: laid out in 'sweeping arcs', the first developments were varied in height and colour to 'lead the eyes towards the mountains'. The idea that public-housing modernism could be intrinsically 'artistic' also informed the first steps in heritage nostalgia for early estates, including a 'Fashionable Sixties' exhibition at Lok Fu by the Hong Kong Arts Centre with the HA in 1995.[135]

Before long, however, the carefully conceived chromatic and landscape harmonies had begun to be taken for granted, as critiques of the standardised approach grew louder. Tony Miller recalled his reactions on becoming Director of Housing in 1996:

> Architects have a proud tendency of squeezing incremental improvements out of their masters. The Harmony was already the new standard block when I came in, and the Concord was under development. I was appalled when I went in to a new estate in Tin Shui Wai, to discover we were essentially rebuilding Sau Mau Ping – a cookie-cutter design on a flat site, you couldn't get more anonymous if you tried. Yet the same team could also produce beautiful estates on difficult, contoured sites, like at Ma On Shan – you could get socially friendly, warm estates. The excuse for the cookie-cutter job was, this one had been forced on them, and they'd been told to crank up the numbers – and the architects weren't happy with it. You could use clustering [of blocks] to compensate for the apparent standardization of mass housing'.[136]

The major individual innovation in housing design during the mid-1990s – the 'Harmony Annex' – stemmed from Patten's policy of enhanced housing for the elderly, reflecting the stresses of shared accommodation within public and private housing.[137] Following Patten's original pledge of a 4,000-unit interim programme and the establishment of an ad-hoc committee in late 1993, the committee recommended a 40,000 programme in 1994, scaled down rather more modestly to 11,400 by 2000–1, the following year.[138] Patten's initial pledge, however, placed the Housing Department in a quandary. John Lambon recalled the high-speed way in which a bold response was developed – simply to bolt lower wings of small flats on to the main blocks – in a way that answered urgent production needs but also potentially brought subtle community benefits: 'We were looking urgently into the "one-person crisis". Stephen Poon didn't like anything except cruciform blocks, but now we had a crisis. So one day he came in and said, "I want to think about an annex block". We suddenly had an inadequacy of one-person flats – and suddenly the Harmony range of sizes had become a crisis. Stephen Poon said, "We need an Annex!" '[139]

The Annex was developed organically in 1994 out of a rural Harmony variant, which was often linked together in chain-like patterns – as also at Ma Hang – and which had been adapted by Penny Ward for New Territories gap sites that were too small for standard towers.

> From not liking the low-rise rural Harmony blocks, Stephen suddenly saw them as a solution to the one-person problem. Rosman [Wai] subsequently developed the Annex up to 20 storeys: it was basically a battery of one-person flats. The Harmony Annex was developed from the Harmony Rural as a solution to the one-person crisis, and suddenly we were back at the era of a single instruction for a 15-storey building: that was made possible by the fact that the Standards Group said we could knock through the basic Harmony at the end. (Figure 12.12)

The fast-tracking of the Annex concept was facilitated by the loose density controls for public housing. Lambon argued,

> The Housing Department's perspective is to get as much out of sites as they can. Its brief is maximum production. Personally, I never understood plot ratios – I relied on my architects to get it done – but how Stephen Poon managed to get another 150 flats in those Annex blocks, I don't know![140]

Poon also saw the Annex project as having unexpected social benefits:

> A key consideration was *social* – to enable the younger generation to stay closer to their grandparents and parents. With the older generation living in the Harmony blocks, the Annex could accommodate the younger generation. They could stay away when they needed privacy, but if their parents needed them they could come to their rescue very easily – you could organize a family gathering very easily. In our Eastern culture, there still remains the idea that young people should support the older generation.

However, because of allocation programmes the concept 'may not have worked out 100%'.[141] In practice, the Annex proved a vital way of boosting the yield of

Figure 12.12 Yung Shing Court, Fanling, completed 2000: Harmony 1 blocks with 21-storey Annexes. 2013 photo (MG).

many sites, including the largest single CRP project, the redevelopment of the Kwai Chung Resettlement estate. Here 8,850 existing units in 42 Mk II and Mk III blocks were replaced by 14,543 flats in a protracted, multi-phase project spanning twelve years (1995–2007), with a central 'civic hub' ringed by Harmony and New Cruciform blocks of various generations, several including Annexes: up to 7,000 of the existing 22,000 inhabitants were re-accommodated in situ.[142]

To follow up on the emergency Annex programme, in 1994 Chris Gabriel was put in charge of a project to develop a long-term small-household and elderly housing type. He toured elderly people's housing schemes in various English cities and met the managers and architects of the Rowntree Housing Trust and other big housing associations. On the basis of their experience he recommended 22 sq m flats with shared communal facilities, and, controversially, enhanced means-of-escape arrangements in 20-storey blocks for the elderly. 'We were the first developer in Hong Kong to propose refuge areas and evacuation lifts. But the Fire Services Department were very anti-evacuation lifts – so we never built any'.[143] A programme was prepared for 'Small Household Blocks' of up to 21 storeys which comprised 22 m^2 flats for two or three persons (designated as HS1) over hostel-style accommodation for single persons (designated as HS3). Private

Figure 12.13 (a) HA exhibition model of Small Household development at Pak Tin, completed 1998. 2011 photo (MG). (b) On Tin House, Pak Tin, trial Small Household development managed by D & S and completed 1998: 2010 photo (MG).

consultants were engaged to develop these after a trial scheme managed by D & S in Pak Tin (completed 1998 and 2000), but the programme proved excessively costly and was eventually abandoned.[144] (Figure 12.13a, b) The Small Household prototypes were closely tailored to infill sites and in some ways, like Ma Hang, anticipated the later switch to site-specific design (Chapter 13).

Equally long term in intention was the Concord, a specifically HOS block type, finalised in December 1996 to keep pace with rising expectations. It was also cruciform and based on prefabrication and modular construction, but slimmer and more elegant than the Harmony in both its main variants – the 41-storey Concord 1 with eight flats per floor, led by Chris Gabriel and Theresa Yim, and the 30-storey Concord 2 with six flats per floor, led by Ken Cheung – each with two flat mix configurations. The Concord would immediately become the HOS mainstay, with around 9,000 completed by the end of 1999.[145] (Figure 12.14a–c)

As previously mentioned, fully furnished mock-up flats were built on a site close to the HD headquarters, and D & S Section conducted visits, firstly for HA members and later for the press and public. Ken Cheung regarded the Concord as 'far superior to any private development – we even created the betterment of a cross-ventilated room with views on both sides, and we had a lovely living/dining/ room design. We wanted to differentiate HOS with an enhanced design ideology for compact dwelling, and we were almost competing with the private developer!'[146]

In the construction field, Messling trumpeted as his last, pre-retirement triumph the finalisation of the Construction Branch's ISO9000 certification, building on the 1990 introduction of the PASS system. Ada Fung recalled that once the ISO certification of a significant number of contractors was achieved, in 1991–2, 'then the contractors said, "Why don't you get certified too?"' Adoption of ISO9000 by the HD itself, Messling believed, would provide a more systematic management framework for the 3,200 staff of the Branch. This was coupled to a move from 'performance' to more prescriptive 'method'-based specification.[147] But after

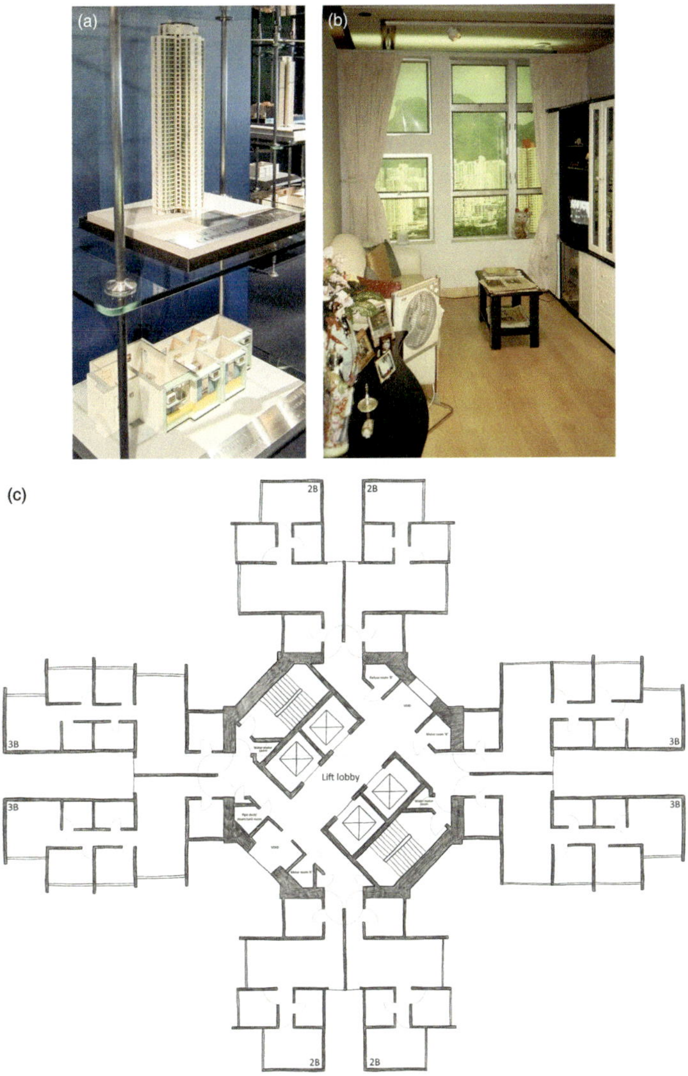

Figure 12.14 (a) Housing Authority Permanent Exhibition: model of Concord 1 block, and of a three-bedroom flat in Concord 1: 2011 photo (cf. Fig. 13.3). (MG). (b) HD mock-up of Concord living room in 1996 exhibition, 'Hong Kong: City of Tomorrow', in City Art Centre, Edinburgh (MG). (c) Typical upper-floor plan of Concord 1 Option 1: an almost 'private-sector' formula of four 2-bedroom and four 3-bedroom flats. Drawing by Joyce Fu, 2023.

Messling's departure, a different perspective also emerged, namely that ISO9000 was exacerbating bureaucracy rather than simplifying it. Gabriel contended that

> we were the first design office in Hong Kong to have ISO9000 accreditation. We burdened ourselves with a system that, though comprehensive and procedure-based, was overly complicated. It generated huge numbers of manuals – it was a case of teaching your grandma to suck eggs, and we later reviewed the manuals to work with a simpler, more efficient system![148]

The new system was intended in particular to facilitate construction enhancements such as the contract-shortening authorised by the Building Committee in February 1994 during the build-up to the LTHS Medium-Term Review Final Report: this comprised a seven-month shortening of pre-contract procedures and two-month shortenings of both piling and construction tendering, and a progressive compression of Harmony 1 floor construction cycles through prefabrication and work-flow planning from eight days (early 1990s) to six days (mid-1990s) to finally four days (1997, in a pilot project at Tseung Kwan O Area 57).[149] Alongside these, the new system was also designed to help the HD cope with sudden, urgent challenges, such as a June 1995 crisis over concrete decay when a top-floor ceiling in a 31-year old block in Kwai Chung Estate, scheduled for demolition in 1999, collapsed without warning. Rosanna Wong authorised an immediate condition check (at a cost of HK$1 billion) of thirty estates scheduled for medium-term demolition: the trouble was found to be largely confined to pre-1973 Resettlement or GLCH blocks, Mk IIIs being the worst culprits. Doubtless scenting a business opportunity, the Hong Kong Concrete Repair Association thundered that 'residents of public housing blocks would have been safer living in ancient Egypt than in some of this territory's estates'. Likewise, four months later, the sudden discovery of unexpected underground caverns in Ma On Shan Area 90, exacerbated by a problematic piling method chosen by Edward Ho's architecture firm, Wong Tung & Partners Ltd, compelled deletion of four 36-storey blocks from the project.[150]

Conclusion: going out with a production bang?

During the final months of British colonial rule, the multi-polar distribution of housing powers and policy-making authority became even more complicated and confusing. The Beijing input into the housing programme, in effect, grew two heads rather than one, after the designation in December 1996 of former shipping magnate Tung Chee-hwa as first Chief Executive of the HKSAR. Tung's argument that 'there has been far too much politics, to the distraction of everything else in Hong Kong, over the past four years', and that citizens were more concerned with 'livelihood' and 'welfare' than 'liberty', suggested the possibility of increased attention to housing.[151] However, although Tung pledged not to undermine the outgoing administration, his March 1997 appointment of property surveyor and Beijing ally C Y Leung to map out a post-July housing strategy triggered a barrage of press criticism. This focused not only on potential conflicts of interest within the real-estate industry, but also on conflicts between Leung's role and a recently announced government task-force review into housing policy, and more generally whether his appointment made Dominic Wong effectively redundant.[152] Wong, however, had been bolstering his position with a flurry of consultative activity, and disclosed in May that he had been meeting regularly for policy discussions with both Leung and Tung, while stressing that 'I am still the Secretary for Housing'. The direct Beijing input via the Land Commission was also still active, but now clearly on its last lap: in February Chinese representatives on the Commission vigorously rebutted off-the-cuff accusations by Financial Secretary Donald Tsang that they had not been 'sympathetic' to pleas for increased land supply.[153]

Later, in January 1997, Dominic Wong decisively secured his position with publication of his fifty-page LTHS blueprint for the years to 2006, *Homes for Hong Kong People – the Way Forward*. Stepping back slightly from the 85,000 commitment, it proposed to enhance advance planning to increase annual land supply within five years from 145 to 260 ha. This would permit a consistent minimum level of 80,000 completions (50,000 public and 30,000 private) each year into the future, while maximising private-enterprise involvement and wider home-ownership, and reserving public rental housing for those 'in genuine need' by methods including means-testing. The most controversial proposal, for higher rents (reviving Wong's original proposal to the HA) was to be discussed with both C H Tung and C Y Leung.[154] Reaction to Wong's new plan was mixed: one Democratic LegCo member branded it 'a roller-coaster rushing downwards faster and faster towards private housing'; the pro-establishment Edward Ho doubted the government's ability to consistently increase land supply; while someone even left a hoax bomb outside LegCo with slogans against Wong and C H Tung.[155] Following that incident, Dominic Wong suffered embarrassment from an unprompted public intervention by his wife, Cecilia, who protested that his 12-hours-a-day dedication to duty was rewarded only by 'sneering, misunderstanding and even intimidation', to which one journalist riposted that, bomb hoax or not, Wong 'has easy access to those rare but desirable two Ps which are an indispensable part of happiness – a pension and a passport'.[156]

Dominic Wong's strategic intervention came in the immediate context of a fresh upsurge in market overheating and 'bullish sentiment', which, he warned, might jeopardise the latest homeownership percentage aspiration of 70% by 2010.[157] His response, in March 1997, was to introduce fresh curbs on speculation on a more restricted scale than in 1994, including a new regulation that all flats must be offered for sale within 6 months of the start of the pre-sales process, and that each batch must comprise at least 20% of the total development – the aim being to prevent developers from creating 'an impression of artificial shortage'. Although the measures successfully prompted an immediate drop in output, developers and apologists hit back against the 'embattled' Wong, arguing predictably that his curbs risked depressing output.[158] Tung, however, also signalled support for reining in high property prices, and Leung hinted that his package would include significant restraints – leading to fresh claims (for example from Lee Wing-Tat) that Wong had been 'sidelined' from prior knowledge of Leung's recommendations.[159]

In this situation of flux, the other chief player in the multi-polar housing scene – Rosanna Wong's HA – attempted to safeguard its position, calling on the government on 16 June 1997 to set up a high-level panel to coordinate and maintain the land supply, arguing that growing rather than diminishing land shortages underlay the decline in public housing output, from 53,000 to 33,000 since 1990. Rosanna Wong stressed she wanted to be involved in 'a mechanism to improve the coordination of government departments in the public housing development process', and that the new Long-Term Housing Strategy must be unambiguously 'public housing-led' rather than dominated by the private sector.[160]

Perhaps appropriately, the final, anarchic word in the confused last few months of colonial rule lay with the unofficials and protesters who had recently so enlivened the Hong Kong housing scene – and focusing, very appropriately, on the arch-populist issue of rent levels. In a completely unanticipated intervention in the final LegCo meeting of the old era, Leung Yiu-Chung of the radical democratic group, The Frontier, tabled a private member's bill, the Housing (Amendment) (No. 3) Bill 1996, which proposed to cap any future increases to the inflation rate. In a chaotic and emotional debate – after a proposal by Lee Wing-Tat of the Democratic Alliance for an 'inflation minus 2%' rent-rise regime had been defeated – an amendment by Chan Kam-Lam of the Democratic Alliance for the Betterment of Hong Kong finally substituted an 'inflation plus 10%' cap. Dominic Wong railed vainly against this 'irresponsible and unreasonable' gesture against his cherished rent-rise policy, arguing it would prevent any move to differential rents geared to 'ability to pay'. More seriously, it risked exhausting the HA's surpluses within three years if HOS sales income were ever to stop – an eventuality that seemed unthinkable at this stage. This seemed as direct a challenge to the executive-led principle as could be conceived. However, it would also be the last, as the Basic Law forbade LegCo members after the handover from introducing private bills regarding government policy, as part of the incoming administration's strategy of 'building a new kitchen'.[161]

As we will see in the next chapter, public housing would occupy a central place within that post-1997 strategy. Yet paradoxically, its central plank – a much-trumpeted pledge by Tung Chee-hwa to build 85,000 housing units (of all tenures) a year – was far from being part of any 'new kitchen'. Instead, it was directly based on the public production drive devised by Dominic Wong at Patten's instigation. And this was also a programme whose confident political re-packaging by the new administration concealed a number of serious structural weaknesses, especially in relation to the housing hegemony of the real-estate 'tycoons' – as would become all too clear within a handful of years.

Notes

1 C Patten, *The Hong Kong Diaries*, Penguin, London, 2022, xxxiv, 6, 49, 335; Dimbleby, *The Last Governor*, 10–11.

2 Patten, *Hong Kong Diaries,* 231–8, 249, 254, 260–2.

3 Dimbleby, *The Last Governor;* C Patten, *East and West: the Last Governor of Hong Kong on Power, Freedom and the Future.*' London Macmillan 1998.
4 SCMP 13-5-1992, 12-7-1992, 9.
5 SCMP 8-10-1992, 29.
6 Blyth and Wotherspoon, *Hong Kong Remembers*, 281.
7 HKRS545-7-352, *Dateline* 8, 1992, on Patten visits. SCMP 29-9-94, 23; 30-8-93, 10.
8 Blyth and Wotherspoon, *Hong Kong Remembers*, 276; SCMP, 8-11-1992, 2; 23-10-1992, 6; 15-8-1992, 1; Patten, *Hong Kong Diaries*, 346.
9 Akers-Jones, *Feeling the Stones*, 215; SCMP 3-3-1993, 23.
10 SCMP 5-6-1994, 3; 8-5-1994, 2; Tsang, AMHOHK, 2007 edition, 255-63. Donald McNeill, 'Airports and territorial restructuring: The case of Hong Kong', *Urban Studies* 2014, Vol. 51(14), 3000.
11 K Wong, K Chau, S Ma, 'The disposal of the Hong Kong land stock under the Sino-British Joint Declaration', *Journal of Property Development*, 1999, 16(4) 323.
12 SCMP 1-1-1993, 1; 4-7-1993, 9. Rise in Patten's popularity ratings later in 1992, Patten, *Hong Kong Diaries*, 260–1.
13 SCMP 4-7-1993, 9; 3-10-1993, 4; 26-9-94, 6; 25-6-1994, 16.
14 SCMP 17-12-1993, 60.
15 SCMP 11-10-1994, 5; 8-10-1992, p29; 25-10-1992, 25; 30-3-1994, 1.
16 HKRS1881-2-19 10-8-1992 DO Southern to Ward.
17 SCMP 3-4-1994, 23; 26-9-1994, 6; 29-9-1994, 23; 29-8-1996, 16.
18 SCMP 6-10-1993, 1; 17-12-1993, 49-55; 7-10-1993, 36.
19 SCMP 9-9-1993, 27.
20 SCMP 10-7-1994, 2; 16-11-1994, 6; 11-5-1995, 3.
21 SCMP 25-6-1994, 16; 29-9-1994, 47; 16-10-1996, 59; 30-3-1997, 10.
22 SCMP 5-11-1993, 56.
23 SCMP 12-4-1994, 6; 20-12-1994, 6; 30-4-1995, 80.
24 Agnes Allcock, 'The Effects of Housing Pressure Groups on Housing Policy', HKU thesis, 1994 2,21-29, 41, 64. SCMP 24-8-1992, 5; 4-10-1994, 1; 5-10-1995, 62.
25 Allcock, 'Housing Pressure Groups', 41; SCMP 6-10-1994, 29; 27-8-1995, 62. Cagemen: SCMP 16-1-1996, 2.
26 Allcock, 'Housing Pressure Groups', 64.
27 SCMP 10-4-1994, 15; 27-8-1994, 22.
28 Allcock, 'Housing Pressure Groups', 21, 46–50.
29 SCMP 20-11-1993, 17; 31-7-1993, 4; 10-4-1994, 15; 7-12-1994, 18.
30 SCMP 23-8-1995, 1.
31 Akers-Jones, *Feeling the Stones*, 231, 203.
32 HKRS696-3-9 Brenda Fung (HA Secretary) to CS Office 5-3-1992. Akers-Jones, *Feeling the Stones*, 203. SCMP 7-7-1993, 1; 30-8-1993, 10; 9-6-1994, 3.
33 Akers-Jones, *Feeling the Stones*, 231; SCMP 23-3-1993, 23; 20-6-1993, 2.
34 SCMP 9-9-1995, 26–30.
35 HKRS545-7-352 11-10-1992 on Bates as acting DD. Information from Chris Gabriel, 2023.
36 Lambon, 2012 interview; Poon, 2009 interview; SCMP 17-8-1992, 15 (on Murray House and Penny Ward).
37 Lambon, 2012 interview; SCMP 11-9-1994, 46.
38 SCMP 30-6-1997, 19; 3-12-1996, 21; 20-5-1996, 19; 28-9-1995, 25.
39 SCMP 20-5-1996, 19; 28-9-1995, 25; 17-10-1996, 6.

40 Rosanna Wong, 2014 interview.
41 Yeung and Wong, *Fifty Years*, 268; SCMP 11-5-1995, 7; 30-4-1994, 44; 28-8-1995, 12; Akers-Jones, interview 2013; Housing Authority, *Annual Report*, 1992/3, 6; SCMP 15-9-1996, 4; 16-1-1996, 2; 4-4-1995, 5.
42 HKRS545-7-352 Eason note of 3-4-1992. Rosanna Wong, 2014 interview. SCMP 15-1-1994, 2.
43 SCMP 17-01-1993, 2.
44 SCMP 10-5-2014, 1; 8-5-1994, 2.
45 SCMP 5-6-1994, 1.
46 Yeung and Wong, *Fifty Years*, 27; SCMP 29-10-1993, 3; 26-9-1995, 1.
47 Rosanna Wong, 2014 interview.
48 SCMP 16-6-1994, 20.
49 SCMP 5-6-1994, 1.
50 SCMP 6-1-1995, 1.
51 Yeung and Wong, *Fifty Years*, 2003, 26.
52 Miller, 2014 interview.
53 Yeung and Wong, *Fifty Years*, 27.
54 SCMP 10-10-1992, 16; 19-6-1993, 24; 7-1-1994, 1.
55 Wong Chau Ma, 'Disposal of the Hong Kong land stock', 330; James Lee, *Housing, Home-Ownership and Social Change in Hong Kong*, Ashgate, Aldershot, 1999, 106; Liu Pak Wai, 'Land Premium and Hong Kong Government Budget', Institute of Global Economics and Finance, *Working Paper 19*, February 2014.
56 Cecilia Chu, *Building Colonial Hong Kong*, 2, 18–19.
57 SCMP 12-6-1996, 1; 3-4-1994, 25; 13-9-2019 'Beijing heaps pressure on Hong Kong developers'.
58 Rosanna Wong, 2014 interview.
59 C K Tsang, *Home-Ownership in Hong Kong*, Routledge, London, 2021, 65; Wong Chau Ma, 'Disposal of the Hong Kong land stock', 329; Y C Richard Wong, Hong Kong Land for Hong Kong People, HKUP, 2015.
60 SCMP 1-8-1993, 4.
61 SCMP 28-1-1995, 13; 25-10-1992, 25; 5-1-1994, 26; 10-4-1995, 36; 19-4-1995, 53.
62 SCMP 24-3-1994, 6; 30-3-1994, 18; 31-3-1994, 1.
63 HKRS696-3-8 22-10-1990, and HKRS696-3-9 25-3-1992 correspondence re HKPCPHP proposal for elected HA members; SCMP 28-1-1995, 13; 5-12-1995, 38.
64 SCMP 27-2-1995, 34; 17-1-1997, 10; 15-1-1997, 51.
65 Patten, *East and West,* 51; Patten, *The Hong Kong Diaries,* 67–8. Cf. the 1907 crisis in London private housing output caused partly by the deliberately 'depressive' effect on speculation of the LCC public rental housing programme: Owen Hatherley, *Red Metropolis, Socialism and the Government of London*, Repeater, London, 2020, 42.
66 Akers-Jones, *Feeling the Stones,* 257; Akers-Jones, 2013 interview; Alice Poon, 'Hong Kong's Land Policy – A Recipe for Social Trouble', *Hong Kong Journal*, January 2011; Information Services Department, *Hong Kong 2001*, Hong Kong, 2001, 202.
67 SCMP 19-5-1994, 6.
68 Wong Chau Ma, 324; SCMP 1-2-1997, 1.
69 HKRS545-7-32 14-10-1992 response to Elsie Tu LegCo question. Wong Chau Ma, 324–333.
70 Miller, 2014 interview.
71 Rosanna Wong, 2014 interview; S Poon, 2010 interview; Akers-Jones, 2013 interview (on sudden rush of land releases).

72 SCMP 3-4-1994, 25; 20-5-1994, 6.
73 SCMP 14-5-1994, 5; 3-6-1994, 1.
74 SCMP 10-2-1995, 3; 18-11-1994, 1; 9-6-1994, 3.
75 SCMP 18-11-1994, 1; 23-2-1995, 18.
76 SCMP 17-6-1994, 7; 11-11-1994, 3; 23-2-1995, 18; 5-6-1994, 3; 30-4-1994, 44.
77 Miller, 2014 interview.
78 SCMP 17-10-1994, 27.
79 R Wai, 2010 interview; Akers-Jones, *Feeling the Stones*, 257.
80 Hong Kong Housing Authority, *The Long-Term Housing Strategy, Final Report on the Medium-Term Review*, June 1994, 12, 30–32. HKHA, *A Report on the Medium-Term Review*, October 1993.
81 HKHA, *A Report on the Medium-Term Review*, October 1993, 6–9, 26, 55–7. HKHA, *Final Report on the Medium-Term Review*, 30.
82 HKHA, *Final Report on the Medium-Term Review*, 30.
83 HKHA, *Final Report on the Medium-Term Review*, 12; HKRS 2145-1-1.
84 Yeung and Wong, *Fifty Years*, 414; SCMP 17-12-1993, 49.
85 SCMP 4-6-1994, 1, 5-6-1994, 1.
86 SCMP 9-6-1994, 1; 9-6-1994, 2.
87 Miller, 2014 interview; SCMP 10-8-1996, 4.
88 SCMP 22-3-1995, 59.
89 SCMP 22-3-1995, 5.
90 SCMP 31-12-1995, 1.
91 Dominic S W Wong, *The 1996 Policy Address, Housing Policy Commitments*, Hong Kong Government, 1996; SCMP 31-12-1995, 1; 22-3-1995, 1.
92 Miller, 2014 interview.
93 Government Information Services Department, *Housing*, 1996. SCMP 31-12-1995, 1.
94 Poon, 2014 interview.
95 Miller, 2014 interview.
96 Patten, *Hong Kong Diaries*, 423–4.
97 James Lee, *Housing, Home Ownership and Social Change*, 266; Information Services Department, *Hong Kong 2001*, Hong Kong, 2001, 202.
98 N M Yip, 'Housing Crises and Interventions in Hong Kong', in Doling and Ronald, *Housing East Asia*, 73.
99 SCMP 15-4-1994, 3; 12-5-1995, 6.
100 SCMP 18-11-1993, 2; 28-7-1994, 6.
101 SCMP 24-8-1992, 5.
102 Poon, 2009 interview; Yeung and Wong, *Fifty Years*, 283; SCMP 17-12-1994, 12; 21-8-1993; 2-9-1993; 12-1-1994, 47; 15-11-1995, 55; 8-2-96, 6.
103 Yeung and Wong, Fifty Years, 373, 187
104 HKRS545-7-352 cutting of 17-12-1992. Yeung and Wong, *Fifty Years*, 182–7, 333; SCMP 25-4-1993, 3; 22-5-1994, 2; 7-1-1994, 3; 4-8-1995, 2; 29-10-1995, 3.
105 SCMP 14-10-1993, 2; 15-8-1994, 3; 7-10-1994, 5; 26-2-1996, 4.
106 SCMP 25-8-1994, 5; 12-11-1993, 24; 2-8-1995, 7; 19-2-1994, 14.
107 HKRS545-7-352 question by Zachary Wong at 24-6-1992 LegCo.
108 SCMP 28-2-1993, 55; 12-12-1993, 3.
109 SCMP 23-7-1994, 15; 24-7-1994, 5; 26-7-1994, 5; 2-8-1994, 3; 21-8-1994, 3.
110 Gabriel, 2009 interview.
111 SCMP 21-8-1994, 16; 16-11-1992, 5.

112 Territory Development Department, Urban Area and New Territories Development, 1993; SCMP 26-3-1993, 45. 'Sad City': R Wai, 2010 interview, SCMP 22-10-1995 ('Nightmare in a Dormitory Town') and SCMP 20-10-2007 ('City of Sorrow'). Patten opening of Tin Shui Wai, SCMP 26-3-1993, 45.
113 SCMP 14-6-1995, 55.
114 HKRS1882-3-19 27-3-1993 SHK presentation by Thomas Kwok and others; 24-4-1992 Y Yuen memo. SCMP 12-6-1996, 62.
115 Lambon, 2012 interview; Yeung and Wong, *Fifty Years*, 92; SCMP 10-11-1996, Agenda 1.
116 SCMP 16-2-1997, 31.
117 Fung Tung, 2010 interview.
118 Patten, *Hong Kong Diaries*, 403.
119 HKRS2145-1-1; SCMP 14-6-1995, 55; 17-12-1993, 59.
120 Government Information Services Department, *Housing*, 1996. SCMP 5-5-1995, 6; 28-8-1992, 25.
121 SCMP 20-9-1995, 57; 24-5-1995, 19.
122 Gabriel, 2011 interview.
123 SCMP 16-3-1994, 60; 7-8-1994, 5.
124 SCMP 23-7-1995, 29.
125 HKRS1881-2-25 notes for 6-9-1993 SDB meeting. SCMP 27-11-1993, 33. Information from Chris Gabriel, 2023.
126 HKRS2145-1-1; SCMP 17-12-1993, 59; 5-2-1995, 2; 29-5-1997, 8; SCMP 29-3-1995, 3.
127 SCMP 6-6-1993, 54.
128 SCMP 5-2-1995, 2; 23-9-1995, 1 (for example in 1995 concerning Lai Kok THA in Kowloon Bay).
129 Patten, *Hong Kong Diaries*, 308–9; SCMP 29-9-1995, 1, 30-9-1995, 1; 28-6-1997, 29.
130 SCMP 28-1-1996, 32; 29-9-1996, 2; 12-1-1995, 19.
131 HA Paper 71/95, File HD(C)DS/328/G, 28-12-1995, 'Development Fund Project, Interim Housing at Sha Kok Mei'; SCMP 7-11-1995, 5; 13-11-1995, 6; 29-5-1997, 8.
132 SCMP 9-9-1993, 28.
133 Ng, 2012 interview; SCMP 17-12-1993, 58–9.
134 Ng, 2012 interview; SCMP 17-12-1993, 49, 58.
135 Tung Chung landscape concept: SCMP 19-3-1995, 68.
136 Miller, 2014 interview.
137 SCMP 30-10-1997 (death of 75-year-old Wong Fai in fight with 74-year-old room-mate at Butterfly Estate).
138 Yeung and Wong, *Fifty Years*, 414; SCMP 17-12-1993, 49; 5-5-1996, 6.
139 Lambon, 2012 interview.
140 Lambon, 2012 interview.
141 Poon, 2009 and 2014 interviews.
142 Irene Cheng, Chris Gabriel, N.M. Chan, S.H. Ho, Polly C.P. Young, 'The redevelopment of Kwai Chung Estate', in CSIRO – Commonwealth Scientific and Industrial Research Organisation, *Proceedings of the World Conference on Sustainable Building SB08 Melbourne*, Melbourne, 2008, 1164-1171.
143 Gabriel, 2009 and 2011 interviews.
144 Gabriel, 2009 interview and 2023 information.
145 Chan and Chan, 'Public housing construction', 352. Gabriel, 2023 information.
146 Cheung, 2012 interview.

147 Ada Fung, 2023 interview. SCMP 26-3-1993; 9-9-1993, 25-9; 25-5-1994, 86; 8-5-1995, 48.
148 HKRS545-7-352, cutting of 11-10-1992; Gabriel, 2009 interview.
149 HKRS2145-1-1; Chan and Chan, 'Public housing construction', 353.
150 SCMP 20-6-1995, 2; 30-6-1995, 7; 2-5-1996, 5.
151 SCMP 9-1-1997, 16; 1-3-1997, 1.
152 SCMP 12-3-1997, 1; 22-3-1997, 6; 23-3-1997, 14; 25-3-1997, 1; 26-3-1997, 18.
153 SCMP 5-5-1997, 1; 1-2-1997, 1.
154 SCMP 25-1-1997, 6; 22-1-1997, 53; 20-2-1997, 16.
155 SCMP 20-2-1997, 16; 25-1-1997, 1–6.
156 SCMP 1-4-1997, 3; 6-4-1997, 48; 11-4-1997, 22.
157 SCMP 22-1-1997, 53.
158 SCMP 2-4-1997, 54; 15-1-1997, 51; 7-5-1997, 55.
159 SCMP 30-3-1997, 2; 16-6-1997, 45; 17-6-1997, 19; 24-6-1997, 8.
160 SCMP 13-6-1997, 4.
161 Yeung and Wong, *Fifty Years*, 32, 203; SCMP 28-6-1997, 10.

Part IV

July 1997 to the present day

13 1997–2005

The Tung administration – building a 'new identity' through public housing?

In Part IV, we will see that while in the constitutional field, 1997 represented a sharp break in continuity, as the Beijing leadership reconstituted LegCo as part of their 'new kitchen', the underlying economic framework of finance-led globalisation remained unaltered. Administratively, too, there was continuity with the outgoing regime's 'executive-led' system – not least in the housing strategy initially pursued by Chief Executive Tung Chee-hwa.[1] This was, in practice, a continuation of Patten's last three years, with its combination of a crash production drive and attempted boosting of home-ownership. Where it differed was not in substance but in its ideological framing, which was far more assertively political, and indeed echoed housing's role in the self-trumpeting nation-building project of Lee Kuan Yew in Singapore in earlier decades. That was hardly surprising, as Tung's strategy was significantly inspired by admiration for Singaporean policies, especially in 'home-ownership for the people', which inspired his announcement of a big HOS boost following a trip there in 1997.[2]

Praised as 'decent and honest' by Patten, Tung, the former CEO of a family shipping firm, Overseas Orient Container Lines, combined Chinese cultural conservatism with capitalist entrepreneurialism.[3] Around this he built a political persona of supposedly greater empathy with ordinary Hongkongers, combined with a Singapore-style agenda of outstripping (or claiming to have outstripped) colonial achievement: he argued in his first Policy Address in October 1997 that 'Hong Kong has finally broken free from the psychological constraints brought about by the colonial era' and should 'set aside past modes of thought', and boasted that 'I hear the pulses of the people better' than Patten.[4] Those decadent 'past modes of thought' had fuelled the housing problem: in October 1997, pro-Beijing politicians, including Elsie Tu, claimed the colonial regime had actively fuelled housing problems by 'encouraging people to spend on dancing and horse-racing'. Placed in charge of an explicitly 'executive-led' system and outspokenly opposed to Patten's 'politicising of society', Tung himself was ironically responsible for the most 'political' framing of Hong Kong housing ever.[5]

This higher-profile approach reflected the 1997 disappearance of what historian Steve Tsang referred to as the 'inhibited political centre' of the colonial regime – the caretaker-government mind-set that MacLehose had called a 'low

DOI: 10.1201/9781315563701-17

posture' – and its replacement by a more assertive attitude. This was fuelled by the big infrastructural projects now coming to maturity, above all the airport project, but was also concerned to rectify social inequality and was both supported and critiqued by a post-1997 surge in civic activism.[6] The new administration attracted contradictory criticisms from the start, ranging from accusations of domineering behaviour, e.g. in its rescinding of the last-gasp rent restrictions introduced by the outgoing LegCo, to accusations that it lacked vision.[7]

To some extent, the rampant house-price inflation of the 1990s had neutralised the lower-profile housing successes of the inhibited-centre regime under MacLehose and successors. It had also briefly embarrassed Tung even before his assumption of office, when he advised citizens in early 1997 not to buy flats for the moment, only to see prices shooting upwards again.[8] Tung's overall housing strategy was to boost public spending on housing – as part of an overall rise in recurrent public spending from $10.9bn to $18.6bn – and stamp out price speculation and dampen house prices,[9] while disavowing Patten's 1994 anti-speculation measures.[10] This would be framed by a more aggressive, higher-profile repackaging of public intervention, above all the state-sponsored home-ownership drive that Patten had expanded adventitiously from 1994–5. These were now elevated into political pledges and gauges of accountability.[11]

85,000 or bust! From ideological projection to practical production strategy

Tung's three central housing pledges all stemmed directly from Patten's strategy, including firstly a three-year waiting-list maximum, and secondly a Singapore-inspired target of 70% home-ownership by 2007, expanding slightly on the Patten pledge of two-thirds home-ownership by 2001 – which was already giving Patten credibility problems in the mid-90s. Financially, the strategy was boosted by the $190bn war-chest of the accumulated Land Fund: all land-sale receipts now went to the government.[12]

By far the most prominent of the three pledges, and the one most intimately bound up with concepts of accountability, was the overall annual output target of 85,000 – a figure that was extrapolated by Tung from Patten's policies. This target was suggested both by his pre-1997 'housing supremo' C Y Leung, and by Dominic Wong.[13] It was a repackaged and 'politically spun' version of the ad-hoc targets previously put together by Patten and Wong in 1995–6, supported by the post-1996 explosion in land supply; these had then been incorporated in Wong's new 'Mk II LTHS' consultation of early 1997, despite the pointed questioning of its achievability by Tony Miller in autumn 1996 on his appointment as Director of Housing.[14] Miller recalled later that Tung's 85,000 target was a 'crude way of laying claim to what was already in the programme – that had been initiated by Patten and cranked up at his insistence', and that Tung took ownership of it without any specific plan as to how to make it work. That appropriation, however, was no accident, but quite deliberate: 'Tung intended it, and made the best of it!' The December 1996 PHDP completions target of 106,000 for 2000/1, already criticised as unrealistic by Rosanna Wong, had soared by June 1997 to over 114,000.[15] Behind the scenes, in practice, Miller successfully reined back the public sector's actual annual output target to 82,000–83,000 units.[16] As a result, only in 2000 was there a significantly higher completions total – a record level of around 89,000.[17]

All this was a formula that, aided by good luck in its timing and skill in its self-promotion, had worked triumphantly for Lee's Singapore: but the outcome for Tung would be very different, owing to its unhappy coincidence with the Asian financial crisis that hit Hong Kong almost immediately after the handover.[18] Subsequently, owing to its high political profile, the 85,000 target was publicly pilloried as the overwhelming, if not sole, cause of the property-market traumas of 1998–2003. But as C Y Leung later pertinently observed in 2010, the property market had not crashed in early 1997 on the announcement of the new LTHS 'Mk II' – nor in 1995–6 when the expanded output targets had first taken shape, building on the scenarios listed in the 1993–4 interim review of the original 1987 LTHS 'Mk I'.[19] As we saw in Chapter 12, the original 1987 LTHS had proposed 1,085,000 new flats by 2001, implying an annual output of 40,000 public-sector and 30,000 private-sector flats.[20] The 1993 Mid-Term Review had evaluated PHDP 66/93 against scenarios which envisaged a 63,000 public-sector blip in 2000/1; the actual figure in 2000/1 would be 71,000.[21] And by 1994, the Final Report of the Mid-Term Review was arguing that the effective demand from 1993/4 to 2000/1 was in fact 606,000 households (76,000 annual equivalent), as opposed to the 527,000 assumed in 1993. The Housing Authority accordingly proposed an additional 50,000 flats, i.e. 10,000 per annum, and the predicted output of public rental housing became 160,000 flats from 94/5 to 97/8. Throughout these years of incremental upwards 'target creep', the PHDP system was still fully in force, and being regularly updated in 1998; the February 1998 LTHS Mk II had less explicit targets, referring to 85,000 'on average'.[22]

All of this had played out, during the early/mid-1990s, against the background of the progressive growth of the oligopolistic power of the largest private developers, especially in the accumulating land-banks and constructing new private-sector flats – a situation that was exacerbated, ironically, by the damage caused to smaller developers by Patten's 1994 anti-speculation measures. The largest, Sun Hung Kai, had built up its holdings especially through Letters A and B and had a 42 million sq ft land bank by 2009.[23] The result was a growing public conviction of the existence of a so-called 'high land price policy', allegedly maintained by government and developers in collusion, allowing the latter to circumvent the high cost of official lease modifications by buying low and selling high.[24]

Patten had argued that he dared not take on the tycoons directly owing to the risk of a collapse in confidence in the economy in the lead-up to 1997. This constraint no longer applied to Tung, but he was just as timid in dealing with them as Patten had been. His initial strategy was to circumvent them indirectly, by using the post-1996 land-supply boom to force down land prices.[25] However, the rush of land only gathered pace after the ending of all the Beijing-imposed restrictions in 1997, and it became clear that this new glut would result in a potential bunching of production around 2000. In December 1998, no less than 650 ha were pledged by government over the next five years for public and private housing.[26] Development of the New Territories was still central to the strategy: the 1998 review stressed that six out of its 16 major planning studies were 'strategic growth areas' in the New Territories: Tung Chung, Tseung Kwan O, North-West and North-East New Territories, Hong Kong Island South, and Reclamation: they could accommodate 790,000 by 2011.[27]

To oversee this public-sector-led process and (inspired by Singapore's governmental land controls) to face down the speculators and the 'artificial' land scarcity caused by their monopolistic hoarding, a new, central coordination mechanism for land supply was introduced in July 1997, the Steering Committee on Land Supply for Housing, or 'HOUSCOM' for short.[28] Chaired by the Financial Secretary – an indication of its importance – HOUSCOM's focal responsibility was land supply and exploitation, including identifying sites and (from October 1997) maximising their developmental densities. At its instigation, the previous development ratio of 5–7 for public housing since 1990 was replaced by a presumption of 7 as a standard: 'every opportunity' would also be taken to maximise densities beyond DR7.[29] It would also oversee overall production phasing, to secure output of 'at least' 85,000 flats every year 'for the foreseeable future', via a rolling 13-year programme divided into three separate segments, supported by a departmental 'accountability system'.[30] An agreement 'hammered out' between HD and other departments would permit fast-tracking of preparatory work, with the aim (suggested by Miller) of bringing forward 10,000 programmed completions from 2000/2001 to 1999/2000, to minimise the threatened production spike.[31]

Thus HOUSCOM was conceived as an enforcement agency for the PHDP in general, and for the 85,000 target in particular. It would also more generally coordinate the government departments involved in housing production: the Housing Department, the Territory Development Department, and the Lands Department. Within the site-delivery and flat-completion stages of production – the LD had almost sole responsibility for the government oversight of the private sector, while the HD and TDD shared responsibility for public housing in various contexts (including New Towns).[32] A complication within this system stemmed from the autonomous role of the Housing Bureau (formerly Branch) and of Dominic Wong as Secretary: according to Miller, the Housing Authority was in practical terms dependent on the Bureau for land supply, which caused recurrent 'anxiety' in the HA–HB relationship; the accelerating releases of land secured through HOUSCOM rapidly led to a further bunching of the programme around 2000–1, as predicted in November 1996 by Miller.[33]

Yet any attempt, even as concerted as this, to overcome the inertia of the high land-value system, was likely to prove problematic, especially as the proportion of government revenue from land sales was actually rising during this period: 1996/7 was a peak year for land sales, and according to tax experts in 1998, up to 62% of government revenue fleetingly came from the property industry, including land-sale proceeds, property-related profits tax, stamp duties, rates, and public housing rents and sales; that revenue had subsequently fallen, reflecting the 65% property crash.[34] However, the entrenched and monopolistic system allowed the developers to manage land-premium conversion to their advantage, buying low and selling high.[35] The Hong Kong government was, far more than Singapore, dependent on high land prices and consequential revenue, not least in the latter's multiplier effect on HA income from the 1980s onwards, allowing the Authority (via HOS sales) to 'internally' finance its expansion in a circular relationship between high land value and public-housing activity.[36] And Brown and Loh argued in 2002 that the SAR government's reliance on the price performance of the property market had actually risen since 1997.[37] In housing, the multiplier-effect of government land income meant there could be no escape from its dominance, and that if anything unforeseen happened to disturb Tung's expansion strategy, the default mode for the government would inevitably be a reversion to the status quo. The earlier, 1990s government restrictions had, in effect, weeded out all small developers and left the largest firms in an even more dominant position: the profits of the four largest accounted for as much as 7% of GDP during the 1990s.[38]

Owing to these factors, housing policy in the Tung years saw increasingly radical fluctuations, exacerbated by growing public participation demands, which protracted the development process: Wai recalled that 'previously, we could just announce a new scheme – or we wouldn't even announce it – no-one would know! Now, there's consultation, and moving beyond that, to pre-consultation. After each day you think – what have I actually done today?'[39] Gabriel recalled that Hong Kong frequently looked enviously at Singapore in this period, particularly the generous size of its flats and with its unified approach, whereas 'the Hong Kong government had this contradictory view: firstly, the government doesn't interfere; yet secondly, 50% of the people are living in subsidised housing.'[40] Ng argued that 'Singapore's political structures are very different. The consultation process in Hong Kong is enormous, compared to Singapore. There, the government says, 'That's it!'[41] Yet as at July 1997, the initial resemblances to Lee Kuan Yew's 1959 strategy of appropriating reforms introduced by the outgoing administration, for his own identity-building purposes, were nevertheless strong. Arguably, the key factor that differentiated Tung's housing programme from Lee's was unlucky timing, which would leave his bold initiative looking like a false start.[42]

Building towards disaster: from financial crisis to housing crisis

These latent instabilities might not have fatally impeded Tung's strategy had the financial crisis not struck at the heart of Hong Kong's new global-capitalist identity – only days into July 1997.[43] The strategy was assailed from all sides, by precipitous falls in land prices (57% in 1998–2003, compared with 44% in 1981–5), house prices, and GDP, which shrank by 2% in the first quarter of 1998.[44] (Figure 13.1) Yet HA production kept shooting up unstoppably for the first three years, from 35,000 in 1998 (21,000 HOS) to 74,000 in 2001 (23,000 HOS).[45] The first six months of 1998 saw more Housing Authority starts than all of 1997. Expenditure on public housing could be reined in somewhat faster: in 1999/2000 it was 12% up in real terms on the previous year, whereas in 2000/1 it was 83% down on 1999/2000.[46]

Figure 13.1 Graph of fluctuations in property prices from 1980 to 2010, correlated with external economic and administrative events. Drawing by Joyce Fu, 2023.

During 1998, the rhetoric of some developers and their apologists rapidly turned against Tung's strategy: for example, Centaline's Shih-Wing-chung completely reversed his policy rhetoric between 1997 and 1998, from arguing in 1997 that the government should boost housing supply to combat speculators, to arguing in August 1998 that all government housing schemes for sale 'should be scrapped'.[47] Reflecting this, the government became increasingly confused during 1998, about whether its main strategy should be 'to keep land prices low or to drive them higher'.[48] But May 1998 saw the beginnings of the loosening of government curbs on speculation, branded a 'total surrender' to the big developers by some critics.[49]

The continuing predominance of the low-price strategy for the moment was suggested by the successful introduction in 1997 of the Tenants Purchase Scheme, a project whose aggressively low pricing strategy and more highly organised maintenance and management provisions ensured that it made a far more immediate impact than Akers-Jones's earlier attempts. A total of 39 estates containing 184,903 flats were rolled out from January 1998 (the first 2,500 receiving up to an 88% discount) until August 2005 – 40,547 of which were still unsold by 2020.[50] Although the Lands Department's control of land somewhat inhibited TPS estate sales by the HD, the scheme's impact benefited from the vigorous personal backing given it by Tung, following which Rosanna Wong firmly encouraged HA members to acquiesce; in November and December 1997 it was welcomed by all the main political parties.[51]

The concentration of this privatisation process in specific estates gave the TPS programme a concentrated character very different from the piecemeal Thatcherite Right-to-Buy in Britain (which in Yeung and Wong's opinion, would have led to market collapse if it had been introduced in Hong Kong), and ensured from the start a considerable overlap with the HOS, as the lowest rung in the ladder of housing self-improvement. In March 1998 commentators began debating whether the TPS was actually knocking out that lowest rung, and whether TPS and HOS were targeting the same market. Ho Lok-sing argued it would set off a 'chain reaction' of weakened demand upwards from HOS to luxury, but Tony Miller insisted in June that any overlap was minimal.[52]

Later, following the TPS's eventual wind-down after 2003, its pros and cons were debated, with privatisation enthusiast Richard Wong insisting it was not to blame for the price crash, and indeed had not gone far enough, but housing minister Michael Suen arguing in the famous 'Nine Tactics' policy speech of November 2002 (see below) that its relationship to PRH was destabilising:

> The irony of TPS… is that as Government keeps on rolling out the existing PRH stock for sale to sitting tenants, it has to continue to embark on a major PRH production to replenish its housing stock. Continuation with the TPS clearly flies in the face of the principle of rational allocation of public resources.[53]

In late 1998 and early 1999, a consensus grew that TPS and HOS were not only in conflict with each other but were both detrimental to the private market.[54] Yet at the same time the Housing Authority was becoming increasingly dependent on the

HOS, whose sales revenues accounted for a rising proportion of HA income, from 46% in the early '90s and 55% in the mid-1990s to 61% around 2000.[55] Despite the criticisms of HOS as an imperfect form of home-ownership by Richard Wong and others, a lively secondary market in HOS resales was already well-developed, as evidenced in a July 1997 analysis of trading-up sales transactions at Lung Poon Court. There, 60% of original occupants had already switched to the private sector following expiry of the original ten-year resale restrictions, invariably making a significant profit even after payment of an average $800,000 premium; and in November a survey suggested 60% of all PRH tenants wanted to become HOS owners. By 1997, the principle was established that the HA would use the HOS to fund its building programme, and its commercial income to subsidise its PRH rents.[56] In October 1998 Rosanna Wong argued that financial reasons would protect the HOS from being abandoned, as its 1996–7 profits of $13.9 billion provided half the HA's income, and during the same years the HA had spent $11.4 billion building homes: 'we need all the income to build public housing'.[57] But increasingly there were cautionary statements, for example from Ho Hei-wah in February 2000, that the government's 70% home-ownership target was 'not a holy target' but 'only Mr Tung's personal wish'. There was growing debate about the relationship of the HOS and the private market, with some arguing the HOS should be expanded and the private sector 'propped up no longer', and others arguing that the government, far from propping up the private market, had 'in fact suppressed it'.[58]

During 1998, the big developers and their media mouthpieces voiced increasing criticisms of the 85,000 target – not yet as an absolute evil in itself, but on grounds that it was inordinately vulnerable to the economic downturn. Both DAB and the Democrats still supported the target in early 1998.[59] But by early 1998, James Lee, CE of the HK Policy Research Institute, was arguing that the 'rigid target' was increasingly seen by public opinion as 'an act of public economy which works against a free market'.[60] So far, the biggest players on the developers' side held their fire: in May 1998 Li Ka-shing denied he was putting 'pressure' on the government, while urging it to 'rethink' its planned output of HOS and Sandwich Class flats. Government officials such as Miller were still more preoccupied with managing the production spike stemming from the Patten plan of 1995–6.[61] Tung's strategy received a strong defensive boost in March 1999, in an intervention by PRC Premier Zhu Rongji, aiming to persuade Li, Kwok and others to accede to Tung's plan to resume land sales to offset the ballooning budget deficit, estimated to reach US $832m by March 1999: Li took the lead in publicly reversing his opposition to restarting land sales, against opposition from members of the Real Estate Developers' Association.[62] 1999 saw the consequent introduction of the land application list system, allowing developers to control the pace of sales rather than the government, and which would continue until 2013.[63]

Tung's high-output strategy was also fleetingly bolstered by a demographic distraction: a succession of Housing Bureau projections between March 1998 and October 2000, predicting a huge rise in housing demand stemming from mass mainland immigration. This projection, of a rise in population to 9 million by 2020 (refined in 1999 to a rise of 1.67 million in three years, requiring 170,000 extra flats), suggested urgent expansion of the public housing drive would be needed, to a level of 730,000 completions over eight years (91,250 annually). Rapidly, however, it emerged that the Housing Bureau figures on which it was based were no more than guesswork.[64] In the event, the total population only reached 7.5 million in 2020. But in reality the underlying trend was in the other direction, towards contraction. Several tax experts argued in 1998 that the government was simply unable to get away from the status quo, owing to its dependence on land income and its multiplier effect, with some 65–70% of government revenue coming from the property industry.[65] Overall, the trajectory of pressure was towards an undermining of Tung's high-output, low land-price strategy.

Here the effect of the CRP was also potentially confusing, in its high continuing level of both demolition and costly construction between 1998 and 2003, which raised the cumulative number of demolished blocks from 394 to 531.[66] May 2001 (October 1999) also saw the establishment of the URA, with its 'high-powered' ability to resume land without going through ExCo. However, it was beset by problems, including slow and controversial progress in an initial high-profile infill redevelopment at Wedding Card Street in Causeway Bay.[67]

There was also continuing debate, throughout Tung's term of office, about the role of the Housing Society. January 1999 saw calls for it to concentrate on building for sale, to give it a new sense of 'identity', and September 2001 witnessed a more controversial bid by chairman Timothy Chung, swiftly rebuffed by the government, to build schemes on the mainland for sale to middle-class residents, followed by a slightly different suggestion by a private think-tank to instead build low-income PRH in Shenzhen – also quickly dismissed.[68] The HS responded vigorously to the calls for specialised housing for the elderly, especially following the June 2004 report of an HS-commissioned HKU study on elderly housing needs, and its first multi-storey towers for elderly residents, Jolly Place in Tseung Kwan O, and Cheerful Court in Jordan Valley, were completed from 2003/4 (see next chapter).[69]

Eventually, following ten months of growing public criticisms of the 85,000 target, and homebuyers' growing blame of Tung and his housing policies for their negative equity, a decisive point in public discourse came in July 2000. Tung let slip in an apparently carefully scripted intervention that the 85,000 target, far from an overriding policy determinant, had 'existed only in name, not in substance' since 1998.[70] Doubtless intended as a subtle way of giving the 85,000 target a soft landing, the intervention was instead widely ridiculed as inept and 'bizarre'. Its public-relations effect was to 'deeply wound Tung Chee-hwa's credibility and authority', not least because both the HA and Dominic Wong had been kept in the dark about Tung's announcement: Wong drily referred questions on the issue to Tung's Information Coordinator (i.e. spin doctor), Stephen Lam.[71] The 85,000 target had been recently publicly reaffirmed both by Tsang (in September 1999) and Dominic Wong (December 1999) and even now, C Y Leung protested that it had not been completely 'abandoned'.[72]

The gradual scaling-back of Tung's pledges can be traced in successive annual *Hong Kong Reviews* from 1997 to 2002. In 1997 the annual target was 'at least'

85,000 from 1999; in 1998 it was 'an average of' 50,000 public-sector flats plus facilitating 35,000 private-sector units; and from 1999 onwards the 'estimated requirement' was 'of the order of' 80,000 per year, reflecting an assumed 1.6% annual population growth.[73] After July 2000 and September 2001, the remaining pledges also rapidly lost credibility, with the 70% home-ownership target now branded 'unlikely to be attainable' (Rebecca Chiu).[74] Miller recalled that 'There'd been an outcry from developers and others about the scale of the housing programme and the impact it was having on property prices – though one could argue that the pre-1997 speculative bubble, or spike, would have burst anyway. But the financial crisis dramatically pricked the bubble in Hong Kong, so from the beginning of 1998, we saw a rapid collapse of private prices – which coincided with the first massive impact of Patten's programme – and people linked the two. They said, "We've got negative equity because of the scale of the public housing programme!" C H Tung found himself locked into a programme of massive proportions, which, even if you said, "Stop!" would still run for four more years'.[75] (Figure 13.2)

Between June and December 2000, reflecting his 'bizarre' handling of the '85,000' issue, a new discourse of Tung as a muddle-headed incompetent, or 'Silly Old Tung' (Lo Mung Tung), began to emerge in the mass media, among cartoonists and among some politicians.[76] Christine Loh of the Citizens Party argued that Hong Kong housing was 'a rudderless boat drifting in stormy waters. The captain is nowhere to be found'.[77] In response, Tung's defenders, including trade unions as well as Li Ka-shing, came out in voluble support, to bolster his chances of re-election to a second term in 2002.[78] The Federation of Trade Unions urged people to back Tung to allow him to 'sweep away all the troubles and reforms left behind by the British Hong Kong authorities, that hindered the development of the SAR', and the pro-government newspaper *Ta Kung Pao* thundered that "In the name of down with Tung", their real purpose is "down with Beijing", and "down with one

Figure 13.2 June 2000 SCMP article attacking Tung's housing policy as being dominated by high land prices and dictated by the property tycoons.

country, two systems".[79] As 2000 shaded into 2001, however, Tung's administration began to suffer a more general loss of public respect. By September 2001 it was commented that although his 'amateur advisers' had been vanquished by his senior civil servants, 'Tungenomics' was still a doctrine without strategic direction.[80] And in late 2001 and early 2002 there were growing claims of his, and his administration's, links to private developers and even of 'nepotism' and 'government-business collusion' – a discourse that would, in the event, become thoroughly entrenched for the next decade and the next two Chief Executives.[81]

The piling scandal: public housing under siege

The place of public housing within this escalating crisis of confidence was complicated. While it certainly suffered from the general decline in the prestige of Tung's administration, it was also a key contributing factor to that decline, in one specific and catastrophic respect – the so-called 'piling scandal' concerning defective foundation works in public housing schemes, which did much to undermine the credibility and political standing of the Housing Authority between 1998 and 2002.

The piling scandal was a cumulative succession of events and pressures, beginning ironically with scandals not in the public but in the private sector. It came in the context of much greater pressures on the HA and contractors compared with even the 1980s maximum-output years: in January 1999, Deputy Director of Housing (Works) Raymond Bates explained that over 300,000 flats were under production, and would significantly exceed the late-1980s maximum of 52,000–54,000 public completions; at peak production later in 1999, the HA would need to be employing 18,000 construction workers, and the standard lead-time for a public housing project had been shortened from 61 to 47 months.[82] Piling contracts, Ada Fung recalled, remained a significant exception to the new quality-controls of PASS and ISO, as piling contractors' design-and-build without professional engineering input was still allowed – nor was there even a list of approved firms.[83] And in the background swirled the wider building pressures of the years around 1997: 'After Chris Patten left, Tung Chee-hwa was trying to make a name for himself and he went for the 85,000 target – although this was unsustainable from a labour point of view. The Chinese had delayed the airport to make sure it was completed after the handover. So labour was being drawn away to the airport, and his 85,000 target was impracticable. Cost was not critical – deadlines were. Every month we'd get dossiers with boxes to fill in, on output. The piling contractors were forced into ridiculous programmes to fulfil their contracts on time: if they were late, they'd suffer huge liquidated damages' (Lambon). Miller argued in March 2000 that HA workforce levels could easily have coped with a 35,000-unit production level, but now the Authority was being asked to supply 50,000 annually, to support the 70% home-ownership target.[84]

According to Poon, however, the piling problems also had a more complex cause, stemming partly from the siphoning-off of professional staff at the instigation of a new administrative deputy director.[85] This left no-one with direct experience of construction available to effectively monitor contractor design-and-build. Poon argued that 'the piling was an entirely separate issue' from the output spike and any consequent shortages of resources within HD, not least as the piling trouble started in a joint-venture project between the MTR and the private sector in November 1998.[86] Only later did it spread to public housing, the key problem schemes being Tin Chung Court, Tin Shui Wai, from August 1999, and Sha Tin Area 14B (Yu Chui Court), from January 2000 – in both cases with two Concord HOS blocks being affected.[87] Other lesser cases included Concord blocks at Tin Fu Court, Tin Shui Wai, and Yat Tung I Estate, Tung Chung. Tin Chung Court had been offered to the public in December 1998 but by November 1999 only 35% of units had been sold; remedial works were completed in 2002.[88]

The early investigations of the piling took place in October and November 1999, involving a total of 106 sites; Miller and Rosanna Wong toured the sites, heading the investigations and organising rectification works.[89] In technical terms, the rectification story was one of bold achievement, in straightening leaning buildings. At three projects, 'we took 40-storey buildings that were beginning to lean over, we went under them and put them straight! – these were the most amazing achievements!' 'What they did was very innovative – York Minster stuff! They kept it very close to their chests – they did significant excavation under the buildings that were leaning, and put new foundations under them and corrected the lean'. Offending contractors such as Hsin Chong or Zen Pacific were disqualified from piling work.[90]

By far the most damaging of the scandals affecting public housing was that of Blocks D and E of Sha Tin 14B.[91] (Figure 13.3) Its piling contractor, Zen Pacific (ZPCCL), began bidding for public housing foundation work in December 1997, looking 'aggressively' for contracts after acquiring 90% of specialist company Ngo Kee.[92] The piling contract was awarded in February 1998 and completed in November, with superstructure construction starting in December. Each 41-storey Concord 1 block was to be supported on eighteen 2.3 m large-diameter piles: in January 2000, the two towers having reached 32 storeys, work was suspended and investigations by engineers C M Wong & Associates found only four of 36 piles were definitely resting on bedrock.[93] By late January 2000 it was clear that the situation was 'desperate' and that the blocks would need to be demolished.[94] Miller recalled:

> Most of the short-piled blocks were on friction piles – they were OK, as you could compensate for it by putting in more piles. But with bored caisson piles, they had to go down to bedrock, or you're in trouble. That was what happened at Sha Tin 14B. One day, the Director of Construction came in and said, "You know those two blocks we completed tests on? You're not going to like this, but we've got movement!" We got two experts in: the contractor got the man who'd saved the Leaning Tower of Pisa, and we had an Australian, who was adamant they couldn't be made to stand up. So eventually, we had to take them down.

Figure 13.3 Sha Tin 14b, Yu Chui Court HOS, 2010 photo (MG): the micro-park in the centre foreground is the site of the demolished Concord blocks D and E.

'That was Hong Kong's Ground Zero – it must have cost in the order of $450 million to build those two Concord blocks – then we had to demolish them!' (Gabriel). Cheng Hon-kwan put the position most succinctly: 'At Sha Tin Section 14B, the buildings were hanging in the air!'[95] Nevertheless, it was telling that, in contrast to 'British housing construction disasters' such as Ronan Point (1968) and Grenfell Tower (2017), the faults were discovered and decisive action taken long before potential residents got anywhere near the buildings!

In its public and political 'reception', the piling crisis had three phases: firstly, a direct crisis concerning the technical defects in 1999–2000; secondly, for much of 2000, one of political accountability, with the HA a lightning-rod for discontent at the lack of 'accountable government';[96] and finally, in 2001–3, a clash of real-estate vested interests, with the HA under assault by the developers. An initial investigation, chaired by John Strickland, cleared Rosanna Wong and Miller, but was widely condemned by 'outraged lawmakers'.[97] And a second, semi-confidential government investigation into Tin Chung and Sha Tin 14B chaired by Stephen Selby, Director of Intellectual Property, was similarly scornfully rejected.[98] The ICAC also became involved in following-up the corrupt on-site practices potentially involved. When, under the banner of accountability, the investigative process escalated in January 2001 into a full-scale LegCo inquiry, with the enthusiastic backing of the Liberals and DAB, the third phase began: a barely concealed power struggle between the HA and the developers:

> A LegCo commission did a root-and-branch analysis of the HA. This was a tainted process – it was chaired by a member of the Liberal Party, who was very closely aligned with the developers, and was used to force us eventually out of the HOS programme.[99]

The first, construction-oriented phase of investigation was addressed internally by the Housing Authority, with Miller and Wong rapidly focusing on criminality on-site, rather than the effects of programming problems such as the production spike: 'The problems were not with the civil servants but the private firms'.[100] Eventually, a number of supervisory staff, engineers and clerks of works were convicted and several went to prison. Lambon argued,

> I'm not sure if the piling contractors were corrupt, or just right up against it, but certainly the clerks of works were putting in inaccurate records. The buildings were nearly complete, and were fully loaded, and the lift contractors could see that the fully loaded building was out of plumb. To test them, we had to load up the building with huge amounts of water on each floor.[101]

Miller pointed out at the LegCo inquiry in April 2001 that the piling scandals had mainly occurred one year ahead of the bunching of contracts: although the HA had contracted-out work since 1977, the key factor in his view was not bunching (although the latter 'may have contributed') but the increasingly onerous effects during the financial crisis of the traditional HA system of 'transfer of risk on to the shoulders of the contractor', compounded by very keen bids submitted in a rising market, and the strong overall impact of the crisis in leaving contractors unusually hard up, and potentially leading to 'fraudulent and criminal activity'.[102] In November 2000, arguing that the post-crisis way forward for the HA was some sort of risk-sharing with contractors, Miller suggested that the problems had stemmed from contractors who had *not* come and confided their problems to the HD. 'It happened because it was production, production, production, and people took risks!'[103]

Progressively, however, anger at the fact that no senior officials were directly blamed in the enquiries, coupled with the growing post-Patten climate of demands for 'public accountability', converted the piling scandals into a political scandal concerning accountability within the executive-led system – an onslaught generally led by the democratic and independent parties with the pro-government parties (e.g. the DAB) following behind. The outcome of this was a crescendo of demands for the resignations both of Rosanna Wong and of Tony Miller, despite the fact that they were not political appointees. Housing seemed to be no longer an autonomous para-political discourse, but a part of a wider political confrontation: in June 2000 Democrat Cheung Man-kwong argued that 'The battlefield has shifted from the

Scandal probe clears chiefs

Inquiry identifies 10 housing staff as incompetence blamed for faulty piling at Sha Tin blocks

Michael Wong

Housing Authority chairwoman Rosanna Wong Yick-ming and other senior officials escaped blame yesterday in an independent report on the public housing piling scandal in Sha Tin.

The report on the scam, which led to a decision to tear down two unfinished 34-storey public housing blocks, identified 10 Housing Department staff, nine by name. But senior officials were cleared by the panel, made up of barrister and engineer Teresa Cheng Yeuk-wah, head of the University of Hong Kong's Department of Engineering Professor Lee Chack-fan and former HSBC chairman John Strickland. Mr Strickland said the decision about who to identify was made after considering "the scope of management responsibility and the scale of the incident".

The nine staff named in the report included a senior clerk of works, a supervisor, an engineer and a contract manager. The report also said, without supplying a name, that the business director (development) "has a special accountability". Mr Strickland said later that the business director was Yuen Tse-chu, who was blamed because he "is the lowest level within the department at which the reporting lines of all the parties responsible for a successful project come together".

The report said staff of the financial gain, with heavy-duty corruption along the way. We ended up concluding the matter was instead, or rather more, one of competence – the parties lacking the skills necessary to do a professional job, painting themselves into corners, and then using all means ... to get out of them, careless of contractual obligations, quality or integrity."

Zen Pacific knew of Hui Hon's financial problems and malpractice in its bored-pile work, the report said. Hui Hon was not qualified to be listed as an authority contractor. Housing Department site staff failed to supervise site works closely, it said.

The Housing Authority has said it will take legal action against Zen Pacific, which did not return calls seeking comment. Hui Hon has been wound up.

Ms Wong said three of the 10 staff had been suspended, six had been reassigned, while Mr Yuen remains in his position. An independent disciplinary committee will be set up to recommend to the Civil Service Bureau action against the 10. They will continue to be paid until the ruling.

Chief Executive Tung Chee-hwa dismissed calls from politicians to sack Ms Wong and other officials. He said they had faced up to the problems and acted quickly to investigate them.

Ms Wong was prepared to make a public apology but said resignation was not the issue.

Housing Authority chairman Rosanna Wong addresses a press conference after the release of the piling scandal report. Dickson Lee

The Home Ownership Scheme development where the piling was faulty.

How the blunders were allowed to happen

Zen Pacific: The main piling contractor knew of financial problems experienced by its subcontractor, Hui Hon, in July 1998, but did not terminate its contract until September that year.

Hui Hon: The firm's key directors and engineers knew about the defective works but did not act.

Housing Department:

- Department site inspectors with little or no experience in bored pile works, were promoted based on unreliable judgments.
- Inspectors received no training and only followed procedure manuals.
- The department's project engineer "was involved in practically none of the inspections and he signed all the certificates required of him".
- The project engineer "did not exercise the judgment expected of a professional engineer".

SCMP Graphic

Figure 13.4 May 2000 SCMP article setting out the findings of the initial Strickland Report into the piling scandal. The small inset photo of Area 14b includes Blocks D and E, behind and slightly left of the white school building: work had previously stopped on them at 32 storeys.

housing area to the constitutional framework. We are not targeting Rosanna Wong and Tony Miller, but the undemocratic political system'. Eventually, in June 2000, Wong resigned, a move soon hailed as a rare example of 'courage'.[104] At that point, the third stage of the scandal began – the start of a LegCo inquiry in 2001, which partly served as a front for the underlying interests of the big developers. Here Miller was 'very tough', Gabriel recalled, in defending the HA's interests against the 'intense political posturing by the big developers, who had the clear support of some LegCo members aligned with them'.[105] (Figures 13.4, 13.5)

Within the housing field, this cumulative onslaught now opened the floodgates of direct criticisms of the HOS as 'unbalancing' the market, and policy measures to rein it in. In June 2000, the sale of HOS Phase 22b was postponed to January 2001, and 16,000 new units destined for HOS were transferred to public rental – a process reflecting the original flexibility of the Harmony series, although most new HOS were by now Concord or New Cruciform Block.[106] January 2001 saw a 20,000 cap on HOS sales and August 2001 a ban on further land allocations and strident demands from Li Ka-shing in late August for 'very urgent' cuts to HOS to counteract steep declines in his companies' profits.[107] September 2001 brought a ten-month moratorium (to be followed by a 5-year, 9,000-unit annual cap) on further HOS and PSPS sales. This announcement, made suddenly by Chief Secretary Donald Tsang without prior consultation with HA members, was welcomed by the DAB and Liberals, but questioned by the Democrats and Frontier, and 'hammered

Rosanna Wong resigns

Chris Yeung, Cynthia Wan and Martin Wong

HOUSING Authority chairwoman Rosanna Wong Yick-ming yesterday stepped down ahead of a no-confidence vote by lawmakers, conceding she had lost the trust and support of the public.

The Legislative Council vote has been called following a spate of public housing scandals.

In a hastily announced press conference at the authority headquarters, Ms Wong admitted that the public no longer supported her nor trusted her reforms of the public housing sector.

"After deep consideration I have tendered my resignation to Mr Tung [Chee-hwa] as chairman of the Housing Authority," said Ms Wong, who also sits on the Executive Council.

A motion of no confidence in her and Director of Housing Tony Miller will be tabled tomorrow. Lawmakers who supported the motion said it was not aimed at forcing her and Mr Miller to resign but to build a system and culture of

Lost confidence

DUSTIN SHUM

Housing Authority chief Rosanna Wong is flanked by authority members and Director of Housing Tony Miller (third left) as she announces her resignation.

by the resignation of Ms Wong if the system remains unchanged."

Ms Wong has agreed to stay on until the end of September.

In a letter to legislators before Ms Wong's resignation, eight director-level officials said that if she and Mr Miller resigned it would only add to the instability within the authority.

Authority building committee member Wong Kwan said political pressure from factions with vested interests had forced Ms Wong to step down.

Professor Lau Siu-kai of the Chinese University said Ms Wong's resignation would boost confidence in the Government and the system.

The Liberal Party said the resignation was "appropriate" but it did not mean an end to housing problems. It urged the Government to press ahead with thorough reforms and formulate a new housing policy to restore confidence.

The chairman of the Democratic Alliance for the Betterment of Hong Kong,

Figure 13.5 25 June 2000 SCMP article reporting Rosanna Wong's resignation as HA chair.

the final nail in the coffin' of the 85,000/70% targets; Tsang even labelled the HOS an 'aberration'.[108] Yet even as late as November 2001, Dominic Wong still claimed that the government was sticking to the 70% home-ownership target, as did the 2001 *Hong Kong Review*.[109]

As Miller ruefully commented in his evidence to the LegCo piling enquiry in April 2001, the HD had the previous year broken all records, with a total completion figure (rental and HOS) of 89,000 units, something which would previously have been a cause for celebration but by now was an embarrassment; and now almost anything the HA tried to do was leapt on by the media as evidence of incompetence.[110] In response, a range of reform policies were advocated. Already, as recommended by Coopers & Lybrand, the Construction and Development branch had been reorganised in April/November 1997 from a discipline-based to project-based approach; and in February 1999 there were cost-cutting proposals for privatisation of estate management on 160 estates, with 630 staff to be offered redundancy in January 2000. More generally, the Tang Report into the construction industry led to the establishment of a Construction Industry Council to regulate subcontractors.[111] To succeed Rosanna Wong, in September 2000 Tung appointed not a politician or a public communicator but an eminent 73-year-old engineer, Cheng Hon-kwan, with the paramount aim of stabilising the constructional reputation of the Authority.[112] (Figure 13.6) Cheng had previously been involved in the investigation of the piling scandal:

> That was why C H Tung came to me, as a structural engineer: he called me in to visit him, and when I departed, having accepted the job, he told me, "You have the most difficult job in Hong Kong! I said, "No – you have the most difficult job in Hong Kong, I've got the second most difficult!" He appreciated that![113]

Figure 13.6 Cheng Hon-kwan, pictured in February 2014 in his office, Room 2015, Hang Lung Centre, Causeway Bay (MG).

Immediately following Rosanna Wong's resignation, in June 2000, an institutional investigation – the Review of the Institutional Framework for Public Housing – was announced by the Chief Secretary for Administration, Anson Chan. Partly, this aimed to bring housing within the scope of a quasi-ministerial political accountability, as demanded by many political groups.[114] Chan's review was tasked with scrutinising the interlinked roles of the Housing Bureau, Housing Authority, Housing Society and Housing Department, while focusing especially on the role of the Housing Bureau and of Dominic Wong.[115] In October 2001 it was suggested by social-administration academic Prof. Anthony Cheung that the government's underlying agenda was to strip powers from the HA and establish a 'clear chain of command', reducing the Authority to an estate-management role: Democrat Lee Wing-tat suggested that Dominic Wong might emerge as a 'Housing Minister'.[116]

The Review also reflected a general public and political feeling that the housing system, as most recently reorganised under Patten in 1994, was now excessively complicated and confusing. There was clear tension between the Housing Bureau and the Housing Authority not just over land supply but more generally. In Miller's LegCo enquiry evidence, there were strong undercurrents of distrust between the two bodies, with the Bureau rarely attending the HA's weekly chairman's meeting.[117] Miller apologised for a 'facetious' comment, concerning his relations with Dominic Wong, that 'occasionally we talk on the phone, occasionally he gives me warm words of encouragement, occasionally he will perhaps caution me for speaking too much or something!' He protested that 'I have a very high regard for Mr Wong', but firmly emphasised that 'I do not have two bosses… My staff report is written by the Chairman of the Housing Authority', and countersigned by the Secretary for Housing.[118]

There were demands that there should be reorganisations or mergers, but there was no consensus yet about what kind of reorganisations might be needed. Some suggested that in any pruning and redistribution of the HA's powers, the chief beneficiary should be the Bureau, but against that was the Bureau's post-1997 'notoriety for its failure to engineer a soft landing for the housing market'.[119] Conversely, in March 2002, one newspaper reported that the Government might abolish the Bureau and transfer its policy duties to the HD, with the HA to remain the key body in formulating housing policy. Rebecca Chiu in August 2000 argued that a completely new, 'high-powered' housing leader was needed to coordinate the 'disintegrated' system.[120]

Public housing design around 2000: the questioning of standard solutions

The built-form of public housing echoed these dramatic political and production vicissitudes only indirectly, by a rising emphasis on cost reduction. January 1999 saw approval by the Building Committee of a new and more economically planned version of the Harmony (the 'New Harmony' and 'New Harmony Annex'), providing, for instance, more small flats to cope with demand for two-person units from elderly and non-elderly couples. There would be slight size reductions combined with 'more efficient' planning in each flat-type, and bay windows to allow tenant partitioning-off of an additional bedroom: the New Annex could now be up to 35 rather than 20 storeys, containing a maximum of 385 rather than 180 small flats. Although the current space standards of 5.5 to 7.0 sq m per person were safeguarded, a $368m saving in construction costs over five years was predicted: costs would average $214m per Harmony 1 block as against $240m previously.[121] And there were demands in 1998 to get away from the necessity for bathrooms to have an external window, on grounds that this dictated an unnecessarily complex and costly 'highly indented cruciform structure'.[122]

Increasingly, design and estate-planning debates reflected official and public suspicion of overlaps between public and private housing. November 2000 saw the approval of a so-called 'Flexible Production Mix' for implementation from 2004/5 onwards, previously authorised by the Strategic Planning Committee (SPC) on lines that would avoid any confusion with 'luxury flats'.[123] Within the HOS, the Concord, with its smaller number of flats per floor, was far more costly than the Harmony: when the first tranche of over 7,000 flats on seven sites was offered for sale in March 1998, the selling price for Wo Ming Court in TKO was $1,950 per sq ft as opposed to $1,350 for nearby comparable Harmony blocks. HD assistant director Cheng Yao-kong framed this positively, arguing that 'the quality is not much different from private properties and we believe it will be welcomed by home buyers'; but the Concord was described as 'shockingly expensive' by property agent Tony Chan of the Society of Hong Kong Real Estate Agents.[124]

More generally, during these years, significant differences of opinion flared over whether private or public blocks were intrinsically cheaper, in design or construction terms. A July 2000 study by HKU professor Chau Kwok-wing, funded (significantly) by the Association of Architectural Practices, claimed that HD-designed 41-storey HOS blocks cost 40% more than PSPS blocks designed by private architects and took 20% longer to build, as 'they lacked the market drive and flexibility to save on construction costs and time'. In a bizarre extrapolation, Chau claimed that using only private architects in public housing since 1953 would have saved $100 billion and allowed 200,000 more flats to have been built![125] The D & S architects riposted by appealing to design quality: 'we eventually responded by direct comparisons of the quality of space and environment in the buildings and the greater convenience and comfort for residents, since we had views out and natural ventilation to public areas'. And in 2010, HD construction director Ada Fung suggested the opposite to Chau's study: that 'public housing will be 35% cheaper than private, because of our economy of scale and standardised methods and rationalisation of use of materials' – a percentage echoed exactly by John Ng in relation to his celebrated Upper Ngau Tau Kok redevelopment (see below). Early 2002 saw an ultimately abortive scheme to transfer the HD's architects to the private sector.[126]

The most significant general trend within housing design was the beginning of a reversal of the previously fierce pressure for standardisation, towards more 'site-specific' housing – reflecting not only the drying-up of large virgin sites but also the increasing influence of noise restrictions and air-flow modelling on layouts.[127] Here a key role, in the governance and politics of housing architecture, was played initially by Tony Miller. During a debate over redevelopment of North Point Estate in 2000, for instance, Miller acknowledged that 'nobody would thank the Authority for building two rows of standard "Harmony" blocks along the waterfront'.[128] In the early 2000s, this cause was also notably championed by architect, HKU professor and HA member Patrick Lau, who argued with increasing force for a site-specific approach: 'Patrick was dynamic, energetic, always saying, "We must build non-standard!"' The first stage in the process was to incorporate standard blocks into more variegated layouts, but it soon extended to individualisation of the blocks themselves.[129] However, the entire movement was, arguably, only possible because of the collapse in production levels, which permitted a potentially more time-consuming approach. It could allow the HD, rather than forcing contractors into a lowest-common-denominator situation, to 'change the contractors' culture'. Previously, according to Ada Fung in 2010, 'It was, "The blocks are standard, that's it!" Now, the contractors have to use their brains'.[130]

On the design front, the retirement of Stephen Poon in 1998 in some ways drew a line under the heyday of the standardised type-plans; yet there was also a remarkable aspect of continuity in this new generation of housing architecture, in that the original mastermind of the Harmony I series, John Ng, actually now emerged as a key leader of the successor phase of site-specific design, as we will see below at Upper Ngau Tau Kok. This multi-generational adaptability won him wide respect across the profession, above all as an 'architect's architect, a very capable designer who has won an enormous amount of prizes – but never too tolerant of policy!' 'John was the "site-specific king" – he never lost sight of his architectural principles.'[131]

A key legitimising role in the overall transition to site-specific design was played by a scheme that was never actually built – the highly publicised ideas competition for a 'green' HOS project of 2,500 flats on the Shui Chuen O site in Sha Tin. This, the first ideas competition ever mounted by the HA, was launched in October 2000, with results announced in March 2001, but cancelled in 2003 after the scrapping of the HOS. The winner, Tom Ip, working with Korean firm Heerim, proposed towers linked by multi-storey sky-bridges around 'green cores', while runner-up Anthony Ng had interlocking blocks and corridors; the HD's own entry came third. Of the other entries, Patrick Lau's featured curved, sandwich-like meanders with ventilation in-between.[132] Chris Gabriel, as CA/D & S, briefed the adjudication panel on practical aspects of the entries and recalled that

> although Anthony Ng was a very highly respected architect, in our view his proposal would have given the estate management teams a lot of headaches, because of its very long connected corridors and links between blocks. Treating corridor access to flats as thoroughfares for such a large development and large estate population would have led to severe management and security problems.

The three platforms of the Shui Chuen O site were eventually developed with eighteen more conventional HD-designed site-specific blocks containing over 11,000 flats in 2010–15.[133] (Figure 13.7)

Other, bolder concept proposals also remained on paper, such as a feasibility study for 75-storey public rental towers carried out by John Ng's group in the early 2000s, as a potential way of exploiting the means-of-escape regulations (which

Figure 13.7 Shui Chuen O ideas competition, 2000–1: the winning entry of Tom Ip and Heerim Architects & Planners Co. Ltd.

allowed up to 75 storeys with two escape floors) to allow potential increases in plot ratios to boost output: although no technical obstacle was discovered to the scheme, which also included additional upper-level fire lobbies, and public communal spaces on each floor, it was shelved after it became clear that changes in zoning restrictions were unlikely.[134]

Tung's second term: the downward spiral of public housing

Despite his eventual re-election in 2002, with decisive Beijing backing, Tung's prestige and authority did not significantly recover. His paternalistic management style and willingness to cover up scandals among helpers became increasingly controversial – compounded by his tensions with Anson Chan Fang On-sang over policy issues.[135] In July 2002, the accountability system previously demanded by protesters was eventually introduced, with principal officials now directly answerable to the CE and the Chinese government – a reform that reflected the potential tension between the 1997 regime change and initial political liberalisation.[136] However, from April 2003, the sudden explosion of the SARS epidemic, with its claimed connection to drainage problems, and Tung's perceived 'indecision' in tackling it until November, brought fresh criticism.[137] Fatally wounded by the July 2003 mass demonstration over Article 23 and consequent government defeat in LegCo, he eventually retired prematurely in March 2005.[138] Further housing-related scandals would also play a part in Tung's final decline, perhaps the most awkward being the initial failure in December 2004 of a REIT-based attempt to privatise HA commercial facilities – following which President Hu Jintao voiced a public rebuke, urging the government to 'earnestly review' its 'standards' of governance and to identify and correct 'deficiencies'.[139]

Against the backdrop of growing public discontent at inequality – Hong Kong having an increasingly high Gini index at 43.5 in 2011 – and the polarised language of political debate, there were increasingly harsh public-participation criticisms of housing provision from around 2000. Now, district boards were almost guaranteed to oppose public housing proposals for their areas.[140] Gabriel argued in 2009 that 'Now nobody wants public housing in their area any more. In the old areas of Kowloon, if you can't get the land, you can't build – in Ngau Tau Kok or Kwun Tong, the district councillors don't want it!'[141] This was not for reasons of Western-style social stigmatisation but for financial reasons:

> They say, when you build public housing, you lower the prices in the area, because the people who will live there are poorer. It's not discrimination about who they are – it's just "When they are here, my price will go down!" It's just about money – it's not about crime, as in America.[142]

Behind the scenes, the demographic pressures of mainland immigration had not gone away, with new arrivals post-1997 often bringing entire families; in November 2003, a mainland developer, China Real-Estate Development Corporation, even briefly proposed to take over 20,000 mothballed HOS flats as apartments for mainland tourists.[143] And the public-rental waiting list was significantly altering in character, with young single people, many the children of existing public housing tenants, crowding the waiting list and overburdening the system: in 2005 it was reported that 44% of applicants in the previous financial year were single, compared to 21% six years previously.[144]

In response to the piling scandal, there were reforms both at the micro-level of housing policy and the macro-level of housing politics. Within the Housing Department, the unambiguous focus was building quality.[145] Even before Rosanna Wong's resignation, in early 2000 a new programme of 'Quality Reform', comprising some fifty separate 'Quality Housing Initiatives', had been launched – with the aim of closing all the loopholes in the PASS/ISO system revealed in the piling scandal. Responding to the LegCo inquiry's criticism of the HD's exemption from Buildings Ordinance inspections, H K Cheng steered through an ingenious face-saving compromise, in the form of an 'Independent Checking Unit', established in October 2000, and responsible directly to Tony Miller. This would act as if it was a statutory enforcement agency, even if it was not. Cheng recalled the initiative's slightly ambiguous character, concerned with both substance and presentation:

> In those days, the Housing Department didn't have to submit plans to the government for approval. We didn't have to comply with the building regulations. That's not quite right – I knew that, as I'd worked with the AO and the Buildings Ordinance Office for ten years. So we set up a division within the Housing Department to work like the BOO – to vet their own designs to comply with the Hong Kong building regulations. We still didn't need government approval, but after that we needed our *own* approval! That's good – to the public, it looked good, it showed up a good image![146]

Chris Gabriel became, in effect, an internal building-control officer, in charge of the ICU and other HD technical-audit functions: 'My job was to apply the Ordinance to all our projects. I had a team of 200: we would vet our projects as if they were new private building projects'. This was overlaid on to the already significant requirements of the 1990 PASS system.[147] Precasting, with its agenda of precision, relied on factories on the mainland, often established by large Hong Kong building contractors, situated at most a two-hour journey away, in cities such as Foshan, and producing panels to strictly controlled dimensions of 2.5 m width and 11-ton maximum weight: these were driven into Hong Kong and either erected immediately or, at most, stored overnight, owing to lack of site space.[148] Increased precision in construction was interconnected with a drive to revolutionise Hong Kong's traditionally poor site safety conditions: a key role, as we will see in Chapter 14, would later be played here by Ada Fung as Deputy Director of Housing (Development and Construction) from 2005 to 2017, in liaising closely with the Hong Kong Contractors Association to secure maximum mechanisation and off-site prefabrication, and virtually eliminating site injuries and fatalities.[149] (Figure 13.8)

Figure 13.8 Ada Fung (Deputy Director of Housing, Development and Construction, 2005–17), seen in 2023 at Taikoo Place (MG).

Switching off the machine: the 'Nine-Tactics' revolution

In 2002, Tung's renewed administration took drastic organisational steps to answer the now deafening demands for change – by engineering an almost complete reversal of the 1997 strategy inherited from Patten. First came administrative reorganisation, based on the 2002 report of the Committee on the Institutional Framework of Public Housing, which recommended a streamlined organisation with a single spokesman for housing matters and a single line of responsibility: the Secretary for Housing, Planning and Lands would become the HA chair and head of an expanded HD directorate – coinciding with the retirement of Cheng.[150] This was not just a reversion to the pre-1988 position of direct government oversight of the Housing Authority, but went beyond that, by dethroning the unofficials from decision-making power – an aggrandisement of administrative authority that chimed in with the growing emphasis on 'executive-led' government.[151] Cheng recalled that whereas during his chairmanship,

> we had our own statutory power to make our own policy, our strategy, and our own financial control – we were not working directly under the Secretary of Housing – after me, they combined the two together: the Secretary of Housing became chairman of the Housing Authority. That was the end of my term – I was very sad about it![152]

And in Rosanna Wong's opinion, 'Now it became even more "government". The Authority members still had power to make decisions. They still had some independence. But the only honeymoon period of *full* independence was between 1988 and C H Tung.' Akers-Jones subsequently went rather further, contending that this outcome was a result of nefarious machinations by officials under the influence of the real-estate 'tycoons':

> They did this review, by a small group of people, which evolved into Donald Tsang's shredding of all policies on public housing. The culprits of that review were Donald Tsang, Michael Suen, Dominic Wong, together with the Deputy Director of Housing Administration: he was the most vociferous and noisiest of the lot – that was in 2002.[153]

And John Lambon agreed that 'Our flats were going up in size and we were knocking at everyone's doors: they had to clobber that!'[154] (Figure 13.9)

Accordingly, along with this administrative reorganisation went cutbacks in public housing, especially for home-ownership. The *Hong Kong 2002* annual review argued that the government now believed home-ownership 'should essentially be a matter of personal choice', and so it should withdraw from its previous role as a direct housing provider and refrain from 'competing with the private sector'.[155] The claims of 'overlap', of course, begged the question of how many HOS buyers would actually have been able to afford increasingly 'unaffordable' private-sector flats, but this was now effectively a political discourse rather than a question of practical market share.

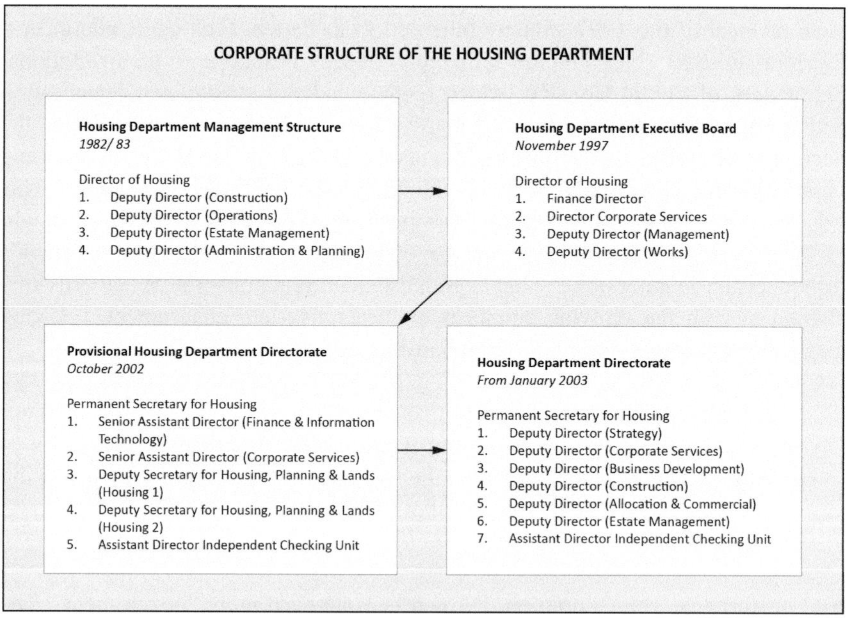

Figure 13.9 Successive versions of the senior management structure of the Housing Department from 1982 onwards, reflecting the shift towards administrative devolution in the 1980s and the return to direct government control in the 2000s – as well as the semi-autonomous status of Chris Gabriel's post-2000 Independent Checking Unit. Drawing by Joyce Fu, 2024 (based on HKHA publications and Wah 2002, fig. 5.1).

The public housing cuts would be the responsibility not of Dominic Wong – who, rather than becoming a 'housing minister', eventually retired altogether in April 2002 – but of his successor. To fill the new 'ministerial-style' Secretaryship, Tung appointed Michael Suen Ming-yeung as Secretary for Housing, Planning and Lands from 1 July 2002. He remained in post until 2007 – during which time, ironically, he was warned by his own staff over an illegal extension to his home in Happy Valley – and thereafter became Secretary for Education.[156] In November 2002, Suen announced that Tung was 'deeply concerned' about the housing situation and had asked the Housing, Planning and Lands Bureau (i.e. Suen's own new secretariat) to 'undertake a root-and-branch review of the SARG's housing policy with a view to restoring the public's confidence in the property market'. To ram home this message, Suen delivered a policy-review speech that signalled the most abrupt policy reversal in Hong Kong housing history. The review was arranged under nine principal headings, as a result of which he was nicknamed in Cantonese 'Nine-Tactics Suen'. He criticised the TPS and argued that home-ownership was a matter of personal choice.[157] He definitively threw the 1997 housing-supply boost into reverse, jettisoning both the 85,000 and 70% pledges while retaining the more modest three-year waiting-list limit, arguing that 'it is superfluous to predetermine a numerical target for provision of assisted housing opportunities'.[158] The three-year pledge had already been met a year early, in 2002, and by 2003 the average wait would stand at 2.3.[159] This wholesale change was praised by the leading housing tycoons and commentators such as Centaline's Shih Wing-chung, who now boldly argued that the high land-price policy was part of the traditional 'fabric' of Hong Kong; that even to tinker with it would lead to 'disaster'; and that Tung's 'greatest mistake' had been to do just that.[160]

With Suen's announcement, Tung's housing-based identity-building project of 1997 was finally abandoned – although some commentators immediately asked what was to stop the government from reversing course again in five years' time.[161] But for the moment, 'the government's position is now to push up property prices in the short term, and allow private developers to control market supply in the long run. The SAR's housing policy has never been so unambiguous'.[162]

All the main features of the LTHS were, in effect, thrown into reverse, in a 180° shift of the paradigm from maximal to minimal – a shift that once again emphasised the dramatic volatility of Hong Kong housing policy by comparison with Singapore.[163] Already, actual production was plummeting from 74,000 in 2001 (23,000 HOS) to 16,100 (4,500 HOS) in 2003. In 2003–4, both spending allocations and production of public housing as a whole were radically scaled back.[164] Rental housing production rapidly settled on an annual target of only 15,000 units and Suen suggested that, eventually, even this modest residual level of new rental housing construction could be replaced by 'recycling' of existing units.[165] By September 2002, HOS sales had fallen to an all-time minimum, and the Housing Authority was told by the Chief Executive to abolish the HOS completely.[166] The TPS and the rental vouchers were 'shot down' along with it (Miller). In 2010, Ada Fung recalled that 'All the previous pledges had gone, all the targets and figures', and that 'we've backtracked to the 70s, when we were only building public rental housing'.[167] Paradoxically, the slashing of output did not make the programme significantly less staff-intensive, as Rosman Wai noted in 2010:

> In 1999/2000 we had a programme of about 100,000 a year, now we are at 15,000. But the architects are still at the same numbers, excluding natural wastage. So although we're not building so many, we're just as busy. We need to face the public – there's lots of public participation, which all takes time – we need to explain the schemes, hold workshops and so forth – because of the District Councils and concerned groups, which operate on behalf of people, and have so much self-interest![168]

Reflecting Suen's self-escalating 'revolutionary' rhetoric, increasingly there was also heady talk about abolishing the Housing Authority altogether. The 2002 Institutional Framework report speculated that the HA 'will in the longer term reduce its executive functions and evolve towards an advisory role in both public and private housing matters'; in 2003 Yeung and Wong argued it was likely to be reduced to something like the old Housing Board. These more drastic reorganisations never materialised, but in April 2002 it was proposed to strip the Authority of control over redeveloping its own sites, like Ngau Tau Kok, potentially selling off the best sites for private housing in more prestigious locations like Ping Shek or Oi Man.[169]

Along with cuts in production went an abandonment of the systematic pursuit of land supply through HOUSCOM. Land supply and prices had fluctuated wildly between the mid-1990s (Patten), the late 1990s (Tung), and the present – an erratically cyclical process that always seemed to be mis-timed by around three years – and now the pendulum swung violently back, towards a calculated neglect of land supply. This neglect would become entrenched throughout the entire term of office of Tung's successor, Donald Tsang – with escalating effects on the viability of the housing drive in those years.[170] More specifically, the size and the density of Tseung Kwan O were scaled back by TDD in May 2003 – partly in a SARS-induced reaction against density – to a total population of 460,000, with reclamation largely deleted. In part-compensation, three additional new towns to house 340,000 (at Kwu Tung North, Fanling North and a 112-ha site at the future West Rail Hung Shui Kiu station) were proposed.[171]

The abolition of the HOS left the HA not just reduced in status but potentially very short of money, compounded by rent concessions during SARS.[172] Gabriel recalled that 'The abandonment of the HOS gave us a tremendous revenue problem. We found ourselves with the possibility of running out of money. Also, our costs were going up, as we were embarking on non-standard designs'.[173] The financial implications of the dismemberment of the HOS gradually sank in between 2002 and late 2004. By February 2003 it was argued that if steps were not taken to sell the HA's commercial properties, it would face a deficit of HK$5.5bn in the next 3 years, rising to HK$12.4bn in FY 2006–7, and significant operating deficits were predicted too. By February 2004 the HA risked falling below the minimum cash balance of $8.7 billion agreed with government, and its revenue had dropped by 60% since suspension of HOS/PRH sales. Thoughts began turning rapidly to possible ways of making good the loss of income from HOS sales – which had accounted for 61% of HA income in 2000 – especially as the Authority was still bound by the 1994 arrangement that it should repay by 2008 the $12.8bn it received from the government when it became financially independent in 1988. Following Suen's November 2002 statement, plans were drawn up during 2003 for divesting the HA's commercial centres and car parks. Ada Fung recalled that 'in 2002 we lost our cash cow, and this was meant to tide us over for a few years'.[174] This was, of course, a short-term solution whose gains could only be used once. However, the Link REIT fiasco of 2003–4, in which privatisation of the $22 billion portfolio, including 151 shopping malls and 178 car parks, was successfully challenged by 67-year-old public housing tenant Ms Lo Siu-lan, deferred its implementation until 2005 – following which public housing estates were left wide-open to the retail activities of the real-estate oligarchy.[175]

The abolition of the HOS also left a glut of unfinished and now unsaleable flats, initially totalling some 20,000, of which around 4,500 were PSPS. Suen ruled that the PSPS units could be transferred to developers after payment of any land premiums – a decision that led to a further embarrassing debacle in 2004 concerning a 2,470-unit development of seven 40-storey towers at Hung Hom Peninsula. Left unoccupied since its completion, this was sold in February on payment of a HK$864 million premium to a joint venture of Sun Hung Kai Properties and New World Development, who promptly announced their intention to demolish and redevelop the entire project as a luxury development commanding far higher profits.[176] Initially, the government stood back and argued it was powerless to interfere in the workings of the market, despite internal dissension within the administration: Dr Sarah Liao, Secretary for Environment, Transport and Works openly admitted that it 'would be wasteful and a violation of environmental principles… I absolutely do not support it', but that she was 'powerless' to intervene. Faced with a crescendo of NGO protests headed by Friends of the Earth, who argued the Hung Hom redevelopment would generate 200,000 tonnes of waste, the developers eventually backed down in December 2004 and opted for refurbishment rather than demolition – but the damage had by then been done, and the episode only deepened the public impression that the government was a prisoner to business interests in general and the property 'tycoons' in particular.[177]

In response to scandals such as this, counter-criticisms of the ending of the HOS began to be heard. Within the public arena, in November 2002 Prof. James Lee of City University weighed in, comprehensively denouncing

> the damage done by the rescue plan to our long-term housing policy, particularly in relation to the scrapping of the Home Ownership Scheme, which is a political sacrifice writ large. In the last two years, reality has been distorted by developers' successful propaganda campaigns. The Home Ownership Scheme has been portrayed as the culprit for a downtrodden property market, while in fact the market was dragged down much more by people's lack of confidence and the government's inability to maintain stability. By killing the scheme, officials effectively amputated the strong arm of a long-established housing

> institution – one that has a proven record of success (keen demand), a high level of sustainability (revenue generation) and, furthermore, has the potential to act as a cushioning institution to combat future housing market irrationality. . . . The free market cannot be left "free" because in some cases it does not work properly.[178]

Earlier decision-makers also offered critical perspectives on the ending of the HOS. Donald Liao questioned it in 2010 from the viewpoint of social cohesion, arguing that 'it is stupidity, creating this gulf between state and private. The people in charge today do not grasp the sociology of public housing. If everything could be taken care of by the private sector, we could retreat – but that won't work!' And more pragmatically, Stephen Poon argued of the organisational consequences that

> it was certainly a mistake to stop the Home Ownership programme overnight. It's all right to diminish capacity, but it's like a big machine running at full speed for many years, and if you switch off the engine very suddenly, you do a lot of damage![179]

These criticisms were paralleled by the beginnings of a very slight rebound in sales policy and a distinct recovery in the land market. Dribbles of HOS flats were released on to the market to gradually reduce the numbers of empty dwellings, which still totalled 12,000 units, mainly Harmony, in the mid-2000s. 2004 saw proposals for more systematic resumption of HOS sales, and 2005 an easing of the HOS sale restriction from five to two years. House prices were already rising again in 2002, and by November 2004 it was argued that private-enterprise prices had recovered by 40% since the outbreak of SARS the previous year, and that the market could even be described as 'heated'.[180] In November 2002 it was being suggested that the recent scrapping of regular land sales might negatively impact land supply in future, and in October 2003, reflecting the beginnings of a property rebound, the government resumed limited land sales.[181] Thus the ink was hardly dry on Suen's reforms when the pendulum began swinging in the opposite direction.

Balancing site-specific and standardised design

Architecturally, in the wake of the 2002 reform, the shift to site-specific design now became overwhelmingly dominant. But this created its own complexities: 'The scarcity of sites, as it developed, meant that the sites became difficult to develop – you got steeper and steeper sites. If you were working within these constraints, what do you do? It had to be site specific.'[182] Gabriel recalled that site-specific design had a financial and dimensional sting in the tail:

> The move to site-specific impacted on cost-effectiveness – it was not as cost-effective as before. We were not the only ones to use standard designs – private developers did too, as it's cheaper. Site-specific design, on the other hand, puts the cost up. Our small 1P/2P flats were reduced to 14 m^2 in 2007 from the original 17 m^2 in the Harmony and Annex blocks. The space-allocation was 7 m^2

per person, and we ended up building 14 m^2 flats for the smallest families – so you're building flats that were almost obsolete from the beginning.

But even the small Harmony flats had provoked disquiet in the late 1990s: Gabriel recalled that 'I remember saying to Tony Miller on an earlier occasion, about the 17 m^2 flats provided in the Harmony blocks, that this might be a case of "designed obsolescence"!'[183] And

> on one occasion in the late 1990s, as CA/D & S, I was invited to attend a meeting with the housing activist Leung Yiu Chung, at his office in Shek Lei Estate in Tsuen Wan, to discuss some problems with the small flats in the Harmony blocks. Rosman Wai accompanied me. Mr Leung led us, or so we thought, to his office. He in fact led us around the base of the block, where we were confronted by a group of smiling elderly people seated in arcs of chairs facing a white board. They wanted to discuss some problems with the small 17 m^2 flats. It was all very good-natured, I used my very limited Cantonese to apologise that I did not speak the language, to which they enthusiastically applauded, and I introduced Rosman who then saved the day and explained our small flat designs. After more applause we were asked to go up to one of the tenants' flats to see at first-hand how an elderly couple had to furnish their flat – single people were not eligible for PRH – and had no option but to use bunk beds. Seeing the husband, at 80 years old, climb into a top bunk was rather sobering.[184]

The post-piling scandal move away from high-pressure contract timetables also potentially increased costs, although, according to Lambon, even as late as 2005–6 costs were still being severely 'screwed down to ridiculous prices' by the HA in new contracts.[185]

Another way round these constraints was to dilute the shift to individuality and retain significant elements of standardisation at flat level. Patrick Lau argued in 2009 that 'Today, the non-standard blocks contain the same number of houses as a Harmony block. The Harmony is just used as a reference now. You can make a combination of the houses, although there are some rules' (Lau).[186] And Ken Cheung noted in 2012 that

> we are moving into site-specific designs, yet we only use standard modular flats. The architect is trying to pull out a different tone, or character, but we're still doing a lot of standardisation in the estate layout, in response to diverse site conditions – it's a psychological balance.[187]

John Ng described the process by which that balance emerged:

> By the turn of the millennium we were going for site-specific blocks. For a period of eight or nine years we were thinking, "OK, let's be site-specific, as when we're going back to the urban areas, the sites are very difficult, and we need to maximise their potential." But somehow we found this wasn't really

> working, as it was far too complicated. So there was a trade-off between site-specific and standard, and since 2009–10 we've been going back to standard modules, but in a non-standard block.[188]

These difficult trade-offs stemmed ultimately from Hong Kong's longstanding restrictions on freedom of action for public-housing designers, owing to its high densities and numbers of flats per floor. Within this constraining context, overall the philosophy inherited from Stephen Poon in effect continued – that of avoiding 'fancy' design features that might offend the proprieties of public-sector design, or implicitly provoke criticisms of overlap, from the private sector. 2003 saw a new principle of 'Functional and Cost-Effective Design', intended 'to maximise cost effectiveness in the construction process' by a review of design standards and finishes in new public rental housing'.[189] John Ng emphasised that 'We're very, very practical – anything which is fancy and fussy is taken away'; and effort was instead devoted to the environment, now increasingly including micro-climate. Ng 'kicked off the microclimate research'… 'If you're using public money, you shouldn't be doing anything extravagant. That's why there are no ornamental features – except at Ma Hang!'[190]

> We could discuss the horticulture direct and do something more ingenious than mere design. We have to provide air paths, so we conduct microclimate studies: at the last phase of Sau Mau Ping, we put the blocks in such a way as to create a breeze corridor, to get the wind going in opposite directions in winter and summer. And we put in wind-powered renewable wind turbines. The private sector may not have this kind of luxury.[191]

Blocks up to 50 storeys were investigated as part of the move beyond Harmony, but generally proved too expensive owing to the need for refuge floors above 40 storeys.[192] The most ambitious exercise in reconciling site-specific and standardised design, the largely abortive 'Flexible HOS' block, will be discussed in the next chapter.

The culminating example of the site-specific phase, however, came in 2002–9: the Upper Ngau Tau Kok redevelopment, one of the last phases of the CRP, designed by Ng and his group in a highly individual form shaped by urban micro-climatology. Overall, the 3.2-ha site, developed at a PR of 7.5 compared with 5.0 on average New Territories sites, accommodated 4,584 flats, neighbourhood centre and retail complex, with block types evolving from Harmony in Phase 1 to site-specific towers over 40 storeys high in Phases 2 and 3: the site-specific blocks were arranged in two zig-zag lines, arranged with micro-climatological layout incorporating cross-ventilation, greening of upper platforms, shading, and a wind-corridor between the two lines to channel the prevailing east wind.[193] The complexity of design and the protracted, seven-year engagement with the local community had to be accommodated within a fiercely constrained budget, all adding up to a 'very, very challenging' process (Ng). The engagement locations shifted progressively from district council meetings to model-making workshops and finally community workshops and briefings with local residents. Contrary to Prof. Chau Kwok-wing's claim (above) of the higher cost of public than private housing design, Ng recalled

Figure 13.10 (a) Upper Ngau Tau Kok Estate, seen in 2015 (MG). (b) John Ng seen at Upper Ngau Tau Kok in January 2015 (MG).

that 'the budget was only 65% of the most humble private development, and you generally can't go over that – we had to go to a committee three times to convince them to go 3% above the budget! But for a development like Upper Ngau Tau Kok, which is going to last at least 100 years, you must have flexibility.'[194] On its completion in 2009, its emphasis on 'local site characteristics' would be generalised for 'all future public housing'[195]. (Figure 13.10a, b)

Upper Ngau Tau Kok won a succession of prizes, including the 2003 Hong Kong Institute of Planners Award, 2006 Green Building Grand Award and the Hong Kong Quality Building Grand Award of 2010 – building more specifically on the HD's 1999 success in gaining an honorary mention in the UIA Sir Robert Matthew Prize for improvement of human settlements. In a direct linkage between housing awards and issues of collective identity, Patrick Lau argued in 2009 that the Matthew award 'says a lot about our history' in having transformed from a refugee society.[196] The claims made for site-specific design also harked back to the time-honoured architectural deterministic claims of the potential role of design in fostering social cohesion. Lau explicitly used this argumentation to contrast the standard blocks of Tin Shui Wai with the individualism of Upper Ngau Tau Kok:

> At Ngau Tau Kok, the new housing blocks are much better, much nicer; this creates real urban spaces. They transplanted a beautiful Banyan tree – they are more interesting. Tin Shui Wai, on the other hand, is a very *bad* example of public housing![197]

At Tin Shui Wai, the claimed deficiencies of alienating design were popularly linked with the alienated 'social time-bomb' said to have been created by large-scale, low-income mainland immigration, and then – stretching the connection further – tied in with specific atrocities of domestic violence, such as the 2004 chopping to death of mother Kim Shuk-ying and her two young daughters (at Tin Shui Wai) or the similar 2002 murder of two children by an abusive father in

Tsz Ching Estate in Kowloon. Here, however, new management devices such as the 'demerit' points system introduced in 2003 were of rather more obvious relevance than architectural design in curbing anti-social behaviour, already generally far lower than in past decades: the controlled-access system was now taken for granted, as part of a general aspiration to 'private' standards.[198]

From nostalgia discourse to housing heritage

The post-2002 radical wind-down in the active production of Hong Kong public housing was parallelled, perhaps unexpectedly, by the first significant emergence of a discourse of nostalgia and even heritage. In the opinion of some historians, an increased popularity of 'heritage values' and community/intellectual protests against redevelopments in the early 2000s reflected wider feelings of identity threat.[199] But within housing, the immediate and specific spur for heritage thinking was the advance of the CRP to take in the remaining Mk I blocks at Shek Kip Mei – in response to which a vigorous heritage debate took place between 1998 and 2005. Here, proposals for specific preservation were balanced with growing nostalgia about the hard but communal life in Resettlement blocks combined with more general rhetoric about the 'miracle' of the public housing system. For example, in a special half-century commemorative issue of the *SCMP* in September 2004, the influential HD senior architect Theresa Yim, who grew up in a Mk I block, wrote fondly of its 'community spirit'.[200] The resulting discourse, in its low-key but distinct positivity about the housing 'achievements' of the last decades of colonial administration, contrasted strongly with the strident self-glorification of the equivalent public housing discourse within Singapore, which trumpeted the heritage of the public housing 'Heartlands' created under PAP rule since 1959.

Overall, given the development pressures within Hong Kong, there was a general acceptance that the growing interest in housing 'heritage and nostalgic preservation of memories' must necessarily focus mainly on recording, or preservation of small symbolic fragments, rather than entire buildings. The last redevelopment in the main CRP sequence was the 3.4-ha Lower Ngau Tau Kok estate, a Mk V 1960s complex redeveloped in two main phases, and seven sub-phases, to provide 4,805 new flats, including temple relocation and a cultural-spine educational walkway, the first phase being completed in 2012 and the second in 2015. As part of the preparations, in 2009 the HA cooperated with Hong Kong Sheng Kung Kui Welfare Council and LNTK tenants to publish a commemorative book, *Memories in Lower Ngau Tau Kok Estate*, for presentation to each tenant moving out, arguing that 'we treasure our memories of the past as we clear the last estate in our Comprehensive Redevelopment Programme'.[201] Previously, in 2002, a community group had systematically collected daily utensils and other small memorabilia prior to demolition, and a farewell party, 'The Last Night of Ngau Tau Kok Lower Estate', was held to mark its 35-year history. And in 2004, events on the estate connected with the annual Yu Lan festival of the Chiu Chow diaspora community were documented as part of Hong Kong's intangible cultural heritage.[202] (Figure 13.11a–c)

Figure 13.11 (a) Lower Ngau Tau Kok II Estate in February 2009, before start of demolition (MG). (b) Lower Ngau Tau Kok II Estate under demolition in February 2011 (MG). (c) 2009 view of staircase in Lower Ngau Tau Kok II Estate pre-demolition (MG).

Figure 13.12 (a) Shek Kip Mei Redevelopment Phase 5, site-specific block under construction in February 2010 (MG). (b) Shek Kip Mei street-scene in February 2019, including low-rise 1970s redevelopment in foreground and small-household block in background, and high-rise site-specific towers behind (MG). (c) Shek Kip Mei Estate, street heritage display seen in 2014 (MG).

The sole, outstanding exception to the confinement of heritage to recording was Shek Kip Mei itself, where the impending redevelopment of the last remaining Mk I blocks – those originally reconditioned and internally amalgamated in the 1970s – stimulated a succession of proposals for preservation of one or more of them, beginning with a November 1999 project for a 'Museum of Housing'.[203] In 2002, rival plans were floated, with the HD proposing to preserve at least three out of Blocks 15–18 because they were close to Shek Kip Mei MTR Station and suitable as a 'tourist hub', but an alternative plan 'strongly advised' by the Antiquities and Monuments Office proposed to preserve Block 41 on its own because of its allegedly more 'authentic' condition.[204] In 2005, with 12,800 still living on the estate, 24 blocks were scheduled for imminent demolition, including 15 seven-storey blocks, and a temporary Shek Kip Mei People's Museum, on the ground floor of Blocks 17 and 18, created out of four flats, was opened during 2005, designed by the Polytechnic University School of Design, and organised by the Neighbourhood Advice-Action Council and Sham Shui Po District Council.[205] (Figure 13.12a–c)

Of this 'People's Museum' exhibition, and the heritage values it expressed, historian Cecilia Chu argued that it was not really concerned with the colonial built heritage in itself, but instead represented an attempt by the SAR government to appropriate the language of 'collective solidarity' and foster an 'image' of hard-working and self-advancing Hong Kong people, whose values were in tune generally with property speculators – in other words, an agenda reflecting the claimed dominance of the property tycoons during the Tung years.[206] However, as we will see in the next chapter, that dominance would soon be challenged: after reaching a climax during the term of office of Tung's successor, Donald Tsang, the tycoons' housing hegemony would gradually start to diminish, as the influence of mainland rather than local capital within Hong Kong soared from the 2010s onwards.

Notes

Many of the SCMP references below are drawn from an online database at the Hong Kong Central Library and do not include page numbers.

1 Tsang, *Modern History of Hong Kong*, 263–4, 272–3.
2 SCMP 9-2-1998, 14-6-1998. Home ownership post-1997: Fong and Lui, *Hong Kong 20 Years after the Handover*, 177–202.
3 Dimbleby, *Last Governor*, 374; Tsang, *Modern History of Hong Kong*, 277; SCMP 28-12-1997, 9.
4 SCMP 9-10-1997, 64; SCMP 27-2-98; Tsang, *Modern History of Hong Kong*, 276–7.
5 SCMP 23-10-1997; SCMP 1-1-1997, 54.
6 HKRS40-547 27-5-1974 MacLehose to Callaghan on 'Hong Kong objectives' (and 28-5-1974 covering letter); Tsang, *Modern History of Hong Kong*, 276–7, 197–210; Tsang, *Governing Hong Kong*, 190–4; Natalie Roseau, 'The shape of things to come – Hong Kong's infrastructural city fabric 1898–2020', *Planning Perspectives*, vol 37:2, 2022, 369–379; Cecilia Chu, 'The myths and politics of housing in Hong Kong – the

controversy over the demolition of the Hunghom estate', *Habitat International,* vol 32:3, September 2008, 375; C Chu, 'The afterlives of modern housing', in Duanfang Lu (ed), *The Routledge Companion to Contemporary Architectural History*, Routledge, New York, 2024, 204–7.

7 SCMP 3-12-1997, 1; 5-12-1997; 9-10-1997.

8 SCMP 28-12-1997, 9; Christine Loh, SCMP 9-2-1998.

9 SCMP 7-10-1999, 17-7-1997, 17-2-1998, 29.

10 SCMP 3-7-1997, 6.

11 Chu, 'The myths and politics of housing', 382.

12 SCMP 9-2-1998, 14-6-1998, 27-2-1998.

13 SCMP 28-9-1997, 16; Rosanna Wong, 2014 interview.

14 Andy Ho, SCMP 3-2-1998.

15 Miller, 2014 interview; SCMP 25-7-1997; LegCo minutes, 13-2-2003, 3578.

16 SCMP 22-4-2001, 4; LegCo Special Committee on Building Problems, minutes 21-4-2001, 45.

17 LegCo Special Committee on Building Problems, 21-4-2001, 44; Akers-Jones, 2014 interview on actual production level.

18 1997 projections of production in 2000–1 and Tung's pledges: Ho-yin Leung, *Crisis Management in Hong Kong*, MPA Dissertation, HKU, June 2002, 37.

19 Alice Poon, *Land and the Ruling Class in Hong Kong*, Enrich, Singapore, 2011, 8 (on Leung article in Ming Pao 23-4-2010); LegCo Special Committee on Building Problems, 21-4-2001, 22 (Mk I-II)

20 HKHA, *Long-Term Housing Strategy, Policy Statement,* 1987, 7.

21 HKHA, *Long-Term Housing Strategy, 1993 Mid-Term Review*, 1993, 11–13; Yeung and Wong, *Fifty Years*, 266.

22 HKRS1881-4-6 11-1997 papers. HKHA, *Final Report of the Mid-Term Review of the Long-Term Housing Strategy*, 6-1994, 12, 32; HKHA, Secretary's Report on Committees, March-May 1998, paper SPC 9-1998; SCMP 15-2-1998, 2.

23 Alice Poon, *Land and the Ruling Class*, 15, 25-32, 118; SCMP 30-5-1998, 52.

24 Alice Poon, *Land and the Ruling Class*, 73, 118.

25 SCMP 1-7-1997, 68.

26 Miller, 2014 interview; SCMP 5-9-2001 (Brooke); SCMP 16-10-1998 (Kenneth Ko).

27 Information Services Department, *Hong Kong 1998*.

28 SCMP 23-7-1997; James Lee, SCMP 14-10-1997; SCMP 24-10-1997, 90; SCMP 11-12-1997, 20; SCMP 9-10-97 p64; Information Services Department, *Hong Kong, a New Era – a Review of 1997*, 183; LegCo Special Committee, 21-4-2001, 32.

29 HKHA, Memorandum for Building Committee, BC 93/99, 18-5-1999, 'Current density guidelines for public housing development'; HKHA, minutes of 9th HOUSCOM meeting 15-10-1997.

30 Information Services Department, *Hong Kong, a New Era – a Review of 1997*, 183; Joint PLC Panel on Housing and Transport, minutes of Special Meeting 17-3-1998, 'Achieving flat production targets'.

31 Information Services Department, *Hong Kong, a New Era – a Review of 1997*, 195; LegCo Special Committee, 24-4-2001, 50, Miller evidence.

32 Joint PLC Panel on Housing and Transport, 17-3-1998 meeting, 'Achieving flat production targets'. Ada Fung, 2010 interview: 'Land supply is what we can control'. Ng, 2012 interview, on targets.

33 LegCo Special Committee, 21-4-2001, 4.

34 J Lee, 'Why we should start housing subsidies now', SCMP 3-10-2001, 3; SCMP 27-11-02, 14 (potted history and critique of land market by James Lee).
35 SCMP 24-6-2000; SCMP 24-1-00, 13; SCMP 15-5-1998 and 28-8-1999 (S Pritchard); SCMP 11-7-1998, JVDK on the 'land premium game'; Poon, *Land and the Ruling Class*, 2011, 73.
36 S Brown and C Loh, *Hong Kong– the Political Economy of Land*, Civic Exchange, Hong Kong, 2002, 1–3, 11.
37 Poon, *Land and the Ruling Class*, 113; Brown and Loh, *Hong Kong*, 1; SCMP, 27-5-1998.
38 SCMP 27-5-1998; SCMP 4-7-2000, 26 (S Pritchard).
39 Wai, 2010 interview.
40 Gabriel, 2009 interview; L C Wong, 2011 interview; Poon, 2014 interview.
41 Ng, 2012 interview.
42 Ada Fung, 2010 interview: systematic comparisons made with Singapore, Japan, and Korea annually. Cheng, 2014 interview; Gabriel, 2011 interview; Ng, 2012 interview; Poon, 2014 interview.
43 SCMP 6-11-2001, 1; SCMP 14-11-2001; SCMP 6-3-2005, 20.
44 Y C R Wong, *Hong Kong Land*, 109; SCMP 4-6-1998.
45 SCMP 15-8-2001, 2; SCMP 22-4-2001, 6.
46 SCMP 21-10-1998; Information Services Department, *Hong Kong 1999*.
47 SCMP 3-6-1998, 16-10-1998.
48 Poon, *Land and the Ruling Class*, 113.
49 SCMP 30-5-1998, 52 (Pritchard).
50 Y C R Wong, *On Privatizing Public Housing*, 1998, 119.
51 Poon, 2009 interview; SCMP 28-4-1998; SCMP 12-12-1997 Lee Wing-tat on scheme as 'shockingly irresistible'.
52 SCMP 24-3-1998 and 15-6-1998 (HLS); SCMP 7-6-1998 (Miller); Yeung and Wong, *Fifty Years*, 263.
53 Y C R Wong, *Hong Kong Land*, 85-6; CB (1) 301/02-03(01) *A Statement on Housing Policy by Hon. Michael M Y Suen, GBS, JP, Secretary for Housing, Planning and Lands*, 13 November 2002.
54 SCMP 14-6-1998; SCMP 14-10-1998, 49.
55 Yeung and Wong, *Fifty Years*, 171.
56 SCMP 30-7-1997; SCMP 3-11-1997, 7; LegCo Special Committee, 21-4-2001, 28.
57 Rosanna Wong, in SCMP 10-10-1998, 6.
58 SCMP 18-2-2000, 6-6-2000, 7-6-2000.
59 SCMP 3-2-1998, 21-5-1998.
60 SCMP 21-4-1998, 14-10-1997, 10-6-1998.
61 Miller, 2014 interview; SCMP 16-5-1998; 3-2-1998; 22-5-98, 31; 27-5-1998, 26.
62 Poon, *Land and the Ruling Class*, 158; SCMP 24-6-2000, 1 (developers Woo, Kwok and Li greeted by Zhu Rongji in Beijing).
63 Alan Smart, *The Speculative City*, University of Toronto Press, Toronto, 2020, 218-23 (Mandy Lau).
64 SCMP 7-5-1999, 9-6-1999, 13-10-2000.
65 SCMP 27-5-98, 26.
66 Information Services Department, *Hong Kong 2000, 2001, 2002, 2003*. HKHA, Building Committee 60-98 minutes, on Sha Kok Mei and Diamond Hill, 20-2-1999; HKHA Building Committee 21-7-1999, scaled down from 579 to 437 ha.
67 SCMP 7-10-1999, 23-9-2004, 26-7-2000, 60.
68 SCMP 18-1-1999; SCMP 7-9-2001, 7; SCMP 9-9-2001, 7; 30-1-2002, 4.

69 SCMP 9-6-2004, 4; L C Wong, 2011 interview, on Housing Society debates/developments of *c.* 2002.
70 Lau, 2009 interview; SCMP 1-7-2000, 1.
71 SCMP 3-7-2000, 40; SCMP 9-7-2000, 13.
72 SCMP 5-7-2000, 1.
73 Information Services Department, *Hong Kong 1997*, 182–3; *Hong Kong 1998*, 193; *Hong Kong 1999*, 208; *Hong Kong 2000*, 200; *Hong Kong 2001*, 193; *Hong Kong 2002.*
74 SCMP 9-7-2000, 6; 14-7-2000, 6.
75 Miller, 2014 interview.
76 SCMP 9-7-2000, 13; SCMP 2-10-2000, 4; SCMP 31-12-2000, 9; SCMP 6-11-2000.
77 SCMP 6-11-2000.
78 SCMP 26-6-2000, 4.
79 SCMP 9-7-2000, 13.
80 SCMP 12-10-2001, 16; 12-9-2001, 16.
81 SCMP 14-10-2001, 1; SCMP 3-4-2002, 1; SCMP 29-1-2005, 15.
82 SCMP 20-1-1999.
83 Ada Fung, 2023 interview.
84 Lambon, 2012 interview; SCMP 19-3-2000.
85 LegCo Special Committee, 24-4-2001, 662–6.
86 Poon 2009, 2010 interviews.
87 Ho-yin Leung, *Crisis Management,* 55–65.
88 Ho-yin Leung, *Crisis Management,* 27–33.
89 Miller, 2014 interview; SCMP 9-1-2000, 9-11-1999, 25-11-1999.
90 Gabriel, 2009 and 2011 interviews; SCMP 9-11-1999.
91 Bernard Hertlein and Allen David, *Non-Destructive Testing of Deep Foundations*, Wiley, Chichester, 2006, 14–16.
92 SCMP 10-12-1997, 9-1-2000.
93 HKHA, *Report of the Investigation Panel on Accountability: Piling Contract 166–1997, Sha Tin 14B Phase 2*, 25 May 2000.
94 Lau, 2009 interview; SCMP 28-1-2000 and 22-1-2000.
95 Miller, 2014 interview; Gabriel, 2011 interview; Cheng, 2014 interview.
96 SCMP 28-5-2000.
97 SCMP 26-5-2000, 18-3-2000.
98 SCMP 28-5-2000, 19-12-2000, 20-12-2000.
99 LegCo Special Committee on Building Problems of Public Housing Units, *First Report,* January 2003. LegCo debate on report: LegCo proceedings, 13-2-2003, 3574. SCMP 11-1-2001, 2; Gabriel, 2009 interview.
100 Miller, 2014 interview; SCMP 9-11-1999.
101 Lambon, 2012 interview; information from Rosman Wai, 2023.
102 SCMP 21-4-2001, 4, 61.
103 SCMP 11-11-2000; Gabriel, 2009 interview.
104 SCMP 26-6-2000, 4; SCMP 9-7-2004, 15.
105 Gabriel, 2009 interview.
106 Gabriel, 2009 interview; SCMP 26-2-2001; SCMP 29-5-2001, 10.
107 SCMP 8-8-2001, 16; SCMP 24-8-01, 2.
108 SCMP 4-9-2001, 2; SCMP 30-4-2001, 1; SCMP 5-9-2001, 15; SCMP 8-9-2001, 2.
109 Information Services Department, *Hong Kong 2001*, 24; SCMP 6-11-2001.

110 LegCo Special Committee on Building Problems, 21-4-2001, 4; SCMP 6-3-2000, 27-5-2000.
111 LegCo Special Committee, 24-4-2001, 662–6; SCMP 25-2-1999, 27-4-1999, 12-1-2000; Lau, 2009 interview.
112 'Old Mr Cheng': SCMP 30-9-2000, 5; SCMP 29-10-2000, 11.
113 Cheng, 2014 interview.
114 SCMP 24-6-2000; SCMP 6-7-2000, 16.
115 SCMP 6-10-2001, 1, 19-6-2002, 15 on 'the plethora of bodies carrying the housing tag'.
116 SCMP 1-10-2001, 10.
117 LegCo Special Committee, 21-4-2001, 4; SCMP 6-10-01, 1.
118 LegCo Special Committee 21-4-2001, 9, 20; SCMP 28-4-2001, 58.
119 SCMP 19-6-2002, 15.
120 SCMP 4-3-2002, 5; SCMP 7-8-2000.
121 HKHA, Building Committee Minutes, 15-1-1999; HKHA, Press Release 25-1-1999. 'More Efficient and Cost-Effective Harmony Block Designs Endorsed'; 17-6-2000 HKHA briefing for June 2000 members' tour led by Chris Gabriel CA/D & S and Theresa Yim SA/16, around Modular Flats Exhibition at Fat Kwong Street HQ.
122 SCMP 10-4-1998.
123 HKHA, memo 9-11-2000, file HD(CR)2/38/201 for HA meeting 16-11-2000, *Moving Towards a Flexible Production Mix*.
124 Billy Wong, 'Home scheme lifts housing block quality', SCMP 26-3-1998, 5.
125 P Moy, 'Government designed flats nearly twice the price to build', 14-7-2000, 6.
126 Gabriel, 2009 interview and 2023 information; Ada Fung, 2010 interview; Ng, 2012 interview. SCMP 4-3-2002, 5.
127 Ada Fung, 2023 interview.
128 Cheung, 2012 interview; Miller, in SCMP 11-3-2000.
129 Gabriel, 2009 interview and 2023 information; Lambon, 2012 interview.
130 Wai, 2010 interview; Ada Fung, 2010 interview.
131 Gabriel, 2009 interview; Lambon, 2012 interview.
132 Lau, 2009 interview.
133 *Public Housing in the New Era: Shui Chuen O Architectural Design Competition*. Hong Kong: Hinge Publications. 2001; SCMP 4-3-2001, 3 (sky gardens, comparison with Singapore). Information from Chris Gabriel, 2023.
134 Ng, 2023 interview.
135 SCMP 28-3-2003, 16.
136 Kai Hon Ng, 'Political context, policy networks and policy change: the complexity of transition in Hong Kong', *The Pacific Review*, vol 20: 1, March 2007, 122.
137 SCMP 7-4-2003, 2, on outbreaks at Block E Amoy Gardens, Lower Ngau Tau Kok, Prince of Wales Hospital, Sha Tin; drainage problems, SCMP 8-5-2003, 4; 6-11-2003, 4; SCMP 29-4-03, 13.
138 SCMP 22-12-2004, 16. Fong and Lui, *Hong Kong 20 Years after the Handover*, 340.
139 SCMP 22-12-2004, 16; SCMP 6-3-2005, 20.
140 SCMP 9-9-2002, 2; Poon, *Land and the Ruling Class*, 2011, 2; SCMP 23-9-2004, 30; SCMP 10-8-2004; Ada Fung, 2010 interview; Lau, 2009 interview.
141 Gabriel, 2009 interview.
142 Lau, 2009 interview.
143 Cheung, 2012 interview; SCMP 21-11-2003.
144 SCMP 25-4-2005, 3; SCMP 26-5-2005, 12.

145 Poon, 2009 interview; Gabriel, 2009 interview. Enquiry questioning versus Miller, SCMP 20-5-2004, 4.
146 Cheng, 2014 interview.
147 C M Tam et al, 'Performance assessment scoring system of public housing construction', *International Journal of Quality and Reliability Management*, June 2000, 467–78; SCMP 23-3-2005, 3. Gabriel, 2009 interview.
148 Wai, 2010 interview.
149 Information from Chris Gabriel, 2023.
150 Ka Fu Wah, 'An analysis of the organisational structure of the Housing Department in Hong Kong', HKU master's thesis, 2002, Fig. 5.1. Information Services Department, *Hong Kong 2001* and *2002.* Reviews, summary of findings and results: Yeung & Wong, *Fifty Years*, 11–13.
151 SCMP 20-6-2002, on Report of the Committee.
152 Cheng, 2014 interview.
153 Rosanna Wong, 2014 interview; Cheng, 2014 interview (on merger: 'They combined the two together after me'); Akers-Jones, 2014 interview.
154 Lambon, 2012 interview.
155 Information Services Department, *Hong Kong 2002,* 200; *Hong Kong 2001*, 206.
156 Michael Chugani, 'A witch-hunt', SCMP 6-6-2011; SCMP 6-11-2001; SCMP 26-6-2002, 14.
157 Yeung and Wong, *Fifty Years*, 11–13; SCMP 18-11-2002, 14; Miller, 2014 interview. Poon, *Land and the Ruling Class,* 11; Y C R Wong, *Hong Kong Land*, 85–6.
158 SCMP 14-11-2002, 17; SCMP 18-11-2002, 14.
159 *The Standard* 10-8-2004; SCMP 18-11-2002, 14.
160 SCMP 25-11-2002; SCMP 14-11-2002, 3; SCMP 9-3-2005, 2; SCMP 15-11-2002, 7 (market and developers' shares happy, in short term, with Suen's Nine Points).
161 Chu, 'Myths and politics', 382; SCMP 14-11-2002, 17.
162 SCMP 22-11-2002, 16.
163 SCMP 16-11-2001, 1; SCMP 14-11-2001. Compare the 1907 defeat of the 'Progressive' municipal housing strategy in the London County Council owing to ratepayer unhappiness at the 'depressive' effect on private speculators of the LCC housing programme: Hatherley, *Red Metropolis*, 42.
164 SCMP 29-11-2004, 2; SCMP 21-11-2002 (on PRH production scale-back).
165 SCMP 21-11-2002, 17.
166 Gabriel, 2009 interview.
167 Miller, 2014 interview; Ada Fung, 2010 interview.
168 Wai, 2010 interview.
169 SCMP 10-10-2002, 16; Information Services Department, *Hong Kong 2002*; Yeung and Wong, *Fifty Years*, 12, 26; *Hong Kong Economic Journal*, 15 August 2002; SCMP 3-4-2002, 1.
170 Rosanna Wong, 2014 interview.
171 SCMP 7-5-2003, 1; SCMP 16-7-2003, 1.
172 SCMP 21-2-2004, 2.
173 Gabriel, 2009 interview.
174 Yeung and Wong, *Fifty Years*, 171; Ada Fung, 2023 interview. SCMP 22-2-2003, 2; SCMP 28-2-2003, 1; SCMP 20-11-2004, 13; SCMP 21-2-04, 2. Information Services Department, *Hong Kong 2003*, 204–7.

175 Yeung and Wong, *Fifty Years*, 173. Y C Chen, 'Neoliberalisation and privatisation in Hong Kong after the 1997 financial crisis', *China Review*, 7(2), 2007, 65-92. SCMP 17-9-2003, 9; SCMP 4-2-2004, 2; SCMP 4-5-2004, 4; SCMP 18-12-2004, 1; SCMP 20-11-2004, 3; SCMP 20-12-2004, 1; SCMP 22-12-2004, 20. Rent levels 1997 to 2004: SCMP 17-3-2004, 3; SCMP 18-3-2004, 11.

176 SCMP 3-2-2003, 12; Cecilia Chu, 'The myths and politics of housing in Hong Kong: The controversy over the demolition of the Hunghom Estate', *Habitat International*, 32(3), September 2008, 383; SCMP 11-2-2004, 18; 2-12-2004, 3; 3-12-2004.

177 Reversal: SCMP 13-12-2004, M3; SCMP 14-12-04; SCMP 1-12-2004, 1, 18; SCMP 10-12-2004, 1.

178 James Lee, SCMP 27-11-2002, 14.

179 Liao, 2010 interview; Lambon, 2012 interview; Poon, 2014 interview.

180 SCMP 8-1-2004, 19; SCMP 1-6-2005, 3; SCMP 21-4-2004, 1 (pressure by DAB legislator Ip Kwok-him and HA member, opposed by Polytechnic University professor concerned could suggest government inconsistency); SCMP 20-10-2005, 1; SCMP 20-11-2004, 1 (Suen on 'adequate' supply, no shortfall likely 2007 and 2008) 'Dribbles' of flats, Gabriel, 2009 interview.

181 SCMP 20-11-2002; SCMP 22-11-2002, 16. SCMP, 5-11-2003, 2. SCMP, 13-5-2005, 20.

182 Wai, 2010 interview; Lambon, 2012 interview.

183 Gabriel, 2009 and 2011 interviews.

184 Information from Chris Gabriel, 2023.

185 Lambon, 2012 interview.

186 Lau, 2009 interview.

187 Cheung, 2012 interview.

188 Ng, 2012 interview.

189 Information Services Department, *Hong Kong 2003*, 205.

190 Ng, 2012 interview. Wai, 2010 interview.

191 Ada Fung, 2010 interview.

192 Too expensive: Gabriel, 2009 interview.

193 HKHA, *Planning, Design and Delivery*, 190–1.

194 Ng, 2012 interview.

195 27-4-2009 press release by Arup East Asia; Hong Kong Housing Authority (lead author Rosman C C Wai), *Planning, Design and Delivery of Quality Public Housing in the New Millennium*, HKHA, Hong Kong, 2010, 190–1.

196 HKHA, *Planning, Design and Delivery*, 190; Lau, 2009 interview.

197 Lau, 2009 interview.

198 SCMP 24-11-2004, 10; SCMP 25-1-2002, 14; SCMP 2-8-2003, 4, SCMP 13-8-2003, 4; Lau, 2009 interview.

199 Hung, *City on the Edge*, 165–174.

200 Geoffrey Somers, 'How we slowly made a home of Hong Kong', SCMP 23-9-2004, 2-8; Gabriel, 2009 interview.

201 HKHA, *Memories in Lower Ngau Tau Kok Estate*, Hong Kong, 2009; HKHA, *Planning, Design and Delivery of Quality Public Housing*, 200.

202 Ada Fung, 2010 interview; SCMP 28-1-2002, 2; Lau, 2009 interview; Cheung, 2012 interview; Dominic Wong Kwok-hing, 'Sustaining the intangible cultural heritage – the traditions of Yue Lan Festival in the Redevelopment of Ngau Tau Kok Estate', HKU MSc dissertation, September 2004.

203 SCMP 21-9-1998, 28; SCMP 28-10-1998, 22-11-99. Shek Kip Mei nostalgia: see e.g. Vincent Yu, *Our Home, Shek Kip Mei 1954–2006*, MCCM, Hong Kong, 2007 (information from Cecilia Chu).

204 SCMP 19-7-2002, 13.

205 SCMP 30-1-2005, 4; SCMP 12-2-2005, 1.

206 Cecilia Chu, 'Heritage of Disappearance? Shekkipmei and Collective Memory(s) in post-handover Hong Kong', *Traditional Dwellings and Settlements Review*, Vol 18: 2, 2007, 43–55.

14 2005 to the present: a frustrated recovery?

Donald Tsang: a vicious circle of housing crisis

In the previous chapter, we traced how the high ambitions and confidence of the new SAR administration under C H Tung, and in particular its aspiration of making public housing and home-ownership the focus of an identity-building strategy, dissipated under the pressures of the Asian financial crisis. Although this had rained hammer-blows on Hong Kong's new 'financialised' economy and society, its effect in housing, by undermining the Housing Authority and more generally creating a power-vacuum, had been perversely to further entrench the hegemony of the real-estate oligarchy. This reassertion of the tycoons' power formed the dominant backdrop for Hong Kong housing during the administration of Tung's successor, Donald Tsang, but significant cracks in that structure emerged under the two subsequent Chief Executives, C Y Leung and Carrie Lam. And eventually, the political turmoil of the late 2010s, and the COVID crisis of 2020–3, drowned out the domestic social-policy debates for a time.

The responses by housing policy-makers and practitioners to this disruptive environment had a distinctly circular character, revisiting the same formulae repeatedly, in permutations that differed largely in detail. At a political level, this circularity partly stemmed from the fact that no incoming Chief Executive could hope to significantly boost housing output during a single five-year term of office, and thus the tendency towards 'back-loading' of land and housing supply to the second half of the rolling ten-year LTHS framework had the effect of repeatedly 'kicking the can down the road' to the next office-holder. Yet, in contrast to the colonial period, there was a constant struggle for public support by each successive executive administration, with housing playing both a political and a social-economic role, not least in its continuing social-wage function.[1]

Initially, the accession to power of Donald Tsang as Chief Executive seemed to build constructively on the autonomy of the SAR system: Tsang, with his civil service administrative background, avoided the paternalistic language and references to cultural tradition that Tung had favoured, instead foregrounding professionals and democratic political mechanisms, and 2010 saw a limited widening of direct elections by Beijing. However, as with Tung, the impression quickly became established that his administration was dominated by vested interests and cronyism.

DOI: 10.1201/9781315563701-18

Figure 14.1 Chief Executive Donald Tsang pictured with Scottish First Minister Alex Salmond, visiting Hong Kong in December 2011.

And while his term arguably saw the high-point of the power of the local business elite, the disunited character of this oligarchy exacerbated government ineffectiveness, while the central government Liaison Office exerted a growing behind-the-scenes role.[2] (Figure 14.1)

In housing, these local vested interests were still seen at their strongest. One senior HA architect argued simply, in relation to the HOS, that 'That's the lesson to learn – to brand your product so as not to overlap with the private sector – or you're out!'[3] It was in land supply that the main effects were felt. In Rosanna Wong's opinion, 'the government never learned on land supply. Because of the crisis, everyone was so nervous about supply. So when Donald Tsang stepped into office, he decided not to build, that there would be no Home Ownership Scheme any longer, and no land supply for seven years. My thesis is that the crisis was nothing to do with the 85,000 – it's because the financial crisis coincided with the backlog. But Donald Tsang was so nervous that he just stopped for seven years. I told Donald Tsang, "You *must* have a regular supply of land for public housing!"' Likewise, Miller agreed that 'from 2002 onwards, the government arguably failed to ensure a forward land supply… the Government had taken its eye off the ball in forming and servicing of land after Suen's nine measures in 2002.'[4]

During Tsang's administration, Suen's 2002 argument that the private sector could most efficiently run Hong Kong housing was given full rein – with results far short of the confident predictions. By 2006/7, the production of public rental housing had dropped to a mere 7,192.[5] As previously high production levels still provided an element of insulation, the negative impact on the waiting list, and the government's last surviving housing pledge of a three-year maximum wait, was not yet visible, with the waiting list standing at only 1.8 years in 2009 and still at 2½ years in December 2011.[6] More ominous, for the private-dominated model, was the parallel decline in *private* output, which dropped to 7,157 in 2009 – a mere 20% of the 2002 level, and overwhelmingly orientated to upper price brackets. The overall home-ownership rate stalled at an all-time maximum of 53% in 2006.[7] Thus the market previously addressed by HOS was now left to its own devices. In the opinion of Ada Fung in 2016,

> When we stopped the sale and construction of the HOS, the private sector also stopped the development of medium-end private housing. They kept building and branding luxury apartments within single-unit blocks in town. So when we removed the HOS out of the equation, the private sector also removed the same market from Hong Kong. Since then, there has been a widening gap between public housing and private housing. Which means there are only public rental housing and the luxury apartments market.[8]

This production/affordability crisis was echoed elsewhere – for example in London's 2000s 'perfect storm' of house-price inflation, population boom, public housing output downturn and privatisations, and the private-rental boom – but in almost all cases far less dramatically.[9]

To be sure, house prices during Tsang's administration fluctuated significantly, but the overall trend was sharply upwards: by 63% in 2003–5, another 32% in 2006–8; then after a 17% drop during the 2008 recession, upwards again by 20% to August 2009, and by another one-third the following year. As Alice Poon argued in 2011, the property bubble had been deliberately 're-inflated' with a vengeance, and the property 'ladder' had been severed. 'If you stop for seven years, the mobility ladder stops, whereas if they keep building, social mobility is no problem'.[10] Housing Authority member Tennessy Hui agreed in 2012 that 'the housing ladder has been broken up and disconnected, with the private and public housing markets disconnected from each other'. In retrospect from 2022, it seemed clear that Tsang had been so 'anxious to stabilise the property market, and halted all land supply measures', and that 'the years of inaction paved the way for the housing crisis that would eventually surface towards the end of his term'. Demand was soaring partly due to planned mainland immigration of 150 people per day, completely outside the control of the SAR Government.[11]

For the time being, counter-measures were confined to demand-side steps, such as quantitative easing in 2008/10, and the 2009 introduction of stamp duty on transactions over $20 million.[12] But there was no shift to large-scale demand-side fiscal subsidies, and so the institutional preference for producer-side stimuli remained. In 2003, Yeung and Wong argued that the cyclical character of the housing market meant a direct producer subsidy could potentially be revived in future. During Tsang's term, the crisis in HA finances followed a volatile course: the 10% MRIR rental cap introduced in 1997 was claimed by some to have condemned the Authority to long-term financial insolvency, yet the revenue from the eventually implemented Link REIT scheme actually pushed its cash balance up to $58 billion by 2007, and an expected $70 billion by 2011 – while in the process permanently truncating 'the cash-cow of our organisation'.[13]

Instead of the HOS, two new home-ownership-based schemes were also introduced, the Buy or Rent and the MHPP (My Home Purchase Plan) schemes.

The former could be tailored to rental or home-ownership, and, according to HA chief architect Ken Cheung in 2012, envisaged

> a simple bare shell arrangement, almost like a rental block. Certainly this will not create private sector resentment, but it will create social confusion, to merge rental and home-ownership: "Why do I have to buy something that looks like a rental flat?"

The MHPP, according to Housing Authority member Prof Anthony Cheung, was an 'interim policy' immediately preceding a potential revival of the HOS, and was 'rife with imperfections'. The last phase of the TPS, Phase 6B, was also released in 2005–6, covering 23,290 flats.[14]

As early as 2006, Suen was hinting the HOS could hypothetically be revived in future, and that one should 'never say never'. Soon the disposal of the 12,000 unsold HOS units gathered pace: with Phase 4 in 2008, for example, released 3,221 units, of which 2,268 were unsold and 953 resales.[15] Blocks left empty for years now had to be rehabilitated, which posed 'a huge problem'.[16] Gradually the tycoons' success in turning the HOS into a social and political taboo was running out of impetus, and many pro-establishment groupings were breaking from it: in 2012, DAB spokesman Ip Kwok-him claimed the DAB had been 'lobbying for many years' for revival of the HOS, and the Federation of Trade Unions' Wong Kwok-kin argued that the unions 'totally support the resumption of HOS'.[17]

Eventually, in his 2011 Policy Address, Tsang yielded to the inevitable, and announced that the HOS would be formally revived, and once again, inevitably, assigned to the HA. It would build over 17,000 completed HOS flats over the four years 2016–17 to 2019–20, and thereafter 5,000 per annum.[18] As late as May 2010, the incoming Director of Housing, Duncan Pescod, was assured by the civil service bureau that 'Housing was a quiet posting', but that was once again about to change.[19]

The new HOS was hailed in mid-2012 by outgoing HA chair Eva Cheng, in terms that explicitly revived the concept of the housing 'ladder', arguing it would be 'another important rung'. From now on the 'ladder' became once again a key trope within Hong Kong housing discourse: in 2016, for example, senior HA architect Rosman Wai argued that 'It is important for a society to have hope. Our housing ladder gives people hope'.[20] Correspondingly, the fear of excessive overlap with private enterprise seemed to be abating: the HA's Subsidised Housing Committee authorised a formal policy of 'narrowing the gap', with selling prices of flats in 'remote' locations such as Yuen Long, for example, being pitched at about the same level as private flats. Construction of the first six 'New HOS' schemes was to be 'fast-tracked', with a view to reducing construction times to 3½ years, but the accumulated land shortages meant that a policy of 'single block squeeze-in' was adopted initially.[21] And by mid-2012, leading HA member Prof Anthony Cheung Bing-leung – shortly to become Transport and Housing Secretary in C Y Leung's administration – was arguing that the 2002 strategy of 'retreating from the housing market' was now 'pointless', owing to the rapid deterioration in the housing situation due to the enormous purchasing power from outside Hong Kong: instead, a supply-led strategy was urgently needed and 'from now on the Government should regard public rental housing and the new HOS as the main tools to solve the housing problem'. In December 2013, anticipating arguments of political pacification used in Hong Kong in 2019, the Singaporean consul-general, Ker Sin Tze, asserted that 'when the majority of the population own their own flat, they will probably refrain from violent protests in the street in order to protect the value of their properties'.[22]

In its overall housing production, the HA's contribution in many ways continued along traditional lines, with a five-year rolling PHDP adapted as needed. However, its personnel was evolving, with a growing percentage of women in leadership and executive positions, following in the previous footsteps of Rosanna Wong, and including not only HA Chair Eva Cheng (2007–12), but also senior architectural staff, such as Ada Fung, Deputy Director of Housing (Development and Construction), Connie Yeung, Chief Architect D & S, or Chief Architect Rosa Ho. Fung's tenure of the Deputy post from 2005 to 2017 was decisive in entrenching a systematised approach to development organisation, in areas ranging from procurement processes and sustainable design to site safety: the annual accident rate per 1,000 workers fell from 24 in 2004 to 6.9 in 2017 (having already dropped from 206 in 1989).[23]

In estate-planning terms, the parallel winding-down of the CRP programme, and overall decline in housing output, had signalled a decisive break from the previous twin-track formula of rolling redevelopment of Resettlement and GLCH estates – exemplified latterly in the giant multi-phase Kwai Chung redevelopment, completed 2007 – alongside large-scale New Town development.[24] As the CRP programme neared its end, at Shek Kip Mei, a symbolic conclusion was heralded in an ideas competition of 2007 for conversion of the last surviving Mk I block, Mei Ho House, with 13 entries from professional bodies and 33 from 'open' groups: they were judged by Patrick Lau and Edward Ho, with projects including 'The Garden of Memories' (a professional entry), 'Lush Growth, Shadows of Bend and Sway (professional), a centre for Cantonese opera (open), or a 'cultural hostel' (open). Eventually, Mei Ho House was converted into a youth hostel.[25] (Figure 14.2a–d)

From now on, clearances would be ad-hoc and piecemeal, as heralded in the controversial demolition of North Point Estate in 2003, the land being returned to the government in 2007 without compensation on grounds of the Housing Authority's then favourable financial position.[26] North Point was a special case, driven by real-estate considerations, but more generally, early HA estates were now for the first time drawn into the scope of redevelopment, on grounds not of 'slum' conditions but of allegedly poor concrete quality. In 2005, the two oldest surviving schemes, Sai Wan and So Uk, were inspected: Deputy Director of Housing Tam Wing-pong stressed that this was 'not aimed at demolishing estates to add to the government's land bank'.[27] By 2011, however, a scheme for rebuilding of So Uk was underway, following participatory workshops with tenants, which encouraged an intangible-heritage orientation including retention of original landscaping, and symbolic

Figure 14.2 (a) Mei Ho House, Shek Kip Mei, in 2010 prior to its modernisation (MG). (b) Mei Ho House, access gallery in 2010 (MG), pre-modernisation. (c) Mei Ho House, Flat 123 (a converted flat formed by merging two single-room, back-to-back units); 2010 photo (MG). (d) Mei Ho House seen in 2019 after its conversion into a youth hostel (MG).

minor structures.[28] Ken Cheung, Chief Architect in charge of the project, argued in 2012 that 'forty years ago, you had very poor concrete quality. That's why it has to be renewed. But we do think about heritage and conservation issues… . retaining the footprints of the Y-blocks, preserving up to the first and second floors.'[29] So Uk was lumped together with Shek Kip Mei and Lower Ngau Tau Kok in another intangible-heritage event, an exhibition in 2009 entitled 'Light and Shade – Life Passé', that celebrated the residents' 'neighbourliness' in the face of the estates' demolition following completion of their 'historic mission'.[30]

From this point, any new redevelopments could potentially provoke serious public opposition. That emerged, for example, when the HA proposed redevelopment of eight blocks at Pak Tin in 2012 as the first of a new, ad hoc sequence of renewals of 'aged' public rental housing estates, here with a proposed net gain of over 2,000 units – a programme which provoked strong 'local community worries' expressed via District Councils.[31] More typical of the ongoing housing programme from now on, however, were infill new developments on rezoned sites, as often in the urban area as in the New Territories, and sharing the redevelopments' emphasis on density and site-specific design. Near Upper and Lower Ngau Tau Kok, for example, the former Jordan Valley Rock Hills, a disused quarry, was carved out into four new PRH sites along Choi Wan Road, on sharply different levels interconnected by lift towers. The first completed, in 2008 (Site 1), was Choi Ying Estate, a 3,995-flat development on a 2.46-ha site, comprising a group of five enhanced 'New Harmony 1' towers, fronted by a gaudy yellow 'iconic' estate portal, but the later phases, such as Choi Tak (by Ng's group), comprised a variety of site-specific blocks, some with curved wing walls to enhance wind penetration along corridors, the entire ensemble being tied together by a U-shaped 'green belt' or 'green promenade' and landscaped gabion-faced embankments to soften the dramatic quarry landscape.[32] (Figure 14.3a, b) Increasingly, overall, the emphasis was once again on increasing plot ratios and increasing building height restrictions for PRH projects in the New Territories towards more 'urban' levels and plot ratios well above 5, initially by 20% from 2014 – permitting substantial increases of numbers at projects at Fo Tan, Sheung Shui and Hung Shui Kiu Area 13.[33]

Figure 14.3 (a) Choi Wan Road, Sites 2 (Blocks 1–4) and 3 (Blocks 5–8), site-specific blocks of 36–40 storeys designed by John Ng's group, seen under construction in August 2009 (MG). (b) The same development in April 2010 (MG).

Housing design in the 2000s – towards modular flats

The block-types used on these sites gradually evolved from standardised to site-specific, rather than transitioning in one jump – the Annex blocks playing a crucial intermediary role. The Annex had already complicated the clean cruciform lines of the Harmony 1, adding, on one side only, something recalling the clumsy stepped profile of the early Harmony feasibility study of 1987. For example, at Phases 3 and 5 of Kwai Chung redevelopment (2001–7), several few Harmony blocks had Annexes.[34] On the other hand, Wai and Lambon's landscaped, linked, low-rise groupings of the same basic type at Ma Hang had already pointed to the potential of a more integrated approach. Paradoxically, as we noted in Chapter 13, the slashing of output did not make public housing design significantly less staff-intensive, given the extra complexities of site-specific design and the ever-growing demands for public consultation. John Ng recalled that 'at Upper Ngau Tau Kok, the impact of design was at least double the normal level. This was the fight we faced – to produce very fast, at very good quality, and meet environmental needs and sustainability demands'.[35] Many permanent staff were redeployed to the Quality Reform process, which required many more site supervisors; and considerable staff time was also absorbed by the 'Dickson scandal' of 2006, in which serious delays on three projects forced the HD to terminate Dickson Construction's contracts and re-enter the sites.[36]

The final iteration of the standard block formula was the new Flexible HOS Block, previously designed in D & S from 2000 for HOS use: a linchpin role was played by Theresa Yim in the concept and detailed design. In an attempt to reconcile site-specific design with elements of standardisation, it was based on a range of 'standard' flat types which could be arranged about a core with variations in the layout of wings and numbers of flats: it was essentially conceived as a design kit to allow blocks to respond to site constraints more effectively. It was never implemented as intended, once the HOS programme was abandoned, but two blocks were built at Shek Pai Wan. This multi-phase development was integrated with the CRP, and its Phase 2 – one of the three contracts involved in the Dickson affair – included two 400-flat Flexible HOS Blocks alongside three PRH New Harmonys (one with Annex) and one small household block, all intended to rehouse tenants from Wong Chuk Hang estate, one of the final estates to be redeveloped in the original CRP: the reassigned contract was at length completed in 2007.[37] (Figure 14.4a, b)

Within the new site-specific developments, the eventually adopted compromise solution retained a freestanding towered formula, adapting the Harmony modular-flat approach to more individualised cruciform or Y-shaped building configurations, in some cases with one wing considerably longer than the others, Annex-style but full-height. Already, by the time of Kwai Chung, the percentage of precast construction had risen significantly, and for locations such as Upper Ngau Tau Kok, with their 'proliferation of non-standard designs' and 'multiple operational implications whenever types were changed', a fresh generation of modular design was developed using BIM software.[38] This would allow 'mass customisation in

Figure 14.4 (a) Model of Flexible HOS Block in the HA permanent exhibition at Fat Kwong Street: 2011 photo (MG). (b) Shek Pai Wan Phase 2, two 40-storey Flexible HOS blocks completed in 2007; 2009 photo (MG).

public rental housing', including a 'library' and 'tool-kit' of small modular flats ranging from one person up to two-bedroom family flats, and provision for volumetric precast bathrooms. And it would continue to back-up the mechanised processes encouraged within the Quality Housing initiatives, as well as responding to the post-SARS emphasis on better and more accessible drainage, and Universal Design principles of accessibility.

Partly returning to the original, Habraken-influenced concept, this Modular Flat Design (2008 version) was first put into action in the redevelopment of Lower Ngau Tau Kok. John Ng recalled that 'the core remained the same, but the block varied'. Post-SARS emphases included minimising re-entrants while retaining efficiency, at over 75%.[39] (Figure 14.5a, b) Contemporary HDB developments in Singapore, as always, provided an instructive contrast, but in a slightly different way from before. Here, modular planning was less critical, owing to the lower density and larger flat size: John Ng argued that 'They have much more flexibility – whereas if you have to have twenty flats per floor, with natural daylight, ventilation and minimising of travel, the limitations immediately affect the housing typology'.

Figure 14.5 (a) Lower Ngau Tau Kok Phase 1 Redevelopment as at July 2011, showing refuge floor in 47-storey block at centre (MG). (b) Lower Ngau Tau Kok Phase 1, progress by February 2013 (MG).

After 2000, Singapore's 1990s embrace of 'decorative' postmodernism mutated into a more flamboyantly 'iconic' approach, above all in the HDB's set-piece Pinnacle@Duxton project of 2001–9, a curved array of linked 52-storey towers with spectacular 'sky gardens' – a more modest Hong Kong echo being Kwai Luen Estate, completed in 2011, with three-storey inset communal terraces, slightly recalling aspects of Tom Ip's Shui Chuen O scheme of 2001.[40] (Figure 14.6a, b)

In the innovative planning of blocks, the Housing Society increasingly took a more active role. 2002 had witnessed the HS's fundamental policy reorientation towards a 'small but flexible' profile, focusing on elderly housing and renewal of earlier estates.[41] The two age-care blocks of 2001–4 (see above) designed by Palmer & Turner at Jolly Place, Tseung Kwan O, and Cheerful Court, Jordan Valley, each had wheelchair access throughout and a nurse's station every two floors. (Figure 14.7a, b) They formed part of a response to the mushrooming of the aged population, leading to two parallel HS projects in the 2010s, the 528-unit Tanner Hill project, North Point, 2013–15, designed by Ronald Lu & Partners in three towers on foundations originally constructed in 2003 for an abortive Sandwich Class scheme, and the 1,000-unit Wetland development at Tin Shui Wai, including elderly flats, hotel, and wellness centre, completed from 2014 onwards to the designs of AGC Design Ltd: 'like a retirement resort… a much bigger version of Cheerful Court'.[42]

Tsang's belated change of course towards a revival of social housing and the HOS, however, coincided with a significant worsening of his own public position

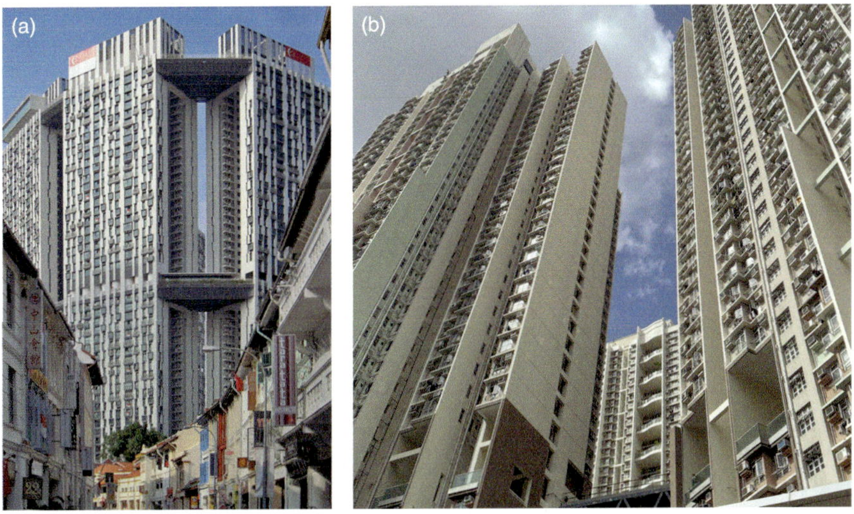

Figure 14.6 (a) The Singapore HDB's Pinnacle@Duxton project of 2001–9, a crescent of linked 52-storey towers with 'sky gardens'. 2011 photo (MG). (b) Hong Kong's more modest echo of the HDB set-piece: Kwai Luen Estate, completed 2011, with three-storey inset terraces. 2023 photo (MG).

and that of his administration, with mounting evidence of corruption and control by the tycoons. His earlier flamboyant image, with bow ties and sharp suits, had now become a distinct liability. At first, the controversies concerned senior officials. 2008 had seen the eruption of a scandal centred on Suen's deputy, Leung Chin-man, Secretary for Housing, Planning and Lands (Housing), who had to back out of his appointment as an executive director of a New World Development subsidiary only four years after his role in the below-market sale of the Hunghom Peninsula project to New World (cf. Chapter 13). Then, in 2014, both tycoon Thomas Kwok of Sun Hung Kai Properties, and Tsang's Chief Secretary from 2005–7, Rafael Hui, were jailed for corruption, Kwok for five years and Hui for seven and a half years, on grounds that the latter had received $34 million to act as Kwok's 'eyes and ears' in government: Kwok's brother Raymond was cleared of linked charges.[43]

By the end of Tsang's term, the spotlight had moved directly to him, with allegations of accepting bribes from tycoons, later investigated by the ICAC. In 2017, Tsang was jailed for 20 months in connection with an alleged conflict-of-interest over a luxury penthouse in Shenzhen, a downfall that shook public opinion in Hong Kong and, although some Democratic politicians stood up for him in court, further undermined the establishment's credibility. Eventually, in early 2019, Tsang was cleared by the Appeal Court, owing to procedural deficiencies at the original trial, but these negative associations clung to the Chief Executive post under successive holders for several years, until eventually drowned out in the 2019 unrest.[44]

Figure 14.7 (a) The Housing Society's Cheerful Court age-care middle-income development, Jordan Valley, 2003–4: 26-storey twin-tower design by Palmer & Turner. 2011 photo (MG). (b) Cheerful Court, main internal lobby, 2011 photo. (MG).

C Y Leung – land-shortage and abortive plans

This climate of public disapproval dogged the administration of Tsang's successor C Y Leung from the outset – although his policies in housing actually represented a significant shift from his predecessor. Leung, a chartered surveyor, had been elected secretary-general of the mainland's Basic Law Consultative Committee in 1985 at the age of only 31, and was rumoured to have been a closet Communist Party member: he rose further in prominence in mainland circles when he served as real-estate adviser to Shanghai party chief Zhu Rongji in 1987–91 and set up his own surveying firm in 1993. Probably the most important change heralded during Leung's administration was a suggestion that the tycoons' power might be subtly on the wane from its climax under Tsang. For example, in Leung's election, his main rival, Henry Tang, strongly favoured by the local establishment, was discredited by leaked corruption and scandal rumours during the election process. In 2012, Leung was accused of the same practices for which he had successfully castigated Tang – illegal alterations to his house – and started his term with low popularity ratings.[45]

On the surface, the property tycoons continued to enjoy a dominant role, not least in view of Leung's own property-industry origins, and the continuing inability of the Hong Kong government to overrule their 'vested interests' – a position that the central government, for now, was content to tolerate, as required under the 'one-country two-systems' framework. But a shift in underlying economic forces was underway: during the 2010s, a huge influx in mainland Chinese capital triggered a growing displacement of the relatively disunited local elite from economic power.[46] This did not signal any diminution of Hong Kong's relative importance within China, or of its character as a global financial city, but instead reflected its growing significance as, in effect, an offshore interface. The dual China–Hong Kong membership of the World Trade Organisation, in particular, allowed China global market access and facilitated renminbi internationalisation without threatening the central government's internal financial and credit control system.[47] It also, in the process, impacted strongly on housing-related areas of the Hong Kong economy: between 2011 and 2017 mainland bidding at government land auctions rose from 1% to 100%, and the construction sector was also evermore dominated by mainland firms. This capital influx drove up prices and rents, pushing the GINI coefficient up to 0.54 by 2016 – the ninth most unequal economy in the world.[48] Correspondingly, the local elites, and Liberal Party politicians in particular, became increasingly alarmed. And a more confrontational shift took place within the political climate after 2012: whereas some of the old democratic activists had supported Hong Kong's return to China, increasingly a new generation of younger radicals began calling for divergence from, rather than convergence with, the mainland.[49]

Having already served as housing adviser to Tung, Leung took office with a reputation as an expert in the field, and in his candidacy platform signalled his desire to radically expand Donald Tsang's halting revival of public housing. Within government, Leung emphasised his seriousness about housing by reorganising the Development Bureau and the Transport and Housing Bureau on his first day of office, creating instead a Housing, Planning and Lands Bureau, and appointing academic and HA member Prof. Anthony Cheung as Housing Secretary. Within the HD, a crash housing drive was anticipated: Chief Architect Ken Cheung, for example, predicted in mid-2012 that Leung 'is likely to ask for double or triple the present 15,000 programme. The target is likely to be 10,000 for home ownership, 30,000 for public rental housing, and to reduce the waiting list from three years to two years.'[50]

To draw up a definitive plan, Leung and Anthony Cheung set in train a fresh iteration of the LTHS, overseen by a steering committee, and working out a ten-year target in the time-honoured Housing Strategy tradition – developed from complex estimates of demand. A September 2013 consultation document proposed a target of 235,000 units over the following five years – an annual average of 47,000 – split 60%–40% public–private. Over the full ten years the total target would be 460,000 units, including 280,000 public housing – a target still in force in 2017.[51] But in the meantime, some immediate measures were introduced to convince the public of the seriousness of the new policy. In August 2012, Leung announced a ten-point short-term plan to boost housing supply, including expanded HOS schemes at Tin Shui Wai and MHPP at Tsing Yi. Anthony Cheung stressed that the new HOS was a permanent policy, not a flash-in-the-pan, arguing that 'There needs to be a continuous supply of HOS flats [and their] pricing has to take into consideration what the public can afford'. At a RTHK forum political representatives expressed mixed reactions, with Democrat Albert Ho branding Leung's ten-point plan a 'panic response' but the pro-government DAB giving it measured support. In December 2012, the first MHPP project under construction, Greenview Villa, Tsing Yi, was released for sale: it comprised 988 flats priced at 70% of similar private flats, and was sold to the public outright, against warnings it risked depressing the market for small secondary-market units.[52]

In 2012, too, demand-side measures were taken to cool overheating of the private market by speculators, above all the imposition of stamp-duty on overseas buyers, through the Stamp Duty (Amendment) Bill 2012, announced in October by the Financial Secretary.[53] But one person's 'ladder' was another's 'contagion': by December 2012, the familiar arguments against use of 'public money' to harm the private sector were already being raised against the HOS revival. The research department at Ricacorp Properties claimed people with a monthly income of $30,000–$40,000 and assets of $830,000 could now afford flats in well-located urban HOS schemes such as Lung Poon Court, with potentially harmful ripple-through effects to the private market in estates such as City One Sha Tin. Inequality and social polarisation were certainly growing in Hong Kong housing, but in complex and sometimes contradictory ways. In 2016, under 20% of public rental tenant households had incomes over median level, compared to 47% in 1976.[54]

But as Leung's plans developed, they came up all the more intractably against the hard reality of the collapse of land supply under Tsang, and the inability of the SAR government to do much about it, other than scrabble for infill sites. In 2014, Miller argued that 'C Y Leung faced exactly the same position [as had Patten] – as from 2002 onwards, the Government arguably failed to ensure a forward land supply. Leung comes in, like Patten, and sees another surplus in property prices, wants to crank up his programme, and sees there's no land!!' And Rosanna Wong argued, also in 2014, that following Tsang's seven-year interruption of land-supply, 'That means, no land, and C Y Leung now has to sort it out – and the backlog will become a big problem.'[55] Beyond land supply, the entire system seemed to discourage any serious reform: in February 2013, for example Michael Suen warned Leung not to push the bureaucracy too hard in pursuing reforms, while conceding it was regrettable that Tsang had been 'not sensitive enough' to avoid becoming embattled in the corruption controversies.[56] And at the beginning of 2015 journalist Stephen Vines predicted that while Leung had 'had success in persuading people that he will make home-ownership more affordable and improve housing for the underclass', his own roots in the property industry, 'a business cabal that speaks with one voice to protect its interests', meant that in practice, 'Leung's plans will have minimal impact', and the 'chasm' between haves and have-nots would only worsen. But the opposition democratic parties equally delayed any longer-term recovery in land supply by political obstruction within LegCo.[57]

Thus within a couple of years Leung's plan was veering increasingly off-course. By December 2015, it was predicted to fall 25,000 short of the 280,000 ten-year public housing target, and in December 2016 the anticipated shortfall (now over an extended timescale to 2027) was 44,000. And the waiting list, far from heading downwards from Leung's 3-year pledge, had risen by September 2016 to 4.5 years, with the waiting list now swollen to 286,500.[58]

All this was partly attributable to land-supply obstructions caused by public opposition, which now affected all kinds of site in the territory, whether from villagers and rural landlords or urban communities. In the short term, one initial expedient was to build 'squeeze-in' towers on small urban or New Territories plots, often rezoned. For example, at Tung Tau Cottage Area East, completed in 2014, featured a single 34-storey site-specific block, on a 'Y' plan not dissimilar to a Trident, but with the central arm truncated.[59] Such sites, however, were highly vulnerable both to local opposition and to myriad other complications: 2016's problem sites included a noise-polluted one near the Tsing Yi container terminal, a site at Tai Po where councillors were pressing for addition of a wet market, and one in Kennedy Town near a former slaughterhouse, with worries about traffic, noise levels and decontamination. Rezonings in the main urban area for 'single block squeeze-in' were often at a micro-scale, as at the Lin Tsui Estate in Chai Wan, a single 37-storey tower of 288 flats shoehorned on to a former HD staff-accommodation site, and completed in 2018.[60] (Figure 14.8) Leung was ready to approve more significant rezonings where circumstances changed, as in the case of a private university site at Queen's Hill, Fanling, which (following a decline in demand for university places) he released in 2013/14 for development as a showpiece project of 12,087 flats in site-specific towers of up to 41 storeys, at a site density of 2,490 ppha, divided roughly 3:1 PRH:HOS. Ada Fung recalled that 'CY was very diligent in helping us find land – we had weekly meetings with him, every Monday – and out of this desperate situation, he offered us Queen's Hill'.[61] (Figure 14.9a, b)

Figure 14.8 Lin Tsui Estate, Lin Shing Road, Chai Wan, 2011–18: 2023 view. A 'squeeze-in' project, fitting a single 37-storey tower containing 288 flats into a tiny (2000 m^2) and precipitously steep site, previously occupied by HD offices, that had failed to stimulate private-sector interest (MG).

Figure 14.9 (a) Queen's Hill Estate, Fanling, rezoned 2014 and completed 2021, including 8,865 PRH units in seven 41-storey blocks, and 3,222 subsidised sale flats (SSF) in six blocks of 24–38 storeys (Shan Lai Court); 2023 distant view (MG). (b) Queen's Hill Estate, upper-level view showing podium landscaping: 2023 photo (MG).

A 2022 critique, however, argued that expedients such as these could not compensate for lack of a secure long-term land-supply: Leung had

> pursued quick solutions to boost land supply by turning dozens of green belt plots around the city over to housing use and further suggesting developing the fringes of protected country parks. But the "not in my backyard" mentality in neighbourhoods has slowed down the land repurposing process, while filibustering by opposition politicians in the legislature delayed plans to secure funding to build new towns and start feasibility studies on reclamation.[62]

In December 2016 Anthony Cheung wrote that 'the hard fact is that in public housing we have virtually used up all "spade-ready" sites in hand. Indeed, some 80% of the sites [to be] processed in the next few years are not spade-ready. These sites are subject to the uncertainties of the various statutory and non-statutory processes' – hence the rising shortfall estimate.[63] The longer-term view was equally ominous, and any suggestion of a 'back-loaded' programme, accelerating in its second half, was evaporating: Knight Frank director Thomas Lam argued that the mid- and long-term land supply post-2020 was the most concerning, with the government facing 'huge opposition' from residents everywhere. Suggested ways round the problem included use of the government fiscal reserve to buy 'private' sites – although in early 2015 Leung was unenthusiastic about the suggestion that the government should take over the 50-year-old, private-philanthropic low-income Tai Hang Sai estate from the ailing Hong Kong Settlers' Corporation.[64]

It was in this context of growing land-supply perplexity that what would become one of Hong Kong's most long-running site controversies began rearing its head: the suggestion, first made in early 2015, that the Hong Kong Golf Club's exclusive course at Fanling could be partly used for public housing. HKU social work professor Paul Yip justified this by arguing that Hong Kong's housing was the least 'affordable' among 360 countries and regions, and the quality of life was actually worse among private mortgage payers, who were paying 30–40% of their income on housing, than public rental tenants (only 10%).[65] Leung's 2014 Policy Address also stressed the restrictions on public housing imposed by the zoning of so much land as country parks, claiming blithely that the housing shortage 'will be coming to an end soon'. Although his Development Secretary, Paul Chan, then immediately shot down the idea that this might require building in those country parks in the future, Leung floated the idea of developing at least the fringes of Tai Lam Country Park, where a 25,000-unit development would generate a whole year's supply target.[66] In the event, despite Leung's high aspirations for output, the reality was frustratingly far more modest. Although private completions increased significantly, from 10,149 in 2012 to 14,495 in 2016, PRH output zigzagged erratically, from 13,114 in 2012/13 to 9,938, 14,264 and 11,416 in successive years. HOS completions in 2016/17 were only 3,017 – amounting to totals far short of the 47,000 annual averages demanded in the 2013 LTHS.[67]

Public housing design in this period continued to develop its balance between standardisation and site-specific individuality. In 2016, for example, Rosman Wai argued that 'There are no more standard blocks. Everything has opened up. Block designs vary. We have typical units as the base, and architects make up blocks according to the site's environment… It's the best distilled from the third and fourth generation of public housing. While repetition is necessary for prefabrication to be possible, it allows us to prefab entire rooms such as kitchens and bathrooms off-site. Approximately half of our design is done in-house'.[68] Strenuous attempts were made to integrate the site-specific towers into environmental schemes that included both heavy landscaping and wind-modelling, the latter being exemplified by the two lavishly planted wind-corridors that traversed the nine 26-storey towers of Hung Fuk Estate in Hung Shui Kiu (completed 2016), and the former by the landscape slope-modelling works at Long Shin Estate, Yuen Long (completed 2017). Ada Fung pointed out that landscape enhancements for residents' 'passive enjoyment' also, ingeniously, helped boost output, by allowing difficult and not easily developable slopes and hillocks nevertheless to be counted as part of sites for yield and plot ratio calculation purposes: 'You could do everything in one go – it was both art and science!'[69] (Figure 14.10a, b)

The most prominent Housing Department urban project completed during the Leung years was the relatively limited-scale, 9-ha public-housing section of the giant Kai Tak airport regeneration scheme. Containing some 13,000 flats in 15 site-specific towers, it was built in two phases and completed in 2014, together with a commercial centre and car park. The public housing element, as so often before, played a pump-priming role for the wider project, as suggested by the HD's effusive branding of the development as a 'Distinguished, Vibrant, Attractive and People-Orientated Kai Tak by Victoria Harbour'. In reality, of course, the public-housing development was actually the furthest part of Kai Tak from the harbour, coming no nearer than 800 m to it, but in compensation it was intensively landscaped and linked into the Kai Tak Avenue Park along the development's north-west side. Its

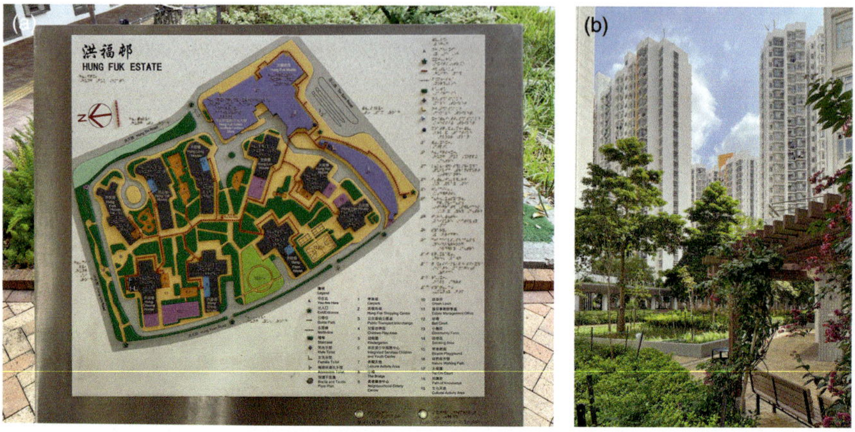

Figure 14.10 (a) Hung Fuk Estate, Hung Shui Kiu, rental development of nine 26-storey towers completed 2015: multi-sensory estate map shows careful planning of estate with wind-corridors, using bus station and commercial complex as a noise and wind barrier at the south end. 2023 photo (MG). (b) Hung Fuk Estate, view of centre of estate showing wind corridor and complex landscape planting: 2023 photo (MG).

site-specific towers comprised a mixture of cruciform blocks not dissimilar to the Harmony 1, Y-plan blocks not unlike Harmony 2, and blocks with one extended wing, slightly resembling the Annex formula – but all built using the post-2008 modular, highly prefabricated approach.[70] (Figure 14.11a–c, 14.12a, b)

In the rural New Territories context of the outer edge of Sha Tin, the development that was eventually built at Shui Chuen O (under Chief Architect Ken Cheung) on the site previously targeted in the abandoned design competition, between the Lion Rock and Ma On Shan Country Parks, struck a more irregularly profiled appearance that ‘merges nature and man-made elements in a harmonious context’, and, inevitably, embodies ‘green living concepts’. Phase 1 was completed in 2014, with five highly site-specific towers, responding to the craggy setting with variegated, stepped profiles a little like that of Sui Wo Court 30 years before.[71] (Figure 14.13)

Following the successive upheavals of the Occupy/Umbrella movement of September–December 2014, and the 2016 ‘Fishball’ unrest, Leung stepped down at the 2017 election, rather than seeking re-election. However, he still intervened significantly in housing debates during the campaign to elect his successor, heavily criticising front-runner and former Financial Secretary John Tsang – the candidate backed by the local elites, like Henry Tang in 2012 – for his pledge to provide public housing for 60% of the population, and arguing there was not enough land available to support it. To this, Tsang countered that land supply could be boosted through accelerated reclamation and urban renewal. More implausibly, Stanley Wong, chair of the HA’s Subsidised Housing Committee, and a member of the

Figure 14.11 (a) Kai Tak Site 1a (Kai Ching Estate), site-specific blocks under construction in 2012: detail of prefabricated elements in yard (MG). (b) Kai Tak Site 1a, prefabricated bathroom being hoisted into position, 2012 (MG). (c) Kai Tak Site 1a, view of nearly completed section of development, 2012 (MG).

2013 LTHS Steering Committee, claimed in support of Leung that Tsang's pledge would require up to 600,000 extra public flats to be built in the next decade, in the process suppressing private supply entirely.[72] By the end of Leung's term in 2017, the counter-claim was increasingly vociferously being heard that the unrest of 2014 and 2016 had stemmed not from 'democracy' discontent but from young people's unhappiness at the high cost of housing – and thus that if the government could contrive to release more land and encourage easier access to home-ownership, the troubles would wither away.[73]

Carrie Lam – housing dilemmas amidst escalating unrest

The appointment of Leung's successor from 2017, Carrie Lam, rather than the more extrovert John Tsang, suggested a Beijing-endorsed return to the ascendancy of old-style administrators, albeit with a slightly more emollient image than that of Leung. The Cambridge-educated Lam had joined the British colonial civil service in 1980, while also cultivating close mainland links and eventually

(a)

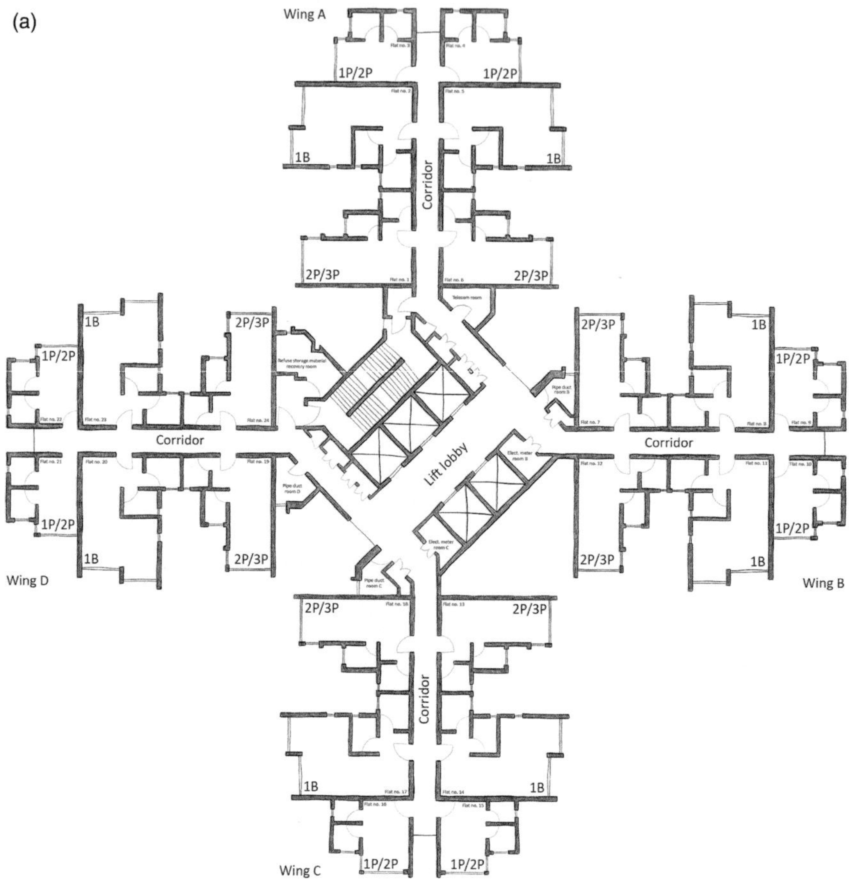

Figure 14.12 (a) Kai Tak Site 1a, typical upper floor plan of site-specific cruciform tower (Block 4). Drawing by Joyce Fu, 2023. (b) Kai Tak Site 1, layout plan of typical one-bedroom (1B) upper-floor flat in Block 4. Drawing by Joyce Fu, 2023.

becoming chief secretary under Leung in 2012. But her victory over John Tsang, the favoured candidate of the local elites, also in some ways echoed Leung's over Tang. More generally, C H Tung's July 2002 quasi-ministerial accountability system facilitated a shift from the traditional Hong Kong administrative ethos to a more politically engaged approach. However, this did not give the HKSAR government any greater effective power in standing up to the real-estate vested interests, which had been hitherto supported by the central government – a double nexus of vested interests not suffered by the earlier colonial governors, whose arm's-length relationship with their supposed masters in London gave them considerable room for manoeuvre.[74]

(b)

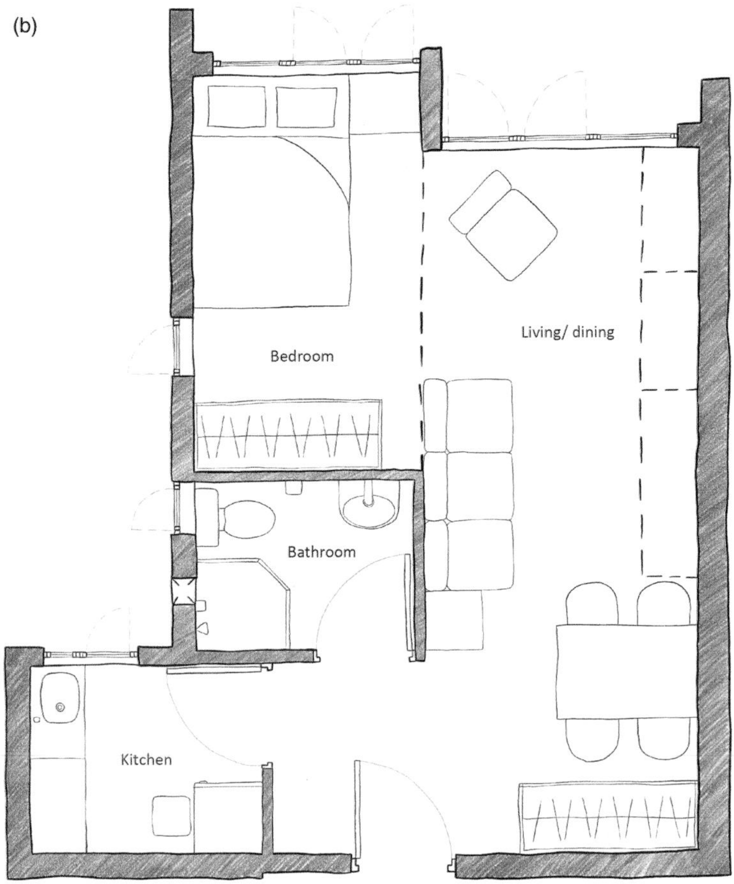

Figure 14.12 (Continued)

Meanwhile there was no let-up in the escalation of popular unrest, following the March 2019 outbreak of demonstrations against the extradition processes in the Fugitive Offenders Amendment Bill, and culminating in the storming of the LegCo building in July, the violent sieges of CUHK and Polytechnic University in November, and the targeting of Chinese state symbols by increasingly radical protesters.[75] Although the onset of COVID-19 in March 2020 dampened down all unrest, as well as sealing Hong Kong off from the outside world, clearly among at least some of the population the decades-long development of an autonomous 'Hong Kong identity' had now begun to veer in directions unacceptable to the central government, and the latter eventually cracked down by the enactment of a National Security Law on 30 June 2020.

We will return later to this escalation of political unrest, and its disruptive effects on the public housing programme. However, in the narrowly defined area

Figure 14.13 Shui Chuen O, view of site-specific development as eventually built in 2012–16 (chief architect, Ken Cheung); 2017 photo (MG).

of housing policy, Lam began her term of office with a significant expansion of Leung's existing housing targets, in a way that was distinctly inconsistent with her pre-election attacks on John Tsang's proposals. Leung's 2014 policy had proposed a 60–40% split of public (including HOS) and private – with the aim of achieving 940,000 public rental units by 2027. But by 2018, the Secretary for Transport and Housing, Frank Chan, was pledging that public output should now account for 70% of all new housing over the next ten years, significantly more than even John Tsang had proposed.[76] At the same time, within the overall total, there was a renewed shift from PRH to HOS, in effect returning to the preferred policy trajectories of both Patten and Tung: in November 2017 Lam was even quoted as saying that a public rental housing stock of only 80,000 units should suffice as a residual pool of dwellings for the poorest. In fact, however, the biggest increase in HOS production resulted ultimately from Leung's building drive. Between 2017/18 and 2018/19, HOS completions shot up from 248 to 9,121. Overall, the yearly average construction (private and public) under Lam was 27,207 – comparable with Leung's 30,469 and Tsang's 26,066 but far below Tung's 48,588. By 2018, the HOS, as a 'brand name', was increasingly subsumed within the new and overarching term,

'Subsidised Sale Flats' (SSF), which included all other kinds of subsidised home-ownership schemes (including that of the HS).[77]

Again developing an existing policy of Leung's, this new numbers drive was underpinned by an ambitious, long-term land strategy, charted by a Task Force on Land Supply that reported in December 2018 under the title, 'Striving for Multi-Pronged Land Supply'. In the 2018 LTHS Annual Progress Report, an updated combined public–private 10-year target of 450,000 units to 2028/9 (315,000 public) was set out, with a warning that sites for only 248,000 had so far been identified.[78] In response, a massive expansion of new land supply was signalled. To circumvent delays from protestors and owners of existing land, its headline element was an ambitious reclamation scheme off the east coast of Lantau, first suggested under Leung, and now known both as the 'Lantau Tomorrow Vision' and the 'Kau Yi Chau Artificial Islands': it could eventually expand to up to 1,700 ha. An extension of Tung Chung New Town was also intended to yield 49,000 flats by 2030 (60% public): ground-breaking began in February 2018.[79] At the same time, the government signalled its intention to embark on a 320-ha quasi-New Town development (termed 'New Development Area') in the North-East New Territories, at Kwu Tung North and Fanling North, to yield 72,000 dwellings (70% public), for which infrastructural works commenced in December 2018: the first stage would be a 68-ha private/100-ha public site, with population intake planned for 2023. This plan would later be expanded further, and re-branded in 2021 by Lam as a fully fledged 'Northern Metropolis', spanning virtually the entire northern zone of the New Territories, and tied in with the central government strategy of 'development integration' of Hong Kong and Shenzhen. The development of this zone would also include the previously suggested part-development of the Fanling Golf Course with public housing.[80] (Figure 14.14) For all these new developments, it was agreed that public housing plot ratios should now be boosted by 30% rather than the 20% authorised in 2014 – allowing typical New Territories plot ratios to rise from 5 to 6.5.[81]

Running alongside all this strategic planning was a more immediate, inexorable continuing rise in housing pressures. The waiting-list time, fuelled by couples getting married and arrivals from the mainland, grew to 5.8 years by early 2021, the largest since 1997–8 (when it had been 6.6 years). And although property prices were now, on occasion, falling – for example by 7.2% in the six months to January 2019 – the affordability ratio of housing was still far above all comparable places (150% higher than London, 350% higher than Singapore). The index had dropped from 85 in 1997 to 20 in 2003, but had recovered to 74 by 2021. By April 2022, following the severe recession induced by COVID, the median price of a home would be over 23 times the median household income.[82] At the same time, the home-ownership rate was beginning to dip, falling to 49.8% in 2019: economics professor Terence Chung argued that a rate of 50% or less was 'most unhealthy' and fuelled social division. Although the TPS had made a significant impact, with 140,000 units sold to tenants by 2019, and the SSF/HOS cumulative total was nudging 400,000 by 2020 (32% of all home-ownership in Hong Kong), demand

Figure 14.14 February 2019 SCMP cartoon of Chief Executive Carrie Lam and Matthew Cheung Kin-Chung, Secretary for Administration, and their Fanling golf course predicament.

was still outstripping production: the success rate in the HOS lucky-dip ballots had dropped from 33% in 2001 to 1.6% in 2018.[83] And private-sector production was still erratic, propped up partly by the publicly organised private housing programmes of the MTR (and URA), which provided 30% of each year's private supply, and 55,000 over the previous decade. Profits from the often semi-luxury-class MTR developments helped support future rail development, under the 'railway plus property' model.[84]

When the 2019 unrest erupted, the widespread discontent at this housing impasse was instrumentalised by the establishment grouping, which argued it was a 'real', underlying cause of grievance for young people, from which the political demands were supposedly an externally fomented distraction – although this argument necessarily, of course, implied a degree of failure in the SAR Government's housing policies since 1997. Gradually, a new political agenda coalesced with central government support, calling for unprecedentedly decisive action on the housing problem as a way of countering the legitimacy of the political protests. But just as in the British colonial period, with MacLehose's 'model-city' discourse, success in that agenda would depend on responding effectively to the old, familiar practical challenges, above all the land shortage. Here the problem of snowballing objections to any category of housing sites immediately raised its head: for example 2020/1 saw 7,200 objections to the proposed rezoning of a greenfield site near Ma On Shan Country Park; and City University property expert Lawrence Poon argued in 2021 that officials had become too 'afraid of objections', leaving brownfield, country park, green-belt and agricultural sites all effectively unusable.[85]

Notwithstanding these warnings, in her autumn 2020 policy address, Lam claimed enough land had been identified to cover housing demand for the next decade, and would permit construction of 316,000 public housing units (including home-ownership) over that period. Medium-term output would be partly covered by an expansion of the 'Lantau Tomorrow Vision'. This might now generate as many as 260,000–400,000 flats by 2034: a three-year expansion study into the reclamation began in mid-2021.[86] Criticisms included claims that this strategy was simply 'new wine in an old bottle' and recycled the '10 Major Infrastructure Projects' of Donald Tsang's 2007/8 Policy Address, and that it was in any case 'back-loaded', with big gains possible only after six years: certainly current construction projects comprised relatively small sites like the 40-ha Anderson Road Quarry.[87] Lam continued to reject Leung's plan to build up to 20,000–30,000 SSF units on a 100-ha site on the edge of the 5,412-ha Tai Lam Country Park, near Kam Sheung Road station – a concept whose original study had been directed by Marco Wu of the Housing Society: C Y Leung would continue promoting the proposal in the following years.[88]

To defend herself against criticisms of 'kicking the can down the road', Lam's 2019 Policy Address had already introduced a tactical expedient to plug the output gap, by a programme of 'transitional' low-rise flats, constructed using 'Modular Integrated Construction' (MIC) assembled out of prefabricated container-like boxes – reviving a concept previously pioneered in the 1996 'interim housing' experiment in the Patten years (Chapter 12), and rather more architecturally substantial than the temporary housing of previous decades. This transitional housing would be targeted not at squatters but at the most urgent waiting-list cases, above all inhabitants of subdivided housing.[89] Already in June 2018, Lam had set out an initial target of 10,000 transitional units to be completed in three years, later increased to 15,000: by February 2021 the government said it had already found land for 14,000 units and the first examples had been not just completed, including four-storey blocks at Nam Cheong, appropriately near Shek Kip Mei, but also demolished again after only two years' occupancy. However, by June 2022, a three-year waiting list was reported even for the transitional flats.[90] (Figure 14.15a, b)

In the political aftermath of the 2019 disturbances, and the 2020 National Security Law, a succession of changes to the electoral committee system and the legislature pointed to a potential reduction in the influence of the real-estate tycoons, reflecting the rise of mainland as opposed to local capital within the Hong Kong economy.[91] 2019 had also seen central government criticisms and 'shaming' of the property tycoons for hoarding land, and some commentators called for the curbing of the autonomy that had allowed these 'vested interests' to flourish. With the removal of the political opposition, other groupings began to play a stronger

Figure 14.15 (a) St James' Concourse Phase 1 Transitional Project, Sham Shui Po (2022–3): infill modular 205-unit project of 2022–3 by the Hong Kong Council of Social Service: 2023 photo (MG). (b) Yan Oi House Transitional Housing scheme, Hung Shui Kiu: view of newly-completed 410-unit, four-storey complex built in 2022–3 by care charity Yan Oi Ltd in 'Modular Integrated Construction'. 2023 photo (MG).

role in housing-policy debates, such as the 'Our Hong Kong Foundation' (a pro-establishment organisation set up by C H Tung) or the Liber Research Community, an independent grouping formed in 2014 to research public-interest issues.[92] Already, Lam had begun to develop a carrot-and-stick response to the challenge of developers' hoarding of both land and completed flats. The carrot, appealing to developers' 'social responsibility', was a pilot 'Land Sharing' scheme finalised in October 2019, under which owners of farmland could be granted increased development densities if 70% of the floor area was set aside for affordable public-sector flats. The financial incentives for this were insufficient to attract developers, and the first application, for a site in Tai Po, was not until mid-2021, with only five applications even by June 2022. The stick was a threat to tax vacant flats, which Lam briefly investigated in 2018 before shelving it two years later.[93]

Even as some new public housing blocks were used as quarantine accommodation in the dramatic clamp-downs on COVID-19, and the pipework design of others was blamed as contributing to COVID spread in 2020, other estates became focal-points of mainland immigration, amplified by existing clan networks.[94] In general, central government figures now showed increasing willingness to comment directly on Hong Kong housing conditions, labelling them a 'deep-seated problem'.[95] Repeatedly, mainland commentators fastened on the small size of Hong Kong flats as a particular disgrace, doubtless reflecting the relatively plentiful land supply in mainland cities and the larger size of equivalent mainland flats (but disregarding the generally far lower quality of the latter). In July 2021, Xia Baolong, newly appointed Director of the Hong Kong and Macau Affairs Office, called for the abolition of cage homes and subdivided homes by 2049, the centenary of the communist revolution in China; but Financial Secretary Paul Chan politely suggested this rhetorical aim could be 'unattainable' in practice, owing to the severe development constraints imposed by land shortages and village demolition objections. Chan agreed, however, that the government must be more firm and resolute in overcoming local protests, and insisted that there was no high land-cost policy to boost government revenue.[96] As a token of concern for the estimated 100,000 people in subdivided flats, a two-year rent-control scheme was announced in 2021, and income limits for Housing Authority tenants were frozen at their existing level in March 2022.[97]

As the end of Lam's term of office neared, increasingly policy debates focused, as so often in the past, on land supply obstacles: residential land-supply was said to be at a 10-year low (and prices at a historic high) in June 2021, and shortages not likely to ease until the later 2020s. Disjointed government structures were once again the focus – including the fact that the housing minister reported to the Chief Secretary but the development minister to the Financial Secretary. With the aim of unifying the government response, in 2020 Chan was tasked with chairing an inter-departmental steering committee on land supply. The 'Northern Metropolis' project, finalised in 2021, pointed to a long-term strategy of finally 'solving' the Hong Kong housing problem, and in particular the unremitting land-supply crisis, by swallowing it up within the wider developmental and demographic framework of 'Greater Bay Area' unification. But in the short term, the housing situation seemed little-changed: in 2022, the current production forecast envisaged an actual decline from 18,500 public-sector completions in 2022/3 to only 14,600 the following year, with output only likely to re-attain 25,000 from 2024–5 onwards.[98]

John Lee – grasping the nettle of housing reform?

With the July 2022 installation of the new Chief Executive, John Lee, we leave the field of housing 'history' and arrive at the present day. Hence only a brief, factual and neutral summary of the housing situation of the early 2020s will be offered here.

The new 'establishment' perspective on housing, as laid down by Lee in April 2022, was that housing was now 'the top priority among all priorities' – a statement that garnered support from all the leading local tycoons, doubtless nervous at the sight of the central government taking on giant enterprises on the mainland, but at the same time seeing potential synergies between the Northern Metropolis strategy and their huge land banks. Overall, the government was still dependent on land sales and related proceeds, which had accounted for 12–21% of all its revenues between 2019/20 and 2022/3, and would play a vital role in supporting the huge cost of the Lantau reclamation and Northern Metropolis projects: yet there was widespread agreement that the 'golden era' of the tycoons was now over, with the growing pressure for Hong Kong housing policy to somehow reflect the central government 'common prosperity' ideology.[99]

As to how that should be done, a strong hint was given at Lee's inauguration, when President Xi Jinping proclaimed that 'What the people of Hong Kong desire the most are a better life, a larger apartment, more business start-up opportunities, better education for kids and better elderly care. What the people call for, we must strive to deliver'.[100] In their responses, Hong Kong commentators tactfully agreed that larger flats were of course desirable, despite the implicitly zero-sum character of this agenda in the context of severely restricted land supply – larger inevitably meaning fewer dwellings. In May 2021 Ryan Ip and Iris Poon of the Our Hong Kong Foundation had highlighted the 'dire' effect of ongoing land shortages in likely further reducing supply by 28% below the LTHS target over the following four years: in reality both the numbers and size of flats, public and private, they argued, would inevitably continue to fall, and the private trend towards 'nano flats' (smaller than 215 sq ft) would continue.[101]

Lee's new Housing Secretary, Winnie Ho, dutifully echoed the central government pressure for larger flat sizes by stressing that while the 'previous administration' had had to compromise on size to increase numbers, henceforth private-sector flats built on government land would be 280 sq ft minimum and the proportion of 'tiny flats' in public housing output would be reduced – although public rental sizes would only increase to 280 sq ft from 2027. The conservative New People's Party (chaired by Regina Ip) argued that the 'real-estate hegemony' that had developed 'since the early 2000s' should now be challenged, to ensure, among other tasks, that the central government's demand for an end to cage homes by 2049 could be met: 'Under Lee, the government will be expected… to eliminate this problem once and for all'.[102]

During 2022–3, clues emerged as to how Lee intended to set about this task. He promised a 'new ideology' of results-based pragmatism aimed both at boosting land supply and at expediting construction on sites once secured – building on his predecessors' ideas rather than making radical departures. As earlier with Dominic Wong, the magic key was seen as above all lying within the government bureaucracy: to coordinate all housing land and production activity through interdepartmental mechanisms, and in particular yet more task forces – with the Housing Bureau, given separate status in July 2022, rapidly assuming a growing executive authority, as had Dominic Wong's Housing Branch 30 years previously.[103] A HOUSCOM-style Steering Committee on Land and Housing Supply would coordinate all relevant work of policy bureaux to come up with policies to unlock private land, while a Task Force on Public Housing Projects would look for ways of accelerating the development process, especially by 'compressing construction' and potentially by moving tenants into new estates before infrastructure was complete.[104] In the latter case, there were echoes of the stampede of the late 1990s, while in the case of land supply there were the long-familiar constraints, including the sacrosanctity of the 44,312-ha country parks, the 16,381-ha Green Belt, and the 1,200-ha Wetland Buffer Area, or the archaic rules governing the 2,400-ha of 'clan land' in the New Territories: it was calculated that developing only a tenth of the Green Belt would yield 1.2 million additional public housing units and double the existing stock. Like MacLehose, Lee proposed to enlist rather than fight the private tycoons by exploiting their New Territories land-banks. It was also suggested by the HA Subsidised Housing Committee chair Cleresa Wong that the waiting list could be trimmed by downgrading new households that had been generated by subdivision of existing households.[105]

The extra land unlocked would be used more intensively. Now resurrected for application in the Northern Metropolis was the 2018 decision to raise public housing plot ratios by 30% from 5 to 6.5 (and private housing by 20%), potentially boosting the yield of the project by 13,100 flats.[106] Also revisited and reinforced was the programme for higher-density redevelopment of 'aged' public HA rental estates: in November 2023 Choi Hung was added to the current list of ten active projects, which would replace 17,000 flats with 32,000 new units, while the HS was also pursuing the redevelopment of four of its estates, including Ming Wah Dai Ha.[107]

But Lee, like all his predecessors, faced the problem that however much construction was accelerated, his housing policies would only reach fruition, at the earliest, in the plan's second five years. In May 2022, Ryan Ip argued that much of the government's planning, as with previous administrations, was 'wishful thinking', and that government acceleration efforts risked being tripped up by 'hidden delays' caused by myriad local issues and obstructions on individual sites. Indeed, despite the administration's avowed intent to pursue both the Northern Metropolis (2021–41) and Lantau Tomorrow Vision (2025–33) projects simultaneously, in the short term once the Tung Chung New Town extension had been completed, there was actually a likelihood that the completion rate of 17,300 flats forecast for the next five years would be followed by sharp decline, if the Hung Shui Ku, Kwu Tung North and Fanling North projects were not rapidly progressed. In October 2022, for example, Housing Secretary Winnie Ho reported to LegCo that labour and materials shortages on the mainland, stemming from the repeated COVID lockdowns there, would compel deferment of 6,800 completions from 2022/3 to 2023/4, notably at the second phase of Tai Po Area 9 (Fu Tip Estate), where only one of nine planned 31-storey blocks had so far been completed, in 2021. Overall, the current ten-year target was over 10% less than the 2018 target of 460,000 – and of course far below the targets of Tung and his predecessors.[108] (Figure 14.16a, b)

To try to short-circuit this process and achieve more immediate results without overburdening the HA, an additional 30,000-unit programme of so-called 'Light Public Housing', mostly comprising prefabricated slab blocks of up to 19 storeys to be completed by 2027/8, was launched in late 2022. Intended for only five-year occupancy and taking advantage of looser planning controls over short-term housing on land zoned for other purposes, Light Public Housing was significantly more substantial than the 21,129-unit Transitional programmes. Within LegCo, the programme was trumpeted in emotively rhetorical terms, as 'not just empty talk' but 'bold… drastic measures' targeted at 'the grassroots'. LPH 'directly addresses people's concerns and difficulties in daily life' and would 'further empathy and promote mutual help', enabling 'each and every family' in poor housing to live 'with dignity'… 'rather than struggling for their lives… in inadequate housing with

Figure 14.16 (a) Fu Tip Estate, Tai Po Area 9: Phase 2 (eight 31-storey public rental blocks) seen under construction in December 2022: the restricted height reflects the lower plot ratio currently applicable on New Territories sites. (b) 'Intake' of new tenants at Fu Tip Phase 2, showing the promotional stalls of home-improvement firms – a longstanding and sometimes controversial 'tradition' in new estates. April 2024 photo (MG).

no way out'. The programme would be overseen directly by the Housing Bureau and designed by the government Architectural Services Department: no less than 10,700 of the 30,000 total would be on a single site at Kai Tak.[109]

Rapidly, the new government's determination regarding all of this was confronted by the perennial controversy over the proposed part-development with 12,000 flats of public housing of the Fanling golf course (see above). This was highlighted by some commentators in August 2022 as 'a test of political will' for Lee, in the face of calls from ExCo Convenor Regina Ip for the project's abandonment on 'ecological' grounds, and claims by some public figures, such as ex-LegCo president Jasper Tsang, of covert lobbying by the Hong Kong Golf Club against the development. Simon Fung, a member of the original 2018 Task Force on Land Supply, branded any suggested back-pedalling as 'ridiculous': 'Now is not the time for discussion, but to get things done'.[110] The outcome at Fanling would give a strong signal as to whether delays and vested interests could now be tackled in earnest by the territory's 21st-century 'home builders'. (Figure 14.17)

As the 2020s began, Hong Kong's political autonomy might have diminished but its economic significance for Beijing as an offshore link to the global economy arguably remained stronger than ever, especially with China's internal economic vicissitudes.[111] Within Hong Kong, having raised the political profile of housing as an alternative to political reform, and having then raised expectations of decisive action, the stakes were now high – perhaps higher even than in the eras of MacLehose, Patten or Tung. Radical government coordination and intervention in housing, and a readiness to override private interests with strong planning

Figure 14.17 The Fanling Golf Course saga (continued): SCMP cartoon of August 2022.

controls, seemed unavoidable if progress was now to be made – despite the difficulty of achieving decisive progress within a single five-year Chief Executive time-span. The challenge would now be whether Lee could marshal sufficient authority within Hong Kong, or backing from the central government, to decisively put such a strategy into effect.

Notes

Some of the SCMP references below are drawn from an online database at the Hong Kong Central Library and do not include page numbers.

1 R Forrest and N-M Yip, 'The future for reluctant intervention: the prospects for Hong Kong's public rental sector', *Housing Studies*, 29:4, 2014, 551–65.
2 Poon, *Land and the Ruling Class,* 14–18; Lambon, 2012 interview ('The private developers became legislators'); Hung, *City on the Edge*, 94, 142, 162.
3 Poon, *Land and the Ruling Class,* 2; Cheung, 2012 interview.
4 Rosanna Wong, 2014 interview; Miller, 2014 interview.
5 HKHA, *Annual Report*, 2008–9, 126; HKHA, *Annual Report*, 2021, Appendix 75.
6 SCMP 28-4-2022 (Office of Government Economist); HKHA, Minutes of Regular Open Meeting, 25-6-2012 (D W Pescod contribution); HA, Annual Special Open Meeting, 7-6-2012 (M Choi and Wong Kwok-kin).
7 HKHA, *Annual Report*, 2008–9, 126; Y C R Wong, *Hong Kong Land*, 13–15.
8 Hong Kong Institute of Architects, *Journal* 72, 2016, 'Occupy Housing', 13.
9 Hatherley, *Red Metropolis*, 158–9.
10 Poon, *Land and the Ruling Class,* 2, 7. Rosanna Wong, 2014 interview.

11 HKHA, Annual Special Open Meeting, 7-6-2012; SCMP 28-4-2022; Gabriel, 2011 interview.
12 Y C R Wong, *Hong Kong Land*, 14, 77.
13 Yeung and Wong, *Fifty Years*, 433; HKHA paper 42/2007, 21-9-07; Ken Cheung, 2012 interview.
14 Ken Cheung, 2012 interview. A Cheung, speech at HKHA Annual Special Open Meeting, 7-6-2012; HKHA, Annual Report 2005–6.
15 SCMP 20-10-2006, 1; HKHA, press release 8-9-2008.
16 Gabriel, 2009 and 2011 interviews.
17 HKHA, Annual Special Open Meeting, 7-6-2012.
18 Lee Ping-kuen speech, HKHA Annual Special Open Meeting, 7-6-2012.
19 Duncan Pescod, speech at HKHA Regular Open Meeting 25-6-2012; Lambon, 2012 interview.
20 Eva Cheng, speech at HKHA Regular Open Meeting 25-6-2012; HKIA, *Journal* 72, 2016, 'Occupy Housing', 64.
21 SCMP 11-2-2012, C2. Yeung Sin-Hung at HKHA Annual Special Open Meeting, 7-6-2012.
22 HKHA, Annual Special Open Meeting, 7-6-2012; SCMP 6-12-2013.
23 Ada Fung, 2023 interview (drawing on 2022 HA statistics); Gabriel, 2009 interview; *Housing Dimensions* 18-3-2011.
24 Irene Cheng et al, 'The redevelopment of Kwai Chung Estate', 1164-1171.
25 HKHA, *Planning, Design and Delivery*, 207.
26 HKHA paper 42–2007, 21-9-2007.
27 SCMP 10-8-2005, 4.
28 HKHA, *Planning, Design and Delivery*, 204.
29 Cheung, 2012 interview.
30 HA press release, 21-6-2009.
31 Alan Leong, remarks at HKHA, Annual Special Open Meeting, 7-6-2012; HKHA Regular Open Meeting 25-6-2012.
32 HKHA, *Planning, Design and Delivery*, 188–9.
33 Duncan Pescod, speech at HKHA Regular Open Meeting 25-6-2012. HKIA, *Journal* 72, 2016, 'Occupy Housing', 16–18 (John Ng).
34 Irene Cheng et al, 'The redevelopment of Kwai Chung Estate', 1164–71.
35 Y Lo, 'Dickson Construction', www.industrialhistoryhk.org; Ng, 2012 interview; Wai, 2010 interview.
36 Ada Fung, 2023 interview.
37 Gabriel, 2009 and 2011 interviews, and 2023 information.
38 Irene Cheng et al, 'The redevelopment of Kwai Chung Estate', 1164–1171. HKIA, *Journal* 72, 2016, 'Occupy Housing', 16–18; Ada Fung, 2023 interview.
39 HKHA, *Planning, Design and Delivery*, 59–61; HKIA, *Journal* 72, 2016, 16–18; Ng, 2023 interview.
40 Ng, 2012 interview; Cheung, 2012 interview. Singapore: www.pinnacleduxton.com.sg; HKIA, *Journal* 72, 2016, 104.
41 L C Wong, 2011 interview.
42 Burns, 2014 interview; HKIA, *Journal* 72, 2016, 65. L C Wong, 2011 interview.
43 Poon, *Land and the Ruling Class,* 14; *Guardian*, 5-10-2015 (on 'eyes and ears').
44 BBC website, 20-7-2018; Fong and Lui, *Hong Kong 20 Years After the Handover*, 2018, 264–5.

45 ABC News website, 26-6-2019; Hung, *City on the Edge*, 89–90, 143. Fong and Lui, *Hong Kong 20 Years After the Handover*, 2018, 264–5.
46 Hung, *City on the Edge*, 78–84.
47 Hung, *City on the Edge*, 53, 64–5.
48 Hung, *City on the Edge*, 78–84.
49 Calls for divergence, see e.g. Tommy Cheung, '"Father" of Hong Kong nationalism? A critical review of Wan Chin's city-state theory', *Asian Education and Development Studies*, vol 4: 4, October 2015. Fong and Lui, *Hong Kong 20 Years after the Handover*, 2018, 270–2.
50 Yeung Sing-hung and Winfield Wong speeches at HKHA, Annual Special Open Meeting, 7-6-2012.
51 SCMP 8-2-2017, News 3.
52 SCMP 31-8-2012, 6-12-2012.
53 SCMP 27-7-2022.
54 SCMP 6-12-2012.
55 Miller, 2014 interview; Rosanna Wong, 2014 interview; L C Wong, 2011 interview.
56 SCMP 8-2-2013.
57 SCMP 22-1-2015, B8.
58 SCMP 21-12-2016, News 1.
59 HKHA, *Planning, Design and Delivery*, 201.
60 Lin Tsui: www.info.gov.hk, article of 12-7-2018. SCMP 22-12-2016 City 1; SCMP 28-4-2022.
61 Queen's Hill: Ada Fung, 2023 interview; 'Public housing set for Queen's Hill', 25-1-2014, www.news.gov.hk.
62 SCMP 22-12-2016 City 1; SCMP 28-4-2022.
63 SCMP 22-12-2016, City 1.
64 SCMP 21-12-2016, News 1; SCMP 18-1-2015, 7.
65 SCMP 30-1-2015.
66 SCMP, 18-1-2015, 7; SCMP 27-7-2022.
67 HKHA, *Annual Report,* 2021, Appendices 75.
68 R Wai in HKIA, *Journal* 72, 2016, 'Occupy Housing', 63–4.
69 Ada Fung, 2023 interview.
70 HKHA, *Planning, Design and Delivery*, 202–3.
71 HKHA, *Planning, Design and Delivery*, 205.
72 *Standard*, 8-2-2017, 4; SCMP 8-2-2017, News 3.
73 Ben Bland, *Generation HK, Seeking Identity in China's Shadow*, Penguin, London, 2017, 72–4.
74 Markus Shaw, SCMP 4-9-2019; Hung, *City on the Edge*, 142-3 on role of Liaison Office.
75 Hung, *City on the Edge*, 185.
76 SCMP 1-11-2017, News 12; SCMP 11-5-2021.
77 Legislative Council Secretariat Research Office: *Housing, Statistical Highlights, Subsidised Sale Flats*, ISSH13/18-19; SCMP 1-11-2017, News 12; HKHA, *Annual Report*, 2021, 11, 75; SCMP 28-4-2022.
78 Legislative Council Paper CB(1) 388/18-19 (03) – LTHS Annual Progress Report 2018.
79 Development Bureau, HKSARG, *Striving for Multi-Pronged Land Supply, Report of the Task Force on Land Supply*, 12-2018; SCMP 6-2-2018, A3.
80 *Building Journal* December 2018, 6-7; SCMP 22-2-2022, 13-8-2022.
81 Legislative Council Paper CB(1) 388/18-19 (03) – LTHS Annual Progress Report 2018.

82 SCMP 11-8-2021, 11-5-2021, 11-1-2019, 25-1-2019, 28-4-2022, 6-7-2021, 11-4-2022.
83 SCMP 11-8-2021, 26-3-2019, 12-5-2022.
84 SCMP 12-8-2021.
85 SCMP 12-8-2021.
86 SCMP 11-5-2021, 12-8-2021.
87 SCMP 22-2-2022, 13-5-2021.
88 SCMP 11-6-2021.
89 SCMP 12-7-2021: also $5 billion for non-profit groups to build temporary housing.
90 www.hb.gov.hk/eng/policy/housing/policy/transitional/index.html (accessed 3-12-2023); SCMP 5-6-2022, 28-11-2022.
91 Hung, *City on the Edge*, 78-90; SCMP 20-3-2021.
92 SCMP 13-8-2021 Part 3; SCMP 17-6-2021; SCMP 28-4-2022.
93 SCMP 22-7-2021, 13-8-2021, 7-6-2022, 15-7-2021, 13-8-2021, 31-5-2022.
94 SCMP 14-3-2022, 15-2-2022, 27-12-2021.
95 SCMP 29-6-2021.
96 SCMP 24-7-2021.
97 SCMP 15-7-2021, 14-3-2022.
98 Hong Kong SAR Government, *Northern Metropolis Development Strategy – Report*, 2021; SCMP 29-6-2021, 6-7-2021, 15-7-2021 (housing production forecast)
99 SCMP 28-4-2022, 19-10-2023, 24-10-2023, 25-10-2023 (Lee policy address).
100 www.scmp.com/hong-kong-25/politics/article/3183808/read-full-english-transcription-chinese-president-xi-jinpings: accessed 12 December 2022.
101 SCMP 13-5-2021.
102 SCMP 23-7-2022, 24-11-22, 5-6-2022.
103 SCMP 28-4-2022, 13-8-2021.
104 SCMP 29-4-2022.
105 SCMP 13-8-2021, 29-4-2022, 7-6-2022.
106 SCMP 19-8-2022.
107 Legislative Council meeting 9-11-2022, paper CB (3)44/2023(01).
108 LegCo Proceedings 26-10-2022, question by S Wong and reply by W Ho; SCMP 28-4-2022, 31-5-2022.
109 LegCo Finance Committee, 8-2-2023 paper, ref. PWSC (2022–23) 35; www.hb.gov.hk/eng/policy/housing/policy/light_public_housing/index.html: accessed 3 December 2023.
110 SCMP 13-8-2022.
111 Hung, *City on the Edge*, 176–9.

Conclusion

Hong Kong housing – a monumental heritage of the Lion Rock Spirit?

The starting point for the Introduction to this book was a sweeping generalisation about late-20th-century mass housing: that in the developed capitalist and socialist worlds, there was a kaleidoscope of vigorous local recipes, with individual countries and cities differing radically from each other in organisation and architecture; but that in developing countries emerging from colonial rule, with their often fragile economies and political systems, it was far less common to encounter strong and enduring 'mass housing cultures'. This book has been a study of a dramatic exception to that rule: the mass housing generated during the decolonisation of Hong Kong.

This was a decolonisation of a particularly unusual kind, not just because the territory's colonial status itself was, and still is, historically contested, but also because of the extraordinary developmental constraints it posed – including perceptions of extreme over-population and land-shortage – and the unprecedented built environment that resulted from those perceptions, dominated by spectacular outcrops of hyper-dense multi-storey towers. In its preponderance of high-density public housing, Hong Kong of course resembled its 'sibling-rival' Singapore, but unlike the latter, the 'normal' outcome of decolonisation, namely self-determination and independence, was expressly ruled out from the outset. Architecturally, too, Hong Kong's housing took a very different form, given its chronic land-supply problems, being increasingly concentrated in dramatically verticalised outcrops of British-style standard towers, rather than distributed as an even carpet of medium-height 'precinct' courtyard complexes. But whether or not Hong Kong was ever a 'proper colony', it and Singapore certainly both in their different ways fell into the established late-20th-century category of Eastern Asian developmentalism: rapidly modernising societies that employed strong state interventions to promote capitalist development, including enforced 'resettlement' of rural–urban migrants, aggressive urban redevelopment, and state-sponsored owner-occupation. In all these policies, mass housing played a self-evidently central role. At the most overarching level, it significantly empowered Hong Kong's extreme and idiosyncratic local contribution to the overarching trans-national narrative of 'Modernization as a Global Project'.[1]

DOI: 10.1201/9781315563701-19

Decolonisation in Hong Kong fell not into a single unitary narrative but into a succession of convulsive leaps. Accordingly, the narrative in this book was also structured into a series of discrete stages, in each case comprising distinct architectural forms and policy recipes – in the former case reflecting international modernism's chameleon-like ability to generate place-specific variants, and in the latter reflecting underlying political and economic forces. As Anthony Giddens argued, 'the structural properties of social systems are both the medium and outcome of the practices that shape those systems'. It would, however, be excessively simplistic to claim that these 'leaps' of decolonisation were straightforward determinants of policy, or to attribute overriding powers of 'control' or 'discipline' of the populace to governmental housing strategies.[2] In Hong Kong, unlike Singapore, government housing policies, and general development planning initiatives, were too variable and unpredictable, too much on the defensive, whether against colonial traditionalists or real-estate tycoons, to have exerted any consistently overriding power.

This convulsive decolonisation process was reflected in the four-part narrative structure of the book.

In Part I, we traced the housing responses of a colonial society cast into relative geographical isolation by the Cold War, a society not yet ready to directly engage with the dynamic of decolonisation, but which instead preoccupied itself more adventitiously with containment of refugees and defensive development of an export-orientated industrial base, in both cases via mass 'Resettlement', while jealously defending its laissez-faire economic system.

Part II related how MacLehose began an implicit reorientation towards the sovereignty question by decisively promoting a new concept of collective identity-building and social citizenship, exploiting to the maximum the scope for government initiative within Hong Kong's 'caretaker' system. For this strategy, radically expanded public housing formed a vital support, especially through the new, Singapore-inspired concept of state-supported home-ownership: the overriding aim was to cement people's sense of 'belonging' while maintaining a low external political profile, and avoiding any 'democratisation' initiatives that might provoke 'the ire of China'.

Part III, covering the last fifteen years of British rule, combined the final stages of decolonisation with a further economic transformation to exploit the opening of China, outsourcing industrial production to the mainland while transforming Hong Kong itself to a global capitalist metropolis. Here housing, as systematised through the 1987 Long-Term Housing Strategy, gradually metamorphosed from an identity-creation device to an integrated support of the 'financialisation' of Hong Kong, a process marked by the emergence of a powerful local real-estate sector able to veto or dictate government housing policy.

Finally, in Part IV, from 1997, the economic and administrative structures set up in the previous years – including public housing and public-led territorial development, as well as the private-sector power of the Hong Kong housing 'tycoons' – began to be brought into alignment with the reality of 'one country, two systems', as part of a gradual but inexorable integration of Hong Kong with the mainland, geographically, demographically and economically, especially under the 'Greater Bay Area' banner.

This process of staged transformation affected all parts of the built environment: for example in the commissioning of cultural centres, there was a similar trend, from social idealism and identity-promotion under late colonialism, towards corporate-capitalistic urban development within a pan-China framework.[3] But public housing, with all its emotive collective significance, spotlighted each stage of the process in its most dramatic form – at least up until the end of the 2010s, when the growing pressures for convergence with the mainland began to suggest that housing might finally lose its talismanic status within Hong Kong society. The gradual absorption of Hong Kong into the Greater Bay Area seems likely to diminish the consciousness of acute land shortage and island-like isolation, as well as gradually diluting the sense of a distinct Hong Kong cultural community. Set against the grand geo-political canvas of 21st-century China, and the pressure of national or regional developmental strategies, Hong Kong's perennial internal housing-crisis discourses of affordability and land shortage are now beginning to seem slightly beside the point, as are the internal housing constraints and challenges facing successive administrations, such as the structural inability of any incoming Chief Executive to significantly boost housing output within a single five-year term of office. Whether or not John Lee's government eventually succeeds in raising housing output or increasing flat sizes, it is clear that the real decisions on issues such as strategic development, demographic change, mainland immigration and land supply are being made elsewhere. Thus it is unlikely that any future equivalents of Murray MacLehose or Donald Liao will have the opportunity to rival their vast achievements, in scale or impact.

The first half-century covered by this book saw the gradual building-up of Hong Kong public housing as an 'interstitial' phenomenon, suspended between two sovereignties; but with the ending of that interstitial status, it is also unclear what might be the ongoing cultural status of the built environments bequeathed by the 'home builders' of that era. Is the present-day built fabric of Hong Kong public housing actually a physical manifestation, on a monumental scale, of the inescapability of Richard Hughes's 1968 conception of Hong Kong as a 'Borrowed Place, Borrowed Time'?[4] It seems undeniable that public housing in Hong Kong owed its very existence, and each of its phases of evolution, to the multi-stage process of decolonisation – but does that correspondingly mean that it itself is ultimately destined to complete oblivion, or complete absorption within the 'patriotic' discourse? The public housing programme itself is still ongoing, however fitfully, and – at any rate following the restoration of the HOS/SSF – is relatively little-changed in organisation and architecture from its position in 1997. And the radical contrast between the compressed intricacy of Hong Kong's public housing landscape and the vast, hyper-Haussmannesque *magistrales* of mainland cities will not be easily erased. In housing at least, it would be rather misleading to divide and polarise the history of Hong Kong modernisation between an idealistic, welfarist late-colonial golden age and a neo-liberal, alienated present: some of the dilemmas and policy remedies of today's 'home builders' are surprisingly similar to those of the MacLehose era.

Figure C.1 Reunion of former HA chairs and directors at the Hong Kong Club, 14 February 2013. From left to right: Albert K W Lee (HD Deputy Director [Estate Management]); Treasa Yan (HD Head, Central Support Unit); Tony Miller (former Director of Housing); Ada Fung (HD Deputy Director of Housing [Development and Construction]); Sir David Akers-Jones (former HA Chairman); Cheng Hon-kwan (former HA Chairman); Duncan Pescod (Permanent Secretary for Transport and Housing [Housing]); Dr Rosanna Wong (former HA Chair); Michael M Y Suen (former Secretary for Housing, Planning and Lands); the author is at the back, behind Wong and Pescod.

Thus the status of Hong Kong mass housing is still arguably one of history-in-progress – for which a diachronic rather than synchronic approach may be more appropriate. But it is also, at least potentially in the future, one of 'heritage'. We noted in the Introduction that built environments begin by being a mirror of the culture and community that spawned them; and, indeed, Hong Kong public housing gives us a window into the heart of government decision-making processes at the various stages of decolonisation, as well as the community structures and identities built up around it (Figures C.1 and C.2). But their monumentality and solidity also give them the power to outlast their parent societies, a power that has manifested itself in the past even in the case of violent ruptures: the Palace of Versailles, for example, survived the Revolution intact, despite being condemned in the process as an 'abode of crime, whose royal magnificence is an insult to the poverty of the people and the simplicity of republican morals'[5].

Clearly, Hong Kong public housing does not fall into that category of apocalyptic rupture, especially given the continuing enthusiasm of all post-1997 Chief Executives (except perhaps Donald Tsang) for the 'housing agenda'. Nor, however, is it a straightforward candidate for transition into 'heritage' status, not least because

Figure C.2 Upper Ngau Tau Kok, part of street heritage display in the estate on the planning of the redevelopment. The main central photo shows a planning workshop of local residents and Housing Department architects in 2007, with John Ng at the centre of the back row. (MG).

of the more general difficulty experienced elsewhere in comfortably assimilating mass housing into heritage. Normally, building types, once historicised, eventually become valorised as potential heritage – as we saw happening on a very small scale with Mei Ho House in Chapter 13. But more typically, even in its European heartlands, mass housing has remained stubbornly resistant to heritage valorisation – even if the Western prejudice against high-rise public housing is inapplicable to Hong Kong for obvious reasons.[6]

In the Hong Kong context, the obstacles to 'heritagisation' of public housing stem not so much from architectural as from cultural-political factors, and in particular from the question of its long-term status as the built legacy of a transient 'interstitial' society. A building programme originally devised and developed by a colonial regime for its own purposes, and shaped jointly by the team effort of both Hongkongers and expatriates, is unlikely to find an easy place within any 'patriotic' historical master-narrative, however strong the practical continuities spanning from MacLehose until today; but there can be no doubt that if there is such a thing as a transcendent and enduring 'Lion Rock Spirit', then Hong Kong's public housing adventure is one of its most resonant expressions – and it is at the

Figure C.3 Wah Fu (I) Estate seen in November 2023 prior to start of demolition (MG).

very least a historically legitimate exercise to set out a detailed record of how it came about, in case it eventually starts to fade into oblivion. The renowned turn-of-century Viennese theorist of architectural heritage, Alois Riegl, argued that the place of monuments was not to be preserved for ever, but to serve as

> a mere perceptible substratum, whose task is to stimulate that feeling which is evoked in modern people by the inexorable ritual of being and passing away, of the arising of the particular out of the general and its inevitable reabsorption back in the general.[7]

Hong Kong's public housing legacy, however vast its scale today, is not exempt from that rule – but it has been the modest aim of this volume to set out an initial basic record, to sketch out a historical memory-landscape, of this monumental collective achievement (Figures C.3 and C.4).

Figure C.4 Donald Liao, seen with Rosman Wai at his home at 55 Kadoorie Avenue in November 2023, the day following the award ceremony for his Gold Medal from the Hong Kong Institute of Architects (MG).

Notes

1 Engerman and Unger, 'Introduction: towards a global history of modernization', 380–2.

2 Economic-structural account: see e.g. Castells, *Shek Kip Mei Syndrome*. Control/discipline interpretation: see e.g. Kockelkorn, 'Peripheralisation'. Anthony Giddens, *Central Problems in Social Theory*, Macmillan, London, 1979, 69.

3 Liu, '*Cultural centers in Hong Kong*', 72.

4 R Hughes, *Borrowed Place, Borrowed Time: Hong Kong and its Many Faces*, Andre Deutsch, London, 1968.

5 M Glendinning, *The Conservation Movement*, Routledge, London, 2013, 68.

6 Cecilia Chu, 'Heritage of disappearance? Shekkipmei and collective memory in post-handover Hong Kong', *Traditional Dwellings and Settlements Review*, 18 (2), 2007, 43–55. M Glendinning, 'Ennobling the ordinary: postwar mass housing and the challenge of change': DOCOMOMO International Journal 39, September 2008, 4–10.

7 Alois Riegl, *Der moderne Denkmalskultus*, Vienna, 1903; Glendinning, *The Conservation Movement*, 143.

Bibliography

David Akers-Jones, *Feeling the Stones – Reminiscences by David Akers-Jones*, Hong Kong University Press, Hong Kong, 2004.

Noel Annan, *Our Age, Portrait of a Generation*, Weidenfeld & Nicholson, London, 1990.

Robert Bickers and Ray Yep (eds), *May Days in Hong Kong: Riot and Emergency in 1967*, Hong Kong University Press, Hong Kong, 2009.

Sally Blyth and Ian Wotherspoon, *Hong Kong Remembers*, Oxford University Press, Oxford, 1996.

Judith M Brown and Rosemary Foot (eds), *Hong Kong's Transitions, 1842–1997*, Palgrave Macmillan, London, 1997.

Stephen Brown and Christine Loh, *Hong Kong – the Political Economy of Land*, Civic Exchange, Hong Kong, 2002.

John M Carroll, *A Concise History of Hong Kong*, Rowman & Littlefield, Lanham,s MD, 2007.

Manuel Castells, Lee Goh, R Yin-Wang Kwok, *The Shek Kip Mei Syndrome – Economic Development and Public Housing in Hong Kong and Singapore*, Pion, London, 1990.

Irene Cheng, Chris Gabriel, N M Chan, S H Ho, Polly C P Young, 'The redevelopment of Kwai Chung Estate', in *Proceedings of the World Conference on Sustainable Building SB08 Melbourne*, CSIRO – Commonwealth Scientific and Industrial Research Organisation, Melbourne, 2008, 1164–1171.

Joseph Y S Cheng (ed), *The Hong Kong Special Administrative Region in its First Decade*, City University of Hong Kong Press, Hong Kong, 2007.

Gary Ka-Wai Cheung, *Hong Kong's Watershed – the 1967 Riots*, Hong Kong University Press, Hong Kong, 2009.

S W-K Chiu, *The Politics of Laissez-Faire: Hong Kong's Strategy of Industrialisation in Historical Perspective*, Institute of Asia-Pacific Studies, Hong Kong, 1994.

Cecilia Chu, *Building Colonial Hong Kong, Speculative Development and Segregation in the City*, Routledge, Abingdon, 2022.

Cecilia Chu, 'The myths and politics of housing in Hong Kong: The controversy over the demolition of the Hunghom Estate', *Habitat International*, 32(3), September 2008, 375–383.

Chen Yun Chung and Pun Ngai, 'Neoliberalisation and privatisation in Hong Kong after the 1997 financial crisis', *China Review*, 7(2), 2007, 65–92.

Jonathan Dimbleby, *The Last Governor – Chris Patten and the Handover of Hong Kong*, Little Brown, London, 1997.

David Drakakis-Smith, *High Society – Housing Provision in Metropolitan Hong Kong 1954 to 1979, A Jubilee Critique*, Centre of Asian Studies, University of Hong Kong, 1979.
David Faure (ed), *A Documentary History of Hong Kong*, Hong Kong University Press, Hong Kong, 1997.
Brian C H Fong and Tai-Lok Lui (eds), *Hong Kong 20 Years after the Handover*, Palgrave Macmillan, London, 2018.
Miles Glendinning, *Mass Housing, Modern Architecture and State Power – A Global History*, Bloomsbury, London, 2021.
Leo F Goodstadt, *Uneasy Partners – The Conflict between Public Interest and Private Profit in Hong Kong*, Hong Kong University Press, Hong Kong, 2005.
Leo F Goodstadt, 'Fiscal freedom and the making of Hong Kong's capitalist society', *China Information*, 24(3), 2010, 273–294.
Michael Ho, 'Privatization of public housing in Hong Kong: A genuine agenda or propaganda', *Habitat International*, (3), September 2004, 481–494.
Pui-Yin Ho, *Challenges for an Evolving City: 160 Years of Port and Land Development in Hong Kong*, Commercial Press, Hong Kong, 2004.
Pui-Yin Ho, *Making Hong Kong*, Elgar Press, Cheltenham, 2018.
May Holdsworth and Christopher Munn, *Dictionary of Hong Kong Biography*, Hong Kong University Press, Hong Kong, 2012.
Robert K Home, *Of Planting and Planning: The Making of British Colonial Cities*, Spon, London, 1997.
Hong Kong Government Information Services (HKGIS), *Events in Hong Kong, 1967: An Official Report*, HKGIS, Hong Kong, 1968.
Hong Kong Housing Authority (editor/lead author Rosman C C Wai), *Planning, Design and Delivery of Quality Public Housing in the New Millennium*, HKHA, Hong Kong, 2010.
Hong Kong Institute of Architects, 'Occupy housing', *HKIA Journal*, 72, 2016, 1–117.
Ho-fung Hung, *City on the Edge – Hong Kong under Chinese Rule*, Cambridge University Press, Cambridge, 2022.
Robin Hutcheon, *High-Rise Society: The First 50 Years of the Hong Kong Housing Society*, Chinese University Press, Hong Kong, 2008.
Information Services Department, *Hong Kong, a New Era – A Review of* 1997.
Information Services Department, *Hong Kong 1998* (and *1999, 2000, 2001, 2002, 2003*).
Y C Jao, 'The rise of Hong Kong as a financial center', *Asian Survey*, 19(7), 1979, 674–694.
Mandy Lau, 'Speculative sub-division of private rental flats in Hong Kong', in A Smart (ed.), *The Speculative City, Emerging Forms and Norms of the Built Environment*, University of Toronto Press, 2020, Chapter 8.
James Lee, *Housing, Home Ownership and Social Change in Hong Kong*, Ashgate, Aldershot, 1999.
Leung Ho-yin, 'Crisis management in Hong Kong: A case study of short pile problems in public housing', Master of Public Administration Dissertation, University of Hong Kong, 2002.
Runhe Liu, *A History of the Municipal Councils of Hong Kong*, 1883–1999, Leisure and Cultural Service Department, Hong Kong, 2002.
C J Mackay, 'Fashion in public administration: The foundation of the Hong Kong Housing Authority and the Northern Ireland Housing Executive', *International Review of Administrative Sciences*, 65, 1999, 87–101
Chi-Kwan Mark, *Hong Kong and the Cold War: Anglo-American Relations 1949–1957*, Oxford University Press, Oxford, 2004.

Chi-Kwan Mark, 'Development without decolonisation? Hong Kong's future and relations with Britain and China, 1967–72', *Journal of the Royal Asiatic Society*, 24(2), 2014, 315–335.

Fujio Mizuoka, *Contrived Laissez-Faireism: The Politico-Economic Structure of British Colonialism in Hong Kong*, Springer, Cham, 2018.

Neil Monnery, *Architect of Prosperity, Sir John Cowperthwaite and the Making of Hong Kong,* London Publishing Partnership, 2017.

Stefan Muthesius and Miles Glendinning, *Towers for the Welfare State – an Architectural History of British Multi-Storey Housing 1945–1970,* Scottish Centre for Conservation Studies, Edinburgh, 2017.

Kaihon Ng, 'Political context, policy networks and policy change: The complexity of transition in Hong Kong', *The Pacific Review*, 20(1), March 2007, 101–126.

Michael H K Ng and John D Wong (eds), *Civil Unrest and Governance in Hong Kong: Law and Order from Historical and Cultural Perspectives*, Routledge, London, 2017.

Ma Ngok, *Political Development in Hong Kong: State, Political Society, and Civil Society*, Hong Kong University Press, Hong Kong, 2007.

Roger Nissim, *Land Administration and Practice in Hong Kong*, 5th edition, Hong Kong University Press, Hong Kong, 2021.

Chris Patten, *The Hong Kong Diaries*, Allen Lane, London, 2022.

Alice Poon, *Land and the Ruling Class in Hong Kong*, Enrich, Singapore, 2011.

E G Pryor, *Housing in Hong Kong*, 2nd edition, Oxford University Press, Oxford, 1983.

Public Housing in the New Era: Shui Chuen O Architectural Design Competition, Hinge Publications, Hong Kong, 2001.

Ian Scott, *Political Change and the Crisis of Legitimacy in Hong Kong*, Hurst, London, 1999.

Alan Smart, *The Shek Kip Mei Myth – Squatters, Fires and Colonial Rule in Hong Kong, 1950–1963*, Hong Kong University Press, Hong Kong, 2006.

Alan Smart and James Lee, 'Financialization and the role of real-estate in Hong Kong's regime of accumulation', *Economic Geography* 79(2), 2003, 153–171.

Alan Smart and Tai-Lok Lui, 'Civil disobedience and the rule of law' in Robert Bickers and Ray Yep (eds), *May Days in Hong Kong, Riot and Emergency in 1967*, Hong Kong University Press 2009, 145–159.

Wing-Shing Tang, 'Hong Kong under Chinese sovereignty: Social development and a land redevelopment regime', *Eurasian Geography and Economics*, 49(3), 2008, 341–361.

Chung-kin Tsang, *Homeownership in Hong Kong – House Buying as Hope Mechanism*, Routledge, London, 2021.

Steve Tsang, *A Modern History of Hong Kong*, I B Tauris, London, 2004.

Steve Tsang, *Governing Hong Kong – Administrative Officers from the Nineteenth Century to the Handover to China, 1861–1997*, I B Tauris, London, 2007.

Raymond Y C Tse and Sivaguru Ganesan, 'Hong Kong', in James Berry and Stanley McGreal (eds), *Cities in the Pacific Rim*, Spon, New York, 1999, 67–88.

Carmen Tsui, 'Housing the nascent middle class: The first high-rise planned community in post-war Hong Kong', *Planning Perspectives*, 73(4), 2021, 735–759.

Carmen Tsui, 'Minimum government assistance: Planning cottage resettlement areas in post-war Hong Kong', *Planning Perspectives*, 38(6), March 2023, 1257–1280.

Elsie Tu, *Colonial Hong Kong in the Eyes of Elsie Tu*, Hong Kong University Press, Hong Kong, 2003.

Gavin Ure, *Governors, Politics and the Colonial Office – Public Policy in Hong Kong, 1918–58*, Hong Kong University Press, Hong Kong, 2012.

Ka Fu Wah, 'An analysis of the organisational structure of the Housing Department in Hong Kong', Masters Thesis, University of Hong Kong, 2002.

Rosman C C Wai, *Design DNA of Mark I, Hong Kong's Public Housing Prototype*, MCCM Creations, Hong Kong, 2019.

Frank Welsh, *A History of Hong Kong*, paperback edition, HarperCollins, London, 1994.

Yue Chim Richard Wong, *Hong Kong Land for Hong Kong People – Fixing the Failures of our Housing Policy*, Hong Kong University Press, Hong Kong, 2015.

Ray Yep and T-L Lui, 'Revisiting the golden era of MacLehose and the dynamics of social reforms', *China Information*, 24(3), 2010, 249–272.

Yue-Man Yeung and Timothy K Y Wong (eds), *Fifty Years of Public Housing in Hong Kong – A Golden Jubilee Review and Appraisal*, Hong Kong Housing Authority/Hong Kong Institute of Asia-Pacific Studies, Hong Kong, 2003.

Maurice Yip, 'New town planning as diplomatic planning: Scalar politics, British-Chinese relations, and Hong Kong', *Journal of Urban History*, 48(2), 361–380.

Melody H-L Yiu, 'Cultural centers in Hong Kong: Welfare provision or economic instrument?', *Architecture and Culture: Journal of the Architectural Humanities Research Association*, 10(1), March 2022, 58–75.

Qian Zhu, 'The production of everyday space for workers: The new village movement in China, 1919–1936', *Positions*, 30(3), 2022, 429–453.

Index

Note: Governors and Chief Executives of Hong Kong (including temporary Governors) are indicated by **bold** type. Illustrations are indicated by page numbers in *italic* type.

For Product Safety Concerns and Information please contact our EU representative GPSR@taylorandfrancis.com Taylor & Francis Verlag GmbH, Kaufingerstraße 24, 80331 München, Germany